MOUNT HOOD

A COMPLETE HISTORY

EXCITING STORY OF AMERICA'S MOST-CLIMBED MOUNTAIN

A COMPREHENSIVE HISTORY OF
MOUNTAIN CLIMBING
ACCIDENTS AND RESCUES
THE FAMOUS BUILDINGS
BIOGRAPHIES OF FAMOUS PEOPLE
RISE OF THE SPORT OF SKIING
DEVELOPMENT OF SKI AREAS
CLUBS AND ORGANIZATIONS
WAGON PIONEERS WHO OPENED THE WAY
THE FOREST SERVICE ON MOUNT HOOD

BY JACK GRAUER

Table of Contents

Cover Photographs

Front, Elk Meadows — 1916 — Photo Homer Rogers
Rear, Mount Hoods Magnificent North Face — Photo Homer Rogers
Inside Front, Summit on New Year, 1932 — Photo Joe Leuthold
Inside Rear, Ole Lien Ascending Chute on New Year, 1932

Photo of author on page 6 by Kenneth Hollingsworth.

Information About the Author

Jack Grauer is an Oregon native, born John Foerste Grauer at Sheridan, Oregon, August 26, 1920, to William Henry and Laura Olive Grauer. His paternal grandparents were Jacob Grauer and Rosa Gutbrod Grauer, both born in Germany. Maternal grandparents were John Augustus Foerste, born in Germany, and Maude Alice Kennedy Foerste, a native of Illinois.

He attended grade school at Ballston, Forest Grove, Silverton, Salem, McMinnville, Sheridan, and Beaverton. He remained in Beaverton to finish high school, then attended Oregon State College at Corvallis. Enrollment in the School of Journalism there gave him the opportunity for experience in writing and editing under the instruction of Professor Fred Shideler. Other teachers vital in his educational pattern were Mrs. Claude Ingalls, Dr. Sigurd Peterson, and Dr. John Kierzek. He was a member of Delta Tau Delta Fraternity.

After a short period of work at Boeing Aircraft Company at Seattle, he enlisted in the US Army Air Corps, spending about 18 months in training in the United States, and an equal amount of time in work as a radio technician in the Solomon Islands, Philipine Islands, and Japan.

After World War Two he worked for the firm, Grauer and Ackerman in the heating and appliance business in Beaverton until 1952. In 1953 a move to Gresham placed him in business with his father in Gresham Hardware Company. In 1956 he entered the linoleum business as a sole owner, operating stores in Gresham, Oregon City, 36th and Hawthorne in Portland, and 15th and Powell in Portland. In 1973 he sold out his business completely.

During the period of living in Seattle, he became aware of the allure of alpine peaks, his first ascent being Pinnacle Peak in the Tatoosh Range at the south base of Mount Rainier. On return from the army he was badly bitten by the ski "bug" and spent most Sundays at Mount Hood from the winter of 1946. That led to a free-lance climb on South Side Route with two other friends, following the tracks of other climbers on the mountain that day.

Late in 1947 he joined The Mazamas, but skiing activity was his main interest until 1954, when he developed a raging case of "climbing fever" that never did subside. His leading began with Mount Constance in the Olympic Peninsula, and The Hermit in the Sierra Nevada Range of California. The following year was his first lead on Mount Hood. Since that time he has led 65 climbs for The Mazamas, as well as assisting the leader on many more. Peaks include all the major peaks of the Oregon Cascades, Mount Rainier, Mount Shuksan, Mount Olympus, Mount Stuart, Glacier Peak, Grand Teton, and Mount Owen. He has made climbs in California, Idaho, Montana, British Columbia, Washington, and Alberta.

In 1956 he was elected to concurrent three-year terms on the Climbing Committee and on the Executive Council of The Mazamas. In 1960 he collaborated with Larry Mills in leading an outing to the upper end of Maligne Lake in the Canadian Rockies, and in the following year led one to The Minarets in the Sierra Nevada. In 1960 he was the chairman of the committee in charge of rebuilding Mazama Lodge, which burned to the ground in 1958. That same year The Mazamas awarded him the Parker Cup for outstanding service to the club.

In 1961 he was re-elected to the Executive Council, becoming president of The Mazamas in 1962. In 1965 he was re-elected to the Climbing Committee, serving as the Chairman the following year. In 1971 he was again re-elected to the Executive Council.

In addition he has been active in the Mazama Climbing School since 1954, having been Chairman of the Basic School and also of the Intermediate School. In every year he has led groups or has been responsible for school training trips. Several times he has served on the Nominating Committee and the Parker Cup Selection Committee and has presided at times as the Master of Ceremonies at the Annual Mazama Banquet. At present he is a member of the Cross-country Ski Committee.

He became interested in the task of compiling a history of Mount Hood, because no significant work has been presented to the public since Fred McNeil published Wy'east the Mountain in 1937. Feeling that much of the data was fast slipping into oblivion, he decided to start the work, while some of the perishable records of The Mazamas are still available and while the old-timers, who developed skiing in the Thirties, can still talk. His personal knowledge of people and places offers a good basis for beginning and for properly interpreting the historical data found.

A Message from the Author

Hopefully, this will be only the first edition of Mount Hood, A Complete History. Time will add other chapters, many of them not even visualized at this time.

However, another, even better reason for a future revision is to correct the mistakes which are bound to creep in. If any reader has additional data to offer, an immediate response will be appreciated. If any stories are deemed inaccurate, I shall be very glad to recheck and discuss the matter with the reader. Please address Jack

Grauer, Box 692, Gresham, Oregon 97030. In the event of my death, please communicate with The Mazamas, 909 NW 19th Avenue, Portland, Oregon 97209. I hope that someone in that organization will carry on the work.

Most of the stories incorporated in this book have been taken from the files of Portland newspapers. A few have been given by the participants in the great and dramatic story of Mount Hood, however cross-checking has been used as much as possible. More often than not the details of any given event are colored in people's minds by time, point of view, and the natural tendency of each individual to picture himself or his organization as the central figure or hero of an event.

So many times the people who have the most interesting story to tell, are the least capable of telling it. Old age has dimmed their memory and tumbled events out of chronological order.

Although this work does not have footnotes for each bit of information, any events that can not be checked back through newspaper sources are noted as quotations from individuals or as unchecked sources. A work complete with all footnotes concerning source material becomes too cumbersome to read and enjoy. On the other hand, all possible dates, times, and names have been incorporated into the book.

Additional sources of information were the minutes, correspondence, and periodicals of clubs. The files of the US Forest Service turned up a good deal of data, a lot of it that was contradictory and needed further checking, but much of it was priceless. The diary of Joel Palmer and Lewis and Clark made it possible to be very explicit about events that happened as long as 170 years ago. The writings of William G. Steel, although not infallible, were quite explicit. The Oregon Historical Society provided considerable data in their Quarterly publication.

Each individual who acquires this book has a different combination of interests. Why not skim through, reading the particular items most interesting to you? Then, come back to it again. Other items will attract your interest. Some data will be completely uninteresting to you, but remember that there will always be some people who devour the parts which you might find dull.

Probably no other mountain in the world has had such an effect on the residents of a large city. Oregonians are remarkably aware of its beauty and presence on the skyline. They make unceasing pilgrimages to visit and revisit Mount Hood. Among the non-climbers there is one universal remark, always stated in the same words, as if read off some invisible script, "I've always wanted to climb Mount Hood just once, just to say I had done it." With the climbers and skiers, Mount Hood is a way of life.

No one knows how many people have climbed Mount Hood. At the turn of the century a valiant effort was made to keep the record, but sheer numbers and confusion made the job impossible. Mount Hood is the most climbed mountain in the world, except for the holy Japanese peak, Fujiyama. Even in early times, the U.S. Forest Service realized that the peak was an unusual recreational attraction, giving climbers and skiers the kind of attention usually reserved for national park areas.

Certainly no other major mountain in the world has been illuminated so frequently and so generously as Mount Hood. And no other mountain in the western hemisphere is visited weekly by such great hordes of skiers, many staying with the sport until mid-summer.

Two books the reader will find very interesting in expanding the background color of the story of Mount Hood are *The Story of Lige Coalman*, published by St. Paul's Press at Sandy, and *Off to Mount Hood*, written by a pioneer motor-stage driver, Dr. Ivan Woolley.

White Man's First Touch

BROUGHTON NAMED MOUNT HOOD

The first recorded view of Mount Hood by white men was October 29, 1792, when British naval Lieutenant William E. Broughton and his crew saw it from the Columbia River near the mouth of the Willamette River. His party had taken two small boats up the Columbia from Astoria Bay. The following day they proceeded upriver to a point near the site of Washougal, naming it Point Vancouver for his commander, Captain George Vancouver.

At the same time he named Mount Hood for Alexander Arthur Hood, famed British naval officer. The location of Point Vancouver has been lost, but it was possible to see Mount Hood from there. Some scholars surmise that it might have been a point on an island which Broughton mistook for mainland, and that the island has worked its way downriver over the past 182 years.

At that time, the British were working feverishly to establish claims to this unexplored northwest coast of America. The Spanish had made an earlier cruise between Vancouver Island and British Columbia and had named such features as the Straights of Juan de Fuca and the islands of Lopez, Orcas, Redonda, and Quadra. Then, on May 11, 1792, the Yankee Captain Robert Gray had crossed the bar and discovered the Columbia River, naming it for his ship, a fur-trading craft. Captain Vancouver, who was under commission from King George the Third to map the rugged northwest coast, thought it wise to send Lieutenant Broughton down to establish claim. It was known that there would be parleys with Spain to establish territorial limits.

Hood's history was a story of success and perserverance. Born December 12, 1724, he entered naval service in 1741 as a captain's servant. By 1746 he was a lieutenant, and kept increasing his rank until he was made governor of the naval academy in 1778. Soon afterward the king made him a Baronet, and he was sent on duty to the West Indies as a rear admiral. In 1782 he became a Baron, and attained the rank of vice admiral in 1783. In 1788 he became a member of the Board of Admiralty, and the following year elevated to the rank of Viscount.In 1815 he was awarded the Grand Cross of the Bath. Hood died January 27, 1816.

LEWIS AND CLARK

The United States began to see the wisdom in placing claim for the unexplored West and the Army organized the Lewis and Clark Expedition to probe beyond the continental divide. Floating down the Columbia River in boats, they were the first Americans to see Mount Hood on October 18, 1805. On October 25, at a point near The Dalles, Clark wrote, "The pinnacle of the round topped mountain, which we saw a short distance below the banks of the river, is South 43-degrees West of us and about 37 miles. It is at this time topped with snow. We called this the Falls Mountain, or Timm Mountain." Timm was the Indian name given to the falls area in the river just above the site of The Dalles. Clark noted that "the mountain was the Mount Hood of Vancouver."

OTHER EARLY VISITORS

A vague story from Hudson's Bay Company reports tells of a trip in about 1818 by two French voyageurs penetrating inland from the Columbia River, probably up the Dog River (Hood River). They reached the ice fields of the "Montagne de Neige." These white men probably stood upon the Eliot, or possibly the Coe Glacier.

The Scot botanist, David Douglas (6-26-1798 — 7-12-1834), disembarked at the mouth of the Columbia River on April 19, 1825. His mission with the Royal Horticultural Society took him upriver to the new Hudson's Bay post at Vancouver. He described in his *Journal* the insurmountability of a peak lying due east (Mt. Hood). Another (St. Helens) lay to the north. Both, he judged to be from 10,000 to 12,000 feet and covered with perpetual snow. His account, written in August, mentioned that there was little diminishing of snow since the first sighting.

Douglas rambled far and long in the Northwest. The Douglas Fir, the world's greatest timber tree, was named for this early scientist. He kept accurate records, but on June 13, 1833, Douglas was nearly killed on British Columbia's Fraser River, when his boat overturned in a waterfall. Douglas lost instruments, specimens, diary, and botanical journal to the savage power of the Fraser. For this reason no detailed accounts remained of the latter part of the summer of 1833, when he possibly attempted to climb the mountain which he had previously declared beyond the ability of man.

The Companion to The Botanical Magazine, published in London, issue of 1835-36, contained a letter to the editor by Archibald McDonald, an official of Hudson's Bay Company. Douglas had told McDonald of his activity in the Northwest after the boating accident. In the company of Pierre Pambrun, chief trader for Hudson's Bay at Fort Walla Walla, Douglas had made sorties to the Blue Mountains and finally attempted an ascent of Mount Hood. If he had met with success, one would presume he would have mentioned the fact. Failure to reach the summit is a safe presumption.

OGDEN AND WYETH

Peter Skene Ogden, one of the great names in the history of the West, explored very close to Mt. Hood in 1825, the very year that Douglas admired it from Fort Vancouver. At age thirty, he was chief trader for Hudson's Bay Company west of the Rockies, later first assistant to Dr. John McLoughlin at Vancouver. On November 21, 1825, he led a large group of trappers from Fort Nez Perce (Fort Walla Walla) on a trip through central and eastern Oregon, back to the Snake River. On December 5, they had reached high ground north of Tygh Valley, ascending Fifteen-mile Creek to a view point due east of Mt. Hood. He described Hood, Mt. St. Helens, and Mt. Nesqually (Mt. Adams) in all their snow-clad glory. Ogden mentioned the tall pines that gave the mountain its majestic setting. Lofty mountains to the south were likened to sugar loaves.

Ogden's party crossed several of the small creeks, coming to White River (known on an 1814 map in the Biddle edition of *Lewis and Clark Journal* as the Skimhoox). He said of White River and Tygh Creek that they appeared to rise from a mountain, not far and covered with snow. Mild weather, which can often be enjoyed in December on the sunny, eastern slopes of the Cascades, caused these streams to run in muddy freshet stage. Ogden's path seems to have closely paralleled the route in 1845 by Barlow and Palmer, suggesting that the contour of land must have led them to follow somewhat the same course.

The "Montagne de Neige" gained the attention of Captain Nathanial J. Wyeth as he boated down the Columbia and saw Mt. Hood on October 20, 1832. It was his first expedition to the Oregon Country, a step towards his hope of building a trading empire in the new country. On his first sighting he saw the "large, snowy mountain" southwest by west. Six days later he passed, looking up the Hood River and declaring it "a more stupendous pile than any of the Rocky Mountains." Wyeth came to Oregon because of the writings of Hall Kelly, only to find ruin. The officers of Hudson's Bay Company were friendly and receptive to him, until he attempted to trade with the Indians. At that point they undersold him and ruined him financially. He was forced to sell his fur operation and leave Oregon.

HALL J. KELLY

One man who was most important in the history of Oregon was Hall J. Kelly, born in 1791, graduate of Harvard University, writer of school books, surveyor, mathematician, and a man of moderate wealth. In 1815 he became enthusiastic about Oregon from tales of the Lewis and Clark expedition of 1805, and of the Pacific Fur Company in establishing Astoria in 1814-15. He was a prolific writer about the Oregon Country as well as an effective lobbyist in Washington D.C., although his visit to the territory was a disastrous disappointment in the year 1834, an incredible story.

He believed in the potential of fur trade, fisheries, and commerce with the Asiatic Continent. In 1827 he formed a society and issued a circular to people who might be interested in migrating to Oregon. In 1830 he published a *"Geographical Sketch of that part of North America Called Oregon."* A year later he wrote a prospectus outlining the glowing possibilities of living in this great land, suggesting a townsite at the confluence of the Columbia and Multnomah (Willamette) Rivers.

His activities in the nation's capitol were dynamic. In 1829 he asked congress for an area 25 miles square in the Columbia Valley, something they could not do, because the United States did not have title to the Oregon country. All during the years of 1830-31-32 he wintered in Washington D.C. to influence men in congress to lay claim to Oregon. There is no doubt that his lectures and writing caused hundreds of wagons to go west, shifting the population balance in favor of the United States, although Hudson's Bay Company definitely gave Britain the upper hand in the 1830's.

Finally in 1833 the great day came for Kelly's own trip to Oregon. He was afraid to go overland because of political enemies, so his first move was with a party to New Orleans, where they all deserted. Next he shipped to Vera Cruz in Mexico, then to California in early 1834. There he joined company with Ewing Young, who picked up Kelly's enthusiasm for Oregon. They started out with a herd of horses that Young had assembled with the idea of starting a ranch. Enroute, horse thieves joined the party and not only stole some of the stock, but somehow succeeded in getting Kelly and Young described as thieves to California's Governor Figueroa.

This resulted in a mad flight to Oregon where Kelly fell very ill. He was nursed by some trappers who took him to the British settlement at Vancouver. The unwarranted stigma of being a horse-thief came right along with him, and Governor McLoughlin could not very well socially receive a criminal, so his time in Vancouver was spent under a cloud. Jason Lee, who had been inspired by Kelly's writings to come to the Oregon country, was impressed favorably with him but could do nothing to relieve him of the stigma.

The man who had placed so much faith in this new state on the Pacific Coast, was unable to visit even Portland or Oregon City. Finally McLoughlin got the chance to ship him out on a whaler, which took him to the Sandwich Islands (Hawaii). He finally reached home in Boston in 1836, a very disillusioned individual. This was heightened by his investment in a cotton mill that went broke and took everything he had. He abandoned his family to live as a hermit until death in 1874.

Ewing Young recovered from the escapade to organize a cattle company that brought the first cattle into the Willamette Valley in 1836.

In Kelly's Geographical Sketch he referred to the Cascades as the Presidential Range, as had Lewis and Clark. His map was inaccurate and confusing, labelling Mount Hood as Mount Adams, although elsewhere he had called it Mount Washington. His map showed Mount St. Helens as Mount Washington.

Kelly was evidently not aware of Mt. Adams, leaving Ogden to first describe it and name it as Nesqually. Other versions of Kelly's map scrambled names still further, labelling St. Helens as Mt. Adams. Mt. Adams must be seen from high ground to identify it. Early river travellers in the lower Columbia saw Mt. St. Helens, but not Adams. Those who travelled the upper Columbia, or the trails parallel to it, could see Mt. Adams, but not St. Helens. Lewis and Clark were probably fooled into believing they were seeing the same peak from the two directions, as were other early travellers.

CAPTAIN JOHN C. FREMONT

The famous Captain John C. Fremont came west into Oregon. His expedition first saw Mt. Hood on October 23, 1843, as they descended the Blue Mountains. He noticed that it glowed in the sunlight from a vantage near the mouth of the John Day River. Fremont followed down to Fort Vancouver, then returned to Fort Dalles. In his journal of November 13, 1843, he made the astute observation that "wherever we came in contact with the rocks of these mountains, we found them volcanic, which is probably the character of the range. At this time two of the great snow cones were in action."

The one was, of course, Mt. St. Helens, which had scattered a half inch of ash as far away as The Dalles on November 22, 1842. Reverend Brewer at Dalles Methodist Mission gave Fremont a sample of the ash.

Fremont was under orders of the War Department. A member of the Cartographic Section of the Army, he was leading a group of 25 men, including Kit Carson. Their 104 animals were mostly pack stock. His mission was to find the Buena Ventura River, which was thought to originate near the Continental Divide and flow south. Leaving The Dalles, he went to Taih Prairie (Tygh Valley), where he referred to Mount Hood as an old friend. He mentioned the mountain several more times as he took his party across what is now the Warm Springs Indian Reservation on the west slopes of Mutton Mountains, down through Indian Head Creek to cross Warm Springs River, thence across Shitike Creek in the vicinity of Warm Springs Agency, across Metolius Bench to a crossing under the bench. Early in 1844 Fremont reached Sutter's Mill in California without discovering the non-existant Buena Vista River.

Fremont did not return to Oregon, but his trip caused the army to send another group from the Cartographic Section north from Sacramento in 1855. Led by Lieutenants Williamson and Abott, they followed up the Sacramento and Pitt Rivers, coming north into Oregon to the Columbia. Their mission was to give a preliminary survey of a railroad route to connect California to Oregon.

Crossing of Barlow & Palmer in 1845

The first claim to crossing the mountain trail south of Mount Hood was by Elvin Thorpe, who was said to have made the trip in 1841 with four white men and six Indians. The story is unsubstantiated, but there is little doubt that the Indians did guide a few white men along the trail prior to the Barlow-Palmer crossing of 1845. The source of information was a statement by V.D. Butler of Bull Run, Thorpe's grandson.

BARLOWS LEAVE ILLINOIS — 1845

March 30 Samuel Kimbrough Barlow, his wife Susannah Lee Barlow, daughter Jane Ellen, and sons William, James, John L. (Doc) left Fulton, Illinois, with the other Barlow daughter, Sarah Barlow Gaines, Albert Gaines, and the two Gaines daughters.

They drove four wagons, one pulled by eight oxen (four yokes), the rest by six oxen, strong young animals that could trot like a horse or pull a moderately loaded wagon 25 to 30 miles per day. Crossing the Mississippi River at Quincy, Illinois, and the Missouri River at Utica, Missouri, they reached Independence, Missouri, where about 5,000 immigrants were marshalling for the trip west. One yoke of oxen was stolen or strayed and replaced at $22. They bought two or three cows for $5 per head for milking along the way. In Oregon these animals would be worth $75 to $100 each.

Under the supervision of Dr. William Welch, elected grand wagon master, about 1,000 wagons were grouped into companies of 40 to 50 wagons. Samuel Barlow was the captain of one of these companies. The story of this giant movement through Nebraska, Wyoming, Idaho, and Oregon is a long, detailed account, involving herds of buffalo, trading tobacco with the Indians for free-

Old Wagon Wheel on Barlow Road — Photo USFS
Mute testimony of pioneer ways

dom to pass peacefully, a destructive stampede enroute, and of maneuvering the wagons over many canyons and hillsides and fast rivers.

There was a great deal of interchanging between companies. The families of Geer, Moore, and Sweet left the party at the mouth of the Malheur River to join the fiasco shortcut led by Stephen Meek. Samuel Barlow emerged from the Blue Mountains with a reputed train of 13 wagons to catch the first sight of Mount Hood.

It was this reoccurring view during the following days that caused a major change in the history of Oregon. Barlow repeatedly noticed the notch or pass in the mountain skyline, just south of Mount Hood, where today Highway 26 runs through Government Camp. The last obstacle before reaching The Dalles was the crossing of the Deschutes River. The water had pushed a gravel bar out into the Columbia, and it gave them a crossing shallow enough to drive the wagons across.

Ahead lay the dreaded trip down the Columbia River. No wagon had ever been driven past The Dalles. From there two boats were ferrying wagons downstream at outrageous prices, making the trip to Oregon City cost more than the wagons were worth. The community at Dalles Mission (Methodist) was jammed with immigrants waiting for boat passage. Human food and livestock feed were scarce and high-priced.

Barlow reasoned that "God never made a mountain without a way over it or under it, and I'm going to try." The missionaries, mountain trappers, and Hudson's Bay Company men shook their heads in disapproval concerning the two trails across Mount Hood which the Indians had mentioned to Barlow. One was a cattle-drovers' trail out of Waucoma (Hood River) up the Dog (Hood) River, and over Lolo Pass. The other ran to the south of the mountain. Barlow remembered the notch he had seen and decided to ride out to survey the area.

Mount Hood from Bonney Butte. The pioneers came up toward the mountain in the valley of White River on the left.

Returning from a 35-mile scouting ride, he made the decision to try to force a road across the mountains. Seven wagons pulled away from The Dalles Mission on September 25, 1845, stopping at Five-mile Creek for a day of resting and washing clothing. William H. Rector, wife and family joined the train. In addition to the Barlow and Gaines families there were those of Gesner and Jacob C. Caplinger, plus three single men, John Bacon, William Berry, and Reuben Gant.

September 26 The party advanced to Tygh Creek, a 25 or 30-mile pull over moderate ground past the present towns of Boyd and Dufur. Some Indian huts lay in the valley, and the grazing was good. The crossing was a short distance up the creek from the present town of Tygh Valley.

September 27 The wagons remained at camp in the valley. A heifer was killed and dressed. Some of the men worked at sharpening tools with the single grindstone and worn-out files. Samuel Barlow and Rector rode out to blaze trail, followed by the able-bodied men who chopped and drug logs or burned them away to make a path for the wagons. William Barlow and Rector's son stayed in camp to help.

September 28 The difficult pull out of the hole at Tygh Creek was made and another camp was established at Stony Branch.

September 29 Joel Palmer arrived at The Dalles with a wagon train to find the same disheartening conditions, high priced food and 50 or 60 families waiting for passage on two small boats. He heard that Samuel Barlow and Henry M. Knighton had ridden out to the south, stirring his interest in crossing the mountains also. But Knighton had returned, declaring the route impractical. Barlow had been gone six days, presumably trying to force a passage across the Cascade Mountains. Palmer decided to follow and persuaded 15 other families to accompany his group, about 23 wagons.

September 30 Samuel Barlow returned to the wagons, spending the night in camp.

October 1 At four in the afternoon, Palmer's train left The Dalles, presumably following Barlow's wagon tracks and probably camping at the same Five-mile Creek for the night. Samuel Barlow and three men rode out ahead from the Barlow train to plot the possible course of the road.

October 2 Palmer's group travelled about ten miles, passing several streams, and camping on one that ran out of the Cascade Mountains. Out ahead, Barlow and three men were still pushing ahead to find a route.

October 3 Palmer and one man rode out ahead of the slow wagons and came to Tygh Creek, crossed the creek, climbed out of the canyon and turned west about 10 miles. This took them across Badger Creek to what Palmer called Stony Branch, where he found Barlow's little train of seven wagons encamped. Barlow was still out on reconaissance. The terrain was rolling grassy slopes with a scattering of yellow pine trees. Here Palmer spent the night.

October 4 Palmer and companion with a scant two day's provisions, rode west into the mountains. From open, higher ground they could see Mt. Hood. Palmer described a trip of this day of about 35 miles, passing several streams and naming one Rock Creek. This may or may not be the present Rock Creek. Grass was meager for the horses. They found the bluffs of White River and followed them north. Camp was made on a high ridge overlooking its canyon.

October 5 Very early in the morning, Palmer and friend descended a very abrupt, difficult slope from their camp about a half mile to the stream, The White River. They referred to the fast, sandy stream as a branch of the *De Shutes* River. Later on it was called the Little De Chutes. Palmer compared the glacial-silt laden river with the Mississippi, noting that its waters were high late in the day and low in the morning, a characteristic of glacial streams. He followed the stream far enough to ascertain that Mount Hood was its source. Provisions were low, and they retraced their step toward Barlow's camp, noting a possible road site down the mountainside to the north of White River, as they travelled. Arriving at Rock Creek, they found their wagon train had progressed to that point. Evidently Barlow's train had followed along, too. Samuel Barlow had not yet returned from his scouting trip.

October 6 This was a day of rest and planning. A decision was made to send most of the loose cattle ahead with a party of people to Oregon City. Palmer sent his riding horse ahead, anticipating little more use for him. He thought that by taking the ridges west, the party would intercept the north-of-the-mountain trail used by a band of drovers that had started for Oregon City from The Dalles on October 1.

This was a bad guess on Palmer's part, but it turned out to be a providential one. He had asked this group to send back provisions and assistance, but because they were not his own people, he felt that the chances were poor of their compliance. He reasoned that his own Advance Party of Drovers (author's terminology) would insure getting help, as well as taking the cattle away from the poor grazing of the mountain area.

Two families decided to leave their wagons and go with this party. One was that of Colonel James Taylor of the Ohio Militia, his wife, Esther D'Armon Taylor, and their children. In the afternoon Samuel Barlow and his three companions returned from their five-day reconaissance trip. William Barlow remembered hearing the crack of his father's rifle and his appearance shortly after. Their route had been much the same as Palmer's. Barlow thought he had come to within 12 to 15 miles of Mount Hood in following up the White River. Barlow and Palmer quickly agreed that they should work together and talked over plans for developing the wagon road.

October 7 The Advance Party of Drovers left early in the morning. A few men were sent to The Dalles for a beef and some wheat. Others were left to maintain the camp and pack provisions. The rest went to work on the road with axes, saws, and flame.

October 10 By evening the workmen had passed the short, 30-degree slope down into the canyon of Klip Creek, and the road was open to the top of the steep hillside leading down into White River Canyon. This hillside that later travellers were to call "Little Laurel Hill" was covered with a species of laurel (rhododendron) too thick to pass through. They fought their way down through it in the afternoon and set fire to the dry shrubs. In the morning they awoke at their camp on the White River to find the slope clean and nearly ready for wagon travel.

October 11 The leaders held consultation. The road crew would open the way up to the bed of White River, then progress up the stream bed as far as possible. Meanwhile Joel Palmer, Samuel Barlow, and Mr. Lock would scout in advance. Palmer stated that they went up the White River about 15 miles. It was actually more like five miles, when they struck a stream coming in from their left (NW). This stream, probably Barlow Creek, they followed a short distance, then left it to cut back to their original course, the White River. A cedar swamp, dense with brush and timber, slowed them severely, although they were on foot, not on horseback. Reaching the White River stream bed, they followed it up about five miles (Palmer thought eight) and intercepted the Indian trail "near where it comes down from the mountain." This would undoubtedly be the site of the Skyline Trail where it crosses White River and ascends the steep slopes leading to the Timberline Lodge area. Indians were known to have made trails on the tops of ridges, as a rule.

Palmer was awed with the grandeur of Mount Hood, visible for the first time from bottom to top. He remarked about the upper part of White River Canyon, with its great moraines, the torrent of water carrying sand down from the mountain, the glacial area and cliffs near the summit of Mt. Hood. Very significantly he mentioned was a grove of dead trees in the bottom that had been killed by water-carried sand being deposited around them.

They followed the trail up a grassy ridge to the timberline area, where there was no vegetation. Shortly after leaving the White River bottom they ran across members of the Advance Party of Drovers, who said they were then encamped on the west side of Mt. Hood. They had lost about a third of the stock and were ready to return to camp, having found a few. Palmer, Barlow, and Lock decided to camp with them and proceded west with them. On reaching Big Zigzag Canyon they followed the trail to its bottom, crossed the rapid, sandy stream, and climbed the trail out of the west side of the canyon. There in the next ravine was the drover camp, abundant with grass and whortleberry bushes (huckleberry). That October night was windy and cold.

October 12 Big Zigzag Canyon stunned and awed them. The slopes were steep, barely sustaining a trail for people and livestock. Palmer described the trail as a zigzag to the right, to the left, to the right, until it reached the stream bed. This reference probably gave the Zigzag River its name. Palmer estimated the canyon as 3000 feet deep, although it would not even be 1000 feet from rim to creek where the trail descends. Their impression of its vast size is understandable, however, because of the massive hulk of Mississippi Head standing at the head of the canyon. Certainly no wagon could pass above that great cliff, although the three decided to find out by walking over the top of it.

Barlow and Lock wore clumsy boots that made walking painful. Palmer was shod in leather mocassins, but holes were developing in the soles. In walking up the west rim of the canyon toward Mississippi Head, Palmer kept ahead, with the other two lagging. They contended that the ascent was useless, as the cliff of Mississippi Head could not be passed over the top. Finally they sat down, awaiting Palmer's signal as to whether the cliff was passable. In 1845 the Zigzag Glacier was much larger and presented an ice cliff about 40 feet in height. Atop Mississippi Head, Palmer signalled, and they came up to the base of the ice, evidently stopping there. Palmer cut holes in the ice for footholds, climbing by this time in bare feet. He continued up, a mile he thought, to sit on some rocks that had fallen away from Illumination Rock, where he stayed a half hour, warming his feet on the warm rock.

He gave up the idea of Barlow and Lock following. They had retraced their steps and crossed to the east bank of Big Zigzag on the trail. Palmer continued climbing, contouring around to the south slopes of the mountain, observing the country around Government Camp area, thinking that a passage through was possible. Palmer's ascent must have taken him close to the base of Crater Rock. This was close enough for him to feel that Mt. Hood was climbable. The descent was alarming to him, as he crossed several blind crevasses that never fail to impress any alpinist, no matter how well equipped. That he saw crevasses at that time, indicates that the Palmer Glacier has shrunk considerably since 1845.

Palmer remarked about the black rock of the summit cliffs, but failed to perceive the volcanic origin of Mt. Hood. He remarked about gray "sandstone." He correctly assayed the direction of Zigzag, Little Zigzag, and the Camp Creek of Government Camp, calling them branches of the Quicksand (Sandy) River. He noted that Hunchback Mountain was visible on the south side of the Zigzag Valley, until its view was obscured by Zigzag Mountain. He identified the Sandy River correctly in the valley that runs off the drainage of the Reid Glacier. Still Creek and Salmon River he identified incorrectly as branches of the "Clackamis," not realizing that Still Creek winds around back of Tom-Dick-Harry Mountain, and Salmon River passes behind Hunchback Mountain to join the Sandy River. But he felt that, if the pass at Government Camp area would not be feasible, then the Still Creek route might be possible.

He saw Barlow and Lock ascending on the east side of Big Zigzag Canyon and met them below on the trail. The next objective was to reach Summit Meadows, which he had seen from above. A rest stop near a spring gave them a chance to eat huckleberries and the ration of *one* biscuit for the day. They found Summit Meadows to be grassy and wet, with Still Creek running through in a southeast direction. From higher they had seen another meadow about two miles further south, which they supposed might be drier.

The hour was late, and the three struck out for camp on the White River. Although Palmer had noted the low notch of Barlow Pass from high on Mount Hood, he failed to orient properly from the meadows, and struck the White River much too high up stream. It was 11:00 p.m. when they hobbled in the encampment of the road crew at the confluence of Barlow Creek and White River.

October 13 A consultation was held early in the morning. The wagon train was down below at Camp Creek. Although the provision party had returned from The Dalles, food was still painfully scarce. Despair prevailed. Cattle had strayed and became lost; Indians had stolen some horses. So many men were needed to preserve the camp, that only a third of the manpower could be devoted to road building. New wagons had arrived, and some families had not sent their cattle ahead with the Advance Party of Drovers. Bawling, hungry cattle and restless horses needed grass.

It was decided that a party would go ahead to Summit Meadows, assaying the road building problems as they went. A second group would continue pushing the road construction up to Barlow Pass. A third group would bring all the wagons to Barlow Creek. A nearby meadow would feed the livestock for a few days. These arrangements being made, the next step was to reconnoiter the route far out ahead, with the thought that it might be possible to get through to Oregon City for badly needed provisions. It might be noted that no mention was ever made of killing deer or elk for food. Evidently they were not bountiful at that time. Huckleberries offered one of the few opportunities to live off the land. Palmer and one other man were elected to scout ahead.

At eight o'clock a.m., Palmer and companion left for Barlow Pass, Summit Meadows, and points west through the Government Camp gap that Palmer had seen from high up on Mt. Hood. This was the first time a white man had crossed Barlow Pass. On arriving at Summit Meadow, Palmer noted that building the road to that point would be practicable, although it would require a great deal of brush and tree cutting.

They then struck out west through the area that was to later be named Government Camp. The swamps and heavy timber of this area indicated an overwhelming amount of road work, too much to do in the last days of autumn. They retraced their steps east. Palmer's journal is vague, but their probable route was around the east end of Multorpor Mountain and down the Still Creek drainage, contouring up to the top of Tom-Dick-Harry Ridge. Palmer mentioned an old Indian trail that is not traceable. They followed the ridge west and angled down to reach a creek, probably Wind Creek, where darkness forced them to camp.

October 14 Palmer's moccasins were again worn out, and walking was painful. They descended, striking Camp Creek, and following it down to somewhere near the site of Rhododendron. The valley did not look very promising for a wagon route, although this is where the Barlow Road was located in 1846. The creek had a rapid flow over a rocky bottom.

Until this day these wagon pioneers had enjoyed the idylic beauty of Mt. Hood's Indian Summer, with lovely sun-filled days and crisp nights. But clouds formed that morning, and Palmer noted that even the birds and squirrels indicated the coming of stormy weather. The reputation of Oregon's unrelenting rain was well known to the travellers, and this caused Palmer to feel great alarm and indecision. The next step was to bring the bad news to those back at camp.

The options were two. *First*, they might take the wagon train back to The Dalles, while White River was still passable. Perhaps they could leave their valuables with the missionaries there and descend the Columbia somehow.

Secondly, a permanent camp might be established there near the mouth of Barlow Creek on the White River. They could build a cabin, leave their belongings with a caretaker, and run for their lives toward Oregon City. This was the choice they actually made, calling the cabin "Fort Deposit."

But Palmer's mind was full of distress that morning, as the two men headed back to the wagon train. Preferring the mountain top to the creek, they ascended Hunchback Mountain again, pulling themselves up on the bushes on the steep terrain. At the end of this hard, footsore day they had walked back to the road builders' camp at Barlow Creek. It is believed that at that time none of the Barlow-Palmer party had ever seen the infamous Laurel Hill, the grade that provided an exit to the upper Camp Creek Valley at Government Camp.

October 15 All personnel at Barlow Creek left for the main encampment near the mount of "Camp Creek" on White River, arriving by 2:00 p.m. There they found the camp crew busy rounding up strayed cattle. The full membership of the wagon party was assembled. Palmer told them of his fears, stressing the need for a decision caused by threatening weather and shrinking food supply. The decision was to build a cabin, "Fort Deposit". Meanwhile, all who could, should run for their lives to the settlement at Oregon City.

October 16 Samuel Barlow and William Rector started on foot for Oregon City to procure provisions and horses. Men, women, and children worked feverishly to prepare for the movement of wagons to the site at Barlow Creek where the Fort Deposit cabin would be built. A few necessities were set aside for their flight along the timberline trail.

Joel Palmer took three people with him for a horseback trip to civilization, Mrs. Miriam A. Thompson, and William Gilbert Buffum and wife Caroline Thurman Buffum. Buffum supplied the horses. It shortly began to rain, and their first night was spent at Barlow Creek.

October 17 After a rainy night, the four continued up White River in a drizzle, reaching the Indian timberline trail. Rain became heavier. When dark overtook them about 4:30 they were at the bottom of Big Zigzag Canyon. They felt their way up the west slope of the canyon, over the ridge to a grassy slope. The men kindled a fire and built a tent out of poles and blankets. This was sufficient for the women and luggage, and the men spent the night shivering in front of the fire.

October 18 The gray light of a rainy morning exposed the sight of an extinguished fire and the tired, gaunt faces of the travellers. The shivering horses had to be driven around a while to make them eat. Palmer remarked that for the humans "there was little to eat, and they were not troubled much in cooking it." They continued west along the trail in fog and heavy, cold rain. Somewhere west of Paradise Park they lost the trail in the fog and descended a wrong ridge (probably Slide Mountain) until stopped by dense brush. The women waited astride the horses in the rain while Buffum went down the ridge and Palmer climbed back up, looking for the trail. Palmer found it up the mountainside a mile or more.

Once more on the trail, they were blessed by a breeze that blew away the fog and gave them visibility. Soon, they saw a large band of cattle grazing and coming up toward them. The drovers who followed had come from The Dalles over Lolo Pass and were camped in the flats below four or five miles, where the trails converged. They bore great news! **A rescue party from Oregon City was at that moment at the drovers' camp** with food for the Barlow-Palmer party.

Palmer and his companions sped down the trail to the camp. But the rescue party was gone! They had been out from Oregon City longer than they expected, and they had despaired of finding the wagon party. They had given a little food to the men in the camp and then started back home with the rest. Palmer prevailed on one of the drovers to mount a fresh horse and overtake them. In about ten minutes he returned and reported that the rescue team had been contacted. They had gone about six miles toward Oregon City, but had decided to camp and make one more ride eastward to find the immigrants.

Palmer and Buffum built a large, warming fire and prepared a blanket shelter for the group. With no more than two small coffee-pots and some tin cups, the women prepared a supper of bread and coffee, the first food since Barlow Creek. The rescue party was composed of Peter G. Stewart, Charles Gilmore, Matthew Gilmore, and a surly Indian.

October 19 There was breakfast, food to eat once more. The drovers pushed on toward Oregon City with their herd. Stewart, Matthew Gilmore, Mrs. Thompson, and Mr. and Mrs. Buffum proceeded on their way to the settlement. Palmer, Charles Gilmore, and the Indian were soon on their way to Barlow Creek with provisions. The heavily loaded horses were slipping on the rain-soaked trails, and fog had cut the visibility to 15 feet.

Climbing to higher elevation, they encountered snow that made it very difficult to follow the trail. The Indian balked. Only the threat of a whip prompted him to stay with the party, but he would not assist in driving the horses. There was no snow on the steep trail through Big Zigzag Canyon. The only difficulty incurred was that of packs coming loose and rolling down the hillside. But on the east side of the canyon snow was heavy and drifted. Crossing Little Zigzag and Sand Canyons presented serious problems and some narrow escapes by the horses. The Indian tried to turn the horses back but consented to continue for the price of an extra blanket.

Soon, however, two Indians from The Dalles met them on the trail, and the surly one announced his intention of leaving the party and going west with them. In the midst of this parley, confusion was added by a group of men from Barlow Creek, driving cattle ahead of them. The Indian took advantage of this diversion of attention to maneuver a pack horse and his riding horse out into the fog and disappear with the other two Indians on the trail west.

They managed to get the pack string across the snow covered heights to a grassy ridge, a relief for horses that had eaten nothing for 36 hours. Gilmore mixed flour with water, baked it on sticks over the fire. The two had some tea, and spent a comfortable night.

October 20 A clear, sunny morning promised a much brighter future. They hurried the pack horses down the trail, down the White River to Barlow Creek, arriving at 3:00 p.m. Hungry people thanked God for the food that Palmer and Gilmore brought. Many families were ready to begin eating their livestock, which would have been a great financial sacrifice.

October 21 Building the large cabin and the wagon-yard for Fort Deposit was the principal activity. William Berry and Albert P. Gaines were the principal workmen on the cabin, being expert with the tools. Others were working as directed. Women and children were sorting out their treasures, deciding what could be carried on the trip to Oregon City.

October 22 Charles Gilmore started the westward trip, taking three families. Other families departed at intervals, when they could make themselves ready. The families of Rev. Theophilus Powell and Sharp C. Senters struck out upon the trail, poorly clad and nearly barefooted, nine people, of whom four were small children. The family of Andrew Hood also left this day.

October 25 Ten men were continuing the construction of the cabin which was well along. All but three families had started for the settlement, those of Barlow, Rector, and Caplinger. Samuel Barlow and William Rector had now been gone for nine days on their trip to Oregon City for supplies, and their families were anxiously waiting. Palmer, with Creighton, Farwell, and Buckley, started their trek on foot. When they had travelled but a short distance from Fort Deposit they met the long overdue Samuel Barlow and Rector coming toward them with horses and supplies. After they had left the wagon train on October 16th, they had walked out to civilization, nearly perishing for lack of food. At Eagle Creek they had stumbled across the farm of Philip Foster, who had the easternmost residence along the trail. Foster's sons, Frank, 6, and George, 8, ran with fright to tell their father that two strange men had yelled at them near the farm.

Foster found Barlow and Rector, staggering with exhaustion and hunger, and Mrs. Foster fed them and bade them rest before continuing to Oregon City. Entering that thriving Provisional Capital city of the Oregon Country, they were refused credit at the American store and the Methodist Mission store. Surprisingly they were granted credit from the last resort, the Hudson's Bay Company, the economic arm of Britain's conquest.

Near Mt. Hood on their return trip, Barlow and Rector met several families and induced them to start back over the trail with the idea of going to The Dalles. Fortunately, these people waited a day, disregarded the advice, and started westward again.

Palmer and three companions travelled up the White River to the point where the trail ascends the steep slopes. There they spent a night camped in the rain, before continuing westward.

October 26 Following the trail upward in rainy weather, the four overtook some of the families who had left Fort Deposit on October 22. At the bottom of Big Zigzag Canyon the Powell and Senters families had spent the night without fuel or grazing for cattle and horses. The coming of daylight had permitted them to find the way up the west slope of the canyon to the encampment of the Hood family. During the night one of the horses broke loose and destroyed their sack of food. The Hoods shared their own scanty food supply, as did Palmer and companions. Andrew Hood supplied Palmer with a wagon cover for a shelter.

October 27 The Powell and Senters families found a heifer, that they killed, and cured its meat. The poor animal had slipped while grazing over rock ledge and crippled itself. About four inches of new snow had fallen during the night.

Palmer's foursome pushed forward rapidly. Descending the trail to lower elevations down toward the Sandy River was a great relief, because their moccasins had worn out again, exposing bare feet. Approaching the junction with the northside trail over Lolo Pass, they met William Buffum, Lock, and Smith (believed to be Simeon Smith), bringing 14 pack horses back to Fort Deposit for valuables. One horse was Palmer's,

COMMENTS FROM WILLIAM H. RECTOR

William Henry Rector wrote a story of his own life, which gives some interesting comment about the crossing of the mountains. This narrative of Rector's life was printed verbatim in Fred Lockley's *History of the Columbia River Valley from The Dalles to the Sea.*

Rector's experience was something like that of Joel Palmer; he came to The Dalles and found that wagons had left to try a crossing of the Cascade Mountains south of Mount Hood. Forming company with a few others, he overtook the Barlow-Palmer group in three days.

Rector's account of the crossing of the plains was most interesting, however we shall recount only one incident. Soon after leaving Fort Hall, the youngest son, William Henry Rector, Jr., almost 5, was run over by a wagon. The wheel hit his leg between knee and ankle; the leg was fractured with the bone protruding. There being no doctor available in the wagon train, Rector and a Mr. Avery set the bone. There was no water available until they reached a campsite that night, and the Rectors stayed over in camp one full day. A few weeks later, when they reached The Dalles, the boy was well enough to walk.

According to Rector's story, it was he who suggested the idea of leaving the wagons at a depository at Mount Hood for the winter. Also he wrote that he had suggested to Joel Palmer that two men push through to Oregon City for supplies and fresh horses. It is on record, of course, that he and Barlow were the men, who went for help.

Barlow and Rector started out for Oregon City with food sufficient for two days. This estimate was based upon the reconnaissance that Palmer, Barlow, and Lock had made on October 12. The trip actually took six days, mostly because they were lost the first two or three.

Rector carried a light shotgun, but there was nothing to shoot for food. At the end of the first day, Barlow commented that he wanted to eat all of his food, just for supper. Rector felt the same way. Barlow suggested that each time they had a meal, that they should eat only half. They both lived up to the idea.

During the second day of travel, October 17, they walked in a light, misty rain. At dark, they descended into a canyon to get water and to try to build a fire. Their matches were wet, and using their gun didn't work any better. Barlow was falling into despair and fear that they would not survive the cold, rainy night. Rector got astride a fallen tree and began rubbing with a dry limb. Soon Barlow was helping, the two sitting face-to-face under a blanket and rubbing on the wood until it was warm. By putting the matches on the warm wood, they were able to dry them enough to start a fire. Rector worked all night getting wood, and Barlow slept.

They spent the whole third day walking parallel to the canyon in fog. Rector then suggested that they follow north on a compass course to hit the cattle trail at timberline. Barlow agreed. Finally they came out of the fog and could see Mount Hood. Barlow insisted that he had been on the spot before, and that it was not over a mile from the wagon camp. Feeling that Barlow's mind had failed him, Rector took control and forced him to go on with him.

Barlow complained bitterly, becoming so weak that he stumbled frequently, as he walked behind in a sullen silence. Rector carried the gun and the axe to relieve him of all possible weight.

Once Barlow asked, "Mr. Rector, if I should break a leg in some of these falls, what would you do with me?"

"I would eat you," Rector answered jokingly, but when he looked around, Barlow was in tears. "Why Barlow, you old fool, I won't eat you. Neither will you break a leg. We will get to the trail early tomorrow."

Barlow insisted that he probably would never make his way out of the mountains. He made Rector promise that if he should become disabled, that he would knock out his brains with the axe and not let him linger. However, Barlow took good care not to fall after that.

Rector stated that on the fourth day they hit the trail and fell in with a party of people driving cattle. He noted that some food and rest made a lot of difference in Barlow's personality. There is no note of the incident of their stumbling onto Philip Foster's farm. Obviously, either one story or the other is not true. Accounts written many years after their occurrence, tend to become twisted and contain important omissions. The episode of the two being found by Foster's children, may be a bit of unfounded folk-lore that has been handed down through the Barlow family.

and they intended to bring back a load of his belongings. The two parties continued in their own directions, except that Palmer's group took back two of the 14 horses that were too starved to be able to climb back over the mountain trail.

They crossed the Sandy River several times until they reached the "forks" where the Zigzag River runs into it. They noted the steep, timbered hillsides, the outcroppings of gray rock, and the deep canyons carved into the mountain walls. They also noted the valley of Camp Creek, where Palmer and a companion had explored on October 14.

October 28 They started early and followed the Sandy River down for several miles, crossing it three times. Finally they struck the wagon road that had been opened from the western end by James Taylor, who had taken his family across the trail on October 7, with the Advance Party of Drovers. Taylor had organized a party of men to return and meet the later travellers at the crossing of the Sandy, (probably near Brightwood). The road builders had then worked back toward Oregon City, having finished about five miles. Palmer found them camped on the north side of the Sandy, a little distance from where the road followed westward up the hill to Marmot and the "Devil's Backbone" west of Marmot. Palmer was out of food, so Taylor's supply of rations was very welcome. They spent the night in the same camp. It rained.

October 29 They ascended the ridge to Marmot and followed down the Devil's Backbone to the Sandy. Many slopes were barren, and the creek bottom had many dead trees, all the result of former fires. Crossing the Sandy in the cold, rapid water was difficult, especially for Buckley, who was too sick to carry his pack. Buckley was almost ready to lose his footing in the swift water of midstream, when Farwell, a strong young man from Maine, saved him. One of the emaciated horses fell in the cold water and died. The other had to be left by the river, where it was picked up in a few days by the road crew.

Being relieved of the burden of tending the horses, the four pushed on as fast as Buckley's strength would permit. The knapsacks were doubly heavy, being saturated with rain. At dark they met a party of men who had been through to the settlement with a herd of cattle and were on their way back to Fort Deposit with pack horses for the three families there. There were actually only two, because Rector, his wife and family had departed from Fort Deposit shortly after October 25 for The Dalles. He had feared that his wife's delicate health would not stand the trip over the mountain. Peter Skene Ogden of Hudson's Bay Company provided Rector with food, and with a group of other wagon pioneers he rafted down the Columbia to Linnton and paddled back up to Oregon City.

October 30 Continuing southwest over rolling prairie country, Palmer and friends came to the Clackamas River and the home of Samuel McSwain. There they encountered some of the families that had been led out by Charles Gilmore. They stayed the night.

October 31 They followed down the Clackamas River to the homestead of Peter B. Hatch, and spent the night.

November 1 After a couple of miles, they came to a crossing of the river, probably near the present community of Clackamas, a place with gentle banks and shallow, rocky bottom. Here a village of some twenty Indian families existed on the providence of a little fish and game available. The homes were of poles and cedar shakes. The Indians furnished canoes for the crossing, and soon the four had covered the remaining two miles to Oregon City. They walked out of the timber on the east side of the city to see simultaneously the splendor of the falls and the welcome sight of a civilized town once more. So ended the westward trip of Joel Palmer.

December 1 No day-to-day records are available after Palmer reached Oregon City and passed out of the scene. Back at Fort Deposit a full month went by. As far as is known, the only remaining people were the Barlow family, the Caplingers, The Gaines, William Berry, and J.M. Bacon. The cabin was tight, with cracks chinked with moss. A great store of wood had been cut, and there was plenty of food for Berry for the long winter.

Snow came, and all except Berry left for the settlement. Berry walked up with them to the top of Barlow Pass. The passage through the Government Camp area was very difficult. Horses had to be pried out of the swamps in the Camp Creek Valley. Snow covered the grass. As far as is known, this was the first group to use this route down Laurel Hill as an escape to Oregon City, the others all having taken the Timberline Trail.

They camped on top of Laurel Hill in a foot of snow. One of Barlow's best horses died from eating the laurel (rhododendron). Mrs. Barlow lamented, "poor old Gray is dead, but I hope his meat is good; we will not starve so long as we can eat horse meat." Samuel Barlow's spirit was low. He saved Gray's harness, and brought it into camp.

The pessimistic Mrs. Caplinger broke down and commenced crying. Only the cheerful Barlow daughter, Sarah Gaines brought any touch of cheer into the grim situation. "We are in the midst of plenty," she quipped, "plenty of wood to make fires, plenty of horses to make meat, plenty of snow to make water, and when it comes to starving, here is your old dog as fat as butter, and he will last us a week."

The next morning William Barlow and J.M. Bacon started for Foster's for more supplies. They took a little coffee, four small biscuits, an axe, and two blankets, descending Laurel Hill "like shot on a shovel". They soon struck the "forks" at Zigzag and followed the Sandy River down the well established trail. That last crossing of the Sandy was a hard one. Rising water had made swimming just about the only possibility. Cutting a tree failed, when the tree broke in two and floated away. They slept under a large cedar, hoping for better inspiration in the morning.

December 21 After a big pot of coffee, and nothing else, because Bacon had dropped the precious biscuits, William Barlow cut a ten foot safety pole. Edging out into the current, he used it to brace against rocks downstream, as he stepped cautiously across the gravel bottom. Once across the stream, he waved goodbye to Bacon and ran the eight miles to Foster's in about three hours. There he found his little brothers, James and John L., tending livestock. He told them to ride fast for Oregon City for men and eight or ten horses, and to be back the following morning.

December 22 Help arrived. Although ill from over-eating, William mounted a horse and rode toward the Sandy at a lope. At dark he met his mother and father and the other two families. He was careful to keep them from over eating.

December 23 The full party arrived at Foster's.

December 24 The day was spent in resting and eating.

December 25 Most of the party travelled to Oregon City, thus ending the gruelling pioneering of the Barlow Trail on the south slopes of Mount Hood.

1846 — A RETURN TRIP

January 1 William Barlow and companion, Eaton, started back for Fort Deposit with sugar, coffee, flour, and bacon sufficient to feed two men until June. Barlow intended to spend the winter with William Berry, the two of them intending to divide the ten dollars per wagon agreed by the owners back in October. Eaton would bring the horses back to Oregon City.

Many people thought that they would not be able to get through, and indeed, on most years they would not. The pair encountered snow five feet deep, with a hard crust about two feet under the surface. They followed the blazed trail left by Sam Barlow, often digging the horses out with shovels, when their hooves broke through. At night they tied the horses to a tree with a nose bag of oats. A campfire cheered the scene. A hole dug in the snow and a wrapping in their Hudson's Bay blankets served as a bed.

January 5 They crossed Barlow Pass and descended to Fort Deposit. William Berry was warm and happy in the snug cabin. Indians had visited and brought him a supply of huckleberries and dried salmon. A man named Foster had come in over the trail from The Dalles and wanted to stay all winter. Foster paid for his share of the food. Berry offered to release Barlow from the agreement to spend the winter at Fort Deposit, giving him enough to pay the expense of the trip.

January 6 Barlow and Eaton started back to Oregon City. A blinding snowstorm made their travel very difficult. At night their matches were wet, and they lighted the fire after several attempts with an old flintlock gun. They fired an old dead tree that illuminated the landscape enough to be able to find the strayed horses. They had left the best blankets with Berry, so the fire was essential to their staying alive that night.

They returned to Oregon City, comprised of a hundred houses, Methodist and Catholic Churches, two grist mills, two saw mills, four stores, two taverns, one hatter, one tannery, three tailors, two cabinet shops, two silversmiths, one cooper, two blacksmiths, one physician, three lawyers, a printing office, one lathe machine, a brick yard, an inoperative foundry. There were about 600 whites plus a few Indians. The aborigines spent most evenings gambling for high stakes, including possessions, wives, or even self-slavery, on a game centered in guessing in which hand the opponent had concealed a small bone.

Building lots sold from $100 to $500 each. Carpenters and masons were busy. William Barlow traded a $250 American filly for squatters rights on a section of land up the Clackamas River, hired a man, and went to work planting a peck of apple seeds he had brought over the plains and packed out from Fort Deposit. William was a very enterprising young man, and he lamented the $50,000 lost by virtue of bad advice given him at Independence Rock at Sweetwater in the Rockies, by a group of men, whom he thought included Jason Lee. Young Barlow was induced by their advice to dump 300 pounds of seedling apples and pears, set in dirt aboard his wagon. It turned out that there were no seedlings on the whole Pacific coast. Henderson Luelling (Lewelling), and his sons-in-law, William Meek and Henry W. Eddy compounded a large fortune out of just such a shipment of seedlings brought out by wagon train in 1847.

White River From Bridge

Samuel Barlow was a tired, beaten man during the last months of 1845. However, on his walk out through the Government Camp area and down Laurel Hill, he blazed the trees and noted where swamps must be corduroyed with strips of wood to make a passable road. When the territorial Assembly met in 1846, he presented a plan to build a toll road that would serve future wagon travellers. With Philip Foster as a partner he was granted a charter and made plans to open the road, as soon as melting snow would permit, from Foster's farm at Eagle Creek to Fort Deposit. A plea for subscriptions was circulated among the settlers, but only $30 was ever received.

The $4000 cost, which Barlow had originally budgeted, proved to be too low. There were more trees to cut, more swamp to corduroy, more grades to cut, more creek crossings to improve, than the 40-man crew could accomplish on that amount of money. Philip Foster had to approve a good many bills for supplies purchased on credit.

William Barlow was one of the men on the crew, for which his father paid him $400 at the end of the season. When they reached Fort Deposit, they found that William Berry had taken good care of the cache. Wagons and household goods were brought out in good order. William Barlow wanted the distinction of driving the first wagon down the new road, but Reuben Gant beat him to it, piloting the wagon of Carmi Goodrich.

Laurel Hill was the most dangerous stretch. Some wagon owners dismantled their wagons and slid the parts down the hill. Trees could be seen fifty years later with scarred bark, where other people had belayed wagons downward by ropes wrapped around tree trunks. When a rope broke, the result was a broken wagon at the bottom of the hill. A technique was developed of driving down in a zigzag path, dragging a 10-inch diameter tree, the branches pointed forward to increase friction. When a driver reached the bottom of the hill, he would find one of these logs blocking the road, where the previous inconsiderate driver had cut it loose. With black thoughts he would need to dismount and move the tree. Naturally, he would then cut his own tree loose for the next unfortunate driver to move.

Once the wagons were taken west from Fort Deposit, the crew was put to work on the eastern section. A toll gate was established at Gate Creek, about ten miles southwest of Tygh Valley, in a location providing grass, water, and wood. Tolls were $5 per wagon, ten cents for each loose animal. There was a certain amount of bartering and promises to pay later were common. At the end of the season Barlow reported the passage of 152 wagons, 1300 sheep, and 1559 mules, horses, and cattle. The improved road speeded travel substantially, Barlow and his son reaching Oregon City in only two days at the end of the season.

A certain amount of maintenance and improvement was done on the road, but its general character varied from rough to barely passable. A standard joke of the time noted that the toll gate was placed at Wamic where money could be collected before the immigrants were able to see the road. Samuel Barlow did most of the toll-collecting himself. He wanted only to get his money back, and in 1848 he leased it to other operators, two of whom were Philip Foster and Joseph Young. At times the road was allowed to regress to virtually impassable condition. Wagons and teams mired into the swamps, resulting in damaged cargo. Barlow was unable to collect on many of the promised payments, so he proved to be a loser on the project.

The toll road operated about 70 years. In 1858 Philip Foster, Samuel Hiple, Francis Revenue, and Stephen Coalman organized the Cascade Bridge and Toll Road Company. Revenue's 640 acre homestead lay on the location of the city of Sandy. He was an immigrant of 1850, and he ran a roadside trading post on his ranch, much the same as did Philip Foster at Eagle Creek. Coalman had arrived in Oregon City in 1852, having survived a precarious raft trip down the Columbia. He drifted to California and Southern Oregon in response to the gold fever, returning to a homestead between Sandy and Eagle Creek in 1858 with two or three thousand dollars in gold. In 1859 he sold and relocated on 160 acres at Cedar Creek, three miles east of Sandy. Coalman spent about 40 years with Barlow Road companies, overseeing the constant improvement and construction needed.

Oregon became a state in 1859, causing reincorporation of the road company as the Mount Hood and Barlow Toll Road Company. Rates were $2.50 per team, $1.25 per saddle horse, six cents for cattle, and four cents for sheep.

In October, 1862, the Mount Hood Wagon Road Company was capitalized at $25,000 to take over and reconstruct the primitive track. Probably lacking in success, this firm was superceded by Cascade Road and Bridge Company in May, 1864, incorporated by Joseph Young, Egbert Alcott, Stephen Coalman, Frederick Sievers, and Francis Revenue. Coalman, who had been superintendent since 1858, supervised extensive improvements in regrading, corduroying swamps, and straightening portions of road. During his 40 year administration, 25 bridges were built over streams, including one 110-foot covered structure over the Salmon River.

In 1882 the road was deeded to Mount Hood and Barlow Road Company, incorporated by Richard Gerder, Stephen Coalman, H.E. Cross, F.O. McGown, and J.T. Apperson. Still more improvement was needed and the Oak Grove Branch begun in 1896, a road that ran from Government Camp — down the Salmon River — up over the ridge near Frog Lake — Clear Lake — down Clear Creek — Camas Meadows, somewhat of a parallel to modern day Highway 26.

Over the years the Barlow road was changed and rechanged so many times, that no one really knows of all the variations. For a half century it was essentially a one-way road. Laurel Hill and Little Laurel Hill were too steep to ascend with a team. Early travellers told of the ruts on Laurel Hill worn down seven feet deep, with only the bare room for a wagon to scrape through. Great boulders in the track caused wagons to lurch at crazy angles from side to side as the desperate drivers fought to keep down the speed of the steep descent.

The toll gate was moved many times. It was located on Revenue's place from 1853-65, Summit House at Government Camp 1866-70, Two Mile Camp three miles east of Rhododendron 1871-78, and Toll Gate one mile east of Rhododendron 1879-1915.

Even after 1900 the road followed the ridge route from the rock corral on the north bank of the Sandy west of Brightwood, up through Marmot, and over the Devil's Backbone to Sandy River and the community of Sandy. East of Brightwood the older route, up the north bank of the Sandy River to the community of Zigzag, was superceded by a track on the south side of the Sandy River. From Zigzag it continued up to Rhododendron, following high ground to avoid swamps. East of Rhododendron it continued eastward on the north side of Camp Creek, then veering north to Little Zigzag River near Twin Bridges Camp and the foot of the Laurel Hill grade.

Today's wide, fast highway runs out of Sandy along the south bank of Sandy River, past Cherryville, through Alder Creek, now crossing a bridge over Salmon River that bypasses the old loop through Brightwood. Just how long travel has been made over this general route is not known for sure, but a story by Thomas J. Dryer in *The Oregonian* of August 6, 1859 gives a clue. Arriving at Sandy, they were told by John Revenue that they could take the "new trail on the south side of Sandy River and thereby avoid the danger and difficulty in crossing it twice." Dryer's party took the suggestion and "found a good trail, barring a few steep and narrow passes." Evidently the trail had been cut through since Dryer's trip of the previous year.

How long it took for the trail to become a road is not known. The old route across the Sandy River near Revenue's was bridged, and traffic rolled over the Marmot Hill in great amounts until after 1900. The old Cherryville Hill on the south bank route was quite an obstacle, and it probably was avoided in favor of the Marmot route by most wagon travellers.

1893 *The Oregonian* of October 17, tells of bridges being swept out by floods over Zigzag and Slate Creeks. The new bridge over the Salmon River was saved, but one side settled considerably. Loss of the bridges should not impair travel, as the early travellers had no bridges in pioneer days.

It was also in 1893 that President Grover Cleveland proclaimed the creation of the Cascade Range Forest Reserve on September 28. Many people had for years objected to paying tolls on the road, but Cleveland's action caused the battle to become heated, with William G. Steel and O.C. Yocum right in the middle of it. They seemed to ignore the fact that road companies had spent a great deal on bridges and cutting and grading; they could not forget the expense and indignity of the tolls.

The Oregonian of Monday, January 16, 1893 carried a letter to the editor from George W. McCoy. He implored that the State of Oregon and City of Portland take action to free the Barlow Road of tolls.

The Troutdale Champion began to promote the idea in its columns. On August 10, 1894, they printed "That toll gate is an outrage upon the public, and nothing but pure gall ever instituted and sustained the thing." The claim was that the Barlow Road ran over unsurveyed government land to which the Mt. Hood and Barlow Road Corporation could never secure a title. "The road is a public road and this company built a gate across it." They reported that W.G. Steel and O.C. Yocum paid for a legal opinion on it, and that Steel was preparing for a legal battle.

It was later reported that the road company gave Steel a pass to keep him quiet. This was refuted by Yocum in a letter from Government Camp date June 6, 1895. Yocum stated that Steel normally requested passage through the gate; if it were not granted, he knocked down a section of fence and went upon his way. Yocum's letter was accompanied by a long legal opinion from attorney J.H. Morrison of Portland, stating that the road company did not have any leases or agreements with any governmental body and were acting illegally.

On August 14, 1895 United States Attorney, Daniel R. Murphy, published in the newspapers a letter he had received from S.W. Lameoux, Land Commissioner of the general land office in the nation's capital. The right to collect tolls was upheld.

Steel took strong exception to this in a public letter of August 22. Two days later a stockholder of the road company rebutted Steel in another letter to *The Oregonian*. On September 4, attorney J.H. Morrison reiterated his stand that it was not legal to charge tolls on the road built over public land. Supreme Court decisions upheld the road company, and the tolls went on.

Shortly after 1900 Portland businessman E. Henry Wemme tried to purchase the Mount Hood and Barlow Road Company. The owners asked $35,000, and Wemme balked. The railroad along the Columbia had eroded the need of the Barlow Road. Wemme finally bought the road for $5,400 and in subsequent years spent $2,000 in improvement. In 1915 he opened the road to free travel, attempting several times to donate his rights to the State of Oregon. After Wemme's death in 1917, the road was willed to his attorney, George

W. Joseph. Joseph held it in trust until acceptance by Oregon State Highway Commission in 1919. A forest corridor in the Rhododendron-Zigzag area commemorates the public-spirited Wemme today.

The highway commission modernized the road for automobile travel from Foster Road to a point two miles east of Government Camp by 1920. Soon model-T Fords were carefully chugging up the formidable Laurel Hill. The Barlow Road had thus become a two way road, although wagon travel to Government Camp was an accomplished fact before the turn of the century.

In 1936 Francis E. Williamson of the Forest Service established some facts about the toll gates from Arlie E. Mitchell, who still lives at Faubion. He said one of the early toll gates was near Bull Run, then near Brightwood, and later at the site of Toll Gate Park on the eastern outskirts of Rhododendron.

A fire destroyed the first gate there. Then a log house was erected. The gatekeeper was John Maronay, who maintained a small trading post along with his toll-collecting duties. The term TOLL GATE meant just that. There was actually a gate in the fence across the road, and it was closed until the traveller paid his money.

In 1900 Arlie Mitchell helped haul timbers for a new building that butted up to the old log cabin. The log cabin was slowly dismantled piece-by-piece for firewood. In 1936 the new building still stood in all its dignity, although tolls had not been collected on the road since 1915. A large wooden gate framed Highway 26, a portal for each vehicle to cross.

Mitchell also said that a French-Canadian had started the Oak Grove Road as a competitor to the Barlow Road. It ran west from Blue Box Pass to Summit Meadow, thence down Still Creek to Rhododendron. The Mount Hood and Barlow Road Company then bought him out and abandoned the Still Creek road.

Loop Highway Finally Encircled Hood

COLUMBIA GORGE ROUTE

Early military officers of the United States Army recognized the value of a road down the Columbia from The Dalles to Portland. A six mile road was completed from Bonneville to Cascade Locks on February 9, 1856, being built over the rocky point west of Eagle Creek. It was operated as a portage road by W.R. Kilborn, who offered transportation with his wagons and teams at all times. On October 23, 1872, the Oregon Legislature appropriated $50,000 to build road from Sandy River to The Dalles. In October 1876, they granted another $50,000. When the Oregon Washington Railroad & Navigation company constructed rail grades in the gorge in 1883, the road was obliterated, with only traces visible in 1913.

March 25, 1910, the well-known E. Henry

Early tractor and grader 1922 — Photo USFS

Wemme and others petitioned Multnomah County to build road from Bridal Veil to the county line near Cascade Locks. On April 29, 1911, after surveys and reports were filed, the county crew built 1.8 miles east of Bridal Veil. Work came to a halt when the railroad objected to digging on hillsides above their tracks. Meanwhile Portland lumberman, Simon Benson entrusted Governor Oswald West with $10,000 to be used in building road at the base of Shell Mountain, a very difficult section. A high route on the shale slopes of this mountain, built in 1876 had been impossible to maintain. Hood River County administered the work made possible by the Benson funds and the use of prisoners from Oregon State Prison.

Lack of engineering skill and proper supervision caused most of the Benson donation to be wasted, however the project revived interest in communities along the way and stimulated authorities in Multnomah County to act. On July 26, 1913, Chairman of the Board of Commissioners, Rufus C. Holman presented a resolution which created the Advisory Board of Roads and Highways. On August 28 the Board of Commissioners hired Samuel Christopher Lancaster as Consulting Engineer. A road was planned 24-feet wide, extra wide curves, curves of at least 100 feet radius, and grades no more than five percent. Surveys were started in early September, and a construction camp placed at Multnomah Falls in October.

The newspapers gave the highway great publicity. Julius Meier headed the Columbia Highway Association. Simon Benson promoted interest in Hood River and gave great enthusiasm to the project. Meanwhile, a newly created Oregon State Highway Commission promoted uniform standards between the counties. John B. Yeon, wealthy lumberman from Portland, volunteered his time free of charge to running the large day-labor force spread up and down the Columbia in work camps. As Multnomah County Roadmaster, he and Lancaster managed completion on time. The paving contracts were let for $1,250,000, and the road was officially opened on July 6, 1915 from Portland to Hood River. On that day a motor party came through from Portland to Cloud Cap Inn. At Mount Hood Lodge, owner Homer Rogers noted that such notables as Simon Benson, John B. Yeon, Rufus Holman, Sam Hill had paused there on their trip.

Modern day travellers can still see signs of the old tunnels of the first highway at Mitchell Point, Eagle Creek, and Oneonta Gorge. The old road exists, virtually unchanged, from Troutdale to Dodson, passing some points near Crown Point, Shepherd's Dell, and Multnomah Falls, that are most picturesque and reminiscent of early days. The Vista House was begun on Crown Point in 1916, a memorial to the Pioneers.

Building road the hard way 1922 — Photo USFS

LOLO PASS ROUTE

With a road to Hood River, agitation became alive to connect Hood River and Government Camp. In 1859 Captain A. Walker had tried to enlarge the old Indian trail over Lolo Pass on the north side of Mount Hood. He had a gang of men working, but did not realize his dream to divert some of the business away from the Barlow Road. After the magnificent Columbia River Highway was completed in 1915, E. Henry Wemme stirred up interest sufficient to cause the Forest Service to survey and construct 3.5 miles of road toward Lolo Pass. A furor rose with the officials of Portland, who jealously guarded the Bull Run water reserve, which lies astride Lolo Pass area. Although water in this area drains into either Sandy River or Hood River, not the Bull Run water supply, the passage over it was fiercely contested for years.

The scope of some of this bitter controversy can be gleaned from the following chronological notes gleaned from historical files of the Forest Service;

December 16, 1910 Forest Supervisor Thomas Sherrard wrote to the District Forester, advocating a road over what is now called Lolo Pass, saying that the fire protection alone would be well worth the expense.

1911 80 men worked at cutting a trail six feet wide. $10,000 had been appropriated, and they worked about five miles in length.

July 20, 1912 T.J. Maupin, pipeline supervisor, wrote to Frank Dodge of the Portland Water Works, deploring the building of a road through the Bull Run Reserve.

July 22, 1912 Frank Dodge wrote a detailed letter to the Portland Water Board, asking that the road not be built. The claim was that it placed tourists dangerously close to the actual watershed boundary and increased the chance for fire to sweep Bull Run Reserve.

February 21, 1913 Thomas Sherrard again advocated the building of a road and the admittance of the public in a letter to the District Forester.

March 12, 1913 The Forester of the United States wrote N.J. Sinnott in the US House of Representatives, advocating the road.

March 9, 1914 The Forester, H.S. Graves, wrote to Johnathan Bourne, Jr., Senator, stating that the road would be a help in fire protection and would not menace the Bull Run Water Supply. However, he felt that limited funds made it advisable to drop the project.

November 12, 1921 District Forester Cecil wrote to the City of Portland, stating that he would back the act of April 28, 1904, which prohibited people from entering the Bull Run Reserve. He also noted that he was aware the city was considering use of water from Lost Lake and the Clear Fork of the Sandy River, which would definitely mean permanent closure to the public of the proposed road over Lolo Pass.

1935 A.O. Waha, Supervisor of MHNF announced that Lolo Pass Road would probably be finished by the end of the summer.

1951 By the end of the year, construction had been completed three quarters of the way to the pass.

1952 Parker-Schram Construction Company had cleared a strip 175-feet wide across 10 miles of the Lolo Pass area, preparing right-of-way for the new Bonneville Administration high voltage power line. The Lolo Pass Road was completed.

1953 Parker-Schram had completed the towers and strung the wire for the power line.

Sunday, October 10, 1954 The first public viewing of the road was arranged by the Hood River Chamber of Commerce. Forest Ranger Milton Andrews of Parkdale opened a locked gate to admit 118 automobiles from the Hood River side. Participants in the special caravan were registered by members of the Crag Rats, when they reached the summit of the pass.

Sunday, July 1, 1956 Lolo Pass Road was opened to free access by the public. A new surface had been applied, making the road much cleaner than it had been when the first caravan passed through in 1954.

TOLLS TO CLOUD CAP

The furor about tolls on the Barlow Road eventually spilled over into dissent about the road to Cloud Cap Inn. In July of 1912, J.C. Howland of Hood River wrote to the Secretary of the Interior, and F.X. Arens sent letters to the Forest Com-

FS Auto 1924 — Photo USFS
At Buzzard Point

missioner in Salem and Washington D.C.

They fell into the hands of the Assistant Forester, James B. Adams, who promised he would investigate. Inquiry was sent down the line from Washington to C.J. Buck, Regional Forester, then to Thomas Sherrard of MHNF. After much conferring, Buck wrote to Arens on September 5, telling him that the tolls were valid, because the road had been authorized as a toll road before 1906. This, however, opened a can of worms in that the tolls had not always been posted clearly on a public sign. There was much quibbling about the exact letter of the law, but the tolls stood. In 1925 the matter became an academic question, when the Forest Service built a new road up to Cloud Cap Inn from Cooper Spur Junction.

THE LOOP HIGHWAY

For several years men of the Forest Service, as well as many others, had discussed the idea of a highway from the Hood River Valley across the eastern slopes of Mount Hood to Government Camp. **Finally in 1915** a party of important officials was assembled to ride across the route and evaluate the problem of building such a road. The Forester of the United States, H.S. Graves, and T.S. Schuyler of the US Department of Highways and Public Roads were two top-level officials who gave the operation much promise.

Prominent in the party was Multnomah County Commissioner Rufus Holman, who had visited at Mount Hood Lodge in August of 1914. After being told that it would only take about 23 miles of road to complete the link, he became very interested and set a program of inquiry in motion. Others in the party were Mr. and Mrs. W.L. Clark, Mrs. Amelia Baker, C.A. Bell, Assistant District Forester Charles H. Flory, Supervisor of Oregon National Forest, Thomas H. Sherrard, Ranger Warren "Barney" Cooper, packer Dee Wright, Leslie Butler of the Oregon Highway Advisory Board, and Homer Rogers.

Not expecting such a large party, the Forest Service had told Dee Wright to bring only six saddle horses and two pack horses. The rest of the horses were furnished at no charge by Homer Rogers from his stable at Mount Hood Lodge. It is rather ironic that Rogers was so eager to see the highway loop an actuality, donating his time and resources to it, yet it was the creation of the highway that diminished his business and drove him into financial ruin a decade later.

The party rode out from Mount Hood Lodge on Thursday, June 24, 1915, making about 10 miles. Their route on the trail had been over Sand Canyon and Fall Creek to Elk Meadow. A beautiful camp at 4,000 feet, undoubtedly at Elk Meadow, gave them a fine base for enjoying the afternoon. Some rode up to the snow line at 6,600 feet. Friday morning they rode on to Government Camp, where they got automobile transportation back to Portland. Holman was enthusiastic about the prospects. The concensus of the officials in the party was that the road should cost about $60,000, and that construction problems would not be at all great.

Holman's idea took ahold so firmly that another trip followed on Thursday, August 12, this time attended by T. Warren Allen, Chief of National Parks and Forest Roads. Allen was amazed by the scenic beauty of the tour and

Bridge at Sahalie Falls under construction 1924 — Photo USFS

reinforced the previous pronouncements of the apparent of ease of construction of the proposed road. He guessed that maximum grade could be held at or under 5%.

The second trip was attended by T.J. Schuyler, B.J. Finch, highway engineer, Jacob Kanzler of Portland Chamber of Commerce, Congressman, C.N. McArthur, Judge M.C. George, Judge Gilbert, District Forester George H. Cecil, Thomas H. Sherrard, E.O. Blanchar, Trueman Butler, Homer Rogers and the distinguished writer from the *Oregon Journal*, Marshall N. Dana. Dee Wright, whom Dana described as the "most talkative government packer in the world," brought 28 horses to Mount Hood Lodge the day before the trip.

As an interesting sidelight, Dana described a little evening hike some of them made from the camp at Elk Meadows on Thursday. Walking to the ridge just east of the meadows, they could see down into the valley of the East Fork of Hood River. There below lay Horsethief Meadow, where horse thieves of the early times had corraled the stock stolen in eastern Oregon and planned for sale in the Willamette Valley. The log fence they had built was still standing at that time.

On Friday many of the group made the early morning ride up to Gnarl Ridge for some sight-seeing. After admiring that awesome view the party turned to the sport of rolling giant boulders down into Newton Canyon. Government officials, judges, and other grown men all joined in the effort to dislodge the great pieces of rock they sent bounding down the slope to smash into bits. This bit of boyish fun accomplished, they returned to Elk Meadow for a breakfast of boiled cabbage, fat bacon, potatoes, bread, and coffee seasoned with condensed milk.

Leaving Elk Meadow, they followed the trail down to Newton Creek and up the East Fork to Bennett Pass, White River, and Barlow Summit, where the Barlow Road took them in to Summit Meadow and Government Camp. Congressman McArthur was glowing over the possibility of the road, promising to do his best in Congress to secure the $75,000 needed. It had been previously proposed that the government authorize the highway money against anticipated timber sales income from the Oregon National Forest. When the trip was over, T.J. Schuyler and B.J. Finch began the detail survey at once.

When the highway was finally located, a lower route was chosen. From Cooper Spur Junction the route descended to the East Fork of Hood River at Polallie Creek, following up the East Fork Canyon to the flats that extend all the way to Hood River Meadows. James Schuyler of the Federal Bureau of Public Roads made the location survey after considerable discussion had been done on the general route. At one time there was serious consideration of running the highway atop Lookout Ridge to the east. In later years a fire protection service road was placed there.

The canyon of the East Fork offered a lot of problems in blasting away cliffs and bridging the twisting stream many times. Governor of Oregon, James Withcomb signed an application for federal financial aid on the road, the first for any Oregon project. Various sections of road were awarded to different contractors. The section from Hood River Meadows to White River was done by Doggett and Davis. Much work was done by hand or with horse teams pulling scoops, as the day of heavy construction machinery had not yet arrived.

The work progressed between the years of 1920 to 1925 when it was finally opened to through travel on June 21. The opening brought great caravans of tourists from Portland, thrilled with the mountain scenery as they passed Hood River Meadows, Sahalie Falls, and over the summit of 4674' Bennett Pass down to the awesome canyon of White River.

White River and its glacier above, form a great gash right up to the base of Crater Rock near the summit of Mount Hood. The view from the bridge is impressive, with tremendous moraines filling the valley floor, the graceful sweep of the south slope of the mountain, and the towering majesty of its summit.

At Barlow Pass, the automobile highway followed Barlow's route to Buzzard Point, where tourists usually stopped to view Mount Hood across the Salmon River Valley. Hairpin turns then descended to the flats where Loop Highway 35 joins present-day Highway 26 to central Oregon. Then, going on to join the road built by the Oregon Highway Commission in 1919 through Government Camp, the full circuit was opened.

Sunday, October 19, 1924 W.B. Van Duzer of the Oregon State Highway Commission made public the road costs, as told in the *Oregon Journal.*

From the Clackamas-Multnomah County line to the Forest Service boundary, the State of Oregon spent $237,669, Multnomah County $170,000, and Clackamas County $62,735. The Loop Highway inside Forest Service land cost Oregon $461,584, and United States Government $467,352. The section of road from Hood River to the Forest Service boundary cost Oregon $315,744 and Hood River County $271,392.

In the same account newspaper reporter, Ernest W. Peterson told of a trip in an *Oregon Journal* automobile, made by special permission around the new Loop Highway. The White River Bridge had already been damaged by the flood that had followed the severe electric storm of September 7.

Homer Rogers' automobile ready to descend Laurel Hill 1925 — Photo Homer Rogers

ALL-WINTER ROADS

Opening of the loop road in 1925 created a demand in Government Camp to keep the road clear of snow from there to Portland in wintertime. The key figures in this drama were two millionaire lumbermen, E.S. Collins and Van Deuser, and the owner of Battle Axe Inn, Everett Sickler. Van Deuser was the head of the Oregon State Highway Commission, uninterested in the winter sports problems at Mount Hood. Collins, a well-known philanthropist, owned land between Government Camp and Multorpor on which he made experiments on the husbandry of foreign species of trees. He often came to the mountain after church on Sunday, out with his wife for a drive in his old clothes. Tall and thin, he would not be taken for a wealthy man by those who saw his rangy attire and thick, wooden-soled shoes normally used by farmhands in cleaning out a cattle barn. To wipe his nose he took opposite corners of a bandana handkerchief between his two hands and pulled it across his nostrils.

Collins always came to Battle Axe Inn to spend 50¢ for a pie. Sickler let him know on several occasions that a clear road would bring a lot of skiers to Government Camp, and Collins was very sympathetic to the idea. He advised Sickler to attend the commission meeting on July 16, 1926, over which Van Deuser presided. The result was an emphatic NO, and Sickler left the meeting on that hottest day of the year a beaten man. Even the red-headed stenographer at the meeting had turned to him and laughed derisively.

But back at Collins' office a few days later, the story turned for Sickler. He related his experience in the Highway Commission meeting, and Collins said, "I think I ought to give Mr. Van Deuser a phone call. You get on the extension phone, but don't say anything."

"Hello, Van," he began, "I understand your commission hadn't decided to plow out the road up toward Government Camp."

"Yes, that's right, Mr. Collins," Van Deuser replied. "We figured that it wasn't justified to just keep it open for pleasure use."

"Well now, Van, don't you think that it would be very beneficial to open up that area in the winter? You know, there are a lot of skiers would like to drive up there, if they could."

Evidently Collins packed quite a lot of influence, because with just a few softly-spoken words, he set Van Deuser to thinking. In a few days it was announced that the road would be kept open for the winter of 1926-27. The first snowplow was a World War One caterpillar with a vee blade in front. It did well in light snows, but in snow-paks over three feet deep it bored in to a complete stop, then started to crawl off to the side of the road.

Starting the tractor in cold weather was a terrible problem. Highway foreman Fred Stultz and his crew spent many an hour building fires under the machine until it became warm enough to start. On many days it was two in the afternoon before the engine would turn over. When the first rotary plow was brought to Government Camp in 1927, the whole picture changed, and skiers could depend on an open road.

A CLASSIC TEST FOR AUTOMOBILES

In September of 1924 Howard M. Covey drove a stock model, six Cylinder Chrysler touring car from Mount Hood Lodge to Cloud Cap Inn in 29 minutes. Taking an automobile up the 6.5-mile road, a rise of 3,180 feet over boulders, roots, ruts, and chuckholes, was used heavily in advertising the merits of Chrysler to the public. The race against time was carefully clocked with a stopwatch. L.H. Rogers, Homer Rogers' father, was the official starter.

Another company met the challenge immediately, dropping the time to 22 minutes. There was strict compliance with the rules, that the automobile must be a stock model with no alterations, and that at least three people must be aboard. Covey returned with his Chrysler to run the 6.5 miles in 21 minutes. The competition then cut the time to 20 minutes and 3 seconds, whereupon Covey reappeared for a run of 18 minutes and 46 seconds.

This activity had taken place on every week of the autumn, until Wednesday, October 8, when W.R. "Dick" Fenton came up in a Buick six-cylinder. Despite a blinding snow storm that had laid three inches of new cover on the road, Fenton roared up from Mount Hood Lodge in 14 minutes and 40 seconds. Using tire chains to combat the snow and slush, he reached a top speed in one stretch of 46 miles per hour, using second and low gears. On one culvert the Buick bounced and left the ground for 20 feet.

The course was beginning to be considered as a classic, such as Pike's Peak in Colorado. The next year the Forest Service built the new road from Cooper Spur Junction to Cloud Cap Inn and the old road began to pass into oblivion.

APPROACHING SOUTH SIDE BY AUTO

1904 Dr. C.B. Brown made an attempt to reach timberline by automobile up the crude dirt track from Government Camp. He was able to get within two miles before conditions became insurmountable. The trip with his son, Hoyt, his brother, J.M. Brown, and Dr. F.M. Yates, began at 6:00 a.m. one Wednesday morning in Portland. It was 5:00 p.m., before they had reached the high point of their automobile trip.

On Thursday, they climbed Mount Hood. On Friday, they drove home, being met by J.D. Kelley in his car at Pleasant Home. Dr. Brown's car, a White, which he nicknamed Samantha, was probably the first to penetrate the track toward timberline.

Snowplow of 1930 era — Photo Alice Harris

Parking soon became a terrible problem. The advent of the rotary plow helped considerably, but the road was narrow, a severely congested area to through traffic. The following summer, the highway department began shoving gravel into all the possible areas alongside the road to widen it for parking. Collins at one time suggested to Sickler that they lay steam pipes under the parking areas to keep them free of snow. This was an idea that never did get any further attention.

ROAD TO LARCH MOUNTAIN

A little section of Mount Hood National Forest that is dear to the hearts of so many Oregonians is Larch Mountain. Just before World War One, a trail was opened, which became the target of many hikes by The Mazamas and Trails Club. In 1933 a road was begun. It took several years to complete it. On August 3, 1939, the finished highway was opened to the public. The rocky pinnacle of Larch Mountain was named Sherrard Point in honor of Thomas H. Sherrard, Supervisor of MHNF from 1907 to 1934.

STRAIGHTENING THE LOOP

Proud Oregonians toured the twisting loop highway for years. After World War 2 the East Fork of Hood River was relocated in the canyon above Polallie Creek, eliminating many bridges and dozens of tortuous curves. A new road below Polallie Creek was constructed down the canyon, eliminating the climb over the ridge to Cooper Spur Junction. Hood River Meadows and Sahalie Falls were bypassed, becoming sideroad attractions known to only a few.

Construction in 1967 of the massive Mount Hood Ski Resort northwest of Umbrella Falls on the headwaters of East Fork caused rerouting of the road as a superhighway. The old Barlow Road section across Buzzard Point was eliminated, and a costly, new stretch was blasted out to contour the steep hillside, approaching Barlow Pass from the north. This allowed all-year travel around the loop as well as access to the two-mile highway leading up to Mt. Hood Meadows Ski Resort from Bennett Pass.

On the Columbia River Highway, now Interstate 80N, superhighway all the way, now follows a route as close to water level as possible. Springdale, Corbett, Crown Point, Latourell, Bridal Veil, Multnomah Falls, Horsetail Falls, and Dodson have all been relegated to scenic road status, the new highway beginning to follow the old at McCord Creek. The water-level route, requiring tremendous earth fills, was begun in 1947. In 1949 it was dedicated, taking the fast through-traffic away from the scenic stretches. In 1950, the new section between Dodson and Bonneville was completed.

Later development bypassed the town of Cascade Locks and the curves around Mitchell Point. In the Hood River Valley the old loop up from Parkdale to Cooper Spur Junction was bypassed with a new section of road following directly up the East Fork of Hood River.

It was in the autumn of 1949 that the new highway across the Warm Springs Indian Reservation was dedicated, saving 33 miles to Madras. A ceremony was held at the Mill Creek Bridge. The following year the road was open to traffic.

In August of 1949 the new highway to Timberline Lodge was opened, cutting out the old steep section above the Timberline Garage, which later became Snowbunny Lodge. The State of Oregon then took over the job of snow removal to Timberline from the Forest Service.

In 1951 a new bridge was built over the White River. At Government Camp a new maintenance complex was begun by the Oregon State Highway Department on the south side of Highway 26 at the junction to Timberline Lodge. The old station at the curve in Government Camp had proved inadequate. The new complex was ready to use in 1952.

Also in 1952 Mile Bridge was eliminated, a narrow structure across the Zigzag just east of Toll Gate Camp, that had slowed traffic and menaced drivers for so many years. At the same time the famous Twin Bridges were eliminated on the Zigzag River at Twin Bridges Camp.

In 1953 Rogers Construction Company was awarded the contract to reroute the highway directly from Zigzag to Rhododendron. Clearing across the swampy area was made, and in the next year the road was built. This eliminated a good deal of winding road between the two communities and included a wide, new bridge at the west end of Rhododendron.

In 1956 funds were released for massive changes west of Government Camp. A bypass around the community was completed the next year, eliminating the need for all of the through traffic to inch through the confusion on the main street caused by skiers, stalled automobiles, dogs, and crowds of pedestrians. Also in 1957 work was begun on a new stretch of road that eliminated the tight loops of Laurel Hill. Great cuts in solid rock followed up the north side of the valley of Camp Creek. Cuts and deep fills created a highway with a gentle grade all the way down to the valley floor.

The old highway up to Twin Bridges Camp, Barlow Campground, and Kiwanis camp, is now merely a dead-end stub road.

From Wemme the highway going west has been rerouted, eliminating hundreds of curves. A large new bridge across Salmon River speeds the motorist along a freeway that eliminates the loop through Brightwood. West of Alder Creek a bold cut takes the highway west-southwest, eliminating old road through Cherryville. Sandy is linked directly to Gresham, avoiding the old landmark communities of Orient and Kelso.

Rails to Mount Hood

1892, July 25 The *Oregon Oracle* monthly extolled the value of a railroad to timberline, where hotels could be built. The editorial exhorted the participation by financiers such as Ladd, Failing, Corbett, and Lewis, assuring that they would find themselves owners of a gold mine.

The *Evening Telegram* of Tuesday, November 15, 1892, gave a communication from W.G. Steel that he had incorporated the Single-Rail & Saddle-Truck Railway Company, or the Bicycle Road Company, and that the stock books would be opened in a few days. The company proposed to build a rail line to Mount Hood for $13,250 per mile. The Bicycle Company had subscribed $375,000, and there were $200,000 cash subscriptions. Only $270,000 of the estimated $845,000 cost was left to be raised.

The *Evening Telegram* reported the next day of the presentation of the plan in full to the Chamber of Commerce.

December 4, 1892 *The Oregonian* told of Steel's great plans and noted that a rail line would be built to Government Camp. A cog railway would thence proceed to Crater Rock, placing prospective climbers only a thousand feet from the summit.

December 13, 1892 *The Oregonian* reported that the Chamber of Commerce considered a railroad of great value, and that the committee would continue the idea.

March 20, 1893 *The Oregonian* noted that a rail line might be laid parallel to the Bull Run Pipe Line. Lee Hoffman, who was in charge of laying a new pipeline, stated in favor of a rail system to carry the 80,000 tons of pipe, fittings, brick, and supplies. Line had been surveyed and right-of-way secured for some distance out of town, but the terminus remained unknown.

July 30, 1893 *The Oregonian* told of the interest in the rail line by farmers. The rail line would use a saddle-track engine running over a standard gauge system with a track in the center elevated two inches. The drive wheel bears on the center rail.

A Wasco County paper reported that an engineer with four years of construction experience on the Denver and Rio Grande Railroad estimated a rail line could be built from Portland to White River Falls for $8000 per mile. The opening up of commerce through the timber and wheat country was stressed. This would place rail service within three miles of the Deschutes River.

July 20, 1893 *The Oregonian* mentioned considerable agitation in favor of a railroad in Damascus and Sunnyside, with public meetings scheduled by the promoters to get subsidy from local residents. Five days later the story was told of the meeting and the presentation by Dr. J.B. Mehanna, president of the rail company. Local people at Sunnyside elected Seth Johnson, president and ________________ Randall, secretary of a group favoring support of the project. Locals expressed willingness to contribute to a rail system, largely in land.

July 7, 1893 *The Telegram* editorialized that the Union Pacific would do better to reroute its line over the south side of Mount Hood, because the Columbia River route is proving too expensive to maintain. This was evidenced by recent washout of trackage.

June 17, 1893 *The Oregonian* however felt that the water level grade along the Columbia, although not profitable, was the only feasible route, and that capital could not be secured to pay for a massive rerouting of the railroad.

August 7, 1897 H.L. Johnson of Mount Scott, who had been working to raise funds for the railroad, announced that he had decided to give up the scheme for the present.

July 10, 1899 *The Oregonian* ran a story by E.G. Jones outlining the practicability of a railroad to Mount Hood and of all the alluring area it would open up to tourists.

July 12, 1899 A letter from W.W. Baker asked some pertinent questions, questioning Jones on some indefinite statements. Jones came back the next day with an enthusiastic reply. A man who signed himself "A Railroad Builder" also replied, stating that no road could be built for less than $18,000 per mile. He did not oppose the building of a rail line, merely set the thinking straight on costs. Two more articles followed shortly, outlining the fine points concerning routes and financial feasibility.

1904 An electric power plant near Bull Run was planned. Water from Badger Creek would give enough power to operate a rail line to Mount Hood. The project of Miller and Miller was planned for completion in time for the 1905 Lewis and Clark Exposition.

1906 The Portland and Mount Hood Railway proposed a franchise for a 46-mile line to Mount Hood costing about $500,000. At Mount Hood would be a 200-room hotel and a 600-room sanatarium. The spokesman for eastern financiers was Dr. Milton G. McCorkle, who said work would start in 1907. He had surveyors looking for a 3% grade, although they had already found a 4% grade that he believed to be too steep.

Meanwhile on the Hood River side, promoters were telling of proposed rail line on the north side.

Rails to Mount Hood was an idea never achieved, despite the tremendous promotion put behind it for so many years. The closest to the mountain that the railroad ever came was to Parkdale in the Upper Hood River Valley. The line was heavily used. In addition to regular train schedules, passengers were also hauled on a rail bus, built to haul 26 people on a White two-ton chassis. It was sent to Hood River on February 19, 1917, to be placed into duty. The few days previous to that, it had been on public display in Portland at the corner of 4th and Stark.

The first rail bus had been put into use only a year earlier on May 1, 1916, to augment regular train service. It was a once-a-day schedule, leaving Parkdale each morning at 7:45, and departing from Hood River at 4:30 p.m. Local residents often referred to the rail bus as the "jitney."

The vast schemes to run a rail line to Government Camp never did materialize in anything closer than a line to Bull Run. As many as 10,000 Portland people often visited Bull Run on a busy day to picnic, swim, and dance. Most of them rode on the rail line that was put in about 1911. Before that time, the closest rail connections were to Pleasant Home or Boring, just after the turn of the century.

A 125-acre park at the confluence of the Sandy and Bull Run Rivers was later given status as Portland city park. The rail lines were eventually removed, and today there is little indication of the Coney Island setting once enjoyed by Bull Run. Gresham is now the eastern terminus of the line. Another line runs out to the Boring area. No doubt some planners have given some thought to the feasibility of a rail system to present-day Mount Hood.

Government Camp, Hood's Only Town

In May, 1845 the United States Congress appropriated $75,500.00 to mount and equip an army regiment to establish posts along the Oregon Trail. It was later decided to divert the effort to the Mexican war. In 1849 Lieutenant William Frost brought an immense wagon train through from Fort Leavenworth, Kansas. 429 wagons, drawn by 1716 mules arrived at Fort Dalles with 250 tons of freight. A part of this contingent travelled by boat to Vancouver, as planned. While the rest were waiting for available boats, someone up high in command decided to send the remainder up over the Barlow Road to Oregon City.

Mules, in poor condition, were pulling heavily overloaded wagons. Many literally starved on their trek over the Barlow Road. As usual, it was late in the fall, with winter threatening. About 45 wagons had to be abandoned, before the train descended Laurel Hill. Wagon parts have been noted near Government Camp. For many years the vicinity was known as the government camp on Camp Creek. Later, capitalizing of the names indicated that the title Government Camp had gained full acceptance.

The meadows along Camp Creek had always been a camping place for some of the early travellers. However, for most of the immigrants along the Barlow Road the favorite spot was Summit Meadows, along Still Creek to the SE of Multorpor Mountain. After the long pull up the White River and Barlow Creek to Barlow Pass, this lovely, open meadow was a very welcome sight to tired travellers, with streams of cold, clear water coming right from the side of Mount Hood. Shrubs, brilliant gold and red in the autumn sun, and pointed alpine trees, lend the beauty of nature's landscape. What a wonderful contrast this was to the hundreds of miles of sun-baked, wind-blown rock and grit east of the Cascades. Many immigrants continued to return to Summit Meadows after they had established homes in the Willamette Valley.

An actual community was not developed until the advent of O.C. Yocum, Francis C. Little, and William G. Steel, all of whom filed for homestead rights. Some immigrant and climbing parties had camped there, but most travellers used Summit Meadow.

Most of the history of the Government Camp area is covered in other chapters. However, some of the present day individuals and institutions should be mentioned.

Charles F. Sperr (pronounced speer) and his wife, Jeanine, entered the scene in 1955, when they bought one of the buildings of the Wy'east Cabins, a motel that was removed on the east end of the community, because of the building of the bypass highway. They moved the structure to the Camp Creek Road on the north side of the village and held possession of it until 1963.

In 1963 Sperr bought Ole Langerud's ski shop building, which had once housed the Hjalmar Hvam business. On the top they maintained apartments. The ski shop on the second floor was maintained for a year or two, then leased out to another operator. On the bottom floor they established the Ratskeller, serving beer and light food.

In 1969 Charlie Sperr left Government Camp to establish Ratskeller West at Cannon Beach. In 1971 the couple were divorced, with Jeanine staying on as the owner of the Ratskeller in Government Camp until 1972. Charlie then opened the

Inn-Between at Wemme, selling it in early November of 1973. He then returned to Government Camp to open up Charlie's Place at Thunderhead Lodge later that same month.

In 1964 Sperr entered into a business arrangement with Robert Finn to buy the old 160-acre Meldrum homestead at Salmon River Meadows on Highway 26, two miles south of the junction with Highway 35. In 1964 a Union-76 gasoline station was built on the east side of Highway 26, on the lower slopes of Bird Butte. On the west side of the highway they platted a residential area, Salmon River Meadows. In 1972 Sperr sold his interest. A number of lots have been sold, and Finn is keeping roads clear in the winter with his own snow plow.

Finn is a contractor in the Government Camp area, owning dirt moving equipment, as well as two large rotary snow plows.

OLE LANGERUD RAN A SKI SHOP

Ole Langerud was born June 21, 1896 at Rollag, a community near Kongsberg, Norway. In 1923 he tried his luck in the Americas by moving to Vancouver, British Columbia, to work in the timber industry. In 1926 he came to Oregon, working as a timber faller.

One of the early ski jumpers at Mount Hood, Langerud did most of the work at the jumping hill at Swim, where the Viking Ski Club and Mount Hood Ski Club first competed. When activity at Swim dissolved, he became active with Cascade Ski Club on the early Multorpor jump hill.

In the Thirties, Langerud was one of the better known skiing personalities at Mount Hood. Much of that time he worked for the Oregon State Highway Department, living in Government Camp.

In 1938 he erected the large building now occupied by the Ratskeller, operating in partnership with Hjalmar Hvam until the years of World War Two. During the war he operated alone, and then Hvam returned. The partnership flourished until 1949, when Hvam retired from Government Camp to pay greater attention to his business in Portland.

When Langerud built the structure, a New York engineer, Carl Lans, happened to be visiting in Government Camp. Lans had been designing irrigation layout near Madras at the time, and was attracted by the Norwegian names of Hvam and Langerud. Before he left, Lans helped Langerud with the engineering on the roof structure of the building.

From 1949 to 1963, he operated the ski shop alone, selling out in 1963 to Charles and Jeanine Sperr, who changed the building into a beer-dispensing night spot, the Ratskeller. Sperrs separated in 1968, and Jeanine stayed on as the operator of the Ratskeller. She sold it to Denny and Susan Reese in 1972.

Langerud has stayed with skiing despite his years. In 1973 he broke ribs in an accident, and in February of 1975 he spent a night in the Gresham Hospital with a dislocated left shoulder. In February of 1974 he was chosen to Skiyente Ski Club for a one-year reign as King Winter. He made trips to Norway in the summers of 1973 and 1974. His home for some time has been in a mobile home at Cooks Motel on the Salmon River near Brightwood.

Government Camp 1892

BOYD FRENCH, SR.

One of the first men in the ski business at Mount Hood was Boyd French, born 1888 at Cashmere, Washington, a community near the skiing town of Leavenworth. French earned an engineering degree at University of Washington and worked as a designer at Boeing for a time. The struggling Boeing company wanted to pay him in stock, and he moved to Oregon.

In the early Thirties, he managed the ski shop at Battle Axe Inn for the Villigers on weekends. Although not a competitive skier, he was one of the first men to bring the Arlberg technique of turning to Oregon, a method that revolutionized sport skiing as well as making possible the previously unknown slalom events. French often acted as course prover for ski races.

French and some of his friends were the forerunners of the Ski Patrol, directing rescue operations for at least a half-dozen years before the patrol was formed. On many Sunday afternoons an excited skier would burst into the ski shop at Battle Axe with the news that his friend lay up on the trail with a broken leg. French became the coordinator for the rescue activity, operating what might be called a defacto ski patrol.

He moved from Portland to Mount Hood in about 1936 with his wife, LaRue, and their children Donald, Richard, Boyd, Jr., and Margie. Life was not easy for the family in the following years. Some summers he spent as operator of Cloud Cap Inn. One summer he operated the curio shop at White River. Winters were spent at Government Camp in the ski business. In 1938, when Hjalmar Hvam moved from the Ski Pole to Ole Langerud's big building on the north side of the street, French took over the building, running a ski rental business and living upstairs. (The Ski Pole was the original Latourette structure of 1934, later bought and enlarged by Darr.)

He was in on the construction of the rope tow at the Ski Bowl in 1936, also in erecting the ski lift at the Bowl a decade later. He ran the ski shop at Timberline Lodge for a year, shortly after it opened.

At least two of the sons were prominent competitive skiers, Boyd, Jr. and Donald. They, along with Richard, all went into the 10th Mountain Division during World War Two. Daughter Margie married James Simmons, prominent in the Ski Patrol. Boyd, Sr. left the hard life of the mountain with advent of World War Two. He moved to Portland and worked as an engineer for Timber Structures through the Sixties. He died in 1973.

THE RAFFERTY FAMILY

John Valentine "Jack" Rafferty was born in Michigan on February 14, 1874, and spent his youth near Grand Rapids until 1906, when he was 34. On February 20th of that year, he married Anna Riely, and the same day left for Oregon. For about two years he worked in the shipping department of Meier and Frank, and Olds-Wortman & King. He then started a truck line and took mail hauling contracts with the US Post Office, at one time running 10 large mail trucks. His son, John Vincent Rafferty was born in 1910, always going by the name of Vince or Vincent.

In 1923, the family moved to Government Camp, where Jack leased Government Camp Hotel from the Latourette family. He became very popular with his clientele, being noted for

Government Camp 1946 — Photo USFS

his concern for the safety of the skiers and climbers who came through the village. A news story in the *Oregon Journal* in 1928 mentioned that Rafferty never went to bed until he had accounted for the last guest. He rented rooms to hundreds of climbers, but he never did climb the mountain, himself. A trip to Crater Rock was the peak of his effort in that sport.

It was on Friday, November 19, 1926, that 18 inches of snow dumped onto the Loop Highway, stalling a Tyrell sightseeing bus, just west of Bennett Pass. The driver was not carrying chains, and terror began to set in with the tourists who filled the bus.

Although he was lightly clad, one of the passengers, Ivan F. Simpson, an actor at the Heilig Theater, walked the 11 miles to Government Camp for help. Rafferty answered the call, making three trips in his auto to evacuate the stranded travellers. The last load reached Government Camp Hotel at 1:30 a.m. on Saturday.

When skiing became extremely popular in 1928 and after, he was often host to groups who were staging awards banquets. Feeling great hope for the community, he did extensive remodelling in the early Thirties to the hotel, which he had bought by that time. This was followed by the disappointment of the hotel being destroyed by a fire in 1933.

But Rafferty was resolved to stay in Government Camp, and he made arrangements with Mrs. Little to take over her home and convert it to a hotel. He stayed in business there, until his health failed in 1940, and he moved to 8949 NE Wygant Street in Portland. He died there July 1, 1943.

Vincent married Lois Beers in 1939. When his father died, he left Government Camp to work at driving truck. In about 1948 he and Lois returned to the village to lease Hill's Place. Fire plagued him, during the two and a half years of his lease. In 1950, the fire that destroyed Battle Axe Inn, did a lot of damage to Hill's Place. Shortly afterward, Hill's again caught fire, doing great loss. The Raffertys left Government Camp and moved to Sandy. Not long afterward, Vincent sold the water company to Maryanne Hill, severing all his ties at the mountain. He and Lois were divorced about 1957. At present he is managing an apartment house in Portland.

John Rafferty's widow, Anna, died in about 1965.

HILL'S PLACE

Charles Leslie Hill was born in Missouri in 1884. He moved to California to work for the Crane Plumbing Company and played some professional football in those early times. Returning to the Midwest, he owned a laundry and cleaning business in Alliance, Nebraska.

His wife's parents moved to Forest Grove, Oregon, and Hill moved his family to that area in about 1923, locating on a chicken ranch on Gales Creek. Hill sold the chicken ranch and ran a gasoline station in Forest Grove for several years, acquiring property for rentals on the side. The crash of 1929 broke him, and he lost all he had. During the years between 1924 and 1929, he spent many summer vacations at Swim, where Boyd Summers had built a store and cottages in 1926.

He sold automobiles in Hillsboro at times, and in the summers came to Government Camp, where he ran a soft-drink and knick-knack stand. At one time his stand was in front of the present Cascade Ski Club, and later he built one on the south side of the street, across from Battle Axe Inn. To lure customers inside, he had a telescope that tourists could use FREE to look at Mount Hood.

By 1932 he had done well enough to erect Hill's Place, a large wooden building which stood across from Battle Axe, the present site of Huckleberry Inn. He and the family operated the cafe for many years, living in the upstairs section.

The Thirties were rough, tough days in Government Camp. Hill was pretty tough, himself, and so was his counterman, Gary Leech. In those times it was illegal to sell beer to Indians. One day an Indian from Warm Springs sidled up to another customer, a man of slight build, and asked him to buy a beer for him. The customer refused, and the Indian backed him into a corner, becoming belligerent. Gary Leech shoved one of his long legs over the counter, followed by the other. He gave the Indian a punch with his fist, then threw him out the door into the parking lot.

The state highway crew had a lot of rough characters in it. One evening, Gary Leech got mixed up with one of them in a fight, Virgil Gill. The battle was going quite evenly in the street in front of Hill's Place, until Gary slipped on the icy surface and fell to the ground. Gill took his advantage and jumped on Leech, breaking his leg and ending the fight.

On another occasion, Charlie Hill was tending the counter one night, when a bus load of drunken Indians from a CCC camp unloaded in front of the cafe. They came in and began to advance on Hill, taking candy and groceries off the shelf. He held them off with a knife, while he backed into the kitchen for his shotgun. Firing one barrel into the ceiling slowed them down, and he convinced them that they should go out the door and leave. His daughter, Maryanne, was asleep in the room just above the blast, but she slept right through the fracas. The hole remained in the ceiling for some time.

Maryanne Hill, born in 1921, went to Grant High School in Portland, graduating in January of 1940. In her senior year she was a princess and contender for Queen of the Annual Portland Winter Sports Festival at Mount Hood. As a result, she received a trip to Mexico City in 1939.

Charlie and Sally Hill after 1951 fire — Photo Maryanne Hill

Growing up in Government Camp, Maryanne became a very proficient contender in ski racing, and later a founder of Skiyente Ski Club. Her college days were spent at Pacific University, where she received her Bachelor of Science degree in Health and Physical Education.

Charlie Hill and his wife were divorced in 1940. In about 1942 he married Salina "Sally" Fox Hill, who is still living. He acquired a cattle ranch near Tumalo, Oregon, where he spent a little time during the war years, when Hill's Place was occasionaly closed. It is said that the ranch enabled him to maintain a supply of meat at the restaurant, when supplies were short during the war.

Fire was always a problem in the restaurants at Government Camp. Maryanne Hill can recall helping her father douse a chimney fire. She handed him buckets of water as he stood and sloshed out the flames. On November 7, 1950, Battle Axe Inn burned across the street. The front of Hill's Place was charred badly, windows knocked out with heat, and upholstery burned on the booths. Vincent Rafferty was leasing Hill's at the time.

BUILDING ALMOST BURNED IN 1951

On Tuesday, March 20, 1951, flames from grease on the stove were sucked into the exhaust fan about 4:25 p.m., and the building was set afire. Flames gained headway, despite the efforts of about 200 skiers and local residents. Two pumpers came up from Zigzag, and two fire trucks from Sandy took 33 minutes to reach the scene. Five hundred feet of fire hose was run to Darr's but a broken water pipe in the community caused low water pressure. Firefighters were helped to quite an extent, by the two feet of snow that lay on the roof.

Shortly afterward, Everett and Irene Worthington took over the business, and later on Charlie Hill was back running the place, himself. In October of 1955 he entered the hospital for serious surgery. From that time on he remained in deteriorating health, experiencing at one time a heart attack, and finally dying from failure of the circulatory system on January 25, 1956.

Maryanne had married Charles Lawton in 1949, having one child, Lesli Ann. The Lawtons were later divorced, and in 1959 she married James Parker, who had been an employee of Marchx Bakery in Gresham. She bought Hill's Place from her step-mother, Sally, in 1961. It was under lease at the time to Bill and Frances Adams, but Maryanne had owned the place only about three months, when Mrs. Adams concluded she could not keep up with the work any longer, and they quit.

Maryanne took over management of the place at times. At one time she planned to lease it to Buster Dunbar, but the deal fell through. W.L. "Dub" Rogers and his wife, Violet, took it over for about five years. When their lease was concluded, Maryanne decided not to renew with them. Hugh Carrins ran it for a few months, followed by Marjorie Lambert, who hired an operator to conduct the business. In May of 1969, Maryanne took over the business and was making some improvements. She had moved the rest rooms from the end of the hall in the southwest end of the building in 1961 to a place nearer the door. Decorating and work upstairs was in progress, when the last fire occurred.

On June 26, 1969, Frank Lieful was working the hoot-owl shift, when he smelled smoke about 2:00 a.m. Going to the beer and wine storage room on the west end of the building, he opened the door to find a fire working up the stairway. He ran for a large extinguisher in the kitchen, and just about had the fire out. He ran for the second one, but when he got back, the flames were just as far advanced as when he first found them. If Lieful had only known, there was a 1½ inch hose connected to a 2-inch standpipe, not over 15 feet from the fire, but by the time help arrived, that source of water had been overrun by the fire.

The problem then was to get the people out of the building, while men of the village fought fire for several hours. Hill's Place was burned to the ground, along with one nearby cabin and the old post office, which had been converted into a tool shed. Cause of the fire has been surmised to have been started in the electrical wiring of the beer cooler. A workman from Meadowland Dairy had just serviced it a few days previously.

Although Maryanne Hill taught school for several years, two years at Kalama, two years at Milwaukie, and 8½ at Lincoln High, she has now become a permanent resident of Government Camp. She and James Parker have been divorced, and she took back her original name. She is at present active in local affairs, as well as owning the water company and serving as a director of the Government Camp Sanitary District.

ROGERS JUMPED ACROSS THE STREET

The Huckleberry Inn was started by Dub Rogers in about 1966, when his lease was terminated at Hill's Place. He also acquired the motel built by the Hughes family, Raymond M. "Bill" Hughes, his wife Olga, and their sons LaVerne and Guy. A shell was built around the motel to create a building within a building. The Huckleberry Inn was built with somewhat the same design, with the roof coming well down toward the ground to create a walkway alongside and guard against the snow.

A bar room was later added to Huckleberry Inn, tying the whole building together with the motel. During the 1973-4 skiing season the management gave primary use of the west ell of the bar room to cross-country skiers. The policy was still in effect during the 1974-75 season.

In late 1974 Dub and Vi Rogers leased the Huckleberry Inn to Paul Goodell and James Osborne.

DEAN AND MARION MANN

This couple entered the business scene at Government Camp in 1951, he coming up in March, and she in May. She was employed for a time at Mountain Inn, later at Hill's Place.

In about 1957 they left the community to run Hoodland Cafe west of Wemme, remaining there until 1965. At that time they returned to the village of Government Camp to buy the Village Store. That was sold in August of 1973. The couple are now separated. Mrs. Mann lives at Sandy.

JOE AND MARYELLEN ENGLESBY

Joseph L. Englesby, a graduate of Washington High School in Portland, came to Government Camp after World War Two. His career there has been a varied one, tending bar at Battle Axe Inn, construction work on the Ski-way, and managing the Ski Bowl from 1961 to 1964. At that time he and his wife took over the ski shop above the Ratskeller, calling it Trollhaugen. In about 1968 he erected a new building on the south side of the street, right across from the new post office. The Trollhaugen Ski Shop was moved into the new building, where they do business at the present time.

In June of 1952 he married Maryellen Loveland, who had lived in Government Camp since her father, Charles Loveland, had built a house north of the present post office in 1937. She spent all her school years in the village. Her father moved away in 1966.

The Englesbys built a new home on Park Street in 1966. In addition to working in the ski shop, Maryellen raises purebred Husky dogs. Joe belongs to Cascade and Schnee Voegli Ski Clubs, officiating at many races during each season.

ECONOMIC FACTS OF LIFE

In 1957 Government Camp was bypassed. Drivers, passing through on the highway, no longer were forced to thread through the impossible maze of skiers walking aimlessly and blindly on the road, or the stalled automobiles, and the jumble of the business district. If present levels of traffic were forced through the town, the congestion would be intolerable.

However, restaurants and other businesses immediately noticed a large reduction in trade. Maryanne Hill reported that Hill's Place dropped 40%, as a result. Restaurant business at the once-prosperous Thunderhead Lodge (Ski-way) has seldom been in the profit column. Despite all the thousands of skiers that mob the community in the winter, only 25% of the restaurant business at Government Camp is wintertime business. The 75% comes from summer tourists, campers, fishermen, and hunters.

Government Camp operators have tried to get the Oregon State Highway Department to mark the signs at both ends of the bypass as a BUSINESS LOOP, indicating that the motorist is not entering a dead-end street. But in 17 years, they have not been able to get this concession.

THE VILLAGE STORE

On the east end of the business community, east of Huckleberry Inn on the north side of the street is the Village Store, at present a grocery, coin laundry, and gasoline station.

Marian Mann says the building was erected for a garage in about 1938 by the Villiger family. After World War Two it served as a cafe called LET'S EAT, as well as a gas station.

In the early Fifties the owners sold groceries. About 1957 Barney and Sylvia DeCamp bought the business, adding more groceries.

The DeCamps sold the operation in 1965 to Marion and Dean Mann, who discontinued cafe operation inside, but opened a drive-in service for about two years on the east end of the building. Upon closing the drive-in window, all food service was discontinued.

In August of 1973, Joanne and Andy Buxton of Madras bought out the business from the Manns. At the time of writing, it is Government Camp's only grocery store.

GOVERNMENT CAMP'S WEEKEND DOCTOR

One of the leading characters of Government Camp from 1940 to 1956 was Dr. J. Otto George, who set bones for a whole generation of skiers, as well as being vitally interested in the young people who visited the village on weekends.

George was born in Kentucky, moving shortly afterward to Oklahoma City, where he attended high school. He then experienced city life at the Art Institute of Chicago, but World War One interrupted his training, when he enlisted. Military duty took him to England, flying as a machine-gunner in a Bristol aircraft with a British unit.

At the end of the war he returned to Chicago, but soon decided to try his luck in the west. In Portland he drove a street car, a job he kept for several years, as he entered and graduated from Reed College. Working full time while attending college was no snap. He not only made his way through Reed, but he was one of the 62 accepted, out of 500 applicants for the University of Oregon Medical School, graduating there in 1930.

He first gained contact with Mount Hood in about 1922, when he got summer work with the Forest Service. Most of his duty was on the Benson Plateau, Larch Mountain, and Roaring River.

After attaining the degree of Medical Doctor, he began to visit Government Camp, spending time at Cascade Ski Club. Latourette had built a building known as the Ski Pole, that was later bought and enlarged by Everett Darr. In the basement of that building, Dr. George set up his first aid room. This was in the years of 1934 and 1935, before the creation of the Ski Patrol. At that time, skiers, who had accidents on the trail up to Camp Blossom, got help by sending a friend down with a distress call to Boyd French, who was operating the ski shop at Villigers' Battle Axe Inn. Sometimes Dr. George went out himself to help drag in the victims on a makeshift toboggan fashioned from a pair of skis.

Dr. George married his wife, Virginia, who had been the second stewardess to ever be employed by United Air Lines. In June of 1935 they left for several years of medical practice at Point Barrow, Alaska, taking along their son, Paul, who was five months old at the time. A daughter, Virginia, and another son, John, were born in Point Barrow, that far-north tip of Alaska. Dr. George's adventures in medicine with the Eskimo people were enough to fill a book.

In 1940, the family returned to Portland, where he established a practice with Dr. Fitzgibbons. He quickly became involved in weekend medicine again at Government Camp. The Mount Hood Ski Patrol was bringing an ever-increasing load of victims into the first aid room.

At one time, he maintained his own first aid facility in one of Charlie Hill's cabins, on the highway between Darr's and Hill's Place. At other times he used the George family ski cabin, back of Battle Axe Inn. Weekends at the George cabin were pretty busy occasions. By that time there were four children in the family, Michael having been born after their return from Alaska.

But the young guests were virtually unlimited. Upstairs there were 20 beds, a dormitory for the girls. Downstairs another 20 beds accommodated the boys. Despite all that capacity, the doctor often had to step around the oversupply of guests, who slept on the floor. For one year, in 1950 or 1951, the whole family lived full-time at Government Camp, Dr. George commuting to his practice in Portland, and the children riding the bus to Welches School.

Two x-ray technicians, Lorraine Smith of Providence Hospital, and Pearl Homier of Emanuel, came to the mountain regularly to help with accident cases in Dr. George's mountain clinic. They stayed in one of the small cabins near the big George residence. Also Sister Marie of St. Vincent's Hospital sent up a half dozen student nurses every week to get additional training. They skied and enjoyed resort life, until the end of the day. Then they usually were busy caring for broken bones and wrenched knees.

George was a promoter and a member of the board of the Ski-way. He favored the use of smaller, faster cars on a moving cable, rather than the system of large busses operating on a fixed cable.

In 1954 the George family left Government Camp. The doctor and his wife moved to Clatskanie, where he has spent two decades as the only doctor in a large geographical area. Besides a demanding medical practice, he has also commanded a good deal of attention in the world of art, showing his work at the Oregon Society of Artists. In the medical world he has attracted substantial attention with a technique for treatment of burns, which he assimilated from the Eskimo culture.

Public Utilities at Government Camp

In 1958 a sewage plant was installed at Government Camp, eliminating the use of many septic tanks. New buildings were all placed on the system, and existing ones were gradually added, as lines were installed.

At the present, the plant serves a little over 200 outlets. The three-man board of Government Camp Sanitary District consisted of Lloyd Musser, Rich Morton, and Maryanne Hill in early 1975.

The treatment equipment of 1958 had not proved fully effective. Winter snow deters proper action of the sewage ponds, and a more elaborate plant was required. On January 7, 1975, a fact sheet was sent to sewer users, outlining future problems.

First, the US Department of Environmental Quality has insisted that a new plant be built. The Sanitary District got cost and specifications. The Environmental Protective Agency will pay 75% of the cost by outright grant. The remaining 25% must come from owners of the sewer outlets in Government Camp. A special election was called for March 18, 1975, to place the $225,000 bond issue before the voters, who rejected it 21 to 3. A rescheduling of the election was slated for the month of May.

Secondly, some very serious discrepancies in use fees exist. The most glaring inequity is the State of Oregon, placing 30.9% of the flow into the system, yet paying only 2.3% of the cost. Houses and condominiums are placing 24.5% of the flow, but they are paying 72.% of the cost of the system. An enumeration of Government Camp users follows:

Source	% Flow	Present Use Fee	% Total Use Fees
Oregon State Public Restrooms (Summit Ski Area)	30.9	$ 384.00	2.3
Multorpor-Ski Bowl	17.4	1,200.00	7.3
Cabins (includes condominiums)	24.5	11,904.00	72.3
Cascade Ski Club	.5	336.00	2.1
Mazama Lodge	.8	240.00	1.5
Reed College	.4	96.00	.5
Huckleberry Inn	19.5	576.00	3.5
Ratskeller	1.8	576.00	3.5
Mountain Shop & Service Station	2.1	384.00	2.3
Summit House & Service Station	1.3	240.00	1.5
Thunderhead	.3	192.00	1.2
Village Store	.3	240.00	1.5
U.S. Post Office, First Aid Station, Miscellaneous	.2	96.00	.5
	100%	$16,464.00	100%

The Sanitary District has plans under way to make payments more equitable among sewer users.

Another source of problem of the Sanitary District is the fact that the State of Oregon Highway Maintenance Station and the US Forest Service Complex at Summit have never hooked on to the sewer system. The effluent of their septic tanks flows to Still Creek. Naturally, the people of Government Camp feel that these two large users should be a part of the system and help pay the expense.

Retirement party for Fred Stultz circa 1936 — Photo Maryanne Hill
Back row from left, Virgil Gill, Ole Langerud, Ed Hocking, Fred Stultz, Jack Greenwood in vest, Charles Hill, John Lake, ???, Roger Wright, Jack Rafferty.
Seated,???, Dick Maronay, ???, Jack Oaks, Gary Leech, ???, Harold Krebs, Vincent Rafferty.
Right row from back to front, Lawrence Anderson, ???, ???, Ted Brunner, Vern Solomon, Bob Painter, Cloyd Lewis, Glenn Wood.

UTILITIES

Hotels in the Government Camp area were the first people to bring in electric power generators of their own. Before and after World War Two the night air throbbed with the varied voices of generating plants of the community.

In 1950 power lines were run up from Rhododendron and REA power reached Government Camp and Summit. Businesses and homes hooked up, and the private plants were silenced for good. In 1951 a line was run to Timberline. Later the lines were run to Swim and a new gasoline station at Salmon River Meadows.

The REA-sponsored Sandy Electric Cooperative finally succumbed to the bad management inherent in all publicly owned businesses and went out of existence in 1956. Portland General Electric Company took over the existing accounts and placed a large facility west of Summit Guard Station.

POSTAL SERVICE

Swim was the site of the post office for many years. When Swim gave its last gasp in the winter of 1929-30, the post office was moved over to Government Camp, even if the government *didn't* like two-word names to designate post offices. Margaret Villiger had the post office for a time. It was then moved into a cabin on the site of the present telephone company building. The cabin was owned by Charles Hill, and he rented it to the government for $24.50 per month. Ted Bruner acted as postmaster. He was later followed by Juanita Hagen. The present postmaster is Dee Rogers.

WATER SYSTEM DATES TO 1907

The water system in Government Camp was originally a ditch, from Camp Creek, that ran right by the door of Yocum's hotel. On September 27, 1907, John W. Meldrum, Georgia P. Meldrum and Franklin T. Griffith, filed water rights to the source in Camp Creek north of Government Camp. It evidently was soon after incorporated, because the Meldrum Flume Company was in control of the water company, with O.C. Yocum signing a document as the president. It is said that the company flumed logs down to the Yocum sawmill by the hotel, as well as supplying water.

On July 28, 1926, Meldrum sold the water company to D.J. Finn. Finn later sold out to John V. "Jack" Rafferty, who passed the property along to his son John Vincent "Vince" Rafferty. Vince sold the utility to Charles Hill.

In about 1951 the water company was sold for $1,500 to Charles Hill, owner of Hill's Place, by Vincent Rafferty. Hill made improvements on the system and spent part of the summer of 1955 drawing maps of the system. The maps were later destroyed in the burning of Hill's Place in 1969.

In 1961, Maryanne Hill, bought the water company for $15,000 from Salina Fox Hill, her stepmother and Charles Hill's widow. Maryanne upgraded the system considerably in 1971, when at a cost of about $10,000 she placed 6-inch steel pipe through the system. The old water pipe had been of wood construction. Only one small section of the old pipe still remains, down by the Swarz cabin below the site of Hill's place. Joe Englesby did the back-hoe work to dig the trenches for the new system.

At present the water system serves about 175 users. Golden Poles Condominium and Multorpor Ski Resort have their own wells. The Mazamas tap a branch of Still Creek.

Hotel de Government Camp, the First

YOCUM STARTED THE HOTEL

In the summer of 1899, O.C. Yocum began erection of the first hotel structure at Government Camp, a two-and-a-half-story structure of 16 rooms. Lumber was cut with a portable water-powered mill from trees cut on his own property. While in Portland for a visit on October 4, he announced that the outside was finished and he would do the inside work during the winter months. He was accustomed to making doors and window casings, cabinets, and furniture by hand.

It was known as MOUNTAIN VIEW HOUSE during the time that Yocum owned it, and perhaps afterward. Through 1907 he acted as the

Government Camp Hotel circa 1916

Government Camp Hotel circa 1927. On the site stands Darr's old Mountain Shop, now abandoned. Across the street now stands Cascade Ski Club. — Photo Everett Sickler

head guide for the hotel, but in 1908 he let Elijah Coalman take over guiding. The water system was a ditch Yocum dug down the hillside from one of the branches of Camp Creek. It was so natural-looking that it often tempted a small child to build a dam and roil the water. This immediately brought forth an irate Ann Yocum, who gave a copious lecture to any adult, child, or animal who might have offended.

In 1910 Coalman bought the hotel and immediately began to build a larger one to the east, again bringing in a portable mill to saw lumber. The old hotel was from then on called the "Annex." Coalman guided in the summer and worked on the building on every spare moment he had. As with Yocum, he spent the wintertime completing inside finish and furniture. The new building was designed for 50 guests and by 1912 it was placed into use in an unfinished condition. The three story building had a high, steep roof to withstand deep winter snow.

Lige had led 47 climbing parties in 1909 and about as many in 1910, giving him great hope for a prosperous business. He had built ahead of his time, however; the roads to Government Camp were not adequate to bring sufficient business. In 1914 the disillusioned Coalman sold the whole hotel operation to Dell Fox and Louis F. Pridemore, along with 57.5 of the 160 acres he had bought from Yocum. The rest of the acreage went to D.C. Latourette to pay off indebtedness.

How long Fox remained in the partnership is not known, but Pridemore stayed with the operation through the summer of 1922, a gracious host who followed Coalman down the path to failure. In September of 1920 O.C. Yocum brought a court suit against Louis and Grace Pridemore, Elijah Coalman, John Maronay, F.A. Updike, and A.E. Latourette. Yocum's agreement with Coalman had evidently not been satisfied by proper payment, because Coalman was in turn not being paid sufficiently by Pridemore. Latourette was the holder of the mortgage. The court action was brought too late to help Yocum, because the taxes were also in arrears. A seizure of the property was made at the Clackamas County courthouse door by Sheriff W.J. Wilson on November 8, 1920. Latourette picked up the ownership for a successful bid of $7,748.65.

The next known operator was John V. Rafferty. Although known to have been there in 1924, it is probable that he immediately succeeded Pridemore, when he left in 1922.

BRANCH AT TIMBERLINE

The Government Camp Hotel went through several generations of use. At one point Rafferty set up a branch called Timberline Hotel about a half mile west of present-day Timberline Lodge, near the old Camp Blossom. A crude track, hardly a road, led up from Government Camp. It was scarcely suitable for any automobile travel, more appropriate for horse and wagon or travel on foot.

Timberline Hotel was 8' x 16', built in 1924 by Dr. Lewis "Bus" Reavis, a dentist who now resides in McMinnville. One side was fronted up by a slanting and rather springy porch. A removable panel exposed a lunch counter where a climber could buy a cup of coffee for 10¢, a rather large price at the time. Three sleeping tents with mattresses and springs accommodated the customers who brought their own blankets. Sleeping bags were almost unknown in those days. The whole operation was under a "manager", who was always some young climbing enthusiast ready to act as a guide, as well as cook the meals and collect for the use of a bed. Typically, the manager would lock up and conduct the guests on a climb of Mount Hood, then return to serve a meal to those who wished to stay. The operation was the first commercial venture at timberline on the south side to enjoy a Forest Service lease. It is notable that "hotel" accommodations on the south timberline were at approximately the level in 1930 as those offered by Mrs. Cooper on the north side in 1889 before Cloud Cap Inn was built.

Some of the managers of Timberline Hotel were:

1925 Dr. Lewis "Bus" Reavis in partnership with Wayne Leland
1926 Dr. Lewis "Bus" Reavis in partnership with Jimmy Leake
1927 Harry Conway in partnership with Phil Kirkley
1928 Harry Conway in partnership with Phil Kirkley
1929 Pearlee Peyton in partnership with George Corns
1930 Harry Conway

At that juncture the venture folded its doors.

Although the United States was gripped by a crippling depression that began in 1929 and persisted in varying severity until World War 2, Government Camp seemed to fare better than average. Climbers and tourists still visited the mountain; interest in skiing was definitely on the upswing with crowds increasing each year. Highway construction circulated a good deal of money in the area, and the CCC brought hundreds of young men into the woods to help the Forest Service improve trails, roads, and camps. On December 7, 1929, Harry Conway took over as manager.

In this spirit of optimism Rafferty decided to remodel Government Camp Hotel in 1931. The first phase was on the interior of the building, revamping some of the work that had been done in Lige Coalman's day. Effort was made to preserve the charm of the old building, reminiscent of the earlier days. Rafferty had accumulated many Indian and pioneer relics that remained in the decor. The great stone fireplace in the lobby was still a central place where the plans for climbs were formulated or tired skiers could relax. One could sit and reflect with the spirits of the old-time mountain men hovering about. Over against the wall had laid the alpenstocks of Will Steel, Ray Conway, Mark Weygandt, O.C. Yokum, L.A. Nelson.

In 1932, the very depth of the depression, Rafferty began to change the outside. The three-story building with its high roof and boxlike outline was given some nice touches to transform it to a chalet-like design. Dormers were added to break up the plain old roof line. A new porch was run around three sides of the structure, capped with attractive observation balconies. Cedar log siding was used to dress up the lower part of the structure with cedar shakes above. *The Oregon Journal* and the *Oregonian* both reported on June 19 of Rafferty's progress, one noting that five men were working on construction.

A year passed; a camp of CCC boys was located at summit, and Rafferty had a good many construction men living at the hotel, men who were working on the Wapinitia Highway to the east of Government Camp. Kern and Kibbe were running a rock crusher that supplied the highway job. Government Camp was humming all summer and fall.

Then came the bad Wednesday of October 11, 1933. It was 11:00 in the morning. Rafferty was under the building doing some plumbing work, when someone yelled **"FIRE"**. A flue from the kitchen stove had caught the attic afire; by the time it was detected the flames had spread across the whole building. There were two large water lines in the hotel for fire protection, but the fire had gained too much momentum. Many men were off shift from the highway crew and the rock crusher. Ranger Hiatt came running from Summit Guard Station, and the CCC boys followed him. Within minutes hundreds of men arrived to fight fire. The Forest Service pumper from Summit under the charge of H.G. Cooper, was the only source of water to stem the blaze.

Early arrivals at the scene made sure that no one was asleep in the rooms, then began to haul out furniture into the street. Gilbert Gilligan was carried out, overcome with smoke. Cecil Finn was overcome by smoke and got blistered feet. Other men on the scene had to literally force George Jacobson and Jack Graves to leave the smoke-filled building.

Within minutes the street was full of furniture, and the problem suddenly shifted to saving the town, not just the building. The Forest Service pumper was empty, drained because the season was over and autumn freezing weather was near. Cooper frantically filled it from Camp Creek and hurried to save surrounding buildings, some which had already caught by flying firebrands. The Mount Hood Hut (Battle Axe Inn) and Mount Hood Chalet (later called Mountain View Inn) across on the north side of the street were both scorched from the intense heat. Only the pumper saved these buildings from igniting. At the back of the hotel (south) was the Cascade Ski Club, a discarded portable building once use by the Portland School District. Although it stood only about 300 feet from the hotel, the firefighters also saved it.

By nightfall all that remained of the hotel was the old fireplace, a dark monolith against the afternoon sky. In the street stood a pitiful collection of furniture, an old Victrola, chairs, pictures, boxes. George Flinn, one of the original workmen on the old hotel structure, stood there and reflected about the early days when he had worked with Lige Coalman and George Maronay to erect it. Gone was the mountain creation of O.C. Yocum; only his old homestead cabin remained, standing down there in the trees toward Multorpor to the south of where the new Highway 26 Bypass runs past Government Camp.

At the time of the fire, Government Camp Hotel and the land belonged to the D.C. Latourette estate. Mrs. Rafferty told the newspapers that only a small percentage had been insured. There was no plan to rebuild the hotel.

A small building appeared on the site, built by Boyd French. This was used from 1936 to 1938 by Hjalmar Hvam as a ski shop. It disappeared when Everett Darr built his ski shop at the same location in 1946.

On the east end of Government Camp the Oregon State Highway Department built equipment sheds, just past the curve in the main street. These buildings were used until 1952, when the department put in a much larger facility on Highway 26 across the road from Timberline Junction. This made them a next-door neighbor to the east of the Forest Service building complex at Summit.

A list of known operators of Government Camp Hotel is as follows:

1900 to 1909 O.C. Yocum and his wife, Ann, operated the first building, known as the "Annex" after the larger building was erected in 1910.
1910 . . . . Elijah Coalman
1911 . . . . Elijah Coalman
1912 . . . . Elijah Coalman
1913 . . . . Elijah Coalman
1914-21 . . . . . Dell Fox and Louis F. Pridemore
1922 . . . . Louis F. Pridemore
1923
1924 . . . . John V. Rafferty
1925-33 . . . . John V. Rafferty

A FANCY OF THE THIRTIES

An elaborate plan drawn by Johnson and Wallwork in March of 1932, showed a massive project for Government Camp. A boulevard skirted the base of Multorpor and Tom-Dick-Harry Mountains. Near the site of the present Multorpor Ski Lift, a large hotel overlooked an 18-hole golf course with a beautiful view of Mount Hood. Camp Creek was shown as being diverted into many pools and canals that threaded through the golf course, giving canoers a large network of channels. The plan evidently died in the 1932 depression.

THE GUIDES AND THE ROPES

For many years the Forest Service furnished and set fixed ropes above the crater for the safety of the climbing public. Just when this practice started is not known, but it probably was during the time the summit lookout was established in 1915.

In 1905 a humorous occurrence took place with the rope that O.C. Yocum had set for his patrons. It was the practice to charge all climbers to use the rope, and one August night before a climb, Reverend A.J. Montgomery overheard a group at the timberline camp say that they would not pay to use the ropes or ladders below the summit.

Montgomery and his party got an earlier start than the other group, and when they crossed a ladder over a crevasse, they pulled it up, leaving no way to cross the chasm. When the freeloaders reached the crevasse, they surveyed the awesome problem and turned back down the mountain. They were heard later to report that they had cancelled their climb because of the bitter cold, 40 degrees below zero, they said.

In 1921 there was still contention about paying to use the fixed rope. One man said he had been asked for money by a man wearing a badge, although it was not Forest Service policy to make such a charge. At the end of the season in 1921 the government men wanted to take the ropes down late in August, but Pridemore of Government Camp Hotel had climbers scheduled to climb over Labor Day, and he prevailed upon them to leave it hanging in the Chute.

A snow storm covered the rope, and by the time the Forest Service was ready to take it down, it was frozen under 14 inches of ice and hard snow. Pridemore was billed $30 for 1,200 feet of manila rope.

The old Dr. Kelly home — Photo Everett Sickler
Oldest house in the village owned by Esther Kelly Watson

White River Curio Shop — Photo Everett Sickler

A BUDDING HOTELIER

Everett Sickler was born September 12, 1901, at Wessington Springs, South Dakota. Because of allergy his parents sent him to live with grandparents in Santa Cruz, California and in Vancouver. His first two years of high school were at Jefferson High in Portland, and the last two at Vancouver.

A turning point in his life was a trip to Yellowstone Park with his parents in 1922. When they were ready to leave, he announced that he had a job and would stay at Yellowstone the rest of the summer. A member of the hotel crew, he helped clean up tents and cabins and carry food for cooks in the kitchen. Pay was a dollar a day, and he lived in a log bunkhouse with 40 boys.

Sickler returned to Vancouver for several years, becoming active in the Klatawa Hiking Club, a group that explored trails up and down the Columbia Gorge and the slopes of Mount Hood. Through Klatawa, he met his wife, Belle Pierce, whom he married September 27, 1925. Ever since his days at Yellowstone, Sickler had the dream of operating a resort hotel, and his visits to Mount Hood pinpointed the location. Belle did her part by attending Oregon State College and concentrating on institutional cooking.

Early in 1925 Everett and Belle took a contract of running the lunch counter at the Hood River Drug Company. It was there that he met Albert Krieg, the contractor who erected Battle Axe Inn.

Sicklers sold Battle Axe Inn to Henry and Margaret Villiger in 1929 and moved to Rhododendron.

Everett and Belle Sickler — Photo Sickler

Everett Sickler got his idea for building his picturesque hotel at Government Camp from a picture in a Johns-Manville roofing advertisement. Becoming acquainted with the German builder, Albert Krieg, in 1925, he gave him a size and asked for a price. Seeing the log construction, Krieg balked.

"Py Gott, I don't tink I want to build out of logs."

"Oh yes, but the logs make appearance of that building," said Sickler.

"Let me tink," replied Krieg. "I have idea. I make it look yust like logs." The idea was later carried out to use log facing for the inn.

"How much will it cost me?"

"Thirty-six hundred dollars," Krieg answered. "But when the walls are up, I need one-third of the money."

"You will have it." Sickler was mentally calculating the money he had left from the bequest of his aunt.

"And when the building is done, I need all the money."

"You will have it." They shook hands, and that constituted the contract for building Battle Axe Inn. Sickler went to Dundee to buy the property from O.C. Yocum.

Krieg brought his sons and a small crew to Government Camp. Disregarding the time-honored tradition of waiting until September to start new construction, Krieg moved onto the site just as soon as the melting of the snow would permit. Planning and layout was made as the building progressed. Sickler had an old Model T Ford cut down to a pickup, which he used to bring many loads of equipment up from Portland. A 32-volt Delco power plant was brought in to supply electricity for lights and the freezer they used for meat and ice cream. Krieg wrapped the job up in short and workmanlike order.

Sicklers operated Battle Axe Inn with Bud and Irene Flurry as the nucleus of a close-knit, family-type group of employees. Finances were hand-to-mouth, and when the month was over, it was always a scramble to pay the meat and grocery bill down at Ruben Hoffman's Sandy Market. Whatever was left went to the employees, and whenever the money stretched further than that, Everett and Belle had a few dollars. As Sickler says, competition was fierce, and Battle Axe Inn ran on enthusiasm, not money.

Bud Flurry was a man with great personality, always attracting people around him. He was an able mechanic, too. In 1926 Sickler brought back

Toboggan run at Battle Axe Inn — Photo Everett Sickler

the Kriegs to erect the 50' x 90' three-story Recreational Building, east of Battle Axe on the site occupied in 1974 by the Village Store. Part of that building was the toboggan slide, a mechanical marvel put together in 1928 by Carl Krieg and Bud Flurry. Sickler got a suggestion from lumberman E.S. Collins on towing the toboggans on an endless cable. Krieg and Flurry erected the system, driven by a Sampson tractor motor.

The toboggan run was a tremendous attraction, and its twin tracks were very busy on weekends. There were lots of accidents as the toboggans left the track. Speed ran as high as 60 miles per hour but naturally depended upon temperature and snow conditions. Insurance was costing $100 per operating day, which made the operation uneconomical and caused closure.

In the winter of 1926 Sickler bought out the whole stock of skis from Marshall-Wells Company in Portland, 18 pair. He turned them over as a concession to Donald Welch. It was a real money maker, but unfortunately Sickler did not benefit directly. Several cabins were built between the Inn and the Recreational Building.

GERTRUDE JENSEN'S INFLUENCE

The story of the inn is interwoven with the story of Gertrude Glutsch Jensen, beginning with her days as a student at Reed College in 1922-23. One of her college friends was a girl named Marcel Villiger, whose parents ran Arlington Hotel for working people near the Portland railway station. Gertrude got to know Marcel's parents and urged them several times to visit Mount Hood. Finally the effort resulted in a plan for a two-car caravan to Government Camp. Gertrude led the way with her mother as a passenger in their Hudson automobile, and Henry F. and Margaret E. Villiger with their daughter, Marcel, following along the primitive road in their Stutz Bearcat.

At that time it was quite an accomplishment for a girl to drive such a road with the wood plank sections and the narrow bridges. When they arrived at Government Camp, it opened up a whole new world to Henry Villiger, a Swiss, who was enchanted with the alpine setting. This was the same type of scenery and trees and shrubs that he had known in Switzerland. The party stayed at Battle Axe Inn, and he struck up quite a friendship with Sickler. This association eventually culminated in the sale of Battle Axe to the Villigers, although negotiations were painfully slow.

The transaction was finally agreed in 1929 at $23,000 with $3,000 down. The balance was to be paid at $350 per month. The daughter Marcel married Alfred Douglas King. They and the Villigers filed articles of incorporation as BATTLE AXE INN, INC. on November 25, 1930 for $3200. King built a cabin in back which is standing today. The depression began to grip the country severely after Villiger bought. Payments got down to as low as $30 per month. Sickler did not want to repossess, because by that time Belle was busy with two small children. She did not have the time to pick huckleberries and bake pies and run the kitchen, as she had done in the past. The Kings and Villigers went along running the operation, assisted by their son, Armand "Gravy" Villiger. This young man's talents in the kitchen were specialized in making gravy, and he therefore acquired the name.

With the recreation annex up the street, Villiger felt that the business was too decentralized. He had the annex moved down to the original building and attached. Fewer employees could run the business, and the cash register could be kept under better surveillance. Most people who recall Battle Axe Inn remember it as it was after the two buildings were consolidated. Henry Villiger died February 25, 1938, and Margaret continued to run the business.

PURCHASE BY MRS. JENSEN

On Friday, January 10, 1947 a story appeared in *The Oregonian*, stating that Battle Axe Inn had been purchased from Margaret E. Villiger, a widow, for $85,000 by Gertrude Glutsch Jensen, a Portland woman prominent in real estate and known for her work as Chairman of the Columbia Gorge Commission. This, of course, was the same woman, who had showed the Government Camp area to the Villigers many years before. Plans were to reopen the 1500-foot toboggan run and tow, that had once been in use near the rear of the hotel. In addition, she would install a cafeteria and build a swiss-style home on the property for her mother, Mrs. Glutsch. Hjalmar Hvam was to manage the ski rental business, and Chester Chin of Chin's Buffet in Portland would manage the cafeteria. Mrs. Jensen's son, Frederick Charles, at that time a senior at Grant High School, was to manage the toboggan tow. The hotel, built on 200 feet of frontage 80 feet deep, was rated at 100 guests.

After a well-done grand opening, all of the plans went awry. Mrs. Jensen became bogged down with repair problems that were overwhelming, and in addition, her doctor told her that her health did not permit her living at Government Camp. In her absence, employee theft and gross mismanagement were financially ruinous. She finally placed the management in the hands of Ivan Hamerlynck in March or April. An accord was finally reached in September for Margaret Villiger to take possession once more, with Hank Junkers from Hill's Place moving across the street to become manager. At last Gertrude Jensen was freed of Battle Axe Inn.

Hank Junkers ran the establishment until his agreement ran out, when it was sold by Mrs. Villiger to Warren Huff.

Battle Axe Inn had emerged from World War 2 as the queen of the old buildings in the community, a picturesque old structure with massive lines. Huff owned and managed the business for about two years when the day of reckoning arrived. It was on a quiet Monday, November 7, 1950, about 4:30 p.m., when someone shouted **"FIRE!"** Battle Axe was ablaze. As usual the firefighting became a community affair, using hose and equipment from neighboring buildings around. A pumper was dispatched from Zig Zag Ranger Station and two more from the town of Sandy. Flames leaped from end to end in minutes, and again the problem was to save the town. The 15 employees and the few hotel guests had to run for their lives. Flames detonated the recently filled diesel oil tanks, and the resulting fireball in the sky was seen 40 miles east on the Wapinitia plains.

The cabin of Doug King, Margaret Villiger's son-in-law, caught fire, but was saved and still stands today. Hill's Place, on the south side of the street, was badly scorched, windows broken, and booths damaged by fire. There was fire damage to the home of Vincent Rafferty, who operated Hill's Place. Ole Lien, Forest Service veteran, had his clothes burned off in the firefighting and was treated for blisters. Everett Darr lost a section of fire hose, and the heat buckled pavement in the street.

The unconfirmed story about the origin of the fire is that someone was using a blowtorch on plumbing on the second floor and was called away momentarily. By nightfall flames had taken Government Camp's largest building, a structure in use 25 years. The picturesque old place had a large fireplace on the west wall, home-made rustic chairs and furniture, and was decorated with many Indian and pioneer artifacts. A curio shop graced one corner of the main floor, and there were sleeping rooms upstairs. The east end of the building, or "annex" housed the lunch counter, taproom, grocery, and laundry, with dormitories above.

Lobby at Battle Axe Inn, a living museum — Photo Everett Sickler

Gertrude Jensen's grand opening at Battle Axe Inn. Mrs. Jensen with corsage. Katherine Cushingway in native Indian costume, Marshall Dana with white hair, Mrs. Dana in black hat. — Photo Jensen

The building was believed to have been only insured to $20,000. Amount of the loss must have been well over $100,000, although the building itself was irreplaceable, a priceless relic of times past. At the time of burning, Battle Axe Inn was the largest building in Government Camp.

Battle Axe Inn 1939 — Photo Everett Sickler

Mountain View Inn (or Tyrolean, or Hut)

When John V. "Jack" Rafferty was burned out in the fire of Government Camp Hotel in 1933, only Battle Axe Inn remained as a hotel. Lena Little, widow of pioneer homesteader, Francis C. Little, had moved her large home down to the highway a short time previously. Rafferty struck an agreement with her and leased the building for a hotel site, calling it Rafferty's and Rafferty's Hut. He later bought the property, as well as the water company. Rafferty ran the hotel until his death on July 1, 1943 at age 68. It is believed that the hotel acquired the name Tyrolean sometime after that.

Harry Albright of Boring reopened the inn on December 2, 1945 and changed the name to Mountain View Inn. On July 6, 1947, Mr. and Mrs. W.E. Dunbar bought the inn for an estimated $55,000.

On the last day of February, 1955, a Monday storm raised havoc, toppling hundreds of large trees every direction and severing the electric power lines of the Sandy Electric Cooperative. Especially great damage was done between Zigzag and Government Camp, shutting power off there for several days. Many buildings had auxiliary power plants, and one was Mountain View Inn, the only hotel left at Government Camp. It stood between Cascade Ski Club and the main street, across the street from Darr's ski shop. Mountain View had sleeping accommodation for about 60 in nine guest rooms and two dormitories. The main floor had a central lobby, a dining room on the west, and on the east side a small beer hall that packed in legendary numbers of wild, noisy skiers on weekends.

The operators of the inn had been limping along all week on their own small generator, hoping that the main power line would be restored for the weekend. About midnight the lights went out completely, and the employees brought out candles for some of the guests to use. Roy Moxness, editor of the *Oregon Teamster*, had just checked in at the desk and went to his room, carrying a candle. His assistant, James Harding, and another teamster official, Charles Rice, were just checking in at the desk, when Rice detected fire. With great shouts they awoke the guests and employees of the hotel. John Backus, the hotel maintenance man, awoke to find the rear wall of the building engulfed in flames. Fire had crept through a tunnel from the hotel to the generator shack in the rear, after the overloaded machinery had quit.

The only fire-fighting equipment was an extinguisher which Rice had in his truck, a futile gesture against the mounting conflagration. Rice and Harding ran from room to room arousing employees and the 16 guests, one family of whom was that of George Bender and his wife, 14-year old daughter Sandra Ann, and 12-year old daughter Jo Ann. Roy Moxness, ran from his room for dear life, then remembering the lighted candle, went back to extinguish it, then once more ran out of the building.

Ena Payne, a widow, owned the hotel. She was able to save the two cash registers and the money from the safe; that was all. Outside, Gene Beckman of the Oregon State Highway Department had brought the rotary plows on the scene, throwing snow to muffle the effect of the heat. Two 500-gallon propane tanks stood by the building. Their explosion would have been disastrous, but Beckman kept them from detonating. The ski shop on the west and Cascade Ski Club on the north were threatened. Hughes Motel on the east was also too close for comfort, but the snowplow was able to keep the fire from spreading. When the excitement was all over, they found that Mrs. Payne's automobile had been damaged by the plow.

Government Camp was left with no hotel, only a small motel. Someone in the community bravely told the newspapers that there were still accommodations for 150 to 200 people, an optimistic estimate that did not sound very accurate at the time. The situation was especially acute, because on February 15, Timberline Lodge had closed its doors to the public until further notice.

Mountain View Inn — Photo Joe Leuthold

The East Side Commercial Club under the leadership of George W. Jackson, started work in the fall of 1952 to remodel the old Timberline Lodge garage at the foot of East Leg Road on Highway 26. About 150 members worked on the project of insulating and lining the walls with plywood and sheetrock.

The goal was to provide a snow play area for children away from the congestion and danger of the major ski areas. Toboggans were purchased for the gentle hill behind the lodge. Rooms inside for warming, eating lunch, and play for small children were arranged.

Snow Bunny Lodge began operations on Saturdays and Sundays, with the building available for youth organizations during the week. Opening date was February 1, 1953. It has been in continuous operation during snow months ever since that time.

Calverley's advertisement as packer and guide — Photo Everett Sickler.

GEORGE CALVERLEY PIONEERED

Born September 14, 1900, George Calverley grew up near Bend. In June, 1920, he went to work for the Forest Service at Summit Meadows, where his brother John was ranger. After a summer with the government he left their service and established a business of horse-packing and guiding. He did Mount Hood summit guiding, as well as taking parties of hunters and fishermen to the choice areas around the mountain.

In 1924 he erected a building at the east end of the private land in the Government Camp area, and started Calverley's, a cafe which his wife ran. In 1928 work for the Forest Service beckoned. He finally served with them 35 years before retiring in 1965. He at present lives on a small fruit acreage at Mosier.

During the years 1925 to 1927 when Calverly was guiding climbing parties, he led 8 or 10 climbs per summer. Fees were $5 per person with a $20 minimum.

George and his brother, Vern, once took humorist Irving S. Cobb on a pack trip down the Skyline Road toward Mount Jefferson for a few days. Anything but humorous, Cobb remained drunk for almost the entirety of the trip. It was in Prohibition days, and he guarded his whisky in silent suspicion, sharing with no one. The Calverleys were very happy to be rid of their client at the end of the week.

Another resident of Summit area in Calverley's time was David Donaldson, who had a cabin to the south, across the new highway #26 cutoff, just west of the Forest Service Summit Guard Station. Donaldson was a retired sheep man and played host in the summer time to sheepherders of the area. Herds of sheep were common in the area as late as the Thirties. Donaldson and Vern Rogers named Veda Lake, using the VE of Rogers' name and the DA of Donaldson's first name.

Toboggan Slide at Summit — Photo USFS

SUMMIT AREA

The area called Summit creates confusion, because it is nowhere near the top of Mount Hood, nor is it at the same place as the original Summit House at Summit Meadows. The Summit of today lies on the most easterly part of the private land of Government Camp and spills over onto the Forest Service land to the east.

It includes the following:
Summit Guard station, USFS.
State of Oregon public restroom.
Darr's Summit ski area.
Oregon highway maintenance station.
West's Summit House.

Original Forest Service activity was at Summit Meadow. When they built the guard station at its present location, they named it Summit, which was probably the start of the name there.

SUMMIT WINTER SPORTS AREA

Development of winter sports facilities at Government Camp area was a result of the massive 1927 New Year's Week search for Brownlee and White. H.C. Hodgkins, a director of the Advertising Club of Portland, headed a campaign to raise money to support that search. White was found, and Brownlee was eventually given up for lost. When it was all over, there was money remaining in the Ad Club fund.

William P. Merry, Ad Club president, began promoting the idea of using the unspent funds to start a winter playground that would keep people from wandering around all over the mountain. When Grover A. Rebintisch took over as president in July of 1927, he appointed Hodgkins to the head of a new Winter Sports Committee. Judge Fred Stadter of The Mazamas was invited to membership on the committee and became an active leader.

Summit Ski Area 1928 — Photo Everett Sickler
From left, Everett and Belle Sickler, Marjorie and Scotty Williamson

They selected an area now known as Summit, just east of Calverley's, which was built on the last bit of private land of Government Camp. The new winter sports site was on Forest Service land, and a nominal usage rental was placed upon it. The committee planned and erected a wooden-structure ski jump, a toboggan slide, ski slopes, and a building east of Calverley's which housed ski and toboggan rentals and lunch counter. An outdoor fireplace gave skiers and tobogganers a place to congregate and get warm.

The opening of the Advertising Club Winter Sports Area was one of the more impressive formal ceremonies held at Mount Hood. On Sunday, December 11, 1927, past-president William P. Merry led a caravan of automobiles to Mount Hood. At 2:00 p.m. the Grant High School band played the Star Spangled Banner to open the program. Ad Club president Rebintisch compared Mount Hood to resorts in The Alps and said that the day marked the beginning of an era of development, as he formally presented the area to the State of Oregon.

Hal E. Hoss, secretary to Governor Isaac L. Patterson accepted for the state, and the colorful

Calverley's in early Thirties — Photo George Calverley
Note the small trees at Summit at that time. The gas pump later became a gas station. The house was later moved to left and is the building now operated by the West family. The old water fountain is gone, but one like it still stands on the east end of the Sahalie Falls Bridge.

mayor of Portland, George L. Baker, was on hand in stylish light-hued sport suit to make the acceptance for the City of Portland. Thomas H. Sherrard spoke for the Forest Service, as did H.B. VanDuzer for the Oregon State Highway Commission. Other notables were Judge Fred Stadter, Chief Rafferty of the Oregon State Police, Chief L.V. Jenkins of the Portland Police, Portland Postmaster J.W. Jones, and commissioners from the counties of Hood, Clackamas, and Multnomah.

The Mazamas staged an outdoor parade of correct sports wear. Mayor Baker got a toboggan and made a "belly-buster" slide to open the run, being pelted on his run by snowballs from local admirers. With that the area was opened to the public. The toboggan run was mobbed, and the Ad Club kept it open until 11:00 that night to let the sliders get their fill. It was estimated that 800 people used the course. Despite the large crowds, not any accidents were reported.

The original expenditure of the Ad Club was about $5,000. The Forest Service Ranger at Zigzag, Raymond Smith, detailed two of his men to take charge of the area, O.G. Johnson and A.O. Day.

The hotels at Government Camp had filled up for the weekend. By mid-day on Sunday there was an obvious shortage of food. When Rafferty, Calverley, Sickler, and Boyd Summers had all tried to borrow food from one another, they finally got together and sent a truck to Sandy for more.

In following weeks the public arrived in great numbers to use the new winter sports hill. On December 26 there were 800 cars parked in the area of Government Camp. The highway department made space for about 2,000 automobiles.

DEVELOPMENT AT SWIM

Another ski area was developing in a neck-and-neck race with the Ad Club area at Summit. It was the jump hill at Swim, where Boyd Summers ran a store, post office, and a few cabins alongside the naturally-warm-water swimming pool.

Experts don't agree about the swimming pool. It is generally believed that a spring exudes water which is slightly warmer than icy snow water. A personal inspection by the author confirmed this. However, knowledgeable people differ on whether Summers heated the water. Albertine West says that a hot water line ran through the cook stove at the resort to heat the water. Others say not.

At any rate, Harold Bangs and Robert Arthur "Art" Parish can recall visiting Swim during Christmas week of 1929. Swimmers were plunging into the water from the snow banks around the pool. At that time Swim was still functioning as the US Post Office for the Government Camp area.

The Mount Hood Ski Club, which had been organized in 1927, planned a ski-jumping hill on the east side of Multorpor Mountain. The outrun ended in the low creek-bottom ground at Swim. Ole Langerud was falling snags and slashing brush in a virtually single-handed job of shaping the hill in the fall of 1927. It was a natural hill without wood structures. The average grade was 59%, although one section was 64%. The experts said that it compared well with the jump hills of the eastern United States. Experience later showed that the morning sun on the east exposure of the mountain softened the snow more than was desirable. But the real problem proved to be the

Swim Resort had a swimming pool — Photo USFS

warm creek water that caused the snow on the outrun to melt out in potholes. A successful jumper was thus forced to dodge an obstacle course of these soft spots as he completed his run.

In addition to the ski jump a toboggan and bobsled hill was laid out with high-banked corners, that gave riders high speeds and great thrills, as they ran the course. Signs of this run can still be seen in the land contours above the historic site of Swim. Also visible are signs of the concrete swimming pool.

Spectators at ski jumps normally paid an admission fee, and the jumps at Mount Hood were no exception. Automobiles were parked up at the Summit area, and the crowds walked down the old Barlow Road, which ran right into Swim.

On Sunday, February 5, 1928, the Mount Hood Ski Club held its first Annual Tournament at Swim, an event that drew a large crowd to Government Camp, filling the hotels with notables. At Battle Axe Inn some of the prominent guests were Henry Corbett and wife, Lewis Mills and wife, Erskine Wood and wife, William Wheeler and wife, Donald Denman and wife, Mrs. Charlotte Thompson, Joseph Durham and wife, and Sidney V.W. Peters. The Snowshoe Club was well represented by C. Edward Grelle, Dr. Eugene Rockey, Dr. Millard Holbrook, David T. Honeyman, and Horace Mecklem.

Government Camp 1928 — Photo Everett Sickler
The large winter crowds began to arrive.

Ski jump at Swim 1930 — Photo Hjalmar Hvam

The real star among the people of distinction was also a competitor in the jumps, German birdman Hans Otto Giese of the Black Forest Ski Club of Germany. Giese flew in from Seattle to Vancouver Field, where he was met by Portland Mayor, George Baker.

Harry Conway was the official starter for the contestants. When the contest was all over, all the winners were members of Mount Hood Ski Club except Giese:

1. .... Ole Haugen
2. .... Kaare Schafstad
3. .... Thor Lief
4. .... Otto Hagen
5. .... John Anderson
6. .... Ole Langerud
7. .... Hans Otto Giese
8. .... C. Woxman
9. .... R.J. Wolfstad

SUMMIT SPORTS AREA

After the contest, awards were made at a banquet at Rafferty's Government Camp Hotel, a congregation of Mount Hood Ski Clubbers, Crag Rats, Mazamas, and many prominent guests. Committee for the tournament had been Chairman Dr. Guy DuPlessis, Perlee Payton, Merle Moore, Frank Siecke, Ted Emerson, Einer Hermensen, Harry Conway, Gordon Johnson, Myron Jones, Otto Hagen, Gerald Lymp, Steward McKenzie, and Herbert H. Vial. Judges were Fred Stadter, Kent Shoemaker, and Guy DuPlessis.

A year later, on February 10, 1929, Mount Hood Ski Club held its second annual tourney at Swim. By this time the club had split, some of its members joining Cascade Ski Club, and others joining Viking Sports Club. The contestants placed as follows:

Kaare Schafstad .... Cascade
Corey Gustafson .... MHSC
Hjalmar Hvam .... Cascade
Thor Lief .... Viking
John Anderson .... MHSC
Einer Hermensen .... MHSC
Ole Langerud .... MHSC

John Anderson was the old man of the mountain, over 50 at the time. He very often proved the course by making the first jump, and most of the time he fell on the outrun.

A week later all the contestants were over on the Multorpor Hill in a tournament sponsored by Cascade Ski Club.

At some time in 1929 Boyd Summers sold out his resort at Swim to the Law brothers. Although Cascade Ski Club had normally been using the facilities at Multorpor, they scheduled a tournament at Swim for January 13, 1930, probably because Law Brothers offered a higher percentage of spectator receipts. This tournament was the last ever held at Swim, for the next day the Law brothers loaded all the valuable detachables at the Swim resort into trailers and headed south.

Everett Sickler can remember their stopping at Government Camp and assuring everyone that they would be right back, but nothing was ever heard from them again. Cascade Ski Club was left in the lurch for some of their money, and Boyd Summers had nothing but promises to pay. Just before the tournament, they were reported to be in the process of building a "tram" in the Swim area. At that point the resort just about died, although on March 8, 1932 Swim Ski Jump was incorporated in a filing at the Clackamas County Court House by Boyd Summers, Ole Langerud, and Fred Herman.

DEVELOPING AD CLUB HILL

At Summit, which was still known as Calverley's, the year of 1928 was a great success on the Ad Club hill. Large crowds were coming to toboggan and ski. From Government Camp through to Summit the state highway department had made space for as many as 2000 cars.

The Ad Club ran the concession a year and decided to give it up. The volunteer help all wanted to be out skiing instead of running the business. Their attorney contacted Adrian J. Johanns, a Westmoreland builder of distinction, who had a sideline in the amusement business. Johanns owned Interstate Amusement Company with attractions at Jantzen Beach. He had become engaged in that business because the owners of Jantzen Beach Amusement Park had called him in to do some construction, and one thing led to another.

Johanns and his brother, John Henry Johanns, decided to buy the facilities at Summit, but they made only a down payment on the $3,000 purchase price. Johanns was afraid to own it outright as an individual, and he would not take title to ownership until he could incorporate Mount Hood Amusement Company. Sure enough, the third Sunday of operation, a woman on a toboggan collided with two boys on another. She broke a wrist, one boy broke a leg, and the other cracked his ankle. Attorney Ralph Bunch took the case and pressed for damages of $900 per injury, a total of $2,700.

This foresight avoided financial disaster for Johanns, and the business went on. The lunch room was discontinued after two seasons, and the building was enlarged, making room for more rentals. His brother, John, got out of the business about the same time.

During blizzards, Johanns was asked by the Forest Service to lead his customers down the highway on Sunday nights. When he locked up, he and his wife would crawl into the seat of their car and show the way for a long line of automobiles behind him. At the bottom of Laurel Hill the worst places had been passed, and one-by-one the drivers would overtake him and leave the caravan.

In April of 1931 a vicious wind storm hit the area and toppled the trees on the hill, all young and spindly, in all directions. The toboggan slide was just about obliterated, so Johanns decided to build a new one. The new slide was made of wood and was long and fast, so he gave it a racy name, Red Devil. The name was hung on the rental shack and was quickly adopted as the name of the whole area.

The Red Devil slide proved more dangerous than the old hill. In about 1935 or 1936 Johanns decided to dismantle it and turn more attention to skiing. At this point the rope tow was erected, which served skiers for many years. It is believed that The Mazamas had put in the first tow on the south side of Mount Hood very shortly before, an installation on Mazama Hill above West Leg Road.

Arthur Pieritz, a superintendent at Crown Willamette Paper Company at Camas, kept the toboggan sliding sport alive by developing a new type he called a "glider." It was easier to steer and much less dangerous. Pieritz rented gliders out of the Red Devil shack on a percentage basis.

The building had been enlarged the second time. Most of the skiers came inside to warm themselves by the big stove and to eat lunches they had brought. Johanns did not want any alcoholic beverages in the place and a sign on the wall said "YOU CAN EAT LUNCH HERE, BUT DON'T BRING ANY BEER." Johanns had a safe in which his customers could leave wallets or purses when they were out on the slopes.

Although the Red Devil sign was taken down when the big wooden toboggan slide was dismantled, the name stuck with the area for years. Wests used it for their rope tow several years later. When World War Two shut down gasoline and tires, help became hard to get, and customers could not reach Government Camp. Johanns decided to quit and sold the business to Everett Darr.

Darr eventually placed a T-Bar tow at Summit, and in 1966 he built a 2,000-square foot day lodge to replace the old building. The new lodge is faced with andesite rock and offers ski rental, snack bar, and warming area.

The State of Oregon built a large rest-room facility at the east end of Summit parking lot in 1964 at a cost of $51,244 plus extras.

THE WEST FAMILY

The West family moved into Mount Hood life when Albertine came to Calverley's to work as a waitress at age 17 from Wapinitia. She worked there in 1927 and 1928, then married Isham (Ike) West, who also grew up at Wapinitia. They returned to ranch life there until discussion with George Calverley resulted in the sale of Calverley's to the Wests on May 1, 1938.

Calverley's had been rented out since the fall of 1937 to Mrs. Cloyd (Peggy) Lewis, who called it

Summit ski area in 1939 — Photo USFS

Peggy's Inn. She also ran Peggy's Place at Zigzag, now known as Barlow Trail Lodge, providing board and room to highway construction men.

Isham West was born August 3, 1903 at Juniper Flat, Wapinitia. He was a descendant of a grandfather who had crossed the Barlow Road in 1847 and settled at Basket Slough near Rickreall. Isham and Albertine were parents of four children, John born 1939, Thomas 1940, Emily 1943, and Robert 1947.

In 1939 they removed the single gasoline pump that had served for years in front of Calverley's and built a gasoline station. In 1940 they moved the original residence and cafe building from its position behind the gasoline station to a new location to the west of the station. At that time the size of the building was increased.

Calverley's in late Thirties — Photo George Calverley

In 1946 Wests built Red Devil Ski Tow on the gentle slope north of their buildings. As with Darr's tows at Summit, they catered to beginning skiers. Wests finally got out of the ski tow business in 1970, using their hill for sliders who rented saucers from them. At present they operate the gasoline and towing business, ski and boot rentals, and cafe.

Wests used the name Summit House for their cafe, taking the same name that Perry Vickers had used in early times for his building at Summit Meadows.

Multorpor—Ski Bowl, Major Lift Area

BEGINNING OF MULTORPOR

Multorpor and Ski Bowl began as two distinctly different areas, not an integrated complex as they exist today. The jump hill on the northwest end of Multorpor Mountain was developed in the fall of 1928, a year after the hill at Swim. The old supervisor of Mount Hood National Forest, Thomas Sherrard, had been a friend of Everett Sickler for at least seven years, when the two had a discussion about the Forest Service providing some recreation areas in 1928.

"There are only two functions for this forest," Sherrard boomed. "One is to provide watershed area. The other is for grazing land." At the time the mountain areas supported thousands of sheep and cattle. Strangely, he did not mention the production of timber.

Multorpor Jump Hill in Early 30's —Photo H. Hvam

"But the public wants trails and ski areas," said Sickler.

"The public can go to blazes," retorted the forester.

However, public interest was swinging toward skiing and climbing. Sherrard had so many comments and requests, that he was prompted to go along with it. He gave Francis E. (Scotty) Williamson at Zigzag the instructions to get together with the people at Government Camp and talk about a ski area. In 1928 Williamson made a field trip with Sickler, Jack Rafferty of Government Camp Hotel, and Boyd Summers of Swim.

They crashed brush at the base of Multorpor Mountain and finally came out on the steep sidehill at one point where there was little timber. The government wanted an area that would disturb as few trees as possible, and the area on the mountainside had little but the snags from a forest fire that had ravaged the area many years before. They agreed that the hill would be good for a jump site. At the bottom of the hill a heavy stand of young trees would need to be cleared out for the runout zone.

It was in such manner that the ski jump was located. Ole Haugen secured rights on the hill and with the help of his brothers Lars and Siebert, he built the first jump course. Sickler and Rafferty donated $25 apiece, the budget for slashing a few trees and smoothing the slope.

On January 6, 1929, the newly founded Cascade Ski Club opened the hill for use with a tournament. 3600 people visited the south side of Mount Hood. Winning jumpers were Martin Arlberg of The Cascadians, Thor Lief of Viking Sports Club, and Hjalmar Hvam of Cascade Ski Club. This was probably the first competition Hvam ever entered in the United States.

On February 17, 1929, Cascade Ski Club held a tournament recognized as an official event of the National Ski Association, their affiliation having been made in January with Western Amateur Ski Association. This step put Mount Hood into the big-time competition. Winners were:

F. Finkenhagen .... Hollyburn
Thor Lief .... Viking
Kaare Schafstad .... Cascade
P. Sanders .... Hollyburn
Otto Hagen .... MHSC
Corey Gustafson .... Cascade
A. Sanes .... Hollyburn
Ole Haugen .... Cascade
Einer Hermensen .... MHSC
F. Fadmark .... Hollyburn
Olaf Lundy .... Washougal
F.W. Seide .... Cascade

The pre-contest favorite, Sanders of the Hollyburn Ski Club of British Columbia, did a post-race exhibition jump of 125 feet, 13 feet longer than his winning teammate Finkenhagen had made. Hans Hoerlein of Hood River came in first in the Class B competition, after which he joined the ranks of the A jumpers.

It was thus that the big jump hill at Multorpor gained great recognition, with Cascade Ski Club playing host every year for several jumping contests. In 1937 engineering was done by Marshall Brothers Engineering and Christian Dahl of Cascade Club to design the hill for optimum use. That fall a CCC crew worked on the hill to shape it as per the new plan. About 1500 cubic yards of rock and dirt were moved by dynamiting and shovelling, and new wood platforms were erected. The new configuration permitted a jump of 225 feet.

Multorpor in 1946 — Photo USFS

BUILDING A SKI TOW AT MULTORPOR

The ski tow at Multorpor was much like the one at Ski Bowl, steep, fast, and hard to ride. It mainly attracted slalom racers and some of the more advanced non-competitive crowd.

According to Maryanne Hill and Everett Darr the tow was built by Raymond R. "Bill" Hughes. The machinery was powered by a Dodge truck engine, and the rope on the steep hill ran over sheave wheels along the course, which precluded the rider holding directly onto the rope. Instead the rider held onto a short piece of pipe with a hook welded on one end; this would grasp the rope and pass through the sheaves.

Hughes' partner in the venture was George Beutler. There was constant wrangling between the two, and Beutler emerged as the operator. Charge was $1 per day or 5¢ per ride. Riders would at times find the tow shut down, Beutler having decided that the skiers had received enough action for one day.

Multorpor ski tow 1947 — Photo USFS

For some time Multorpor Tow was run by George Beutler, his sister, and his niece. In April of 1950 an electric storm struck the tow house, which also served as Beutler's home. The building burned and took the tow out of commission. Everett Darr can remember walking over to Beutler's with his wife and Joe and Laurita Leuthold.

"What are you going to do, rebuild?" Darr asked him.

"No. It's all right; I'm not going to live much longer anyway," Beutler said. In another month he was gone, dead from cancer.

The Forest Service put the area up for bid to a new operator. It was finally awarded to a new partnership formed by Carl N. Reynolds and Everett Darr. They installed a modern T-Bar in the autumn of 1950, and it opened for business in January of 1951, under the name of Multorpor Mountain Company.

Carl N. Reynolds and his wife, Mary, lived at Palo Alto for many years, where he was associated with Stanford University. Their family ties reached back into Government Camp history. His great grandfather was Clinton Kelly, who crossed the Barlow Road in 1848. The Dr. Kelly home built in Government Camp around the turn of the century, still stands, and is in the hands of Esther Kelly Watson.

Reynolds was willed property by two aunts, Mary Shaver Perrot and Cora Shaver, lots up the east end of Pompeii Addition. Mary Shaver had been a waitress at the old hotel in 1900, and O.C. Yocum gave her a plot of ground in 1911, as he had done with several employees.

The Reynolds family revisited Government Camp in 1948, an encounter with local people there, that led to their eventual heavy investment with Everett L. Darr in the Multorpor area.

Beutler had built a new warming hut for the Multorpor Hill in 1949. This was the principal asset which Darr and Reynolds had to buy in acquiring the area. Over the next decade, additions and improvements were made on the building. In 1961 an A-frame addition was incorporated into the structure to give greatly increased space and a snack bar.

Also in 1961, Multorpor Mountain Company made their greatest move. They erected a large new lift on the east face of Tom-Dick-Harry Mountain. With several new ski trails cut onto the slope, Multorpor developed a whole new dimension to its ski facilities.

SKI BOWL STORY

In the Ski Bowl the Forest Service built a warming hut on the shelf between Lower and Upper Bowls in 1937. The building was a 29' x 32' structure with a series of stone stoves for warmth. Skiers could buy coffee, snacks, and soft drinks, an arrangement that lasted until 1964.

Skiers Walking Into Ski Bowl
Circa 1938 — Photo Maryanne Hill

In the last good autumn days of 1937 the Mount Hood Winter Sports Association was finishing the first ski tow in the Ski Bowl. Boyd French and his son, Boyd, Jr., used an automobile engine to power a 2,100-foot rope that gave them about 1,000 feet of tow with top terminal on the shelf of the first steep hill behind the warming hut.

The tow was fast, and riders held on with special hooks that could ride over the sheaves without excessive hazard. This required a special kind of skier, so that Ski Bowl was not overcrowded in those years by beginners.

In 1946 "Sandy" Sandberg installed a lift in the lower bowl with wooden towers. Its course was laid out on the west side of the cleared slope. Management was under Boyd French and Herb and Kenneth Underdahl.

In 1954 Russell McJury, Shepard Wilson, and William Rosenfeld bought the Ski Bowl operation from Sandberg, soon afterward installing a new Riblet double chairlift in the Upper Bowl. They opened it for business the first week of January,

1955, the latest piece of equipment at the time, capable of moving 800 skiers per hour. The old lift with the wooden towers was still in operation in the Lower Bowl, and they used the combination until they sold out to Darr and Reynolds in 1964. Selling scuttled the plan that they had made to run a new chair lift all the way from the highway to the east end of Tom-Dick-Harry Ridge.

TWO AREAS BLEND

Multorpor Inc., a new corporation, was formed in 1964, when the new owners took over. Carl N. Reynolds became the president, Everett Darr the vice president, and Mary L. Reynolds the secretary treasurer. This purchase by the owners of Multorpor soon opened up a most interesting combination for the skier, who could buy a ticket at either resort, good for the full area. Darr and Reynolds made the announcement on March 4, 1964.

By the 1964-5 season trails had been opened up from the top of the Multorpor chairlift, running to the bottom of the Ski Bowl, as well as to the center of the Ski Bowl. In addition, skiers could ride the lift to the top of the Upper Bowl, then run the "Skyline Trail" back to the upper terminus of Multorpor Lift. This gives the area the following approximate capacities:

Multorpor T-Bar	800 per hour
Multorpor rope tows	1,000 per hour
Multorpor Chairlift	1,200 per hour
Upper Bowl Lift	800 per hour
Lower Bowl Lift	1,200 per hour
Bowl rope tows	500 per hour

In 1965 Multorpor Inc. built a new 3,575 foot Riblet double chair on the east side of the Lower Bowl. It has 716 feet of rise to the 4,300-foot level. It was dedicated early in 1966.

For the 1966-7 season, the owners installed a very effective night lighting system in the Ski Bowl at a cost of $35,000. In 1967 they added a new day lodge to existing facilities at Ski Bowl.

House on the Summit of Mount Hood

Bushnell Osborne, Jr., graduate of the Yale School of Forestry, in 1914 climbed Mount Hood to evaluate the summit as a possible site for one of his "Firefinder" stations, an invention he had perfected only three years previously. Lige Coalman had already reported many forest fires as he saw them in his climbs, and he was very interested in Osborne's device, a map with a pivot point at the position of a given lookout station. Sighting across the map on a compass azimuth ring, the lookout can easily determine a bearing. By taking a reading from another station, the district fire control ranger can pinpoint a blaze exactly.

The Forest Service decided to use the Firefinder on the summit of Mount Hood, and similar stations were set up on Mount McLoughlin, Mount St. Helens, and at Anvil Rock on Mount Rainier. Mount Jefferson was considered but turned down because of the small, hard-to-attain summit area. An agreement was made with Lige Coalman to begin the use of the Firefinder in the summer of 1915. Coalman proposed the plan himself in a letter to Forest Service Supervisor, Thomas Sherrard in June. A quick conference resulted in acceptance and government packer Dee Wright brought up a mile of insulated quarter-inch cable for a telephone line, dropping it at the Turtleneck at the top of the moraine west of White River Glacier on Sunday, July 23, 1915.

A special 12' x 12' tent was made for the job from two thicknesses of the heaviest canvas, reinforced with leather at seams and stress points. The top was a tapered cone, supported by a six-inch cedar post, 14-feet long, which Coalman carried to the summit. Iron fittings at the top allowed guying the tent to the rocks. Wright began bringing up loads of equipment, including the tent, to the base of Crater Rock. From there Coalman, Osborne, and Ranger George Ledford planned to carry everything on their backs.

A fortunate thing happened just at the time the big load was ready to carry. Coalman stood sorting out piles of equipment into 60-pound piles, when he looked up to see a stocky man descending the fixed line from the summit.

"You are Lige Coalman," he said as he approached. This Coalman admitted. "They told me at Cloud Cap you were working here," he

Osborne backfiring 1916 — Photo USFS

First Lookout Station on summit 1915 Lige Coalman on Left — Photo USFS

continued. "I need a job."

"Nothing you can do," said Coalman. "All the work here is packing. You can't pack."

"Try me," snapped the stranger, who identified himself as Olson.

Coalman handed him a 65-pound load, took a 50-pound one himself, and they set out for the summit. Coalman admitted later that the little man set a pace hard to keep up with, although he was pretty winded at the top. For three days they moved material up the mountain, then Olson moved on. He had been a sailor and had spent several years in difficult Alaskan terrain.

ERECTING THE TENT

A floor was built for the tent, and a kerosene stove furnished a bit of heat. Soon after the station was set up, Coalman and the Firefinder system proved their worth during an electric storm which caused several spot fires. One day he saw a fire on the south side of Mount Adams and sent a warning of it to Columbia National Forest in Washington. Fortunately this one was merely a group of Mazamas cleaning up their camp at Cold Spring after a climb. In six weeks, between July 10 and August 25, Coalman located 131 fires, positively proving the value of the installation.

Every day a trip down to the cache below Crater Rock had to be made for kerosene, food, or building materials. This needed to be done in early morning or late evening, when Coalman was not needed for constant fire vigil. The stove was smoky, and the tent cold. The lookout, over 6'2", was forced to spend a considerable amount of his time on hands and knees. So when the Forest Service asked him for a suggested cabin design, he responded promptly. They decided immediately, and lumber was delivered to Government Camp.

Lige precut and bundled the boards for packing up onto the mountain. He excavated a foundation three feet deep and 12-feet square, right near the highest point. Dee Wright packed the four tons of lumber and hardware in eight days, using 14 of the biggest mules he could find in the government stables.

Ranger Ledford set up a camp near the cache and sent up a husky crew of "pack rats" to carry the heavy loads to the summit. On September 6 the crew took the first loads up. Late summer brought on the worst possible climbing conditions with bare ice showing after all snow had melted. Huge crevasses crossed its surface. Even the guides were refusing to take clients to the summit.

At the end of the Hogsback stood a 25-foot ice slope to be climbed hand-over-hand on the fixed

Dee Wright, government packer — Photo George Calverley
Barn boss Jack O'Halloran in background.

line. Then, a walk along a ridge of ice from two to three feet wide led up another hundred feet, with a crevasse yawning at one side and a long drop into a rocky basin on the other. Then, a four foot jump over a crevasse led to the base of a ladder over a crevasse twenty feet wide. The ladder hung by a margin of four inches on either end, swaying and rolling like a ship in distress as the climbers crossed it. After that, a 500-foot climb over black ice on a 55-degree slope, aided by a fixed rope brought them to another catwalk to cross for 60 feet. Then, only one more flimsy ladder bridging a wide crevasse was the only obstacle to the final summit slope.

The "pack rats" worked one day and found that by working hard they could make $5 per day. They asked Coalman to increase the rate per pound from 2¢ to 3¢. The night was cold, the camp uncomfortable; mutiny was in the air.

Coalman telephoned below, and Ledford rode up on his horse, not having the authority to raise the rate. After an argument at the cache, Coalman took the responsibility to raise the pay, hoping that Sherrard would back him up. Even so, four men quit later in the day, four the following day, and three more soon after. This left only Coalman, his assistant Roy Mitchell, Marshall Davis, George Maronay, and the two Swiss guide brothers, Hans and Heinie Fuhrer. It took a week to complete the job. It is said that Coalman took 120 pounds of nails and hardware up on the last load. The route led directly up the Hogsback to the summit, as it has done at times in history, crossing a crevasse that was wide and very deep in the late summer. Rocks rolling from above compounded the problem on negotiating the slope. Lige's ladder was barely minimal, made out of scrap lumber with widely-spaced rungs to save precious material. The fixed rope from the summit was tied to the top of the ladder to secure it, but there was considerable creaking and groaning as the men gingerly crossed the hungry crevasse.

Soon hammers were ringing in the high air. A 10-inch frame was laminated from 2" x 8" boards for the well-braced base. Coalman framed up from that and filled the base with heavy rock. Then, a doubled floor was laid and a laminated 10-inch center post ran to the center of the cupola. They knew this could be no ordinary construction to withstand the high winds and pressure of snow and ice. Walls were double-thickness outside with a layer of building paper between, and the same construction inside.

Time ran short before the winter storm. One blast forced Coalman and Mitchell to crawl 300 feet back to their tent in freezing sleet. By morning the tent was a pyramid of ice. The two were pinned there for three days, the tent becoming smaller and smaller under encroaching walls of ice. First unable to stand, they later had not even space to kneel. They merely laid in their sleeping bags and waited, eating a little now and then to stay alive. The telephone was outside, but no rescue party could have come to their aid anyway.

The wall dropping off to the Eliot Glacier was only 14 feet away. What if the guy wires had broken? The six-inch center pole was bent far over and needed propping. Finally the storm eased off. They cut through two and a half feet of ice to reach the outside. On the windward side the ice had built up to a four-foot thickness.

Returning to work, they finished all the cabin but the cupola. It was the last of September, and another storm was threatening. Fuel and food were about gone. As the storm began to bluster around the summit, they prepared to run for life. The first item was to remove the fixed rope running up across the crevasse from the Hogsback. Mitchell started down to untie the bottom after freeing the top end. Cutting steps with his ice-axe he broke the handle and returned to make a new one. At dusk both men started down in the storm, Mitchell below cutting steps when he broke the handle again.

He then took the alpenstock and Lige was left to depend upon the nails of his boots to keep footing. At the crevasse the line was gone. With the storm cutting visibility, they searched for the ladder and an anchoring rope, often groping on hands and knees on the top lip of the crevasse. Working too far west in the gloom, Lige was whipped off his feet by a gust of wind as he stood ten feet above the lip. He sat down as he slid downward, remembering quickly the configuration of the crevasse. On the upper side a shelf broke the vertical fall. So as he hit the lower lip, he pushed himself back hard, hit the shelf to break his fall and slid off it the remaining 35 feet to the bottom. Quick thinking had saved him from a long, direct fall, but even so, he lay there at the bottom of the crevasse on a stormy autumn night with sprained ankles and sprained knee.

With a towel in his pack he bandaged his legs. Mitchell had meanwhile located the place where the rope should have anchored the ladder, but the rope had dropped into the crevasse. Lige was able to retrieve it and got it into Mitchell's hands after several casts. Mitchell was then able to descend to the shelf in the crevasse and help them both to reach the lower side. Walking was very difficult for Lige as he battled the deep snow. At timberline they were lost and swung west to find the trail to Government Camp. By chance a lucky swing of the alpenstock by Coalman struck the telephone wire, giving them location. They reached Government Camp Hotel at 2:00 a.m. where he recuperated for three weeks from the sprains.

LIVING ON THE SUMMIT

Once the building was complete a new dimension was added to Mount Hood. The $632.92 which it cost the Forest Service in no way reflects the gruelling work, the hazards, and near misses with disaster encountered by the builders. To so many climbers, the presence of a Forest Service lookout on top became a routine, expected thing. Many an adventurer reached the summit tired and listless to find a cup of coffee waiting. But few considered the price of such a nicety, that was the result of a summit guard such as Lige Coalman carrying up water and the kerosene to heat it on his back.

Many interesting references to the summit cabin are found in the chapter on Lige Coalman. Another that is indicative of his hospitality is the story of a climb led by T. Raymond Conway, written for the *Sunday Oregon Journal* by Vera Taylor. Others in the party were Mary Knapp, Agnes Lawson, Margaret Griffin, Harry Wolbers, Linn Johnson, and Albert Brown. On Saturday, September 1, 1917, they left Portland by automobile to travel through several miles of burning forest east of the Rhododendron Toll Gate. The crackling of the nearby fire was ominous as they drove along.

Arriving at the camp at timberline, they slept in, while another party got up and left for the summit well ahead of them. With a full day to make the summit, they did not leave camp until 10:00 a.m. At the White River Glacier they took a detour and explored into a crevasse, marvelling at the huge icicles hanging from the ceiling and the deep, indigo blue of the ice. At Crater Rock, Coalman welcomed them and led them to the summit about 6:30, where a blustering wind threatened their footing.

Coalman made dinner for the group, and afterward he put a record on the phonograph. The cabin whined and creaked in the wind, as it tugged on its foundations, but inside the group of nine danced foxtrots and one-steps until the moon had risen high in the sky. Finally, blankets were spread on every available bit of floor, and the party went to sleep. In the morning, Coalman was making breakfast at 6:30.

The group explored the summit area and sat in the sun on Mazama Rock. At 1:00 p.m. Coalman descended with them to the crater, and the full party climbed Crater Rock, its second ascent in history. The first climb had been made by Coalman in 1912. Descending the rock, they went to its base, where he found a break in the telephone line caused by a falling rock. He waved goodbye to the group as he retaped the splice, then turned to climb his lonesome way back to the summit cabin.

MOVIES ARRIVE ON TOP

The first weekend of September, 1922, a motion picture company of 14 worked its way up to the summit by Cooper Spur Route. Starting early from Cloud Cap Inn, they filmed scenes for "The Crystal Ascension" as they climbed. In the afternoon a storm hit, and the party was forced to cut steps up to the top. The cameramen came first, turning back to shoot scenes, as the others came over the top.

The ascent had taken 14 hours, and many of the party were in fatigue. The fixed line had by that time become encrusted in ice, and Lookout Charles A. Phelps took them in for the night. Their rations had dwindled to only a few chocolate bars, and there were no blankets for them. The feminine star, Irene Marvin, was made as comfortable as possible. In the morning it was decided that the north was too dangerous to descend, and the party left by the South Side Route and a very long return trip to Cloud Cap Inn.

The group included F.H. Kiser, head of Kiser Studios, Inc., Director Broderick O'Farrell, Dolph Thomas, Jack Barry, Lloyd Jones, Jack Fenton, Lewis Kiser, Charles Carver, Leslie Morgan, Thille De Fontenay, E.J. Taylor, Mel Wharton, and William Moody, guide from Cloud Cap Inn.

WEATHER STRUCK QUICKLY

A terrible, harrowing experience was had by lookout Charles A. Phelps on Sunday, September 7, 1924. A pleasant day was just about over. At 4:30 p.m. he could see that a lightning storm played around Mount Jefferson, fifty miles to the south. In just two hours it had reached Mount Hood, clouds creeping up the east slope to envelop the summit.

For an hour a vast number of lightning bolts crashed and roared around peaks and crags nearby. About 20 minutes after the storm hit, lightning struck the cupola, jumped to the firefinder, smashed a window. For the next 15 minutes he fought to extinguish the burning cupola, then found that the telephone was knocked out. After he returned to the living quarters below, a second bolt struck the cupola, a ball of fire that left sulphurous smoke so thick he could not see or breathe.

He thought about the 50 gallons of fuel on the lower floor, gasoline, coal oil, and alcohol, and decided to run for his life. Grabbing a sweater and his ice axe, he stepped out to find the wind blowing so hard he could not stand up in it. It was getting dark. Heavy snow and sleet were sweeping almost horizontally with the gale. He crawled the 300 feet to reach the fixed line in the chute. By that time his clothing was wet, and the storm had torn loose the rope.

He moved carefully down the Chute in the dusk. Suddenly the heavens lit up as a bolt of lightning hit the cliff above him, sending down an avalanche of rock onto the slope. To avoid the expected bombardment of rock he threw himself into a depression in the snow, but it was only about three feet long, not enough to protect his feet and legs. When the avalanche had passed over, he found that his left leg was badly sprained, and his feet were dangerously cold. A few stones still clattered above.

Groping downward, he could see the menacing blackness of the crevasse below, and with more rock coming from above he was forced to take the shelter of a niche in the ice of the very top lip. There were times when he decided to venture out to return to the cabin, but each time rock rolled from above and drove him back. Finally, the storm broke at about 5:00 a.m., and he hobbled up to the cabin to get warm and make coffee.

Closing the cabin, he began to limp down the miles to timberline, a frightful ordeal for the left leg with torn tendons. At Timberline Cabin, Forest Service men met him and took him on down to the doctor. Phelps wore a plaster cast on his leg for a long while. Exposure to cold and dampness all night on the glacier caused rheumatic problems in his feet and legs.

WANTED: FRESH EGGS

Life was never very easy for the man at the lookout station, but it did have its humorous moments. At the last of July, 1932, climber Paul Callicotte brought the news to *The Oregonian* that Mack Hall was really hungry for fresh eggs up there on the summit and would pay 35¢ per dozen.

Seeing the news in the paper, Barney Young, 20, bought a dozen eggs and headed for the summit on the evening of Wednesday, August 3. Hall was very pleased to get them, when Young came knocking on his cabin door at ten minutes before midnight. At 12:45 a.m., Young left to descend the mountain, reaching the end of the road at timberline at about 2:30. This had been his 12th climb of Mount Hood. The next morning, after getting one hour of sleep, he was back on his job as a bank messenger, telling all his friends that he hadn't broken a single egg.

Thursday morning, Ed Miller of Hood River provided for the lookout and brought up two dozen eggs while guiding up a group of climbers. The following day Paul Callicotte and Hubert North came up from the south and brought eight dozen. Later on Friday, Ben Moores and Wilfred Playton, two Crag Rats, were considerate enough to bring up a dozen each for Hall.

At the last reporting Hall was wondering what he was going to do with 13 dozen eggs and hoping that no one brought more. He then began complaining that he really needed a haircut and hoped that a barber would climb the mountain.

1933 was the last year of use. Ray Lewis went through the yearly ritual of coiling the fixed ropes hanging on both sides of the summit and storing them in the cabin on the Wednesday after Labor Day. He then closed the door, not realizing that it would be forever. The summit lookout station was never manned again.

However, the Forest Service frequently mentioned building a new cabin on the summit. On September 29, 1938, Harold Engles, Ranger at Zigzag said that the dilapidated cabin, its windowless cupola sagging, had been moored and braced for the winter, and that they hoped to replace it the next summer. He also noted that the ropes had been taken down and climbers should stay off the peak. The chute was bare ice, and the big crevasse was 100 feet deep and impassable.

In 1940 Engles sent materials to Crater Rock to rebuild the summit cabin. Experience with the masonry house in the crater had been a failure. Walls of the hut built in 1934 had cracked by the following year, and by 1940 only two-foot stubs showed where the wall had been.

The new structure on the summit was to be all of wood with no windows. Sleeping bays and rest rooms located off a 15' x 15' main room would give shelter to climbers hit by storms. The building was to have no heat.

The lumber was sent up on snow cats, then highlined into the crater. Climbers who have thought they saw old machine parts on the side of Crater Rock are not mistaken. A Model B gasoline engine was used to drive a winch. At first the workmen used a quarter-inch cable, but it broke repeatedly, so a half-inch cable was brought up. The heavy cable burned out the clutch on the engine. One of the exciting moments on the operation was when Sinclair hit ice with a snow cat, skidded, and turned it over.

Some of the men who worked on the job were George Henderson, George Lasher, Cloyd McKinnon, Lewis Hayes, Boyd French, Jr., J. Fred Tolley, Edison Mills, Wilbur E. Butts, Robert M. Lasher, Albert H. Stone, Howard C. Stone. Irwin Hull did some horse-packing on the job. A high-peaked tent was set up on the remnant walls of the 1934 stone hut in the crater, serving as a bleak headquarters for the crew.

The operation was cut short by a vicious storm in September, that drove the men from the camp. The lumber was left in the crater, covered with tarpaulins. If it had not been for one-too-many fires during the summer, or that sudden storm, the new house would have been built. The following year Ranger Harold Engles tried again to activate the project. He proposed to do the carpentry work himself, and to have the whole crew organized on a standby basis, wherein they could answer a fire call within 30 minutes.

The project did not materialize, and later the whole concept was abandoned. Some of the lumber probably still lies stacked in the crater north of the Devil's Kitchen. Heavy snows of recent years have not exposed the little "crater lake" that once was visible in that area each summer. Coalman used the water in the lake as a ground for his lightning rod and telephone line.

Today only a couple of wooden posts mark the site of Coalman's old summit cabin.

WHO MANNED THE CABIN

The summit cabin was manned as follows:

1915 .... Construction
1916 .... Elijah Coalman
1917 .... Elijah Coalman
1918 .... Elijah Coalman
Mark Weygandt
1919 .... Elijah Coalman
George Maronay
1920 .... Al T. Maas
W.C. Kelly

1921 .... Al T. Maas
Clem Blakney
1922 .... Charles A. Phelps
1923 .... Charles A. Phelps
1924 .... Charles A. Phelps
1925 .... Fred Schmeling
1926 .... Dean VanZandt
1927 .... Robert G. McVicar
1928 .... Robert G. McVicar
1929 .... Robert G. McVicar
1930 .... Robert G. McVicar
1931 .... Robert G. McVicar
1932 .... Mack Hall
1933 .... Ray Lewis

TIMBERLINE CABIN

Near the head of Sand Canyon a cabin was built in 1916 by Lige Coalman for a Forest Service operating base at timberline. The cabin was used as a refuge from bad weather by climbers over the years. In the late Twenties skiers began to climb to timberline during the winter and use the building as a place to bunk. It was used a great deal by The Mazamas and especially by the Wy'east Climbers before they built their own cabin in 1934.

The area around the cabin was sometimes known as Camp Blossom, actually a confusion. Camp Blossom had been located at the end of the old wagon road, a little further east, named for early-day visitor Judge Blossom. The camp had been a favorite camping spot of Judge M.C. George, a prominent member of The Mazamas. In 1907 George came up the road to find the camp jammed with the Sylvester mapping party of the US Geological Survey. Judge George just kept going and chose a site at Sand Canyon, which was known for a long while as Camp George. Later Timberline Cabin was built there.

Ron Thompson, Recreational Assistant at Zigzag Ranger Station stated that Timberline Cabin was built partly from the lumber of an older cabin at Camp Blossom, about a quarter mile to the east, on the headwaters of Still Creek. The older cabin had been built by Judge Blossom, himself, after he built a wagon road to timberline in 1888. Blossom would at times serve tea to climbers on their way to the summit or returning from it. Everett Darr told Thompson that the old Blossom road made a good ski trail in the early Thirties, for the Wy'easters and Mazamas who stayed at Timberline Cabin.

The only present remains of Timberline Cabin consists of a concrete fireplace footing. In the protection of some nearby trees a few stones reveal the site of the old outhouse.

Timberline Cabin February 14, 1932 — Photo Joe Leuthold
On snow Walt Staehli. On wall James Mount. In doorway, Curtis Ijames

Typical Plank Road — Photo Maryanne Hill
Summit Meadows in the Thirties.

To comprehend the importance of this great building one must understand the politics and economic philosophy of the early Thirties. America had suffered severe economic collapse in 1929. By the year 1932 unemployment was desperate, and the voters elected flambouyant and personable Franklin D. Roosevelt to the presidency. Rather than to try to repair the sick economy, so that once again it could flourish, Roosevelt took drastic steps that eventually replaced the free enterprise economy with the socialist welfare-state economy and society under which we live today.

In late 1935 he had only one more year to go before facing election. Price controls had come to an inevitable failure. Plowing under grain and killing livestock had not succeeded in driving farm prices up. Millions of men were being fed by the Works Progress Administration, a government labor system that employed large gangs of men, mostly on make-work projects. Great dams were under way in the Tennessee Valley, as well as Bonneville and Grand Coulee dams on the Columbia. The government was printing money and adding it to the national debt. Knowledgeable economists, business executives, and money managers realized that these policies were resulting in instability and fear on the part of free enterprise. However, they were but a few people. Roosevelt, a master showman, was playing to the masses, and the more printing-press dollars he passed around, the more votes he bought at the polls.

This being the political climate, the Portland Winter Sports Association made high level requests to the federal government for a hotel facility at Mount Hood. Portland businessmen Jack Meier, Charles Bierli, Dr. Paul Dutton, George W. Joseph, Walter W.R. May, James Mount, Berger Underdahl, and John Yeon were some of those who helped promote Timberline Lodge. The public was evidently not aware of the efforts, for there was no mention in the newspapers. On December 12, 1935, Ferdinand A. Silcox, Chief of US Forestry Service, spoke at the convention of Western Forestry and Conservation Association at the Portland Hotel. He made no reference to the project. Yet three days later on December 15, *The Oregonian* ran a surprise front page story.

WPA WILL BUILD MT. HOOD HOTEL

Roosevelt Puts Approval on Wanted Project

BIG RECREATION ENTERPRISE TO INCLUDE ALL FEATURES OF HIGH-CLASS RESORT

"Mt. Hood. Oregon's all-year playground, will be the scene of the most outstanding recreational development ever undertaken in the United States, as the result of approval yesterday by President Roosevelt of a WPA project for $275,513, it was announced at the Portland office of the works progress administration."

The long news story continued to state that the hotel would accommodate 300, with roads, trails, parking, ski jumps, ski and toboggan runs, swimming pool, amphitheatre, water system, tennis courts, barns, garages, a very large package for even the low prices of that day. It is quite evident that any planning or price projections were very minimal. The government strategy was to present a vast, attractive package with a very low price tag. The approved application had three sponsors, the State of Oregon, the Regional office of US Forest Service, and Mount Hood Recreation Association of Portland. A local pledge of $10,000 was a stipulated condition. The Forest Service would supervise and control the facility.

Again, it is important to know the climate of enthusiasm that was being generated at the time. On November 21, 1935, A.O. Waha, supervisor of Mount Hood National Forest reported that short wave broadcasts from station PF-153 at 3385 kilocycles, located at Summit Guard Station, would send 8 a.m. and 4 p.m. data on temperature, weather, and road conditions, using the talents of Paul Williams, winter sports ranger. On December 12, Count Felix Schaffgotsch, a wealthy Austrian skier, visited Mount Hood with Jack Meier, John Yeon, and Otto Urbach, an Austrian exchange student teaching skiing at Reed College. The Count gave the newspapers enthusiastic approval of skiing potential at Mount Hood.

On the very day that the Timberline Lodge story broke in the papers, December 15, another new story announced that the fifth annual Winter Sports Carnival was well under way. The carnival was to culminate in a Friday parade in downtown Portland on January 24, 1936, a dance on Saturday night at Battle Axe Inn, and a Pacific Northwest Ski Tournament at Multorpor Mountain on Sunday, sponsored by Cascade Ski Club. Portland residents voted for a queen of the carnival among a slate of 22 entrants. By the time

Looking south over Timberline Lodge — Photo Joe Leuthold

Eileen Troland, daughter of a local Norwegian skier, had been elected as queen, the winter sports fervor had been whipped into a frenzy by the promoters. On New Year's Day over a thousand visited Government Camp, where it rained. Many hiked to timberline for good skiing conditions. When the big carnival weekend arrived, an unprecedented 10,000 visitors jammed Government Camp and its limited facilities. Hermod Bakke of Leavenworth, Washington, won the Class A jumping competition, with Hjalmar Hvam running second.

With this setting of wild enthusiasm, the raising of the money for the sponsor's guarantee was made possible. Organizations involved were Portland Winter Sports Association, Mount Hood Recreation Association, Chamber of Commerce, and East Side Commercial Club.

January 2, 1936 It was announced that Stanley Stonaker of Underwood and Company, Los Angeles, was coming to Portland to confer with US Forest Service architects on hotel design, expedited by F.A. Silcox, himself. The project would employ 500. Hewing logs, quarrying stone, and making shakes would begin by January 6. Plans were that the private operator-lessee would provide bus service to the lodge. In winter only busses might use the road, but in summer, visitors could drive up the road in their automobiles.

January 8, 1936 E.J. Griffith, WPA administrator for Oregon, announced that federal funds were ready for release upon receipt of the $10,000 sponsor guarantee. He appointed Lorenz Brothers, Portland, as contracting supervisors, and preliminary designs had begun. The site was selected, about 1000 feet east of the eventual site, on the rim of the Salmon River. Completion by autumn was hoped.

January 14, 1936 Thirty seven members of the Chamber of Commerce pledged from $1500 to $2000.

January 16, 1936 Mount Hood Development Association was reformed from the remains of the existing Mount Hood Recreation Association. Jack Meier was president; Walter R. May, vice-president; James Mount, secretary; Berger Underdahl, treasurer. The amount of the sponsor pledge was raised to $20,000.

January 24, 1936 East Side Commercial Club joined the crusade for funds. The Chamber of Commerce asked members for contributions from $10 to $100.

January 25, 1936 Shakes for roof split and accumulated at Camp One-and-one-half on the North Fork of the Clackamas River near Estacada, a Civilian Conservation Corps branch reopened by the WPA for that purpose.

January 27, 1936 Lorenz Brothers were placing lists of needed materials on bulletin board of Bedell Building, eliminating the call for bids usually required.

January 31, 1936 Lorenz Brothers announced the type of building. Contracts would be on negotiated contract.

February 20, 1936 Twenty five men were cutting shakes, 1¼-inch thick. Snow removal planned for March 1.

February 23, 1936 Newspaper presentation showed artist's drawing and description of the lodge.

February 27, 1936 James Mount, secretary of Mount Hood Development Association, told members of the Progressive Business Mens' Club that the $270,000 hotel would make Oregon famous as a winter sports playground. He announced the sale of $20,000 in 4% bonds.

March 8, 1936 A large newspaper story showed an artist's sketch. Plans called for miles of hiking and horseback trails, showers and dressing rooms for hikers and skiers, tennis courts, a vast swimming pool to be converted to a skating rink in winter, and complete guide service.

Wednesday, March 11, 1936 126 buyers had purchased $8510 in bonds.

Sunday, March 15, 1936 $275,513 in WPA funds had been allocated for the project. In addition, $20,000 must be subscribed in local bonds. A supplement of $10,000 was being requested to use solely for art adornments.

Thursday, March 19, 1936 Only $3,300 remained to be sold of the $20,000 bond issue.

Later in the spring the site on the edge of Salmon River Canyon was re-examined. With 18 feet of snow on the ground, great snow cornices overhung the canyon, and the planners realized that a site about 900 to 1,000 feet west would be more suitable. A survey party established a new site in May, working over snowdrifts to make their locations.

June 1, 1936 A photograph in *The Oregonian* by George Henderson showed a dragline clearing snow for the hotel site. On the same weekend the Mount Hood Loop highway was opened.

Sunday, June 14, 1936 The $350,000 Mount Hood Timberline lodge was honored by a cornerstone ceremony by E.J. Griffith, Oregon W.P.A. administrator, and Major James Frankland, regional forestry engineer. Jack Meier served as chairman for the program sent over the National Broadcasting Company network by radio station KGW in Portland. Winter sports Queen Eileen Troland and her court were present.

The road was not open to the public. Visitors were given free bus rides to timberline from a parking area near Summit. Note that the newspaper story almost used the name Timberline Lodge. It could have been the wording in the news story that gave the hotel its ultimate name.

Ski competition of national caliber was held on this day in the Mazama Cup Race run from Crater Rock to timberline. Hjalmar Hvam and Boyd French, Jr. of Cascade Ski Club took first and second place in a combined race, slalom and downhill. French had the best downhill time, but his combined score was slower than Hvam's. Other racers were Bob Donaldson of The Mazamas, Roy Tangen of Cascade Ski Club, Jack Walker of Portland, Adams Carter of Harvard, and many top runners from Seattle and Vancouver, British Columbia.

Junior skiers of high school age ran a steep course into the Salmon River Canyon. Competition at that age level was just beginning.

Wednesday, July 29, 1936 Allen Johnstone, one of two national W.P.A. officials from Washington D.C., visited the new hotel site as a part of his swing through the west. All exterior work was expected to be finished by November 10.

August 16, 1936 Captain C.G. Jones, construction engineer on the hotel, told newsmen that 380 W.P.A. workers were on the job. The roof on the west wing was taking shape with 50-foot rafters raised 34 feet above the wall level. Stone walls were being laid up, a construction that weighed six tons per running foot of wall.

Henry Steiner, log building craftsman from Brightwood, was in the process of bringing 30-foot logs from Mount Adams to be hewed into hexagonal-shaped, three-foot diameter pillars.

Newspaper accounts mentioned that the hotel was designed by architect W. Turner. Max Lorenz was the builder. Landscaping was to be handled by E.U. Blanchfield and F.E. Williamson, Jr.

Machinery on the hotel and road construction included 35 trucks, four caterpillar tractors, and two large shovels.

September 7, 1936 It was noted that a "snowcat" had been developed by I.F. Davidson, who was working at the hotel site. The machine would be able to climb 40% grades, carry its own weight, and run 25 miles per hour. This is perhaps the first mention of the machines that have since become standard equipment around ski resorts and mountain areas everywhere.

September 13, 1936 The Forest Service announced that it was extending Alpine Ski Trail on up to the site of the new hotel. Previously it had run from Government Camp to Phlox Point.

September 14, 1936 On a Monday visit, Harry L. Hopkins, administrator of the W.P.A. inspected the new lodge. The first snow of the season fell on the new roof.

Thursday, January 7, 1937 With all of Oregon in freezing weather, Timberline Lodge was experiencing vicious, 70-mile winds and low visibility. When the 86 men of the construction crew started down to the camp at Summit Meadow at 4:00 p.m. the trucks wallowed down the road about three quarters of a mile before stalling in the drifting snow.

It was finally necessary to leave the trucks and run for life back to the lodge. With wind pelting their faces with stinging particles of snow, they fought their way back uphill in an effort that very nearly proved tragic. It was necessary to hang onto a rope to keep the group together.

Calls for snowplows were answered, but it took hours for the snow removal machines to clear the road. It was midnight before the crews were all safely returned to Summit Meadows.

Meanwhile at 11:00 p.m. the repair garage at Summit caught fire and quickly burned. Heat from a home-made oil stove ignited oil on the floor and quickly took the building with all contents, including a caterpillar tractor and several trucks. Loss was valued at $10,000. Water pipes were frozen at Summit, and almost all the wood supply was depleted.

August 23, 1937 C.J. Buck, Regional Forester, announced that an operator would be selected on a bid basis before October 15. The operator was to pay $1000 per year plus half of the profits, as agreed by the Forest Service and Mount Hood Development Association.

Operator must provide climbing guide service, skiing instruction, proper insurance, horses and wrangler, dining service, and keep the road open in winter time. It was the stipulation concerning the road that kept the bids from coming in as the forest service wanted them, and October passed without selection of an operator.

Sunday, June 13, 1937 Timberline Lodge held its first open house showing to the public. About 3,000 people visited the building and were spectators at the Golden Rose Ski Race, run from Crater Rock to timberline. E.J. Griffith addressed a banquet at the CCC barracks at Summit Meadows, attended by tournament skiers and guests of the Oregon Winter Sports Association.

June 19, 1937 It was announced that Timberline lodge had cost $955,642 to date. $246,893 had originally been allocated. Notice that the name was beginning to gain acceptance in speeches and news references, although the name Timberline Lodge had not been officially decided.

September 28, 1937 The formal dedication of the lodge was made by President Franklin D. Roosevelt. Advance publicity had created great interest and enthusiasm for the presidential visit. Although rooms were not ready to occupy in the lodge, two were made ready for the Roosevelts, who never did use them. Plans were made for parking a thousand automobiles, and additional telephone lines were run in to provide for radio broadcasting and secret service needs.

On the morning of the great day, the Roosevelts' private rail car entered the siding in Portland at 6:30 a.m. The president was then whisked to Bonneville Dam for its formal dedication scheduled at 9:30 a.m. The trip was made in Horace Mecklem's open four-door Packard, the president waving to the crowds as he rode in the open car with his wife and Charles Martin, Governor of Oregon, and his wife.

After the formal opening of the dam, the motorcade proceeded to Hood River and thence up to Timberline Lodge, where the president arrived at 1:12 p.m. Shortly after, another car

F.D. Roosevelt dedicated Timberline — Photo USFS

Roosevelt party enroute to Timberline Lodge, passing through Parkdale. — Photo David Cooper, Jr.

arrived with Mr. and Mrs. John Boettinger, son-in-law and daughter of the Roosevelts, and their children, Sistie and Bussie Dahl. The president was supported by his military aide, Colonel Edwin M. Watson. Mayor Carson of Portland was in attendance, and Governor Martin made the introduction for the speech on the parapet over the front door.

The address, of course, had little content other than the usual platitudes of praise for the party in power at the White House, but it was radioed over major networks to every part of the United States. Fifteen forest guards in lookout stations blinked back messages by heliograph to Timberline, acknowledging the radio speech.

The Roosevelts, the Boettinger family, and the Martins sat down to lunch in the dining room. After lunch the president took quick leave, bundling up in auto robes in the open car, and travelling quickly to Portland and on to Seattle.

A humorous sidelight is connected with the presidential visit. One prominent outdoor figure of Mount Hood, whose name can not now be revealed, made a trip into Roosevelt's room. Secret service men caught him unscrewing the seat off the toilet and threatened arrest. When they asked him why he was doing this, he replied that he wanted to frame the president's picture. Struggling to keep from smiling, they decided to forego any legal action because of bad publicity it would make. Roosevelt was a very much hated president by most of the influential classes of people, and he was very sensitive to any adverse news that might damage his image.

October 30, 1937 The Forest Service indicated that it would keep the road open at all times of the year.

November 13, 1937 The building project was mostly complete, but no successful bidder to operate the lodge had been received by the Forest Service. Local people were worried. The Chamber of Commerce proposed a community organization to take over the venture.

November 17, 1937 The Forest Service tested a snow-cat that would be used to pull a sled with 20 to 25 passengers, a possible answer for times when the road could not be kept open.

November 13, 1937 A large crew of CCC boys were busy laying an auxiliary water pipe line to the lodge from a spring 1½ miles below. The ditch was three feet deep, below the freezing line. The system needed pumping to bring the water up hill. The primary system was by gravity and fed by a spring on the ridge above Salmon River Canyon about a third of a mile north of the lodge.

Sunday, November 21, 1937 The lodge was visited by Sir Arnold Lunn, editor of the British Ski Year Book. About 200 cars had brought up a crowd of 1,000 for his speech and for the opening ski race of the year. Lunn made his 20-minute

An interesting little sidelight on the leasing of Timberline Lodge is told by Everett Sickler. When Sickler was operating Battle Axe Inn, long before anyone dreamed of Timberline Lodge, he had some ideas of building a skiing and climbing chalet at timberline. Sickler and Scotty Williamson of the Forest Service toured around the area one summer and got some ideas about a site. Williamson's activity was authorized by Thomas Sherrard, Supervisor of MHNF.

Sickler placed an application with the Forest Service and drew plans for a Swiss-style building. On the bottom floor was planned a warming hut for skiers and climbers. Food was to be a simple menu, such as soup and coffee. The second floor was to be a men's dormitory, and the third floor a women's dormitory. The whole operation was meant to be a satellite of Battle Axe Inn. Sickler's sale of Battle Axe at a later date and the development of the depression eliminated the whole plan, and he forgot all about it.

But when Timberline Lodge was announced, Sherrard contacted Sickler, saying "I have your hotel for you."

"What do you mean?" asked Sickler.

"The government is building a hotel. Do you want to run it?"

By that time Sickler was all out of the notion of running any hotel, much less an immense operation such as Timberline Lodge.

Clearing the road to Timberline 1938 — Photo Joe Leuthold

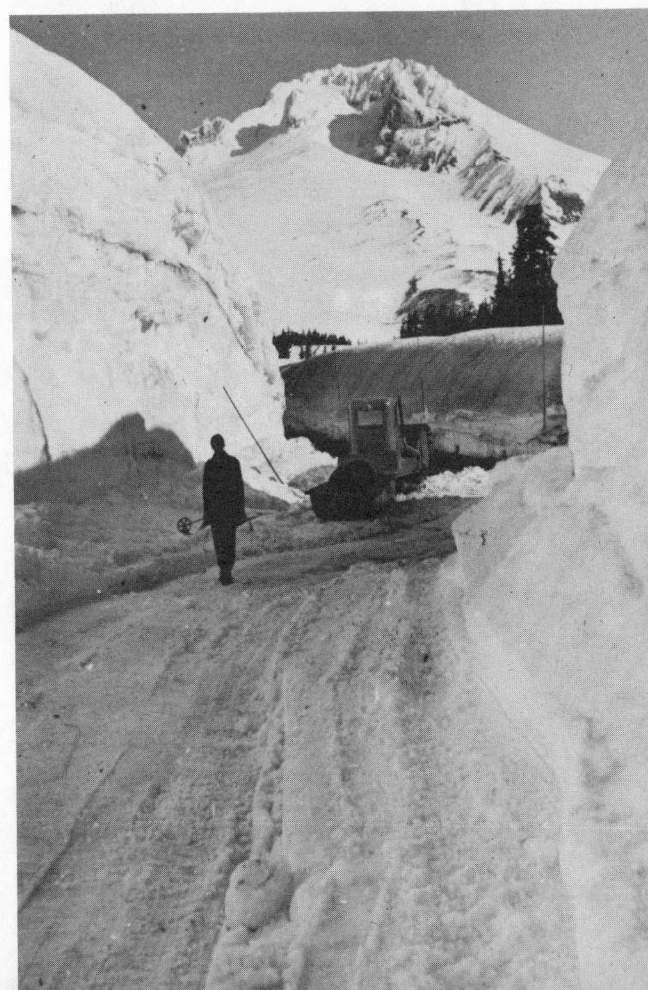

talk on the parapet in front of the lodge in perfect weather. He marvelled at the all-year skiing potential and encouraged American skiers in world-wide competition and acknowledgement. He suggested that a tram to Crater Rock or to the summit would bring Mount Hood to its fullest ski fame.

The opening race was named the Arnold Lunn, a classic that has lasted over the years. Hjalmar Hvam took the honors, and Don French won the junior competition.

January 5, 1938 Timberline Lodge Inc., a $72,290 corporation of local people to operate the hotel, was announced to the public. The prominent leaders were Horace Mecklem, E.J. Griffith, and J.V. Horton, Legal incorporators were Herbert L. Swett, R.R. Morris, and Frank C. McCulloch, $12,290 was earmarked to retire bonds of Mount Hood Development Company, and the remaining $60,000 to buy equipment.

The Forest Service granted a ten year permit at $250 per year, plus a share in profits after the $72,290 plus interest was repaid. The hotel manager had been appointed, C.E. (Larry) McLean, hotelier with experience at the Waldorf-Astoria in New York, the Book-Cadillac in Detroit, as well as some western hotels. Plans were made to open for business in just one month, on February fifth.

OPEN FOR BUSINESS

Friday, February 5, 1938 Fires crackled in the fireplaces, dining tables were decked with spring flowers, and the staff worked in businesslike precision, as a parade of 150 influential guests registered for the opening weekend of Timberline Lodge. The Multnomah Hotel in Portland sent up its executive staff to give the hostelry a flying start, Gordon Bass on reservations, Morris Bertoglio on staff training, and Mildred Marshall in charge of the office. Permanent personnel were learning and would take over on the following Monday. Larry McLean managed with an expert eye and affable manner.

Transportation was by bus from Government Camp. Timberline Lodge Inc. held an official directors' meeting. Attending were President Jack Meier, Vice-president Horace Mecklem, Secretary-Treasurer Harvey Black, Directors Forrest Berg, Aubrey Watzek, William Healy, and A.A. Comrie. In every way, this new hotel had the backing of the very prominent people of Portland.

A banquet was held, followed by a program by the WPA officials and two-and-a-half hours of music and vaudeville.

On Saturday, a ceremonial passing of the key to the hotel was made from E.J. Griffith of WPA to Fred Brundage, the acting regional forester, who gave it to Barbara Johnson, Miss Oregon, who passed it to W.J. Haffam of Timberline Lodge Inc. Manager McLean reported heavy future bookings for the rest of the season. Super-

Timberline Lodge drew large crowds in 1938-39 — Photo Joe Leuthold

visor of Mount Hood National Forest, A.O. Waha, stipulated that automobiles could be taken up the road Monday through Friday, but that on weekends all visitors must come to the lodge on the shuttle bus from Government Camp.

Boyd French was placed in charge of the ski shop sales and rentals. A visit had been made by Otto Lang to determine whether he wished to bring the services of the Hannes Schneider Ski School to the lodge.

It was on this opening day that the public had its first real chance to view the unusual artistry that had gone into the building. When President Roosevelt had dedicated Timberline Lodge in September, there was yet much work to be finished.

The art work had been coordinated and supervised by Margery Hoffman Smith, using the labor of some who were talented artists and artisans, but many of the workers began their jobs completely untrained. Espirit de corps was very high, and the crew had made every effort to produce a work of beauty.

Hooked rugs were made by the dozens from old uniforms and army blankets, dyed in spruce green, gold, avocado, and other earth tones. When the job was complete, 119 of them had been made. Upholstery fabric was woven by hand loom for the massive and distinctive furniture being built by crews of men that were learning as they worked.

Women who did not have the talent for making rugs or weaving, were put to the task of making 100 pairs of curtains from sail cloth, appliqued with intriguing floral designs. They also made 152 bedspreads for the guest rooms.

A metal shop set up on SE Boise Street in Portland fabricated massive metal work and iron hardware to blend with the Cascadian architecture of the structure. In another shop, Fred Baker supervised the work on the distinctive lighting fixtures, now considered classics in their setting. In still another shop, most of the carved wooden art work was done.

When all of the finished work was ready to take to Mount Hood, it was finally realized just how many tons of cloth and wood and iron there were to truck up to the new building. This resulted in some increased budget costs at the last moment. However, the result was a collection of artisanry that is unparalleled in our country. The following description of the lodge is written from the 1975 viewpoint, but it tells the story of an artistic building.

A LIVING ART MUSEUM

Timberline Lodge has been visited by millions of sightseers, interested in viewing its unique Cascadian architecture and the works of art that have been fashioned into beams and boards, doors and grilles, walls and floors. From the first exposure to the public in the Thirties, the public has been aware that the lodge is something different, a heavily-used building that is in itself a living art museum.

The main front door is seldom used. It is a massive piece of work in hand-hewn Ponderosa pine, that opens onto the parapet of stone, which covers the door to the ski lounge on the lower floor. That main door is five feet wide, 10 feet high, and weighs 1100 pounds. Four hundred of those pounds are the massive, hand-forged iron ware, hinges, latch, and knocker. The door was built with such delicate balance, that it can be opened with a light touch.

From the parking lot, a set of concrete steps leads up to the door of the ski lounge, well protected from the weather by an entrance alcove. Most visitors assume that this is the main door, as they view the carved Indian on its surface, a work of James Duncan. In winter time the lower steps to this entrance are covered with a large semicircular tubular tunnel, that keeps snow off the area. This practical, but ugly, protection is removed for summer use.

As one steps into the lower door, he sees the mass of the great hexagonal stone fireplace, 14 feet in diameter. This fireplace rises 92 feet to the peak of the building, constructed with 400 tons of stone. Three firepits are placed in the ski lounge, and the three alternating sides of the hexagon are used for fire pits in the main lounge above.

A huge compass circle of brass is set into the floor, just inside the door. The ceiling is not high; its beams are Ponderosa pine. The viewer begins to notice the Indian symbols that are used in many areas of the building.

To the right is the ski grille, barred in off-hours with great wooden gates. A set of steps leads down to the sunken floor of the room, giving it the airy feeling of a higher ceiling. The walls are decorated with carved and painted murals, done by Douglas Lynch, depicting the early sportsmen who enjoyed the area around Timberline. The Indian theme is brought into the room with the lighting fixtures made of wood and enhanced with hand-made iron work.

Past the ski grille, a hall leads past the door of the men's rest room to a short flight of stairs. To the right is an outside exit, but to the left in a stone dungeon is the most interesting bar room anywhere, the Blue Ox. Inspired by the legend of Paul Bunyan, the walls are decorated with stained glass murals of the famous logger and his blue ox, Babe. Virginia Darce was the artist who did the glass work. The room also boasts a mountain in full-wall scale, done in bas relief by Florence Thomas. Chairs and tables are of design sufficiently massive to be worthy of Paul Bunyan, himself.

Returning to the fireplace in the ski lounge, one notices the seating of woven rawhide mounted on pine plank construction, usually occupied by skiers or their wet clothing left to dry. To the left of the lounge is the stair going upward, but first a mention of the gift shop and ski shop is in order. They face the opposite sides of the long hallway which runs out to the west end of the building.

Mounting the stairs, one cannot help fondling the carved sleeping bear of the newell post, polished by literally millions of hands. This is one of many such carvings of native animals such as the beaver, coyote, wildcat, and badger. These were sketched by Howard Gifford, then designed by Ray Neufer and Florence Thomas. Cedar posts were used, and some of the first attempts were discarded and recarved to achieve the best possible effect.

At the top of the stair, past the hotel desk, the visitor is suddenly confronted with the vast grandeur of the main lounge. Again, the central column of the great fireplace captures the eye, sweeping up to the high peak of the ceiling. Beams and wood are of a natural, weathered finish. Around the hexagonal room, six tremendous Ponderosa logs form the support for the balcony and roof.

Chairs and davenports are of oak, ornamental iron, and handmade Oregon flax and wool. Paul Bunyan would be at home in this setting of great dimensions. The fireplace has curtains made of chain mesh, and the great stones on its face show the scratches of recent glaciers of Mount Hood. Stone of several colors in the hearth, was taken from Oregon quarries near Stayton. On the east side of the lounge are the ten-foot gates of wrought iron, guarding the dining room. These heavy gates stand over seven feet in height, yet they are delicately balanced, as is the great front door. They were made without bolts or rivets by Mr. Dawson, who also did other iron work in the lodge.

There is an interesting story concerning the rails used for fireplace grates. In 1937 Japan was buying large tonnages of scrap steel in the United States, steel that was later thrown back at American soldiers in World War Two in the form of bullets, ships, and tanks. Rails, discarded from the Lackawana Railroad, had arrived in Portland, awaiting shipment to Japan. Buyers for the Timberline project were scrounging in junk yards, when they found them, and sent them to the shops for fabrication as fireplace equipment.

Turning right (south) one faces the front door. Over it is another magnificent mountain lion, carved by Florence Thomas. The main lounge also shows the marquetry of Aimee Gorham, with coyote and cougar done in woods of varying color and grain. Near the main stair the hardships of the wagon pioneers are immortalized in redwood carvings.

The Cascade dining room, 36' x 58', beyond the scrollwork of the iron gates, holds 150 guests. Twelve-foot drapes, in the same autumn colors used in the lounge, hang at the north and south windows. The room has its own fireplace, done in pioneer motif with a built-in oven. Above it is a carving of Oregon animals by Eric Lamade. Serving stands around the room are decorated with a fox head.

Taking the stairway upward from the main lounge, one comes to the hexagonal balcony. Quaint little alcoves, with bench and desk, offer a place to write letters. To the north, great windows show the splendor of Mount Hood, as is true in the lounge below. Further around to the east is a cocktail bar, then on the south is a windowed alcove, looking out over the vast mountain land to Mount Jefferson on the horizon.

Paintings were used profusely in the lodge. Karl Feurer, assisted by Dora Erickson, George Jeffrey, and Martina Gangle, painted 113 watercolors of native flowers, trees, and shrubs. These hang in halls and alcoves throughout the building.

The work of C.S. Price, who has since become famous, is represented by **Landscape** and **Plowing,** oil paintings that hang in the balcony. **Dishwashers** and **Musicians** are works of Darrell Austin. Charles Heaney did **The Mountain.** Two pictures by H.S. Sewall are hung across from each other in the Cascade dining room. They tell the story of wood and metal work in the building of the lodge. When the new wing is finally opened, some new paintings will be brought forth, done originally for the lodge, but never shown more than once. Some have never been shown at all. All have been in storage all these years.

Unlike most hotels, Timberline Lodge was decorated with no two guest rooms alike. Some examples are the **Blond Room** done in Oregon pine. Orange and gold upholstery and bedspread are color-coordinated with rugs of burned orange and black.

The Trillium Room has walls of knotty pine. The native trillium is worked into design of draperies and bookcase doors. In the **Skunk Cabbage Room** that native plant is embodied in light green leaves and yellow flower, against the teal background of the drapery. Indian or pioneer motifs grace many of the rooms. In the **Zigzag River Room** the window curtains are decorated with fish and ripples of gold and yellow. Paintings on the walls pick up color from other appointments in all the rooms.

The superb color coordination by Margery Hoffman Smith is evident throughout Timberline Lodge. The job was especially challenging for her, because of the makeshift nature of so much of the material used. Old army uniforms and blankets can be dyed in only a subdued color range.

1932 — Hogsback was low, did not run to summit as it does now.

September 30, 1938 Representatives from Timberline Lodge Inc., outdoor clubs, and towns of the Mount Hood vicinity asked the Oregon State Highway Commission to take over the road to the lodge. Jack Meier stated that 49,799 automobiles had used the road since November of 1937. He told the commission that the gasoline tax generated by travel to the lodge would pay for snow removal costs. A plan was underway to allow drivers to pull up in front of the building to eject their passengers and then drive below to park automobiles.

Horace Mecklem reported that 220 people had invested $39,000 to start the lodge. Profit on the operation was to be divided by first giving 6% to the stockholders. The remainder was to be divided with 80% to the Forest Service and 20% for improvements. It might be well to mention at this point, that profits were so rare over the years, that the original stockholders never did realize more than about 10% of their investment.

July 24, 1939 The Forest Service announced a 25¢ fee to enter main lounge and lobby and to give visitors a guided tour through the building. It was noted that since February, 1938, over 300,000 people had trooped through the building, and the Forest Service was worried about excessive wear. This was followed by editorials and protests and a dropping of the fee shortly afterward.

November 3, 1939 New operators for the ski shop were announced, Mr. and Mrs. Emanuel Treyve, who had been in ski manufacturing business in France. Boyd French had left Timberline to manage the tow at Ski Bowl.

November 26, 1939 The ski lift which had been under construction all summer was given a Sunday premier at 10:00 a.m. Herman Brunke of Cascade Ski Club was the first rider on the "Magic Mile" up to Silcox Hut. The hut at the headhouse was not complete, but complete enclosure was planned within two weeks. A fire burned in the fireplace of the partially done building.

Skiers were walking up and sliding down snow-covered ravines in the vicinity of Silcox. There was enough snow on the cat road to allow skiers to get almost to the bottom lift house before removing skis. Conditions were stormy most of the day. The Magic Mile was 4950 feet long with 991 feet vertical rise. It carried 255 passengers per hour and took 11 minutes to reach Silcox Hut. A diesel generator at the lower terminal sent electric power through an underground cable to the head house, where electric motors turned the bull wheel.

July 3, 1940 Manager of the Timberline Lodge, Arthur V. Allen, announced that fireworks would be displayed from the top of the ski lift and also from a site near Illumination Rock. Sunset rides on chairlift would precede the fireworks.

Newton B. Drury, director of the National Park Service, stated that there were no plans afoot to change Timberline Lodge and vicinity to a national park status.

Snow buried Timberline 1939 — Photo Joe Leuthold

Autumn, 1940 Fred VanDyke and his wife, Anna, took over the management of the lodge. Anna had immigrated from Switzerland in 1921, he in 1922. They married the following year. She had worked in the business department of hotels in the Murren Valley and in the Seiler Hotel at Scheidig, where the railroad enters the Jungfrau Tunnel.

March 12, 1941 Timberline Lodge Inc. announced a deficit of $1,657 for the first three years of operation. Clackamas County had levied tax of $5,647 on the building, which had not been paid, but showed as an operating expense in the books. Without the tax the operation would be in the black. Summer months were proving to be the most profitable.

October 23, 1941 The corporation filed suit against Assessor Rufus E. Ward and Sheriff Fred Reaksecker for an injunction against taxes of 1939, 1940, 1941. The plea was that the Forest Service was operating the lodge for public benefit, and that taxes should be stricken.

April 30, 1942 Lyle F. Watts, regional forester for Oregon and Washington, in conjunction with Timberline Lodge Inc. announced that the hotel would be open during the summer. War had been declared on December 7, 1941, and shortage of tires and gasoline had cut travel. Fred VanDyke was manager of the lodge.

August 28, 1942 Fred VanDyke reported that the lodge would close on Labor Day for the duration of the war. Summer business had been about 50% of usual because of decreased travel during wartime.

October 1, 1942 A verbal agreement had been made with the United States Navy to use the lodge as a rehabilitation center for officers. The VanDykes had a full staff standing by, ready to receive the new guests.

November 30, 1942 Some sort of legal difficulty had caused the Navy to decide against using the facility. At this point VanDyke closed Timberline Lodge for the duration of the war. A small gasoline generator was used for electric power, instead of the large, throbbing diesels that had run for five years. Just enough heat was used to prevent freezing. Draperies were mothproofed and stored. Chairs were removed from the ski lift and the cables lashed together.

Heavy snows closed the road and left the VanDykes marooned without food. For years Brule and Lady had been the dogs "on duty" at Timberline. Being snowed in a short while caused the giant St. Bernard, Brule, to gain weight alarmingly, as he was normally accustomed to romping up and down the hills for miles in the snow. When the snowplows reached the lodge on December 10, four men lifted the 200-pound dog aboard a Forest Service truck and took him to the veterinarian, who found it advisable to put him to sleep. Lady stayed on with the caretakers, Mr. and Mrs. Volley Reed.

Ole Lien and Colonel Hartwell W. Palmer acted as guards at the Lodge during much of the long war closure. Both were remarkable outdoorsmen and thought little of hiking out across country to Zigzag for supplies or the sight of another human face. Post-war skiers remember both men directing traffic in the parking lot at times.

Both were well educated. Palmer had worked for the Forest Service as an engineering aide. In 1937-8 he had prepared an intensive report on the trails, streams and vegetation in a resource analysis of the south side.

Timberline dogs, Brule and Lady — Photo Leuthold

AFTER WORLD WAR TWO

September 19, 1945 A.A. Comrie, President of Timberline Lodge, Inc., announced plans to be open by December. Maintenance had been performed over the years of wartime closure by the caretakers and an occasional work crew from the Conscientious Objector Camp at Wyeth. Now, a general review of building and equipment was under way. Fred VanDyke was busy hiring cooks and waitresses. Custodian, Colonel Hart W. Palmer, was busy with a great many details in the building.

Saturday, December 1, 1945 The lodge opened for business once more. On Sunday, post-war skiing got off to a good start. Timberline had 375 cars, and 350 more were parked at Government Camp. Glen Asher, chief of the Ski Patrol, announced appointment of Dean Beckley as First Aid Chief at the lodge.

The ski lift still needed some repair work before it could be placed into operation. Snow removal on the road from Government Camp was still the responsibility of the Forest Service.

The paintings of C.S. Price had been stored in the damp basement during the war, a little worse for neglect. Rugs and curtains and upholstery were beginning to show their age.

March 22, 1946 William Temple took over management of the lodge.

October, 1947 The operation showed the first profits since the lodge was built.

July 1, 1948 The Forest Service issued a new 10-year permit at $5,000 per year plus a percentage of gross sales.

November 16, 1948 President R.L. Orem of Timberline Lodge Inc. reported after-tax profits of $9,465, noting that completion of the new road to the lodge and the proposed tramway should bring more visitors up, as well as to allow employees to live at Government Camp.

November, 1949 A loss in operation had occurred. William Temple resigned, and the old Aero Club manager, George B. North, took the job as manager.

1951 The lodge showed a profit, the first since 1947.

May 4, 1952 Timberline Lodge Inc. announced the sale of the business to Elston Ireland, Portland restauranteur, and Portland theatre operators, C.R. McFadden and his son, John R. McFadden. An estimated 500,000 visitors a year were noted at the lodge, 100,000 being skiers.

By November, the new ownership was purring along well. John McFadden, his wife, and infant son had moved into the lodge, so that he could best pursue his duties as the new manager. James Duncan, one of the original construction engineers, was busy with the tools, refurbishing the ski rental and the Blue Ox Bar, which had been closed for two-and-a-half years. A 60-foot tunnel had been built to keep snow away from the chairlift terminal. Chairs in the lobby, worn threadbare by thousands of visitors, had been sanded, refinished, and reupholstered. Rooms had been converted to additional dormitory space, with a $2.50 per night rental.

Silcox hut, closed for some time, was scheduled to reopen to serve sandwiches and coffee. The forbidding chains that had hung so long across the access to Timberline Lodge's main lounge, were gone, and an atmosphere of friendly welcome was in evidence.

The partnership of Ireland and the McFaddens ran into rough sailing, as partnerships often do. Problems arose among the employees, who were almost all single, as the lodge had no accommodations for married couples. In addition, after every payday a gambling game was allowed to go on, and most of the help were broke. Ireland, who lived in Portland, was often approached for loans that were seldom collected.

Late in the fall of 1953, Charles W. Slaney bought out the McFaddens. Shortly afterward, on December 16, he also bought the Ireland interest in the Timberline Lodge operation. Ireland reported later that the transaction had proved very costly, because his business advisors had permitted Slaney to take possession of the premises prior to receiving the agreed amount of money. Ireland said that Slaney never did pay, and although he won a court decision against him, no funds were ever received.

Employees and Forest Service personnel have since remarked that during Slaney's control, the lodge was more neglected in routine maintenance and repair of mechanical equipment, than in any other time in its history. Aside from general observance by visitors, the public was not aware of any real problem at the lodge, until February of 1955, when the lid blew off the situation in the form of a news story in the Portland papers, announcing closure of the establishment for lack of payment of power bills.

THE LODGE WAS CLOSED

February 17, 1955 It was a grim Thursday at Timberline Lodge for the operators, Charles W. Slaney and his wife. The Sandy Electric Cooperative shut off the power at 1:45 p.m. and closed him down for non-payment of over $7,000 in past due power bills. Power costs had been running from $600 to $800 per month, and the Co-op demanded $2,800 to forestall closure.

Leverett G. Richards, *Oregonian* reporter, visited the lodge and found Slaney busy loading a truck with liquor and groceries to take to one of his other operations. He had at first determined to stay open by firing the heating system with wood, but the enormity of the problem finally struck home, and he and his wife were busy salvaging what they could. Guests began leaving in the afternoon, some from distant areas. Mrs. Slaney stood at the desk on the second floor paying off the help with a final paycheck. The 65 employees suddenly found themselves without work.

There was a full booking of the lodge for the coming weekend, guests that must be turned away. The Forest Service cancelled Slaney's permit as of the effective date April 11. The principal reason was for "unsafe and unsatisfactory operation of the ski lift." A few days previously, some of Slaney's employees permitted the lift to get out of control and damage the equipment. Lloyd's of London, who insured the lift, responded by cancelling the insurance required by the Forest Service in their permit agreement.

Darkness fell on an empty lodge. The Forest Service sent in their men to protect the property, including Lloyd Olsen, supervisor of Mount Hood National Forest, district ranger Ralph Wiese, and assistant district ranger, James Ralph. Forest Service veteran, Ole Lien, was shown in a photograph, cigar in mouth, lighting a candle needed to navigate down the dark halls. Ian McAndy manned the short-wave radio, the power interruption having severed the phone service. Standby electric generators were being used sparingly to supply power to the heating system sufficient to prevent freezing of water pipes.

February 20, 1955 6000 skiers visited the south side, almost all avoiding Timberline Lodge area by staying on the lower slopes.

March 5, 1955 Supervisor Lloyd Olson spoke at a Toastmaster Club in Portland and stated that the Forest Service hoped to open a lodge on weekends, so that the ground floor could be used. This would mean that the public could use the snack bar and the rest rooms. Outside the lift, and possibly a portable tow might be put into operation. The chair lift needed survey on the damage.

Slaney would have until May 15 to remove his equipment from the lodge. His attorney, Reuben Lenske, indicated willingness to vacate the building at once. The Forest Service reported that 40 individuals or companies had showed interest in bidding on future operation.

KOHNSTAMM BUYS TIMBERLINE

Thursday, April 28, 1955 After sifting through 150 applications from those who wished to operate Timberline Lodge, the Forest Service announced the selection of Richard L. Kohnstamm of Portland. Regional Forester J. Herbert Stone stated that Kohnstamm had been awarded a 10-year permit and would take over the operation about June 1. Attorney Scott M. Kelley represented the successful applicant, who was a graduate of Brooklyn College and Columbia University, and had been a group worker at Neighborhood House in Portland since September of 1953.

The Internal Revenue Bureau expressed intent of forced sale of the lodge equipment to pay the tax lien of $19,625 against the former owners. Tom Johnson, who had been operating the cafeteria in the interim since Slaney's departure, planned to continue until the end of May.

Kohnstamm, a skiing enthusiast who had visited European alpine resorts with his wife, said he planned to add a mile-long chairlift below the lodge, arrange mountain climbs, establish golf affiliations, and schedule fishing trips for guests.

Taking over the building was a forbidding job. As Kohnstamm went through the lodge, he found torn and dirty draperies, bedding and upholstery. Floor rugs were packed outside, more like mud cakes held together with fabric binder. Mechanical details on heating equipment, kitchen, and ski lift had been neglected. Considerable work and money were needed to bring the lodge back to standards.

Some of the draperies, upholstery, and rugs were missing. Others had been slashed or torn by vandals. Residents of Government camp had seen some of the material at the local dumping ground, dirty but relatively intact. It is no wonder that previous to Kohnstamm's management, there had been suggestions by some, that the government should burn the lodge, which had sunk at times to a very poor state of repair.

During 1955 work was begun on a new ski lift in the Pucci Glade area. The towers ran west of the cabin of the Wy'east Climbers and east of their long-gone neighbors, the Nile River Yacht Club. It was an ultra-modern double chair facility, that made the old Magic Mile lift seem very primitive, indeed.

May 27, 1958 Richard L. Kohnstamm announced the beginning of construction of the long-awaited swimming pool, to be completed by August. Pacific Pools of Seattle was building the 30' x 60' unit, which would hold 116,000 gallons of heated water. The system used to heat it was almost as large as the heating plant for all the rest of the lodge.

A 12-foot fence screened the parapets around the pool and kept strong winter wind from striking swimmers. Admission was free to lodge guests and $2 to others.

May 2, 1958 The fourth annual Austrian weekend was planned for Timberline Lodge. Lodge employees wore alpine old-country costumes. Folk dancing was added to the usual entertainment, and Swiss yodelling champion Christina Roffler was the featured entertainer.

On Saturday and Sunday at noon the "Camp Ten" buffet was held near the 9,000 foot level, with snow-cats hauling the celebrants up to the large tent set up on the slopes below Crater Rock. Wine, food, and music brought a holiday air to the high slopes of Mount Hood.

1960 A new water system was completed at Timberline Lodge, and construction was started on a new sewage plant, just off the lower end of the parking lot.

December 9, 1962 Timberline Lodge celebrated its **25th anniversary** with a party that attracted 6,000. Most of the guests were skiers who spent the day riding the new $275,000 Magic Mile chair lift free of charge, running in 33 inches of wet, packed snow in 65 degree temperature.

At 11:00 a.m., Darrell Jones, Clackamas County Commissioner, officiated at a ceremony in which he broke a bottle of champagne against an anchor pole in conjunction with Edward P. Cliff, Chief Forester of the United States. The two then climbed on a special silver chair on the 900-person-per-hour Riblet lift and rode to the top, a vertical rise of 1,089 feet.

Jones, Chairman of the Association of Oregon and California Counties, was proclaimed by Cliff as being the person largely responsible for freeing money to build the lift and other mountain recreation facilities. It might be noted that the Magic Mile was the only post-war lift at Timberline built with public money. The earlier lift in Pucci Glade and the lift later built to the east of Pucci were built by Richard Kohnstamm's RLK Company.

At 1:00 p.m. a luncheon in the dining room of the lodge was held for special guests, George Henderson being the master of ceremonies. Chief Edward Cliff delivered the major address. Another speaker was Sir Arnold Lunn, who in November of 1937, had delivered a speech on the steps of the lodge, telling Oregonians of the bright future of skiing at Mount Hood.

Emilio Pucci, famed Italian clothing designer, flew in from Europe to attend the banquet. Pucci had developed a ski area below the lodge called Pucci's Glade, while he was a student at Reed College. The $150,000 ski lift that was built in 1955 was named Pucci Lift **(pronounced poochie).** Another speaker at the party was Dr. Merrill H. Stiles, president of the US Ski Association. Stiles commented on the merit of skiing as one of the best ways to avoid heart trouble in later life.

The first skiers to ride the new lift were Carole Mattson, Ernest McDonald, and Ray Howerton, making the 12-minute ride to the upper terminus at 7,057 feet.

In 1964, a good deal of profitable room space was added by buying Thunderhead Inn at Government Camp to house a good part of the 116 employees of the lodge. Hourly bus service was provided to transport employees.

The third floor of the lodge was remodelled in October to gain 15 more rooms. The lodge was completely closed to facilitate the building program. Richard Kohnstamm remarked that during the past year the lodge had been turning away about 75% of the people who asked for rooms on weekends.

Monday, January 3, 1966 Timberline Lodge was snowed in by a raging three-day blizzard, that had turned the New Year's celebration of the previous

Saturday into a series of impromptu games by the marooned guests. The musicians slated to play New Year's Eve had not been able to reach the lodge.

The snowplow crew under direction of Gene Beckman of the Oregon State Highway Maintenance, had barely been able to stay even with the tremendous fall of snow on the Timberline Road, but the public was not allowed to use it. Four rotary plows, six heavy truck plows, two graders, and a D-8 cat were in use.

On Sunday the lifts were still closed, and guests turned out in unprecedented number for the Catholic Mass at the lodge. About a hundred guests were taken down to Government Camp in the lodge bus, leaving their cars behind to be dug out of the snow later. They managed to dig out five automobiles in the afternoon, but many were hopelessly buried beneath 10-foot drifts. Snow clearance work could not begin until the automobiles were first found.

On Monday the D-8 cat finally reached the lodge to help in the search for parked cars. Pucci Chairlift was running, but most of the guests had gone home. At Government Camp six feet of snow had turned the highway into a bleak, narrow lane, and owners were hunting for their automobiles, then digging them out. The storm was the heaviest since February of 1948. At that time guests were marooned for 12 days at Timberline Lodge.

Tuesday, May 24, 1966 At Salem the Oregon Tax Court overruled the State Tax Commission, setting lower cash values for tax purposes on the RLK interest in Timberline Lodge. The Commission had previously set the values at $402,000 for 1962, $601,000 for 1963, and $581,000 for 1964.

The tax court reset the figures much lower, $71,330 for 1962, $185,450 for 1963, and $175,000 for 1964. Judge Edward Howell noted that the State Tax Commission had failed to give consideration to the restrictions involved in RLK Company's special use permit with USFS. A similar lowering in value was made at the same time for Multnomah Falls Lodge, also owned by the USFS.

Sunday, November 13, 1966 The 30th anniversary was celebrated at Timberline Lodge by the formal opening of Number 3 lift, located east of the Pucci Lift. It was a 900-foot vertical rise from the 5,000-foot level, a 5,150-foot ride. George Henderson was first to ride in the $200,000 installation.

The parking lot had been enlarged to accommodate 1,800 automobiles, and seven new ski runs had been opened, making a total of 20 in the area. Manager Richard Kohnstamm unveiled three new Thiokol snow cats that would be used in packing ski slopes.

Officials of the Jaycee Ski School joined the party to celebrate their own 20th year of operation on Mount Hood. Skiing was prevented by too many rocks that still showed through the five inches of new snow that covered the ground.

April 7, 1969 The USFS was asking for a congressional appropriation of $3 million to update Timberline Lodge. Proposals included a day lodge to comfortably handle 4,000 to 5,000 skiers per day at $1,225,000, a building for housing employees that would cost $565,000, and a garage for trucks, busses, and snow cats at $96,000. A new wing proposed for the east end would cost $450,000.

July 22, 1970 Congress authorized $101,000 to finance the garage, to be started later in the summer. The $3 million proposal of the previous year had not been written into congressional bills. The garage job was completed in 1971.

June 25, 1971 Approval was made by a House of Representatives Appropriations Committee of $961,000 to finance a convention wing on the east end of the lodge. In the summer of 1972 work began on the wing, which would add 19,500 square feet to the floor space of the lodge. By August 15, 1972 the excavation was complete, and concrete was being poured. Thompson Construction Company had a 100-foot crane on the job, moving materials.

The wing included a banquet hall, meeting rooms, and storage space, and was scheduled for completion January 1974, but heavy snowfall compounded problems during the winter of 1973-74. By the first week of March of 1974, the snow had piled up to a depth of 320 inches behind the lodge. All during February, crews were busy shovelling snow to keep damage at a minimum, but they could not keep ahead of the record accumulation. The snow was turning to ice on the north side of the building, damaging siding and window casing, both on the old dining room and on the new wing.

Assistant Ranger Warren Olney said that the new wing had changed wind patterns, causing the snow to build heavily on the northeast corner. The passageway from the new building to the old was being pushed out of position.

On Thursday, March 7, 1974, Walt Aeppli, head engineer at the lodge, said that he had never seen so much snow in his 17 years of duty there. Snow was higher than the bullwheel on Pucci Lift, and crews were being assembled to dig out the chairs by hand. The rope tow above the lodge was buried to the top of the poles, and the Magic Mile was being dug out.

September 7, 1974 Wright Mallery, Supervisor of MHNF announced that the snow had done $300,000 damage on the lodge and the new wing. The main dining room had been damaged, and the passageway from it to the new wing had been torn away. The passageway was rebuilt with a copper roof, heated with steam coils to prevent formation of ice.

The sprinkler system in the wing had frozen. Plans were made to fill it with compressed air, which would be replaced automatically with water, in case of fire. The loading dock was rebuilt and strengthened, and a stairway on the southeast end of the new wing was rebuilt. Dick Woodrow of the USFS recreation office commented that about $80,000 per year is an average need in maintaining Timberline Lodge. Availability of money is always at the mercy of congressional appropriation.

Weather takes a severe toll on siding and window casings. Rewiring and plumbing are often needed. The USFS estimated that over 800,000 people had visited Timberline Lodge in 1973.

For the new wing, art work was brought forth, paintings that had been done for the original building. Some had never been seen by the public, and others had been shown once, then stored for over 36 years.

BUCKING HEADS WITH USFS

June 23, 1974 *Oregonian* told of the battle going on between Richard Kohnstamm and the Forest Service over the renewing of a lease for Timberline Lodge. At the time he was 49 years of age, having put 20 years into the operation, as well as $262,000 in operating losses, and the further investment of $500,000 in new chairlifts and a swimming pool.

He had proposed to the Forest Service that they award him a 30-year contract. In return he would spend $4,000,000. Improvements would include a new Blossom Chairlift for the ski school, Salmon River Chairlift for advanced skiers, a summertime chairlift to the 8720 foot level, doubling of parking facility, and build a 60-room hotel down below the parking areas. It was noted that congress has approved money for a day lodge to be built below the west side of the parking lot.

It is well to note that Kohnstamm would need complete assurance of a viable plan, in contrast to the money-losing arrangement to date, because he would need a positive plan to present to the future stockholders, who would advance the $4,000,000.

In the first days of October, 1974, the Forest Service placed Timberline Lodge in the hands of the public to decide the future of the building. In a 100-page document that outlined the impact on the environment, four possible courses of action were given:

1. To proceed in much the same manner as in the past, using the same lifts, parking, and lodging facilities. The new east wing might be converted to a day lodge for skiers, which would take some of the pressure off the use of one main doorway in front.

2. To eliminate skiing or restrict it to the use of lodge guests only. Under this concept all lodging might be discontinued and the building made into a museum, which would entail removal of all ski lifts and closure of ski trails to Government Camp.

3. To add medium development to the area. This would entail a day lodge that would give skiers a place to eat, buy lift tickets, use rest rooms, and take refuge from bad weather. Three lifts would be added, one into the steep Salmon River Canyon east of the lodge, one at the head of Blossom Trail west of the lodge, and an all-year lift that would take skiers up Palmer Glacier to the 8700-foot level. Parking area would need improvement.

4. To develop the area to a maximum. This would add an additional 60 rooms in an area that would probably be tucked under the parking space directly in front of the lodge. It would also add a large day lodge near the main parking lot. Parking facilities would have to be greatly increased and bus service augmented. Eight ski lifts would serve the sportsmen.

Plan number One leaves operator Richard L. Kohnstamm with a plan that has proved economically unsound for years.

Plan number Two would also be unsound financially, if the lodge were to keep guests. If the building reverted to a museum, the area would tend to become a romantic backwater similar to Cloud Cap Inn, deteriorating in old age and visited by dwindling numbers of curiosity seekers.

Plan Three is favored by the present operator Kohnstamm. He has already invested $500,000 in improvements and has lost an additional $262,000 in operating Timberline Lodge over the past 20 years. The three additional lifts and new day lodge would involve Kohnstamm's spending another $4,000,000 plus an outlay by the Forest Service of $2,500,000. His new day lodge would probably be tucked under the driveway in front of the present building. It would be a three-story structure that would house a ski shop, lift ticket sale, ski patrol and aid, fast food service, rest rooms, and gift shop. Tunnels would connect to the present lodge, which could then assume the quiet and dignity that hotel patrons wish.

Plan Four would run an estimated $7.8 million, to accommodate 8,000 skiers and 4,000 sightseers at one time, a population that boggles the mind. It would undoubtedly require a faster, more dependable system of transportation from Government Camp to alleviate the parking problems.

Unless Plan Two is used, the parking problem is one of urgent need. A $200,000 project to build a retaining wall along the incoming (northbound) one-way road on the east, would increase capacity from 900 automobiles to about 1050. The real significance would be that the full capacity of the lot could be kept alive by blowing the snow over into the Salmon River Canyon with rotary plows. As it is, snow builds up in cornices that threaten the inbound road, and snow removal problems cause the existing 900-car capacity to shrink to about half.

The Forest Service scheduled a public meeting for early November to explain the options and answer questions. Written comments were given a deadline of November 20. The final draft, including these comments, was to be finished in March of 1975. Wright T. Mallery, supervisor of Mount Hood National Forest, indicated that one of the four plans would be selected by the end of May, 1975.

SKI TOWS & LIFTS

In the winter of 1938-39 a little Sweden portable rope tow was used on what was later known as Otto Lang Hill just north of the lodge. It was mounted on a toboggan and not overly powerful. Ariel Edmiston recalls one day when he was conducting a ski class at the bottom, and the tow slid off the hill, toboggan and all. The class had to scramble for safety. The following year a more powerful tow was installed in a permanent manner. There was also a rope tow in Pucci's Glade below the lodge.

In the summer of 1939 work was begun on the longest chair lift in America, the old Magic Mile, with terminal houses designed in architecture to match Timberline Lodge. The large warming hut, snack bar, and head-house facility at the top was named Silcox Hut after Ferdinand Silcox, Secretary of Agriculture.

On May 21, 1939, the lift was given a preconstruction dedication by Crown Prince Olav and Princess Martha of Norway. The prince placed a bolt and screwed a nut onto it to secure the first tower. The Forest Service was represented by Assistant Regional Forester Jack Horton, MHNF Supervisor, A.O. Waha. E.J. Griffith represented the WPA and Jack Meier the Oregon Winter Sports Association.

From the very first the new lift attracted long lines of skiers, and when World War Two was over, Timberline Lodge was one of the most up-to-date ski areas. A more powerful tow was installed on Otto Lang Hill, and the "Betsy" ski tow was placed just east of the lodge to accommodate the crowds of beginners. For the experts a very fast tow was placed down into Salmon River Canyon. It took a good skier to catch the rope and hold on, and as he reached the top of the severe slope, he shot up into the air as if

Riding Magic Mile lift 1941 — Photo USFS

Magic Mile lift in 1941 — Photo USFS

catapulted to land on a platform area.

In 1955 the first truly modern equipment was installed at Timberline, when a new lift was run downhill from a point just west of the west end of the building, giving the area a high-capacity operation over slopes that were protected by the trees from the wind. It was named Pucci Lift after Emilio Pucci, who had popularized the area below the lodge while he was a student at Reed College. The name Pucci's Glade had lasted through World War Two and was used by postwar skiers.

The $150,000 lift was financed by RLK Company. It ran west of the Wy'east cabin, passing over a knoll very near where the old Nile River Yacht Club had stood years before.

In 1957 the Betsy Tow east of the lodge was given night lighting, the first on the mountain other than a short-lived attempt at Summit in the late Forties.

In 1961 a new Magic Mile Lift was begun, using Oregon and California Counties money administered by the USFS. The lower terminal was placed west of the lodge. A vertical rise placed the top at 7,057 feet. An intermediate exit point was also established. The new Magic Mile ran very close to the old Lone Fir Lookout, built in 1933, so the Forest Service scrapped the lookout, which had not been used in fire detection for many years. The new lift was completed at a cost of $275,000 in 1962, and the old Magic Mile towers were dismantled.

In 1966 the new Number 3 Lift was built east of the Pucci Lift, giving about 900 feet of rise from the 5,000-foot level. It is 5,150 long and carries about 750 skiers per hour. The run is a bit unusual, following gentle undulations at the top to suddenly plunge down a steep slope to the lower terminus at the bottom.

In 1970 the USFS spent $71,000 to renovate the Magic Mile lift.

Ski-way, an Aerial Tram Experiment

Skiers were thrilled in 1947, when an aerial tramway between Government Camp and Timberline was announced. The tram was to be an adaptation of the "sky-hook" cable system used by northwest loggers to move large timber out of the woods. The Mount Hood Aerial Transportation Company was formed and a Forest Service permit issued to cover the operation.

The skiing public supplied some of the money through sale of stock. The three-mile cable system was to be supported on towers. The lower terminal was located on Highway 26, just west of Government Camp, at a point where the builders could get a straight shot at a top terminal just west of Timberline Lodge.

In 1948, construction was begun. A large building was placed on the lower end, complete with restaurant, rest rooms, and waiting lounge. The tram cars could come in to a docking area under the roof on the top floor of the building. A wide swath of skiing space alongside the towers was cut

Looking Down the Tram Line from Timberline — Photo Maryanne Hill

on the slopes down from Timberline Lodge. On the lower sections the existing ski trails were adequate. Since the ski trail normally took the skier to Government Camp, a new one had to be cut to the west to arrive at the new tram house. This section was never made to be very pleasing, a narrow track with a v-notch to cross, and the last distance had small obstacle hills in the way. Cross-country skiers would be pleased with such a run, but not down-hill skiers.

By 1949 the lower terminal was complete. The towers were up and the cables laid out to raise. Opening was scheduled for the first of the new year, but delays arose. The really significant event was that in the summer of 1949 a new road to Timberline Lodge was opened, cutting out many miles of bad curves. Drivers would no longer have to take the steep grade up from Snowbunny Lodge. The new Timberline Highway started at the parking lot just east of Summit, and followed a much gentler grade. The new road helped to kill the tramway.

Despite much publicity, the tram did not open for the ski season in the spring of 1950. But when the snow had melted, skiers were promised that it would be ready to operate in the fall. The management announced each month that it was almost ready, but the opening date finally came on January 3, 1951.

The skiers responded at once, but they did not come back to use the tram heavily. Fare was 75¢ to Timberline Lodge, but the same trip on the shuttle bus was only 50¢. Since the tram was no faster than the shuttle bus, there was very little incentive to ride it. Either way, the trip up took close to a half hour. Had the operators been able to offer an all-day ticket, the crowds might have been larger, but the all-day lift ticket at Timberline Lodge was from $2.50 to $3.00, a price hard to compete against.

The tram cars were modified city busses. Speed of the car on the cable was not very fast, but when it reached a tower, it was forced to slow almost to a halt in passing the cable suspension system.

The original concept of the tramway was that of a moving cable. Roebling Cable Company sent a representative to confer with the board of directors, agreeing to donate $80,000 toward the cost of construction. One of the key figures of Ski-way was Merle Hoover, head of Mount Hood Stages, the operators of the Trailways bus system. Hoover was adamant in the concept of using tram cars, which were very similar to design to a bus, and which would move on a fixed cable.

Roebling's representative stated that the concept of a bus moving on a fixed cable would not result in a profitable system, and in one meeting he finally left under a condition of strained relationship. Hoover's plan was used, and the speed of the ride to Timberline Lodge left a great deal to be desired. After a period of operation, it is said that some consideration was being given to changing over to a moving cable.

The tram operated about two years before closing down with great losses to the stockholders. The restaurant at the lower terminus continued to serve meals, and the building remained as the stop for Trailways busses at Government Camp. In the summer of 1961 the towers were removed from the mountainside, leaving the Ski-way tram only a memory.

In 1962 William Simon and Zanley Galton bought the building and altered the top loading area into a series of 21 rooms that could house 60 guests. A swimming pool was built on the west end of the building, and the restaurant was upgraded. In the basement a bar was established. The name was changed to Thunderhead Inn.

August 21, 1964, Richard Kohnstamm bought the inn to provide living space for most of his Timberline Lodge staff. The public was still served in the bar and restaurant.

Thunderhead Lodge remained in the ownership of Dick Kohnstamm's RLK Company. In the last part of November, 1973, Charles F. Sperr took over Thunderhead Lodge, maintaining a dining room on the second floor. In the basement the bar offered the music of a live band, a small dance floor, and pool table. In the autumn of 1974 it was obvious that the dining room was not a paying proposition. Dancing in the basement was discontinued, and the pool table was moved onto the dance floor. In the evenings Sperr plays piano and sings along with Bill Spencer or other visiting vocalists. A cook-your-own steak operation is maintained on the east end of the bar area.

In the fall of 1974 Thunderhead Lodge ceased to be a housing facility for RLK Company and became a motel. As of March, 1975, consideration is being given to making the building into a condominium, leaving only the bar on the lower level open to the public. In such a case, the second floor probably will be converted to more living units.

Ski-way to Timberline — Photo USFS

Mount Hood Meadows, Newest Ski Resort

For many, many years the old ski veterans and Forest Service recreation personnel had eyed the east slopes of Mount Hood, inaccessible because the Loop Road had always been closed in wintertime. The Oregon State Highway Commission finally formulated plans to straighten and widen the highway, eliminating the narrow curves that were quaint and scenic, but next to impossible to keep clear with the snow plows.

On February 12, 1964, the public was made aware that the Forest Service had plans to develop a ski area on the headwaters of the East Fork of Hood River, up above Umbrella Falls astraddle the Timberline Trail. Richard E. Worthington, Assistant Supervisor of Mount Hood National Forest announced that a feasibility study was under way. A group from Hood River men had helped make the study possible by raising $3,500 and incorporating as Hood River Meadows Inc. President was L.R. Steeves, vice-president Dr. J. Allan Henderson, secretary Roland B. Leavens. One of the directors was Jack L. Baldwin, who for years had been associated with the Cooper Spur Ski Area.

A Portland newspaper ran a large story with a pictoral map showing the location of the new area to be called Hood River Meadows. Minimum investment would be at the $300,000 level. The better weather and drier snow of the area was stressed. Completion was to be effected in about four years, to coincide with the Oregon State Highway Department plans to straighten the highway.

When William Rosenfeld, Russell McJury, and Shepard Wilson sold out their Ski Bowl interests in 1963, thoughts for entering another area entered their minds. Rosenfeld advanced the idea to industrialist John Gray, that the Hood River Meadows area would be a good one to bid with the Forest Service when the bids were invited. On February 28, 1966, they formed a group to investigate the proposal and put in their bid. This they did, securing a Forest Service permit on July 19, 1966 to build two lifts, a T-Bar, a rope tow, and an ultra-modern day lodge. Ironically, the Hood River Group who had put up the money to further the original studies, did not get the bid.

In the summer of 1966 the Forest Service ran about two miles of new highway up to the new resort site from Bennett Pass on Highway 35. In late summer the chain saws were howling on the slopes below Timberline Trail.

In 1967 Mount Hood Meadows Development Corp. began to function in the actual construction of the resort. The corporation was formed by Franklin Drake, Mitchell Drake, John Gray, William Rosenfeld, and Preston C. Hiefield Jr. The construction contract was awarded to Donald M. Drake Construction Company.

By late May of 1967 over-the-snow removal of trees on the 300-foot-wide slalom hill started up the project once more. By early summer snow had melted enough so that construction began on the day lodge and maintenance shops. Fire danger was so high in September that the Forest Service stopped work on the area for eight days. Upon resumption, footings were poured for ski-lift towers, all done by helicopter to avoid damaging the delicate alpine ground cover. Towers were then set by helicopter, taking only ten to fifteen minutes apiece to put in place. Today the only evidence of that construction is a concrete bucket lying in a ravine above timberline, dropped on an aerial run and never retrieved. The buildings, including large structures for the lift terminals, were all complete by late autumn. Paved parking area gave space for about 330 automobiles. On October 12, *The Oregonian* reported that Keith Petrie had been hired as General Manager.

By December of 1967 skiers were using the new resort, however all traffic had to come in from Hood River. State highway construction was not completed on the sections of road toward Government Camp until the summer of 1968. From that time Highway 35 was maintained as an all-winter road, and the skiers poured in from the south side.

When the area opened, the earlier name of Hood River Meadows was dropped in favor of Mount Hood Meadows. The first manager was Keith Petrie, former forestry executive, who had been prominent for years in Wy'east Climbers, Mount Hood Ski Patrol, and MORESCO. Other ski operators at Government Camp winced when the elaborate facilities were installed at the Meadows, fearing a public stampede to the area. However, the skiing public was quickly disenchanted by the long waiting lines on the lifts, and before many weeks had passed, the crowds were well dispersed once more. Great promotion by the new resort had merely increased the total number of skiers.

The #3 or Red chairlift was added in a location on the south side of the ski area, with a compass heading uphill of west-northwest or about 293 degrees. In 1972 the original T-Bar, which had stood just west of the day lodge, was torn down and the #4 Daisy chairlift was installed to give riders access to a longer and higher course.

In August of 1974 the new #5 Texas lift was built on the high, barren slopes above timberline, serving a vast area that funnels down through all of the other lift areas in many courses. The bottom of Texas is near the top terminal of the original #1 Blue lift at timberline. The top lies just under a rock buttress at the 7800-foot level.

The day lodge and parking lot at Mount Hood Meadows lie at 5,370 feet elevation. The parking lot has been enlarged to accommodate about 1,000 automobiles. Since the area lies in Hood River County, problems exist in public transportation from Portland. The Tri-Met system of busses serving the counties of Clackamas, Multnomah and Washington, can not leave those counties. Therefore, the area must be served by private automobile, special group-chartered busses, or a possible future service of shuttle busses from Government Camp. To avoid these problems a series of busses has been arranged to serve the area from several different pickup points in Portland.

Lifts are as follows:

#2 Yellow . 550' vertical 1400' long NNE of lodge
#1 Blue . .1200' vertical 4700' long NNW of lodge
#3 Red . . 550' vertical 2300' long WNW of lodge
#4 Daisy . . 650' Vertical 3500' long NW of lodge
#5 Texas . . . . . 900' Vertical 3500' long above #1

The #2 yellow lift serves a hill appealing to skilled skiers, although it has a more gentle canyon run on the northwest side that can be negotiated by intermediates. The #1 blue lift takes the skier on a high run to the very edge of the timberline trees. The trails leading down vary from expert to intermediate, with some of the open slopes below the lift line being steep enough to challenge the finest skiers. #3 red chair lift is an ideal area for intermediate skiers. Its slopes are more gentle and undulate just enough to keep the skier alert. #4 Daisy replaced a T-Bar that served the beginning skier. The new lift takes the beginner higher on the mountain, but deposits him on slopes easy to return upon.

Construction and grooming of slopes have both entered an era of great sophistication. Erection of the #5 Texas Lift in 1974 is a perfect example of what is being done on ski hills all over the country. To reach ground for some of the tower footings it was necessary to bulldoze and plow down through snow that still lay 25 feet deep in mid-summer. Concrete was poured by buckets suspended from a hovering helicopter. After the concrete had matured, towers were brought in by helicopter and quickly set by small crews. This allowed steel fabrication in accessible areas, before the towers were moved on to their eventual sites. It took two days of flying time to pour the concrete, three and a half hours to set the towers.

John Rogers and his assistant Rich Morton managed the construction job. Business Manager Mike Durbin was foreman of the surveying and layout. Some of the other men who worked on the operation were Ski School Director Rene' Farwig, Steve Bratt, maintenance technician Walt Nathan, and lift operators Ken Anderl and Dick Furrow.

Grooming of slopes in summer had been aided by use of a Vermeer stump grinder, a machine that reduces stumps to a pile of chips broadcast over the terrain. Chips add to ground cover and help prevent erosion, an attempt to maintain the mountain meadow vegetation of the area. The usual use of snow cats and rollers is made in the area. The management bought a Kaasbohrer Pisten-Bully cat with Mercedes-Benz diesel engine from Germany in 1974, as well as a Thiokol 1200 cat. Both machines have very wide treads that chew up crusted snow and reduce moguls on the slopes to smooth ski paths. A three-gang expanded-metal roller can be pulled behind the cats to break up wind crust or broken snow. The snow cats run regularly to the top of Texas Lift, where it was previously a feat to drive a machine.

In the future, Mount Hood Meadows plans to build a chairlift #6 from the top of the Yellow Lift NNE of the lodge, running down to the edge of Hood River Meadow. This would bring hordes of people into the lower area to park and ride upward, a concept that has horrified conservation groups and outdoor clubs. At present Hood River Meadow and the wooded area north to Clark Creek are visited only by small groups of cross-country skiers, who are very sad about seeing it turned into the usual Coney-Island-on-skis found around any major lift area. There has been an appeal to the Regional Forester by the Sierra Club over the decision of the Supervisor of MHNF. The Regional Forester upheld the decision after a 120-day period of mandatory waiting. Then, the Sierra Club appealed that decision to the Forester in Washington D.C., where the outcome rests.

Mount Hood Meadows Ski Club is an active group, most of whom buy season passes for the whole family. President is John Mathews. The club holds PNSA status and conducts the Meadows Slalom, Meadows Snowflake (downhill), Kandy Kup Kandahar, Champagne Slalom, a spring vacation Team Training Camp, and a Summer Racing Camp. Several social events during the year give the club cohesion. A courtesy patrol was started in 1974 to help bewildered "bunnies" and to try to control skiing out of control, dangerous to the skier as well as the others on the slopes.

The Mount Hood Meadows Ski School is run as a part of the whole operation under the direction of Rene' Farwig, born in Spain of German lineage. Farwig started his racing career in Bolivia, becoming a national champion and representing that county in the 1956 Olympic Games. He has won the South American championship several times and competed in FIS events in Europe and North America as well. He wrote the Advanced Skiing Maneuvers section of the American Ski Technique Manual, third edition. A resident of Parkdale, he has a wife, Jeannie, who coaches Mity Mites at Mount Hood Meadows. Their children, Rene' Lyn, 12, and Steve, 8, are racing competitors on the Meadows team.

Steve Bratt, 26, is assistant to Farwig, a native of Boise, Idaho. He belongs to the Professional Ski Instructors of America and is a certification examiner for the PNSIA. His home is also at Parkdale. Mike Durbin, for a time the business manager, is manager of the ski shop. John Rogers is the manager of mountain operations and is responsible for outside activities, as well as maintenance of the Day Lodge. Mike Gandee of Parkdale runs the rental and repair shop.

Manager of Mount Hood Meadows is Norman McKinnon. Previous managers have been Keith Petrie, George Hall, and Dennis Reese.

Ownership of Mount Hood Meadows is a partnership. The General Partner is the previously mentioned Mount Hood Meadows Development Corporation. In addition there are limited partners as follows: Theodore Lilley, Jr., Joseph Canell, Winston R. Fuller, John B. Fewel, William B. Rosenfeld, Phillip Miller, Drake Investment Co., Elizabeth Brooke, John Gray, Trusts for five of children of John Gray, Robert C. Warren, Bruce M. Hall, S. Eberly Thompson, Sr., and S. Eberly Thompson, Jr.

Rhododendron, A Town Once Called Rowe

Henry S. Rowe, mayor of Portland from June 4, 1900, to January, 1902, built Rhododendron Inn in 1905 on the 160-acre homestead he had purchased from Henery Hammond for $1,200. Construction and design was done by the man who had been chief of Portland Fire Department in Rowe's administration, Lee Holden. Holden took over as the operator of the hotel after its completion in 1910, but lasted only one season. It was during that year the post office was established as Rowe, Oregon.

In 1912 Emil and Suzette Franzetti, hoteliers from Europe, bought the hotel and initiated a program of extensive improvement. They added a 60'x100' dance hall, a 50'x100' concrete swimming pool, tennis and croquet courts, bridle paths, and hiking trails. The original building had 14 guest rooms, kitchen, dining hall, and lobby. They built an annex across the highway with eight more rooms, kitchen, and dining room. Near the annex were several cottages, and many more guests could be accommodated in tent houses. The Franzetti mode of operation was in the formal, European style, which attracted the more affluent Portland trade.

In 1916 Suzette Franzetti was suddenly widowed when Emil was killed in the turnover of his automobile in soft sand near the Zigzag Ranger Station. For seven years she ran it by herself and finally sold for an undisclosed price to William F. Cash and his wife on about April 9, 1924. Mrs. Cash had recently been the cateress for the tea room at Olds, Wortman, and King in Portland, and had hotel experience at Seaside and at Campbell Hotel, Mallory Hotel, and Multnomah Hotel. At the time of the sale, the property amounted to six acres,

On Friday, July 18, 1930, a defective chimney started a fire in the annex. Hotel staff and guests helped fight the flames until the Forest Service arrived with a pumper from Zigzag. The pumper threw water on the cabins, store, and post office to keep the fire from spreading. Merchandise and equipment were removed from the store and post office, but the buildings were saved.

In 1948 the old hotel was sold to Thomas Rex, who changed the name to Rex Inn. During the six months previous to February, 1949, it had been closed to public use. The winter of 1949 was severe. Hydrants and many inside pipes were frozen in Rhododendron. Late in the day on Wednesday, February 2, came the alarm **FIRE!** A blow torch was being used to thaw pipes and was the probable cause of fire. By the time the Forest Service and Sandy Fire Department could arrive with pumpers to take water from the creek, the building was gone. Fighting fire resolved itself into the usual problem of a struggle to save the rest of the town. Fortunately the day was windless, and no other buildings burned. The hotel was the largest building in the community.

Rhododendron Inn — Photo Everett Sickler

An early visitor to the north slopes of Mount Hood was Thomas Lamb Eliot, Portland minister who brought the Unitarian faith to the West. He reached the timberline area in an exploration of 1875, returning in following years with botanist, Professor Louis F. Henderson, to study the glacial structure of the mountain and to catalogue the plant life.

South Side Route climbers had previously seen Lost Lake from the summit of the mountain. It was rumored that two brothers from the Hood River Valley had visited it, Joe and John Diver. In August of 1880 a party was led by Ezra L. Smith with the objective of locating the lake. The party included Thomas Eliot, his brothers Edward and Christopher Eliot, Professor Henderson, surveyor Newton Clark, William Ferguson, Lyman Smith, William Smith, Milton D. Odell, William Hudson, and ________________Pitts. Smoky atmosphere hampered their search, but suddenly the deep lake was found on August 21, reportedly seen first by Ferguson from a ridge. Eliot suggested that they name it Lost Lake until an authoritative Indian could be found. Later search showed the Indians had forgotten.

So far as is known, Eliot never did climb Mount Hood, although he ascended Mount Adams in 1878. The Eliot Glacier commemorates his name. Its chaos of seracs and crevasses undulates over two spectacular ice-falls, and lies against the towering rock buttress of the very summit of the mountain. Its terminus lies between two immense lateral moraines, the lowest terminal ice buried under mounds of glacial rock not far above Cloud Cap Inn.

PLANNING THE FIRST ROAD

In the summer of 1884, Captain Henry C. Coe, Oscar L. Stranahan, David Rose Cooper, and James Graham approached Mount Hood with development in mind. On the hot, dry day on which they neared the north slopes, a forest fire burned ahead of them, cleaning out the brush and trees almost to Elk Beds, an old elk wallow about five miles north of the site of Cloud Cap Inn. This was fortunate for them, because from the toll bridge near Mount Hood Post Office there were no roads, only crude "way trails" for explorers such as Dr. Eliot. Most of the area was trackless wilderness covered with timber and heavy underbrush predominating in impenetrable willow thickets.

On the second day they had ascended to a campsite at a spring about a mile and a half below Elk Beds. Inspired by the sound of the nearby forest fire, they called it Roaring Camp. Bedded down that night, the men were asleep, when Cooper awoke with an uneasy feeling. He rose and moved his blankets to another site. In less than five minutes the top of a burning snag tree crashed to the ground, striking the very place where he had been sleeping. A premonition had saved his life.

The four men explored the timberline area and returned to Hood River Valley with great ideas of building a road to bring tourists to the beautiful north side. Hood River people had long admired Mount Hood, and there was a great urge to make it accessible. Graham dropped out, but Coe, Stranahan, and Cooper wove their way into the fabric of history by forming the Mount Hood Trail and Wagon Company under a Wasco County charter to build a toll road and operate a passenger service.

A DIFFERENT VERSION

The source of most of the information for the preceeding paragraphs was taken from the writing of William A. Langille. The *Oregon Journal* published a story on Marion Cooper on March 12, 1939, by R.G.Rumbaugh, some of which cannot be double-checked.

She reported that six men, not four, made that original trip to timberline. They were Coe, Stranahan, and Cooper, as previously reported, and Henry Thomlinson, George Winner, and Will Langille. The presence of Langille, the author feels, should be discounted; he was only 14 in that year of 1884, and he surely would have mentioned himself in his own historic resume. If it had been his father, James, he would also surely have mentioned him. Thomlinson and Winner are unknown quantities.

Mrs. Rumbaugh also stated that Coe, Stranahan, and Cooper, along with three unnamed men, gathered around the campfire in September, following the building of the road. (This would be 1885). They planned to climb to the summit of Mount Hood, and Cooper chose the Cooper Spur Route. Once on top, they each chose a prominent geographical feature to bear his own name. This ascent has never been noted elsewhere, and it is a very good guess that it was an ascent to the top of Cooper Spur.

Road construction began in later summer. Winter snow covered the project, completed in summer of 1885. Roaring Camp was used as a base for the road work, the spring furnishing water for horses and men. The new road was no highway; it was extremely steep and direct. Most early tourists chose to walk the final stretch. Sections of the old route can still be seen today, faint under the encroaching forest.

Oscar Stranahan's son, Bert, an effusive raconteur of times past, drove the struggling horses that pulled the democrat wagon across unbridged creeks and up the steep hills, meanwhile entertaining guests with his rare wit that spared no man. The family is perpetuated in Stranahan Falls on Eliot Creek, visible from Inspiration Point on the Cloud Cap Road, and also in Stranahan Ridge. The Forest Service erred in recent years by putting up a sign at Inspiration Point pointing to Wallalute Falls, rather than the correct name of Stranahan. The error was compounded by labelling the falls on the Forest Service maps as Wallalute. Wallalute Falls are actually on Compass

Creek, west of Stranahan Ridge, but the Forest Service erred and labelled them Branch Falls. Many such mislabellings have resulted in name changing; perhaps this one will. Stranahan Ridge will be found by hikers on the Timberline Trail, the second one west of Eliot Creek, just east of Compass Creek. Following up the ridge, one comes to Langille Crags.

Dr. Thomas Eliot placed Henry Coe's name on Coe Glacier. He named Cooper Spur for David Rose Cooper. Coe Glacier, the second of the two large glaciers of the north side, lies due north of the summit of Mount Hood, engulfing the base of Pulpit Rock, and sweeping down toward Elk Cove. It is more remote to visitors than Eliot Glacier. Coe Creek on the Timberline Trail was always one of the nightmare crossings for horses and hikers traversing the treacherous moraine and shifting gravel. The Forest Service by-passed the old crossing by running a much safer, lower passage in the Sixties.

Dr. Eliot conducted a ceremony on Cooper Spur to perpetuate the name of the well-known surveyor Newton Clark upon the Newton Clark Glacier. However, information given to Percy Bucklin indicates that the name was probably already allocated by a party of government surveyors with whom Clark was working.

David Cooper spent much of his time leading groups of visitors on hikes to Eliot Glacier and Cooper Spur, a prominent shoulder of the mountain that presents the hiker a striking view. To the south and east are Mount Jefferson, the plains of Central Oregon, and Newton Clark Glacier. To the north one sees Mount Adams, Mount Rainier, Mount St. Helens, and stretches of the mighty Columbia River. Directly below the north side of Cooper Spur the Eliot Glacier has plucked away the rock to form a vertical cliff, and the hiker can admire the treacherous beauty of yawning crevasses. Cooper had a most spectacular showcase for his leadership of early-day tourists.

Rodney L. Glisan wrote in 1907 of the trip he made in 1888 to the north side. Dave Cooper took the party on a long trip across Cooper Spur and across the wide Newton Clark Glacier to the point where they could look up and see Crater Rock and the awesome canyon of the White River Glacier. This was a long and demanding trip for novices such as Glisan had been at that time.

Cooper's wife, Marian, was the warm and friendly hostess of the first "hotel" at timberline. Facilities in the gully near Tilly Jane Camp included cook tent, dining tent, and sleeping tents. In the fall the hotel was simply folded up and taken down the hill until the next season. There were 10 children in the family, the "baby" David Robert being born in 1894, but in the days of the tent hotel, the family was smaller. Warren (Barney) Cooper, and his brother James, split wood and stoked fires, while the two oldest daughters, Wyoming (Noma) and Teena, were waitresses. The boys made trips down to Tony Creek to keep trout on the table, and occasionally they shot a deer for hotel fare.

Through an interview with Mrs. R.G. Brumbaugh, Mrs. Cooper noted that she was not always the hostess at the tent camp. Others were Oscar Sandman's wife, George Winner, Mrs. C. Hagerdorn, and Mrs. Sandman's daughter Emma Edick, who later became Mrs. Henry Thomlinson.

Mrs. Cooper recalled some of the amenities of the camp hotel. Two cows gave them plenty of milk, whipped cream, and butter. Her son, James, and George Perkins came up from the valley at times with elk meat, which they put in a snow igloo for safe keeping. James usually stayed on the homestead at Parkdale with Noma, Tena, Lizzie, and John. Warren, who later became a Forest Ranger, stayed at the camp with his mother and the babies, Mae, George, and David.

Cooper's tent hotel — circa 1888 — Photo David Cooper, Jr.

White dishes and white oilcloth gave the camp a civilized appearance. A good cook stove made it possible to bake bread and pastry. Each sleeping tent had a bed, a chair, table, and candle.

In 1888, an early blizzard caught her in the kitchen tent, which was tied to trees with ropes. Frequent trips outside to get more firewood for the bonfire were needed. After one trip, she returned to find the axe and rope missing, a paralyzing mystery. All through the night the gale blew the drifting snow through the camp. At daybreak, she heard the crunch of footsteps and saw the outline of a man in the firelight. She grabbed a club to defend her camp, then realized that it was John O'Leary, a sheep herder, who used the high pastures. He had taken the axe and rope to get his favorite horse free of a crevasse. He was unsuccessful, and the horse was never recovered. There is no note as to which glacier claimed the poor animal. O'Leary stayed in camp to keep the fire alive, until help arrived.

In 1886 another of the inevitable forest fires burned up the Middle Fork of Hood River. It forced Mrs. Cooper to grab her children and run for life amid smoke and falling firebrands, taking refuge on the lower part of Eliot Glacier until well past dark. The fire swept the ridge where Cloud Cap Inn was later built, giving it the name of "Ghost Ridge".

Another pioneer name is bestowed on Barrett Spur, the high volcanic ridge west of Coe Glacier. Dr. and Mrs. Perry Barrett were early explorers of Eden Park, the floral wonderland on Mount Hood's northwest slopes between Vista Ridge and Cathedral Ridge.

Newton Clark Glacier was named for the early Hood River surveyor of that name. According to information given to Percy Bucklin by Newton Clark's son, W. Louis Clark, the name was given by government surveyors while both father and son were working with their party high on the east slopes of Mount Hood. They were camped in the meadows near the present-day Mount Hood Meadows. Newton Clark suggested that they spend a day of rest in climbing up that side of the mountain. The trip ended on top of Steel Cliffs, probably the first time anyone had been there since the Dryer climb of 1854. The adventuresome Clark participated years later in a climb in 1887, said to be the first ascent of the north side of Mount Hood.

Another enthusiast of the north side was Eliot's son-in-law Reverend Earl Morse Wilbur, a charter member of The Mazamas.

In August and September of 1922 the Oregon Nature Lovers' Club of Hood River did further exploring in the area once known to the Barretts. Mr. and Mrs. C.E. Graves and Mr. and Mrs. F.W. Rockhold of that group made several hikes into the remote northwest timberline area and established several names in use today. Eden Park, lying along two branches of Ladd Creek, is one. Eden Park is flanked by two great ridges which they named, Cathedral Ridge on the south and Vista Ridge, which separates Eden Park from Wiyeast Basin. Wiyeast was given the parklike area at timberline that lies just west of Barrett Spur; it perpetuates the old Indian name for Mount Hood.

In January of 1923 the Oregon Nature Lovers' Club ceased operation, and some of its members formed another club in Hood River called the Wiyeast Club. This was evidently short lived and had no connection with the Wy'east Climbers.

Cloud Cap Inn, Precious Building Relic

Great development was in the wind in the spring of 1889, when two Portland men, William M. Ladd, banker, and Colonel C.E.S. Wood, attorney, announced that they had bought the original road and organized the Mount Hood Stage Company, with plans for a hotel building and a much improved road. It was Wood's wife, Nannie, who named the hotel, Cloud Cap Inn.

Road improvement began near the toll bridge, down on the East Fork of Hood River about a mile south of Mount Hood Post Office, close to the location of the original Baldwin homestead cabin. A new bridge was built over East Fork at the old fording site, and several more were added across minor streams on the way up to the mountain. At Elk Beds Spring a stage station with cabin and barn was built to shelter the relief of coach horses needed for the severe pull up the last steep miles.

Chinese laborers were hired to dig and fill on the grades. "China Fill", a problem and challenge to early motorists, was a 22-percent grade on a curve over a small ravine just below Cloud Cap Inn, the new hotel. "China Hill" was another section of road below the old Mount Hood Lodge site, northwest of present-day Cooper Spur Junction. The old road did not follow today's highway from Parkdale to Cooper Spur Junction. Instead it ran on the ridge between Evans Creek and Crystal Springs Creek.

Architectural plans for the proposed Cloud Cap Inn were made after careful esthetic site evaluation by Whidden and Lewis, a firm that later designed the famous 1905 Lewis and Clark Exposition Forestry Building on NW Vaughn Street in Portland. By March the area was accessible by horse and wagon, the snowpack being unusually low in 1889. After the new road was sufficiently improved, a forest camp was installed, and men began to cut and hew a stockpile of amabilis fir logs near the lodge site.

Then work on the fine, old building began, with heavy log walls, a thick roof of cedar shakes, and two mammoth fireplaces of native stone. To keep the structure from blowing off the ridge, cables were fastened to buried foundations. Water was piped in 1200 feet from Tilly Jane Creek.

Kitchen, baths, and beds were installed, and Cloud Cap Inn was opened as a modern hotel August 6, 1889. The first guest, Malcom Moody of The Dalles, brought along five friends in his own coach drawn by four horses. Operation of the Inn was by Lewis H. Adams and wife. Adams had owned the stages and wild, outlaw horse teams used during the construction period.

Few guests arrived before Cloud Cap Inn closed for the winter, one marked by raging storms and very deep snow. The owners worried that the snow might crush the structure, or that the wind might strip away the roof. In February, Will and Doug Langille visited the building on homemade skis to check conditions. They reached Elk Beds Cabin the first night and Cloud Cap the second. Most people thought that weather at that elevation would be too cold to endure. The Langille boys found a little drifted snow inside, but the day was pleasant; water dripped from the eaves.

In March manager Adams and wagon driver Theodore Dallas hiked to the Inn in the company of photographer, A.B. McAlpin. McAlpin took winter scenes on 18" x 22" plates, which helped popularize the idea of winter travel to the remote area. Snowdrifts blocked the road until July 12, 1890.

Hotel service was deluxe, including the ultimate in transportation from Hood River. When the Portland train arrived there each noon, the horse-drawn Cloud Cap Stage was waiting. A ten mile ride took the guests to a lunch stop at Joe Divers' ranch on the Little Luckamas (Louis Rhodes ranch in 1927). Then four fresh horses pulled the coach to Elk Beds, where Theodore Dallas waited with six strong, wild horses, straining at their bits to terrify the passengers with a lurching, careening start. The fast start up the final six miles diminished as the steep hill settled the horses down to a brisk walk. Guests stepped into Cloud Cap Inn just five-and-a-half hours from the railroad station at Hood River.

Unfortunately, Malcom Moody's great enthusiasm for the new hotel was not contagious. At season's end in 1890, only 88 guests had signed the register. Owners Ladd and Wood had spent over $50,000; the mounting deficits prompted them to sell the livestock and close down. Sarah, wife of James Langille, agreed to take over Cloud Cap Inn in 1891. Service was simpler, and the transportation under Olinger and Bone was scaled down, bringing the Inn into an era of profitability.

Cloud Cap Inn 1890 — Photo Homer Rogers
From left, Kenneth Beebe, Mrs. William Wade Beebe, Gerald Beebe. In top hat, Syl Riker. Third from right, the famous artist Bierstadt. To his right J. Thorburn Ross. On right end, mountain guide.

CONSTRUCTION STAFF OF CLOUD CAP INN AND IMPROVED ROAD

____________Whidden, Portland . . . . . . Architect
John Hamilton, Portland . . . . . . Superintendent
James Turner, Portland . Foreman of woods crew
Thomas McKay, Hood River . . . . Bossed Chinese crew, a railroad contractor
______________Brown, Portland . . . . Foreman of construction
James L. Langille, Hood River . . . . Brown's assistant, later took over
William Ehrck, Hood River . . Masonry contractor
Lewis H. Adams, Portland . . . . . Transportation
Old Country Chinese . . . . . Cooks and road crew

Two of Sarah Langille's sons, Will and Doug, **(pronounced Doog)** were active in helping with the chore of running the operation. Both were mountain guides, Will being much more active and prominent. Mrs. Langille, sometimes called "Lady of the Mountain", was usually known as Tantsana by friends and guests. Tantsana's warm hospitality set a tone for the lodge that made the visit of any guest a truly memorable experience. Even for the least adventuresome, a trip to Cloud Cap was very rewarding. Beginning with the exciting coach ride up the mountain roads, the guest was next blessed with the comforts of the hotel, then the good meals and the party atmosphere before the fireplace. On clear summer days the impressive, rugged view of Eliot Glacier carried one's mind to a level of philosophical bliss.

Activity of the climbing parties added excitement and ceremony. To so many of these climbing guests the ascent of Mount Hood was a once-in-a-lifetime experience. At the snow line Will and Doug coiled the climbing ropes and cached them; then the party marched triumphantly down the open slopes to Cloud Cap. Occasionally the tenderfoot guests were accommodated with a trip down by horseback. On arrival at the registry desk, the successful climbers were permitted to solemnly note the word SUMMIT by their names. The guest then took his personal card, which everyone had in those days, and thumbtacked it to the ceiling for future generations to see. This was done by throwing the tacked card upward with a silver dollar behind it to drive home the tack.

A typical trip of the era was reported in the *Sunday Oregonian* of July 9, 1893. A group of Portlanders had spent the Fourth of July at Cloud Cap, taking the last few miles in a horse-drawn sleigh. At lower elevations the roads were good. The party consisted of Mr. and Mrs. E.T.C. Stevens, Mrs. Russell, Mrs. John Effinger, Miss Wilson, Miss Clementina Wilson, Bruce Wilson, Miss Flanders, Miss Sallie Beck, Miss Hewett, and Miss Millie Trevett.

An 1893 brochure of Cloud Cap, extolled its facilities as written by Will Langille, manager. He noted that climbers have the choice of four different routes, south, east, north, and northwest. He strongly urged a circuit trip of the mountain, run by competent guides across nine glaciers. This trip was to be done in ten hours. He advised ladies to bring strong ankle boots and short woolen skirts. Will made the trip with G.W. Graham in

Sarah Langille at home at Cloud Cap Inn — Photo Mrs. Ivan Langley

1892.

No record is available of such further whirlwind trips around the glacial belt of Mount Hood by Langille or any other guides for the tourists of the day. One might assume that such activity was merely an idea seldom undertaken by clients.

In 1894 owner Ladd bought telephone wire and equipment to connect Cloud Cap Inn to the outside world. Will Langille ran the wire and made the installation.

In 1897 Will left the guiding to his brother Doug and followed the lure of gold to mining operations at Nome, Alaska. Doug, who was seven years younger than Will, quickly stepped into the position of head guide for the next three years. In 1900 he quit to join the US Geological Survey at age 25. Sarah Langille then employed Peter Feldhausen and Hans Furrer, European guides, to serve climbing clients until 1903. Furrer is believed to be a different individual than the Hans Fuhrer, who guided from Government Camp Hotel in 1916-17.

Feldhausen contracted tuberculosis and went south. Soon afterward, he began a hike from Mexico to Canada along the backbone of the Rockies. After the trip, he was declared free of the disease and began guiding at Jasper National Park in Canada. Furrer joined him, and the two tried in vain to get Mark Weygandt to join them.

Mark Weygandt went to work for Sarah Langille in 1904 as head guide. He stayed with her several years, and worked for Horace Mecklem after 1907.

When her two sons left Cloud Cap for greener pastures, Sarah Langille turned for help to Horace Mecklem, her nephew. He came from the east coast to work for her in 1901-2. In 1905 he married a New York girl, Olive Slate, in a ceremony at Waughwingwin Lodge west of Hood River. The newlyweds promptly moved to Cloud Cap, where he waited tables, kept books, cut wood, and guided occasionally for climbing parties. Mrs. Langille gave up the Inn after 16 golden years of operation, and Mecklem took over in 1907 for several prosperous years. In later life Mecklem was to become a very prominent business and civic leader in Portland.

He arrived at Mount Hood just in time to witness the first automobile trips to the north side. E.Y. Judd, a Mazama from Pendleton, tried the Cloud Cap road in 1901 with a three-cylinder car, said to be the only gasoline propelled model on the west coast. It ran at 18 miles-per-hour top speed on the level with a 12-horsepower engine. Accompanying the auto all the way were two wagons to gas the vehicle, carry baggage, and repair breakdowns, and two men on horseback to quell the stampedes of local farm horses. The third cylinder stopped 12 miles out of Hood River, was repaired, and the auto finally made the top of Booth Hill with the driver walking and steering alongside. The breakneck speed of 20 mph down a subsequent hill caused failure of the water pump. Judd gave up near Elk Beds and rode to Cloud Cap by wagon. Consoling Tantsana assured him that he would have made it, if it had not been for the snow.

In 1907 Portland auto dealer, H.M. Covey drove a one-lung Cadillac with high-tonneau seat and blunt nose right up to the door of the Inn. Mecklem drove an accompanying car that made it only to the curve of the China Fill and foundered in the heavy volcanic ash. This car, a Pierce-Arrow, originally belonged to the Failing sisters, one of the first ever to be delivered in Portland. The following day Covey drove victoriously back to Hood River. Furious ranchers along the way

H.M. Covey drove the first car to Cloud Cap Inn 1907 — Photo Homer Rogers

threatened to lynch him, if he ever returned, because the Cadillac had caused seven teams of farm horses to run away.

Mecklem put the Pierce-Arrow into regular passenger stage service from that time on, but the China Fill was the top limit. Use of the motor car cut travel time from Hood River from eight hours to three. In the very first load of paying passengers was the inveterate enthusiast, Malcom Moody, bringing along the Lang sisters from The Dalles.

Just when Mecklem stopped management of the inn is not known, but at some time Dorsey B. Smith came into the picture. It is on record that he was the manager during the summer of 1912. It is also known that Homer Rogers expressed difficulty in dealing with Smith in 1917, indicating that Smith may have operated the hotel for quite a number of years before Rogers' regime.

Homer Rogers bought Cloud Cap Inn for $5,000 from William Ladd on May 9, 1919. The use of the 12-acre lodge site was secured from the Forest Service on an annual permit basis. Rogers (1881-1974), a 1903 graduate of Yale University, had alpine experience in the Swiss and French Alps, belonged to The Mazamas, Sierra Club, and American Alpine Club. His family home was in another hotel established in 1913, Mount Hood Lodge, at 2800-feet elevation just north of the old Roaring Camp.

An advertising brochure showed Mount Hood Lodge offering all year sleeping rooms or tents, gracious meals, horseback trips, mountain ascents under Mr. Rogers, timberline hiking jaunts, and the use of Rocky Butte Camp near the snout of Coe Glacier. The building boasted a windmill atop the observation deck, a 2,500-volume library, Steinway piano, a Victor phonograph with many late records, and a 250-power telescope for scanning the mountain's rugged north side. Rogers hired William Moody and George Miller as guides during his regime.

Rogers operated the two hotels simultaneously, but he made few improvements at Cloud Cap Inn. In the early Twenties the federal government was spending large sums on the building of the Mount Hood Loop Highway and had plans for a new road to the Inn. In 1923 the Forest Service notified Rogers that he must make improvements or lose his permit on Cloud Cap. On November 8, 1924, a newspaper story quoted an unnamed Forest Service representative in Washington D.C. declaring that Rogers' permit would be revoked and he would be paid for his investment. This was in response to many letters from the public in support of Rogers. The Forest Service did make it clear that Rogers would be welcome to bid on the construction and operation of a new structure.

PLANNING FOR A NEW HOTEL

In 1925 a press release by Colonel W.B. Greeley, chief of US Forest Service, announced allotment of $85,000 to build 9½ miles of standard grade road to Cloud Cap Inn. He reiterated that Rogers must make improvements or lose his permit. He cited the Paradise Hotel at Mount Rainier and indicated that a new, modern hotel at Cloud Cap site was being considered.

August 19, 1925 Newspapers carried the story that Homer Rogers had sold Cloud Cap Inn on August 17, and would operate only to the end of summer. A civic committee had bought it, headed by Chairman J.C. Ainsworth. Dorsey Smith would operate the old inn until a new one could be built. The others were E.S. Collins, Franklin T. Griffith, Rodney Glisan, The Oregon Journal, H.B. Van Duzer, W.B. Beebe, and L.R. Wheeler, all of Portland; E.O. Blanchard and Leslie Butler of Hood River.

At last a full scale movement was under way for the first-class development of the north side. The Forest Service was at work on the new road, now valued at $175,000, to be complete in 1926. The following civic meetings and drum beating by the press are fascinating, because they so closely parallel the promotion of Timberline Lodge a decade later in 1936. Why did the strong campaign to rebuild Cloud Cap Inn fail, when the similar crusade for Timberline Lodge succeeded? It is all a matter of conjecture, but perhaps the reader may form his own conclusions.

January 31, 1926 The committee announced a company to be capitalized at $150,000 with an initial amount of $100,000 to be raised promptly to accommodate the first stage of development. Seattle architect E.A. Doyle made preliminary plans for a massive stone building with 32 rooms, dining hall, and lounge. More extensive sleeping areas could come when indicated by demand.

March 10, 1926 L.R. Wheeler of Hood River told the Portland Chamber of Commerce that the first $25,000 had already been underwritten. Forest Service Supervisor T.R. Sherrard reported that the new $200,000 road would be soon finished. He noted that 400,000 people had driven around the new Mount Hood Loop Highway in 1925. Dorsey B. Smith assured that a two-month season would be sufficient for economic success. B.W. Huntoon of Bellingham, Washington, gave a glowing report of raising $250,000 for a new lodge at Mount Baker.

March 22, 1926 Using the pioneer name, Mount Hood Trail and Wagon Company, Ainsworth, Beebe, Glisan, Van Duzer, Wheeler, and Butler filed articles of incorporation — 3,000 shares, $150,000 capital stock. Subscription was declared an accomplished fact. W.S. Basinger, Union Pacific Railway passenger traffic manager, stated that the UP would feature Mount Hood in advertising, making it a nationally known resort. The railroad would issue coupons good for stopover at Hood River and round trip transport to Cloud Cap.

April 30, 1926 The new hotel was declared assured at Chamber of Commerce meeting.

May 2, 1926 A prospectus was announced as planned and soon to be in the hands of the 30 businessmen seeking subscriptions.

May 4, 1926 An office was established on the 6th floor of the Oregon Building.

May 10, 1926 The Chamber of Commerce heard Henry J. Rhoades, president of Rainier National Park Company tell of Portland's great opportunity in a new Cloud Cap Inn. During 1925 Rainier had 175,000 visitors. Paradise Hotel was proving a sound investment with $80,000 of net earnings the past year.

May 13, 1926 The sales office reported that many small investors were requesting stock in less than the prescribed $3,000 minimum.

May 29, 1926 The new road was opened to Cloud Cap. Permanent surfacing was proposed immediately by the Forest Service.

June 14, 1926 Announcing that $75,000 had been subscribed, the committee tried to whip enthusiasm to a frenzy, in order to raise the last $25,000. Chairman Clay S. Morse hoped for completion by the weekend, in order that construction could begin in two weeks. Hood River people had subscribed $10,000. Those contributors in Portland, who had pledged a total of $65,000 were:

C.F. Adams	Franklin T. Griffith
J.C. Ainsworth	Eric V. Hauser
W.B. Beebe	George F. Mason
Ralph H. Burnside	William P. Merry
E.S. Collins	L.R. Wheeler
W.C. Culbertson	A.L. Mills
A.E. Doyle	Clay S. Morse
J.O. Elrod	H.J. Ottenheimer
Peter Kerr	Ira F. Powers
F.C. Knapp	Joseph Shemanski
R.L. Glisan	Dorsey B. Smith
Guy Talbot	Lorenz Brothers
J.N. Teal	Meier & Frank
A.R. Watzek	Nortonia Hotel
Columbia Gorge Motor Systems	Olds, Wortman & King
Failing Estate	The Oregonian
Hazelwood Restaurants	Wilcox Investment Co.
Josephy, Haney & Littlewood	Knight Packing Co.
Journal Publishing	Keller & Boyd

June 15, 1926 Chairman Clay S. Morse remarked that tourist agencies and railways had not included Mount Hood in itineraries, because of lack of first class hotel facilities. The new hotel would be expected to fill the day it opens, putting Mount Hood on an equal basis with resorts such as Mount Rainier, Yellowstone, Yosemite, or Grand Canyon. Two luncheons were held on this day, one for 46 members of the fund raising committee, Dorsey B. Smith presiding. The other was a Rotary Club group which dedicated themselves to the project. New subscriptions were received by Dr. W.W. Youngson, S.S. Pier, and Chief of Police L.V. Jenkins.

June 17, 1926 After a half day of canvassing, the committee gathered at The Chamber of Commerce for luncheon. Morse assured success. Pier and Glisan were speakers.

June 18, 1926 Another luncheon. Morse reported a third of the last $25,000 had been subscribed. T.H. Martin, general manager of Rainier National Park Company gave glowing investment reports to the group.

June 22, 1926 Another luncheon at the Chamber of Commerce. Still only a third of the $25,000 had been raised. Committee workers voted to say on the job. Other financial drives were said to be competing with the Cloud Cap Hotel project.

August 20, 1926 Despite the lack of success in raising the full amount of funds, the Cloud Cap Inn Company seemed very assured in going ahead with the new building. Their contractor, Max Lorentz, who later built Timberline Lodge, planned to build the basement and foundation later that autumn and have a stock pile of materials needed for the next spring.

Pietro Belluschi, representing architect Arthur Doyle, conducted an on-site inspection of the plans for the board of directors on August 14. Attending were the president Leslie Butler, and directors L.R. Wheeler, J.C. Ainsworth, Rodney L. Glisan, Harry Joyce, Eric W. Hanser, Jr., Sim Winch, E.V. Littlefield, and John Veatch. Also present were the mechanical engineer, O. Goodwin, and Dorsey Smith and Thomas Sherrard.

Newspaper stories at a later time indicated that the Forest Service did not intend to let any construction go ahead without accumulation of the full sum of money. Soon the whole story became overshadowed with the promotion of a tramway.

With that the mighty drive to raise funds for a new hotel died. The newspapers gave up on publicity, and Portland business men turned to other problems. Dorsey Smith ran the old inn, waiting for the time when Mount Hood Trail and Wagon Company could proceed with the hotel building project.

GRANDIOSE SCHEME FOR A TRAM

In the summer of 1926 a virulent new ingredient was added. Promoter L.L. Tyler, backed by Philip and Henry Buerhner and Thornton Ladd, proposed to the Forest Service a giant plan to build a cable railway from Cloud Cap Inn to Cooper Spur, and a cable tramway from Cooper Spur to the very summit of Mount Hood. The estimated cost of $350,000 was to be covered by a stock promotion.

The development would include a power house and waiting room on Cooper Spur and an observation building on the summit. Two giant steel towers would support the cables for the summit tramway. Cloud Cap Inn would be replaced with a four-story hotel.

The scheme was finally brought to a public hearing on April 15, 1927, attended by Chief Forester, Colonel William B. Greeley, from Washington D.C. Tempers were very hot at the hearing, especially among The Mazamas and other groups wishing to save the wilderness. Surprisingly, several very prominent Mazamas favored the project, Kenneth Beebe, John Lee, Earl Marshall, Rodney L. Glisan, Charles Sholes, Carl P. Richards, and Dr. Edwin T. Hodge. However, the club as a whole took the official position of strong opposition, declaring the promotion an unconscionable rape of a prime, scenic wilderness area. Prominent Mazamas who fought the development were Judge Fred W. Stadter, Louis W. Waldorf, Merle Manley, Martha Nilsson, Nelle Heiser, Frank Redman, John D. Scott, Merle S. Moore, and Rex Bunage. As a result of the hearing, as well as of his personal inspection of Mount Hood's north side, Colonel Greeley vetoed the application.

The promoters were not to be so easily denied and immediately formed the Mount Hood Committee to carry the battle to Washington D.C. and lay it right on the desk of the Secretary of Agriculture, William M. Jardine. The committee consisted of C.M. Granger, the US District Forester, F.A. Elliott, Oregon Forester, Rodney Glisan, Dr. Edwin T. Hodge of University of Oregon, Dr. George W. Peavy of Oregon State Agricultural College, R.E. Scott of Hood River Chamber of Commerce, R.H. Richards of Farmers' Co-op of The Dalles, John B. Yeon, and Julius Meier. One other member of the committee was John Denny Scott of The Mazamas, in a unique position, because he was the only member in opposition.

The Mount Hood Committee held meetings in the office of its chairman, Julius Meier, Meier and Frank executive, who later became governor of the state. John Scott, an electrical engineer by profession, presented a strong case against building a tram. He advised the committee of the very small number of clear days in any given summer, when the view would not be obscured by smoke or clouds. A veteran of climbing, Scott knew the conditions personally, whereas the others had lesser amounts of knowledge of the mountain. The Mount Hood Committee was so enchanted with the prospects of money rolling into the area, that they could think of nothing else. The vote was completely in favor of the tramway, except for Scott's NO and Granger's abstainment.

It was at these mettings, however, that other vital conservation decisions were effected. A vote was made to recommend to the Forest Service that Mount Jefferson be set aside as a primitive wilderness area and to turn the proposed Syline Road west at Breitenbush Lake, instead of running into Jefferson Park, a lake-studded gem of the Cascades.

The committee took the proposals to Washington D.C., where it became buried in detail. In the summer of 1929, Secretary Jardine sent three experts to evaluate the problem:

Dr. John C. Merriam, President of Carnegie Institute

Dr. Frank A. Waugh, Amhurst College

Frederick Law Olmstead, Planning and Landscape Engineer

Their report reached Jardine's desk about May 1, 1930, recommending two-to-one against the building of a tram. Then Jardine resigned, and the new Secretary of Agriculture, Arthur M. Hyde, reversed the decision and granted a permit.

The permit stipulated that all structures must be designed architecturally as to hold to a minimum any adverse effect they might have upon the use and enjoyment of the area by the larger numbers of people who prefer to distribute themselves throughout the timberline zone (in other words, the non-riders).

Tyler, the promoter, submitted two hotel designs to the Forest Service. Plans were rejected, and all effort ceased. Gloom of the great depression had cooled the optimism about raising money through stock promotion. Thus was Mount Hood saved from the fiasco of having her most beautiful face, the north side, marred with the industrial ugliness of the proposed tramway. Many engineers have since commented on the folly of installing heavy construction on the fragil volcanic structure of Mount Hood's summit. Mountain rescue experts have often shuddered at the potential danger of sudden summer storms and jammed equipment, that could turn a casual joyride on a tramway into a disastrous nightmare.

OLD AGE COMES TO CLOUD CAP

Turning momentarily from grandiose plans to the actual reality of running a small, outmoded lodge, let us go back to Dorsey B. Smith. In 1927 he placed the management of Cloud Cap Inn in the hands of Noyes Tyrell, who ran other businesses, the largest being Tyrell's Tavern at Bonneville, an eating house that often served from 2,000 to 2,500 patrons on a busy Sunday. Building Bonneville Dam flooded the site. Tyrell also ran Tyrell's Trips, a busline operation that later became Mount Hood Scenic Trips Inc.

Tyrell ran Cloud Cap Inn until about 1932, after which it stood empty about a year. William E. Jones was head guide from 1932 on. Boyd French, Sr. leased it about 1934 and stayed on until World War Two interrupted operation. On February 3, 1942, the Mount Hood Road and Wagon Co. sold the building for $2,000 to the Forest Service. Dorsey B. Smith acted as a representative of the corporation, thus ending his many years of association with the inn. Smith, who had been born in Tennessee in 1872, died September 10, 1942. He is survived by a son, Dorsey VonBehren Smith of Pasadena, California. Boyd French occupied the building as a residence at some times during the war.

After cessation of the war in 1946 the Forest Service made attempts to find a lessee-operator. French took it for a short while, then closed it as a hotel for good.

In 1950 the Forest Service had strongly considered tearing down Cloud Cap Inn and erecting a marker to show its old location. Hunters had used some of the interior for fireplace wood, and the doors had been allowed to swing open to the storms of winter.

The Crag Rats heard about the plans of the Forest Service and immediately asked to use the building as a clubhouse and also as a base for their well-established program for snow survey. The proposal was lost in the shuffle of paperwork in Washington, when suddenly an order was sent to MHNF to raze the building.

This immediately spurred the Crag Rats to great activity. Senatorial backing was secured, and the old building was saved from extinction in the bare nick of time, because the Forest Service men **did have their orders** to take action in destroying the building.

The Forest Service then granted permission in 1954 for club use by the Hood River Crag Rats, who made extensive repairs, rehung doors, replaced windows, reactivated the water system. Since that time there are a few Crag Rats using the building every weekend.

On March 6, 1955, *The Oregonian* carried a story. Donald M. Sharpe of The Dalles and Roy Webster, a fruit grower of Hood River, announced plans for a ski lift. The lift would be about a mile long and 1000 feet vertical and reach from Inspiration Point up to Cloud Cap. They hoped to raise $150,000 for the project in their own towns. The Forest Service had agreed to widen and improve the road during the next two years. Sharpe and Webster hoped to have the lift operating in the winter of 1956-57. Three ski trails were planned. If the venture proved successful, they would build a lodge with dormitory facilities at the bottom of the lift. They planned to use Cloud Cap Inn in the summer time. No further word was heard of this project.

November 25, 1974 David G. Talbot, state parks superintendent and state historic preservation officer, announced that Cloud Cap Inn had been placed on the list of historic places. About 65 of these exist in Oregon. At the same time the Vista House at Crown Point was included.

The Crag Rats made extensive repairs and restoration in 1974, including protection against thoughtless vandals.

THREE LOST PHOTOGRAPHERS

1889 C. Fritz, H. Crosley, and Ernest Skarstedt, three photographers who arrived by train in Hood River, planned a trip to Cloud Cap Inn. A Hood River resident advised them that they would find it much more interesting to travel via Lost Lake, which would require only one more day to Cloud Cap. They were further tantalized by the information that only one photographer, Jackson from Denver, had ever visited Lost Lake. The guide services of a Mr. D. were recommended, and they left for his home eight miles south of town in a horse-drawn livery rig, filled with two day's supply of groceries.

Not finding Mr. D. at home, they continued 2½ miles to Hood River Falls and camped. In late evening, the guide came along with two pack ponies and got them out of bed to select a safer camp site. It seemed that several rattlesnakes had been killed on the site recently.

On Wednesday morning, they rose at 5:00 and travelled the 16 miles to Lost Lake by noon. Their stay was at an uninviting, old cabin at the lake. Many photographs were taken, and they set out on Thursday for the easy trip to Cloud Cap Inn with little food remaining. At 8:00 p.m. they reached the first creek and dined on two crackers and a little cheese for each man.

Friday morning they satisfied their hunger with cold water, hoping to reach the hotel by noon. By noon they had struggled through the steep forest to timberline and ate a dozen sardines, the last of the food. By 6:30 in the evening, they could see the roof of the inn through their field glasses. It developed that the guide had never been any closer than the spot where they had eaten the sardines. Crossing Coe Creek proved to be an impossible task, and successive attempts through the brush found them encamped forcibly by darkness.

Saturday at 4:00 a.m., they started once more. After an hour, Mr. D. advised them to leave the horses and walk for the inn, where food could be purchased. At noon they staggered into the area of Ghost Ridge and saw the welcome sight of the white tents of the hotel camp. The building at that date was in the stage of construction, and the area hummed with the noise of workmen sawing and pounding and teams of horses pulling loads onto the site.

The superintendent of the Mount Hood Store Co., Mr. Hamilton, gave them a meal. The guide went back in the afternoon for the horses and equipment, returning with them a full day later.

Cooper Spur, North Side Ski Area

World War Two came to an end and cast up the tireless L.C. (Jack) Baldwin Jr. once more on Hood River's doorstep about Christmas 1945. Anxious to get on the skis again, he soon made a trip with Harry Ethel to try to start the little tow west of Cooper Spur Junction. The tow was not very popular, and despite the efforts of the Hull brothers, who took it over as a private venture, it soon went out of existence.

Attention turned to the tow on the jump hill. Jack Baldwin, Harry Ethel, and George Howell rejuvenated the old equipment. The tow motor was on the center of the hill, with tow area running both above and below the 12' x 16' shack, an unusual arrangement. The installation was somewhat underpowered, but the ski club used it well for several years by not overloading the slope. Too many skiers, holding onto the rope all at once, could halt the tow.

Myron, Wes, and Ted Weygandt, sons of the old guide, Mark Weygandt, brought three army surplus Weasels to the area. The amphibious vehicles ran well on snow and were used to shuttle skiers from Cooper Spur Junction to the ski hill for a suggested 50¢ fare. Runs in the Weasel were also made to Cloud Cap Inn, eleven miles up the road. The return on skis could either be made on the road or on the Howell Trail. In about 1949 Ski Club built a warming hut and enlarged the hill as related in the chapter North Side Skiing.

In 1956, the Hood River Junior Chamber of Commerce built a loop road, running up from Cloud Cap Road to the bottom of the ski hill and back down again to Cloud Cap Road. This road, much improved now, is the one in use today, operated on a one-way traffic system. B. Clemmons, brother of Jack Baldwin's wife, Virginia, arranged a timber sale with the Forest Service, wherein he was paid for his work with logs in return for the road construction work. At the same time, the tow motor was moved to the bottom of the hill, dragged down with the use of Clemmons' "Cat" tractor. The Oregon State Highway Department agreed to keep the road plowed out to the bottom of the loop road, which gave skiers only about a quarter of a mile to walk.

The old tow house was left in the center of the hill, unused until about 1955, when it was moved down below to house a new engine bought for the slope that year. The tow was lengthened to 1000 feet. The old equipment was used to make a second tow about 200 feet long. That year the highway department agreed to plow out the loop road. By this time the tow facilities had become a private operation by Jack Baldwin and George Howell. So many of their nights and weekends were spent working and reworking all of the mechanical devices involved in operating a rope tow. The ski club members did their part by manning the warming hut, providing ski instruction and ski patrol personnel.

The ski hill had an uncleared strip of trees down the center, separating the two tow areas. In about 1957 the Forest Service gave the edict that the trees must be cut. Once again the club members went into action, cutting trees, pulling stumps, and levelling ground. The sumps were piled in a shambles over on the west side of the slope. 1958 Baldwin and Howell installed a Chevrolet V-8 engine. In 1959 Russ and Myra Ward, who ran Cooper Spur Inn, put in a food concession at the warming hut, relieving club members of the job. In 1960 George Howell moved to Portland, buying Hjalmar Hvam's sport shop. It made a longer trip for him to come up on weekends to work on the machinery.

In 1957, the Oregon National Guard used the loop road as a training maneuver, bringing in their machinery to widen the road and greatly increase the parking area. In 1963 Forest Service records showed a 1200-foot main tow and an 800-foot bunny tow in operation. In 1964 the partners modernized their equipment with a powerful new Chrysler engine. That year there was so little snow, that the tow was never run, a complete financial disaster.

In 1968 Mount Hood Meadows opened their new lifts, with their highway open from Hood River side only. During the 1967-68 season the patronage of the Cooper Spur area began to drop drastically as skiers found it very easy to reach the spectacular facilities at the Meadows. The ski club dropped out of all participation, and Baldwin and Howell carried on the disappointing operation. In 1970 Howell sold out to Baldwin and quit.

Baldwin then collaborated with Phil Tyler and Robert O. Lee, a retired vice-president of Georgia Pacific Corporation. Lee and Baldwin were friends through the American Alpine Club and had made some gargantuan jaunts across the hostile jungles of the Yucatan Peninsula in Mexico. The three formed Cooper Spur Ski, Inc. with Baldwin as president and made plans to elevate the status of the ski hill. In 1971 they installed a Hall T-Bar lift on the west side of the slope capable of handling 1,200 skiers per hour. It is 1,100 feet long with 250 feet vertical rise. The clearing on the hill is 1,000 feet wide and 1,400 feet long. A snow cat serves the area. The buildings include a warming hut with food concession run by Mr. and Mrs. Manard Philly, a ski rental shop, and a ski patrol shack that was the old motor house left on the center of the hill in 1954. The new lift was placed into operation on Christmas night of 1971 after many 14-hour work days by Baldwin and associates to get it ready.

The new facilities were financed by Small Business Administration loan, a bank loan, private money, and Hood River Improvement Corporation. Lighting opened the area for night skiing. Area was increased from 20 to 40 acres. The Forest Service permit allows for future development two airline miles above the present area. A master plan includes two more T-Bar lifts, a chairlift, and a large day lodge. At present, the size of the hill is small enough, so that parents can keep track of children with little effort. Weather is a big factor on the northeast shoulder of Mount Hood. At Bob Lee's farm four miles below the ski area, Lee counted 107 consecutive days in 1970-71 when the sun shone at some time during the day.

Cooper Spur Ski Area is often referred to as a family ski area, where family members of varying abilities can keep track of one another. There is always a group of racers training on a slalom course they set up on the steeper parts of the hill. Less able skiers can find routes off the T-Bar that are a little less demanding. In 1972 there was a noticeable trend on Mount Hood toward cross-country skiing away from the lifts. By 1974 this trend had bulged to the point of becoming a big factor in skiing once more. On any given weekend several groups of cross-country men and women are seen taking the trail that leads out of the middle of the ski hill toward Tilly Jane Camp above.

Perry Vickers, First Alpine Guide

In May 1865 Perry Vickers came to Vancouver, Washington, from the east. Vickers, a man whose bearing and education revealed a high-born early life, was believed to be a veteran of the Civil War. He was a generous extrovert, always eager to help, but he had a hot temper. In Vancouver he was seeking employment and fell into the companionship of three strangers, spending a couple of days of congenial time with them. They were suddenly approached and arrested by military officers from Fort Vancouver on the charge of stealing horses, and placed in the military jail for two months awaiting trial.

Vickers felt that he might be judged guilty because of association, and he pried boards loose on his cell and ran. Although hampered by an "Oregon Boot", a seven-pound clevis attached to his ankle, he escaped pursuers hot on his trail and ran for the Columbia River, running and stumbling through brush over a mile. He groped along the river bank for a rock to break the iron clevis. The voices and noises of pursuers forced him to wade out into the river, then swim the mile of open water to Oregon. There, in a farmer's yard, he found a wagon wheel wrench and an iron bolt to use as makeshift hammer and punch and removed the torturing iron.

In the morning he was given breakfast from a pair of wood cutters, and made his way to Powell Valley, where his brother lived. His brother gave him clothing and food, advising him to escape to eastern Oregon over the Barlow Road. Two days later he spoke to a rancher busy building a rail fence, Stephen Coalman, who happened to be the Barlow Road superintendent. Vickers first declined Coalman's offer of employment, indicating that he wanted something east of the mountains. Then Coalman offered work on the road, smoothing grades, cutting deadfall logs. Vickers accepted, and about the first of June, he went with Coalman, working from camp to camp, clearing the road.

On a Sunday's day of rest, when they were camped at Summit Meadows, Vickers hiked up Still Creek to timberline. Thrilled by the magnificent close-up view of Mount Hood, the pointed mountain trees, the stream-fed beds of flowers, he returned to the work camp with the statement that he would climb Mount Hood some day. Throughout the rest of his life, he was so greatly inspired with the alpine setting, that the mountain became his first love, the subject of poetry he wrote, and of conversations he held.

The refugee confided in Coalman concerning his escape. When the road was cleared through to the Strickland place on Gate Creek, Coalman suggested that Vickers return to the Willamette Valley, promising legal defense, if needed. At Summit Meadows they made a preliminary survey of a squatter's claim, as they returned home. Vickers spent the rest of the winter of 1865 working at Coalman's ranch at Sandy and with his brother at Powell Valley.

He filed a squatter's claim, and by June of 1866 he had begun construction of Summit House, a peaked structure 20' x 20' x 32' high. It was sturdy enough for the winter snow, and had a great fireplace laid on one end. Construction was managed while working for the Cascade Road and Bridge Company. When winter approached, and the road crews went home, Vickers stayed on until January, finishing the inside, building and stocking an attached woodshed, sleeping rooms upstairs, and cooking facilities. Furniture was hand made. He then left for Sandy on a pair of home-made snow shoes and spent the winter as he had the past one.

He then stocked Summit House with food and supplies and made his living as host to immigrants. The grass in the meadow was cut to feed hungry stock. Camping facility for travellers was always available, but for friends, he insisted on sharing his home. The immigrants who could not pay found Vickers a man with a big heart. He was always willing to ride out and help someone with a broken wagon or a sick child, no matter what the hour or the weather.

There is no record of the date of Vickers' first ascent of Mount Hood. It could have been as early as 1867. In 1870 he illuminated the mountain on July 4th, up high enough for view by Portland. Everyone in the city was so engrossed in local events that they missed his attempt, a large bonfire.

In 1873 he proposed to the Celebration Committee in Portland that they supply him red fire, and that he would illuminate the very summit of Mount Hood. The committee vacillated. They thought the cost too high, and they all agreed that no man could survive on the summit over night. So on Saturday, August 16, he set out to prove them wrong. At 5:00 a.m. he left Summit Meadows with a 60-pound pack crammed with blankets, food, notebook, thermometer, telescope, and a few folds of magnesium wire. He reached the summit at 1:00 p.m., making frequent notes of the temperature, which never did fall below 28 degrees Fahrenheit, a truly significant discovery concerning mountain environment.

At the appointed hour of 9:30 p.m. he touched off the magnesium. Its brilliant light could be seen on the summit by the people who awaited the event at Summit Meadows. There were about 25 people, some of whom were James Powell, Senator David Powell, Linnemann, Williamson, McCall, and Barnes

Vickers became the first man to guide parties up Mount Hood, and his name was known well in Portland. His fee was $25, a substantial sum for that day. Strangely enough, he was never pursued by any of the officers from Fort Vancouver, in spite of his fame. Perhaps Stephen Coalman deterred them. The years passed peacefully, as Vickers became an institution on the mountain, for climbers and travellers alike.

The winters came and went at Summit Meadow, some more severe than others. In 1880 the snow piled up to a depth of 12 feet, a crushing load for Summit House. Vickers braced the building to prevent collapse of the roof. John Roberts of Gresham saw blazes on the trees made 18 feet off the ground during that winter when the lone resident found it necessary to leave the cabin. On one trip Vickers just about did not make it back and was getting ready to eat his dog, when he was finally able to get inside by going down the fireplace chimney. On milder winters he kept his trail open by dragging a log along behind his horse.

September 13, 1882, Stephen and Elizabeth Coalman came up with their 9-month son Elijah, to pick huckleberries in the meadows. Naturally, Vickers insisted that they take the best accommodations, the downstairs bedroom at Summit House. Elizabeth woke during the night, hearing moans of a sick child in the tent of Barclays, an immigrant family sleeping just outside. She tried to help, but by morning the infant boy was dead.

Near Summit House was the 1847 grave of "Baby Morgan" marked by a large rock. Vickers suggested that they bury the Barclay child nearby at the foot of a tiny pine tree, unknowingly selecting his own grave site. They fashioned a small coffin, and Vickers laid the child to rest with a few simple words.

By the summer of 1883 Elizabeth Coalman had been taken away by an early death. Stephen rode up the Barlow Road with 18-month Lige sitting on the saddle in front of him. Heavy rain fell and they spent four days at Summit House. Rivers were swollen, and when they were ready to return, Vickers rode down to help Stephen cross the Salmon River at Brightwood. The water was so high that even the horses must swim. Vickers tied Lige on his back and swam the strong current, while Coalman rode one swimming horse and led the other, landing well downstream from Vickers. They hurried to John McIntyre's on the west bank. John's wife, Winifred, put warm clothing on Lige and fed them all a warm meal. Lige started his adventurous life at an early age.

MURDER AT MOUNT HOOD

Then, in August 1883, the day of judgement arrived for Perry Vickers. Down at Columbia Slough, Steele, a cook at Hensley's Mill stole a double-barrel shotgun from Adam Fisher, one of the neighbors. Fisher and his son rode over to get help from Pleasant (Pleas) H. Roork, Justice of the Peace at Powell Valley. Roork was able to find that Steele had crossed the Revenue Bridge at Sandy and taken the road over the Devil's Backbone to the Bates farm.

Roork and Fisher headed for Eagle Creek to get the Clackamas County Justice to endorse their Multnomah County warrant. Then they were off in pursuit. At the homestead of Philip Moore they found that Steele and an old man had spent the night and had traded the shotgun for a Sharp's rifle, probably at least a .44 caliber large enough to knock down a buffalo. At John McIntyre's place at Salmon River Fisher was showing so much fatigue, that he was not able to go on. Roork deputized McIntyre, and they rode on toward Government Camp.

Vickers had also been host to Steele and had been suspicious of him. He persuaded Roork and McIntyre to eat a meal before resuming the chase. Vickers was known to be a dead shot, and they included him in the posse. Near Cornelius Gray's trading post at White River, 12 miles south of the Barlow Summit, they saw two campfires on opposite sides of the road. The time was about 11:00 p.m.

The three held a conference. One would announce that he would ride ahead to find pasture for the horses, while the others would choose a place to camp. But Steele was not fooled by this talk. Two of the party returned to the fire on the right side of the road; Vickers turned to the one on the left. As he swung his leg over the horse to dismount, Steele fired on him at close range with the Sharp's rifle, striking him in the stomach.

Vickers drew one of his Colt revolvers and emptied it quickly at the thief, but his own horse was in his way. Steele disappeared into the timber, leaving his hat, coat, and blankets where they lay. At the trading post Cornelius Gray heard the shots and came running with his rifle, two other men close behind. Roork and McIntyre were expected to give gun cover to Vickers during the maneuver. But according to information passed down to Lige Coalman from Stephen Coalman, Vickers had seen them riding away and confronted them with their cowardice as he lay dying. Gray was quoted as a witness to the remarks.

The dying man thought of the laudanum which he kept back at his own place to kill pain for occasional injured travelers, but Gray had nothing to give him to mitigate the pain of the large-caliber bullet wound. One of the men rode out to get medical help and summon Stephen Coalman, Vickers' closest friend. A long, terrible night passed for him, and he told them how to dispose of his belongings. He wanted to be buried back near Summit House at the meadow where the Barclay baby lay. *The Oregonian* reported his death at 7:00 a.m. on Sunday, August 19, 1883.

They loaded his body onto a wagon and took it to Summit Meadow. Coalman made a fast ride to the meadow from his home at Cedar Creek, east of Sandy. Samuel Welch and Steve Mitchell cut a tree and split boards for a coffin. O.C. Yocum, a very religious man, came over from Government Camp and performed a simple service at the graveside. Today a white picket fence surrounds the small site with three graves and the tree, now grown to 22 inches in diameter.

Coalman kept Vickers' overalls with the bullet hole in the waist band. He hung them in the workroom at the ranch, figuring that someday they might be used as evidence in the murder. In about two years, vigilantes hung a horse thief who confessed killing a man in the Cascade Mountains. Coalman eventually burned the overalls, much to the relief of his son, Lige, who felt their presence uncomfortable.

Vickers was believed to have considerable money, possibly buried near the house. Many a shovel of dirt was turned in searching for it, but no find was ever reported. Mrs. J.C. Duke recalled watching him make sour-dough biscuits when she was about 11. Someone made a purchase, and he stopped to wipe his hands on a towel, then make change from a flour sack below the counter. The sack was full of silver with a sprinkling of gold pieces. He cautioned the child not to say anything about the cache.

John Roberts of Gresham once commented about the character of Vickers. He noted that Vickers was a good friend, if he liked a person, but he would draw his Colt pistols quickly in an argument. One traveler at Summit Meadow refused to pay for a meal, and the store-keeper instantly drew and put two bullet holes in his clothing. Payment was made very quickly after that point.

Two bits of information about Perry Vickers are related by George Calverley. The first does not dovetail at all with the more accepted accounts and originated from Mr. Woodcock of Smock Prairie, a land agent at The Dalles and father of Jimmy Woodcock. Woodcock's story is that Vickers was actually killed in an incident of hot temper near Iron Creek on the Bennett Pass Road. Vickers was riding along when a stranger reared up out of the brush and scared his horse. Angry words followed, and Vickers, though fast on drawing his pistols, was not fast enough.

The other rests in information told to Calverley by Jimmy Scoggin, a rancher at Fossil, who often drove cattle and horses through over the Barlow Road. Scoggin remarked that Summit House was not a safe place for a lone man with any money in his pocket, and that there had been mysterious disappearances of bankrolled lone travelers who stopped at Vickers'.

CAMPBELL AT SUMMIT HOUSE

Vickers had never applied for homestead claim at Summit Meadow. His building was occupied by Horace Campbell, a squatter. Campbell was a religious eccentric and was widely known as King David. He erected a tepee-shaped building to the rear of Summit House. It had a central fireplace and a smoke hole in the top. It was used by the last wave of immigrants to come west over the road. King David had a brother Hector who drove stage. One or possibly both men spent winters at Salmon. Horace at one time had plans, or possibly illusions of building a resort hotel. Shortly afterward, such plans were echoed by Will Steel and O.C. Yocum.

Another occupant of Summit House was Frederick Sievers, one of many. In time, the buildings disappeared. First, the travelers burned the furniture, then the log structures were burned piece by piece until only a sagging gate remained for some years. Today all is gone.

O.C. Yocum, First Hotelier

YOCUM ANCESTORS

Heinrich Jochems came to New Amsterdam (New York) from Holland in 1661. His descendents spelled the name variously as Joachim, Jochem, Yokum, Yocom.

Oliver Cooper Yocum's father was Jessee Yocum, born in Kentucky, June 19, 1815. He married Minerva Cooper in Sangamon County, Illinois, December 29, 1836. Jessee was commissioned Captain in the 64th Regiment, fighting in the Black Hawk War. One of the men serving under him was Abraham Lincoln.

By 1847 Jessee and Minerva took their children west by wagon train and settled on a donation land claim on Sections 16 and 17 just north of Bellevue, Oregon, a tiny crossroads community east of Sheridan. His brothers, Thomas J., Henrich, Joseph P., and James, settled on claims right around him. Better education for his children lured Jessee to Lafayette, then the county seat, where he ran a hotel. By 1870, he had moved to Dayton, a city he thought showed great promise because of river travel and talk of railroads to come. By that time, Jessee was a farmer again, the father of 12 children. He bought and sold a great deal of real estate, passing away in 1899.

A man of legendary talents, Oliver Cooper Yocum was a pioneer who left his mark on Mount Hood. Travellers on Highway 26 can stop a few feet west of the Mirror Lake Trail and admire the sight of Camp Creek cascading over the cliffs, Yocum Falls. High on the west side of Mount Hood stands Yocum Ridge, a narrow arete of ice-covered rock lying north of the Reid Glacier. This bold, sweeping buttress has tantalized mountaineers ever since men began to climb the difficult routes. The falls and the ridge memorialize the Yocum name.

O.C. Yocum was the fourth in a family of 12 children. He was born September 16, 1842 in Illinois, being almost five when he came to Oregon in the great wagon migration to the west. He attended school at Bellevue and Lafayette. At 17 or younger he was clerking in the family hotel at Lafayette and apprenticed as a saddle maker. Pioneer children learned many skills; this showed dramatically in his later life.

No accurate record is available of his early life. He clerked in stores, studied the law, and worked on his father's farm. He became very interested in Shakespearean drama and in 1865 toured as a tragedian with a theatrical group visiting some of the primitive, rough-and-ready Idaho mining camps, a very hard life as the acting profession goes.

On June 18, 1867, he wed Ann M. Robertson, 16. Ann was born in Iowa, April 15, 1851, crossing the plains at age two to southern Oregon. In 1863 her parents resettled at Dundee. The newlyweds followed along behind his parents to Dayton, where he did some building, cabinet making, and grain buying. The 1880 census showed him as a warehouseman at Dayton. When the Willamette Valley Railroad began narrow-gauge operations from Dayton to Sheridan in 1877-78, the railroad company located their office in a house which O.C. had built at First and Main Streets.

In 1881 he sold his house to his mother, Minerva, and moved to Portland, becoming a photographic printer, then a photographer. He worked for I.G. Davidson, then formed a partnership with a Mr. Severance, and later was a partner of Henry C. Hayes. Ann continued with her lifelong occupation as a dressmaker, although she worked with him in the photography firm at times. Their residences were at several locations in East Portland.

YOCUM CLIMBED MOUNT HOOD

Shortly after moving to Portland, Yocum felt the lure of Mount Hood and took the road to Government Camp, the route he had followed with his parents as a child in 1847. On July 16, 1883, he climbed the mountain for his first time, going with a faculty group from Willamette University. The first camera to be taken to the top of Mount Hood was on Yocum's back that day, a cumbersome 50 pounds with all the film and accessories included. Yocum fondly kept that old 8" x 10" camera until he died.

He must have felt great attraction for Government Camp. Perhaps he stayed around several weeks, but more probably he made another trip or two back. On the 19th of August he was in the area and was called over to Summit Meadows to give the last rites for Perry Vickers.

With Vickers gone, O.C. Yocum took over the function of guide, taking up people free of charge, whereas Vickers had charged a $25 fee. Both men possessed a love of the alpine scenery and were pleased to explain the nature of glaciers, the moraines, and the hot volcanic crater area, or to point out a whistling marmot standing guard by his burrow. Yocum was always willing to escort the parties of would-be mountaineers who came to Government Camp. Where judgement was concerned in guiding parties, his record was superlative, never losing a customer and passing along the benefit of his experience to those who took his place.

In addition to identifying trees and flowers, suggesting the proper clothing for climbing, he

Oliver C. and Ann Robertson Yocum — Photo Alice Harris

provided the service of feeding his guests at his climbing camp near timberline, a short distance west of present Timberline Lodge. One remarkable day he guided three parties of climbers from the camp to the summit and back. Before dawn he started the first party, leaving them on the summit to return to the camp to meet a second group. He then took them up to the summit and the first group back to camp. He then took a third group up and brought the second and third groups back to camp, arriving there as the last dim light faded in the summer sky.

For a number of years Yocum worked in the photography business in Portland during the wintertime and spent some of the summertime at Government Camp. He finally changed his occupation to surveying in the early Nineties to get away from the smoke and damp climate in Portland. A job with a government party took him to northern Washington on a survey of the Okanogan Valley.

It is indefinite as to when he built his first cabin. Most probably he started with an improved campsite and finally ended with some sort of shelter. On July 2, 1892, he applied for a homestead claim at Government Camp. The adjoining plot was claimed by William G. Steel on March 22, 1892, and the two were required by law to maintain a residence. They followed the letter of the law by erecting a cabin on the line, so that each could bunk on his own property. About 1930, long after the homestead rights had been proved, it was discovered that they had erred, and the cabin had been built entirely on Yocum's property.

Later he put up a large house, which is known to have been standing at the time The Mazamas organized in 1894 and held an encampment on his property. In fact, it was being used as a boarding house, and Mrs. Yocum served many meals to the adventurers who crowded Government Camp that summer.

LIVING AT MOUNT HOOD

The Yocums spent the summer of 1895 at Mount Hood and never did go home to Portland until October 1899. He went down then to Portland and to Oregon City to process final papers on his homestead. In Portland he told newspaper reporters that he hardly recognized the city where he had been so prominent only a few years before. He had a lot to say about the climate at Government Camp, claiming it to be better than Arizona for those who shared his pulmonary weakness. Mrs. George Prosser went up to Government Camp to keep Ann company while O.C. was in town.

In 1886 enthusiasm for bicycles rose to unprecedented height. Yocum became a part of the scene with his bicycle at Government Camp, a very poor place to ride. In August, 1897, Elijah Coalman, then almost 16, joined Yocum for his first climb of Mount Hood. Lige was helping his father on the maintenance of Barlow Road, having been a frequent visitor at their home over the years. The boy, who later became a climbing legend of Mount Hood, proved so apt at mountaineering that Yocum began to use him as an assistant party leader. Lige climbed five more times in that season.

Another assistant was George Prosser, who lived with his wife and two daughters for many years in a small cabin built on land given him by Yocum in appreciation for his service.

Life became a pattern for the couple at Government Camp. Summers were busy with guests at the boarding house and climbers who wanted a guide for Mount Hood. After taking full-time residence there, he began to charge for guide service, $5 a head. Any building or outside repairing needed to be done in summer and fall.

Winters were long and lonely. He became proficient in Spanish and Greek during the mountain years. Interior woodwork, cabinetry and furniture took long, painstaking hours to complete. A little trapping for pine marten, and other fur-bearing animals took him out on long treks away from the settlement. Every month he walked the many miles down to Salmon Post Office to get the mail. Taking a stack of *Oregonians*, he would read the oldest issues first, gradually catching up on current news.

A HOTEL WAS BUILT

In 1899 he erected his hotel. On October 4, he made his first trip to Portland in five years. At the time, the hotel was finished outside and ready for completion inside during the winter months. Lumber was cut right there on the property with a portable, water-powered mill he had secured.

Yocum's deed was effective April 21, 1900, signed by President William McKinley and recorded at Oregon City in Book 71, Page 64. It involved the east half of the northeast quarter, plus lots 1 and 2 of section 23, Township 3 South, Range 8½ east, a total of 161.84 acres.

With a hotel erected, he then turned to platting a townsite, using the name Government Camp. The United States Post Office objected to a 2-word name; he came back with the name Pompeii, and local wags asked if Mount Hood would be changed to Mount Vesuvius. Pompeii was registered at the Clackamas County Court House in Plat Book 7, Page 2 on June 28, 1907, notarized by John T. McIntyre of Salmon Post Office and surveyed by John W. Meldrum. The name of the community soon reverted back to Government Camp.

Mountain House, as the hotel was called, was located on the south side of the Barlow Road, the Second Street of the Pompeii Plat. It was approximately on the same site as the old Darr building on the southeast corner of the highway and Multorpor Road. Second Street later became U.S. Highway 26 before a bypass was put around Government Camp in 1957.

After 1900 a little interest in skiing developed.

A highly publicized trip by Mazamas L.L. Hawkins, Martin Gorman, and T. Brook White brought these adventurers on skis (referred to at the time as Norwegian snow shoes) to the Yocum residence on about Wednesday, February 11, 1903. The three presented a masterpiece of press-agentry to the newspapers upon their return, exciting the interest of others to follow in succeeding years.

Lige Coalman related a tale of visiting Yocum in January 1904, and finding the old guide alone and ill. Coalman went forth to kill a deer for him and went through a series of hardships too intricate to describe in these pages.

During 1904 and 1905, Yocum's niece, Katie Yocum, a daughter of his brother, James, lived at Mountain House and helped with the kitchen and dining room work. In the summer of 1905, Fred Kamph and his sister, Claire, climbed Mount Hood under his guidance, and Katie accompanied them.

The trip from the hotel is about eight miles one way, and Katie had very sore leg muscles, although the two girls stopped at Crater Rock. Ann Yocum got out a bottle of alcohol to rub Katie's legs, but it seemed to have little effect. It turned out to be plain water; O.C. and Fred Kamph had drunk the alcohol and replaced it with water. Fred's acquaintance with Katie developed into a lifetime association; they were married December 12, 1905, at The Dalles.

The Lewis and Clark Exposition of 1905 drew visitors to Portland from all over the world. Some stayed on to climb Mount Hood. Business was more than O.C. could handle, so he let his understudy, Lige Coalman, take full charge of a party for the first time. Business was more plentiful than both of them could handle.

Yocum devised a promotion in about 1905 to develop the community. He proposed to about 20 Portland businessmen that they pay $100 for a 100' x 100' lot. He would then give them title to the land plus give them $100 worth of lumber for building a house. Some of the sales were the following, listed at Oregon City in Book 99, Pages 514 through 520:

R.E.L. Simmons	Lots 1-2 Block B
Charles H. Wentz	Lots 3-4 Block B
George W. Hoyt	Lots 1-2 Block C
George L. Campbell	Lots 3-4 Block C
William F. Hawley	Lots 7-8 Block 4
Ralph Stern	Lots 3-4 Block 6
	Lots 1-2-3-4-5-6-7-8 Block 7
Dr. J.K. Locke	Lots 3-4 Block 3
W.G. Manning	Lots 3-4-5-6 Block A

In 1908 the old guide hung up his equipment and turned the business of guiding over to Lige Coalman. It had been 25 years of experience on Mount Hood, and he had 66 colorful years behind him. The guide service prospered under Coalman; he took 47 parties to the summit in 1909 and about the same number in 1910.

Yocum and Coalman came to an agreement March 19, 1911, wherein the younger man bought the hotel and 160 acres. This spurred Lige to start work on a new, larger hotel designed for 50 guests. All during 1911 and 1912 he worked on the building in between guiding jobs. George Flinn and George Maronay helped with the construction of the high, steep-roofed building designed to withstand winter snowloads. Lumber was cut on the site with a portable mill, just as it had been on the first building.

By this time Yocums had built and occupied another house, but it is a pretty safe bet that Ann Yocum was helping in the new hotel when business demanded it. The progress of the hotel is part of the story of Lige Coalman from that point on. A significant letter from Ann Yocum to her grand nephew at Sheridan was written in February 1911, indicating a business proposition that would make a vast change in their lives.

Surely enough, a short time later O.C. Yocum took a position with North Pacific Dental College in Portland. He studied pharmacy and worked in the pharmaceutic department there until he retired in 1916 at the age of 77. Leaving Portland, they moved near Dundee.

In 1920 it became evident to the world that the transaction with Coalman had not culminated well. Coalman had sold the hotel and 57.5 acres to Dell Fox and Louis F. Pridemore. On September 6, 1912 Yocum deeded the 57.5 acres to Coalman with notation of an outstanding mortgage by A.E. Latourette. Coalman had not enjoyed the greatest of prosperity in the hotel, and evidently Pridemore and Fox were not very successful either.

In September of 1920, Yocum as plaintiff, sued Elijah Coalman, Louis and Grace Pridemore, John Maronay, F.A. Updike, and A.E. Latourette, trustee, securing a decree of foreclosure on the hotel and 57.5 acres. But too much debt was evident, and the foreclosure did not help Yocum. W.J. Wilson, Clackamas County Sheriff seized the property for non-payment of taxes and sold it at the court house door on November 8, 1920.

This placed the property in the hands of A.E. Latourette, including the balance of the 160 acres Lige had bought from Yocum originally. Latourette was forced to bid the property, paying $7,748.65 at auction, to protect the outstanding debts he had due.

This meant that most of the Yocum property had been dissipated, although he did retain ownership of a few good lots. Fred Kamph's son, Frank, recalls that in 1923 Yocum asked him to run a fence around the property that lay across the street from the hotel. He foresaw a boom in winter sports that would make the property valuable. He would have been astonished, if he had known the ultimate value of the land. Frank was a boy of only 16, and couldn't be motivated to put forth the effort.

In 1925 Everett Sickler bought 200 feet of frontage for Battle Axe Inn, some of the last of the Yocum property. The last days of O.C. and

Ann Yocum were spent apart, she staying with relatives at Dayton. He was cared for by his niece, Mrs. Newton (Minerva) Branson at Bellevue on the old home place his father had homesteaded in 1847. Their 60th anniversary of marriage was observed with a large gathering on June 18, 1927. The following March 16th he died.

This man who contributed so much to the formation of Government Camp, to The Mazamas, and to the sport of mountaineering, was one of the most versatile individuals to immigrate to Oregon. In *Believe It Or Not*, Robert Ripley noted that Yocum had been a photographer, guide, actor, store clerk, lawyer, chemist, surveyor, postmaster, pharmacist, saddler, farmer, grain buyer, hotel keeper, and lumberman. Ripley forgot to mention carpenter, cabinet maker, trapper, warehouseman, and real estate subdivider.

Ann Robertson Yocum died on July 6, 1931.

MOUNTAIN VIEW HOUSE

MRS. A. M. YOCUM, Manager

Experienced Guide Furnished

Location of New City of Pompeii

E Coalman

OLD GOVERNMENT CAMP

Rowe Post Office

Mt. Hood, Oregon, F 18 1911

My Dear Nephiew

Your Card is received we are truly glad
that we have a Nephiew O C Yocum, and
that he thinks enough
to him. I your Aunt
to you to day and your
your Uncle received a
Proposition yesterday
so I knew he would
to day. perhaps if the
may be able to pay yo
a visit some time the
we have both been
last three weeks. we ha
am afflicted with Neura
suffering tortures with m
quite a lot of Company
winter. it is quite the
for the Skii riding. the
here now. and they wi
when they go: the sno

Mt. Hood, Oregon, February 18, 1911

My Dear Nephew,

Your card is received. We are truly glad that we have a nephew, O.C. Yocum, and that he thinks enough of his uncle to write to him. I, your aunt, will write a few lines to you today, and your uncle will write later. Your uncle received a letter with a business proposition yesterday, which he is considering, so I knew he would not take time to write today. Perhaps if the business goes through, we may be able to pay you and other friends a visit sometime the following summer. We have both been quite sick for the last three weeks. We had the grippe, and I am afflicted with Neuralgia for the past week suffering tortures with my head. We have had quite a lot of company at several times this winter. It is quite the fad to come up here for the ski riding. There are two young men here now, and they will take our mail out when they go. The snow is six feet deep now. We have a few traps out, but the marten are very scarce. We have only one so far this winter. Beaver are plenty, but we are not allowed to catch them. They are protected by law. Write and tell us how old you are, and where you go to school. I think it is a shame for relatives to know so little of their familys. Also tell me how your grandmother has been this winter and give her my love when you see her. Also remember me to any the rest of the relatives. Now you must try and come and make us a visit. When the road is open for travel next summer, bring your father and the rest of the family. I don't think your uncle has seen your father since he was a little boy. Now I must close with love to you all.

Sincerely your aunt,
A M Yocum

BICYCLE BOOM OF THE 90'S

In Portland numerous bicycle clubs sprung up along with grand plans for riding routes in all directions. It became quite common to ride to Mt. Hood, although much of the trip was anything but riding. Mud holes and hills, loose sand, and large rocks meant a lot of walking and pushing.

George Prosser and his wife made several trips to Portland, sometimes making the round trip in one day. Yocum, of course, was the owner of a "wheel", which he used around Government Camp or down the road to Salmon. In 1911 when he moved back to Portland, he gladdened the heart of his grand nephew and namesake, O.C. Yocum of Gopher Valley near Sheridan, in announcing that he was sending him his bicycle. The nine-year old boy was quite let down when the machine was uncrated and he found the gear ratio was very low, appropriate for the hills around Government Camp.

L.L. Hawkins, Mazama friend of Yocum, came to the mountain in 1896 with companions from a wheeling club. He got Yocum to agree to build a bicycle path to Toll Gate east of Rhododendron, where John Maronay was to take over and extend it to Welches. Hawkins reported that 250 people were encamped at Welches at the time, showing the need for a path. Welch agreed to McIntyre's, who would continue to the Ware ranch. Ware would continue to Cherryville. The Larnon boys would then build a section to Firwood, and road supervisor T.A. Meinig would complete the plan to Sandy.

George Prosser in Late Thirties at Yocum-Steel cabin — Photo Maryanne Hill

Occasional mention of the plan was made in the newspapers. Yocum made experiments with sand and concrete surfaces. The path was to be two feet wide through a six-foot clearing. Despite considerable agitation the plan died with a last gasp of promotion indicated in a news story of 1899.

Elijah Coalman, a Legendary Mountaineer

Perhaps the greatest of the mountain men in the story of Mount Hood was Elijah (Lige) Coalman, who made 586 recorded ascents, built and manned the summit cabin, guided so many climbing parties, and took charge in an unbelievable succession of searches and rescues.

His family history goes back to great grandfather Elijah, born in 1745 in England. He came to America in 1760 and served in George Washington's continental army, later settling in Pennsylvania.

Grandfather Elijah was also a Pennsylvania farmer, served in the United States Army in the war of 1812. He was wounded in the battle of New Orleans and returned to life on the farm. He moved westward to Ohio, married, and reared five daughters and three sons. The eldest was Stephen Davis Coalman, born in Ohio, May 9, 1834, a man who was an important figure in the shaping of the Barlow Road. Stephen was the father of Lige Coalman.

His older sister married LeRoy Curry (Curry County, Oregon) and went with her new husband by sailing ship around the dangerous Cape Horn passage in 1842 to San Francisco. They made their way to Gold Beach, Oregon, where they established a business of canning and drying salmon. A second sister and husband Henry Edson followed them to Gold Beach via a hazardous crossing of the Isthmus of Panama in 1845. In 1848 Edward Boles married a third sister and took the Oregon Trail by wagon to settle in Oregon City.

Stephen worked as a tailors helper for an uncle, Dick Cheedle, through 1846-47, after working on the family farm. From 1848-50 he drove towing teams, pulling barges on the Erie Canal. His fourth sister married Leslie Dillon, who in 1851 joined the great migration west, and Stephen joined them. They wintered in St. Louis, and started in a wagon train in April 1852 for California and the lure of gold. Stephen, a strapping young man of 18, was one of the forward scouts, the men who looked for water, wood, and grass and signs of Indians who might steal horses or even attack the wagon train.

At the Rockies they met disgruntled immigrants returning east with gloomy reports about the far west, but they intended to go on. At Fort Hall, Idaho, great indecision developed, some families driving their wagons to the gold country in California, and others following the trail to Oregon. Stephen went to Oregon City. The Dillons continued to California, tried their luck at gold at Yreka, then finally drove north to join the elder sisters at Gold Beach.

Arriving at The Dalles in early November, Stephen and a scouting partner elected to take a raft trip down the Columbia. They bought lumber and built a raft, embarked for Portland on short rations with the help of two Indian guides who offered to help portage at the rapids in exchange for their precious rifles and ammunition, that they had carried across the Oregon Trail. Possessions were tied on in waterproof sacks, and twice the raft tipped over. They landed at the mouth of the Sandy River, then backpacked their meager possessions to Foster's and on to Oregon City. Visiting his sister, Mrs. Edward Boles, he worked at an Oregon City sawmill to save money for a trip to the California gold fields. When spring warmed in 1853 he set out on foot alone for the gold camps at Yreka. Working as a day laborer in the mines showed no more promise than it had to Leslie Dillon, so he took the trails north to join his three sisters at Gold Beach. Following the Illinois and Rogue Rivers, he saw many camps where placer miners were doing well, whetting his desire to prospect for gold.

Work at the salmon cannery gave him enough money for horse and saddle. News that Mrs. Boles was ill in Oregon City, caused him to go there, and this was probably the time when he bought property on Sandy Ridge.

Gold fever took him south to Gold Beach once more. In the spring of 1854 he located a gold claim on the Illinois River and spent three years there. In 1858, whites had stopped salmon migration in the Rogue by overuse of nets, and thoughtless atrocities were perpetrated on Indians near Jacksonville, causing a state of alarm and the calling up of volunteers.

Stephen left his cabin to answer the call and enlist. On returning that evening to get his clothes and blankets, he found the cabin reduced to coals. A group of Indians had gathered, eating biscuits made from his pan of dough. In the confrontation he shot an Indian and escaped on his horse. This was possibly the first Indian killed in this sporadic war, which seethed in southern Oregon for a long while. Eventually troops from El Presidio in San Francisco were called to assume the battle.

The day after his cabin was burned, Coalman induced an armed group to return and help him dig up the gold he had buried there, some two or three thousand dollars. That, with his pack horse, still grazing nearby, was a grubstake to return to Sandy and build a log house on 80 acres on Sandy Ridge. In 1859 he sold and took a 160 acre plot at Cedar Creek, three miles east of Sandy on the south bank of Sandy River.

ELIJAH COALMAN BORN

A homestead neighbor there, named Daniel Harnett, came from Ireland to Toronto, thence to Sandy. Following him, his sister, Elizabeth, finally traced him to the ranch at Sandy, where she kept house for Harnett four years. Stephen Coalman married her in January 1880. Their only child, was born on November 26, 1881.

Elizabeth Coalman's early death in May 1883 left Stephen with 18-month old Lige to bring up, a great problem to the man who spent summer and fall superintending the Barlow Road. He hired Steve and Ellen Mitchell to run his farm and keep Lige. Eventually Mitchells had nine children, so the boy became part of the large family, but his early years were lonely.

At age six he was pronounced consumptive by a homeopathic pill doctor from Cherryville. Parents feared tuberculosis and kept their children away from Lige, leaving the lonely child only the company of Indian children and his horse and dogs. Later Stephen took him to a Portland doctor, who correctly diagnosed the boy's cough as a bronchial problem and suggested that he be taken out of school. As a result, three or four years of schooling was all that he ever got. Stephen Coalman took over the job of teaching him reading, writing, and arithmetic. The teaching was evidently well done, because as Lige grew older he was a voracious reader and took great interest in science, philosophy, and religion. At thirteen he was attending Sunday evening meetings of Christian Endeavor Society at Pleasant home, joining 15 or 20 teenagers each week in Sandy to walk the six miles each way to the meeting.

Lige also had the standard training of the pioneer farm boy of the time. On the farm at Cedar Creek Stephen Coalman kept horses, cattle, hogs, poultry, sheep. In the fields he raised corn, wheat, berries, pears, apples, peaches, berries, and a large garden. Salmon were plentiful in the Sandy River, and deer, elk, bear, and racoons supplemented their diet. Wheat, after primitive threshing, was taken down the road to a miller who ran it through two large mill stones, bringing forth flour, middlings, shorts, and bran.

Shopping was done occasionally for tools, guns and ammunition, clothing and footwear, rice, coffee and tea, salt, baking powder, and spices. Beeswax or the tallow from butchering livestock, were the material for candles. The great fireplace lighted the room for the young children as they studied before early bedtime. Stephen ran a water power sawmill on Cedar Creek, and was building the two-story, six-room house when Elizabeth died.

In such an environment, a man grew up with the ability to build a house, thread a pipe, sew leather, plant fields, repair machinery, doctor a man or an animal. Lige Coalman was no exception. Later jobs, even as a boy, led him through a vast string of experiences, all taken naturally in stride.

He was molded in the morality of the day. At age of six he rode into Sandy with Stephen in the wagon. On the steps of the saloon-hardware a half dozen men stood alert, one a sheriff deputy with double-barrel shotgun. A man approached, grabbed for the barrel, and the deputy shot him. The stranger, a horsethief running west from The Dalles, tried to rise, then sagged to the ground. Stephen Coalman helped lift him to the porch, where he soon died and was covered with a piece of canvas. A coroner's jury, for which Coalman was a witness, exonerated the deputy the next day. For Lige this was a grim reminder of the code of frontier justice.

Pioneer honesty was vastly different from present-day theft and vandalism, and he learned an early lesson from the neighboring Nelson family. When Lige was twelve, he made a walk to the Bull Run River to fish with the Nelson boys, Ned and Bee. Fishing was good, and they started home early across the Tavelli homestead. This Italian family had been burned out by a forest fire in 1889, and they had abandoned their acreage for work in Portland. Daffodils, planted years before, were in full May bloom at the desolate site of the burned home. The boys agreed it would be nice to dig some and take them to Mrs. Nelson.

On arriving home with them, they were confronted by Mr. Nelson, who termed their acquisition as stealing. Dinner was ready on the table, but Nelson made the three boys walk six miles back with the flowers. At midnight they returned and devoured the meal that Mrs. Nelson had set aside for them. This was a vividly learned lesson for Lige.

He was a dead shot with the sling shot, and one day he thoughtlessly killed a half dozen chipmunks that were storing hazel nuts for the winter. A little later he noticed another chipmunk chipping and fussing over something in the trail. It was one of the dead young ones; this was the mother in distress over the killing. Lige felt tears in his own eyes and never again killed an animal needlessly.

COALMAN'S FIRST CLIMB

Trips to Mount Hood in the summer were frequent as Lige grew older. In 1896 Oliver C. Yocum, Mountain Guide, who ran the Government Camp Hotel and guided parties of alpinists, took 16-year old Lige on a climb of Mt. Hood. It was his introduction to the mountain, where his name was to become a legend among the great climbers.

This first ascent for Lige was an unnerving one. The slopes above Crater Rock were glare ice that day, and Yocum had to chop steps. On the descent, always more dangerous than the ascent, the party approached the big crevasse when Lige slipped. This resulted in an involuntary glissade down the steep ice, and the boy had to jump the crevasse. Of course, he immediately resolved to never climb again, as have so many thousands of mountaineers experiencing their first scare.

Yocum encouraged him, and a few days later he was back on the mountain assisting in taking up another party. Lige made five climbs that year. Stephen Coalman had been bringing the boy up over the Barlow Road ever since he was a baby; they knew Yocum well. At the time of that first climb, Stephen had Lige working on the road; the climbs were sandwiched in between other duties. During the summers of 1887 and 1888, Lige assisted Yocum quite regularly.

In May of 1899, he was 17 and wanted to try life on his own. Walking to Portland, he got a job with the railroad, laying track out of Wallula, Washington toward Idaho. Food and water and beds were bad. He aspired to the life of railway engineer and maneuvered a job on the train crew. Soon after a locomotive tipped over, scalding the engineer and fireman. Lige watched their pitiful remains being removed in wash tubs, and lost all enthusiasm for railroading.

He had $110 coming in wages earned. While the company was preparing payment, Lige decided to try the life of the hobo, enroute to Tacoma. Riding the brake beams blasted his face with gravel, and he dropped off at Kiona. Then, secreting himself between the baggage car and passenger coach, he was caught by the conductor and flung from the moving train. Recoiling from the effects of torn shirt and trousers, bleeding face, and skinless elbows, he retreated to a hobo jungle. A few days later he braved the possibility of 30 days imprisonment at hard labor and hid in a piece of four-foot pipe that was moving by flatcar to Seattle's Cedar River water project. He nearly froze, then almost suffocated when the train entered the Tunnel at Easton, west of Ellensburg. He bluffed a brakeman with an inoperative revolver found in a trash pile, then bribed him with a dollar to continue riding. Later he desperately climbed into a car of flour with a broken seal, a potential penitentiary offense if he were caught. A brakeman resealed the car, and Lige had to pry his way out, landing in Seattle without detection.

A longshore job in Seattle gave him money to ride to Tacoma and collect his paycheck. He made the trial run of the S.S. City of Seattle to Juneau, Alaska as a boilermaker's helper, worked for Simpson Logging Company at Kamiliki near Shelton, drove team and did concrete work at the Cedar River Dam project, worked on gun emplacement at Point Wilson near Port Townsend. June of 1900 he came back to the homestead, broke, but full of experience for an 18-year old man.

In July he teamed up with George Maronay to purchase the Portland-Sandy Stage Line from Firmes Walklie, the operator of the John Revenue Hotel. The covered stages had three seats and were drawn by a pair of horses. Each weekday a stage left Portland, picking up passengers at leading hotels and the mail at the post office. Crossing the Morrison Bridge, it detoured to Division Street, touched at Montavilla, Rockwood, and Gresham by lunch time. By night it had arrived at Sandy via Powell Valley, Orient, Pleasant Home, Cottrell, and Kelso, a very tedious trip that now consumes no more than three quarters of an hour.

The United States Government subsidized a part of the cost of the line to secure mail service. Coalman had to make up the rest in carrying passengers and freight. The freight might be almost anything that someone needed in a hurry. Living was meager and became much more so when a rail line extended interurban service to Boring by autumn of 1901. Coalman and Maronay sold the line, keeping one wagon and four horses.

The two went in on another venture on Maronay's homestead at Juniper Flat near Wapinitia. It was midwinter and no hope of crossing Barlow Road, so they loaded their equipment on the sternwheeler Bailey Gatzert, disembarking at The Dalles the 4th of January 1902. At their hotel they ran into Ed Bruns, a friend from Sandy, and the three decided to make the trip to Wapinitia together. On leaving town on the next cold, windy morning, they stopped at a hardware store. The owner was just opening and was building a fire in the stove. Minutes later the stove exploded, and the three men fought fire furiously alongside the owner. It took quite a while for the local volunteer fire department to douse the fire. It is very probable that the three travelers saved the whole town of The Dalles from going up in flames in the strong wind.

Out south of Dufur they ran into an area of large mud puddles, frozen hard in the winter wind. It took one man to drive the horses, but the other two amused themselves by skating on the ice with their shoes. Coming to a very long stretch of ice, Bruns made a monumental run, hit the ice at high speed, and fell. His head struck the ice with a sickening, loud thud. He did not return to full consciousness, so they wrapped him in blankets and hurried him to a doctor in Dufur.

The doctor diagnosed it as concussion and the trio spent the day at Dufur with Bruns lying in a hotel room. In the evening the doctor gave him a sedative, and by the next morning Coalman and Maronay found their partner stiff-necked and woozy, but ready to go again.

On January 11, they dropped Bruns off at his homestead in the care of a neighbor and proceeded to Maronay's place. After the first night they woke to find the weight of snow on the blankets, fine powder that had sifted in profusely as they slept. It took some time to sweep the snow out of the cabin before they could build a fire, and the rest of the day was spent in chinking cracks.

By spring they had the 160 acres fenced with poles cut from oak trees and driven with a wooden maul. Lige searched the country for a suitable piece of ground to homestead, but never did find one. He did some plowing for a neighbor. On June 15 they loaded their possessions in the wagon and headed west to open the Barlow Road, cutting away fallen trees and repairing obstacles as well as possible. Taking the Oak Grove Branch road, they passed by Frog Lake. After several days they had to return to Wamic for food and supplies, then pushed on to Government Camp and the toll gate near Rhododendron. George's parents, John Maronay and his wife, were keepers at the toll gate and had already left the winter home at Sandy to assume the summer job.

The summer of 1902 Lige worked for Robert Jonsrud at the Sandy Blacksmith Shop. It is an educated guess that he assisted O.C. Yocum to some extent that summer in guiding on Mount Hood. No record is made of his guiding activity in 1903, but he undoubtedly did some.

Charlie Freeier ran a sawmill about 15 miles east of Summit House. On a visit there, Lige became involved in a wild game of cops-and-robbers in October of 1903. Two counterfeiters were at the moment engaged in a poker game with a father and son, stock herders at a meadow close by. At Freeier's suggestion he and Lige entered the game to get evidence. The counterfeiters were exchanging their own money for real coins as the game progressed.

After a time Lige rode to reach the sheriff deputy at Wapinitia. The story is a muddled one full of missed connections, inoperative telephone line, but the result was two-and-a-half days without sleep and 160 miles in the saddle for Lige. Between Tygh Valley and Wapinitia he suffered the chilling shock of the icy water, as his horse plunged into a deep hole in fording a stream, but he just kept riding and trying to dry out from the little heat he got from the horse. He rode the 20 miles from Wapinitia to Freeier's between 10:00 p.m. and 4:00 a.m. There he got hot food and plunged into bed.

The real surprise in the affair came with his return to Summit House which was run by "King David" Campbell, a religious eccentric. Campbell had been hit on the head by the counterfeiters, who robbed him. This left him without funds to live the winter at Summit House, and he had to return to Portland.

Lige Coalman was learning the art of guiding all the while on his climbs with O.C. Yocum. In 1903 and 1904 he spent a good part of his summers in guiding on Mount Hood. The clients would walk up to timberline the night before and Yocum provided them with tents and blankets and coffee in the morning. They always started at the first light of day, hoping to get the best climbing conditions in the crater and then to avoid the soft afternoon snow as they descended the lower slopes of the mountain.

In January 1904, Lige hiked up to the Yocum place, using the skis the old man kept cached at Laurel Hill. Ann Yocum normally spent the winters there, but that time she was down in the Willamette Valley, and O.C. was ill with influenza. Yocum asked Lige to kill him a deer, and the ensuing day and a half of stalking game and being stalked by wolves in the Salmon River is hard to imagine in these times of tamed wilderness.

In 1905 Mount Hood was visited by many people who were lured to Oregon by the Lewis and Clark Exposition. The business was too much for both Coalman and Yocum, and they were busy that summer at $5 per person on guided climbs. From that time on there was no doubt about Coalman being a full-fledged guide. In 1908 Yocum turned the whole business over to the younger man.

One patron asked for a trip around the glaciers at the 9,000 level, a round-the-mountain circuit that had been touted by Will Langille many years before. Yocum showed Lige the problems in crossing Reid and Sandy Glaciers in a private field trip one day, pointing out the routes he had used. Lige did not take the guiding job, but circling the mountain did pique his interest.

He and a friend decided to try the trip. From Illumination Rock they descended to the Reid Glacier, a heavily-crevassed body of ice that at times presents problems in crossing. Out in the center stood a 50-foot island of rock. Above lay the seracs of the hanging glacier, poised in fanciful shapes peculiar to ice falls. It was picture-taking time, and Lige set up a tripod. Just at that moment a serac broke loose, bombarding them with massive blocks of ice. Dodging behind the protective rock, they were able to save their lives as the great torrent of roaring ice flew past them.

Ice and rock were falling down between them and Yocum Ridge, blocking their progress to the north, so they retreated to Illumination Rock and crossed Reid Glacier at the 7,000-foot level. That night they camped in the canyon north of Yocum Ridge and listened to the roar of avalanches brought down by the hot September weather.

The next day they wound through the crevasses of the glaciers on the north side, having special difficulty in finding a way through the maze of blocks and seracs on the Eliot Glacier. That night was spent at Cloud Cap Inn. In the morning a cloudy sky covered their ascent to Cooper Spur and over a difficult crossing of Newton Clark Glacier. Overhead the signs of a thunder storm began to appear.

At 3:00 p.m. they started across White River Glacier on the way to the completion of their tour at Triangle Moraine. Not finding suitable snow bridges, they climbed down 40 feet into a crevasse to cross on the rocky bottom. Hail and rain were falling and a lightning flash illuminated the whole crevasse for an instant.

Suddenly the glacier heaved and the noise around them was terrifying. The daylight above them disappeared as the crevasse closed above. The sulphur odor of the fumaroles entered their nostrils. When the noise subsided they kept on walking along the bottom and emerged at the end safely.

They found that lightning had struck Steel Cliff, knocking off tons of rock onto the glacier. The shock had closed the crevasse just in time to save their lives from the devastating rockfall.

The great vitality of Coalman was demonstrated by one day he spent in 1910. He and a climbing client ate breakfast at the hotel in Government Camp. They then climbed to the summit of Mount Hood and down to Cloud Cap Inn, where the client wanted to go. After lunch at Cloud Cap, Lige climbed back over the summit and arrived for dinner at Government Camp at 5:00 p.m.

LIGE BECAME HOTELIER

In 1910 Lige bought Mountain House and most of the Yocum acreage from O.C. and began a new hotel for 50 guests just east of the old building. It was on January 1 of that year that he took a wife, Elvina Nystrom, 23, who was born in Sweden and worked as a waitress for the Yocums. Four children resulted from that marriage, Elrod born in 1910, Elvin born in 1912, Roy born in 1914, and Louise born in 1916.

Work on the hotel progressed well in 1910 and 1911. Wintertime was a good chance to catch up on the interior finishing work. George Flinn and Lige's old friend, George Maronay, were part of the heavy construction crew in the summer. By 1912 they began to use part of the hotel, ready or not.

By 1914 Coalman had decided that running a hotel was not for him and sold to Dell Fox and Louis F. Pridemore. In addition to guiding mountain parties, he turned his attention to the Forest Service, becoming interested and involved in the new Osborne firefinder. Coalman proposed to the government that he man a lookout station atop the mountain. The full story is told in *A House on the Summit.*

In 1916 Elijah Coalman participated in an advertising stunt by the makers of the Paige Fairfield automobile in taking a 6-46 model (6 cylinder, 46 horsepower) to the 8500 foot level on the south side. The car was in charge of W.S. Barnes, sales manager of Paige Motor Sales Company, and driven by James Foley.

The usual mud holes and snowdrifts were surmounted by pushing and pulling, and on June 25 they got the car above timberline on its own power. In addition to Lige's help on the job, they then added George Maronay and Warren L. Wilkens to the party. Sections of track were laid on the snow, allowing the driver to advance a few feet, then track was reset for another advance.

By July 1, they had left the car on a 44% grade. On July 3, a storm hit the mountain and encased the automobile in ice. The fiasco finally ended with the driver unable to advance on a 50-degree angle at 8500 feet in elevation. Needless to say, the trip down was also laborious, but somewhat faster. *The Oregonian* of July 9, carried a large advertisement showing the triumphant Paige at the peak of its climb.

In the summer of 1916 the Forest Service employed him to build a cabin at Camp Blossom near Timberline. Known as Timberline Cabin, the structure enjoyed great use as a base for climbing parties. Later in the 1930's it was used in winter as well by skiing groups, who needed shelter at the timberline level.

A GLACIAL LINEMAN

In mid-June 1916 the Forest Service directed Coalman to run a wire from the summit down to the residence of Ranger Barney Cooper, son of David Cooper, Sr., which was near Cloud Cap Inn, giving much better communication with the north side. In September Lige went down to roll up the wire for winter storage. The wire was coupled every 250 feet, and one coupling occurred about 100 feet below Crescent Crevasse.

He tied a large rock to the lower end, so that when he uncoupled the top end, the whole 250 feet would not be drug into the crevasse. When he disconnected the coupling above, the end of the wire slipped away from him and slid toward the crevasse, stopping after snarling in loose rocks. Twenty-five feet of the upper end was left exposed. Walking downward to it, he chopped two good footholds with his ice axe and began to coil the wire around his hand and left elbow.

Suddenly he glanced below and realized that the rock he had tied to the bottom of the wire had loosened from the heat of the sun and was moving. There was a lot of slack to be taken up as the wire pulled easily out of Crescent Crevasse. Anticipating a sizeable jolt when the wire became taut, he desperately tried to throw the wire off his arm, but it was wrapped too tightly around elbow and hand. He braced for the jerk, but it pulled him off balance, spreadeagled and sliding helplessly toward the crevasse. He made a one-handed attempt with his ice axe in his right hand.

The arrest held at the last moment, just short of the lip. But here was a dilema. The weight of the rock and the wire was pulling downward, but the coil of wire around his arm lay under him, giving him the friction needed to merely remain in place. Cautiously he released one strand of wire; the resulting jerk started his slide once more. When he stopped, his toes were hanging out in air over the lip of the crevasse, cutting his friction even more.

Lying there with his chin on the ice, his right hand on the axe, he moved his left hand carefully, finally encountering a small rock well-imbeded in the ice. Staking everything on that small rock, he removed the protecting axe from the snow with his right hand and struck a new blow with the pick. Taking a new prone stance which allowed him to move his right hand, he began to remove the loops one-by-one, taking great care to avoid any more jerk in the line. Once free of the wire, he then advanced in painful, fearful slowness, inching from one pebble to the next, striking new holds with the pick of his axe. With his feet once more back up on the ice, he could then stand erect. The Crescent Crevasse was cheated of its victim that day. Lige went below and rolled up the wire that had pulled him treacherously down.

August, 1916 Lige Coalman followed the telephone line down from the summit cabin to find a break in the wire at Still Creek, where Indian ponies had become entangled. The same day he had been down at Cloud Cap on the north side for some line work, and he was very tired that night. Instead of returning to the summit as usual, he bedded down at Camp Blossom.

A climbing party was being organized there for the next day, and Coalman offered to guide them up as he returned to his cabin. A newspaper reporter named Osborne joined the party, intending to take pictures and bring back a story about mountain climbing. During the night he became nauseated and decided to return to Government Camp. Lige took the party up and spent the rest of his day on firefinder duty.

That night the staff at Government Camp Hotel noticed Osborne's car still there. The search was on! The hotel called Osborne's paper, and they sent up three carloads of people to search. The Forest Service diverted men onto the search, which went on all the following day and night. Lige scanned the slopes with field glasses, although fog had rolled in shortly after the search began. Osborne had been out two full nights. By noon on the next day the weather was breaking, and Lige saw a man through the glasses, staggering and falling near Mississippi Head.

He phoned for permission to leave the summit and shot down the gulley between Crater Rock and Castle Crags, arriving at Osborne's side in minutes. It was a descent of great skill and great abandon, requiring not only muscles of steel, but finely-honed coordination and judgement. In the slopes too shallow to glissade he was known for his peculiar kangaroo lope. Lige was able to signal searchers below with a mirror in the sunlight.

The tattered reporter was near collapse. He was confused in thinking that he must cross to the other side of the mountain to safety. It wasn't long until he was riding down from timberline on a Forest Service horse.

The Hood River News reported that John W. Osborne was a member of the staff of the *Portland Spectator*, and that Coalman had reached his side in just 23 minutes.

START OF LIGE'S DOWNFALL

During the summer of 1916 Coalman had an accident that damaged his heart. In ascending the summit above Crater Rock, he was carrying about 90 pounds of kerosene on his back, when he broke through a small crevasse and fell downward about eight feet. His chest struck the ice, and being driven by the weight on his back, it suffered a very sharp blow.

There was no immediate reaction, and after he overcame the first shock, he climbed back out onto the slope and took the kerosene to the summit. As he stooped over to light the oil stove, everything went black and terrible pains shot through his chest. For two hours he described the pain as "the torture of hell without being able to die." However, he finished the season and went on as normal with his other work.

In October of 1916 the Forest Service employed Coalman on the survey for the Skyline Road that runs south off the Wapinitia Highway toward Ollalie Lake. The survey party was in charge of K.P. Cecil, forestry engineer. The party worked in wonderful autumn weather for a time, but snow storms later turned the operation into a rout when food ran low and accident victims had to be evacuated on stretchers.

The weekend of July 14-15 of 1917, Coalman was given considerable space in the newspapers. He and L.F. Pridemore of the hotel had prearranged with the *Oregon Journal* that a phone call from him on the summit to Portland would signal the *Journal* to turn off their tower lights. Then, in 15 minutes, he and T. Raymond Conway would ignite red fire for an illumination. The whole program was tied in with a convention of the National Education Association in Portland and a climb from the north side on the following day by Mazamas and NEA delegates.

During the day a party of climbers, resting at Crater Rock on their way to the top, saw Coalman emerge from the cabin, run across the summit to the top of the Chute, give a tremendous leap into the air and land on the steep snow. He then did a controlled glissade for 600 feet, stopping at the top of the Big Crevasse. He then clung to the fixed line that hung down the slope, swung across the crevasse, and was once more on his way with great kangaroo leaps to the Hogsback, where he leaped into another rapid glissade.

In just six minutes he had reached the group, a trip that usually took about an hour for most climbing parties, greeted them, and took off for timberline, running, jumping, and glissading. He disappeared into the trees three miles below, then shortly appeared, walking quickly up the mountain. It was some rolls of telephone wire he had gone after, no doubt needed to repair the system for that evening's activity. At Triangle Moraine he stopped and began to string out the wire, stopping a time or two to splice in a new roll. Laying a new section a mile long in a short time, he then hurried on up to the summit to greet the climbing party, a round trip of five hours and 20 minutes.

The climbing party was exhausted from the climb, and Coalman set about preparing them some food. The party consisted of guide Hans Fuhrer, five men, and Estes Snedecor, who was making his second ascent of the mountain. Snedecor was remarkable for having his right leg amputated at the hip and being athletic enough to climb on crutches. On reaching the Chute he had laid the crutches aside and pulled himself bodily up on the fixed rope, hopping here and there as the situation dictated.

The illumination was staged as scheduled, and the group spent the night at the summit cabin. The Mazama party got away to a late start the following morning for the climb from their camp on the north side. Leader R.W. Ayer held the group back as a big thunderstorm lashed the mountain, then passed over at about 4:45 a.m. He and George T. Brown brought 85 climbers up in the party, only 27 of whom had ever climbed a peak before.

Coalman was very busy making tea for all of the guests, using water carried from timberline on the south side. If there was any indication of heart problems at that time, he surely was not telling anyone. However, he did later indicate in his resignation letter to Thomas Sherrard, that he did experience trouble at times, and that in 1918 he had difficulty on the last 2000 feet of the mountain.

It was two weeks later on the weekend of July 28-29, 1917, that Hans Fuhrer was guiding a party down the summit slopes. An accident occurred (covered in Tragedies and Searches) that again sent Coalman screaming down the slopes to administer first aid at the bottom of the Hogsback.

On duty again in 1918, he experienced an **accident that meant the end of his career** on Saturday, July 27. Having a dead telephone line to Cloud Cap, he called the ranger station at Summit Meadow for permission to leave the lookout, and headed off down Cooper Spur Route. He traced the line down to a point in the trees above Cloud Cap Inn, where a bad connection had been made. He then descended to the inn and checked with his test set to find the line in working order.

By that time it was 6:30 p.m., too late to go back to the lookout, so he walked down to Homer Rogers' Mount Hood Lodge. Sunday morning the Rogers family breakfasted late, and he did not get away until 10:00 a.m. It took until 3:00 p.m. to reach the top of Cooper Spur, retaping about 40 wire splices as he went. A little later he reached Crescent Crevasse, not yet open, but dished with a slight depression about two feet deep.

Leaving the crevasse, he climbed upward only 150 feet when an ominous noise above signalled the breaking of a very large ledge of rock that quickly broke into a massive avalanche of rock and gravel, fanning out into a 300-foot front. Falling rock quickly cut the fixed rope, then came flying all around him. One flat stone slithered down and came to a slow stop above him. Then two huge boulders of perhaps four feet in diameter appeared taking courses on both sides of him.

At the last moment the boulder on the right veered toward him, struck the flat rock in front of Coalman, and broke into five large pieces that fanned out as a bursting artillery shell. He was unable to dodge all of them, and a five-inch chunk struck him on his left chest as he was attempting to move sidewise to avoid it. That was all he knew. When he regained consciousness, he found that he had slid back to Crescent Crevasse and by looking at his watch, he knew that he had lain there in its depression for at least a half hour.

He rose to his feet. Aside from a sprained hip, all seemed well, and he started slowly up. Rocks were still rolling occasionally, and he detoured east a bit. He was just about across the top of Newton Clark Glacier, when he encountered some steep slope in a heavily-broken jumble of ice. In attempting to climb that, he was stricken by heart pains and finally hobbled back down to Cloud Cap Inn.

Judge Gilbert had come up to stay at the closed inn, and Coalman stayed with him. Since he was feeling better, he saw no reason to tell the judge of his problems, merely mentioning that an avalanche had prevented his climbing to the summit. It should be noted that his very life was undoubtedly saved because of several letters and his glasses in a case in his left breast pocket had absorbed some of the shock of the striking rock. Lige had shoved the glasses into the case, when he first heard the rock break loose above.

On Monday morning he felt quite normal, aside from a numbness at the point where the rock had struck his chest. He started for the summit. On reaching the severed rope, he pulled the cut section behind him until he could tie it to the top portion once more. After a hard day he retired in the summit cabin, feeling no soreness. As sleep overcame him, a sharp pain ran through his left side, "as though a bullet had pierced my heart." Breathing was excruciatingly painful.

He dressed and rang Government Camp on the telephone. There was no answer. He lit the oil stove and walked the floor the balance of the night, fighting severe pain for every gasp of breath he got. At 4:30 a.m., Roy Henson, District Ranger at Zigzag, finally answered the telephone. He told Henson that he was going below to Crater Rock at 5:00 a.m., and that he would need help. Closing the cabin, he started down, but the snow was frozen hard. He got back to the cabin and waited.

Later he again made telephone connection, but was too stricken to talk. Communication degenerated to Henson asking questions and Coalman answering by turning the telephone crank for ring signals. Henson finally went up with a party to take Lige down on Tuesday.

On Wednesday, July 31, Coalman wrote a long letter of resignation to Thomas H. Sherrard, Supervisor of Oregon National Forest, telling him in full of his problems with the telephone line. The Forest Service engaged Mark Weygandt to man the lookout for the last part of the summer.

In 1919 he returned to duty at the summit cabin, no longer shouldering 100-pound loads and galloping up the chute. George Maronay carried up the oil and food, as well as hanging and recoiling the telephone lines. All went well until the end of the season on September 10. Cloud Cap Inn threw a party to celebrate the closing of the season. Lige and George slammed the door on the lookout cabin, closing it for the year and started down Cooper Spur Route.

Early snows had loaded the upper slopes of the mountain to a dangerous level with loose snow. The two men made it down to Crescent Crevasse when the whole summit area avalanched with a terrible roar toward the Eliot Glacier, missing them by 150 feet. The accompanying wind of the avalanche generated minor flow of snow directly above them, burying them completely. They had shoved their alpenstocks in as deeply as they would go, enough to avoid being swept right along in the river of flowing snow. Observers at Cloud Cap saw the whole occurrence, but saw no sign of life, as the two men very carefully dug themselves out to avoid further movement of the snow mass.

The party at Cloud Cap Inn took on the proportions of a wake, with their friends being considered dead. When Coalman and Maronay finally appeared, the group had a real reason to rejoice. About 25 people helped them celebrate their salvation with dancing and singing around the fireplace that lasted into the night.

Lige and George intended to head for Government Camp via Elk Meadow, Bennett Pass, White River and Summit Ranger Station. Waiting a day for better weather, they ran into snow above Elk Meadow. Visibility dropped to nothing, and they lost the trail. Lige thought it would be well to climb toward Bonnie Butte where he knew a trail. But that meant miles of bushwhacking down to East Fork of Hood River and up the steep ridge on the east. Leaving the river they broke out of the fog but were pounded by wind and sleet. Maronay wore a truss to correct a hernia and had to be helped along over small obstacles as he tired. Finally, Lige found a telephone wire along the trail, three miles north of the Bonney Butte shelter.

Maronay was close to collapse, near the end with hypothermia as the two made their way along the gale-swept ridge, three miles in two hours. Another hour was spent in looking for the shelter, but it had been levelled to ashes by careless hunters. It was vital that Maronay be kept afoot.

At 3:00 a.m., Lige found the Forest Service emergency cache of tools and food located some 300 feet from the cabin site. His key opened it, and they had an axe, matches, kindling, and a lantern. A big fire in a sheltered spot soon had them warmed considerably and eating beans and corned beef.

Using a dry cell bettery in the cache, Lige tapped out a code on the Forest Service phone line. They were met with three horses down the trail, although the exhausted Maronay could hardly ride. Lige helped the ranger close down the summit cabin a couple of days later, the last of his duty with the Forest Service on Mount Hood.

After the summer of 1919 he returned to live on the ranch near Sandy, and took a job as foreman for a time on the Minsinger Ranch at Marmot. Times were difficult following World War One, and the Coalman Homestead was claimed by Clackamas County for non-payment of taxes, although the Mitchell family bought parts of it back later.

Lige had a job in 1922 with Star Sand and Gravel in Portland. He bought an acre on NE 71st near Sandy Boulevard and the family lived in a tent while he worked on a three-room shack for their home. The minister of Unity Presbyterian Church got him interested in a Sunday school class that led toward boy scout work and association with the Young Mens' Christian Association. He became leader of ski trips and hikes and fishing trips for teen-age boys. In the summer of 1924 he worked in the hotel at Government

Camp and did his last mountain guiding.

Smelt dipping trips to the Sandy River were largely responsible for the YMCA becoming interested in buying land for a boys' camp, named Camp Collins for E.S. Collins, lumberman who bankrolled the project. Coalman became so interested in YMCA activities that he took a job with the organization in 1925. The next year he became an employee at their camp at Spirit Lake near Mount St. Helens. True to form, this versatile pioneer in an alpine setting found a wealth of heroic adventures at his new home. He did return to Mount Hood on the New Year search of 1927, when Brownlee was lost without a trace on the south side.

Coalman had the custom of celebrating Christmas with J.C. Meehan and his wife. Meehan was the general secretary of the Young Mens' Christian Association, the group that ran the camp where Lige worked at Spirit Lake.

Mrs. Meehan had come to the lake in advance, just in time to witness several days of deluge that flooded the Toutle River, sending down a chaos of logs and boulders that obliterated sections of the new river road. On December 23, 1933, Lige fought his way downstream, struggling over piles of driftwood and climbing above bands of cliff to reach the community of St. Helen, 26 miles below the lake. There he met Meehan and the two started back to the camp at Spirit Lake. It took 48 hours to make the return trip.

On Wednesday, December 27, a rainfall of 3.9 inches fell, followed by 2.8 inches the next day. It was several days before Lige could escort the Meehans back out to St. Helen and accompany them to Portland. Shortly after the first of the year he returned to the lake with a representative of the Bureau of Public Roads to survey the destruction on the new highway.

In 1937, Coalman gave up the hard job at Spirit Lake at the age of 56. On April 1, 1938, he took a job with the YMCA at Berkeley, California. His wife did not follow, but divorced him. His job alternated between the YMCA office and their camp on the Gualala River in Sonoma County. In his camp work in California he also encountered more of the dramatic adventure that always seemed to follow him.

In 1960 his wife returned to him in his retirement at Santa Rosa, where he died June 29, 1970. His ashes were scattered on his beloved Mount Hood.

William Gladstone Steel, Mr. Mazama

The man most influential in developing the community of Government Camp, the sport of mountaineering, and The Mazamas, was William Gladstone Steel, born at Stafford, Ohio, September 7, 1854, the youngest of 10 children. His parents moved to Pittsburgh in 1865, Kansas in 1868, and Oregon in 1872. Four of his brothers moved to Portland at that time, James, John, David, and George. His father settled in Portland to become a partner with a McLernon in a grist mill on Front Avenue at the foot of Vine Street.

Will went to North School in Portland, but he was not able to graduate from Portland High School, which stood at Broadway and Morrison. He was forced to go to work and spent five years learning patternmaking at Smith and Watson Iron Works. During this time he joined the Philomathean Society, a group of young men who learned parliamentary procedures, debated, and wrote essays. The group was organized October 3, 1875, and undoubtedly had a great influence on Steel.

In 1878, D.H. Stearns, owner of the *Portland Evening Bee*, gave him a job as circulation manager. In the fall of 1880 he went to Albany to establish his own newspaper, the *Albany Herald*. It was the first Republican paper there and swung the vote away from the Democratic Party for the first time in Linn County. He soon sold the newspaper and moved to Portland to become a substitute letter carrier. Within four years he was superintendent, but when Grover Cleveland was inaugurated as president in 1885, Republican Steel soon found himself involved in a heated and long political wrangle, and out of a job.

One of Steel's early friends was Charles H. Sholes, who came to Oregon in 1883. When Steel lost out in the US Post Office, he went into the real estate business, being temporarily associated with Sholes. Steel first climbed Mount Hood in

William G. Steel at Mt. Rainier 1905

1885. This was perhaps the year in which he finally found Crater Lake. Crater Lake (Deep Blue Lake) had been discovered in June, 1853, but the news was not widespread. Steel had heard about it in Kansas, but when he began asking about it in Oregon, no one had ever heard of such a lake. Finally, he found a source of information and made a trip to southern Oregon to stand on the rim and see the infinite blue of the water himself.

In 1885 he began a movement to make the lake part of a national reserve, sending letters to magazines, and sending thousands of circulars to editors all over the United States telling of the lake in an extinct crater. A 112-page book, *The Mountains of Oregon*, was sent to the president, cabinet members, congress, and newspapermen. This was done at great personal expense. Steel took a petition to Grover Cleveland himself. On January 30, 1886, the President issued a proclamation setting aside 10 townships. The same year a request for US Geological Survey operations was granted, conducted by Captains Clarence E. Dutton and George E. Davis. Steel was asked to join the effort and was placed in charge of boat building.

Boats were built in Portland and taken to the lake, where depth soundings were made. On June 18, 1886, Senator Dolph introduced a bill in the US Senate that would give Crater Lake national park status. Opposition was heavy, so Dolph proposed giving the land to Oregon in trust for a park. Steel objected on the grounds that the state would not maintain it properly. An impasse developed. Senator Tongue renewed the project when he entered Congress. Finally on May 22, 1902, Congress declared Crater Lake a national park after 17 tireless and expensive years of promotion by Will Steel. Many trips to Washington D.C. were made at his own expense.

In 1887 the Oregon Alpine Club came into being, Steel being one of the founders. The club let in too many who wanted to do their climbing with a telescope from Portland, and its interests became far too divergent. It finally foundered and sunk under its own weight, being a financial burden on Steel as it went.

In 1889 Republican Benjamin Harrison replaced Cleveland, and Steel's brother, George, became Postmaster in Portland. He induced Will to abandon the real estate business and become superintendent of letter carriers once more.

It was in 1892 that he really began to be a factor at Mount Hood, applying for a homestead claim at Government Camp. Shortly thereafter several of his mountaineering friends filed claims, including O.C. Yocum and Francis C. Little.

It is true that he had been active and prominent in the limited scope of mountain activity of the years since Steel helped on a much-publicized illumination in 1887, the year Oregon Alpine Club was initiated. But after the homesteads were claimed, he spent much more time at Government Camp. It was necessary to build a cabin and live in it a certain part of the time. He and Yocum collaborated by building one cabin on the property line, using it in vacation times. During this era he climbed often and became an authority on Mount Hood.

UNFULFILLED SCHEMES

1893 Incorporation of the Mount Hood Improvement Company was made March 18, for $5,000 by W.G. Steel, George H. Lamberson, and F.C. Little. A hotel was proposed for Government Camp. A sawmill hauled up in the autumn of 1892 would be set up, using water power that would also drive an electric power plant. The corporation proposed furnishing guides, climbing equipment, food and lodging, to improve trails, and to operate a store. Negotiations were under way for a stage line that hopefully could deliver passengers from Portland to Government Camp in one day. So reported *The Sunday Oregonian.*

STEEL'S CABIN ROBBED

1893 On Thursday, July 13, Will Steel returned from Government Camp to restock his supplies. Camping out, instead of using the cabin as usual, he and a companion went on an exploration trip. On returning they found a thief had taken food, arms, and ammunition. Steel was on his way back to Government Camp on Friday morning.

Steel's brothers George and James became interested in building Fulton Park, then built an electric rail line to the subdivision. This led to the building of a line to Oregon City. As early as 1892, Will was promoting a rail line to Mount Hood, a dream never fulfilled. He was also involved with rail lines to Coos Bay and other points in southern Oregon. There were many years that he was involved in so many companies in railroads and real estate, that it is impossible to keep up with the succession of events. He was the corporate secretary of Coos Bay and Oregon Central Railway in 1892, and he had held the same position with the Drain Natural Gas Company in 1890.

In 1894, Steel and others organized The Mazamas, this time avoiding the pitfalls that had killed the Oregon Alpine Club. The initial effort of the club was to be a tremendous climb, open to all, to give a backlog of new members. Press coverage was something of the scope of the coverage given to World War One, and it continued that way for thirty years, largely because of the newspaper contacts of Steel. When the tremendous group of alpinists assembled at Mount Hood in July of 1894, he was very prominent in all the arrangements and operation. As might be expected, he became the first president of The Mazamas, but shortly after organization he was absent in Washington D.C. promoting the idea of Crater Lake NP.

In August of 1892 a number of prominent Portland people formed the Multorpor Republican Club, a name that member Will Steel immediately took to Government Camp and gave to the mountain that stands just south of the community. The name uses the first syllables of Multnomah, Oregon, and Portland.

In 1897, the call of Alaskan gold was too strong to keep Will Steel in Portland, and he was off to Dyea to write syndicate letters from the wild north country. At Dyea there were thousands of men waiting to go over the trail to the gold fields, and the postoffice was in a state of impossible confusion under the direction of a lady who had no comprehension as to how to handle large volumes of mail. Steel took over as unofficial postmaster and undid the snarl. Charles Sholes had also gone north, and the two men organized a delivery system to those who wished their mail at 25¢ per week. Soon ten clerks were working, and they established an express service to carry money, gold dust, and valuables to Skagway. Their safety was guaranteed by the fabled Soapy Smith, who introduced them to all the gamblers and saloon keepers of the community and placed a hands-off status on the express operators. They also took over the telephone line from Dyea to Skagway.

When the spring thaw came, Dyea suddenly died. A $3,500 lot was sold to Steel at $150, and two weeks later he sold it to another man for $50. Flour at $100 a sack suddenly dropped to 25¢ a sack. Condensed milk at $1 a can went to 5¢. Steel came home broke, but he did establish a friendship with Lydia Hatch, whom he had hired to work in the express office. On February 16, 1900, they were married. Back in Portland he was again spending all the money he could muster to promote Crater Lake. He remembered going without meals to afford the price of a telegram to Washington.

To give an insight into the character and integrity of Steel, Charles Sholes told a story after his death about a real estate deal at the turn of the century. Collaborating with two other realtors, he was about to consumate a very large deal, good for a million dollars profit. To prevent an option on coal land from running out, Steel put his personal guarantee on the obligations of his corporation. The day before the close of the transaction, a cable from London announced the collapse of the house of Baring Brothers, and Steel was obligated for $25,000. It took him until 1932 to pay off the debt, which most men would have avoided.

In 1901 Steel had been prominent on the 1901 Mazama outing at Mount Hood. However something happened on the outing or later that year that made him resign from the club. It was over three years before he rejoined. Earl Bronaugh, the corresponding secretary of The Mazamas, wrote to him on July 14, 1904, on behalf of the Executive Council, expressing regret about the incident, which had caused him to resign.

There are other instances that showed the fiery temper of Will Steel. On October 16, 1903, F.A. Bancroft, Portland Postmaster, wrote a letter of suspension to him, "owing to statements you have made to the various clerks and individuals in the office, and the threats you have made to put me out of office, I hereby suspend you from the service." And he did. But soon afterward Bancroft was the subject of investigation, and was forced to resign. John W. Minto was appointed the new Postmaster. Oregon's Senator Mitchell figured in the argument, and he and Steel conducted a very acid exchange of frank letters, each telling the other of his low moral character.

After 1900 he was active in real estate, often pointing out in his writing how Portland was growing and was destined to become the dominant city of the Pacific Coast. He became very much interested in the community of St. John, named for James St. John, and became president of Peninsula Development Club in 1909. At that time he was also president of Klamath Lake Navigation Company. Also in 1909 he led a movement to unite all of the Steel family of the United States in a meeting he set up on August 26, at the Alaska-Yukon Exposition in Seattle.

In 1910 he was a kingpin in the move to organize a hospital in north Portland, a project that was still fighting hard for existence in 1912. In December of 1912 W.F. Arrant, Superintendent of Crater Lake NP was leaving office, and vast support was given all over the state to give the job to Will Steel, although he was a member of the Republican Party. Referring to him as the "Father of Crater Lake", editorials up and down the state stated their support of him. Early in 1913 he was given the position. It paid only $1,000 a year, later $1,500.

All through his career he had been a prolific writer, publishing *The Native Son* and *Steel Points*. *Steel Points* appeared with a Portland issue in October, 1906, *Crater Lake* in January, 1907, *Mount Hood* in April, 1907, *The Olympics* in July, 1907, and *Oregon Place Names* in March, 1917. In addition to these there were many works published as *Steel Points* in the newspaper. In 1905 Steel named Mississippi Head on Mount Hood in honor of the Mississippi delegation to the National Editorial Association meeting in Portland, during which he illuminated Mount Hood with red fire with the aid of A.J. Capron and E.G. Jones.

During these years he was conducting people up and down Mount Hood in substantial numbers. He was always patient with the slowest climber, pacing himself to the weakest. Many who believed themselves too tired to go on, were encouraged to make the little extra effort to get them to the summit.

In October of 1908 the Governor appointed him to the board of three commissioners of Geographic Names. Steel continued in this position until 1916, although the collection of data on geographic names was a hobby for many years before and after his period of service on the board. The names of hundreds of cities, rivers, mountains, and every county in the United States were investigated and listed in a monster file believed to now be in Washington D.C. as a gift of Steel.

In 1917 he promoted an outdoor organization in Medford, The Grizzlies, and was the president. Later that year he took a job as editor of the *Rogue River Courier* at Grants Pass. On January 22, 1919, he was elected as Secretary of the Commercial Club at Medford. On March 1, 1920, he took the job as Executive Secretary of the Eugene Chamber of Commerce. The following October 12, he resigned to take a position of field secretary of the Oregon State Motor Association, setting up a new office in Medford, then proceeding soon afterward to do the same at Eugene. On March 25, 1925, Judge Charles E. Wolverton appointed him as Commissioner for Crater Lake NP. In 1927 the *Medford Mail Tribune* reported that he was planning to walk from there to Crater Lake, scoffing at the idea of walking over a little snow, a hearty attitude for one of 73 years. Steel died at Medford October 21, 1934.

Mount Steel in the Olympic Peninsula commemorates him, as does Steel Cliff on Mount Hood, which name was suggested by *Oregonian* reporter, E.L. Coldwell. No one could make a good guess on how many speeches he made at civic clubs, churches, and any other group that might assemble. He usually showed films and told of the beauties of Mount Hood, Crater Lake, Cascade Pass, and the Olympic Peninsula. It is probable that no other Oregonian ever held the presidency to so many organizations. And certainly no individual ever gave more of his own time and money to preserve for posterity such a priceless treasure as Crater Lake National Park.

Adolf Aschoff, First Supervision of MHNF

Adolf Aschoff, one of the most colorful characters in the history of Mount Hood, was born at Celle, Hanover on May 21, 1849, the son of a manufacturer who descended from Russian royalty. He was educated for the clergy but did not feel attracted to the profession. At 17 he became involved in trouble with a Prussian army officer. Young men at the time in Germany were required to enter military service for a period of time.

Aschoff escaped by hiding in the water of a lake with only his face exposed for a day and night. Student friends effected his rescue, and he left Germany covertly as a political exile. Arriving in New York in 1869 he made his living for a time with his cleverness at wood carving. By 1871 he had drifted to Kansas to file on a homestead and take a wife. In 1882 he came to Portland, going on to his final home at Marmot 1883.

He had acquired many influential friends in his short stay in Portland, so that when he built resort cabins at Marmot, business came his way quickly. A hotel followed, that was enlarged in 1902 to 23 rooms. About 1890 he established a post office and became postmaster.

Running a hotel and resort in those days also entailed feeding and stabling horses for relief on the stage and freight wagons operating on the road. Aschoff was often involved in transporting wagon loads of vacationers off to see the sights at Government Camp. This led to his climbing Mount Hood and his friendship with William Steel and O.C. Yocum. When The Mazamas held their organizational climb in 1894, Aschoff attended and became a prominent charter member.

The Aschoffs reared nine children there at their home at Marmot, which explains how Adolf could be postmaster, storekeeper, hotelier, mountain guide, and still hold the position of Supervisor of Cascade Forest Reserve North. He had a good deal of family help.

On May 19, 1899, he was appointed Ranger on the Forest, and in time became Supervisor with many rangers under his direction. His employment with the Forest Service ended January 1, 1906. Many details of his interesting career can be found in the chapter about the Forest Service.

An accomplished musician on the piano, he played until late in life, composing several works of his own. His artistic ability was phenomenal. He worked with paint, sketched quickly and effectively, and cut amazingly accurate silhouettes in diminutive size with paper and scissors. His museum was full of art works and the heads of game animals he had stuffed.

He had a great affinity for communicating with important people. His correspondence included such figures as President Theodore Roosevelt and many notable people in Europe. When he was rebuked by Doug Langille, Inspector with the Forest Service, for writing unneccessarily to head office, it probably dampened his zest for government work and possibly caused his eventual resignation.

Aschoff was of medium height, quite stocky. Witnesses saw him hold a 100-pound bag of flour at arm's length with either hand. This led to a fiasco on October 22, 1906, when he decided to give an exhibition and lift a man of over 200 pounds with his neck. He put his head between the man's legs and lifted him right off the ground, but when the feat was finished, his head drooped on his chest. He could raise it only by using his hands.

At St. Vincent's Hospital they found that he had broken a vertebra and torn a tendon loose. Dr. Eugene Rockey put him in a plaster cast, and he remained helpless for some time, until the neck healed.

In 1924 The Mazamas honored him with a life membership and a testimonial banquet at the Portland YMCA, a display of mutual admiration. He had always been an enthusiastic member of the club, and The Mazamas often scheduled weekends at Marmot, sometimes crowding the hotel with as many as 200 people.

On his 80th birthday in May of 1929 he entertained a large Mazama group, that time alone, because his wife had died the previous year. On March 1, 1930, Portland papers announced the the old man was selling his place to Percy T. Shelley and moving into town. On May 16, he died. The white community church in Sandy swelled with people at his last rites. The Mazamas came out in force.

On July 4, 1931, the Shelley family lost their worldly belongings when the old hotel and cabins burned to the ground. The museum, post office, and store on the south side of Marmot Road were saved. Today everything is gone. Only a few old boards and some ancient apple trees mark the spot.

The Langille Family, North Side Pioneers

James Langille was born March 24, 1841, at River John, Nova Scotia, of Scotch ancestry. He worked as a millright and shipfitter near his home, but the urge to wander became very strong. In 1869 he was involved in the silver strike at White Pine Mountain, Nevada. Other work was in New England, and it is known that he made an early trip by ship to Panama, thence by another ship to California, where he settled for a time at Gilroy in the Santa Clara Valley.

In 1880 he moved his wife and three sons to Chicago, where he obtained a very good position with the Pullman Works in their new rail car factory. By 1883 he decided to move on again to the Hood River Valley, travelling on the Northern Pacific Railway, except for an incomplete gap in the Rockies that were negotiated by horse coach. His wife, Sarah, took the rails to San Francisco and came up the coast on the *Queen of the Pacific.*

Finding all the good land in the lower valley gone, he finally chose a homestead a mile north of Mount Hood Post Office, 160 acres that fronted on what is now Highway 35 and ran west to the river. On this land he erected the first sawmill in the upper valley. At the time the only other homesteaders were Tieman and Baldwin.

James Langille was a gregarious, generous, warm-hearted Scot with red hair, a contrast to his proper English wife. He became interested in the developments at Cloud Cap Inn in 1889 and became assistant foreman on the job. Brown, the first foreman, quit, and Langille took over the duty until the job was complete. After that time his life was divided between work on the homestead and further wandering. He and his wife became estranged and were not together from about 1891.

In the last year of his life he had visited Nova Scotia, then headed west. He was visiting relatives in Mound Valley, Kansas, when he died February 11, 1911.

Sarah Harding Langille was born January 24, 1844 at Tuskat, Nova Scotia. She married James Langille in about 1867. Much of her married life was spent alone at home with her children while James worked at various jobs in the United States.

With the help of her sons, William, Herbert, and Harold Douglas, she took the management of Cloud Cap Inn in 1891. Lewis Adams, the previous manager, had evidently been too free with expenses, putting the inn so far in arrears, so that the owners demanded a change. Sarah came in and made the operation pay, staying in the position for 16 summer seasons.

Although she was very austere and proper, of English ancestry, she proved a very gracious hostess, known to her sons and many of the hotel visitors as "Tantsana", a name the children had gleaned from the book "*Story of an African Farm*" which she had read to them in years gone by. The hotel was a warm, cheerful place under her regime.

When she finally retired from Cloud Cap Inn, she moved to 683 Wasco Street in Portland. On June 16, 1924, she died. Her son, Harold Douglas Langille, spread her ashes atop the lonely Langille Crags on the west side of Eliot Glacier.

William Alexander Langille was born in Nova Scotia, August 18, 1868, the eldest child of James and Sarah. He attended public school there and in Chicago, moving to Hood River with the family in 1883. He was involved with building Cloud Cap Inn and the first road to it in 1888-89.

Mountaineering became a great interest with him. During the 1889 season he and his father took off enough time from the Cloud Cap project to attempt a climb by the Newton Clark Glacier to the top of Steel Cliff, thence along the route known as Wy'east. That climb was not successful, but the following year he did push the route to a conclusion, topping the mountain with inn manager, Lewis H. Adams, and photographer A.B. McAlpin. In 1891 he attempted the route again with Fred Josselyn, Will Smith, Horatio J. Green, and his cousin, Anne Lang of The Dalles. Miss Lang slipped, and an heroic rescue just short of the summit cancelled the climb.

It is believed that Will first climbed Mount Hood by South Side Route. In 1891 when his mother took command of the inn, he became a regular mountain guide, the first on the north side to take parties to the summit. In 1893 he and his brother Doug pioneered a July climb of Cooper Spur Route, one that has become very popular over the years.

In 1893 Will climbed solo over the Eliot and Coe Glaciers to Horseshoe Rock, Queen's Chair, and the summit. For some reason this route did not become accepted until Mark Weygandt "discovered" it in 1916. In July 1896 he led a group to retrieve the body of Frederick Kirn from the

Newton Clark Glacier, where it had fallen from the Cooper Spur Route.

Will and Doug established permanent "lifeline" fixed ropes on the routes they regularly guided. In addition, climbers were tied in to a climbing rope. These and other precautions allowed Will to retire from guiding in 1897 with no casualties after fifty ascents.

Will Langille felt the call of the wild and headed for Alaska. In January of 1900 he left Dawson for the 1500-mile trip over Yukon ice to Nome, a 35-day trip. He prospected and mined there until 1902.

Mining proved unprofitable, and he applied for a job with the US Forest Service. In February 1903 he was appointed as Forest Examiner in the US Bureau of Forestry under Gifford Pinchot, the Chief. His first assignment was to report on the forest potential of the Alexander Archipelago, which consists of most of the islands of Southern Alaska. No power boats were available for charter, so all the work was done on a five-ton sloop. His report indicated 75 billion board feet of lumber in the archipelago.

At the end of the 1903 season he was sent to Mount Whitney Military Reservation in California to appraise forests on the eastern fringe of the Sierra Nevada Range. On December 5, he returned to Washington D.C.

In April 1904 he was on his way to Prince William Sound on an inspection that resulted in the creation and naming of Chugach National Forest. President Theodore Roosevelt requested an evaluation of forests at Norton Bay near Nome, but there were only small stands of isolated spruce, and it was not designated as a National Forest. On returning to Prince William Sound he cruised the Kenai Peninsula, part with a native, part alone. He then retired to Seward to write reports for a month.

In December he started a trip with a friend from his Nome mining days, buying a good team of dogs and an eight-foot basket sled. Before they left for Fairbanks, they were visited in turn by the saloon keepers of Seward. The result was that 13 different bottles of brandy or whisky had been left as gifts inside the dog sled, a regrettable waste, because neither was a drinking man. It took them until April, 10, 1905 to reach Fairbanks, where a telegram directed Will Langille to go to the coast.

He left alone with a 75-pound pack on his back, taking nine days to reach Circle City on the Yukon River. From there he took a steamer to Dawson and Wrangell. Upon opening his mail he found that he had been appointed First Administrator for Alaska under the newly formed United States Forest Service as a part of the Department of Agriculture.

Langille set up his headquarters at Ketchikan. A staff of men, including a finance officer, was assembled. For transportation, a 64-foot launch was built. The new Forest Service had new rules to administer. Langille found that the Indians, speaking Chinook jargon, were not too difficult to handle. But lumbermen and mill owners balked and objected to the new policies on cutting and payment for timber stumpage.

In 1909 a serious controversy arose between mining and timber interests in Cugach National Forest, the Ballinger-Pinchot feud. As Supervisor of the forest, Langille was required to rule on mining claims. Finally a series of timber and mining experts were called into the area to make evaluations. Hearings in Washington stirred up a great deal of bitterness in the Taft regime, resulting in the dismissal of Gifford Pinchot in 1910. Langille resigned in 1911 and returned to the family farm at Hood River for a short while.

During that time he met Marie Slate, sister of Olive Slate, the wife of Horace Mecklem. Marie had been visiting her sister, and Will met her on a trip to the Portland train depot. In 1912 they were married and made a 14-month trip to Saõ Paulo, Brazil. Will surveyed the forests of that area for marketable timber, but reported back that although the forests were dense, the trees were too varied and scattered.

Will and Marie Langille had three daughters, Elizabeth who married Webb Trimble of Seattle, Jean who married Dr. Ivan I. Langley, and Helen who married Clyde P. Carroll, Jr. Shortly after Helen was born in 1919, Marie Langille took her three children back to her home in New York for a three-year stay. For several years he evidently marked time at the farm. It is known that he built a boy scout camp and cabin at Wahtum Lake in 1918.

There are notes of his building road to Lost Lake. The Forest Service records show his using 50 men for 720 man-days in June of 1922, and 60 men for 458 days in July, a very high labor turnover. The wages paid by the Forest Service were not high enough to keep men on the job very long. In 1923 the road was completed.

There is also a note that he joined the first climb by the Hood River American Legion, held in 1921.

From 1924 to 1926 Will Langille worked with the Oregon State Board of Forestry as an inspector. From 1927 to 1932 he was a highway deputy with the Oregon State Highway Maintenance office at The Dalles. In 1932-3 he worked for the department at Mr. Devers' office in Salem. Then until 1935 he worked with the CCC program. From 1935-1938 he was engaged in the Recreational Development Program in which Silver Creek Falls was acquired and established as a park. From that time he was with the Oregon State Highway Parks Division until retirement in 1951, after which time lived with his daughter, Jean.

In 1938 he climbed Mount Hood South Side Route at the age of 70. It was his 54th ascent of the peak. He died August 21, 1956, a man who left a permanent impression on Mount Hood.

Herbert B. Langille was born January 1, 1871 in Nova Scotia. Herb had little interest in mountaineering and did not climb Mount Hood very many times. He graduated from Stanford University, being one of the first students there. Later he was an instructor in electrical engineering at the University of California. He died of a heart attack on a San Francisco street in February, 1950.

Harold Douglas Langille was born September 19, 1874 in Nova Scotia, the most happy-go-lucky of the three boys. He helped Will with guiding at Cloud Cap Inn and took over as the guide when Will left in 1897. He led the north side Mazama party on the day of organization on July 19, 1894. Doug **(pronounced Doog)** ceased guiding at age 25 in 1899, but by that time he had climbed a hundred times, twice Will's record.

Doug joined the United States Geological Survey, working under the geographer Henry Gannett. East of Muir Pass in California's Sierra Nevada Range lies a jagged mass of granite named Langille Peak, overlooking the alpine beauty of Diamond Meadows. This job soon led into work with the Department of Forestry, as he was working as a Forest Inspector based in Washington D.C. in 1904.

In 1911 he was known to be working in private industry, managing the Portland branch of J.D. Lacey Lumber Company of Chicago.

About 1930, Doug's wife was killed in an auto crash on the highway to Seaside. After that time, he more-or-less retired and went into prospecting for gold. It was in the early Thirties, that he was living in a mining camp in Idaho. One night he chased a porcupine in the dark with a shotgun. He hit the porcupine, but he had forgot that the powder magazine stood right in the line of fire. The magazine went up with a mighty roar that partially deafened him and caused a good deal of arthritis in later years.

About the last decade of his life was spent travelling in Mexico, following various mining operations. He remarried and his new wife, Jean, went with him. Doug died on July 11, 1954; his ashes were taken to Langille Crags by a party of 15 Crag Rats, led by their Big Squeek Norman Hukari and the veteran Mace Baldwin. Doug's wife Jean stood at Inspiration Point and pointed out the approximate area where she wanted the ashes placed. On September 4, 1955, the Crag Rats took a bronze plaque to the crags and cemented it to a large rock.

The Cooper Family of Cooper Spur

The Scot, David Rose Cooper, was one of the men, who originally visited the north side of Mount Hood with the idea of opening it up with a road. According to Marion Cooper, his wife, the two came from Scotland in 1873 to settle in southern Oregon. During their trip across the United States, one of their daughters, Wyoming (Noma) was born in Wyoming, the second child in the family.

The Coopers lived in southern Oregon until 1883, when they came to Hood River with horses and wagon. All during the stay there, Dave Cooper had heard of the wonders of Mount Hood, and even before he came to the valley, he wanted to blaze a road to the mountain. Their land claim was in the upper valley, just north and east of Parkdale, their son, John, only a month old at the time they settled on it. The house was located on the East Fork of Hood River in a grove of oaks and one giant pine. That tree was later cut and a 12-foot section sent to the Chicago World's Fair to show the size of Mount Hood trees.

Other families settled nearby, James Graham, a cabinetmaker, James Langille, another cabinetmaker, and Oscar Stranahan. The following February, the community received their mail, a whole sack full brought up on snow shoes. At the site of what is known as Mount Hood Post Office, just south of them, a post office was opened in the home of Oscar Fredenburg. Food was in short supply. Flour ran short, and the men kept meat on the table by killing deer and elk.

It was in the summer of 1884 that Cooper, Stranahan, Coe, and others went to explore at Mount Hood, following Cooper's urge to bring a road to it. A log cabin was thrown up, and the building of the road began. In the spring of 1885 the snow stayed late, but finally the melt came, and the job was completed, a rough road, which ran directly up the ridge to the present site of Cloud Cap Inn. At that time, sheepherders were said to have been using the area during the summers for about 20 years.

Finding the log house collapsed by heavy snow,

Cooper family circa 1884 — Photo David Cooper, Jr. Standing at rear, Teena, Noma, James, Warren. Front, Mae, Elizabeth, mother Marion, father Dave. George on Marion's lap. John on Dave's lap.

Cooper decided to put in a tent camp. Warren (Barney) Cooper helped his mother, who not only cooked for the guests, but took care of as many small babies as she might happen to have in any given year. Dave rotated his duty between the mountain resort and the family homestead, which was usually in the care of the older children.

Dave acted as the first guide on the north side, taking groups to the top of Cooper Spur or out onto the Eliot Glacier. He is known to have taken groups across the Newton Clark Glacier to overlook the White River Canyon.

One of Marion's babies was David Robert Cooper, born in 1894, who still lives with his wife in Parkdale. David, Jr. grew up around Cloud Cap Inn, working at various jobs. When the Snow Shoe Club built their lodge in 1910, he helped Mark Weygandt and Bill Jones on the hauling of the logs. The logs were hand-hewn by Jones and hauled to the site with horse teams.

Along about 1916 and 1917, Dave, Jr. was working for Dorsey B. Smith of Cloud Cap Inn, driving coach down to the Turnaround. Above the Turnaround was the China Fill, a very steep grade of sand, that Dave swears is unnegotiable for four-wheel-drive vehicles today. The China Fill was put in place by Ladd, when Cloud Cap Inn was built, eliminating a short section of switchback. Although it is of record that Mr. Covey drove a Cadillac to the door of the Inn in 1907, Dave, Jr. insists that any automobiles that ever got there, did so with the help of a team of horses.

Below the Turnaround, a regular bus service was run to Hood River by Oscar Stranahan's son, Bert, who had driven the wild teams up from Elk Beds 20 years before. So it was Dave's job to make connections with the Stranahans. The stable was located down the ridge about a half mile below Cloud Cap Inn. Dave's living quarters were up near the Inn in a small log cabin, which he shared with the cook and Mark Weygandt.

During these years he often climbed to the summit and developed quite a friendship with Lige Coalman. His first climb had been at the age of 12 with Walt Ford. As Dave's ability grew, Coalman sometimes called him on the telephone line to help with some emergency. On many occasions he climbed Cooper Spur Route, just to sleep in the summit cabin.

Dave, Jr. entered military service in the army in World War One. After being released from the army, he was involved in the construction business, working for L.M. Baldwin, father of L.C. (Jack) Baldwin. In 1924 he worked for Doggett and Davis, road contractors who had a contract for a section of the Mount Hood Loop Highway between Hood River Meadow and White River. In that year, the Forest Service advertised bids on the new road from Cooper Spur Junction to Cloud Cap Inn. Cooper bid the job and got it.

In 1925 he employed large crews in the construction. The major barrier was the grading and filling around the deep canyon of Tilly Jane Creek, near the bottom of the road. With modern methods, two or three machines would be able to do such a job in short time, but it was a matter of hand work then. A narrow-gauge track was set for mine cars to move rock and dirt. At the peak of production, Cooper had a hundred Swedes filling and dumping the small cars. The crew worked around the clock, using a portable generator at night for light.

Warren (Barney) Cooper was one of the older children in the family. His interest ran to work in the woods, being associated with such men as Adolf Aschoff and W.H.H. Dufur of the Forest Service. Barney was listed as the District Ranger of Hood River District back in 1905, although he had already served in that line of work for several years. He continued as District Ranger until 1920, using his own ranch as headquarters. When high government officials made the preliminary survey of the Loop Road in 1915, Barney took them over the Forest Service trail that was in common use through Elk Meadow.

The original David Cooper spent most of his time on the farm after the building of Cloud Cap Inn. He and Coe and Stranahan had sold the rights to the toll road and hotel facility to Ladd and Wood, in order that they might build with Cloud Cap. He died in 1922. His wife, Marion, born 1850, lived at the family farm at Parkdale for years. She died December 10, 1939.

Warren M. "Barney" Cooper — Photo USFS

Dave, Jr. later became a turkey farmer of distinction, running a large farm in southern Oregon. His improved breeds won dozens of Grand Champion awards at state fairs and Pacific International Livestock Exposition. At present, he has an apple orchard at Parkdale.

Mark Weygandt

Mark Weygandt was born at Excelsior, Illinois, December 16, 1881, the son of Lewis and Lois Weygandt. At the age of 15 he joined two other brothers on a bicycle trip from the family home at Boscobel, Wisconsin, to The Dalles. That trip in 1897 took 31 days of pedalling across the pioneer Oregon Trail route. From The Dalles they took the river steamer to Portland and stayed at the time with friends before going to eastern Oregon for summer work in the wheat fields.

In 1898 he moved to Hood River to live with his uncle, George Weygandt, on the farm that was later bought by Homer Rogers. Homesteading was an attraction, but Mark was too young to qualify. Meanwhile his father, Lewis, had moved to Oregon and took up a homestead very high in the Hood River Valley, a 160-acre plot that lies east of the old Goldsbury Ranch now occupied by Robert O. Lee. Mark eventually got 80 acres of his father's homestead.

Wesley and Mark Weygandt — Photo Wesley Weygandt

For two or three summers Mark followed the wheat harvest in areas around Pendleton, Condon, and John Day. But he developed a very early interest in Mount Hood, guiding for Sarah Langille as early as 1900. When her European guides left Cloud Cap Inn in 1903, he stepped into the position of head guide and stayed on for years.

J. Wesley Ladd, Rodney Glisan, Dr. Herbert Nichols, and several other prominent Portland business men had been coming to the north side for winter ski trips. As a guide, Mark Weygandt became very well known to them, and when they organized into the Snowshoe Club in 1904, he fell into the position of taking them to Cloud Cap Inn and providing their food and supplies. The arrangement worked so well that the club erected a lodge on the ridge just north of Cloud Cap, securing a 99-year lease from the Forest Service.

Weygandt took full charge of the 1910 construction project for the Snowshoe Club, hiring David Cooper, Sr., David Cooper, Jr., Bert Sandman, and Russell Gobin. He was then appointed caretaker of the club and supervised their annual winter outings every year until 1926.

In 1910 he married Beulah Jones. Also in that year he began guiding a series of fall hunting trips to eastern Oregon for the Snowshoe Club members and their friends. The party would go by rail to Arlington or Pendleton, then board a motor bus to travel to some ranch-house that Mark had spoken for. He knew many ranchers from his days in the wheat fields, and he talked them into offering his clients board and room during the hunting trip. Usually horses and wagon and riding horses were also reserved for the members of the hunting party.

The hunters would then spend several days picking out their buck deer and getting to know his habits, making sure that no two had chosen the same deer. Then the day before departure for home, they all hurried out to shoot and dress their deer. It was then wrapped in cloth, and the party sped to the train, trying to get the meat to Portland before it spoiled. In later years, ice was arranged for on the train to prevent spoilage.

Thus Mark Weygandt introduced the idea of hunting in eastern Oregon to Portlanders, a sport that now draws thousands across the Cascades every hunting season. He kept up the program until about 1930, when better roads eliminated the need of a guide's services.

Weygandt was a very fast climber in his youth. One story of 1903 records him in leaving his home at the ranch one morning and reaching the summit of Mount Hood by noon. Sarah Langille once watched him climb to the top from Cloud Cap in 110 minutes and descend in 35. In 1916 he rediscovered the Sunshine Route that had been climbed once solo by Will Langille. After making notes for years and carefully watching the route, he finally began to take parties up it in 1923. On July 31, 1931 he led a party of 247 on an American Legion climb of Cooper Spur Route, the largest group to ever reach the summit up until that time.

When the Hood River Ski Club ran their first race, probably the first ever staged on Mount Hood, Weygandt came in first from the run to Kirby Camp from Cloud Cap Inn.

He was employed in 1915 in the construction of the cabin on the summit, and when Lige Coalman was seriously injured in 1917, he took over the job as summit fire lookout for the remainder of the season.

Mark Weygandt has been credited with 588 ascents of Mount Hood, seventy of which were on the South Side Route. He made it through his guiding career without a fatality and very few accidents. One accident that did occur on one of his climbs was the Labor Day accident of 1933 in which Esther Gilman broke her leg. Miss Gilman later became his daughter-in-law, marrying Wes Weygandt.

Mark had so many different working arrangements in guiding that his activities are impossible to trace. At times he worked for Cloud Cap Inn, at others he worked as an independent guide, and on occasions he had guiding concessions. He did hire several men to do guiding with him from 1905 to 1927, Orville Thompson, Earl Newman, Shorty Rice, Ed Kile, Felix Kile, Ed Hardman, and Alva Hardman. He worked at times with George Miller.

Mark and Beulah Weygandt had four sons, Wesley, Theodore, Richard, and Myron. Wes did a limited amount of guiding after his father retired. Wes, Myron and Ted offered snow-cat transportation on the Cloud Cap road for a few years after World War Two.

Mark Weygandt retired to his home at 9933 E. Burnside in Portland, where he died August 8, 1944.

Fred Stadter

Fred W. Stadter was born at Hedrick, Iowa, December 20, 1877. He was appointed Assistant City Attorney for the City of Portland in 1913. He joined The Mazamas in 1920, becoming one of the dynamic leaders of the club. He served two terms as president in 1926-7 and 1927-8.

Following observations of a previous outing, in 1926 he discovered the Stadter Buried Forest, fossil trees that date back several thousand years, and whose trunks protruded from a glacial ridge high above the headwaters of the Sandy River. The area is at the 6,200-foot level on the north side of the north fork of the south fork of Sandy River, a remote place that is seldom seen. The geologic implications of Stadter's find are discussed in great detail in the 1931 Mazama Annual by Dr. Edwin T. Hodge. Since that time other fossil trees have been observed on the side of a moraine deep in the south part of White River Canyon.

Stadter was elected a municipal judge in 1925, after which time all of the many newspaper accounts of his activity at Mount Hood always referred to him as Judge. He was very active in early skiing at Summit, Swim, and Multorpor, usually presiding at dedications and award dinners.

In 1927 he was the leader of the climb of Sunshine Route on which Dr. Stryker became the first casualty on a Mazama ascent.

His retirement from professional life was in 1934. He died February 26, 1959.

Fred McNeil

Fred H. McNeil was born in the state of Illinois and started his career in journalism there in 1910. Two years later he joined the staff of *The Oregon Journal*, a lifetime association.

He was not long in entering outdoor activities, joining The Mazamas in 1914. A news story of August 8, 1917, told of his being lost overnight on Mount Jefferson with Pascho Ivanekoff, Portland tailor. The two were on the Mazama Annual Outing and took a wrong turn in the trail, finally ending up in the Jefferson Park area, whereas the base camp was at Pamelia Lake. He fell asleep too close to his campfire and burned off parts of his trousers. Searchers finally found him the next day after Ivanekoff had stumbled into base camp, but McNeil was too weak to walk until they brought him food.

Soon after, his name appeared as the writer of a news story about the placement of Prouty's ashes in a memorial service at Three Sisters. In years to come McNeil's name appeared on many stories about Mount Hood, which became his specialty.

In 1918, as a member of the US Army Engineers, he wrote from France. He had been promised a leave for November 4th, and planned to visit the Dauphine Alps. The Armistice was signed a week later.

He took a great deal of interest in the wave of skiing enthusiasm that surged at Mount Hood about 1928. He became the Secretary of Cascade Ski Club, the president of Pacific Northwest Ski Association, and recording secretary of The Mazamas, all at the same time in 1931. In addition he became an important part of Wy'east Climbers and of the Mount Hood Ski Patrol.

In 1937 his book was published, *Wy'east, The Mountain*, a story of Mount Hood that outlined its history in an interesting readable narrative. The book has long been out of print and is a collector's item.

Fred McNeil died December 28, 1958. His ashes were scattered on a remote west ridge near timberline on July 13, 1959, and the spot was named McNeil Point. Far below on the Sandy River near Old Maid Flat the Forest Service built a camp and named it McNeil Forest Camp.

Homer A. Rogers, Owner of Mount Hood Lodge

Homer A. Rogers was born in New York in 1881, the son of Lebbeus H. Rogers, an affluent merchant, inventor, traveller, writer, entrepreneur (1846-1933). Homer spent his college preparatory years at a private school in France, then returned to America to attend Yale University and graduate in 1903.

After college he turned his efforts toward the business world. One of his assignments was the liquidation of a large mercantile establishment in St. Louis. In 1909 he yielded to the lure of the apple-growing business in Oregon. Orchards were well established in the lower Hood River Valley, and promoters were touting the possibilities of the upper valley in the Parkdale area. In 1909 he bought property on the road to Cloud Cap Inn, just north of the old Roaring Camp, about three miles south of Parkdale.

Homer Rogers was typical of the wave of high-born easterners who invaded the upper valley at that time, all highly educated men with educated wives, an entirely different breed from the wagon-train pioneers who had homesteaded the land. These college men from Princeton, Yale, Harvard bought land high up in the valley, most of it too high in elevation to raise apples well. It was once remarked as a joke, that the Upper Hood River Valley had more members in the University Club than did Portland

When these people settled on farms, they found they knew little about raising hogs, horses, and apples. One by one they starved out and left the valley in defeat. Homer Rogers lasted longer than most of them. Sidney Babson and Ewer were about the only ones who were able to build fortunes and remain.

Homer Rogers came back with his family to develop his farm in early 1910, staying with the Candee family, just north of the acreage. Soon he had a house under way, living in a tent while the construction was in progress. In May he was out grubbing in the orchard and planting trees. Within a year he was daydreaming about lecturing in the eastern United States and abroad about the marvellous mountain setting of Mount Hood. Trips to nearby Cloud Cap Inn had completely captivated him.

Mountaineering was not new to him. In France he had made many, many ascents in The Alps, progressing to climbs that guides would lead, only if they knew their client to be highly skilled. It was only natural that he was soon taking friends onto the glaciers of Mount Hood.

Trips to Portland by the train were very frequent, and he developed a group of very affluent friends through groups such as the University Club. One early friend was the dynamic attorney, Frank Branch Riley, one of the most gifted speakers in Oregon's history, and who was the last living charter member of The Mazamas. (Died February 23, 1975)

Rogers found that the life of chasing hogs or cows, nursing trees in a zone susceptible to frost, and riding herd on an endless succession of hired men, was a little dull and was proving unprofitable. By 1913 he decided to turn the family home into a small hotel, which he called Mount Hood Lodge. He sold "memberships" to well-to-do

Skiers at Mount Hood Lodge 1916 — Photo Homer Rogers

friends in Portland to apply against food and lodging. Families came up to ski in the wintertime, and for a while he offered the services of a European ski instructor. With a more rugged guest he might take a 15-hour round trip on skis to Elk Meadow or Cooper Spur.

In summertime he led horseback groups to Elk Meadow or Barrett Spur. At times he led ascents of Mount Hood or trips across Eliot or Coe Glaciers. He maintained a high camp near Elk Cove named Rocky Butte Camp. In general the list of clientele was much like a social registry. There were times when aristocratic guests arrived from Portland as the result of Rogers' salesmanship to be very disappointed in the accommodations.

The Lodge was a mixture of American farm and cultured home. On one side of the building was a hugh wood range, but there was a Steinway piano to compensate for it. Some sleeping quarters were in tents outside, yet the living room boasted a voluminous library filled with 2,500 books that were up to the minute. The Victrola had hundreds of records to fill the room with the voices of world-reknown masters.

In 1917 Rogers made a trip to Chicago, New York, Buffalo, Boston, Philadelphia, Washington, St. Louis, Denver, and San Francisco. He sold shares in his hotel operation, showed pictures, and invited many to visit the Hood River Valley and enjoy Mount Hood.

Mark Weygandt was a near neighbor and at times worked for Rogers on the ranch. At times he did some guiding for Mount Hood Lodge. At Cloud Cap Inn it is not clear who was the manager after Horace Mecklem, but there is some indication that Dorsey B. Smith may have held the position. There is also indication of friction between Smith and Rogers in 1916.

Rogers negotiated with William Ladd for a long while to purchase Cloud Cap Inn. Finally Ladd agreed to sell and the deal was made on May 9, 1919. This gave Rogers two hotels to run, and he stepped up his promotion and advertising accordingly.

The financial picture never did brighten much, however. Ever since Rogers had built the house on the farm, life had always been a struggle to find enough money to pay the grocer, the bank, the phone company. Large sums of money came and went, but little remained as profit. He was very thrilled when the Loop Highway was proposed. But instead of bringing him business, Portlanders then just drove right around in one day, and hotel business was actually hurt.

Likewise, when the government ran the new road to Cloud Cap, they then demanded a larger hotel to replace the old inn. Rogers was barely eking out with the old one. Replacing it with a large investment was completely out of the question, and the government forced him to relinquish ownership. At Mount Hood Lodge business dropped to an impossible level, and the farm was eventually lost for non-payment of property taxes. The building and ranch were bought by Grover McKee, and later acquired by Tom Feely.

The hotel burned, was rebuilt as a home, and burned again. Rogers' daughter Kate, Mrs. Jerry McCarthy, repurchased the 190 acre ranch in 1945 for $5,000.

Homer joined Frank Branch Riley on several transcontinental tours in the early Thirties. Riley extolled the beauties and commercial possibilities of Oregon, Washington, and British Columbia, while Rogers skillfully operated the stereoptican projector that showed impressive pictures, incorporating slowly blending colored backgrounds. At that time colored slides, as we know them today, were not developed.

Both of these men were very polished gentlemen and moved in the best society. On one occasion they attended a state banquet in the nation's capitol. Rogers was seated next to the wife of the ambassador from France, and he kept her well entertained during the evening with his fluent command of the French language.

His father spent much of his time at Mount Hood Lodge after it was built. His financial support from time to time undoubtedly saved Homer from bankruptcy. L.H. Rogers wore a great white beard that gave him the appearance of Santa Claus. Many of his hours were spent in building trails and bridges along the creek, developing a garden area he called Venice. These trails were popular with hotel guests. L.H. Rogers did not weather the depression and lost the fortune he had once possessed. In 1933 he died.

Homer followed the insurance business in Portland with Metropolitan Life Insurance Company, prospering with his pleasing and persuasive personality. In later years he ran the Freedom Book Store, then retired. His last days were spent in the Milwaukie Care Center, where he died in 1974.

Donald G. Onthank, Mazama Patriarch

Born at Vineland, New Jersey, September 22, 1892, Onthank was brought to Oregon by his parents to live in Hood River in 1903. His first climb on Mount Hood was August 25, 1912 with Frank Dudley, brother Karl Onthank, and Chet Huggins, who took his car. Leaving home at Hood River at about 2:00 a.m., they drove to the turnaround about a mile below Cloud Cap and started for the ascent of the Cooper Spur Route. He recalls that the snowfields astraddle the route were still a glacier, being noticeably crevassed. They tied into a rope just past the top of the spur and climbed roped all the way to the summit. Returning to the automobile, they drove back to Hood River, being possibly the first team to ever drive up, make the climb, and drive back in the same day.

Onthank worked as a young man for the Pacific Power and Light Co., working and supervising line construction, testing meters and equipment, and reading meters throughout the whole Hood River Valley. College took him to the University of Oregon, where he graduated in 1916.

In 1917 he moved to Portland and made his first Mazama climb, an event that was to change the lives of hundreds of people. Late that summer he took a job as an accountant time-keeper at Camp Lewis. The government was feverishly building the military base, with about 5000 men at work constructing barracks, drill fields, shooting ranges, and warehouses, a major military installation where nothing had stood before. To escape the stifling dust in the area he took a trip one weekend by bus to Mount Rainier, hoping to climb.

It was mid-September; the Park Service had closed all climbing on Labor Day, and he had to content himself with a hike up towards Camp Muir. The day was overcast with a low cloud cover that looked more menacing as he ascended the trail up past Inspiration Point. Finally at Anvil Rock he came upon a group of workmen who were building a fire lookout building out of native rock. The weather had deteriorated severely, and he found them all huddled inside their living tent.

They were well aware of the oncoming storm, and they told him to get out of there RIGHT NOW. But first they quickly gave him some letters to post, and he was on his way. Wearing only street clothing, he soon found what mountain weather can to a human being. He groped his way down the trail in the fog, half running most of the time to keep warm. Back at the hotel desk at Paradise the clerk was incredulous that Onthank had just been at Anvil Rock.

Onthank's first foray on the south side was not a summit climb, merely a climb to Crater Rock and across to the Zigzag Glacier in 1925. At that time the Zigzag was a massive body of ice, not the shrunken remnant that it is today. Readers will recall that Joel Palmer in encountering the glacier in 1845, found it to be a great wall of ice overlying Mississippi Head. In 1926 Onthank returned to the south side, better prepared to climb. Meeting Fred and Bea McNeil on the bus, he got better acquainted with them and joined forces for the summit climb.

In 1927 he was an active participant in the Sunshine Route climb that ended in the death of Dr. Stryker. Don was quite demoralized by the accident, having been only spared from destruction himself by the shortness of the climbing rope. He decided to solo the south side and went to the timberline camp one Saturday night two weeks later. Rising at 2:00 a.m., he ate a fast breakfast and headed for the top, arriving at 6:00 a.m. The wind was cold, and he felt that he was forced to come back down. Later that day as he lounged on the porch at Government Camp Hotel, he wished that he had stayed longer to enjoy the hot summer day on top.

He recalls the mass assault of 1933, when Mazamas climbed four routes to meet at the top for the annual climb. He followed Everett Darr up the first club climb of Wy'east Route. On reaching the summit he met Leon Darling, who had brought a group on Sunshine Route, intending to descend Cooper Spur Route. Darling confided that he had some inadequate climbers and asked for Onthank's help in descending. All was agreed and Darling took the rear of the first rope. By the time the first string had passed, the bottomless tapioca snow was left as a mushy groove for Don's string to follow. Even for good climbers to keep stable footing would have been difficult. But time and again one of the novices would sit back too far toward the slope and slip, pulling the others down with him. Onthank, keeping control with his alpenstock jammed deep into the snow, was the only protection on those very-steep upper slopes that lead out onto the Eliot Headwall and destruction. Many times he thought his time had come, but he was always able to hold.

Don Onthank has become known over the years as "Mister Mazama" to so many members. Serving as president in 1938-1939, he also spent many years of duty on the library, local walks, publications, and membership. He eventually spent more hours in the clubroom offices than most businessmen spend at their own business offices, undoubtedly to the neglect of his livelihood, the insurance business. Attending council meetings for years on end, he overheard the often-dry proceedings with little or no comment, only speaking when no other person could come up with an appropriate comment or suggestion.

Probably no other person has done so much to keep alive the incredible feeling of responsibility by Mazama leaders, a factor that has kept safety paramount within the club. Likewise he perpetually encouraged new people to step forward into leadership, the factor that has kept the club young and dynamic. Finally his efforts were all along the line of the dominant theme of the club, mountaineering; his effort was not squandered on divisive sidelines such as dances and social functions, or the ownership of clubroom and mountain lodge property.

So many people owe to this man the gratitude for steering them properly toward the right clothing and food and equipment, and even companions, when they wanted to climb Mount Hood and came groping for advice. His impact on Mount Hood, as well as on northwest mountaineering has been immense.

Ole Lien, USFS Rescue Expert

Born July 31, 1898, at Beloit, Wisconsin, Ole B. Lien was the son of Halvor Lien, a railroad employee. Halvor followed railroad work and moved to Astoria in 1907, then Oregon City in 1909. In 1912 he homesteaded at Two Rivers, a locale now inundated by dams on the Columbia between Pasco and Othello, Washington.

In 1915 he died leaving his wife with five children, 16 head of cattle, and four horses. Mrs. Lien moved her family back to Oregon in 1916, taking a boat down the Columbia to Portland, and settling at Tigard. Ole graduated from High School there, then entered teacher training at the University of Oregon. His education was cut off just short of graduation.

His first job was with Pacific Coast Cone Company in Portland. On September 1, 1923, he went to Government Camp for a picnic. On arriving he met Lige Coalman, who offered him a position on a climb of Mount Hood for a $4 guide fee. Ole accepted, thus beginning a long career of climbing, said to be well over 400 climbs.

From about 1929 there was a great rivalry at Mount Hood to be first on the summit each New Year. Ole Lien figured heavily in these escapades, being in the first party on six consecutive years. Beginning May, 1929, he and James Mount began to climb each month of the year. Mount quit after 16 consecutive monthly climbs, then resumed later, but Lien kept up the effort until he had achieved 31 consecutive ascents. In January of 1933 he began a new series of 14, missing only four months in five years.

He was a member of The Mazamas from 1924 to 1960, a very notable member of Wy'east Climbers, and a stalwart of the Mount Hood Ski Patrol. His only accident was a 200 foot slide down the Chute on the South Side Route of Mount Hood, self arrested just in time to avoid a crevasse. There was never a major accident on any climb of which he was a member, although many, many times he helped evacuate victims of ski and mountaineering tragedies.

Ole Lien 1933 — Photo Joe Leuthold

In the late Twenties he worked for B.P. John Furniture Company, remaining there about ten years. Employment with Everett Darr at the Mountain Shop in Portland occupied him a short while; then he began his career with the Forest Service. For 15 summers he manned the fire lookout station at Lone Fir. After Fred VanDyke left Timberline Lodge at the beginning of World War Two, Lien and Colonel Palmer shared the duty as caretakers. It was not uncommon for them to walk to Zigzag from the lodge at that time. They kept the building dark, with only enough heat to keep pipes from freezing, and spent most of their time in one small area.

In an economy wave October 13, 1949, the Forest Service for a while placed him on temporary status, with two or three days of work per week. He augmented his income by working for the management of Timberline Lodge. Thousands of skiers can recall seeing Ole or Colonel Palmer directing traffic in the lower parking lot.

During his climbing career he made over 400 ascents of Mount Hood, a great many of them in the company of Rafferty's dog, Ranger. Later Lien had a small dog named Butch, part pekingese, which climbed with him.

As a resident of Portland he was a member of United Bretheren Church. Having a very good tenor voice, he took vocal lessons and sang with Rosaria Chorus, King Chorus, and his own church choir. One of his favorite selections was "Trees." When he began work with the Forest Service he lived in various government shacks and houses at Government Camp and Zigzag, too far from Portland to continue his singing.

On November 7, 1950, the day that Battle Axe Inn burned, Ole was living at Government Camp. He hurried in to help save equipment and make sure there were no people remaining in the building. The fire levelled the inn in less than an hour, and burned most of the clothing off him. He had to be treated for burns afterward. Lien figured in the news again in 1955, when Slaney went broke and Timberline Lodge was locked to the public. A news photo showed him in the darkened hallway, cigar in mouth, and using a candle to find his way.

Retirement from the Forest Service came on December 22, 1960. He moved to Portland for a time, living in hotels, then occupied his sister's vacation cabin on the banks of the Sandy River just west of the Brightwood bridge. The disastrous flood of 1964 swept the cabin away, and he moved to a house on NE 29th between Alberta and Prescott in Portland.

In April of 1972 he suffered a stroke. His sister, Ingrid Malo, was alerted by the owners of a nearby cleaning shop who had not seen Ole taking his usual daily walks. Mrs. Malo found him unable to move in his bed. That began a 10-month stay at Emanuel Hospital, where he was treated for ulcers and other complications. Ole Lien died there January 26, 1973, at age 74. His hospital bill of $18,038 was paid by Forest Service insurance.

Ole had one brother, Nils, who died as a young man, and three sisters, Hilma Gaarde, Esther Fischer, and Ingrid Malo. His funeral service was commemorated with the rendition of "Trees."

Everett L. Darr

It was New Year's Day 1927. Battle-Axe Inn crawled with mountain men, loggers, hiking clubs, police, rangers, and seekers of excitement, as the building was being used as search headquarters for lost climber, Leslie Brownlee and a lost skier, Calvin White. One of the curious who came to Government Camp that day to view the water-soaked searchers, who came into Battle-Axe and flopped down on the floor in exhaustion, was Everett Darr.

Almost 20, he had finished school at Portland's Lincoln High School in 1925 and had begun work as a secretary in the Oregon office of the Portland Cement Association. Darr was born in Memphis, Tennessee, March 3, 1907. His father, who had been a plantation owner and lost his holdings in the depression of 1907, died shortly after Everett's birth.

Visiting the mountain that first day whetted his appetite to try skiing, and the following week he was back again to rent a pair of skis. He reminisces about paying 35¢ for using a pair of skis for one hour, a double-grooved set 7½ feet long, appropriate for jumping and little else. The bottoms were waxed with hot painted paraffin, and Everett complained that he couldn't walk up hill on them.

"That is to keep you here. We don't want you walking away with them," the man behind the counter told him, remembering Calvin White's nearly fatal ski trip to timberline the week before. This exposure to ski rental was the first for Everett Darr, the man who would later himself sell or rent many thousands of skis.

Once exposed to the rugged mountain life, he found himself bitten by the ski "bug" and later by the fascination of climbing. By 1931 the Wy'east club had formed as an aftermath of the Lincoln High School Hiking Club, to which he had belonged. Although not a charter member, he joined shortly after its formation, assimilating the Wy'east all-weather approach to enjoying Mount Hood.

Skiing in those days included jumping and cross-country. Rope tows were to come a little later. But most of the sport skiers took the trail to the timberline area, had lunch, then explored the slopes returning to Government Camp. Darr helped the Wy'east group with the construction of their cabin just below Pucci's glade at timberline, a haven in the wilderness usually reached long after dark every Saturday night, and a base for exploration in the higher country.

Darr got his first taste in the building of ski tows in 1935 when he worked with the Ski Committee of The Mazamas in erecting a tow on Mazama Hill, a respectable slope at the end of the Alpine Ski Trail, that leads down toward Westleg Road above Mazama Lodge.

Joining The Mazamas in 1931, Darr began to take part in their climbing activity, dividing his time with Wy'east Club. The following year with James Mount and Ralph Calkin, he made the first ascent of the Wy'east Route that runs from the top of Steel Cliff over onto the steep eastern face, high on the mountain. The lower part of this route lay a little south of the Newton Clark route that Will Langille used for a normal route in the days before Cooper Spur was climbed.

Labor Day weekend of 1933, Don Burkhart, Mazama and charter member of Wy'east Climbers, led John Thomas and Davis McCamant on a climb of the east face of Mount Jefferson. When they had not returned on Tuesday, Curtis Ijames and Perlee Payton organized a rescue party including Darr, Ralph Calkin, James Harlow, Ray Atkeson, Barry James, Clyde Hildreth, and Ed Lenz, all competent mountaineers. On Thursday, four searchers climbed the route to the summit, establishing that the three mountaineers had not arrived there.

Friday, Darr was searching high on the steep ice with Grant McConnell, Mount, and Calkin, when he spotted a glimmer of a yellow knapsack. Simultaneously he and McConnell saw a crampon protruding from the snow. They dug the bodies from the snow; Darr can remember to this day carrying the frozen corpse of their dear friend, Burkhart, down the glacier to Jefferson Park and sleeping there in the tent with his corpse that night. The following day packhorses took the bodies out ten miles to the roadhead at Ollalie Lake.

On Labor Day weekend in 1935 he was an accident victim himself while leading a Mazama climb on Three Fingered Jack in the Central Cascades. In the chimney on the summit pinnacle, a rock gave way under his foot, and he dropped 30 feet in two 15-foot bounces to sprain his ankle and cut his face and body. The climbing party got him safely around the gendarme and carried him out to the car.

Despite his great activity with Wy'east Climbers, Everett Darr found time to be very prominent in climbing activity with The Mazamas, leading many climbs and serving on the Climbing Committee in 1934-35-36. In 1936 he was committee chairman.

Eventually he became much better known for his business activity at Mount Hood. When he and Ida Zacher were marred in 1936 they began to collaborate on designing a new backpack. They made and sold a great many and began to manufacture sleeping bags as well. In 1937 they opened a store at 628 NE Broadway in Portland to facilitate sales. Although it was a sideline at first, business was so active by 1938, that he resigned his position with the cement association to spend full time in the store.

Times were difficult in 1937, and Glen Asher was laid off at B.P. Johns Furniture factory. He proposed that Darr put in a line of skis for him to manage. The department did well, and in time they sold all types of ski and mountaineering clothing and equipment.

In about 1944 Darr made an agreement with Adrian J. Johanns to buy the Summit Ski Tow. Johanns claimed that he had $8,000 invested in the facility at the time, but agreed to sell for less. Although the experts used the steeper hills, Summit had a great appeal for the beginners, just as it does today.

Another acquisition of property was made in Government Camp. Darr wanted to buy the 200' x 200' business frontage at the site of the old Government Camp Hotel, on the corner of the old highway main street and Multorpor Road. He went in to see Lyman Latourette, city attorney of Portland, who owned the property. Latourette told him that he might as well buy the 55 acres that lay between the lot and Multorpor Ski Area; the price would be the same — $5,000. But first he wanted to be sure that the buyer was genuinely interested in Government Camp, not just a speculator. Darr qualified.

The property had on it a long, narrow building lying alongside what is now Multorpor Road, finished inside by Hjalmar Hvam in about 1936, the object of much difficult hand work and scrimping along with the least possible materials. The building had been used by Boyd French since Hjalmar Hvam had moved his ski business across the street with Ole Langerud. Darr decided to move some of his own skis in for rentals. It was wartime, and no new skis were available. He had only the equipment from the Mountain Shop in Portland. During the early part of the war he went to Washington D.C. to serve as a civilian with the 10th Mountain Division and other alpine training units.

He returned from duty with the military service in the middle of the war. Ida had been keeping the store open in Portland, and he came back to help. On weekends they operated the shop at Government Camp in a limited manner.

After the war, business at Summit and at the Mountain Shop in Government Camp was so demanding, that he sold the store in Portland to George Dunning in 1947 and moved his family to Government Camp. In the same year he put a crew to work building a large new addition to the building in Government Camp. Wartime shortages made nails and hardware very hard to procure; even lumber was in tight supply. Even so, the addition was put up at very low cost in comparison to today's prices. Working on the job were Glen Asher, Leo Burgess, Reuben Meier, and Robert Hvam. For almost 20 years that building was the focal point of Government Camp, with busses bringing in loads of teen-agers to rent equipment, buy wax or goggles, and eat doughnuts made in the machine across from the front door. At the end of the day a few of them would end up with broken legs in the ski patrol room that Darr supported at the east end of the building.

In 1965 the Oregon State Highway Commission built a straight by-pass that cut out the curve by the Ski Bowl and gave through traffic the chance to avoid the provoking congestion of automobiles and pedestrians in Government Camp. One junction of this by-pass is at Summit, the other just east of Ski Bowl. On the latter Darr erected a gasoline station and a large, new ski shop and restaurant. The building is a handsome 48' x 62' two-store stone structure. The walls of the coffee shop are made of Ichnolite, a fossil stone from Malheur County, Oregon, that shows prehistoric worm borings on its surface. In recent years Everett and Ida Darr have followed the hobby of finding and polishing agatized material. Their shop now displays hundreds of polished agates set in many interesting ways.

Joe Darr, their son born in 1941, grew up in Government Camp and became very prominent in ski competition in the west. At present he is the manager of the Multorpor Ski Area. Another son, Pete, and daughter, Lori, are also active in the family business.

Hartwell W. Palmer

A well known personality around Timberline Lodge was the Colonel, a real colonel from the calvalry with 40 years of US Army duty. He had enlisted on October 18, 1893, in the Iowa National Guard and worked up the line of command.

In 1937 he joined the Forest Service as an engineering aide and did an analysis in detail of the trails, streams, and vegetation of the south side of Mount Hood. Timberline Lodge opened for business in early 1938, and that summer he operated the horse concession there. Later he was the lecturer and chief guide at the lodge. When the Forest Service put Timberline Lodge in moth balls for the duration of World War Two, Colonel Palmer stayed on with Ole Lien and tended the building. It was not at all uncommon to see one or the other in Zigzag or Government Camp, having hiked down from the lodge to get groceries or reading material.

When the war was over, the Colonel took charge of the traffic control at Timberline Lodge, and thousands of skiers knew him as the tough old man they had better not cross. He also acted as an observer with the United States Weather Service. He was interested in the history of Mount Hood and each year conducted a ceremony at the grave of the Unknown Pioneer Woman on the Barlow Road below Buzzard Point. Upon his retirement with the Forest Service on January 17, 1954, he pursued his hobby of collecting historic data. In 1962 he celebrated his 88th birthday at a party at Timberline Lodge.

One of the truly great skiers of the United States and a well-known personality around Mount Hood is Hjalmar Hvam, born at Kongsberg, Norway, where a youngster could step out the door and walk to any one of a dozen ski jump hills in five minutes. Little children grow up on skis there. Discontent with his baby skis, he learned to borrow the longer ones of his older brothers while they were in school. It was only natural for him to enter children's jumping tournaments, although his father thought it was too dangerous and disapproved. Hjalmar was born November 16, 1902; at the age of 12 he had won his first tournament.

At 21, he moved to Saskatchewan with his brother, Ingvald, doing summer farm work and attending school in the winter. He was encouraged to become a teacher, but the two moved on to British Columbia, working in sawmills and lumber camps near Vancouver. The next move was to Portland in 1927; Hjalmar stacked boards for Multnomah Lumber and Box Company. In Oregon, he got the chance to try on skis again.

On the Sunday between Christmas of 1928 and New Year of 1929 the chance came up to visit Government Camp as the guest of Ole Haugen. Haugen, who was the old man of Cascade Ski Club, had leased the Multorpor jumping hill from the Latourette family; his two brothers, Lars and Siebert, had spent several days building jump platforms out of snow and grooming the landing run. The day of the tournament was plagued by a snow storm. Gloomy contenders stood watching the heavy snowflakes fall, not making any moves toward jumping.

"Isn't anyone going to jump?" Hjalmar asked Kaare Schafstad, one of the jumpers.

"Not in this weather. I don't think anyone would jump today, if they paid him five dollars."

"I'd almost be willing to pay five dollars."

"Then go ahead," Kaare told him, however he was not willing to loan Hjalmar his skis.

He was able to borrow a pair from the old man of the hill, John Anderson. It had been five years since he had "boards" on his feet, but all the old skills came back instantly. The wind whistled past his face on the upper run, then he hit the takeoff and leaped outwards through the heavy falling snow, his body poised in the classic jumping form so common on the hills at Kongsberg. He hit the landing run and glided to a smooth turn and stop.

The spectators and contestants alike knew a real competitor when they saw him. Hjalmar had an invitation to jump in the tournament the following week. He, at first, demurred but then accepted, becoming a legendary champion in his own time, and competing under the colors of Cascade Ski Club for many years.

Norwegians are naturals at cross country technique, but the running of slalom courses through control flag "gates" was a new idea to Hjalmar. Some of his friends in Cascade Ski Club encouraged him to try out the sport in 1934, and he entered the Oregon Slalom Championships. He borrowed a pair of downhill skis, different from either jumping or cross country types, from Harald Lee, the club president, and entered the race. Hunching down low on a long, straight run, he picked up speed, veered up a wall under a cornice, then down to catch the turns through two gates. Ahead lay the "flush", several closely spaced turns.

"I had to jump like a goat to get through that flush," he recalls, but he won the best time on

Hjalmar Hvam and his wife, Vera 1936 — Photo Hvam

two runs of the course. From that time he quickly picked up finesse in his most recently acquired form of skiing.

On April 19, 1936, he entered the Silver Skis Race, a 3.18-mile course on Mount Rainier from 10,000-foot Camp Muir down to Edith Creek at 4,500 feet. There were 51 contestants that day, and by the time Hvam made his run, the course was strewn with broken skis, poles, and hats. He gave the 1,500 spectators a thrill as he dodged obstacles, including one of his competitors who had fallen on the track. The Silver Skis race was later discontinued because of its dangerous nature.

In 1936 he swept the field at Mount Baker, an unheard of feat, winning first place in Slalom, Giant Slalom, Cross Country, and Jumping. In each category the competition was fierce, with specialists present who excelled in only one event. He was not able to join the United States team in the winter Olympic Games in 1936, because he had not yet completed citizenship requirements.

Percy Bucklin of the Hood River Crag Rats told of being a gate keeper on a control-point in one of the cross-country races at Government Camp in the Thirties. Stationed by the large ditch at the foot of Multorpor Mountain, he watched the competitors come roaring off the hill, check their speed, and side-step through the wide ditch. Then came Hjalmar Hvam, not checking his speed. "Surely he won't try to jump it," Bucklin mused, for the ditch was too wide. Hjalmar boomed up to the edge at high speed, stuck his poles down and executed a perfect gelandesprung. Landing on the other side, he flashed off across the meadows with no loss of momentum. It was such perfect technique that won him a room full of skiing trophies.

Good skiing has always required clamping the boot firmly to the ski. Early bindings were "bear traps" with inflexible front clamps and strong cables to hold down the heel. Broken legs were common, and for several years Hvam had been considering the idea of a releasable safety binding, but some mechanical features were never resolved. Hjalmar won the Golden Rose Race in June, 1937, at Timberline Lodge. After the race, he and a friend were jumping a cornice, when Hjalmar fell and broke his leg.

Coming out of the ether, he jumped up in the hospital bed, the idea for the safety binding at last clearly fixed in his mind. A nurse brought pencil and paper, and the sketch was made at once. There were several refinements in the course of field testing; he patented the first safety bindings in 1939 and made a change in 1940. Hvam sold over 15,000 safety bindings before leaving the business because of the harrassment of modern business life. The binding is no longer made, although it has a much better safety record than any of the other types, all of which are more complicated and costly and operate on a different principle. Hjalmar's bindings have an automatic detenting system which increases the holding power as the user "edges" his skis, so that the ski does not fall off while the skier is rounding a turn.

Unfortunately, safety bindings did not save him from future fractures. The broken leg did not set properly, and in 1938 he broke it again. In 1939 he broke it the third time on a gentle run into a snowbank. After that the bone set properly, and he had no further trouble.

It is regretful that he never was able to compete in jumping at Holmenkollen in Norway, considered to be the ultimate in tourneys. In 1952 he managed the United States jumping team for the Olympic Games; during that trip he was able to make many unofficial jumps on the hill.

Hjalmar's early working days in Oregon fell at the time of the great depression that began in 1929. By 1930 he began to get summer work with the Forest Service, continuing with it until 1937. Work was on trail construction, reforestation, fire patrols, and work in various guard stations. He helped put the "life line" rope on Cooper Spur and on the south side Chute for two or three years, then helping to coil it in the fall for storage in the summit lookout cabin.

Hjalmar recalls a day in 1937 when he was on duty at Phlox Point Guard Station at the end of the timberline road. A lone climber from the eastern states left his car there and climbed Mount Hood. At dark the car was still there. Hjalmar called Boyd French, Jr., the guard at Lone Fir, and the two hiked up the mountain on that warm, moonlit night to find the missing climber. On top of the mountain, they found him huddled in the summit cabin, waiting to view the splendor of the sunrise. The two forest service guards had some splendid comments for the thoughtless climber who had neglected to tell them of his plans.

Winter work for several years was catch-as-catch-can in machine shops, lumber yards, and retail stores. In 1934 he ran a sporting goods department for Lipman Wolfe Company. In 1935 he worked on percentage with Jim Smith in a tennis and golf shop near 5th and Stark in Portland. In 1936 he took the ski concession at Olds, Wortman and King. In that year he married Vera Anderson.

It was in 1936 that he opened business at Government Camp. Lyman Latourette had a long, narrow shell of a building erected on the site previously occupied by the old Government Camp Hotel Annex. It was a breezy structure with many cracks to let in the winter wind. With the help of his brother Robert, Hjalmar tightened up the building and finished the inside for a ski rental shop. The rental business was only a weekend operation, and Robert helped out when Hjalmar was out of town on competitive meets.

When Ole Langerud put up the big two-story ski shop on the north side of the street in 1938, Hjalmar moved over with him, and the two were partners for years. When World War 2 closed down travel he left Ole alone in the ski shop in 1942 and took employment with Monarch Forge and Machine Works. The war over in 1945, he renewed his partnership with Ole and also established a new ski shop in Portland in 1946. This was at 21 NW 23rd Place, in a new building just under the cliffs where Burnside Street enters the canyon leading over the west hills. In 1949 he left business at Mount Hood, concentrating on the Portland store. Vera worked with him, selling and keeping books. In 1960 they sold the store to George Howell, retiring to their 15-acres just off Scholls Ferry Road south of Beaverton.

Hjalmar Hvam, tall and moustached, is thin and trim at 72 as he was in the days when he stacked lumber. It takes a very good skier to even keep up with him as he carves sweeping turns on the steep walls of the Ski Bowl. He shoots a competitive game of golf several times a week at the Portland Golf Club. In 1971 he took second place in combined events at the U.S. National Alpine Championship tourney conducted at Sun Valley, Idaho.

Joe Leuthold, Outstanding Mountaineer

Joe Leuthold was born February 21, 1906 at Stans, Switzerland, coming to the United States with his parents at age nine. In crossing the North Atlantic the family recalls seeing the iceberg that sunk the liner Titanic May 7, 1915. So many passengers gathered on one side of the ship, that the captain found it necessary to prevent listing by dispersing the crowd.

At an early age Leuthold started work for Portland automobile dealers, Wentworth and Irwin, becoming a body and fender man. His first climb was on Mount Hood on August 4, 1929 with Alec Gill, Charles Beck, and Walter Staheli. He became a member of Wy'east Climbers, soon being known as a skier and climber. He was involved in the building of the ski tow on Mazama Hill in 1935, reputed to be one of the very first tows. When the Ski Patrol was organized, Joe was one of the first members.

A member of the Climbing Committee of The Mazamas, he became chairman in 1939. During the years he made 208 total ascents, 64 being on Mount Hood. This piled up a tremendous number of leads during his career. In 1938 he and William Wood, a fellow Climbing Committee member, co-led the first Mazama winter climb, an unfortunate venture that finally resulted in the death by hypothermia of two climbers, Roy Varney and Russell Gueffroy. In the years from 1938 to 1940 he participated in and led many rescues and searches for skiers and climbers.

Leuthold achieved several first ascents of northwest peaks, such as Bonanza Peak, Tupshin Peak, Wy'east Mountain, Riddle Peak, White Goat Mountain, and Mount Flora. In Oregon he was in the first party to ascend St. Peter's Dome with Eldon Metzger, Everett and Ida Darr, Glen Asher, and James Mount. The ascent on June 23, 1940 culminated many grueling weekends of frustrating, slow movement on the lower bands of treacherous, flaking rock. The following week he returned with Metzger and the Darrs, Ralph Calkin, Virginia Cresmers, Grant and Jane McConnell, Herb Rasor, Ralph Wiese, and Don Onthank.

After a most illustrious record as a soldier with the 10th Mountain Division in Italy, Leuthold returned to Oregon and went to work for his old friend, Everett Darr. He ran the Summit Ski Area for Darr since 1948, as well as helping new lifts and tows in summertime.

On June 23, 1946, Laurita Abendroth became his wife. Their daughter, Toni, born in 1958, has become well known in US skiing competition.

The Mazamas in post-war years knew him as a friendly and competent climb leader, always willing to help someone. He was very much the same in kindly cooperation as had been the legendary Elijah Coalman of forty years before. He carried a large pack full of equipment, but his friends always noticed that his pockets bulged with items that would not fit in the pack. There was always some food or an article of extra clothing for another climber. In 1964 The Mazamas presented him with a plaque, not just for climbing, but for LEADING the 16 major northwest peaks.

On December 12, 1965, Joe Leuthold died of brain cancer after several months of illness. His

Joe Leuthold 1934 — Photo Leuthold

funeral was attended by a host of friends, a great many from The Mazamas and Wy'east Climbers. On April 21, 1968, he was commemorated by a bronze plaque indicating his membership in those two organizations plus the Ski Patrol and MORESCO. A group of forty friends attended a ceremony at Timberline, then boarded four snow cats to take the plaque to Illumination Rock where it was cemented into place on the south side of a small needle of rock that stands alone in Illumination Saddle. The work was done by Charles Lake, Multorpor Lift manager and his brother William Lake. Laurita and Toni took part in the ceremony. 82-year-old John D. Scott attended the trip.

In December 1970, the Oregon Geographic Names Board denoted the chute above Reid Glacier as Leuthold Couloir. The hour-glass-shaped chute was previously known as West Side Route, and before that as the Avalanche Route.

Percy Bucklin

A Hood River resident, he was born in Rockford, Minnesota, March 13, 1899. His parents moved to Hood River in 1911. His first climb on Mount Hood was in 1919 with Mace Baldwin guiding. He served in the US Army during World War One, returning to become a life-long member of The American Legion.

Bucklin was one of the organizing members of the Hood River Ski Club. Skiing activities over the years led him to be Secretary-Treasurer of the Pacific Northwest Ski Association (PNSA) at the time of its organization in 1930. He served often as judge in jumping competition and as a race official in many down-hill and slalom events.

A member of the Crag Rats since the moment of their inception, he participated in many rescues, searches, and climbs with the club.

His occupation was a banker, working for the First National Bank of Hood River until 1937, when it was sold to the statewide First National Bank of Oregon. He stayed with that firm until retirement, becoming manager and assistant vice-president at the Hood River branch.

Percy Bucklin circa 1921.

Gnarl Ridge Shelter — Photo USFS

Oregon Alpine Club, First Mountain Club

Early trips to Mount Hood for illumination resulted in the storing of some equipment at the drug store of John M. Breck, Jr., a crippled man who walked on a crutch, nevertheless who attained an early reputation as an experienced mountaineer. The drug store became a focal point for the alpinists in Portland, such as Will Steel, O.C. Yocum, N.W. Durham, Martin W. Gorman, F.C. Little, J. Francis Drake, Charles H. Sholes, Charles H. Gove, Dr. J.M. Keene, Dr. Charles F. Adams, and others.

Some of the men in the group formulated the plan for Oregon Alpine Club. A preliminary meeting was held in Steel's office on September 14, 1887. O.C. Yocum, then an East Portland resident, was chosen temporary chairman. An open meeting was called for Friday, September 23, at which time formal organization was made. Original structure was as follows:

Geologist	Prof. Thomas Condon
Ontologist	Capt. S.S. Douglass
Entomologist	Prof. O.B. Johnson
Botanist	Prof. E.L. Henderson
Mineralogist	Prof. Herbert Lang
Room Committee	George H. Himes
	Dr. Osman Royal
	William G. Steel
Membership	William G. Steel
	George H. Himes
	George Breck
	Capt. S.S. Douglass

Initiation was set at $1 and monthly dues at 50¢. It was the idea of Steel, Yocum, and the other mountaineers, **that the club should be limited** to those who had climbed a glacial peak. The newspaper notice about the organizational meeting brought out 75 people. However, mountaineering soon began to be of second rank interest in the group, many of whom were "telescope climbers", viewing Mount Hood from a Portland office building.

On October 5, a special meeting was held to effect incorporation, and a serious discussion was held concerning purchase of a collection of Eskimo artifacts to place in a museum that the club would operate.

One of the first efforts of the club was to attempt the curbing of wanton slaying of deer and elk. The practice was illegal, and the club proposed a $100 reward for information leading to arrest and conviction.

The club began to present lectures by mountaineers, explorers, and all sorts of interesting personalities of the day. On March 16, 1888, the club moved into new rooms in the Portland Savings Bank Building, overlooking a panorama of three peaks. The main room 28' x 25' was floored with a velvet rug.

One of the functions of the club in those times was to publicize Mount Hood, Portland, and the Northwest to the populated eastern states. This seems wantonly wasteful to residents today, who do not want hordes of tourists trampling down their wilderness. The Oregon Alpine Club probably arrived at its pinnacle of glory, when it presented the noted author, Charles Dickens in May of 1888, closely followed by the humorist Robert J. Burdette.

CLUB PLACED SUMMIT BOX

In the summer of 1888 the club placed the first summit box atop Mount Hood. It was soon crushed by a shifting rock rolled by vandals and replaced. Trips to Mount Hood for heliography and illumination, as well as for climbing for pleasure, all fell within the activities of the Alpine Club. The group received many, many columns of print in the newspapers covering every move they made at Mount Hood, every reading, lecture or concert in Portland. Through 1888 and 1889 Steel and the Oregon Alpine Club did a lot to tighten up the enforcement of the game laws, especially near Grants Pass and other southern Oregon communities. The scientists of the club entered their works at the Industrial Fair in Portland in 1889. A museum building was under planning.

On November 12, 1889 the club adopted a new constitution, expanding its field of activity and interest. President D.P. Thompson appointed new committees. Game Protection was under J.W. Whalley, R.E. Bybee, and H.T. Hudson. Museum was under B.J. Bretherton, Dr. Cardwell, and John Gill. Exploration was in charge of William G. Steel, Martin W. Gorman, and Edward Casey. The Portland Camera Club was taken in en toto and became a committee under W.W. Bretherton. Discussion was held on renting a dwelling for clubrooms and museum or in building a new one.

An October, 1889 *Oregonian* feature told of the Olympic Peninsula, an area about 2500 square miles, a rugged mountain wonderland that had never been trodden by a white man. In 1890 many stories filled the papers about trips to the periphery of the Peninsula, and one account on June 5 told of a six-month trip by S.C. Gillman and his father C.A. Gillman an ex-lieutenant governor of Minnesota. The pair had crossed the rugged area in a daring trip that began in December. An August story told of a six-man group of men under James H. Christie.

The Oregon Alpine Club was busy planning a trip to the Peninsula in conjunction with the US Army. Lieutenant J.P. O'Neill, later a general, headed the contingent and debarked at Lilliwaup Creek on July 2. The party included Colonel Lindsay, Professor L.F. Henderson, B.J. Bretherton, S.E. Ingraham, Sergeants Yates, Marsh, and Hoffner, and Privates Bariens, Krause, Kranichfeldt, Hughes, Higgins, Fisher and Danton. Leader O'Neill had previously penetrated well into the Peninsula in 1885 from Port Angeles.

The expedition cut trails and explored the Skokomish, Duckabush, Quinault and Qillayute

River areas. Much of the purpose was to assay the value of the area for timber and mining. On October 5, the Hoquiam Board of Trade held a very fancy banquet for the victorious party at the Hoquiam Hotel. Back in Portland, the celebrated Army lieutenant gave lectures and was guest of honor at a great banquet at the Marquam.

An 1891 story in January tells of the intent of the club to sell stock at $25 per share to raise $10,000. This would allow the splendid museum collection to be displayed, rather than being stored in boxes. An elegant clubhouse on a prominent hill was the goal, where a $1000 telescope could be used to advantage. On April 15, Secretary B.J. Bretherton mentioned a new organization, the Alpine Association, which when properly funded would replace or buy out the Oregon Alpine Club. But it was all too late, and the club was already virtually bankrupt.

The Oregonian of December 28, 1891 ran a story on Oregon Alpine Club with the headline **"DIED A NATURAL DEATH."** It stated that the club had not held a meeting for a year and recounted the formation with Steel, Yocum, Breck, and Gove. It reported that Steel had paid $1000 out of his own pocket to keep the club going at the last of 1890. Steel said, "I can't keep up the club any longer."

On January 22, 1891 the newspapers stated that the club had suddenly sprung to life. President George B. Markle announced the purchase of a lot between Morrison and Oak somewhere around Eighth Street. A club house and museum were projected. Three days later Markle sent a wire to congressman Binger Hermann in Washington D.C., offering the services of a thousand well-equipped mountaineers to the U.S. government in the event of an impending war with Chili. In three more days an article in *The Oregonian* chided Steel and Markle. The war had not materialized, and the editors consoled them about their loss of chance for glory.

In April 1891, the stockholders of Oregon Alpine Club Association met in Steel's office to elect directors and adopt a seal and badge. The seal used a goat's head and alpenstock, fish rod, and rifle. Louis W. Akin who later suggested the mountain goat for The Mazamas, was a member of the committee along with Steel and John Gill.

Evidently the movement became so dead that the newspapers deigned to report on it. Most of the active and prominent members began to plan the club which succeeded it, The Mazamas.

The Mazamas, Eighty Years on the Ascent

A PUBLIC ANNOUNCEMENT

Portland, Oregon, March 12, 1894

"On Monday evening, March 19th, a meeting will be held in the office of Sholes, Lake and Mullon, in the Portland Savings Bank building to consider a plan for organizing a Mountain Climbing Club on the summit of Mount Hood, during the coming summer, and spreading a banquet at the time. The list of charter members will be limited to those then and there present, and, no one will be permitted to join thereafter, except such as have climbed to the summit of an acceptable snow-capped mountain. All mountain climbers and lovers of nature are cordially invited to be present and participate in the proceedings. If you cannot be personally present we would be glad to hear from you and consider any suggestions you may choose to make."

W.G. Steel
C.H. Sholes
J. Francis Drake
F.C. Little
O.C. Yocum

At this meeting, Martin W. Gorman, a member of the organizational Executive Committee, was appointed to make research on a name for the club, with the idea of using an Indian or native name for Mountain Goat *(Halpocerus Montanus).* In Mexico it was *Mazama*, *Mazame*, *Macame*, *teuthlamacama.* The Klickitat Indians called *Pow-yan-in;* the Nitlakapamuks — *Swhoy-clatz;* the Cheyenes — *Ohonawa'ksan or Hohona'u-wakaska;* the Arapahoes — *Atta;* Klamaths — *Ko-il;* and so on through a wealth of unpronounceable native names. The Executive Committee agreed on the euphonious Spanish name, Mazama.

From that day forward, The Mazamas have blended their history with that of Mount Hood. In the United States only the Appalachian Club and Sierra Club are older mountaineering societies. The club has maintained an amazing vitality over the years, due in fact to the continued interest in mountaineering and the constant encouragement of new and enthusiastic young people to become involved with the leadership. Numerous other alpine clubs have been spun off The Mazamas, as members moved away and wished to enjoy a local club to satisfy their needs. Some of these are The Seattle Mountaineers, Chemeketans of Salem, Obsidians of Eugene, Angoras of Astoria, Skyliners of Bend.

The date of the charter climb was set on Thursday, July 19, 1894. On the previous weekend, wagons began to roll out of Portland toward Mount Hood. Some went to Cloud Cap Inn on the north side, but most of the aspirants converged on a big encampment at Government Camp. A photograph looking toward Multorpor Mountain shows the Mazama camp, American flag flapping in the breeze, wagons parked in front of huge wall tents, and tethered horses switching flies with their tails.

An entertaining manuscript by Lucia S. Drum Fear tells of her travelling with four other girls up from Portland, arriving by wagon on Saturday. On Monday they hiked up the track to "Camp

Mazama" at timberline and returned. By that evening 106 people had gathered in the clearing at Government Camp. On Tuesday they took short hikes to tone their muscles for the coming climb. By that night 250 were gathered around the campfire for an old-fashioned bean bake and singing.

CAMPED AT TIMBERLINE

On Wednesday everyone moved to timberline. In mid afternoon, Charles Sholes and three men left with their equipment and pulling a toboggan with a load of red fire for illumination. Enroute to Crater Rock they left part of the load. By Wednesday night, 228 people were at Camp Mazama, but others arrived later, and some were camped in little groups away from the throng.

At 10:00 p.m. the singing around the campfire came to an end when notes of the bugler were heard, playing "*America.*" Then came "*Nearer my God to Thee*", and the sounding of "*Taps.*" Most enjoyed a good night of sleep until reveille at 2:00 a.m. Mrs. Fear recalled the ominous weather, a thunderstorm that rumbled and crashed out to the south, although overhead it was clear.

The overall climb was divided into small teams, and hers left timberline at 2:45. The camp was a mass of activity, some groups not leaving until 8:00 a.m. Weather was sporadic; her group was enveloped in a cloud at 6:00 with hailstones falling. By 9:00 the sun was showing, and her group was high on the mountain.

STORM SPOILED "BANQUET"

The first group reached the top at 9:00 a.m., the last, five hours later. Mrs. Fear's group topped out at about 11:30, but no one stayed long. The bitter wind and threatening clouds were not condusive to dallying on the summit. **The Mazamas did have their organizational meeting as planned,** and the club came into official existence. However, the "banquet" planned for the summit was abandoned for the old mountaineers' game of "run-for-your-life", as often happens when weather turns bad. Seldom were more than 25 on the summit at once, although during the day 155 men and 38 women climbed Mount Hood. One hundred seventy one made it from Camp Mazama on the south side and 22 climbed Cooper Spur Route from the north. Of these, 105 signed for membership and became charter members of The Mazamas.

There are so many sidelights to the organizational climb. Max M. Shillock who travelled by horse and wagon with his wife, Grace Clark, Dr. Andrew C. Smith, and J.H. Hawley, complained bitterly to the press about the bad conditions at Government Camp. Meals at the Yocum dining room were 25¢, but the waiting lines were very long. Oats for the horses were scarce, but hay sold for an incredible $30 a ton.

The camp lay deep in stifling dust kicked up by horses and wagons. The horses attracted swarms of flies. Mr. Shillock felt that he had undergone quite a harassing trip. He, his wife, and Dr. Smith were some of the successful climbers of the summit.

J.C. Foster in another group told of an incident that happened near Cherryville. Finding a campsite, they unhitched tired horses and laid out their sleeping equipment. The campfire was built at the base of a large fir tree. In an hour flames and smoke were seen coming out of the tree about 60 feet above ground. Not knowing which way the tree would fall as it finally would give in to the flames, the party decided to move. They hitched up the horses and drove another mile toward Government Camp.

On the way back home they saw that the tree had fallen right where their beds had been. No

Mazama camp at timberline, July 18, 1894.

mention was made about any effort to extinguish the fire or protect the whole forest from catching fire. The early outdoorsmen often gave little or no thought to saving the environment.

STEEL ELECTED PRESIDENT

Will Steel arrived on the summit at about 2:00 p.m. with a large telescope and mirror for signalling Portland, but his efforts were not successful. He did think that he saw a flash from Portland. At 3:00 p.m. he was involved in the organizational meeting on the summit, being elected the first president. Vice presidents were Reverend E.M. Wilbur, H.D. Langille, Professor Chalres H. Chapman, and A.H. Johnson. Charles H. Sholes was chosen secretary; Francis C. Little, treasurer; Fay Fuller, historian. Other members of the Executive Council were Mrs. Ida McElvain, Della Watson, and E.C. Stuart.

The ascent of the north side was scheduled to start at 5:00 a.m., but it was 9:30 before the weather was sufficiently promising. With H.D. (Doug) Langille and Jones as guide and assistant, the party of 22 left the lodge and proceeded rapidly up to Cooper Spur, riding horses or holding onto their tails.

At the top, H.D. Langille had 1000 feet of fixed

July 19, 1894, Mazama climbersarrive at summit on Cooper Spur Route. Ungainly figure crossing cornice was painted out in picture that hung on the clubroom wall. — Photo C.C. Lewis

rope set. On the steep slopes approaching the "lifeline" they held on to a moving hand line tied to Langille's waist. Using an alpenstock and an ice-axe, he would advance a few paces, drive them in fully, and brace himself by leaning into the slope. Then the full group would move up, and the guide would move to another stance. It was 3:00 p.m. when they reached the summit, which held up the long planned meeting on the summit. Just as they reached the snow cornice at the top, C.C. Lewis of Monmouth snapped a classic photograph of the party, a picture that has many times appeared in print. It was amusing, however that the framed copy on the clubroom wall in Portland was retouched to remove the climber scrambling ungracefully over the cornice.

In the Cooper Spur Route party were Frank E. McClure and Griff Perrott, who brought up three carrier pigeons, Jane, Grover, and Frances, owned by Bretherton. Jane was released at once, and the other two were sent home after the meeting was held. The following Monday, Mr. Bretherton had no word from his wandering birds.

From the summit could be seen smoke signals from points in the Willamette Valley and eastern Oregon. One particularly clear series from Arlington was noted. Since the food for the "banquet" on the summit somehow failed to arrive, and the weather at times was too cold for comfort, the crowd did not build up very much during the day. Temperature ran at about 34 degrees, and when the sun was not showing, the cold, raw wind cut to the bone.

Climbers from the south were in small groups. There were stragglers by the dozen who dropped out, some to eventually resume the climb. Groups descending from the summit were often discouraging the upward groups, advising them to go back. Many did just that, failing after most of the climb had been made.

Captain H.L. Wells had ascended with the idea of spending the night and taking black tar for smoke signals during the day and setting off the red fire at night. The red fire, of course, had never arrived at the summit. The men who pulled the toboggan had spent a cold windy night near Crater Rock. They were too tired to descend to the moraine and pick up the cache of red fire to take it to the top. Wells decided to go down with the rest. T. Brook White was delegated to set off the illumination on the moraine. Thousands of eyes in Portland and down the valley turned toward Mount Hood that night, but it was thought to be detected by only a few in the bad atmospheric conditions, although the illumination at 10:30 lasted a minute and a half.

As an aftermath of the massive climb of Thursday, a group of Mazamas made another ascent on Monday, July 23, on which Ida McElvain became the first woman to spend the night on the summit. The incident is covered in the chapter *Early Climbs of Mount Hood.*

After the giant organizational outing and climb, The Mazamas fell into a pattern of visiting different areas to explore each year. In 1895 it was Mount Adams. In 1896 Will Steel organized a trip to Crater Lake. In 1897 they conquered the summit of Mount Rainier. In 1898 Mount St. Helens was the target.

In every case the outings were covered by many pages of newspaper stories, complete with pictures and cartoons, not only in Portland, but in other cities of Oregon and Washington as well. It was in 1899, however, that Steel planned a trip to the Northern Cascades, a trip that in those times was about the utmost in high adventure.

THE LAKE CHELAN OUTING

In 1899 an ambitious plan was made to visit the peaks west of the head of Lake Chelan at what is now known as Cascade Pass. On Sunday, July 9, a group had reached Seattle, ready to catch the Monday afternoon run of the Great Northern Railway over Stevens Pass to Wenatchee. In those days there was no rail tunnel under the pass. Arriving at Wenatchee at 2:00 a.m., they were carried over the sand dunes to the edge of the Columbia River, where all hands grabbed their packs and duffel bags and filed up the gangplank of the steamer Selkirk.

The personnel list was lengthened at that point with Mazamas from Walla Walla, Pendleton, and

Mazama officers October 1895

DeSmet, Idaho. All staterooms were filled, and some slept on the deck. At 4:00 a.m., the boat got underway, bucking the strong current of the river for the 12-hour trip up to Chelan Falls. By Tuesday evening the party had been transported up the three miles from the river to Lakeside (now called Chelan) where they stayed in the hotel. On Wednesday they took the lake steamer to Stehekin, passing up the narrow lake bounded on both sides with towering peaks.

Descent of Skagit River in Indian Dugouts

Mazamas Climbed and Named Sahalie Peak in 1899

After a day at Stehekin, they moved to a camp about ten miles up the Stehekin River on Friday, then moved on to Bridge Creek on Saturday. Packer M.E. Field served the party with meals at $1 per day, freeing party members from kitchen chores. Field was also the owner of the hotel at Stehekin. If the reader wonders about the existence of roads up that remote river valley in such early times, it was because of a farm or two and considerable mining activity.

Mr. Buzzard, owner of a tract of land near Rainbow Falls, presented to the club a two-acre tract of land for use as a lodge site. What ever happened to the gift is not known.

By the evening of Sunday, July 16, 25 Mazamas were encamped in magnificent Horseshoe Basin east of Cascade Pass, surrounded by some of the most awe-inspiring peaks in the United States, Sahalie Peak, Magic Mountain, Mount Buckner, Mixup Mountain. There, at Purcell's Cabin, they were 27 miles from Stehekin.

Monday at daylight, the party under the leadership of Dr. E. Weldon Young of Seattle, started out to conquer one of the unnamed peaks to the north of Cascade Pass. They ascended to Doubtful Lake, and just beyond, Dr. Young slipped while unroped on steep snow. He saved himself from a plunge over the cliffs by grasping shrubs on the edge, limiting his injury to a bruised lip and nose. His fall did cause some climbers to reconsider the seriousness of the situation, and only 17 proceeded toward the summit.

Will Steel aided Young on the climb, setting a 160-foot fixed line at times on the long, steep approach to the summit pinnacle. Off to the side a more primitive Mazama stood with her kid on a high rock ledge and watched the human party climb upward. At last they reached the narrow arete of rock that commands the view of Horseshoe Basin to the east and Boston Basin to the west. Soon they had climbed the steep rocks of the pinnacle and stood on the summit, the first people to climb it.

NAMING A MOUNTAIN

Young raised the American Flag, Miss Ella McBride broke a flask of brandy over the rocks, and the peak was named Sahale. Other climbers were Rodney Glisan, Fred Rutledge, Eleanor Gile, Ashahel Curtis, Dr. C.K. Smith, Lewis McArthur, A.S. Pattullo, Kate Young, L.E. Anderson, Maude Parker, Vesta Baldwin, Will Dougan, F.G. Frazier, and Fay Fuller. Misses Parker, Baldwin, and Young, and Messers Curtis, Frazier, Dougan, Anderson, and McArthur were elected to membership by virtue of their qualifying on the climb. They then sang *America* and began to descend the pinnacle.

Once back at the camp at Horseshoe Basin they were hardly aware of the significant climbing history they had made that day. New arrivals in camp cause additional excitement, Mr. and Mrs. H.L. Pittock, E.T. Parsons, and R. Burnham. Around the campfire three more new members were admitted, Dr. J.P. Sweeney, Burnham, and E.Y. Judd. Pittock related details of his first ascent of Mount Hood in 1857.

It is interesting to note that in the party, Portland and Seattle people were about equal in numbers, a factor that caused The Mazamas considerable anguish seven years later, when the Seattle Mountaineers were founded, and the Seattle people dropped their support of the Mazama organization.

After a day of rest, the camp began to break up. Some went back down toward Stehekin, but 12 went over Cascade Pass, supported by a packer with 25 horses. The people marvelled at the manner the animals climbed up over the steep snow, but when they began the sharp descent into the awesome and magnificent valley of Cascade Creek, they had great fears that some of the horses would slip and fall over the cliffs below. One horse who had his saddle slip and turn, kicked up his heels and ran down, but when he saw the cliffs below he quickly stopped and corrected his behavior. Clouds shrouded the pass on this Saturday crossing, spoiling the view of Cascade and Johannesburg Peaks.

That night they spent at the two story log cabin of Gilbert Lander (Gilbert Cabin), eating food prepared on a cookstove for a change. After dinner they held a big dance, with Rodney Glisan cutting a fine figure. On Sunday the weather was clear and the party saw the striking views of glaciers and waterfalls before leaving for the west on horseback. It was 8:00 p.m. when they reached Marblemount.

They visited the Indian village nearby and bought out the local supply of hand-woven baskets. Two very large canoes were hired to take the party down the Skagit River to Hamilton, baggage and all, with two squaws weaving more baskets as they rode. Passing an occasional Indian village, they gave the Mazama yell, perhaps causing the aborigines to wonder if they were seeing some supernatural return of their royal ancestors. By noon the Indian paddlers had negotiated the 40 miles to Hamilton, and the group caught the noon train to Seattle.

MOUNT HOOD OUTING 1901

A very significant outing by the club had a base camp about a mile above Government Camp, set up by Will Steel on July 13, 1901. One important visitor was Henry Fielding Reid, head of the department of geological physics at Johns Hopkins University. Regarded as the world's leading authority on glaciers, he made trips with small groups to measure and flag the terminus of some of the glaciers of Mount Hood. He then indicated that The Mazamas should carry on with annual observations, so that the movement of the bodies of ice might be recorded as scientific data. That has been done over the years, incidentally.

Reid gave a preliminary talk about glaciers at the campfire, followed by a trip on July 15 to White River Glacier. Reid led a group of 35 across the crevassed ice, aided by Ella McBride. He took triangulations and photographs to evaluate his study. The party later split up, Dr. E. Weldon Young and W.A. Gordon leading two different groups back to base camp. Mark O'Neill led a party over to the Zigzag Glacier, as did Fay Fuller. Reid was busy exploring the depths of the canyon and did not start out of it until 6:00 p.m. By the time he neared timberline, following direction by star positions, Ranger Adolf Aschoff was out looking for him with a lantern.

Another prominent guest was Henry Gannett, chief geographer of the US Geological Survey. Gannett was in the area on official business of surveying the timber of the area, determining the age and condition of the trees. At a campfire program given when Reid was still out on his glacier trip, Gannett gave a lecture on the growing habits of trees in relation to the supply of moisture. He stated his conclusion that the Earth's atmosphere is growing warmer, which tied in with Reid's comments of the previous evening. This is common knowledge now, but at that time it was merely a theory.

Spanish-American war hero, Colonel L.L. Hawkins was one of the colorful figures of the camp. With his binoculars and small bugle slung around his neck, he presented a very military figure. Most of his trip from Portland had been by bicycle, but the last five miles he did on G.W. Berrian's handsome gray horse.

Will Steel, O.C. Yocum, Adolf Aschoff, Judge M.C. George, C.C. Lewis, H.L. Pittock, Charles H. Sholes, Fay Fuller, Ashahel Curtis were some of the more prominent of the participants of the outing.

On Wednesday, July 17, Yocum took a party of 26 to the summit. Meanwhile Reid and a small party explored Zigzag, Reid, and Sandy Glaciers. At the evening campfire the previously unnamed glacier was named Reid after a motion by Will Steel and a hearty endorsement by the members. Reid noted the fossil trees that were later named the Stadter Buried Forest.

On Monday, July 15, Bethel Rawson, a member of the DeMoss Troup, was involved in a non-Mazama climb which resulted in an evacuation including a good many of the outing members. The incident is fully covered in Tragedy, Search and Rescue.

On Friday, July 19, a mass assault of the summit was made, 119 climbers reaching the top. The crater held considerably more snow than it does today. The route continued up the Hogsback to the Big Crevasse, which was passed by a long detour around the left (west) end, then swung right again to pass by Geer Rock. On the summit, president Mark O'Neill called a meeting to order to honor the eighth anniversary of the organization. Colonel Hawkins delivered a tribute to Professor Joseph LeConte, who had died on July 6 in California.

Local newspapers carried full page accounts on the progress of the Mazama outing, complete with remarkably good cartoons of many of the prominent members in humorous poses. Complete lists of the climbing parties were given, and all the little details of camp life were reported to the public in Portland.

On the north side, H.B. Langille had returned for a visit to Cloud Cap Inn and planned to take a small group of climbers up that side. The Mazamas on the Cooper Spur Route were a little slower, and by the time they reached the summit, all of the climbers on the south side had departed.

The outings of The Mazamas in early years were of such great interest that a large book would be needed just to tell the story. In 1902 the club went to Mount Adams, in 1903 to Three Sisters, and in 1904 a great excursion was made to Mount Shasta in northern California. Even at that late date the argument still raged "Can Shasta be seen from Hood?" Will Steel and a party climbed Mount Hood to answer an illumination from the top of Mount Shasta at 9:30 p.m. on July 31. If the men on Mount Hood saw no fire to the south, they were to light red fire at 9:45. Naturally that is exactly what happened, because in no way can Shasta be seen from the top of Mount Hood. Unfortunately, the whole matter was befuddled by the fact that a haze of smoke lay across the land, limiting visibility to about 75 miles.

Charles Sholes at Mt. Rainier 1905

In 1905 members of The Mazamas, The Sierra Club, and The Appalacian Club joined forces to visit Mount Rainier. In that particular trip the ladies turned out in strength in the Mazama contingent, outnumbering the men about two to one. The pioneer climber of Mount Rainier, General Hazard Stevens, was a member of the outing. Controversy still raged as whether to call the mountain Tacoma or Rainier.

In 1906 The Mazamas headed for Mount Baker (Kulshan). Initial news stories filtering back from the base camp told of defeat by crevasses and unstable rock slopes. Finally on August 7, a group of six made the summit, Fred H. Kiser, Martin Wanlich, C.E. Forsyth, C.W. Williams, L.H. Hildebrand, and Ashahel Curtis. They found that they had been beaten by one day by a miner, C.C. Cornell, and his partner J. Stewart. On Mount Shuksan the results were better; on reaching the summit they found no evidence of any other climber having ever been there.

In 1907 the challenge was Mount Jefferson with a camp in Hanging Valley (Jefferson Park). L.H. Hicks, John Lee, W. Vollman, and S.M. Stanniers reached the summit to place a Mazama summit box. Stanniers slipped, but Lee saved him with the climbing rope from a fatal fall.

A LEGENDARY RESCUE

In 1908 it was Mount Saint Helens, wherein developed one of the most unbelievable mountain rescue stories of all times. John Anderson, a sawmill worker from Little Falls, Washington, his partner Perry Olson, and his foreman Henry Hanson, climbed to the summit from Spirit Lake in an independent group on Tuesday, August 5. They were not experienced or well equipped, but they descended a distance to explore on the south side. A rolling boulder suddenly appeared and struck Anderson, breaking his right leg in two places.

His companions carried him all the way down the south side to timberline and made him as comfortable as possible. Then Olson went for help around the base of Mount St. Helens to Spirit Lake. The Mazamas were relaxing around their campfire there, when Olson came staggering out of the brush for help. A rescue party, quickly organized by S.E. Forsythe and George Williams, set out for the injured man, spending most of the night crossing mountain torrents, struggling in and out of numberless canyons, crossing ridge after ridge in the unmarked wilderness.

Two Mazama boys, Francis Benefiel and C.W. Whittlesey, had also climbed on Tuesday. They had seen the tracks going to the south, and figuring that they would lead to a camp with plenty of food and shelter for their following day, they descended to timberline to find the injured Swede. Beginning to think for themselves, they pushed out to the crest of a high ridge and built a large signal fire. At 3:00 a.m. the men of the rescue party reached them, and soon all stood at Anderson's side.

They figured it was impossible to carry the 170-pound man around the base of the mountain. The exit south to the Lewis River lay beyond a moat of unknown canyons. The plan developed quickly; **they would carry him over the summit!** Placing him on a stretcher made of canvas and alpenstocks, they began to carry him upward. Twelve hours passed with no food and only the little sleep they got when they pitched forward in exhaustion. Finally at 4:00 p.m. they at last had him back on the summit!

Then came the descent down the north slope, lowering him as gently as possible with ropes down the vast, steep slopes that were traced with the many crevasses of St. Helens. Frequently he had to be shielded from rolling rock. As night descended they had reached timberline and proceeded down a canyon, but the wrong one. A second relief party came up from the Mazama camp and found them at 3:00 a.m., guiding them on in to Spirit Lake for a painful five miles.

At the camp they were met by Dr. Otis F. Akin and nurse Emma Harding of the Mazama party. They laid the haggard Anderson on a table, still smiling bravely after his ordeal. After hot applications to soothe his leg the doctor made a few manipulations and announced that a perfect reduction of the broken bones had been made. The leg was splinted and bound, and the brave Swede laid in the bed of a wagon for the 48-mile trip to the train at Castle Rock. On February 28, 1913, the Washington legislature honored Forsythe's effort by naming the glacier on the north side for him.

In 1909 the club returned to Mount Baker and Mount Shuksan, this time to avenge the defeat that Baker had struck them with in 1906. The team of Benefiel and Whittlesey did one route. E.V. Batstone, Walter Armstrong, R.B. Hess, and a stranger climbed another. After a considerable time of admiring the fumaroles, the second group attained the summit to meet the duo and descend with them.

NORTH TO MCKINLEY

In 1910 three men carried the Mazama Banner to Mount McKinley in Alaska, C.E. Rusk, Joe Ridley, and F.H. Rojec. A.L. Cool of Chelan, Washington, was the fourth member of the expedition which hoped to prove whether Dr. Frederick A. Cook was actually the first to climb the peak. They reached the point declared by Cook to be the summit, but declared it was at least ten miles from the real summit. They were not able to see the flag planted on the summit by the Thomas Lloyd party three months previously, but they accepted the story that his group had actually been successful. It was generally accepted that Cook had not been the conqueror of McKinley. The expedition was financed by Henry Pittock, *The New York Herald*, The Mazamas, and many individual subscriptions. Leader Rusk came back with many ideas on how to achieve success, but he did not return to Alaska to conquer the "roof of North America."

PROUTY ON FIRST ASCENT

Local Mazamas went back to the Three Sisters once more in 1910, ascending six peaks in the area. H.H. Prouty, later a Mazama president, appeared on the scene, climbing the pinnacles like a goat. In honor of his climbing a first ascent on North Sister's summit pinnacle, it was named Prouty's Pinnacle. A group including three women climbed the next day to take up a summit box, but due to the difficulty it was assumed that it would be many years before another woman would try it.

In 1911 the club set their sights on Glacier Peak, going again to Chelan and taking the lake steamer to Stehekin. From Buck Creek Pass they followed up Agnes Creek to Suiattle Pass, making a total of three climbs on Glacier Peak as well as climbing several unknown peaks that have names today.

NORTH SIDE OF HOOD

The 1912 outing was at Tilly Jane Camp on the north side of Mount Hood. H.H. Prouty and George X. Riddell made a trip to Barrett Spur and climbed to the summit of Mount Hood via Cathedral Ridge. Later, Ridell broke the speed record to the summit from Cloud Cap Inn in 1 hour and 52 minutes. What were said to be the first motion pictures of a mountain climbing party in action were taken of one group on Cooper Spur Route. On July 19, an electrical storm treated members to thrills when sparks jumped from alpenstocks and ladies' hatpins.

In 1913 a trip in the early part of the summer to Oregon Caves took a group of 110 through the devious caverns. **E.J. Davidson, who discovered the caves in 1874** while chasing a bear, accompanied the group on their tour. From Grants Pass they travelled 26 miles by car, hiked eight miles to a base camp, then another two to the entrance of the caves. The Annual Outing was held in August at Mount Adams. One climb was made easily, but the second on August 13 was met by weather unseasonably cold, frozen streams, a howling gale, water frozen in canteens, precipitation falling to form verglas on the rocks. A large number made the summit, despite the conditions. After the outing 10 of the party walked the 51 miles across country to Mount St. Helens. President Frank Branch Riley was prominent in the party in leadership on the mountain, speeches and song leading around the campfire.

In 1914 The Mazamas visited the north side of Mount Rainier, pioneering a new route to the summit over Winthrop Glacier. First an ascent of the route was made by George X. Riddell, A. Boyd Williams, and park ranger Thomas O. Farrell. A bivouac was required at 9,500 feet between the Carbon and Winthrop Glaciers.

A second ascent of the mountain was made by H.H. Prouty president of the club, Francis Benefiel, Riddell and Williams, over Winthrop Glacier to Steamboat Prow and up Emmons Glacier. These scouting climbs were followed by a climb of 75 with 71 successful, the largest group to ever stand on the top of Rainier. Excitement occurred at one point. John A. Lee and Frank Branch Riley had just crossed a snow bridge over a crevasse seven feet wide, 200 yards long, and virtually bottomless. Next on the rope, Ethel Freeman stepped on the bridge, and it caved under her. Lee and Riley stopped her fall.

In 1915 it was Mount Shasta again with Fred McNeil writing news releases from the Mazama camp. In the autumn when it was time to elect new officers, politics entered the fight for presidency. William P. Hardesty, an engineer with the City of Portland, vied with attorney Frank Branch Riley in a campaign that was spread all over the Portland newspapers. Riley won 202 to 141.

PROUTY'S LAST CLIMB

A return to Three Sisters was made in 1916 on a trip plagued with fog and snow in mid-August. H.H. Prouty led a group of four to the top of North Sister, performing some expert maneuvers on the steep summit snow field. He was surprised to find the big summit chimney so changed by falling rock, that he did not recognize it at first. One person, L.H. Weir, August 29, 1914, had climbed since the Mazama first ascent in 1910. The second week of the outing Prouty became ill and left the camp. At McKenzie Bridge he fainted twice. On September 11, he died at St. Vincent's Hospital of gastric and heart problems. Age 58, he had been divorced and was engaged to Edith Ellis. In November his son Carl, 28, began action to break his will, declaring that Prouty had poisoned himself with bichloride of mercury tablets.

Frank Branch Riley 1916

In 1917 the outing was held at Mount Jefferson with base camp at Pamelia Lake. A total of 46 reached the summit. Dr. W.E. Stone of Purdue University and his wife traversed around to the north side and climbed the north ridge to the pinnacle, a very dangerous ascent. The daring professor fell to his death, while his wife watched, the following year on a climb in the Selkirk Range in British Columbia, and she was trapped for several days on a ledge until rescuers came for her. On a side trip from Pamelia Lake, Edward F. Peterson, Arthur S. Peterson, and John Penland ascended to the base of the pinnacle of Three Fingered Jack, which had not been climbed.

In 1918 it was a trip to the Wallowa Range. In 1919, 150 went to Paradise Valley at Mount Rainier, and 93 climbed to the summit. In 1920 The Mazamas held their outing at Mount Baker. In contrast with previous trips to the mountain, great success was found. On two 100% climbs, 46 reached the summit. E.C. Sammons was president, having returned from the battlefields in Europe a lieutenant colonel.

In 1921 the club converged on Crescent Lake to climb Diamond Peak and W.C. Yoran led an ascent of Cowhorn Mountain. The outing then moved south on foot to Diamond Lake, where some climbed Mount Thielsen, then marched on foot to Crater Lake. Ex-president William G. Steel, who had for a time held the position of superintendent of Crater Lake National Park, welcomed the club to southern Oregon. Steel had been directly responsible for the creation of the national park, had placed the first boats on the lake, made depth soundings, and had been instrumental in the building of the hotel on the rim.

It was about this time in history that The Mazamas began to branch out onto additional trips in addition to the Annual Outing. In the early years, transportation was so primitive, that it was a major undertaking to visit Mount Adams, St. Helens, Mount Jefferson, or any other major peak. With the advent of the automobile the club began to make several climbs per year, but the Annual Outing remained as a great tradition, an ingathering of the clan to be led by the president.

In the Thirties the concept of the week-end climb began to take hold, and a Climbing Committee added a new scope to the club. At the end of World War Two, which was much more of a total war than World War One, climbing activity mushroomed. It was then that the concept of holding more than one outing was begun. Smaller outing groups began to visit interesting climbing areas in the Fifties, leaving the Annual Outing at times a rather passe' adventure into areas that could easily be visited on a week-end, avoided by the better climbers. This caused an era of resentment on the part of those who treasured the high adventure of the earlier Annual Outings. But the era passed, and the number of outings increased. Just to give an example, in 1973 outings were Harold Deery's trip to Hoh headwaters in the Olympic Peninsula, the Swiss Alps with Peg Oslund, a canoe trip on Barkley Sound with Trish Evenson, a whitewater trip on the Rogue River with Spike Paget, a run of the Salmon River in Idaho with William Oberteuffer, climbing near Park Creek Pass with Russell Lamb and Joe Throop, the north side of Mount Rainier with Robert Millus, the Trinity Alps with Thomas Crowder, Monte Cristo area with John Salisbury, the Wallowa Range with Doug Evenson, and Garibaldi Park in British Columbia with John Neal. In addition a January trip to Aconcagua, highest peak in South America, was led by Carmie Dafoe.

In 1974, Harold Deery led an outing in the Glacier Peak Wilderness, Thomas Crowder had one at Mount Olympus, an outing in the Trinity Alps with Verle Duckering, Nootka Sound with Trish Evenson, south-central Norway with Lillian Clark, Enchantment Lake Basin with John Neal, Boston Basin with Joe Throop and Charles Jensen, and a boat trip down the Green and Yampa Rivers of Utah.

The scope of the climbing and outing programs is beyond all imagination of the club's founders, who normally spent two hard days reaching Mount Hood by wagon. It is no small wonder that in 1974 there was no Annual Outing, yet only a handful of members would know that unless told.

A revolution also occurred in skiing. In addition to the well-established sport of downhill skiing, a hundred or more Mazamas are out each weekend enjoying the newly-revived cross-country skiing. After the original skiing, cross-country, died out until in the Fifties, only a few occasional Norwegians toured the back country. Then, from a small start, it began to grow in popularity to a sport with a wide base of acceptance. A great many Mazamas find it an extension of their outdoor activity of hiking and climbing in the summer. Parties of adventuresome skiers tour the forests, ridges, and canyons, enjoying the sociability of a small close-knit group, getting away from the sophisticated crowds around the ski lifts.

MOUNTAIN LODGE, AN EARLY AMBITION FOR THE MAZAMAS

From the very first, there was discussion about building a mountain lodge. When the club visited the headwaters of Lake Chelan in 1899, they were offered a two-acre plot for the purpose at Rainbow Falls north of Stehekin.

There was much talk about building one at Mount Hood about 1905. Adolf Aschoff, Mazama member and Forest Ranger, issued a permit for the construction of a lodge near timberline, an act that caused him to be called on the carpet by Forest Inspector Daniel Bronson.

J.O. Hannum, who later built Homestead Inn near Cooper Spur Junction, offered The Mazamas a free plot of ground in 1916 for a mountain home. He made a special trip from Hood River down to Portland on October 28, to restate his previous offer. As in the cases before, nothing was done by the Executive Council to proceed with any construction.

In April of 1919, a committee was appointed under the chairmanship of L.A. Nelson of the West Coast Lumbermen's Association to investigate costs and to find a site in the Columbia Gorge near Bonneville. The Executive Council voted to proceed with a lease from the Forest Service on a plot a mile and a half from the highway near Wauna Point Trail. The building was to cost $620 and be built under the jurisdiction of Nelson, George X. Riddell, John A. Lee, George Meredith, and Eugene Dowling. Not a word was mentioned about it in the Annual at year's end, so it is evident that the project was scuttled and the committee disbanded.

Attention once more focused toward Mount Hood. A site near Twin Bridges, just below Laurel Hill was chosen. It could be reached on foot from Rhododendron by members coming up for the weekend, and once they had arrived, it offered many interesting side trips to Government Camp, Hidden Lake, and Paradise Park. Going any further would have meant a great deal of effort.

The committee consisted of Richard W. Montague, John A. Lee, and architect Jamieson Parker. In August of 1923, the Executive Council ratified the plan, and a contract was let to Lorenz Brothers for about $3,000. The building was just across the Little Zigzag River. It was close to the highway, but that was of no importance, as snow closed the road all winter anyway. Water supply was from the river.

The ground floor housed a 20' x 33' living room with a large stone fireplace, a kitchen, and a wood room. In front a 9' x 33' porch ran across the front of the structure. The upstairs area gave the women plenty of sleeping space, and the men slept down below on the living room floor.

The second week of October about a hundred members went up to cut the winter's wood supply. The fireplace was still under construction, and the bridge over the Zigzag had not yet been built. That winter, and for the following eight years, crowds of Mazamas trooped to the Twin Bridges lodge to enjoy skiing, snow-shoeing, and hiking.

A typical trip from the first lodge was made on the weekend of March 17, 1930. Of the 40 members present, 11 made a moonlight climb to Mirror Lake on Saturday night, taking skis and a toboggan. The night was cold and the lake frozen solid.

Climbing up the side of Tom-Dick-Harry Mountain, they skied and tobogganned downwards and out across the ice of the lake. Wind in 50-mile gusts pushed them across the lake, when they opened their coats for sails. The party included Conrad J. Sieberts, Ben W. Newell, Gertrude Ross, Martha Jensma, Louise Rea, Mildred Morris, Richard P. Quinn, Gladys Thorne, Alfred G. Ross, and William J. Reid, Jr. Miss Morris and Quinn, who met for the first time on that trip, later were married and are members of The Mazamas in 1975.

Christmas Party at Laurel Hill Lodge
Circa 1929

LODGE AT GOVERNMENT CAMP

Changing times made short work of the first Mazama Lodge, when the highway department decided to keep the road open in wintertime to Government Camp in 1926. With the traffic whizzing by the door, Mazamas were restless to build a lodge higher up on the mountain. The Lodge Committee chose a site northeast of Government Camp, land still occupied by The Mazamas to this day on a Forest Service lease. A new building was all under roof and dedicated on November 1, 1931.

The new lodge was made of 30-inch weathered cedar logs on the ground floor and frame construction on the second floor and third floor loft. The south wall of the 30' x 40' living room had a great stone fireplace that was imbedded with stones sent by 21 outdoor clubs of the Pacific Coast. Each was engraved with the name or symbol of the donor club. In the center of the fireplace was a large piece of black obsidian supporting a white mountain goat carved by Carl Sakrison.

The contractor was William Lens; designer Roscoe A. Johnson. Dr. Paul E. Spangler headed the Building Committee. C.L. Marshall handled outside engineering, surveying, road building, and planning the water system from a spring 500 feet

Mazama Lodge built 1931, burned 1958 — Photo Donald Onthank

north of the building. Financial matters were handled by E.M. Adams. A.O. Soderberg assisted on building problems, and Verne L. Ketchum did engineering on the building and acted as superintendent for the club.

Dorms held a hundred people. There were two large rest rooms, two kitchens, one for use by those who cooked their own food at odd times. A ski-waxing room guarded the rear entry. The basement housed a furnace and large wood supply. In later years an electronic generator was set in a shack east of the building, until the Sandy Electrical Cooperative ran poles up to serve Government Camp area.

The act of asking the many outdoor clubs of the Pacific Coast for memorial rocks for the fireplace resulted in representatives visiting the new building for a Halloween party and dedication. Out of this association was born the Federation of Western Outdoor Clubs, a far-reaching conservation group. The Mazamas were vitally interested in the FWOC as an active member, until federal tax laws forced them to leave the organization.

The lodge was maintained by the use of hired caretakers. Their lives were lived in beautiful serenity during the week, followed by Saturdays and Sundays of bedlam as noisy skiers crammed into the building to eat and dance and finally climb up to the dormitories. The weekday quiet was usually more than most people could take for over a year, and the turnover of caretakers was a constant process.

The last caretakers were George and Helen Bertrand, a very personable couple who were members of the club. George was a Quinault Indian, a great cook, a tremendous raconteur who could entertain groups endlessly with his patter. Helen was tall, friendly, artistic, a sister of another Mazama member, Earl Reitsma.

The caretaker quarters were upstairs; the lodge was not heated during the week. On the morning of Thursday, December 4, 1958, their son, Mike, had just left to catch the school bus. Helen and her mother, Mrs. Ruth Reitsma, 63, who was spending a few days at the lodge, were down below in the small kitchen making coffee, when they smelled smoke. They called George, who was still in bed. A short in the wiring in the bathroom in the caretaker area had started a fire.

By the time George could get any water, the fire had already gained headway. Mrs. Reitsma ran toward Government Camp for help, her last act, for she succumbed to a heart attack from the hurry and excitement. In a short time Mazama Lodge was levelled by fire.

BUILDING A NEW LODGE

President of The Mazamas appointed Betty Parker, Ariel Edmiston, Grant Kirk, Thad Gable, and Fred McNeil to a new committee to assay the possibility of rebuilding. Donations began to roll in, although there was some opposition to rebuilding. Betty Parker's committee sifted out the many suggestions as to what type of building members wanted.

In January, 1959 the Executive Council appointed a Planning and Building Committee with Jack Grauer as chairman. John W. Storrs was selected as the architect, and several months went by as the plans were changed to suit the pocketbook. In summer plans were submitted to contractors for a 56' x 50' building. Builder James Wright was the low bidder, but the cost was out of range. Consultations with the builder and Storrs resulted in cutting the building size to 56' x 40' and simplifying the plan for a cost of $48,052. The Council approved the contract on August 3.

With summer almost over, it became a race to erect the building before winter, the usual pattern of construction at Government Camp. It was with emotional trauma that Mazamas saw the chimney of the old lodge felled in preparation for excavation. Club members dug ditches, installed fuel oil and gas lines, painted, installed furnace and kitchen equipment. Weather was good in the autumn, and roads remained open. Aubrey Watzek donated funds for a mammoth fireplace in memory of Rodney L. Glisan. Al Weese, Dick Uffelman, and Jack Grauer hauled loads of stone from a quarry out on Mud Creek Ridge near Trillium Lake.

Bill and Nick Bush hauled in the large window frames and painted them. Dick Hall, Jim Craig, Don Eastman, Jim Lindsay, Bob Lee, Ed Soderberg, and Jack Grauer set the oil furnace and ran the sheet metal ducts. Gil and Vivian Staender ran metal vents to the rest rooms. Gifford Martin and John McCloskey fabricated the kitchen cabinets. Colin Chisholm and Dean Caldwell dug ditches, and Betty Parker turned to with a shovel to divert water that poured through the basement wall. Gwen Dimm and Viola Lynch wielded paint brushes, while Bill Lynch laid floor tile. Bob Platt II and Bob Platt III, the Gable family, Thad, Mae, Michael, and Harold, Grant and Frances Kirk were there, and many, many more.

For the Christmas holidays came the first guests. A sewer line plugged and flooded the basement floor. More orderly times followed. Adolph Zimmerman continued his work on cabinetry and finishing wood work. A pump was placed in the basement to assure good water pressure in case of fire. Club plaques from other outdoor clubs were received and placed on the wall north of the fireplace. The Mazama goat had been rescued from the old lodge and took its place on a piece of burnt cedar from the old building.

On July 25, 1960 a great gathering of Mazamas dedicated the new lodge. Marge Lynott christened the new building with a snowball from the summit of Mount Hood, and a speech was made by David Brower, Executive Secretary of the Sierra Club. L.A. Nelson dedicated the fireplace, which had been a gift of Aubrey Watzek, to the memory of Rodney Glisan. Members barbecued two pigs and two sheep in an outdoor pit.

On Sunday, July 26, Bob Lynott and Dean Merten led the Dedication Climb for 183 participants. The previous evening some members of the Climbing Committee had gone up to establish a base camp and set off flares at Triangle Moraine, the crater and the Chute. When the climbers came up on Sunday, they were greeted with hot coffee.

A generation of climbers and skiers has matured in the new Mazama Lodge, not realizing that many of the older members feel that nothing can compare with the old log building that burned in 1958. A few can still remember the old lodge at the foot of Laurel Hill.

PORTLAND CLUBROOMS MAINTAINED SINCE 1914

No regular office or clubroom for The Mazamas was maintained until they were established on the second floor of the Northwestern Bank Building on Saturday, November 28, 1914. Previously, space had been available at the city hall in Portland for about a decade.

In June of 1919 a move was made to the third floor of the Chamber of Commerce Building, where business was conducted for seven years. In 1926 a penthouse suite in the Pacific Building on Yamhill between 5th and 6th was arranged. Over 1400 attended the open house held on May 7 and May 8 to formally open the new rooms. Wall displays and pictures gave the new home an atmosphere the club wanted.

Space was available for the library, which had been under a new committee for about a year previously. Moving to the Pacific Building gave the club the opportunity to begin the regular Wednesday evening open house and meeting that has continued all through the years since, with the exception of summer months.

All went peacefully until 1956 when the owners of the Pacific Building decided they wanted the penthouse for other purposes. Their dissatisfaction was perhaps augmented by the night-time elevator traffic to the roof, which required each person signing in and out with the elevator operator. A search for new clubrooms was initiated. Club president John Biewener found one possibility and went to survey it with Jack Grauer one day during lunch hour. This finally resulted in club leasing the property at 909 NW 19th, the corner of NW 19th and Lovejoy in Portland's film colony.

Club members again came to the front and moved the furniture and office equipment and records, outing equipment, and library. A new ceiling was put in the room. The corner office was outfitted as a library and conference room. Another was made as a map room, and a third is used for office space. On March 6, 1957, The Mazamas were in their new home.

However, **club rooms became a great point of interest** for a few years. In 1954 Robert T. Platt had been appointed head of a committee to establish the feasibility of building and owning clubrooms rather than to lease them. A tentative site was presented at 52nd and SE Ankeny, and a building fund of $2,700 was amassed. Neighbors objected to a zone change in the residential district, and many club members felt that even if legal restrictions could be eliminated, it would not be wise to build. Soon a group of members, who wanted action, formed a group outside the structure of the club and began to be very adamant.

By 1956 the building fund had collected $5,300 and political pressure was being applied to elect members to the Executive Council who would favor building. The Council was told on November 11, 1957 that member Harrie Jennison had bought a site at SE 48 and Belmont with the idea of holding it until the club could buy it. The fund grew to $10,000. The club did not buy the property, and Jennison later sold it for a profit.

When the lodge burned at Mount Hood in 1958, the proponents of building a clubroom in Portland attacked the problem with renewed vigor, feeling that money and effort should be put into a city location. There was even an attack upon the validity of the idea that mountaineering was a primary function of the club. This really did polarize thinking within the members of The Mazamas and caused feelings to be expressed strongly and bitterly at meetings. A poll of members was sent out in January, 1958, on whether to rebuild Mazama Lodge at Government Camp. The poll sent a mandate for rebuilding, and the council dissolved the Clubhouse Building Committee and closed the $12,000 fund to further addition.

The bitterness caused a few resignations from the club, but the conflict caused restatement that the club is a **Mountaineering Club,** and that other functions are secondary. It is only the fact that the club has maintained a singleness of purpose, that has let it survive to be the second oldest mountain club in the United States.

William G. Steel, first president of The Mazamas, who had witnessed the Oregon Alpine Club pass into oblivion, knew the problems of diversions of interest, such as sponsoring concerts, holding dances, running a museum, and promoting a large number of social, non-climbing activities. He warned in the very first sentence of his presidential address in 1894, "*Every organization that becomes a permanent success is called into existence for a purpose, and succeeds only as long as it adheres to that purpose.*"

In 1963 a new policy was undertaken at the clubrooms, the employment of a paid secretary to do bookkeeping on the membership rolls, maintain address files, answer the telephone, and do correspondence. It soon became a full time job for Helen Diehl, who became a friend to hundreds of club members until she resigned in December, 1972. Jeanne Hauser trained with her and took her place in January, 1973. In March of 1974 the position was filled by an ex-president and past chairman of the Climbing Committee, John Salisbury.

THE CLIMBING COMMITTEE

Climbing in the early days could not be undertaken without making a trip of considerable difficulty. It took two days just to go to Mount Hood, before the advent of the automobile. Reaching Mount Adams, Mount Shasta, or Glacier Peak took several days. When The Mazamas held the Annual Outing, every climber and climb leader did his best to attend, because it was the only opportunity.

As time passed, The Mazamas began to sponsor some activity each weekend, usually a hike out from some point along the rail line. The Local Walks Committee handled the planning and also managed the few climbs that might be included into the schedule. But climbing activity built up greatly in the late Twenties. In addition to staging an outing and an Annual Climb of Mount Hood, the club was scheduling as many as 10 climbs per summer by the year 1933.

The club vice-president, Cyril H. Crockett, proposed that a separate committee be formed to take charge of mountain climbs. A mountain climbing study group began meeting informally at the clubrooms in 1933, John Scott, Paul Spangler, Cyril Crockett, Russell Collins, Lynn Darcy, Everett Darr, Leon Darling, Art Johnson, Ray Lewis, Everett Morrison, Curtis Ijames, Al Maas, James Mount, Donald Onthank, Perlee Payton, Carl Richards, and some others. The group included a good part of the leadership of the Executive Council, and several of the men were also members of Wy'east Climbers.

Early in 1934 Carl Richards proposed that the bylaws be amended to create a Climbing Committee. The Executive Council would not authorize the necessary special election, but they appointed a temporary committee for the balance of the fiscal year, ending in October. John Scott was the chairman of the new nine-man group. Beginning work in June, they organized and successfully ran 12 climbs in the summer of 1934, creating so much enthusiasm, that a bylaw amendment in the October election was passed easily.

For the 1953-54 year, the committee was expanded to its present strength of 12 members. A larger climbing program and a much larger climbing school was the reason.

The function of the Climbing Committee has remained most important over the years. It plans the climbing schedule, supervises climbs, selects and approves leaders, and lays down rules for all club climbing. At times they have removed individuals from the list of leaders, in instances where they believe that certain of his characteristics might create hazard. They not only ask that a leader be a proficient climber and route finder, but in addition he must be tolerant and sympathetic to the slow and less capable. He is expected to be hard-headed in turning down applicants for climbs, whom he knows will not have the stamina or climbing prowess to successfully perform.

The Climbing Committee has engendered leadership for The Mazamas, and most members of the Executive Council have served upon it. Each winter the committee holds an invitational banquet for past and present members.

It becomes very obvious that the climbing program of The Mazamas has mushroomed far beyond the craziest dreams of the founders. In the 1972-3 season, which actually includes the climbing activity for 1973, the schedule includes 18 winter climbs, 12 cancelled because of bad weather. A total of 2,082 individual summits were attained by 2,532 individuals who made attempted climbs. On outings to Argentina, Trinity Alps of California, Monte Cristo Range in Washington, north side of Mount Rainier, European Alps, Park Creek Pass in Washington, Garibaldi Park in British Columbia another 381 summit ascents were made out of 403 individual starts.

CHAIRMAN	YEAR	SCHEDULED CLIMBS
John D. Scott	1934	12
John D. Scott	1934-5	16
John D. Scott	1935-6	
Everett L. Darr	1936-7	12
Roy Varney	1937-8	10
John D. Scott		
J.E. Nelson	1938-9	18
Joe Leuthold	1939-0	14
Al L. Gerding	1940-1	15
Glen Asher	1941-2	12
Donald G. Onthank		
Lu Norene	1942-3	6
Randall B. Kester	1943-4	5
Harry Moss	1944-5	7
William S. Bush	1945-6	17
Donald G. Onthank	1946-7	27
George Dunning	1947-8	23
Harold A. Scharback	1948-9	24
Warren A. Wilson	1949-0	26
Dale L. Caldwell	1950-1	27
Colin G. Chisholm	1951-2	40
Thaddis T. Gable	1952-3	37
John H. Biewener	1953-4	55
John H. Biewener	1954-5	38
Richard R. Pooley	1955-6	35
Jack Janacek	1956-7	35
William H. Oberteuffer	1957-8	52
Thomas P. Gibbons	1958-9	59
Dean Merton	1959-0	80
Erwin O. Rieger	1960-1	75
Erwin O. Rieger	1961-2	83
Allison L. Belcher	1962-3	105
Neil Baldwin	1963-4	128
L. Lisle Walker	1964-5	156
Carmie R. Dafoe, Jr.	1965-6	151
Jack Grauer	1966-7	157
John Salisbury	1967-8	184
Albert E. Weese	1968-9	208
Donald C. Eastman	1969-0	191
Richard W. Laird	1970-1	228
Ray Sheldon	1971-2	244
Ray Snyder	1972-3	222
Robert Hyslop	1973-4	200
Richard LaPore	1974-5	

A program such as this is based upon a wide base of participation by club members and upon a large group of dependable leaders to conduct such a large number of hazardous missions. As climbing interest has grown within the club, the number of ascents of Mount Hood has increased by very little. Modern transportation has made climbing available in surrounding states on a weekend basis. Scheduling of at least 6 climbs per weekend is common, more than were planned for a whole year, 50 years ago. The number of climbs in the third column refers to the number scheduled, for the most part not including outing climbs.

No matter how far afield the present-day Mazama may roam, all have a great affection for Mount Hood and consider it their home. Most active climbers ascend the peak every year or two to renew their memories and to condition themselves early in the season for more tiring trips.

OFFICERS OVER THE YEARS

	President	Vice-President	Recording Secretary
1894	William G. Steel	H.D. Langille	Charles H. Sholes
1894-5	William G. Steel Leander L. Hawkins	T. Brook White	
1895-6	Charles H. Sholes	William A. Langille	Earl M. Wilbur
1896-7	Henry L. Pittock	Fay Fuller	Earl M. Wilbur
1897-8	Melvin C. George	Emmett M. Parker	Martin W. Gorman
1898-9	William G. Steel	Dr. E.W. Young	L.H. Lamberson A.S. Patullo F.E. Donaldson
1899-0	T. Brook White	George H. Stone	F.E. Donaldson Mark O'Neill
1900-1	Mark O'Neill	Francis R. Cushman	Martin W. Gorman
1901-2	Mark O'Neill	Roland Grant	William R. MacKenzie
1902-3	Rodney L. Glisan	Roland D. Grant	William R. MacKenzie
1903-4	Charles H. Sholes	Martin W. Gorman	George W. Berrion
1904-5	H.H. Northup	Frank W. Cushman	Charles H. Sholes
1905-6	Charles H. Sholes	Hazard Stevens	L.E. Anderson
1906-7	Charles H. Sholes	J.P. Sweeney	Margaret Fleming
1907-8	Charles H. Sholes	L.J. Hicks	Margaret Fleming
1908-9	Martin W. Gorman	L.J. Hicks	Eleanor M. Gardner
1909-0	John A. Lee	Dr. W.C. Adams	C.W. Whittlesey
1910-1	Hayward H. Riddell	Charles H. Sholes	Martha O. Goldapp
1911-2	Edmund P. Sheldon	Harley H. Prouty	Martha O. Goldapp
1912-3	Edmund P. Sheldon	Harley H. Prouty	Martha O. Goldapp
1913-4	Harley H. Prouty	J.E. Bronaugh	Gertrude E. Faber
1914-5	J.E. Bronaugh	Frank Branch Riley	Eleanor Garder Sheldon
1915-6	Frank Branch Riley	George X. Riddell	Beulah F. Miller
1916-7	William P. Hardesty	A. Boyd Williams	Jean Richardson
1917-8	Roy W. Ayer	William P. Hardesty	Jean Richardson
1918-9	Edgar E. Coursen	Harriet E. Monroe	Jean Richardson
1919-0	E.C. Sammons	George X. Riddell	A. Boyd Williams
1920-1	A. Boyd Williams	Leroy E. Anderson	Laura H. Peterson
1921-2	Richard W. Montague	Alfred F. Parker	James A. Ormandy
1922-3	Richard W. Montague	Alfred F. Parker	James A. Ormandy
1923-4	Richard W. Montague	Alfred F. Parker	Robert W. Osborn
1924-5	Alfred F. Parker	Martha E. Nilsson	W.P. Foreman
1925-6	Frank M. Redman	Martha E. Nilsson	W.P. Foreman
1926-7	Fred W. Stadter	Louis W. Waldorf	Martha E. Nilsson
1927-8	Fred W. Stadter	Louis W. Waldorf	Nelle Heizer
1928-9	John D. Scott	Merle W. Manly	Nelle Heizer
1929-0	Kenneth Beebe	L.A. Nelson	Ann W. Shepard
1930-1	L.A. Nelson	Rex H. Bunnage	Lynn J. Darcy
1931-2	L.A. Nelson	Rex H. Bunnage	Fred H. McNeil
1932-3	Rex A. Bunnage	Paul E. Spangler	Jean A. Young
1933-4	Paul E. Spangler	Cyril H. Crockett	Vivian Patterson
1934-5	Lynn J. Darcy	Kenneth Beebe	Vivian Patterson Brugger
1935-6	W.P. Foreman	Aubrey Watzek	Bessie H. Pancake
1936-7	Edward J. Hughes	Donald G. Onthank	Bessie H. Pancake
1937-8	Edward J. Hughes	Donald G. Onthank	Bessie H. Pancake
1938-9	Donald G. Onthank	Oscar A. Wilson	Bessie H. Pancake

1939-0	Oscar A. Wilson	J. Clark Rhodes	Bessie H. Pancake
1940-1	Roy K. Terry	J. Ed Nelson	Julia Wilson
1941-2	J. Ed Nelson	K.N. Phillips	Inez McCabe
1942-3	Charles A. Whittlesey	Wagar G. Carey, Jr.	Bessie H. Pancake
1943-4	Dwight J. Henderson	Dr. Guy A. Woods	Bessie H. Pancake
1944-5	Wagar G. Carey, Jr.	Martha K. Darcy	Jeanette Carlstad
1945-6	Dr. Guy A. Woods	Randall B. Kester	Jeanette Carlstad
1946-7	Robert T. Platt II	Jeanette Carlstad	Betty H. Huntress
1947-8	Harry W. Moss	D.P. Lamb	Emma Jo Stewart
1948-9	J. Clark Rhodes	Betty H. Huntress	Randall B. Kester
1949-0	Al L. Gerding	William S. Bush	Randall B. Kester
1950-1	Randall B. Kester	Dale L. Caldwell	Gwen B. Francisco
1951-2	Virlis L. Fischer	Colin G. Chisholm	Martha Ann Platt
1952-3	Colin G. Chisholm	Thaddis T. Gable	Martha Ann Platt
1953-4	Martha Ann Platt	Thaddis T. Gable	Margaret Oberteuffer
1954-5	Robert J. Boden	C.A. Nelson	Margaret Oberteuffer
1955-6	Alfred Schmitz	Clarence D. Phillips	Marianne G. Ott
1956-7	John H. Biewener	Thaddis T. Gable	Phyllis Neuberger
1957-8	Thaddis T. Gable	George J. Francisco	Marianne G. Ott
1958-9	George J. Francisco	Jack Grauer	William H. Oberteuffer
1959-0	Robert E. Lynott	William H. Oberteuffer	William S. Bush
1960-1	Neil Baldwin	William Hamilton	William H. Lynch
1961-2	James D. Dickey	Edwin J. Dolan	Helen V. Wirtanen
1962-3	Jack Grauer	Donald C. Eastman	Helen V. Wirtanen
1963-4	Erwin O. Rieger	Richard R. Pooley	Dorothy M. Harrington
1964-5	Donald C. Eastman	Harpel W. Keller	Dorothy M. Harrington
1965-6	Clinton Harrington	Walter D. Eriksen	Dorothy M. Harrington
1966-7	Clinton Harrington	Betty L. Parker	William H. Oberteuffer
1967-8	James K. Angell	William H. Oberteuffer	Chad Karr
1968-9	Chad Karr	Dorothy E. Bergstrom	Harry S. Buckley
1969-0	Carmie R. Dafoe, Jr.	John N. Salisbury	Albert B. Combs
1970-1	John N. Salisbury Carmie R. Dafoe Jr.	Erwin O. Rieger	Albert B. Combs
1971-2	Kenneth M. Winters	Roy Kinzie	Richard W. Laird
1972-3	Richard W. Laird	Dorothy E. Bergstrom	Ray G. Sheldon
1973-4	Kenneth A. Hague	Robert R. Stites	Ray Snyder
1974-5	Kenneth M. Winters	Ray Snyder	Linda Shockey

MAZAMA MEMBERSHIP

1894	107	1935	549
1895	122	1936	596
1896	141	1937	661
1897		1938	698
1898		1939	690
1899		1940	690
1900	234	1941	670
1901	188	1942	642
1902		1943	635
1903	197	1944	643
1904		1945	720
1905	213	1946	871
1906	184	1947	918
1907	190	1948	911
1908	183	1949	852
1909		1950	870
1910		1951	901
1911		1952	939
1912		1953	972
1913	197	1954	1020
1914	311	1955	991
1915	419	1956	1052
1916	454	1957	1098
1917	366	1958	1114
1918	411	1959	1065
1919	467	1960	1143

1920	560	1961	1223
1921	618	1962	1274
1922	658	1963	1315
1923	687	1964	1448
1924	665	1965	1488
1925	653	1966	1677
1926	810	1967	1814
1927	712	1968	1996
1928	701	1969	2195
1929	643	1970	2333
1930	627	1971	2473
1931	657	1972	2562
1932	612	1973	2619
1933	505	1974	2667
1934	519		

A constantly increasing membership has at times been a worry to officers of The Mazamas. Likewise there have been times when a decreasing membership brought about sharper pangs. In the winter of 1906-7 The Seattle Mountaineers organized as an auxiliary to The Mazamas, there being so many Washingtonians active in the club.

That arrangement lasted about a year, and the alpinists in Seattle decided to declare their independence from The Mazamas, a very natural course of events. This cost the club a great deal of strength and some prestige. There are no membership records available for several years, mainly because finances were too short to publish an annual from 1907 to 1912, but membership did sag in those years. The year 1907 was one of depression, that took its toll of any activities that cost money.

The year 1917 shows a loss of membership because of World War One. World War Two showed no increase. The depression years beginning in 1929 caused the number of members to dwindle until the mid-Thirties.

Mazama membership requires the climbing of one peak with living glaciers, a limiting factor not used by The Sierra Club or The Seattle Mountaineers. Some Mazamas have proposed raising the requirement to **three** peaks. It is very possible such a requirement might cause the membership to drop to a level that could not be supported economically.

Early members of the club showed a good percentage of professors, doctors, judges, and prosperous business men. As the common man in the common job has come to a position of commanding more money over the years, the mix has changed to more of a true cross-section of Oregon citizens. However, interest in mountaineering and the outdoors usually centers in active, motivated individuals, who normally do not fall within the lowest economic brackets of life.

Snow Shoe Club, Elite North Side Group

The Snowshoe Club grew out of a group of guests that Wesley Ladd invited on a winter outing to Cloud Cap Inn in 1904. They included Walter Honeyman, Richard Ball, Dr. Herbert Nichols, Rodney Glisan, Henry Corbett, and John Kallock.

The idea proved so popular, that the group returned on an annual basis over the years. Most of them graduated to the use of skis eventually, but the name snowshoe stuck as part of their title.

Rodney L. Glisan told of the fourth annual visit to Cloud Cap Inn in 1907. The party of ten left Portland by rail coach the morning of January 19 and arrived at Hood River before noon. After a meal at the hotel they bundled into two four-horse sleighs and headed up the valley, arriving at the homes of their guides, Bert and Bill. Each guide put five of the snowshoers up for the night. In the evening the guests at Bert's house followed the sleigh tracks in the moonlit night to pay a social call at Bill's, a half mile distant.

The following morning they continued their sleigh ride across the East Fork of Hood River and up the ridge to the top of China Hill, where guide Mark Weygandt lived. At that point, they donned snowshoes and plodded single file up the gentle grade, stopping at Elk Beds to adjust foot straps. The telephone wire was visible in places, where Will Langille had run it years previously. By late afternoon they reached Cloud Cap and soon had a fire throwing out heat and light. A cache of food had been left in the fall in anticipation, and the guides had made a special trip in addition, to bring up perishable food.

The Inn shook and groaned that night in the gales of wind that blasted the ridge, and they felt secure in knowing that the heavy cables had been placed to anchor the building to the solid rock foundation. On the 21st the group descended the ravine for water (probably Tilly Jane Creek) and renewed acquaintances with the old trapper, Offield, who lived in a cabin there. His wall displayed the drying skins of many marten, although he claimed it to be an off-year for trapping. That evening the wind died, and on the morning of the 22nd they could see Mount Hood plainly through the windows of the Inn.

They rode toboggan most of that day and experimented with using skis on the next, making the return trip altogether too brief to Weygandt's place at China Hill. Downhill, the horses made fast time, arriving back on the streets of Hood River that afternoon (January 23).

A JOB FOR MARK WEYGANDT

Mark Weygandt was put in charge of guiding and also of taking food up to Cloud Cap Inn for the group. Steaks and fresh vegetables were served on the dining table, and it took a substantial crew of back-packers to carry the loads up the hill. Most of the able-bodied farmers in the Upper Hood River Valley worked at the job at one time or other. Weygandt was given a good budget, and he paid the packers well, $5 a load. Some of them managed to get in two trips in one day.

At that time $5 was a very handsome wage, and the men in the community all looked forward to the men of the Snowshoe Club coming to the north side for their annual Winter Outing. To some it was the only bright spot in an area that was generally financially depressed.

Some of the early packers who worked for Weygandt up until about 1915 were Robert Leasure, William Jones, Ed and Sam McConn, Ed Hardman, George Hanaman, Frank Peeler, Alva Hardman, and William Edick, who later served many years as Sheriff of Hood River County.

There was some overlap, but the group who packed the groceries during the next ten years were David Cooper, Jr., George Cooper, Harry Routson, Orville Thompson, Marion Shearer, Felix and Lloyd Kile, George Monroe, Phil Parrott, and Shorty Rice.

Then there was a group that worked up until about 1930, Frank and Jess Hudson, Cecil Tomlinson, Will Jones, Ernest Monroe, and Earl Newman.

The Snowshoe Club became so pleased with their annual pilgrimages to Mount Hood that they made a 99-year lease with the Forest Service and

Snow Shoe Club Winter Outing circa 1908 — Photo Wesley Weygandt
Mark Weygandt in upper left. The trapper Offield lower left. Wesley Ladd seated at card table in light-colored garment.

Snow Shoe Club Winter Outing circa 1948 — Photo Wesley Weygandt
Front row from left, Dr. W. Ronald Fraser, Dr. H. Hiner Nichols, unidentified man, Bill Rosenfeld, Ernest Monroe, F. Faber Lewis.
Back row, Robert L. Beebe, Jack Meier, Jack Bennett, R. Blake Honeyman, Eric M.L. Kollaratek, Lester Anderson, Robert B. Wilson, Ronald J. Honeyman, Lee Hoffman, Wesley Weygandt.

put up their own building in 1910, a structure north of Cloud Cap Inn on the ridge. Mark Weygandt was put in charge of construction of the building, using the help of David Cooper, Sr., David Cooper, Jr., Bert Sandman, and Russell Gobin.

Once they owned a building, they appointed Weygandt the caretaker, a job he held until 1926. It was the job of the caretaker to warm up the lodge a few days before the Winter Outing, and to fully arrange for all the provisions and a cook. In 1926 Will Jones took over the job until 1934, then Ned VanNuys until 1938, Ernest Monroe until 1955. Since that time Phil Tyler has held the job.

The story of a winter outing in 1925 is somewhat characteristic. The group employed a crew of six to do the cooking and other work. On reaching the lodge, it was necessary to dig 10 feet down and a tunnel of 25 feet to reach the door. The guests fought a raging snow storm to reach the area.

Members attending were J. Wesley Ladd, C.E. Grelle, E.C. Sammons, Dr. Herbert Nichols, Richard W. Montague. T. Raymond Conway came along as a special guest, bringing his moving picture camera to film the members in action on the Eliot Glacier.

Since World War Two, the backpackers have become a thing of the past. Mark Weygandt's sons, Wes, Ted, and Myron used their weasel to bring in the food and provide a taxi service from Cooper Spur Junction up to the club lodge. When they retired, they sold a machine to the club, but today the job is handled by Jack Baldwin and the crew down at Cooper Spur Ski Area, who use snow-cats to support the Snowshoe Club members.

Crag Rats, Hood River Rescue Specialists

The American Legion climbs originated in 1921 with a group of hiking and camping friends of Legion Post #22, who had previously belonged to Company 12 of the Oregon National Guard coast artillery. A little later on, the Hood River Guides were formed, roughly the same group. The Guides marched in the Portland Rose Festival a year or two, further cementing the relationship. The Guides Ski Club was an outgrowth of Hood River Guides.

An E.C. Loveland was rescued at one time after an injury on the Sunshine Route. The search for Blanchar Baldwin in 1923 caused considerable thought as to the need of a search and rescue club at Hood River. The whole idea culminated in 1926, when A.L. Andy Anderson called a meeting for August 3 to consider a club. But first, let us step back to 1923 for a more complete story on the Baldwin search.

The need for a search and rescue group at Hood River was born of a moment of personal anxiety for L. Mason (Mace) Baldwin in 1923. He took his wife, Alda, and son, Blanchar, on a summer picnic near Parkdale on Middle Fork of Hood River. His brother-in-law, Jess Puddy, and another young man decided to fish Tony Creek nearby, and Blanchar wanted to walk along. Blanchar, almost nine, soon tired and started back to the campsite. Crossing a foot-log across Middle Fork, he became confused. Crossing another log that did not reach across, he jumped for shore. Blanchar spent the whole night out, his parents fearing he had drowned.

Jess Puddy rounded up some help in Parkdale, while Baldwin built a large fire and combed the area. At daylight men arrived to help. Finally crossing the log that did not reach, they soon found the boy sleeping beside a log on fir boughs. David Cooper, Jr. was the one who saw him first. It was a happy ending, but the incident was strong in the minds of Puddy and Baldwin. Three years later when they heard about Jack Strong being lost, the urge was strong to repay the effort that had been made to find Blanchar.

On August 13, 1926, Mrs. W.H. Strong of Gresham was camping at Paradise Park with her daughter and sons, Raymond, Winston, and Jack. The boys went fishing down on Lost Creek, and Jack, 7, became separated from them. The older brothers searched all the way down to the Sandy River, returning back up the north side to Clear Fork Ranger Station. There they told the story, and the Forest Service put several men out on search the following morning, a Friday. Mrs. Strong took her little girl, on Friday morning, down the trail to Twin Bridges. By noon, Mr. Strong, working in a lumber mill down in the valley, had been notified. After a few phone calls, millmen and loggers left their jobs to hunt for Jack Strong. On Friday night, Mazamas and Trails Club members were alerted, and the Saturday papers carried an appeal to woods-wise people to help search.

Forty infantrymen from Vancouver rolled into Clear Fork Station in army trucks. State Police, Portland Police, and deputy sheriffs entered the search which was finally headed by T. Raymond Conway at headquarters and Judge John H. Stevenson in the field. Tyrollean Max Muller brought his dogs, Dolf and Bora. The 16-year old daughter of Hood River sheriff Glen Sloat ranged the course on a 17-hour cruise with her bloodhounds. Searchers had early evidence that Jack had descended Lost Creek and cut back uphill along the Muddy Fork of the Sandy River.

Mace Baldwin, Percy Bucklin, and Jesse Puddy arrived from Hood River to do their bit. From Twin Bridges they hiked to Paradise, then across the canyon of the Sandy River below Reid Glacier to the timbered slopes of lower Yocum Ridge. Puddy did a lot of shouting, which was finally answered by Jack Strong. There in the trees they found him, alive and well. He had been living on huckleberries. Bucklin took his revolver out and fired two shots, an interval, and two more shots. Far below in a canyon a Portland policeman answered with two shots, the signal that they knew the boy had been found.

The men were quite proud of their success and didn't want some other group to get credit for it. The wife of Andy Anderson had often joked about their being up in the crags so much that they were just like crag rats. So when they finally arrived in the valley with Jack Strong, the news reporters asked if they belonged to a club.

"Oh, yes."

"What one is it?"

"The Crag Rats — from Hood River."

"We have never heard of that," querried the reporters. The Hood River men had just barely heard of it themselves, having assembled socially only a few days before on August 3 to discuss the idea of a club.

The club scored brilliantly again that year when they went to search for Calvin White, Jr. when on Friday, December 31, 1926, he left a group of five boys on skis, stopping in a tired condition with two of the others. White had better wax than the other two and led out far ahead on their trip toward Government Camp. They arrived there, but he did not, thus launching a massive search that finally culminated in his being found in Zigzag Canyon by Crag Rat William Cochran. Cochran had been working one side of the canyon and John Annala the other, following clues they had received on the morning of Monday, January 3, 1927.

Again in 1927, the club happened on a dramatic rescue, when a string of Mazama climbers fell on the Sunshine Route, fatally injuring Dr. Stanton Stryker on July 17. At least five other members of the Mazama party had to be evacuated after the shocking accident. A group of Crag Rats were skiing on Eliot Glacier at the time and took over the rescue.

In 1929, Phil Hukari responded to a call from Mount Rainier on a retrieval of the body of Forrest Greathouse, frozen in solid ice a hundred feet down a crevasse.

CRAG RATS IN MOTION PICTURES

In 1929 talks with Fox Movietone News brought a crew to Mount Hood to shoot film of the club members using their expertise on the Eliot Glacier. By Saturday, August 17, packer Walter Davidson had moved 1200 pounds of cameras, sound equipment, and wet batteries up onto the moraine, ready for the final trek the following morning into the serac area of the upper glacier.

But when the horses started out with their loads on Sunday morning, it became quickly apparent, that pack animals were not the answer. They floundered on the ice, and one horse slid into a crevasse. The loads were removed and the animals sent back. The unfortunate horse was rescued, unharmed, and returned to the moraine.

Summit party 1919, Crag Rats of the future — Photo Percy Bucklin
Back row, Alda Baldwin, Mace Baldwin, Unidentified, Hans Hoerlein.
Front row, Newton Clark, Lilly Fisher, Charles Crew.

At that point the Crag Rats decided to take over the heavy packing job on their own backs, taking the grueling weight up into the ice fall.

By noon the equipment was all in place and the Crag Rats became movie stars as the cameramen ground out about 2,500 feet of film of them, cutting steps, walking down into crevasses, and crossing spectacular snow bridges.

When the day was over, and the equipment had been returned to solid ground, the Fox representatives, Charles Pifer and Marshall Hall, treated the men in the Crag Rats to a dinner party. Fox was very appreciative that the Hood River men had saved the operation from being a total fiasco. Film was sent all over the United States, taking the climbing group into hundreds of theatres.

The Crag Rat Hut on the northwest corner of Hood River was proving to be a little small. In June of 1957, plans were made to add a 20' x 24' addition. On August 22, they voted to assess the membership $30 each to finance it. By December, $1,012 had been accumulated, but it was a long wait until the building was begun in January of 1958. Six months later they had almost all the exterior done, the hardwood floor in the hall, and the chimney laid up through the ceiling. On March 1, 1959 the Hut was declared finished for a total outlay of $1,906 and a great deal of member effort.

In January of 1965, an offer to buy the Crag Rat Hut for $60,000 was made by the Texas Oil Company for a service station site. The new freeway system built through Hood River had left it perched on a bluff, right above the roar of traffic. The offer was accepted and the deal consumated by early autumn.

New property, a spectacular view site 400' x 400' atop Winchell Butte southeast of Hood River was chosen. Contractor Phil Tyler drew plans and was awarded the contract to build for $37,240. The club paid for many extras and did some of the finishing, especially in the basement area. Club members hauled over 50 tons of lava rock from the Trout Lake area near Mount Adams.

By September of 1966 the new Hut was virtually complete. On December 4, they held open house and showed the building to over 500 visitors. Today the building is probably the most impressive clubhouse owned by any mountaineering club in the nation.

In March of 1953 the club bought an army Weasel for over-the-snow use. An assessment of $10 per member was made to pay for it. Maintenance problems were too great, even for a group that boasted many mechanically-minded farmers in their membership. In March, 1956, the machine was traded for a double-ended steel-hulled life boat, which was named Warfarin.

Warfarin needed scraping, painting, and a motor, and she lay stored for some time at Nichols'. Finally in December of 1958, she was launched sans paint and motor. The club finally decided she was poison and traded her off.

The Crag Rats founded their club on the premise of need for an active search and rescue group. Below lies a list of some of their operations from 1953 to present. Some were strictly Crag Rat activities, not shared by any other rescue group, but most were done in the cooperation with other groups. Since 1955, most operations have been done under the MORESCO organization. All have been done with the sanction of the sheriff of the county involved. On rescues and searches on the north side, most usually the Crag Rats and Alpinees are the only groups involved.

1953 Search for Ralph Day, never found. Search for Bruce Houck, murdered.

1954 Search for W.A. Benson. Search for Robert and Douglas Bartlett and Robert Poot. Rescue of body of William Morley, Jr. on Mount Jefferson.

1955 Search for Henry Baker whose plane crashed, never found. Search for a fisherman. Search for two women at Larch Mountain. Rescue of Frank Gillett on North Sister.

1956 Search for two boys on Larch Mountain. Search for boy on Gilhooley Mountain. Josephine Sedgewick, found drowned. John O'Brian, drowned in East Fork, not found. Search for Lynn Wattier, skier at Timberline. Search for body of Donna Bacon in West Fork. Search for lost fisherman. Search for elderly man. Search for lost fisherman. Search for Alice Nielson.

1957 Search for 5½ year old Ricky Craig at Mount Adams. Search for Luella Leather at Mount Adams. Search for two boys on Yocum Ridge. Rescue of Robert J. Boyle, Jr. from Beacon Rock. Rescue of Mike McGuire and Dave Bishop stranded on Adams Glacier. Rescue of bodies of Don McKay and Joe Quigley on St. Peter's Dome.

1958 Search for Martin family, not found. Search for downed plane east of Wyeth. Retrieved body of Harold Walter who died at Brooks Meadows. Retrieval of body of Francis E. Foss, killed in fall into Punchbowl.

1959 Search for three boys east of Hood River. Search for Alford Deford in Yacolt area. Search for girl 13. Search for deer hunter. Saved Louis Auila, parachutist who landed in Hood River. Search for four fliers in jet collision.

1960 Search for Boy Scout group. Search for Horace Henry, berry picker found dead. Search for Robert Sykes, hunter. Search for Beverly Allen, boy friend murdered, she not found. Retrieval of Owen C. Redwine, Ernest E. Pautz, and Clark Hay, killed in airplane crash. Fighting fires in cliff area in Snake River Canyon.

1961 Search for Rodney McMillan, skier at Timberline. Search for man at Mt. Adams. Search for Lorne Bailey, teenager, south of Mount St. Helens, not found. Rescue of Clarence Hamme, Jr., fisherman on cliff on East Fork. Rescue of Colin and Doug Chisholm on Eliot Glacier. Retrieval of Melvin Brewer body from plane wreck.

1962 Search for Clifford Altman near Bear Paw Camp. Rescue of Steven Knutson on Eliot Glacier. Rescue Jake Dias at Mount Adams.

1963 Rescue Dr. Gloekler, Dr. Hanschka, and Robert Schoemaker on Eliot Glacier.

1964 Search for Ricky Herden, 13, at Mount Adams. Rescue Don Graves in ski accident.

1965 Search for Albert Pisani. Search for Daley. Retrieve Elmer Alex Johnson, died at Badger Lake.

1966 Search for lost climber on south side. Rescue three Lewis and Clark students on Eliot Glacier. Retrieve L. Lisle Walker from Mazama Glacier on Mount Adams. Rescue Charles Gibson on Eliot Glacier. Retrieval of Robert Nield body, solo climber on Mount Jefferson.

1967 Retrieve body of fisherman in East Fork.

1968 Search for plane crash. Search for lost hunter. Rescue of Simonitch party on South Side Route.

1970 Search for two girls on horses. Rescue girl who fell off trail near Lolo Pass.

1971 Rescue of Harry Carson family on Eliot Glacier. Rescue of Muriel Demory, fell off trail at Sentinel Peak.

1972 Retrieve James Black, drowned in East Fork. Retrieve Tom Matheny, fell on Eagle Creek Trail to death. Rescue Louis Frenz, fell off top shelf of Punchbowl.

1973 Rescue teenage boy trapped in Dynamite Cave near Trout Lake. Rescue Pam Kiel on Cooper Spur Route.

For many years the first climb up the north side was always made by Crag Rats, usually an ascent in May or early June. They kept the record from 1946 to 1963, when another party preceded them by an hour, although the Crag Rats passed the other group and were back at Cloud Cap first. On that 16th of June a third party also climbed the north side.

In recent years the north side of the mountain is swarming with skiing and climbing groups, especially since the advent of cross-country ski popularity. Small groups are involved in winter climbing on almost any good weekend in winter time, as well as summer. Although this has not led to problems yet, the Crag Rats and Alpinees are aware of the potential for serious accidents that might go unnoticed until all the victims have died of exposure. The Cooper Spur Route, which has suffered so many summer accidents, is especially vulnerable to avalanche hazard or uncontrolled slides on ice.

Crag Rats can easily be distinguished on the mountainside in their caps and shirts of black and grey checkered wool. The garb makes them very distinctive in a group.

On July 28, 1966, they voted in their last Honorary Member, David Falconer, veteran climber and staff photographer for *The Oregonian.* Other mountaineers so distinguished have been T. Raymond Conway, L.A. Nelson, and Ted Emerson, all of who were prominent in search and rescue operations on Mount Hood.

In September of 1966, the Crag Rats were approached to be a sister club with the Sapporo Alpine Club of Japan. After consideration they accepted, and on June 15, 1967 a group of eight Sapporo members visited them on the return trip from a successful ascent of Mount McKinley. The Japanese were taken to see Cloud Cap Inn and were very impressed with the north side of Mount Hood.

On August 10, 1958, Bob Brown of television station KPTV, documented the club's rescue efforts in a film made on Eliot Glacier. Bill Gale made a realistic slide into a crevasse for the sake of the cameraman, and Rob Hukari and Glenn Marsh rappelled in to give simulated first aid. The affair took a humorous turn for a while when their club mates lost interest in pulling them back out. The film was shown several times on television, giving public education on the hazard of climbing and on the technique for rescue.

In January of 1972, Blanchar Baldwin died in an automobile accident. As a boy in 1926, he had spurred the initial interest in forming a search and rescue club by becoming the object of search. In later life he had been a valued member of the Crag Rats.

Traditional functions of the club have been an Annual Banquet, Annual Steak Fry in November, Winter Outing in February, Annual Picnic in September, and Summer Outing in August. Monthly social events at the Crag Rat Hut include wives.

For many years, the club has contracted with the Soil Conservation Service to make snow surveys at Tilly Jane, Greenpoint, and Red Hill, three major drainage areas of the Hood River Valley.

The publication of the Crag Rats is Rat Tales, begun at the end of 1934 for a single issue. A rough draft was prepared in 1935, but never printed. Regular publication on a quarterly basis started in 1953, and has continued ever since, except for the past three years, when issuance slipped to an annual basis.

The president of the organization is known as the Big Squeek, although a Hood River newspaper referred to the first one as the Head Rat, when the club was formed in 1926. The Little Squeek is vice-president. Other officers are a secretary, treasurer, and three trustees.

The club took over Cloud Cap Inn in 1952 or 1953. A winter outing was held in March of 1953, using the club's newly-acquired Weasel to pack the provisions. In the summer the old water lines were primed and drained again to eliminate air locks, and finally water once more flowed through the lines from the source on Tilly Jane Creek. In December, Wilson Appelgren donated a gas range for the kitchen.

In 1957 the water line was revamped and Harold Wells built drinking fountains in the north and south yards, embellished with chunks of agate and petrified wood he had collected throughout the state. The following year, the fountains had to be replaced with less glamorous stone, because tourists had stripped away the old one, piece by piece for souvenirs. In 1960 they

LIST OF BIG SQUEEKS

Year	Name	Year	Name	Year	Name
1926	L. Mason (Mace) Baldwin	1943	Dan Pierson	1960	Les Hukari
1927	L. Mason (Mace) Baldwin	1944	Gene Annala	1961	John Arens
1928	A.L. (Andy) Anderson	1945	Arne Udelius	1962	William Pattison
1929	T.J. Annala	1946	Arne Udelius	1963	Bernie Wertgen
1930	Harold Davis	1947	George Sheppard	1964	Ned Marshall
1931	Paul Hoerlein	1948	Wilson Applegren	1965	James Struck
1932	W.T. Hukari	1949	Robert Hukari	1966	Eugene Euwer
1933	William Sheppard, Sr.	1950	Robert Sheppard	1967	Robert Lynch
1934	Percy Bucklin	1951	Glenn Marsh	1968	Marcus Thrane R.B. Leavens
1935	Arvi Annala	1952	Robert Moller	1969	Al Lichens
1936	George Iliams	1953	Elwood Samuel	1970	Wolfgang Sterr
1937	Arne Hukari	1954	Norman Hukari	1971	Don Graves
1938	L. Mason (Mace) Baldwin	1955	Ross Hukari	1972	Don Miller
1939	Eino Annala	1956	William Sheppard, Jr.	1973	Les Hukari
1940	Harold Wells	1957	Don Marsh	1974	Dr. W.T. Edmundson
1941	Jess Crenshaw	1958	William Bryan	1975	Jerry Bryan
1942	William Cochran	1959	William Gale		

found the foundation on the northwest corner of the building had collapsed. The floor was jacked up and temporary repairs made. The following summer a concrete pour was made to properly mend the break.

At both the Red Hill Cabin and Cloud Cap Inn, the Crag Rats find a very hard life in trying to protect their property from thieves and vandals. On October 3, 1957, Bill Bryan and Ellwood Samuel went to Cloud Cap and found that someone had broken in. Driving down the road, they met a car driving up with three boys. They gave evasive answers, but Samuel told Bryan "I know they have been in the building. That one is wearing my sweater."

They took the boys down to the sheriff. The judge put them out on eight months of parole, providing they restored stolen goods and paid for the damage. Since that time, break-ins have been very frequent. In 1960, the Forest Service gave permission to block the driveway with a steel cable at Cloud Cap. During the 1974 season, the building was entered more than once. There is little of value to steal at the building, but the damage to windows and shutters is costly.

North Slope Ski Club

The Hood River Guides were the parent organization of both the Crag Rats and the Guides Ski Club. Hood River newspapers spoke often of Guides Ski Club from its inception in 1925, until the winter of 1928-29, when reference was made to the name of Hood River Ski Club. From then on, that name was in effect.

The American Legion had kept alive the friendship of World War One men. Some of the founders of Guides Ski Club were Percy Bucklin, A.L. Andy Anderson, and Hans and Paul Hoerlein. These men had all lived in the Midwest and brought skis with them to Hood River before the war. Ole Severson had learned skiing in Norway, participating in national competition there. These men were joined by Donald Larson, Harold Loomis, Willis "Doc" Eby, Harold Haggen, and John Annala.

At that time no skis were available on the Pacific Coast, as far as they could find. Andy Anderson sent for a catalog from Northland Ski Co. in St. Paul, Minnesota, and the group began to build their stock of equipment. The skis, that the first four originally owned, had merely a front toe strap, but the catalog showed a harness that fitted to the ski by using two metal toe clamps. Soon the whole group was skiing around the north slopes with these new harnesses mounted on the 8-foot pine skis of that era. A plain pole about 7 feet long was used for balance; on steep hills the skier dragged the pole between his legs to slow his speed.

They used their climbing boots, but skiing tore the soles loose. The next step was to order leather Norwegian ski boots from the catalog. The local shoe shop measured their feet and told them what size to order. Poles were the next acquisition, real ski poles with baskets on the ends such as are used today. Then came the shift to maple skis, and finally hickory, as equipment became more refined. Turns were all made by the telemark system. When the stem-christiana and the christiana turns were introduced at Mount Hood, the demand quickly changed to shorter skis, more like 6'6" to 7'0", instead of the 8-footers they had been pushing around.

Much of the activity centered around Homestead Inn, a hotel that stood on private land owned by J.O. Hannum just east of the present day Cooper Spur Ski Area. It is said that in 1924 Hannum had been instrumental in getting the state to run the Mount Hood Loop Highway south out of Parkdale to Cooper Spur Junction, before it curved down to the East Fork near Pollalie Creek. He was a county commissioner and had built Homestead Inn about 1922; running the highway upon the shoulder of the mountain was of much advantage to him in drawing business to the hotel. The other hotel was Mount Hood Lodge, run by Homer Rogers over to the west on the old road to Cloud Cap Inn. The diversion of traffic placed him in a position of great advantage over Rogers.

It is generally believed that the first competitive skiing was a race staged by the Hood River Ski Club in 1925 on a course from Cloud Cap to Kirby Camp. The race was won by the mountain guide, Mark Weygandt. In the following year the club held its first annual ski carnival, featuring a race from Cloud Cap to Homestead Inn.

In the summer of 1926 the ski club brushed out the hill west of Homestead Inn and used the inn as an exclusive headquarters the winter of 1926-27. It was closed to the public, and only the club members were eligible to enter. It was in that summer that the road to Cloud Cap was finally surfaced and the old road from Elk Beds to Cloud Cap was considered abandoned.

In 1927 weather conditions were difficult, and the Ski Carnival was held at the Goldsbury Ranch to avoid slogging the last five miles to Hannum's in heavy snow. The county plowed the road only as far as the end of the mail route at the Blodgett ranch, now occupied by Jerry and Kate McCarthy. The old Goldsbury ranch lay on the old, abandoned road, a short distance north of Homer Rogers' Mount Hood Lodge. Above the ranch a mile was Elk Beds, and it was only five miles to Cloud Cap Inn. Out behind the barn the Echo Mountain Ski Tow serves a short private hill. Bob Lee claims it is the oldest tow on Mount Hood.

That 1927 Ski Carnival featured ski jumping, a

cross-country race and a ball game, with one team on skis and the other on snowshoes. The Mount Hood Ski Club from the south side came over to enter the competition.

BUILDING JUMP HILL

It was probably in 1927 that Hannum told the boys in the ski club one day that they should cut a swath in the trees for a jump hill on his place. They selected a steep area on a long hill and went to work during the summer months. Several weekends of hard, sweaty work were put in, when one day into the First National Bank walked Stanley Walters, ranger at Parkdale. Pulling at his little curved pipe, that had a silver cover to keep sparks from flying into dry forest area, Walters asked Percy Bucklin, if he had been cutting brush and timber up on the hill behind Homestead Inn.

"Sure. That's our new jumping hill," replied Bucklin.

"Who gave you permission?"

"Hannum. It is on his place."

"No, you are cutting on Forest Service land," said Walters.

Walters, a meticulous and conscientious man, somehow got the problem squared away with the beaurocracy, and the ski club got a permit on the ski jump hill. That hill has been used as a ski area all through the years, many times expanded in size.

It was in the summer of 1927 that club members worked over the old road for a ski run, cutting out some fallen trees and banking a few turns. Down lower, they turned onto the new road to Cooper Spur Junction, much as they would today in following down from Cloud Cap Inn.

Before the jump hill was completed that fall, the benefactor of the club suddenly passed out of the picture. J.O. Hannum died suddenly on a Labor Day trip nearby, on Monday September 5, 1927. The ski jump was finally finished in October.

Some of the club members were jumpers; others were cross-country skiers. The jumpers used thick, 8-foot, double-grooved skis that were balanced with more weight to the front. Everyone jumped occasionally, but the less experienced took shorter flights. Jumping on a pair of lighter skis tended to crack the ends on the impact of landing, so they didn't indulge too often with the wrong type of ski.

The cross-country men took off for the higher of Cloud Cap or to Cooper Spur or onto the Eliot Glacier. The Forest Service let them use the cabin at Tilly Jane Camp, where many a Saturday night was spent before the fireplace. A trail up Sand Canyon led 3½ miles to Tilly Jane, just as it does today, and the ski club members were often seen on Saturday plodding up the hill on snow shoes, dragging skis behind on a light cord. The old-time skis were notched on both tips to accommodate the cord. Another trip was to Lost Lake, starting in the flats just above the lumber mill at Dee.

The first wax was paraffin, good for downhill, but much too slick for walking uphill. By the mid-Thirties klister wax became available, as skiing equipment was introduced into sporting goods stores. This allowed uphill walking and leaving the snowshoes home. Before making the downhill run, the skier would remove all the sticky klister and use a faster wax for the descent, much the

J.O. Hannum's Homestead Inn, torn down in the Thirties — Photo Wes Weygandt

Tilly Jane Ski Shelter built 1939 — Photo USFS

same as modern day cross-country skiers do.

On February 12, 1928, the Mount Hood Ski Club from Government Camp held a winter carnival at Argonne Camp on the North Side. Winners in the jumps were Kaare Schafstad, Lindbergh, and Dr. Guy DuPlessis. In cross-country, Otto Haugan and Burglund. Lindbergh and Burglund were Hood River men. A tug-of-war on skis, with 50 men pulling for Hood River and 50 men pulling for Parkdale, resulted in a win for Hood River.

On February 25, 1929, the Hood River Ski Club held a tournament on the hill above Homestead Inn. Winners were Kaare Schafstad of Cascade, Hjalmar Hvam of Cascade, and Hans Hoerlein of Hood River SC. In Class B it was Ole Haugen of Cascade, Vic Miller of Hood River, and Gordon Johnston of Minneapolis Ski Club.

In 1930, the competitive ski clubs from Bend, Seattle, Leavenworth, Cle Elum, Hood River, and Government Camp put together the Pacific Northwestern Ski Association at an organizational meeting at the Multnomah Hotel on November 23. Fred McNeil, an official of Cascade Ski Club was named president, and Percy Bucklin of the Hood River Ski Club was elected treasurer. This organization gave a great deal of acceptance and stature to Mount Hood skiers.

SHARING A CABIN WITH USFS

The Forest Service built a guard station at Tilly Jane Camp in 1931, a building which still stands. The Crag Rats had proved a very good record of cooperation with the Forest Service, and District Ranger Stanley Walters made them an unusual offer. The government would use the cabin in the summer, but during the winter the Crag Rats would be permitted to use it. Since Crag Rats and Hood River Ski Club were for the most part the same group of people, the building was immediately visualized as a winter ski rendezvous.

Skier ascending Ghost Ridge

— Photo Joe Leuthold

On Labor Day weekend of 1931, a large group of Crag Rats worked on a stone fireplace for the building under the direction of George Zells. Some very large pieces of stone were hauled down from the rock area on the loop of the road, just west of Cloud Cap Inn. By the end of the weekend, the men had the fireplace built up six feet into the air, leaving the rest of the chimney to be completed in following weeks.

The skiers used the building heavily during the years following, parking their cars wherever snow blocked the road below, and hiking up the trail to Tilly Jane. Sharing with the Crag Rats and Hood River Ski Club evidently worked out well for the Forest Service, although today's regulations would probably make such an arrangement out of the question. The cabin was often well buried, and the weekend guests found it necessary to tunnel in 15 or 20 feet to gain entry.

On January 17, 1931, the Hood River Ski Club filed articles of incorporation at Salem to avoid possible legal problems. Some of the early additions to the club were the Annala family, Toivo, Eino, Sulo, and Arvi; and there was the Hukari family, Arne and William.

In the fall of 1931 McNeil wrote to Bucklin telling of the great success that Cascade Ski Club had experienced by holding an open public meeting and showing ski films. Membership for a dollar was then suggested, and the club had greatly increased its ranks. The Hood River Ski Club decided to do a little proselyting on the strength of Cascade's success. On December 16, they set up an open meeting at The Dalles.

Weather turned icy, and it took two hours for the two carloads of Hood River skiers to reach The Dalles in a sleet storm. About 25 people had given up and left, but there was still an audience of 50 very eager to hear the message about skiing. Bucklin showed some movies the club had taken on their trips. Although only a half dozen of the audience had ever been on skis, almost everyone wanted to try the sport.

As a result, when Cascade Ski Club held a big PNSA tournament in January of 1932, the Hood River Ski Club was noticeably absent. They were too busy entertaining and training their new recruits from The Dalles to take off and leave their own area.

Homestead Inn was a casualty of the depression. Hannum turned the lodge over to the ski club for winter use. By 1934 he was gone and the building was cold and dark, never to be used again. It was torn down and the logs used elsewhere; only the remains of a fireplace show the old location. The seedling trees of that day are now tall and dense.

As youngsters and new members entered the scene, the older club members gave lessons. Most were teachers at times, but the more prominent were Percy Bucklin, Andy Anderson, Paul Hoerlein, and Donald Lamson.

Competition grew popular in the Thirties. Hood River High School began to award major sports letters to skiers, and from 1937 on, the school was competing in a skiing circuit with Bend, and the Portland high schools, Grant, Lincoln, and Washington. Races were often run from the top of the jump hill down to Cooper Spur Junction. The bottom part on the flat road was usually an advantage to the Hood River skiers, as the other teams were accustomed to steeper terrain for the full race.

The Hood River High School team often went to Government Camp to be gatekeepers, being driven over by Waldo Arens in a camp truck owned by Bob Bartol, Hood River Chevrolet dealer. They parked it at the Ski Bowl and slept in it overnight. Bob Moller recalls two of the famous racers in 1939 Olympic tryouts coming through his gates in the slalom race. Dick Durrance roared through at high speed in breathtaking performance. Then the Austrian-born Friedl Pfieffer came flicking down the course, his turns lightning fast and graceful, but with a light touch that hardly made a noise.

The club moved the bus up to Timberline Lodge the next day for the downhill competition. The race course was high up on the mountain, beginning near Triangle Moraine. Wax, of course, was a great secret among racers, often being the slight edge that won or lost a race. Friedl Pfieffer was working over his skis in the basement of the lodge and dropped his slab of wax, a green colored mixture. Jack Baldwin reached over to pick it up for him, hoping to put his thumbnail into it and examine the texture. But the wary Pfieffer reached over and whisked up the wax before young Baldwin could reach it.

Some of the high school slalom competitors were John Arens, Jack Baldwin, George Howell, James Leonard, Robert F. Moller, Mike Franz, and Chandler Smith. Bend contenders were Gene Gillis, Sam Peoples, Bert Hagen, Clif Blann, Janet Farnham, Neil Farnham, Herb Francis, and Phil Hosmer. From Portland there were Don French, Ellis Bischoff, Dick Lewis, Tom Terry. So many of these student racers grew up to assume dominant positions in the mountain world later.

Competing meant travelling to Government Camp or Bend. Sometimes Waldo Arens took the boys over in his big Buick. The racers on the home team would put the others up in their own homes, so a great deal of friendship was built in those days.

Not all competition was among the school set. Percy Bucklin recalls a team of Finns from Astoria that came to Cooper Spur Ski Area to compete in jumping. It was during the prohibition era, but someone warned that the rambunctuous Finns would expect some alcohol to drink. Norman Shrumm, who drove the gasoline-powered passenger car on the rail tracks up to Parkdale, made the arrangements. He got a gallon of saki from the Japanese workmen on the rail line.

The day of the jumps the Hood River hosts poured small portions of the saki to the smiling Finns, who tossed it off as if it were water. The hosts kept telling them to go easy, that the saki was powerful, but the Finns understood little English; they merely kept smiling and drinking. When they were ready to jump, they could hardly walk and had to be helped and steadied on the takeoff. Once off and running, they bounded out through the air in perfect jumping form, landed straight and true, then pitched face forward into shambles. Undoubtedly, the judges counted off somewhat for their final form, even if circumstances were extenuating.

Jump Hill suffered a shocking event on December 19, 1936, when Victor Howell bounced off a stump and struck the square-sawed edge of another. The impact crushed his chest and killed him instantly. Victor was an older brother of George Howell. The ski club brushed out and improved the Sand Canyon Trail to Cloud Cap in 1939, and named it at that time the Howell Trail in memorium.

In 1940 the jumping competition for the Winter Olympics was held at Lake Placid, New York. Norway, superb in jumping, sent 15 contestants to that event. When it was over they travelled west, putting on exhibitions of their skill at Alta, Utah, and at Multorpor Mountain. Percy Bucklin tells of an amusing encounter they had with the pet bear that was an attraction at the bottom of the hill. The bear was kept on a chain and liked to beg food from the skiers, being able to take a bottle of pop and drink it like a man. One of the skiers offered him some food in his right hand while holding some more in the left. Bystanders were warning him to be careful, but English was falling on Norwegian ears, uncomprehended. The bear lunged for the nordic jumper, who turned to evade his reach. The claws of the animal caught his belt and stripped his trousers right off him. Percy Bucklin, a witness, didn't know what the Norwegian said, but whatever it was, he certainly said a lot of it.

Residents of the upper valley formed the North Slope Ski Club. In 1938 they put in a ski tow about a quarter mile west of Cooper Spur Junction. This rope tow was only about 150 feet long with 50 feet vertical rise. The tow motor was built from an old Star engine by Norval Shurtliff, a mechanic for Oregon Lumber Company at Dee. About 1940 the Hood River Ski Club put a small tow on their jump hill, built by Arthur Bibb and Harry Ethel, a log-truck operator.

In October of 1939 the CCC boys completed a hill improvement project at the Cooper Spur Ski area. Of even more significance was the ski shelter finished at the same time at the Tilly Jane area. The building is a large log lodge behind the Legion Camp area, complete with a large circular fireplace on the ground floor and sleeping space on the floor above. Wintertime skiers find it a good haven after slogging up the ski trail from Jump Hill.

Up until the opening of the Loop Highway on an all-year basis in 1968, Hood River was very much isolated from the popular south-side ski areas. As a result, the local ski clubs were able to keep up a good level of interest. In 1949 the Hood River Ski Club made a big push to improve Jump Hill. Bob Moller recalls the cooperative effort made in clearing more of the slope. Members who had farms brought up crawler and wheel tractors, some with blades to level the ground, others with chains to pull the stumps and roots left from the clearing. With the help of Ole Severson, whose sons Carl and Norman had been jumpers on the hill, a good supply of low-priced or donated lumber was arranged for a warming hut. Severson was a lumber broker in White Salmon and had connections with Oregon Lumber at Dee, Parkdale Lumber Co., and Neal Creek Lumber Co. Moller hauled many loads up to the area with his farm truck.

The warming hut was built at the bottom of Jump Hill with solid 2"x4" "corn crib" wall construction, and is still in use today. In 1949 the area got a Jaycee Ski School staged by the Hood River Junior Chamber of Commerce, similar to the school activity being run at Government Camp by the Portland Jaycees. Bob Donaldson of Timber Structures came up to conduct the school, and they were even blessed by some appearances by Hjalmar Hvam.

After the war it became more difficult to keep two ski clubs alive. Hood River Ski Club and North Slope Ski Club consolidated, using the name of the latter.

The north side has always been patrolled under the National Ski Patrol organization, unlike the south side which went independent after a severance with the national group in 1962. At present the patrol is under the direction of Kenneth Raasch, who also acts as head of the ski school. The patrol usually averages about 15 members, including the apprentices.

American Legion Climbs

American Legion Post #22 of Hood River started in 1921 to sponsor climbs each July on Cooper Spur Route. A group of men from Company 12, Coast Artillery of the Oregon National Guard, were key men in the post, and they had formed the habit of taking overnight hikes. Kent Shoemaker proposed that they climb Mount Hood, and he was immediately selected to fulfill his suggestion. Ned Van Horn, Robert L. Foust, George Wilbur, and Harold Herschner served on the committee under him. Wilbur had been the commanding officer of the old company.

169 on early Legion Climb — Photo Wesley Weygandt

Mark Weygandt acted as guide for the first Legion climb in 1921. Will Langille was back in the valley again during that time and went on the climb. He had pioneered the route with his brother Doug back in 1893. Photography was covered by Fred Donnerberg and Dr. V.R. Abraham. It was from this group of people and some others such as Andy Anderson and Mace Baldwin, that the Crag Rats came into existence in 1927.

The first climb was a success, with no accidents, a record followed through until the Legion climbs ceased after World War Two. A New York woman, Mrs. Beatrice Crawford Newcomb, made it to the top, but she was so ill she spent the night in the summit cabin and was shepherded down the next day by Clem Blakney.

The climbing committee succeeded in getting Governor Ben Olcott and Secretary of State Sam Kozer to join the climb. Olcott had been the only governor of Oregon to climb Mount Hood while in office, except for Governor Geer in 1900.

The second Annual Legion Climb was made Sunday, July 16, 1922, in ideal weather. The climb was preceded by a big campfire program attended by such dignitaries as Portland's Mayor George Baker and his wife, Secretary of State Sam Kozer, and Colonel C.C. Hammond. Unlike some of the programs in later years, the campfire program was disbanded early, and a positive attempt was made to insure that the climbers got some sleep. A large forest fire near Wyeth deterred many visitors, because they felt visibility would be poor on the mountain.

The climb included 102 people who registered on the summit after a hard ascent. There was a good deal of rolling rock that bruised some of the climbers, although no accidents were serious. On the summit the climbers mingled with a group of 70 Mazamas from the south side. Only 12 people of both groups had ever made a previous climb.

One story the Crag Rats tell about the American Legion Climbs is that of the missing mayor, George Baker. The climb had gone well up to Tie-In-Rock on Cooper Spur Route. Suddenly someone realized that His Honor was missing, and so was Bill Brazeau, a horn player with the Knights of Pithias band. There were a good many gloomy fears of the mayor being lost in a crevasse, until one of the climb leaders found the two of them over toward Newton Clark Glacier, sitting behind a rock enjoying a bottle of moonshine.

In 1925, Mark Weygandt took the Legion Climb up the newly-developed Sunshine Route, which the guide claimed was almost free of any danger. Saying that he had climbed it a few days previously in smooth soles without an ice axe, Weygandt, used no climbing ropes, only setting about 500 feet of fixed line in one steep area.

On the Legion climb of July 20, he guided a party of 86 climbers, about half of whom were women. Many were in smooth-soled shoes. It was the fifth Annual Climb and Weygandt's 588th ascent. All went well, but when The Mazamas experienced a death, and the injury of several others in 1927, many people began to think back, and he came under considerable criticism. The Crag Rats began to lead the Legion Climbs thereafter.

LEGION HAD PROBLEMS ALSO

Sunday, July 14, 1929 Following a big Saturday night program with a broadcast over radio KGW, a large party of 199 climbers started out in the black of night for the summit. At Tie-In-Rock they lost two of them, two brothers who were turned back because they had smooth shoes, instead of the caulked boots required.

The two boys had more enthusiasm than good sense, because they decided to join another Crag Rat party that was touring Eliot Glacier below. The *Hood River News* reported that they **slid** down to the Eliot Glacier. This caused the author to read the passage again. **Yes, they slid down,** and that means they glissaded, either sitting or standing. This was a remarkable feat, even though it was done in brash ignorance.

Down below, the Crag Rat leaders watched with their mouths open, not believing anyone could be so casual with his life. Then the two ran with abandon across the glacier to the Crag Rat group, jumping crevasses and neglecting to test suspicious areas for hidden crevasses. One had lost his ice axe, when they reached the party.

The stern Crag Rat leaders put the boys in their line and insisted that they stay there. This quickly produced some complaining, one remarking that "I'm sure not coming back to this side of the mountain anymore!" The other members of the party silently hoped that he meant what he said.

In 1930 the campfire program was of a local nature until 10:30 p.m., when the Portland Chamber of Commerce came on with a program that was broadcast through the western states by the National Boradcasting Company through affiliate KGW. The next day, while the climbers were busy ascending Cooper Spur Route, Percy Bucklin was busy running a ski race for the Hood River Ski Club, and another group of Crag Rats was filming a simulated rescue.

In 1931 "Big Chief" L.A. Nelson was welcomed at the evening campfire. Before dawn about 150 started the climb. High on the mountain a few moments of terror were experienced by Don Lamson, when his string of four slipped and slid along in an avalanche, finally holding in a successful arrest. Once on top Mount Hood, the American Legion members held a meeting. It was cut rather short because of bad weather. Bucklin was holding another ski race, down below on Eliot Glacier.

In 1932, A.L. Anderson led the Annual climb, diminished to only 64 people, because of the depression. H.G. Ball led another group from the Legion Camp on a tour of Eliot Glacier.

A near-tragedy occurred high on the mountain and was averted by quick thinking of Ed Goodrich, anchor man on a string of four descending climbers. An avalanche of rock and snow swept from above, bombarding the party and forcing them to strain on their alpenstocks to keep from being swept away. Goodrich saw it coming and got them to dig the shafts into the snow in time to be effective.

All four were pummelled and injured, but a doctor in the party pronounced them in safe condition. The other members of the rope team were Edna Redmond of Hood River and Mr. and Mrs. George Bailey of Yakima. Goodrich and Bailey were not able to walk back to Legion Camp on their own; Goodrich had been struck in the knee and Bailey suffered a head injury and the fracture of a small bone in his foot.

The 1933 climb on July 16, was threatened by bad weather. Bob Fuller led a group the day before of about 50 men who planned to illuminate points on the summit, Cooper Spur, Horseshoe Rock, and Eliot Glacier. It was to be a spectacular display of high candlepower illumination and bombs, rockets, and other fireworks. But the weather assaulted them with rain, snow, and sleet, driving them off the mountain, and threatening the climb on Sunday.

Although it snowed about a foot during the night, the weather eased, and Chairman Kent Shoemaker sent out a party that put 105 climbers on the summit. The camp kitchen was run by

Vera LaCombe, who had performed the job for several years.

In 1938, a special effort was made to invite prominent people to the encampment at Tilly Jane. O.E. Palmateer of Salem, the State Commander of the American Legion, appeared to take nominal charge of the climbing party of 89 that reached the summit. The climbing party broke over the top to greet the group of nine who had spent the night on top, including Bob Tomlinson and Rusty Fowler of Radio KGW, who made a short wave broadcast over the National Broadcasting Company's red network. Kent Shoemaker and Jess Crenshaw were prominent among the Crag Rat leaders.

The 1941 climb was called off a few days ahead of the scheduled date of Sunday, July 22. Leaders Gene Anala and Mace Baldwin took the group on a tour of the crevasses and seracs of the Eliot Glacier, instead, perhaps a more interesting trip than a summit climb. Glowing reports by the participants were received by the newspapers.

On Saturday Jess Crenshaw led the flare gang up to illuminate prominent points on the mountainside. Richard R. Pooley and Phil Brown formed a part of the crew, acting as radio men. A crowd of 4,000 gathered for the ceremonies and view of the illumination at Tilly Jane Camp.

Despite cancellation by the Crag Rats, two other groups decided to climb Sunshine and Cooper Spur Route on Sunday, one a group of Tacoma Mountaineers. Both made it to the summit without encountering the expected avalanches, but all decided to descend by the South Side Route, being afraid to risk the descent of Cooper Spur.

In 1946, the Legion climbs were resumed. In the party of 135 climbers were Supervisor of MHNF Clare Hendee, and W.M. Parke and Wayne Gurley of the Forest Service.

In 1947, preparations were made for the climb. A party of Crag Rats went to Timberline Lodge the week before with 1,000 feet of rope to carry to the summit for a handline down Cooper Spur Route. They socialized until 2:00 a.m. at the lodge, then talked the lift operators into starting the ski lift. The crew rode to Silcox Hut with the rope strung out between the riders on the chairs. Then came the long job of packing one continuous coil, apportioned to the members of the party.

The following Saturday was the day to string the handline down the steep north side. They packed a load of pickets up the mountain, pieces of 3/4-inch pipe seven feet long, with a ring welded to the end of each piece. On the way up one of those pickets was plunged into the snow about every fifty feet. Then the plan was to string the rope down from the top, tying it off on each picket.

On the way up, several small avalanches rolled off the slope, causing some anxiety. At Tie-In-Rock George Sheppard and Arne Udelius left the party and remained to handle the situation at the bottom end. Bill Bryan can recall indications of avalanching, as the party proceeded up to the summit. Once on top, they had a bite to eat and prepared to descend with the rope.

Meanwhile another group of climbers left the summit and began to descend Cooper Spur Route. The first person kicked off a block of snow off the cornice. It rolled down the slope and triggered an avalanche that swept the top four feet of snow off most of the northeast slope of the mountain. At Tie-In-Rock Sheppard and Udelius watched in fearful awe as blocks the size of refrigerators and automobiles came bounding down the mountainside.

Minutes later all was quiet, and above them they could see a four-foot shelf where the snow had calved away from the highest snow fields. This was obviously a threatening mass, hanging precariously there, ready to go at the least provocation. They were able to communicate by shouting. The decision was made for Sheppard and Udelius to return to Cloud Cap Inn, while Bryan's group on the summit would take the South Side Route down to safety. Needless to say, the Legion climb for the following day was cancelled.

In 1948, a big celebration was held at Legion Camp. It was estimated that 3,500 people attended. On Sunday, July 26, the party started up the Cooper Spur Route with 126 climbers. The Climb Chairman was Jack Baldwin, the leader Ed Puddy.

When they reached the 9,500-foot level there had been some small avalanches, and there were signs that larger ones might be incipient. After a council of war, the leaders decided to turn the party around and not risk the hazard.

In 1949, the same process of taking the ropes up the South Side took place. Myron Weygandt was the general chairman and his brother Wesley headed the mountain detail. On Saturday, July 31, the flare party went up to the summit to stage the illumination for the crowd of 3,000 people at the campfire program.

Al Combs recalls that as they descended, an avalanche caught his string and carried them downward in the darkness toward Newton Clark Glacier. They finally came to rest in the jumble of the avalanche fan. It was very difficult to dig out in the dark and get back to the camp.

Thus, for the third year in a row, the Annual Legion Climb was cancelled. The next morning they could look up at the Cooper Spur Route and see the fixed rope hanging in a great arc on the mountainside. The pickets had been torn loose and hung at regular intervals from the rope.

In 1950, the Annual climb was held on August 6. Attendance at Legion Camp was down to about 1,000 people, and only 34 people made the climb, including the leaders. Since the snow was not considered safe on Cooper Spur, the ascent was made by South Side Route. The climbers left the camp at 3:30 a.m. to drive around to Timberline Lodge.

In 1951, Myron Weygandt acted as the climb chairman. About 60 climbers, plus their leaders, ascended Cooper Spur Route, but they descended South Side Route to insure greater safety. A crowd of 1,500 at Legion Camp watched the impressive illumination Saturday evening, said to be the best ever produced on the Legion climb weekends. The committee used 24 parachute flares with 100,000 candlepower illuminating capacity per flare.

In 1952, Jack Bingaman was the General Chairman of the Legion Climb. Again some excitement entered the picture on Sunday, July 6, when a group of climbers took up 300 pounds of rope and 60 pounds of stakes in preparation for the club at the end of July. The group consisted of a few Alpinee's and a number of guests, mostly untrained in mountaineering. Participants were Bob Harris, Jack Bingaman, Dick Isenberg, Bob Peshall, Nevin Gudeneau, Richard Getchell, Bill Mohr, Ronald Getchell, Roger Getchell, Leonard Murphy, James Platz, James Long, Donald Burnett, and Bill Payne.

According to the recollections of Don Burnett, the group did their work and descended to Lunch Rock. There was some indication of avalanche danger. Seven of the group, all novices, started down in one rope, when an avalanche began to carry them downward. Fortunately, its route swept them down the ridge, not off to the Eliot Glacier.

Riding atop a great stream of avalanching snow, they crossed one crevasse, then another, on their wild slide. The crevasses were substantial in width and depth, but the snow filled them up, allowing the string of climbers to ride across the top unharmed. Burnett can recall flying through the air to land on the lower lip of the second crevasse, and then the party stopped. None of the group was seriously injured, but some of them had to be cut out of the rope with a knife. Up above them, the fixed rope and stakes had been torn out.

On the date of the climb weekend, later that month, Myron Weygandt was in charge of the flare crews during the Saturday evening program. One flare group went to the top of Mount Hood, John Thomas, James Merritt, Joan Merritt, Newt Lineberger, Paul Lineberger, James Platz, Hans VonRosam, Hans Jacobsen, Gunnar Mathiasen, Martin Johansen, Ronald Walton, and Knut Syverson. At Lunch Rock, three more stood by for their part in the illumination, Bud Oliver, Bob Peshall, and Nevin Gunderian.

Climbing on the north side was judged to be too dangerous, so the participants in the Annual Legion Climb left the camp at 11:40 p.m. for the drive to Timberline Lodge. Seven leaders and 17 climbers began the climb of South Side Route, but they were forced to turn back about 8:00 a.m. below Crater Rock because of bad weather.

In 1953, the Annual Climb was scheduled for August 1-2 under the chairmanship of Myron Weygandt. Entertainers at the campfire program were Lloyd Smith and the Western Valley Boys of Eugene. Only a few hundred people attended, and the next morning only about 30 started out on the climb. About a dozen reached the summit.

At the next meeting of the American Legion Post the committee reported that the weekend had resulted in a financial loss. It was evident that interest in the Annual Climb and encampment had been dwindling in recent years. So the 1953 American Legion Climb was the last one ever held.

The end of the Legion climbs was truly the passing of an era. The Hood River Community had become very much involved in the annual program. By the year 1948 over 2,000 people had participated in the climbs, and the crowds around the campfire on the eve of the climb always ran into the thousands. Serving 10,000 meals to the festive crowds was not uncommon during a climb weekend. Kent Shoemaker had followed through with the organization every year until World War Two. After that, Jack Baldwin took over and led the group.

Campfire programs were lavish with lots of funmaking and professional entertainment. Crowning of the queen was one of the first items in each program. The relatively small number of climbers had a very difficult time getting any rest while the great multitude whooped it up into the night. Despite the sleepless ordeal, the climbs had drawn large numbers of participants, until the last few years.

Wy'east Climbers, a Mountain Fraternity

Undoubtedly the most close-knit, courageous, self-giving, hard-living, hilarious group to know the slopes of Mount Hood is the club known as Wy'east Climbers. It is a mountaineering fraternity, selective, restrictive, elite.

In about December of 1930, a small group of active hikers and climbers on a hike up Larch Mountain discussed the idea of a mountaineering club limited to an enthusiastic few. A few days later they held an organizational meeting with the following result:

President	Don Burkhart
Secretary	Ray Atkeson
Historian	James Harlow
Charter Members	Ralph Calkin
	Barrie James
	Alfred Monner
	Norman O'Connor

New Year's day of 1931 they made a snowshoe trip to Government Camp. A few days later they framed a constitution and named themselves the Columbia Hikers. By the time a month had gone by, the name was not liked very well, and many more suggestions were made. Finally someone came up with the name Wi-yeast, which labelled one of the basins on the north side, an Indian name of legend. On April 14, 1931, the name Wy'east Climbers was adopted, the spelling changed slightly.

By the fall of 1932, they decided that all must have first aid training and in October and November took a course under instructor Aitken of Sanderson Safety Supply Company. In December, the full group went ahead with advanced training with Sloan of Pacific Telephone Company. This prompted them to take a toboggan, blankets, and splints to Crater Rock for a permanent cache. On June 4, 1933, six members and three guests made the necessary trip.

January 1, 1934 Wy'easters converged on the summit from both north and south to make the first climb of the year. On the South Side Route were Everett Darr, Bob Furrer, Ray Lewis, and Ole Lien.

On the Cooper Spur Route were Ralph Calkin, Hank Kurtz, Joe Leuthold, and Curtis Ijames. They had to walk from Homestead Inn, which stood about a mile above Cooper Spur Junction. The party left Cloud Cap Inn at 5:00 p.m. in very deep snow. Ijames quit at Cooper Spur, and the party braved the possibility of avalanches to reach the summit at 2:00 a.m. on New Year's Day. They descended in the dark because "we could not see what was below us."

Winter headquarters were in the old Forest Service Timberline Cabin, west of present-day Timberline Lodge. It was smelly and dirty, and it often took hours to dig down through drifted snow, just to get inside. Despite all the bad conditions, Timberline Cabin was becoming more and more popular with a swelling number of new skiers that were showing on the slopes. The Wy'easters were stockpiling kerosene and getting in a winter wood supply for an unappreciative group of interlopers to use. For this reason, they began to agitate the Forest Service for a site to use for a cabin of their own.

On July 1, 1934, Dale Cowen, chairman of the cabin committee, took a small group and with the help of Francis E. Williamson of the Forest Service, selected a site for a Wy'east cabin. The cabin is still there in a glade, a quarter mile east of Phlox Point Cabin. Today's skiers on the #2 lift at Timberline Lodge, flash right by the little building, hardly realizing its identity.

By July 4th, they had the legal problems squared away and a crew in charge of Joe Leuthold had the foundation started and a tram constructed for bringing materials downhill. James Mount had commandeered 20 sacks of cement from some friendly donor. Bernard Heims of Lipman Wolfe Co. drew the plans. The building had a half-basement for wood storage, a ski-waxing and entry room just inside the front door, and an 18' x 18' living room.

From the first, the Wy'easters were very competitive in getting their team first to the top each January. One of the regular performers in that department, Ole Lien, was made a member of the club. On April 29, 1934, James Mount and Ralph Calkin circled Mount Hood on skis for the first recorded time. They left Cloud Cap Inn at 8:30 a.m. and returned at 6:00 p.m., a harrowing trip in storm and fog. Small avalanches on Reid Glacier gave them some minutes of worry.

On June 3, 1934, James Mount, Ralph Calkin, James Harlow, and Everett Darr climbed West Side Route, now called Leuthold Couloir. That day they referred to it as Yocum Ridge Route, and a little later as Avalanche Route, as suggested by Everett Darr. The climb of that day was a floundering struggle through waist-deep powder. Harlow narrowly missed one avalanche by fast foot work, and Calkin and Harlow soon after barely missed another. Open crevasses were deceptively filled with bottomless, loose powder, a dangerous combination of conditions. Soon the pattern emerged wherein every man wanted to lead. No one wanted to be caught in someone else's avalanche. Swimming in the loose powder was the only means of preventing sinking at times.

WY'EAST PRESIDENT KILLED

On Labor Day of 1933, the first president, Don Burkhart had been killed with two other climbers on a fall on the east face of Mount Jefferson. Wy'easters had gone to the rescue and retrieval of his body. In 1934, a memorial service on June 17th was held by the 16 members of the club on one of the pinnacles of Ollalie Butte. Don Burkhart's father, mother, and sister were escorted to the base of the rock cairn the Wy'easters had built there in his memory. About a hundred members of The Mazamas and Trails Club of Oregon followed solemnly and heard a stoic but expressive speech by Wy'east president, Curtis Ijames. He then placed a cedar wreath at the cairn, held a moment of silence, and "Taps" was sounded by an unseen bugler in the rocks. The audience filed down the long trail silently. Joe Leuthold said a silent prayer of thanks to providence that day; he had been invited to climb with the Burkhart party that fateful Labor Day, but was not able to accept.

1934 was largely used for building the Wy'east cabin, although on August 28, Curtis Ijames and James Harlow went to Crater Rock to help in first aid in the VonNorman fumarole tragedy.

In the Thirties most people worked Saturdays and it was always a matter of driving madly up to Mount Hood late in the day to work on cabin construction Saturday night and all day Sunday. The construction work was sufficiently complete to allow the group to stage an illumination of Mount Hood on January 26, 1935.

After the snow fell and covered the road, getting to the cabin each Saturday night was a matter of putting on the skis at Government Camp and slogging up the trail in the dark. Nestled in its own little glade, the building was at times hard to find, and many an hour was wasted by some member searching all over the timberline slopes before he found it. A very hilarious set of instructions on how to reach the cabin were written by Leon Darling, but it did not help Russ McJury very much, because he got lost the month after they were published. It seems that there were trail signs to follow, but on the lower slopes they were 18 feet above the ground. On the higher slopes, close to timberline, the signs could only be found by digging for them, providing one could guess on which tree the sign might be nailed.

On March 16, 1935, the members got a chance to use their first aid training right at their own cabin. Joe Leuthold opened the trap door to the basement to go down for some wood, and he posted a guard to warn passersby. Somehow the guard was diverted, and a guest, Miss Caroline Norton walked by. In a series of moves wherein she stepped over to latch the front door, she fell through the open trap door, first striking her side and then falling into the basement. Ralph Calkin and Joe Leuthold hurried to Government Camp for a toboggan. They got her to Government Camp, and a Forest Service truck took her to the hospital with a fractured spine.

On July 3, 1935, Everett Darr and Grant McConnell visited the rock shelter in the crater north of the Devil's Kitchen to check on the first aid cache left two years before. Some material had been taken, and the blankets had been used by climbers and not put back in their place. Climbers had left them to mildew on the floor and had walked on them with nailed boots and crampons. Darr and McConnell took the blankets back to Wy'east cabin for cleaning. The members decided to maintain the cache for one more year, in spite of the vandalism.

In July of 1935, Everett Darr, Ida Zacher, Joe Leuthold, and Dale Cowen took the Wy'easters' efforts to the North Cascades in Washington, climbing North Star and Chewawa. An attempt on Mount Goode resulted in failure and a night on a ledge in heavy fog, 1,000 feet above base camp. They also tried and failed on Bonanza Peak, attacking the cliffs on the west side.

In September, the club put a pipeline in for water to their cabin and carried brick in for the chimney. Finishing touches were made on wallboard and cabinets.

Having skipped a New Year's climb in 1935, they made an effort on December 31, to place the first party on top of Mount Hood in 1936. Three men and a woman headed out from the cabin in a blizzard, arriving at the crater shelter cabin at 5:30 a.m. The weather was too forbidding to merit a try for the summit, and they descended to Lone Fir Lookout by compass. Reclaiming their skis at that point, they made a fast run back to Wy'east Cabin.

On May 24, Ray Lewis climbed South Side

Wy'east cabin construction. Sending down the stove. — Photo Joe Leuthold

Wy'easters putting on the roof 1934

Route and encountered Leuthold, who had ascended Wy'east Route. Leuthold had his skis cached at Triangle Moraine, and when they arrived there, he suggested they ride his skis down together. Lewis held onto Leuthold with one hand and the two ice axes with the other. He reported that on the first down that Leuthold slid 20 feet on his face while Lewis flew through the air waving the tomahawks. No casualties.

The men of the Nile River Yacht Club had built a cabin in the next glade west of the Wy'easters. This prompted a keenly-fought slalom race in which Wy'east won by taking the first five places in runs by Darr, Lewis, Leuthold, Calkin, and McJury. It was the first of the "mug" races, featuring a traditional chamber pot.

On June 28, Russ McJury made a solo ice climb to the summit, 3,000 feet straight up on the Eliot Glacier, coming out on the NE side of the summit. The same day Ralph Calkin and Joe Leuthold climbed up Steel Cliff from the crater shelter cabin amidst the fall of numerous rocks that were falling all during their climb. Everett Darr and James Harlow climbed the Chute, but made hard work of it by digging the fixed line from under two feet of snow and ice as they ascended.

Having been beaten on Bonanza the previous year, in 1936 Everett and Ida Darr went back up Lake Chelan to try it again. They camped at Holden Lake and explored the east face of the mountain extensively. Ida took off on her own to climb Martin peak, a difficult ascent just east of Holden Lake.

On August 9, 1936, the club was involved, as were many members of The Mazamas, in leading the largest party to ever ascend Mount Hood, the Mantle Club group led by Lynn J. Darcy.

Joe Leuthold and Ralph Calkin did a classic New Year ascent of South Side Route in 1937. They passed Lone Fir Lookout at two minutes past midnight and skied through a heavy accumulation of powder snow to the Hogsback. In the Chute they waded waist deep and topped out on the summit at 6:00 a.m. in a penetrating wind at five degrees below zero. Despite the bitter conditions, they waited to see the sunrise before descending. Another party followed about an hour behind them.

PRIME MOVERS OF PATROL

By April of 1937 some patterns began to emerge as to the need of a ski patrol. Although nothing was mentioned in print about forming one, it was noted that 20 skiers had broken legs or torn ligaments during the ski season, about one broken leg per weekend. A better and wider trail to Government Camp was being promoted with Forest Service officials.

On May 2, Leuthold and Darr skied around Mount Hood to join the ranks of the mythical "Side Hill Gougers," a very select group of skiers.

In the summer of 1937 a very determined group returned to Bonanza Peak in the North Cascades, Joe Leuthold, Ida and Everett Darr, Curtis Ijames, and Barrie James. The first foray was to cross Holden Pass and approach the Company Glacier on the north side of Bonanza Peak, a severe trip around the buttresses of the mountain. They climbed to the top of the Glacier in one of the most brutal ice climbs of their careers, only to find impossible cirque walls of crumbly rock barring the way to the summit.

Abandoning that hard-fought attempt, they retreated to Holden Lake and planned an assault of the Isella Glacier (now known as Mary Green) on the east side where Darrs had explored in 1936. The ascent was wild, but successful as they found the key to the route in getting off the glacier high up on its southwest side, a tongue of ice that gave them access to the rock terraces on the summit. Darr lost out, however, becoming ill when they reached the rock, and Ida remained with him until the other three returned in success.

Barney Macnab with trophy cup — Photo Joe Leuthold

Wy'east first aid cache at crater 1933 — Photo Joe Leuthold
It was stored in the stone cabin after it was built in 1934.

Such was the first ascent of Bonanza Peak.

In the fall of 1937 a 1500-watt power plant was placed at the cabin. The steep side hill on the east was groomed for a ski slope, a steep run that present-day skiers often use when they ride Pucci Chair Lift. Additional bunk space was made inside the building. On October 19, the club was incorporated.

Timberline Lodge opened for business on February 5, 1938. Everett Darr and Barney Macnab had talked previously with Forest Service Supervisor A.O. Waha about the need for a ski patrol. Hank Lewis was chosen to head the organization under the direction of Harold Engels, using the talents of Wy'east Climbers and Nile River Yacht Club. Every ski hill and run was patrolled once an hour. Curtis Ijames worked out a first aid kit to be carried by each patrolman. Thus these skiing groups stepped forward to fill the need as Timberline Lodge began to draw crowds of skiers each weekend.

On April 9, Wy'east and Nile River drank communally from the "mug" and went out on the hill for a Saturday night ski race with the use of floodlights from the cabin generator and a couple of gasoline lanterns. Everett Darr made the first run; then the generator died. Leuthold tinkered with the engine, got it going, and the race was on. Wy'east barely squeaked through in points to win the tournament. Actually, the fast time of Russ McJury was the deciding factor. He came down the course so fast that the timers at first thought the stop watches were defective.

By the end of the 1938-39 ski season, the ski patrol had handled 462 injuries. A few new members began to filter in, other than Wy'easters and Nile River men. It was largely due to the success of the Mount Hood Ski Patrol that the National Ski Association formed the National Ski Patrol.

On April 1, 1939, the club handled a Mount Hood Illumination for the Winter Sports Association.

On September 6, 1940, Joe Leuthold, Everett and Ida Darr, and Eldon Metzger left for Lake Chelan to make first ascents on Tupshin Peak, Riddle Peak, White Goat Mountain, and another they named Wy'east Mountain. Metzger and Leuthold pioneered Mount Flora, and the Darrs were first to climb Devore Peak.

Wy'easters maintained a strong interest in 1957 of their original concepts. President Keith Petrie held the position of Rescue Director with MORESCO, the mountain rescue organization for Oregon. With Frank Fassold, David Hitchcock, Donald McKay, and Richard Pooley, he attended the Mountain Rescue spring training conference at Mount Baker on June 15-16. Four members of the club were active on the ski patrol, and seven more were doing occasional duty.

The club and the climbing world in general were severely shocked when Donald McKay and Joseph Lloyd Quigley were killed on St. Peter's Dome in the Columbia Gorge. McKay had led up a pitch above a cave in the north face on the Dome, while Quigley belayed from the floor of the cave. He slipped, and when the first piton did not hold in the rock, the whole string of hardware pulled out. When McKay hit the end of the rope, his weight pulled Quigley out of his belay stance, and the two hurtled through space to fall to their death on the rocks below.

One might say that the golden early years of Wy'east Climbers were interrupted and ended by World War Two. This is not to say that the club lost vitality, because many new climbers were brought into the organization to keep it thinking young, Ross and Keith Petrie, Richard R. Pooley, David Nelson, James K. Angell, Earl and Jamie Levin, Richard Dodd, John McCormick, Ray Conkling, Al Kirnak, Albert E. Weese.

The old race to be on the summit first on New Year gradually lost its interest as at times many other groups have vied for the distinction. The Mount Hood Ski Patrol grew to a vast size and is no longer a Wy'east province. However, members are still required to hold a first aid card and most are actively interested in Ski Patrol and mountain rescue activities. Both the skiing and climbing communities owe a great debt of gratitude to the Wy'east Climbers for spearheading the formation of Ski Patrol and MORESCO organizations.

Present day Wy'easters enjoy Mount Hood on a more relaxed pace of climbing and skiing. Just as in the early days, many of them also maintain memberships in The Mazamas, and several belong to American Alpine Club. In the Thirties many of the most active Wy'east Climbers were very prominent in Mazama activities, many taking prominent leadership roles and even serving on the Climbing Committee of The Mazamas. This is no longer true, although Richard R. Pooley served on the 1974 Climbing Committee.

Mount Hood Ski Patrol, a National Example

When Timberline Lodge was finished in November of 1937, the skiing community knew that just as soon as the Forest Service secured operators to open the lodge, the slopes from Timberline to Government Camp would be jammed with skiers. Everett Darr of Wy'east Climbers and Barney Macnab of Nile River Yacht Club made a visit to A.O. Waha, Supervisor of Mount Hood National Forest, to lay the accident problem before him.

Waha told them that there was no budget for patrolling ski slopes. The only skier in his whole organization was Ralph Engles, Ranger of the Zigzag District. "We have just the man for you, Hank Lewis," they told Waha. Lewis had been an enthusiastic member of Wy'east for several years and had a good background in first aid. Finally Waha agreed to give him Forest Service pay of $5 per day to work on weekends. All other help was to be volunteer.

One weekend in the last of January, Hank Lewis helped a Forest Service man in a green jacket, splint a broken leg of an accident victim and pack him into the Summit Guard Station. When introductions were made, this turned out to be Engles, Hank's new boss.

"So you are the one who is going to run the patrol," commented the ranger. "Meet me tomorrow morning at Timberline Lodge at nine." He gave Lewis one of the "tin buzzer" badges, the type worn by temporary Forest Service personnel. Lewis skied back up to the Wy'east cabin, but he didn't meet Engles at 9:00 a.m. Heavy, hip-deep snow fell during the night, and the road was not open for the ranger to come up until much later.

On February 5, 1938, the lodge was finally opened for business. Lewis had enlisted the help of all his friends in Wy'east and Nile River Yacht Club, and the ski patrol was in business. Skiers swarmed up the road to Timberline and ran the trails back to Government Camp. A special problem were the young men who brought girl friends up and assured them they could make it down the trail.

FIRST ACCIDENT

One of the first calls for the patrol was an accident near Lone Fir Lookout, a girl with a broken leg. Hank Lewis, Henry Corbett, and a third man left Timberline with one of the Wy'east toboggans. When they had found her and splinted her leg, Hank straddled the front of the toboggan, holding onto the curved front, with Corbett and the other man skiing behind and holding onto ropes. Just after getting started, the two men collided and let go of the ropes, leaving Hank bent over the front of the toboggan in a ridiculously impossible position, picking up high speed on the steep slope.

To add to the problem, they had loaded her in head first, believing that the head should be lower than the feet. Hank Lewis could see his glorious career as Patrol Chief coming to a tragic and shameful end, before it even started. With great effort he managed to steer around parallel to the slope in a snow plow turn and bring his precious cargo to a stop. His two brakemen did a better job on the balance of the trip after being reprimanded in the best skier's vernacular.

So it came to pass that the Mount Hood Ski Patrol was in full operation before it was legally organized. On March 2, 1938, a preliminary meeting was held in the Corbett Studio on the roof of the Pacific Building. Barney Macnab appointed an organization committee of himself, Jack Dukehart, James Mount, Ralph Wiese, Rod Norwood, Robert Kron, Robert North, Robert Donaldson, Fred McNeil, Willis Caldwell, and Everett Darr. Later a nomination committee was appointed, Norwood, Kron, and North.

They nominated a slate of Barney Macnab for president, James Mount for vice-president, Everett Darr for secretary-treasurer, Henry Lewis for Patrol Chief, and Ralph Wiese for First Aid Chief. A rules committee was appointed, Dukehart, Lewis, Kron, and Verne Robertson. An examining committee consisted of Mount, Lewis, and Donaldson, for the purpose of listing requirements for accepting members into the patrol. Darr and District Ranger Harold Engles were appointed to an advisory committee.

On March 8, they met again and voted the slate of officers in. Frank Bigler was selected to chair a committee for selecting an emblem design, and James Mount to head the Examining Committee.

On April 28, the last meeting before October 5th was held. Ralph Wiese noted that all members without first aid cards should get them and advised that a course was starting May 4 at the central fire station.

In the annual meeting on October 5, Macnab announced that he had been appointed Northwest Director of National Ski Patrol. Hank Lewis noted that he was unable to get quarters at Government Camp for a first aid station and that the Forest Service would not run a phone to Mazama Lodge. Jack Dukehart was elected president. A discussion was had as to whether the patrol should sponsor competitive races.

On October 20, the National Patrol volunteered to supply Mount Hood Ski patrol with blanks to record injuries treated. The following day a design for Ski Patrol badges was accepted and an order placed. The badge was similar to a Forest Service badge, but smaller, and had the patrolman's number stamped on it. On October 27, it was decided to refrain from holding any races for at least a year.

November 3, 1938 Ralph Wiese discussed the need of first aid kits. Badges were distributed to the members. Orange and black arm bands were authorized for patrolmen on duty only. Ranger Harold Engles told about trail improvements and mentioned new quarters for the patrol.

Toboggans for the patrol were a problem from the start. At first the Wy'east toboggans were used. Then the carpenter at Timberline Lodge built two for the patrol, but he was evidently so influenced by the grand and massive scale of the lodge, that he built them in the same manner. They were quickly shelved, one going to Lone Fir for emergency work. Toboggans from a warehouse down in Government Camp were then used for a time.

November 25, 1938 Fred "Flannelmouth" Fisher, an attorney in Nile River Yacht Club, was detailed to investigate the legal liability of the patrol and patrolmen. Toboggan designs were discussed; Hank Lewis expressed the feeling that limber units for rough trails were of advantage.

January 10, 1939, found the patrol planning a big benefit dance at Timberline. Hank Lewis noted a free transportation agreement with Tim O'Conner, allowing one patrolman to ride up on each bus to Timberline. J.V. Rafferty was offering patrol space at his hotel in Government Camp. On January 24, plans to use room 26 at Timberline Lodge were announced.

March 23, 1939 Ralph Wiese gave a report of the accidents treated to date. The total number was appalling. It was also mentioned that there had been no accidents on the north side during the ski season. Alfred Monner noted the need for instructors at the ski school at Government Camp.

October 4, 1939, the annual meeting was held. John Benninghoff was elected president over his objection. Everett Darr asked for more recognition for the patrol. He suggested quarters at Timberline, better transportation to Timberline, discount on meals at the lodge, free rides on the tows.

December 1, 1939 Benninghoff resigned because of business obligations. December 14, Vice-President Kron reported that Benninghoff's discussion with Supervisor A.O. Waha had produced results. The patrol would be given free rides on the big (Otto Lang) tow and have the use of a Forest Service truck between Government Camp and Timberline. Whether or not to discontinue the patrol ski school under direction of Robert Kron was referred to the Executive Committee.

January 3, 1940 The new president, Ralph Wiese presided at an executive meeting. Walt White and James Simmons were elected to the patrol and Fred McNeil resigned. It was made a requirement for membership to hold an advanced Red Cross first aid card.

January 24, 1940 Plans were under way for the annual dance. It was decided that because there was no first aid station at Government Camp, the individual patrolman would be responsible for his patient until he joins his party or leaves for Portland.

February 7, 1940 Joe Leuthold explained a system of voluntary service by advance signup. He also warned of the bad effect of patrol members wearing arm bands in the Blue Ox Bar when off duty.

March 18, 1940 The Mount Hood Ski Patrol gained national recognition when Life Magazine ran a spread of several pages, showing patrol members in action. Additional plaudit was received from the publication of full-page stories about the patrol in the magazine sections of Portland newspapers.

May 13, 1940 First Aid Chief Stapleton reported 307 accidents for season. President Wiese said the accident rate had dropped from 4.5 to 3.97 accidents per thousand.

October 4, 1940 At the annual meeting L.W. Anderson was elected president, and James Simmons First Aid Chief. Bob Webb of *The Oregonian* mentioned that his newspaper might run the ski school and take the load off the ski patrol. James Simmons advocated joining the Winter Sports Association, but the action was finally rejected by official motion.

January 5, 1941 A Sunday tournament pitted ski patrolmen from various areas in the northwest against each other in a race from near Lone Fir Lookout to Pucci Glade. John MacNamara and Bill Cameron of Yakima won first place.

The team from the Mount Hood Ski Patrol proved fastest over the course, but their techniques in handling the simulated patient were graded down, placing them at the bottom of the list of contestants. A team from the Girl Petrels, Christina Latta and Marian Dukehart, took fifth place in the competition. Weather was cold with six inches of new snow falling during the day.

October 16, 1940 The opinion of Joe Leuthold was that transportation would be by bus, rather than by a Forest Service truck. He recommended that signs be placed at the top of the ski trails to prevent use of trails after the evening sweep. He also mentioned approaching the Forest Service about a telephone half-way down the trail.

November 28, 1940 President Anderson resigned. Ralph Hadfield was elected to replace him. Albert Weisdanger and Marshall Stenerson were admitted as members. On December 18, it was resolved to put a Ski Patrol First Aid Station sign in front of Dr. Otto George's hospital at Government Camp. This was east of what was later Darr's Mountain Shop. It was resolved to adopt the blue Ski Patrol emblem furnished by the National Patrol Association. On December 30, Fred Fisher gave the legal advice that patients should not be taken to Dr. Otto George, unless they wished the service of a physician. He advocated renting a cabin at Government Camp.

January 22, 1941 Word from Harold Engles of the Forest Service was that he had ordered blankets and cots to be placed in the office of Dr. Otto George. A week later the dance was reported to have netted $202. The ski school had 400 students and only 17 instructors.

March, 1941 The patrol had handled 333 accidents since November 9, 1940. Nile River Yacht Club offered to help build a first aid cabin.

October 1, 1941 At the Annual Meeting, Glen Asher was elected president, and Harold Thomas as First Aid Chief. James Simmons, the retired First Aid Chief, reported 448 injuries, 89 of them being fractures. The Oregonian Ski School had graduated 50 out of 600 students who had registered. Ski Patrol members felt that the school had helped reduce the number of accidents.

A general meeting was held on **March 24, 1942,** with about 15 members present. The attrition of World War Two was beginning to show. The Forest Service Reserves were being organized, and the ski patrol members were urged to volunteer for this service. The formation of a women's auxiliary to the patrol was discussed. Some women had already been helping in first aid and toboggan handling. Dean Beckley was elected to First Aid Chief to replace Harold Thomas who had gone into military service. The minutes indicate that since the 1941 Annual Meeting, Lu Norene had given up the position of vice-president and had become Patrol Chief to take the place of Hank Lewis. Andy Anderson came back as vice-president.

On April 9, 1942 a report was made by James Simmons concerning the state of the Mount Hood Ski Patrol records, correspondence, minutes, receipts for expenditures, committee reports, and bank account. From his examination, he reported a "jumbled mess". The membership file was incorrect and incomplete, and expenditures had been made without proper notation. He noted that three of the five officers had been called to military service, and that the remaining two had neglected the book work in favor of taking care of actual problems at Mount Hood.

He recommended that the savings account be closed in favor of a checking account, that membership files be brought up to date, and that patrol equipment be inventoried properly.

No Annual Meeting was held in 1942, but on November 19, a regular meeting was held at Everett Darr's Mountain Shop at 628 NE Broadway in Portland. The secretary, Ralph Hadfield, conducted the meeting in the absence of both president and vice-president. Everett Darr was elected as the new president, and Dean Beckley re-elected as First Aid Chief. Formality normally required by by-laws was ignored, because so many members were absent in the war.

Barney Macnab told about the system of airplane crash squads advocated by the National Ski Patrol System. Fred Cleator of the Forest Service said that although he did not feel that the Forest Service Reserves should be responsible for this activity, he was willing that the Ski Patrol contact individual members in case of an airplane crash.

February 17, 1943 an Executive Meeting was held at the Mountain Shop, attended by Darr, Hadfield, Norene, and Matthews. The Patrol was not active as a unit, and there had been only one broken leg during the season.

November 23, 1943 election of officers was made from nominations from the floor. The whole slate of officers was re-elected. Dr. George's cabin was slated for use as the Ski Patrol first aid station.

January 25, 1944 an Executive Meeting was held and Charles Thurston and Amos Smelser of Zigzag Ranger Station were elected to membership. A work party at the patrol cabin, an area set aside in Darr's Mountain Shop in Government Camp, had been held on the previous November 30. It was decided that only members of the Ski Patrol could use the cabin.

November 20, 1944 the Annual Meeting was held at the Mountain Shop in Portland. New members were voted in, Al Gerding, Randall Kester, Leighton Roy, Tom Becktol, and Adrian Aldrick. Kester was then promptly elected president. Lu Norene was re-elected Patrol Chief, and Dean Beckley re-elected First Aid Chief. Owen Matthews had entered the military service and had forgotten to turn in the supply of emblems, arm bands, and badges. Ward Gano of the regional office of the Forest Service and Barney Macnab led a discussion on an Aircraft Rescue Unit in charge of Lieutenant Schilling at Payne Field, Everett, Washington. A disaster truck complete with snow-cat had been placed at the disposition of the Ski Patrol to use in a major aircraft crash.

Darr's shop at Government Camp was to be used partially by the Ski Patrol. Dr. George planned to keep his hospital open for the winter. The Forest Service noted that they would like to see a pay telephone installed at Government Camp. A Forest Service phone was in operation at the junction of Glade and Blossom Trails, with connection to Timberline Lodge and Summit Guard Station.

December 29, 1944 Ole Lien was elected to the Ski Patrol. Lu Norene resigned as Patrol Chief, and the position was left vacant.

January 2, 1945 A series of Red Cross First Aid classes was started in conjunction with the Climbing Committee of The Mazamas at the Mazama clubrooms. Dr. Leighton Roy taught the class, which was slanted toward ski and climbing accidents.

The Forest Service provided toboggans and the US Army planned transportation, rations, and first aid supplies at the Portland Air Base, in case the Air Rescue Unit should be called out. Ski Patrol members were asked to assemble camping equipment for overnight bivouacs in snow.

WARTIME CURTAILED ACTIVITY

With the road to Timberline Lodge snowed shut during the war years, few skiers ventured beyond Government Camp, but there were always enough to require the need of Ski Patrol activity. Getting a toboggan back up the slope was a long pull by hand.

Gasoline rationing limited travel to the actual necessity of getting to one's place of employment. A trip to Government Camp was a luxury. Skiers and patrolmen alike, pooled their gasoline ration stamps to make occasional trips. The ski tow at Summit ran once in a while; otherwise all skiing was done on a walk-up-and-slide-down basis. Accidents were minimal, too. In 1943, there was only one case of a broken leg.

October 3, 1945 an Annual meeting was held and Randall Kester re-elected to presidency. **World War Two was finished!** New members began to show their faces.

March 7, 1946 At a General Meeting it was resolved into the by-laws that women would be able to join the Mount Hood Ski Patrol. It was also resolved that the organization should be incorporated under the laws of Oregon as a non-profit corporation. A Ski Patrol dance was planned for March 9 at Timberline Lodge. Harold Johnson and Ethel Fullman were elected to take over the jobs of Patrol Chief and First Aid Chief from Glen Asher and Dean Beckley, who resigned.

October 2, 1946 James Simmons was elected as president of Mount Hood Ski Patrol. First Aid Chief Ethel Fullman reported 373 accidents in the 1945-46 season. About 230,000 people had visited Timberline Lodge and Government Camp. The Ski Patrol joined the Pacific Northwest Ski Association and the Oregon Winter Sports Association. Randall Kester announced the award of green star emblems for wartime activity on the patrol to Tom Bechtol, Dean Beckley, Everett Darr, Harvey Fullman, Al Gerding, Kenneth Gray, Randall Kester, Ole Lien, L.B. (Barney) Macnab, Lu Norene, Dr. Leighton Roy, Charles Thurston, and Fred Wildy.

Everett Darr offered a room in the newly-constructed addition to his Mountain Shop at Government Camp for use as a patrol room. The offer was accepted.

THE JOHNSON SPLINT

Patrol Chief Harold Johnson, who became First Aid Chief in 1950, became dissatisfied with the old board and blanket splints always used by MHSP. Johnson had joined during the war, and came up with the idea of a light splint made of plywood with holes bored in the edges for lacing. Muslin stapled across the bottom, joins the two sections of plywood and cradles the leg, a light and simple splint. Larger holes are bored at the bottom to ease pressure on the ankle bone, and a piece of foam pads the full leg.

The splints were made in the Johnson basement by Ski Patrol work parties. It was not long before the idea and design was disseminated and used by other ski patrols around the Northwest.

January 23, 1947 Darrell Currier, the Ranger at Zigzag, was voted in as a patrol member. Discussion was going on as to where patrol members might find sleeping accommodations at Government Camp. Stuart Mockford suggested procurement of a surplus house. Mazama Lodge was considered. Some members slept at the first aid room, but it was far too small for the demand.

Various systems of signs on the ski trails were being considered. One was to mark each trail with different-colored signs, to eliminate confusion as to the site of a reported accident. It was finally decided to use orange and black on all trails, with a letter prefix for the trail. Thus A-2 would be the second sign down Alpine Trail, and G-4 would be the fourth sign down Glade Trail.

A toboggan race to be sponsored by Mount Hood Ski Patrol was scheduled for March 9. The Ski Patrol dance was set for March 29.

The Timberline Ski Club was in the process of organizing, and wanted to help the patrol. It was suggested that they might furnish instructors to accompany untrained groups of skiers coming to the mountain. Many of the skiers in these groups lacked fundamental training.

James Simmons was elected to represent the patrol on the Central Mountain Emergency Committee. On February 25, his representation was augmented by adding Barney Macnab and Tom Bechtol.

February 25, 1947 it was noted that both the Patrol Chief and First Aid Chief were being paid by the Forest Service.

March 6, 1947 Stuart Mockford promoted the idea of the Ski Patrol establishing a ski school.

April 8, 1947 Twenty patrol backpacks were donated by Everett Darr. The president warned members to ski in control, and that a patrolman wearing an armband makes a very bad example by cartwheeling down a slope.

October 1, 1947 At the Annual Meeting, Tom Bechtol was elected president, James Simmons Patrol Chief. Ranger James Langdon introduced James Ralph, the new Forest Service man on Recreation at Summit.

A former decision to use Mazama Lodge for dormitory facility was augmented by the offer by Dr. Otto George to use his hospital beds as dormitory facility on Saturday nights.

Chet Bohlman, Junior Chamber of Commerce Director of Sports, and Secretary to the Oregon Winter Sports Association, visited the meeting, announcing that the Junior Chamber would sponsor a ski school during the coming season. The patrol was asked to furnish some instructors. He also announced that the Winter Sports Association planned to sell ski license plates during the coming year.

Problems of the era included the proper filling of accident report cards. Another was the replacement of skis broken during patrol work, which finally resulted in the expulsion of Craig Ashford for buying a new pair of skis at Darr's and billing the patrol.

October 3, 1947 a system of four squads was set up for service on succeeding weekends by Patrol Chief James Simmons. Squad Leaders were Stuart Mockford, Russell Fullman, Donald Walker, and Randall Kester.

The Pacific Northwest Ski Association was running a group of proficiency tests for skiers, with ski clubs administering the testing. The Mount Hood Ski Patrol decided not to offer any testing facility to the public, but they would test members of the patrol.

February 17, 1948 it was noted that a first aid station had been set up at West's at Summit.

June 21, 1948 Ethel Fullman reported 701 accidents for the 1947-48 season, 403 being toboggan cases. During Christmas holidays there were 117 accidents. 167 cases were on the ski trails, and Summit, where the beginners congregated, was the second most prolific in injuries.

Joie Smith reported on the Annual Toboggan Race at Stevens Pass on April 17. The only women entered in the race were from Mount Hood, and they placed fourth.

October 6, 1948 the Annual Meeting elected Stuart Mockford president, Ralph Hadfield for Patrol Chief, and Ethel Fullman First Aid Chief. The Forest Service planned to pay only the Patrol Chief. It was expected that Timberline Lodge would pay the First Aid Chief.

A by-law was enacted shortly after, that applicants must serve at least eight weekends of apprenticeship, accompanied by regular members. Each applicant must be sponsored by three active patrol members, who shall assist in training and indoctrination. He must demonstrate his skiing ability, familiarity with the terrain, and ability to administer first aid and handle toboggans.

November 23, 1948 discussion was made on the National Ski Fund, which the Mount Hood Ski Patrol had decided not to support.

January 6, 1949 Stuart Mockford presented a plan and a cost estimate of $27,500 for a ski patrol cabin at Government Camp. The plan was approved.

January 19, 1949 Zigzag District Ranger James Langdon told the General Meeting that the Forest Service was not pleased with the efficiency of the Ski Patrol and the shortage of patrolmen. He suggested that a Junior Patrol might help. He said that if the Mount Hood Ski Patrol could not function properly, it would be necessary to require tow and lift operators to hire paid patrolmen.

Discussion then centered on proposed patrol cabin. Stuart Mockford suggested that they settle the idea as to whether a cabin was needed and wanted. James Langdon pointed out that buildings at Summit had been offered the Patrol and had not been accepted during the past three years. In spite of his comments, a vote was taken to the effect that a cabin was needed. James Simmons stated that the problem was in raising $50,000 for the cabin and $600 per month to run it. Mockford thought it should be built down toward Sky-way tram house, but Langdon said that the Forest Service would not be favorable to giving land to the purpose. Everett Darr said that Mockford's estimate of $27,500 should be multiplied by two.

March 3, 1949 at the Red Cross Auditorium in Portland the General Meeting members of the Patrol heard a talk by Andre' Roch, avalanche expert, the same man who had made the first full ski ascent and descent of Mount Hood with Arne Stene and Hjalmar Hvam in 1931. Roch in 1949 was a safety engineer for the Swiss Government. He showed slides and a moving picture on avalanche rescue.

Stuart Mockford stated that he believed the cabin building program should be shelved for the year, and that a small building be erected at Summit.

May 4, 1949 some discussion was made on possible mountain climbing activity by the Patrol. James Ralph told them that when the Forest Service placed the fixed rope in the Chute, all patrol members would be welcomed to help.

The Patrol had been unsuccessful in getting either Timberline Lodge or the Forest Service to pay the First Aid Chief. Ethel Fullman was paid $251.40 out of Patrol funds.

October 5, 1949 At the Annual Meeting, Donald Walker was elected president, Keith Miller Patrol Chief, and Jerry Lown First Aid Chief.

March 16, 1950 it was announced that Mount Hood Ski Patrol had placed third in the Annual Toboggan Race at Tollgate with the team of Gene Davis and Robert Gillam. Joie Smith and Nancy Leman placed fifth, and Harold Johnson and Ralph Hadfield placed seventh. It was resolved to ask for the race to be held at Mount Hood in 1951.

October 4, 1950 At the Annual Meeting, Bob Gilham was elected president, Bill Keil Patrol Chief, and Harold Johnson First Aid Chief.

During the 1949-50 ski season the National Ski Association used a campaign of "nickel a day — nickel a night", asking contributions from skiers who rode tows and lifts or stayed at lodges. The Mount Hood Ski Patrol had been promised a third of the proceeds collected at Government Camp. The NSA had not responded with a return of funds, so the MHSP decided to check into commitment of funds before participating during the following season. A week later the Executive Committee decided to go along with the collections temporarily.

Dr. Otto George advised the Patrol that his office at Government Camp would have a registered nurse on duty and X-ray equipment. Another doctor would be present on weekends when Dr. George did not appear.

Harold Johnson, inventor of the Johnson Splint, asked for a work party to his basement to make up 50 more splints.

December 13, 1950 Bob Gilham resigned, and Gene Davis was elected president.

January 24, 1951 Larry Morrison succeeded Bill Keil as Patrol Chief.

A discussion brought out the fact that some

patrolmen were not working, merely riding the lifts, and were hard to find when an accident required a run down the trail. A general shakeup was in order.

October 3, 1951 At the Annual Meeting at the Red Cross Auditorium, Paul Shreve was elected president, Larry Morrison Patrol Chief, and Jack Stoddard First Aid Chief.

After several months of discussion on changing toboggans to a newer style, the Patrol voted to purchase some of the Eric Shaw type. Joie Smith was told to secure one.

March 26, 1952 Henry J. Morton of Pacific Northwest Ski Association outlined the "nickel a day — nickel a night" format to the Patrol. The money was to be divided in thirds to National Ski Association, PNSA, and local ski patrol.

October 9, 1952 At the Annual Meeting new officers were Bill Keil president, Harold Johnson Patrol Chief, and John Ries First Aid Chief.

February 11, 1953 the Toboggan Committee reported that Trodse Ski Club had generated $130 from a dance for the benefit of the Patrol. It was voted to buy four toboggans and place plaques on them acknowledging Trodse's efforts.

March 12, 1953 a low-cost log cabin was proposed to be built just east of Darr's Mountain Shop. Darr would lease the ground at no cost. The need for a lodge committee to enforce rules, arrange supplies and heat, and pay costs, was discussed.

October 7, 1953 At the Annual Meeting, Jack Stoddard was elected president, Al George Patrol Chief, and Donald Jessup First Aid Chief.

November 18, 1953 Ralph Wiese discussed a new Red Cross procedure in treating frostbite. Warming should begin with lukewarm temperature, not cool temperature. This was one of the first references to today's standard procedure of immersing frostbitten limbs into water warmed to the 106 to 110 degree range.

Later in the month, the Annual Toboggan Race for ski patrolmen in the northwest was held under chairmanship of Harold Johnson. A pre-race banquet was held at Zigzag Inn on Saturday, March 13.

Donald Jessup resigned as First Aid Chief, and Pauline Johnson was elected to replace him.

October 13, 1954 At the Annual Meeting, Bill Keil was elected president, Bud Siegel Patrol Chief, and Donald Richardson First Aid Chief.

It was decided to give one of the old toboggans to the Cooper Spur Ski Area. Jim Ralph noted that the accident rate had been reduced in the Summit area when Darr began the practice of packing the snow slopes in 1953.

Buildings at Summit were suggested for use as dormitories by Ralph Wiese of the Forest Service.

October 19, 1955 new officers were elected at the Annual Meeting, David Hitchman president, Donald Richardson Patrol Chief, and Ronald Lewis First Aid Chief.

James Simmons outlined the new Mountain Rescue Council of Oregon to the Patrol members. Mrs. Louise Moreley, mother of William Moreley, Jr., a climber killed on Mount Jefferson in 1954, had donated $100 and promoted the formation of the organization. MORESCO then replaced the Central Rescue Council which the Ski Patrol had supported. Mount Hood Ski Patrol voted to join MORESCO.

A new first aid room was being built at Ski Bowl as a part of the facilities there.

Keith Petrie advocated the wearing of bibs to identify patrolmen in all areas. They had been used the previous season in the Ski Bowl only. The following January 4th, it was decided to use bibs at Timberline.

February 29, 1956 Ian McAndie announced a new dispatch method at Timberline Lodge. Previously two patrolmen had taken the chairlift every 15 minutes, but now patrolmen would have a free all-day ticket and wait their turn on the lifts with the other skiers. Pucci and Magic Mile Lifts were affected.

April 11, 1956 three of the toboggans had been converted into "shays" with handles and baskets.

October 3, 1956 At the Annual Meeting, Ross Petrie was elected president, Al Donnelly Patrol Chief, and Keith Petrie First Aid Chief.

Bibs were to be worn by patrolmen at Timberline, Multorpor, and Ski Bowl, giving the patrol dispatcher more control. Injured skiers could more easily see a patrolman in bibs.

Richard Kohnstamm of Timberline Lodge offered to publicize the Patrol. He felt that shovelling and packing in the morning might help prevent accidents. Darr, Kohnstamm, and Russ McJury of the Ski Bowl joined Val Quoidback on a committee to study an incentive system for patrolmen, wherein a patrolman would get a free lift pass for working a specified number of weekends.

December 12, 1956 the idea of a "Hill Captain" was initiated, wherein the man in charge of a given area would be responsible for the full day, checking patrolmen in and out. A new type of shay was ordered from California for test during the season.

February 6, 1957 First Aid Chief Keith Petrie explained that the Red Devil Tow at West's was on private land, and Darr's Summit area was on Forest Service land. People injured at Red Devil should not be taken to the first aid room at Darr's, unless an emergency situation existed. Boy Scouts were being used as auxiliary patrolmen at Summit.

March 13, 1957 the operators' committee came up with an incentive program for MHSP members. A member on patrol could receive a free pass for a wife or girl-friend on the same day and in the same area where the member was working.

October 16, 1957 At the Annual Meeting at Red

Cross Auditorium, Bill Kruger was elected president, Keith Petrie Patrol Chief, and David Hitchcock First Aid Chief. A $30,000 first aid hospital for Government Camp was being discussed with Jack Meier. The building would also give storage and dormitory space.

February 12, 1958 at the suggestion of John Hardiman the MHSP voted to buy five akjas for the use during the next season. This was the beginning of the use of the akja (snow-boat) that later became the standard rescue vehicle at Mount Hood. The akja had been first noticed in a mountain rescue film, which showed its use in Bavaria. After borrowing one, it took only a day's use to convince the Patrol that it was the most efficient vehicle for transporting accident victims. Handles fore and aft permit the patrolmen to easily maneuver on trails or slopes. A wheel can be attached to the bottom for use over bare ground. The MHSP spread the use and popularity of the akja to other ski areas.

March 4, 1958 the MHSP showed at the time, 71 active members and 11 apprentices.

October 1, 1958 At the Annual Meeting, James Coughlan was elected president, Keith Petrie Patrol Chief, and Howard Veazey First Aid Chief.

December 3, 1958 Jack Meier was having a deed drawn for the lot for the Ski Patrol building in Government Camp. Five more akjas were ordered.

There was a discussion about the relationship of MHSP with the National Ski Patrol. A strong letter to NSP representative Val Quoidback was ordered.

March 26, 1959 floor plans for the proposed building by architect Royal Chaple were examined.

April 8, 1959 The Annual Meeting was held and Keith Petrie elected president, Donald Jenkins Patrol Chief, and Howard Veazey First Aid Chief. Change of the date of the Annual Meeting was made through a by-law change passed on February 11.

A long discussion was held concerning the problems with National Ski Patrol. The possibility of forming an Oregon Section of NSP was considered a good solution.

April 1960 The Annual Meeting elected Stan Foss president, Howard Veazey Patrol Chief, and John Hardiman First Aid Chief.

April 19, 1961 The Annual Meeting elected Stan Foss president, Howard Veazey Patrol Chief, and Donald Jenkins First Aid Chief.

June 7, 1961 Stuart Mockford discussed the plans for a proposed MHSP building. A Building Committee was appointed, Lee Daniels, Harvey Osborne, Ray Conkling, and Frank Potter.

October 11, 1961 Keith Petrie announced that 11 akjas had arrived. All Oregon Patrols were using them by this time.

January 10, 1962 Stan Foss was replaced by Tudor Marks as president.

February 14, 1962 was the day that Mount Hood Ski Patrol severed connections with the National Ski Patrol System! A rift had been brewing since the autumn of 1961, when NSPS laid down a rule that each patrolman subscribe $2 for liability insurance. The price was fair, but the leaders at Mount Hood balked at the compulsory compliance.

The Executive Committee sought out advice and sentiment from the patrol members, the lift operators, and the skiing public. Randall Kester, a former president, advised that the adoption of such compulsory insurance might leave the Patrol vulnerable to suit, according to the Oregon law.

A rather humorous part of the battle concerned the award that Mount Hood Ski Patrol had been awarded for the past year by NSPS for being the top ski patrol in the nation. The men at Mound Hood had been the largest patrol operating at any resort area, and their high standards had won them the coveted award. But upon severance of membership, NSPS asked that they send the award back.

One of the founders of the MHSP was Barney Macnab, who held a position with the national for many years. He spoke at the meeting, giving a history of MHSP and NSPS, taking the position of opposing the severance of membership.

Once the cleavage had been made, the local group put renewed effort into maintaining MHSP as a first-class unit. Gone was the nickel-a-day contribution system on lifts and tows. Many members felt that they were more efficient without the need to dissipate their energy on national meetings and worry about compliance with the system.

April 18, 1962 The Annual Meeting elected Lee Daniels president, Keith Petrie Patrol Chief, and Howard Veazey First Aid Chief.

September 5, 1962 Maryanne Hill presented the MHSP with a building near Hill's Place at Government Camp. President Daniels ordered that a letter of acceptance be sent.

April 17, 1963 The Annual Meeting elected Lee Daniels president, George Crisp Patrol Chief, Robert Lewis First Aid Chief.

April 15, 1964 The Annual Meeting elected George Anderson president, Howard Veazey Patrol Chief, and Robert Lewis First Aid Chief.

July 15, 1964 Jack Mitchem presented a letter to the Executive Council Meeting from the Bend Ski Patrol. The Bend unit felt that MHSP should rejoin the national system to which they had belonged so many years. No action toward rejoining was taken.

December 16, 1964 at a General Meeting the Patrol and Forest Service discussed the proposed new Ski Patrol cabin. The cabin at Hill's place was still being used.

January 13, 1965 a Ski Patrol Chalet Committee was tentatively selected with Lee Daniels and

Keith Petrie as co-chairmen. Members were Dick Volpel, Howard Veazey, Art Israelson, and Earl Levin. They planned to apply for a special use permit from the Forest Service. Construction was intended for the summer of 1965.

March 31, 1965 The Chalet Committee reported a conference with Peter Wingle of the Forest Service. The government acknowledged the responsibility for patrolling trails and maintaining facilities for the victims of accidents on the trails. Two possibilities existed. The Forest Service might build a minimum shelter for their own needs, or they might cooperate with the Ski Patrol on the funds to build a larger building. Only generalities were touched, because the MHSP had not advanced any definite proposals.

April 21, 1965 At the Annual Meeting at the Portland General Electric Service Center, John Garren was elected president, Jack Mitchem Patrol Chief, and Bill Rossi First Aid Chief. In this election, it was not a "railroad" style with one nominee per post. All offices had at least two nominees; the First Aid Chief had three.

Art Israelson presented the proposals for a Ski Patrol Chalet. Ross Petrie outlined the drawbacks and problems involved. The membership having been presented the problem, a general panel discussion ensued. The recommendation for a chalet was defeated.

It was resolved that a committee of Israelson, Keith Petrie, and Frank Fassold work with the Forest Service in securing a satisfactory first aid structure. It might be noted that the use of the First Aid Room at Darr's was scheduled to end at the close of present ski season.

December 2, 1967 the dedication of the new Ski Patrol Building, erected and owned by the Forest Service, brought the dream of many years to realization. From almost the time the patrol organized, there had been plans and talk and unrealized schemes to secure a building that the Ski Patrol could use as a first aid station and wardroom. The new building on the north side of the road just west of Government Camp gives office, treatment area, and wardroom on the lower floor, as well as some dormitory space. The top floor has dormitory and space for storing akjas and other patrol equipment.

THE PRESENT SKI PATROL

Members follow rules and instructions from a manual written in 1964 by Ernest McDonald. Richard R. Pooley revised it in 1966, 1967, and 1968, and Steve D. Snider did the same in 1969. Pooley and Pete Landis brought it up to date again in 1971.

To become an apprentice, an applicant must have the desire for public service, have a valid advanced first aid card from the American Red Cross, pass a skiing test, attend Akja practice and other training meetings. When submitting application cards, they must also tender a photograph and pay $20 for the issue of equipment.

After an apprentice has covered the requirements, has patrolled a minimum of 10 times on various ski areas, and has evidenced a genuine interest, he can be voted in to membership. A member must patrol two weekend days per months from November through April.

Elective offices are president, vice-president, secretary-treasurer, three trustees, Patrol Chief, and First Aid Chief. The trustees are senior advisors on patrol business in the executive and general meetings. The Patrol Chief is the line officer for all operations. The First Aid Chief manages first aid standards, operations, and supplies.

Appointed officers are Assistant Patrol Chiefs (3), Apprentice Training Director, Public Relations and Educational Director, Ski Clinic and Training Director. The Assistant Patrol Chief is normally responsible for one major ski area, such as Timberline Lodge or Mount Hood Meadows. He is in contact with the area operator and is responsible for keeping his patrolmen in line in the area. While on duty he represents both the Patrol Chief and the First Aid Chief. He aids in the choice and direction of Hill Captains and oversees their management of patrolmen.

Resupplying first aid cabinets, maintaining akjas, supervision of training, supervision of first aid missions, and hearing the personal problems of patrolmen are all part of his duty. Should a search be necessary, he is expected to organize and head it.

Hill Captains also receive much responsibility. A Hill Captain must be a veteran of two years of active duty on the patrol. He assigns duty to the members of the patrol, checks out bibs, notes akja placement, assigns lunch breaks and lift areas, gives akja tests, supervises accident treatment, and returns accident reports to the Ski Patrol first aid station at Government Camp at the end of the day. He must note the absence of patrol members who have signed up for duty, and validate the duty on the cards of patrolmen who were on the job.

Patrolmen are asked to ski in pairs. They have the right to break into the lift lines, preferably using "single" seats available. Rocks or sticks in the snow are to be marked with warning flags. Patrolmen are not authorized to drive snow cats in any of the ski areas, the operators furnish personnel for this purpose. During ski races, patrolmen are asked to be present. Patrol members are expected to be neatly dressed, polite and helpful to the public. Wild, uncontrolled skiing on their part is definitely forbidden, and they are not to appear in public bar rooms while wearing Ski Patrol bibs. Hill Captains are expected to maintain standards of the behavior of the patrol members.

Occasionally, a member of the skiing public will be so reckless as to endanger everyone around him. A patrolman is authorized to reclaim his lift pass in the presence of the lift operator. This is seldom exercised, as the offenders usually correct their skiing when warned by a patrolman.

Since the patrolman is not paid and skis without charge on the ski lifts and tows, there is always a delicate relationship between the Patrol and the area operators. The Assistant Patrol Chief, or possibly the Hill Captain, normally handles all the discussions with the lift owners concerning activity of the Patrol. A patrolman on duty receives a pass for his wife or friend while he is on duty. It is especially important that the privileges of the free pass are not mistreated, and it is a duty of the Patrol executives to be sure there is no abuse.

If MHSP was not the first ski patrol in the nation, it was certainly one of the very earliest ones. Since the beginning, the badge has been the same, a small silver replica of the Forest Service insignia, bearing the name of the MHSP and the patrol member's number.

Other identification has not been so constant. Members who were members of NSP had the rust-colored rust parkas to wear, a distinctive garment. Arm bands were the traditional marking for many years for MHSP members. It was in 1956 that bibs were initiated at Timberline, soon to be adopted for use all over the mountain. The first idea for bibs was red and white, but the color scheme was dropped because of conflict of insignia with the American Red Cross. Blue bibs with white lettering were used for a long while, but the

OFFICERS OF SKI PATROL

DATE ELECTED	PRESIDENT	PATROL CHIEF	FIRST AID CHIEF
March 8, 1938	Barney Macnab	Henry Lewis	Ralph Wiese
Oct. 5, 1938	Jack Dukehart	Henry Lewis	Ralph Wiese
Oct. 4, 1939	John Benninghoff	Henry Lewis	Dean Stapleton
	Ralph Wiese		
Oct. 4, 1940	L.W. Anderson	Henry Lewis	James Simmons
	Ralph Hadfield		
Oct. 1, 1941	Glen Asher	Henry Lewis	Harold Thomas
		Lu Norene	Dean Beckley
Nov. 19, 1942	Everett Darr	Lu Norene	Dean Beckley
Nov. 23, 1943	Everett Darr	Lu Norene	Dean Beckley
Nov. 20, 1944	Randall Kester	Lu Norene	Dean Beckley
		resigned 12-29-44	
Oct. 3, 1945	Randall Kester	Glen Asher	Dean Beckley
		Harold Johnson	Ethel Fullman
Oct. 21, 1946	James Simmons	Harold Johnson	Ethel Fullman
Oct. 1, 1947	Tom Bechtol	James Simmons	Ethel Fullman
Oct. 6, 1948	Stuart Mockford	Ralph Hadfield	Ethel Fullman
Oct. 5, 1949	Donald Walker	Keith Miller	Jerry Lown
Oct. 4, 1950	Robert Gilham	Bill Keil	Harold Johnson
	Gene Davis	Larry Morrison	
Oct. 3, 1951	Paul Shreve	Larry Morrison	Jack Stoddard
Oct. 9, 1952	Bill Keil	Harold Johnson	John Ries
Oct. 7, 1953	Jack Stoddard	Al George	Donald Jessup
			Pauline Johnson
Oct. 13, 1954	Bill Keil	Louis "Bud" Siegel	Donald Richardson
Oct. 19, 1955	David Hitchman	Donald Richardson	Ronald Lewis
Oct. 31, 1956	Ross Petrie	All Donnelly	Keith Petrie
Oct. 16, 1957	Bill Kruger	Keith Petrie	David Hitchcock
Oct. 1, 1958	James Coughlan	Keith Petrie	Howard Veazey
April 8, 1959	Keith Petrie	Donald Jenkins	Howard Veazey
April, 1960	Stanley Foss	Howard Veazey	John Hardiman
April 19, 1961	Stanley Foss	Howard Veazey	Donald Jenkins
	Tudor Marks		
April 18, 1962	Lee Daniels	Keith Petrie	Howard Veazey
April 17, 1963	Lee Daniels	George Crisp	Robert Lewis
April 15, 1964	George Anderson	Howard Veazey	Robert Lewis
April 21, 1965	John Garren	Jack Mitchem	Bill Rossi
1966	John Garren	Jack Mitchem	
1967	Bob Seelye	Earl Levin	Roger Krage
1968	Bob Seelye	Earl Levin	Roger Krage
1969	Richard R. Pooley	Pete Landis	John Fahey
1970	Richard R. Pooley	Pete Landis	Larry Foster
1971	Buster Bowman	Verne Lawrence	Richard Pope
1972	Buster Bowman	Verne Lawrence	Bill Blakeslee
1973	Norman Lilly	John Wilberding	John McCormick
1974	Norman Lilly	John Wilberding	John McCormick

Mazamas on Eliot Glacier 1912. Cooper Spur Route is on ridge above.

Base Camp at Tilly Jane in 1912.

white soon lost its clear-cut readability. In the early Seventies the bibs were changed to blue with orange lettering. One thing is sure; many an hour in MHSP meetings was used up in discussing methods of identification.

The annual Ski Patrol Dance was begun in the early days and has continued all through the years. Funds generated are used to buy equipment. The dance is usually held the first Saturday in March. It was held at Timberline Lodge for many years, but it became too difficult to manage there; also, MHSP has felt that the dances contributed to overuse. Members sell tickets to the skiing public.

An awards banquet, held in late spring, acknowledges unusual efforts of individuals on the patrol. This banquet is usually held at Bowman's Golf Course at Welches. The Rod Morrison memorial plaque is given to the outstanding apprentice of the year, and the Jerry Edgar award is made to the outstanding hill captain. The Barney Macnab service award is presented to the outstanding senior patrolman. New officers are installed for the fiscal year.

One function of MHSP, not usually considered by the public is the problem of lift evacuation. Failures of machinery or of power supply has caused lifts to stop enroute with some of the riders in chairs very high above the ground. The Ski Patrol holds a practice each year in the technique of safely removing passengers from the chairs.

The procedure is as follows: a patrolman climbs the lift tower on the uphill side of the chair and throws a rope over the lift cable. On the end of the rope is a harness or sling, which the passenger is able to grab as a patrolman on the ground pulls the rope downward on the cable. Once the passenger has the harness, the patrolman instructs him on how to wrap it around his body. At that point the patrolman takes a belay stance with his end of the rope on the ground, and the passenger throws his ski poles down to be retrieved later. Skis are left on the feet, not thrown down.

The passenger must then trust everything to the rope and leave the chair, not an easy thing to do for those who are not accomplished mountain climbers. Once the passenger has been talked into the idea of leaving the chair, the patrolman lets him down gently to the ground. There are instances where the rider is frozen with fear and can not make himself slip off the chair. In such a case, the patrolman must climb up the rope and lift the passenger off into space, while another patrol member belays from the ground. Ascent is made with Jumar ascenders, which are mechanical devices for the climbing rope, or with the more primitive method of using rope slings that are attached to the rescue rope with prusik knots that slide along when unweighted.

LIST OF MEMBERS
MOUNT HOOD SKI PATROL

The first 50 were charter members, coming mostly from the ranks of Wy'east Climbers and Nile River Yacht Club. The Mount Hood Ski Patrol number is on the left. The number after the names of some members is the National Ski Patrol designation. This list contains the names for all time; the majority have dropped their membership, and many are dead. Incomplete records make it impossible to list the membership between 1940 and 1943.

1 . . . Barney MacNab—17
2 . . . . . Robert Duncomb
3 . . . . Ray Lewis
4 . . . . . . Everett Darr—19
4½ . . . . Ken Gray
5 . . . . . L.W. Anderson—4
6 . . . . Tom Dean
7 . . . . . John K. Dukehart
8 . . . . Don Fredericks
9 . . . . James Judson
10 . . . . Ed Klee
11 . . . . . . Jerome W. Clark
12 . . . . Nelson B. Paris—31
13 . . Ralph O. Calkin—165
14 . . . Willis Caldwell—26C
15 Vernon G. Robinson—82
16 . . . . R. Val Peterson
17 . . . . George G. West
18 . . . . P.Y. Paton
19 . . . . . Ernest Markewitz
20 . . . . A.K. Johnson
21 . . Kenneth P. Curry—27
22 . . . Henry W. Lewis—78
23 . . . . . Harold Laman—29
24 John G. Benninghoff—25
25 . . . . . Richard M. Givens
26 . . . . Charles S. Kingsley
27 . . . Henry J. Corbett, Jr.
28 . . . George F. Patten, Jr.
29 . . . . Robert J. Kron—28
30 . . Alfred A. Monner—33
31 . . . . Donald McJury—80
32 . . . . Ray W. O'Brien
33 . . . . Ralph A. Wiese—42
34 . . . . Wayne Loomis
35 . . . . Glen M. Asher—385
36 . William M. Wood—191
37 . . . . K.T. McGrath
38 . . . . W.L. Dawson
39 . . . . . . Eugene Mathews
40 . . . . Lindsay Wilson—32
41 . . . . . . Einer Linstad, Jr.
42 . . . Herbert J. Rasor—81
43 . . . . . . Robert A. Burke
44 . . . . not issued
45 . . Vincent S. Rutherford
46 Alva Ray Huckins, Jr.—77
47 . . . . Harold Maroun—76
48 Atlee Schimelfenig—431
49 . . Stuart Mockford—252
50 . . . Joseph Leuthold—30

1939

51 . . . . Neal McCarthy—79
52 . . . . Dean Stapleton—83
53 . . . . not issued
54 . . . . Curtis C. Ijames
55 . . Frederic A. Fisher—33
56 . . . Ralph Hadfield—193
57 . . . Jimmy Peranto—192

1940

58 . . . . . Peter White—1068
59 James M. Simmons—166
60 . . . . Harold Engles
61 . . . . Marshall Stenerson
62 . . . . Clair Gullickson
63 . . . . . John M. Kindberg
64 . . . . Royal Gaines
65 . . . . Walter White—1069
66 . . . Walter E. Thompson
67 . . . . . Veron Rutherford
68 . . . . Robert F. Cook
69 . . . . E.P. McKean-Smith
70 . . . . . Harold P. Thomas
71 . . . . William Schultz
72 . . . . O.P. Larsen
73 . . . . . Paul V. Livingston
74 . . . . Lu Norene
75 . . . . Robert W. Page
76 . . . . . . William W. Cook
77 . . . . George E. Helt

78 .... Dean Beckley
79 ...... Lloyd L. Carlson
80 .... Walter Hadfield
81 .... Stuart L. Salter
82 .... Bob Allon
83 .... Russell Fullman
84 .... Harold Johnson
85 .... Frank Bigler
86 Owen Matthews III—837
87 .... Everett E. Downing
88 .... Kenneth Arthur
89 .... Volley Reed
90 ... Albert Weisendanger

1943

91 .... Fred Cleator
92 ..... Fred Hanson—808
93 .... Fred Wildy
94 .... Harvey Fullman

1944

95 ...... Charles Thurston
96 .... Amos Smelser
97 .... Al Gerding
98 .... Randall Kester
99 ..... Dr. Leighton Roy
100 ...... Thomas Bechtol
101 .... Adrian Aldrick
102 .... Ole Lien
103 .... Kenneth Gray—742
104 ..... James P. Langdon
105 .... Lloyd Gillmor
106 . Craig Ashford—*revoked*
107 ... Carlisle Brad Geisler
108 .... Bob Paget
109 .... Keith Petrie—1012
110 .... not issued

1946

111 ..... Ethel Fullman—25
112 ...... Constance Smart
113 .... Peggy Norene
114 . Eleanor King Wiese—49
115 .... Fred Brown
116 .... Mason DeNeffe
117 .... Don C. Walker
118 .... Keith Miller—1011
119 .... Darrell Currier
120 ...... Stanton E. Lyon
121 ...... Dr. Otto George
122 .... Paul Shreve
123 .... not issued
124 .... not issued
125 .... Betty Nelson
126 . Shirley Marks Schwage
127 ... Pauline Johnson—55
128 ...... Thelma Jacobsen
129 .. Ann Robel White—48
130 ...... Ellen Stone Fox
131 .... Marion Stone
132 ...... Ed Niedermeyer
133 ...... Robert Wiseman
134 .... Buster Bowman
135 ... Richard Platt—1070
136 ...... Robert Callicrate
137 .... Freddie Loll Tasher
138 Dorothea Maxwell Hughes
139 Gerie Gretchner Fullman
140 .... Helen Gerding
141 .... Milly Gilmore

1947

142 .... Bill Callicrate
143 .... Ian McAndie—1072
144 ..... Lewis A. Coleman
145 .... Robert Gillam
146 .... Larry Semler
147 .... James J. Ralph
148 .... Robert Isler
149 .... Bill Wilkerson
150 .... Robert Reeves
151 .... John Ries
152 .... Dr. John Goldsmith

1948

153 .... Larry Bissett
154 .... Jerry Fullman
155 .... Ralph Hill
156 .... Dean J. Merten
157 .... Ross Petrie
158 .... Jack Ross
159 ...... Forrest Siemroth
160 ..... Joie R. Smith—64
161 .... Donald Thurber
162 .... Richard Volpel
163 .... Fred Wieden
164 .... Archie Winters
165 .... Bert Holtby
166 .. Val Quoidbach—1000
167 .. Donald Bascom—1001
168 .... Gerald Hancock
169 .... George Hibbert
170 .... Dale Holm
171 .... Jeanne Holm
172 .... Harold Kosko
173 .... Jerry Lowen
174 .... Hal Heacock
175 .... John Hoefling
176 . Marion Howard Sutton
177 .... Bill Keil—1183
178 .. Laurita Leuthold—73
179 .... Mollie Murphy
180 .... Don Slaney
181 .... Verne Sutton

1949

182 .... Malcom Hardy
183 ..... Douglas Anderson
184 .... Robert Coy
185 .... Donald Criswell
186 .... Roy Kirkland
187 .... Arthur Lorber
188 .... Fred Mohr
189 .... Larry Morrison
190 .... Ronald O'Brien
191 .... Jerry Taylor
192 .... Betsy Walker
193 .... Bill Henry
194 ...... Floyd Henderson
195 .... Gene Davis
196 ...... John D. Howard
197 .... Eddy Skach
198 .... Robert Skach
199 . George Van Hoomissen
200 Beverly Thompson Miller
201 .... Ed Harvey
202 .... Tex Carter
203 .... Bill Nitzel
204 .... Imogene Calkin
205 ..... Donald G. Condit
206 ...... Bernard Shadoun
207 ..... John C. Stoddard
208 .... Ted Price
209 .... Donna Gaylord

1950

210 .... Ty Kearney
211 .... Jane Peterson
212 .... Roy Stigum
213 .. Dwight C. McKenney
214 Donald Richardson—1495
215 . Neva Richardson Ralph

1951

216 .... Chris Blanchard
217 .... Estel Brown
218 .... F.R. Nelson, Jr.
219 .... Ed Brownlee
220 ...... David Hitchman
221 .... Darryl Kelly
222 .... Bud Leopold

1952

223 .... Fred Gullett—1494
224 ...... La Jean Crossett
225 ...... Carolyn Tamiesie
226 ..... Everett Soderberg

1953

227 .... Donald Case
228 .... Donald Jessup
229 .... Ronald Lewis
230 ... Floyd J. Lyne—1490
231 .... Bill Lewis
232 . Rob Quoidbach—1002
233 .... Herbert Underdahl
234 ...... Al George—1491
235 .... Diane Gillis
236 .... Duane Houston
237 .... Bill Kruger
238 ... Jack Mitchem—1828
239 .... Donna Runyan
240 ...... Marilyn Chandler
241 .... Walter Aeppli
242 .... Ray Conkling

1954

243 .... Terry Baker
244 .... Al Donnelly
245 .... Barbara Fessler
246 .... Graham Newell
247 .... Bill Plywalski
248 .... Lynn Pearson
249 Louis "Bud" Siegel—2071
250 .... David Anderson
251 .... Wayne Peterson
252 ...... Karl Bialkowsky
253 ...... Morris C. Foutch
254 .... Bill LeFevre
255 .... Marilyn Miller
256 .... Charles Lawton
257 .... not issued
258 .... Don Kistner
259 .... Carl Peterson

1955

260 ...... Marion Peterson
261 .... not issued
262 .... Barbara Petrie

MOUNT HOOD SKI PATROL

263 . David Hitchcock—2072
264 .... James Merritt

1956

265 .... Joyce Harris
266 ...... Delbert Johnson
267 .... Malcom McNeil
268 .... Fred Curtice
269 .... John Tanner
270 .... Robert Wachsmuth

1957

271 .... James Coughlin
272 .... Len Nadeau—1855
273 .... Charlene Petrie
274 ..... Pat VanOttingham
275 ..... Jerry Edgar—2377
276 .... Ronald Hespe
277 ..... Leonard Conkling
278 .... Stanley Fink
279 .... Donald McKay
280 .... Harvey Osborn
281 .... John Powell
282 .... Ruth Smith
283 .... J. Walcott
284 .... David Griggs

1958

285 .... Juanita Hagen
286 .... Thomas Scott
287 .... Carol Scott
288 .... Martha Siegel
289 .... Paul Edgar
290 .... John Hardiman
291 ...... Arthur Israelson
292 .... Donald Jenkins
293 .... Tudor Marks
294 .... Michael Smith
295 . Howard Veazey—2187
296 .... David Wiley
297 .... Joanne Wiley
298 .... David Yoder
299 ...... Inez Zink Smyth
300 .... Philip Siegel
301 .... David Nelson
302 .... Richard Ragan
303 .... Frank Fassold
304 .... George Padon
305 .... David Bowe

1959

306 .... Wayne Hill
307 ..... Robert Cummings
308 .... Stanley Foss
309 .... Lee Daniels
310 .... Nancy Daniels
311 ...... Michael Folkstad
312 .... Larry Foster
313 .... Rod Morrison
314 ...... Ernest McDonald
315 .... Bruce Kirkland
316 .... Brice Lausch
317 .... Kurt Kessler

1960

318 .... George Crisp
319 .... Larry Steward
320 ..... Sue Kerseg Nelson
321 .... Clifford Hawks
322 .... Roger Schloe
323 .... Shiro Yoshida
324 .... Harold Gable
325 .... Carl Hanson
326 .... Morgan Howell
327 .... Bob Powne
328 .... Judy Veazey
329 .... Thomas Carter
330 .... Charles Edgar
331 .... Fred Hardiman
332 .... Pete Landis
333 ...... Gary Richardson

1961

334 .... James Kluge
335 .... Larry Powell
336 .... Glen Brown
337 ...... James Charleton
338 ..... Marge Dauelsberg
339 .... Al Hildebrandt
340 .... Earl Levin
341 .... Robert Lewis
342 ..... Thomas Markham
343 .... Mel Patch
344 ...... Warner Pfaender
345 .... Russell Peirson
346 .... Frank Potter
347 .... Donald Smith
348 .... Arthur Stubbs
349 .... Peter Wingle
350 Dale Christianson—2180
351 .... Ed Dennison
352 .... Ted Kramer

1962

353 .... Steve Phinney
354 ...... Bob Vandenberg
355 .... Butch Walker
356 .... Dick Workman
357 .... Mark Whitney
358 .... Alan Andrus
359 .... Jan Bekoy
360 ...... Charles Hartmere
361 .... Bert Nauman
362 ...... George Anderson
363 ...... Richard Criswell
364 ...... Larry Dauelsberg
365 .... Dan Foss
366 .... George Hawkes
367 .... Joyce Hawkes
368 .... Alan Hulse
369 .... Ralph Lewis
370 ..... Donald McKinley
371 ...... Kent Richardson
372 .... Eric Schoenfeld
373 .... Rob Smith
374 ..... Roger Williamson

1963

375 .... Gary Hertz
376 .... Richard Grant
377 .... Jack Elliott
378 ..... Jay Ollenrenshaw
379 .... George Hadley
380 .... Michael Nowak
381 .... Roger Newell
382 ...... Peter Adelsheim
383 .... George Funkhouser
384 .... Michael Lewis
385 .... Jean DeGraff
386 ..... Michael Lockhart
387 .... Steve Mathews
388 .... John Smith
389 .... Thomas Young
390 .... Nick Bush
391 .... Robert Gilsdorf
392 .... Merle Lynch
393 .... Albert O'Brien
394 .... John Schulz
395 .... Carter Smith
396 .... Donald Sullivan

1964

397 .... Charles Erwin
398 .... Gene Jensen
399 .... Jeff Cohen
400 .... Kaye Darby
401 .... John Garren
402 .... George Lage
403 .... Ernst Massey
404 ..... Jacqueline Michel
405 .... Richard Pooley
406 .... Bill Rossi
407 .... Roger Peyton
408 .... Karen Brault
409 .... James Bray
410 .... James Cain
411 .... Duane Ellis
412 .... James Eaton
413 .... Carol Hardiman
414 .... James Simmons, Jr.
415 .... Ray Steiger
416 .... Sue Goodman
417 .... Steve Gunn
418 .... Mary Ann Norman
419 ..... Clyde Rutherford
420 ...... Barry O'Donnell
421 .... Steve Draper
422 .... Thomas Tinker
423 .... Keith Davis
424 .... Bill Hurst
425 .... Pat Lockhart
426 .... Heidi McIssac
427 .... Robert Seelye
428 .... Judy Weinstein
429 .... Lucy Cohan
430 .... James Gillam
431 .... Robert Pierce
432 .... James Dixon

1966

433 .... Bruce Giffin
434 .... Chuck Gibson
435 .... Richard Pope
436 .... Robert Smith
437 ... Richard Scheideman
438 .... John E. Fahey
439 .... Robert Haggart
440 .... Richard Hill
441 ...... Kathryn Kuebler
442 ... K.R. "Mike" Michel
443 .... Jerald Powell
444 .... Rob Ward
445 .... William Lapsley
446 .... Denny McMillin
447 .... Florence Edgar
448 .... Cameron Bangs

449 Chuck (Bill) Wainwright
450 .... Al Smith
451 .... Ken Harding
452 ..... Gordon McAllister
453 .... Steve Snider
454 .... John Wear
455 .... Don Skei
456 .... Joe Williams
457 .... Jamie Levin
458 .... Dick Lozier
459 .... Pat Dowling
460 .. Bill Blakeslee (7-1-66)

1967
461 .... Don Stendal
462 .... Pete Unger
463 .... Rick Ward
464 .... Bill Concannon
465 .... Mike Currier
466 .... Roger Krage
467 .... Roger Squier
468 .... Jim McGugin
469 .... Dick Allen
470 .... Andy Bakker
471 .... Jim Brischle
472 .... Sue Fahey
473 .... Gene Faltus
474 .... Betty Golding
475 .... Mike Herz
476 .... Vern Howell
477 .... Pete Keister
478 ...... Verne Lawrence
479 .... Norm Lilly
480 .... Arlen Madsen
481 .... Trudy Madsen
482 .... Don Malm
483 .... Martin McLain
484 .... Allan Papp
485 .... Pat Parrish
486 .... Jean Robinson
487 .... Jim Robinson
488 .... John Shuholm
489 .... Nick Steffanoff
490 .... Albert Weese
491 .... Roy Larson
492 .... Bill Zeigler

1968
493 .... Jim Lee
494 .... Bob Nagel
495 .... Scott Miller
496 ...... Hans Sittenthaler
497 ...... John Wilberding
498 .... Dan Mandrones
499 .... Bob Kern
500 .... Ken Calkins
501 .... Charles Adams
502 .... Ellen Avery
503 .... Al Bickford
504 .... John Blakesley
505 .... Bill Brown
506 .... Dan Chaney
507 .... Bob Chuinard
508 .... Molly Cohan
509 .... Bill Cummins
510 .... Mike Galvin
511 .... Mike Gehrman
512 .... Ron Getchell
513 .... Paul Golding
514 .... Bob Gray
515 .... Tony Krivak
516 .. Monica Larsell Foster
517 .... Bob Martin
518 .... Gary Parrett
519 .... Bill Pattison
520 .... Joel Schick
521 .... Buzz VanRooy
522 .... Frank Wilson
523 .... Nils A. Arneson, Jr.

1969
524 .... Erwin Burge
525 .... Joel Policar
526 .... Bob Steinle
527 .... Martha Chaney
528 .... Pat Larson
529 .... Jack Lofton
530 .... Sam Smith
531 .... John Becker
532 ...... John Cavanaugh
533 .... Mike Cloud
534 .... Sam Coleman
535 .... Chris Davidson
536 .... Anne Golding
537 .... Nancy Haack
538 .... Norm Hukari
539 .... Dave Jensen
540 .... Oliver Jones
541 ...... Roger Jorgenson
542 .... Allan Kearney
543 .... Dave Larsell
544 .... Dick Lawrence
545 .... Doug Lindley
546 .... Mike Marble
547 .... Randy Morgan
548 .... Tom McGurr
549 ...... Franz Oberbauer
550 .... Glen Owen
551 ..... Lloyd Rosenfield
552 .... Nancy Stangell
553 .... Chris Vanderlinde
554 ...... Tom Winterrowd
555 .... Dave Yamasaki
556 .... Kris Talbot

1970
557 .... Ruth Ann Cole
558 .... Martha Avery
559 .... Nick Langus
560 .... Paul Kunkel
561 ... Gordon Winterrowd
562 .... Mike Holland
563 ...... Craig Shambaugh
564 .... John Austin
565 .... Bill Brett
566 .... Dave Burge
567 .... Ed Davis
568 .... Ted Day
569 .... Brent Dowty
570 .... Peggy Driskel
571 .... Steve Durham
572 .... Craig Fossati
573 .... Dave Gardner
574 .... Ron Handel
575 .... Art Hanseler
576 .... Dick Hanson
577 .... Larry Hayes
578 .... Jim Herman
579 .... Bill Huhta
580 .... Jay Johnson
581 .... Myers Jones
582 .... Robert Karsten
583 .... Jeff Krausse
584 .... Laurin Larsen
585 .... Greg Leo
586 .... Charles Michel
587 .... Jane Miles
588 ...... John McCormick
589 ...... Dante Petruzzelli
590 .... Tom Rocks
591 .... Marvin Sannes
592 .... Dick Semmes
593 .... Jim Shanklin
594 .... Rosina Spray
595 .... Robert Tidd
596 .... Victor Wiessner
597 .... Bob Wilson
598 .... Bill Younce
599 .... Dick Layman

1972
600 .... Gail Pope
601 .... Bob Gustafson
602 .... Scott McAllister
603 .... David Gillespie
604 .... Becky Ward
605 .... Lowell Burns
606 ...... Charles Carlbom
607 .... Jim Fielding
608 ..... Richard Garfinkle
609 .... Julie Goodman
610 .... Kristen Hanson
611 ...... Bernard Hartnell
612 .... Calvin Hartnell
613 .... Gary Hembree
614 ..... Victoria Hembree
615 .... John Holmes
616 .... Frank Hurlbutt
617 .... Jerry Johnson
618 .... Terry Johnson
619 .... Tina Johnson
620 .... Katie Larsell
621 .... Lloyd Clee
622 .... Bruce Miller
623 .... George McCully
624 .... Paul Norris
625 .... Heinz Rudolf
626 .... William Talich
627 .... John Thomas
628 .... Glen Tripplett
629 ..... Robin Wainwright
630 .... Ryan Wiley
631 ...... George R. Wilson
632 ...... Robert C. Wilson
633 .... Steve Wymore
634 .... Roy Zora
635 .... Marne Palmater

1972
636 .... Julie Meiier
637 .... Jerry Takasumi
638 .... Jim Taylor
639 .... Jean Bangs

640 .... Calvin Bridge
641 .... Del Allen
642 ...... Robert Anderson
643 .... Jim Angell
644 .... Lee Ast
645 .... Jim Averill
646 .... William Barlow
647 .... Bill Bryant
648 .... Brian Cannard
649 .... Norm Church
650 .... Patty Cochran
651 .... Jean Cumming
652 .... Thomas Calvin
653 .... Liz Iverson
654 .... Bill Hiatt
655 .... Dave Hillman
656 .... Holly Hirschberger
657 .... Michael Hudson
658 .... David Illias
659 .... Patricia Illias
660 .... Jane Iverson
661 .... Steve Iverson
662 .... John Keyes
663 .... Jess Kriegel
664 ..... Sheryl Lamberton
665 .... Leland Lane
666 .... Matt Larson
667 .... Lori Lee
668 .... Bill McNally
669 .... Cliff Moore
670 .... Marcia Morgan
671 .... Eric Olson
672 .... Julie Odea
673 .... Cosmo Palomba
674 .... Tom Rooney
675 .... Craig Senders
676 .... Steve Swink
677 ...... Douglas Tesdahl
678 .... Tom Tillman
679 .... Russ Tromley
680 ...... George A. Wilson
681 .... Glen Morrison
682 .... Michael Olson

1973

683 .... Omar Hansen
684 .... Sharon Taylor
685 ...... Meyer Avedovich
686 .... John Bader
687 .... Charles Bailey
688 ...... Bruce Bankhead
689 .... Craig Bates
690 .... Tracy Bay
691 .... Linda Besant
692 .... William Bogden
693 .... Irving Jones
694 .... Ed Galen
695 .... Stan Goodell
696 .... Einer Greve
697 .... Jim Groat
698 .... Jerry Harris
699 .... Stan Harryman
700 .... Floyd Hunsaker
701 ...... Gregory Marshall
702 .... Nancy Marshall
703 .... John Mason
704 .... Dale Monroe
705 .... Richard Olson
706 .... Judi Skei
707 .... Jeanice Smith
708 .... Don Wolsborn
709 .... Allen Mills

1974

710 .... Frank Adams
711 .... Harold Appel
712 .... Ron Beltz
713 .... Cliff Bisch
714 ..... Steve Bonnington
715 .... Craig Bowe
716 .... Bill Breitenstein
717 .... Bill Christansen
718 .... Mary Cochran
719 .... Laurie Dignan
720 .... Lynn Freer
721 .... Dave Germann
722 .... Andy Grove
723 .... Dave Hatfield
724 ..... Peter Heitkemper
725 .... Don Herman
726 .... Tom Herman
727 .... Judy Hitchcock
728 .... Dave Leonard
729 .... Dale McDonald
730 ..... Kathy McPherson
731 .... Lloyd Mohling
732 .... Bob Nagel, Jr.
733 .... Karen Owen
734 .... Craig Petrie
735 ..... Clarence Potts, Jr.
736 .... Joel Stevens
737 ..... Nancy Stochosky
738 .... Bob Stochosky
739 ...... Karen Thornton
740 .... Dennis Tripp
741 ...... Dave Warrington
742 ..... Raymond Webber
743 .... Dave Wedeking
744 .... Jim Wolf

Moresco, Serving in Mountain Rescue

Search and rescue on Mount Hood became more and more needed through the years. Men such as T. Raymond Conway and L.A. Nelson came to the front when help was needed, but no official organization existed. Aside from the Crag Rats, no rescue group existed in an established manner. The searches for Brownlee and White on New Year's Week in 1927 accentuated a need, but it took a few more accidents to draw the matter to a head.

In October of 1933, John Scott of The Mazamas announced the formation of a group with himself, Roy Beam of Trails Club, and James Mount of Wy'east Climbers, representing the three clubs. Ray Conway was to head the group. This group existed for years, cooperating with other groups such as the Crag Rats. It carried various names such as Central Rescue Committee and Emergency Rescue Group. The Ski Patrol was a valued contributor in time and expertise. This era came to a close in 1954.

William Morley, Jr. disappeared from the summit of Mount Jefferson on Labor Day, 1954. When his climbing companion looked around, Morely was gone, and a search was set up that finally located his body far down the Milk Creek Glacier. The terrain of the glacier is steep, inaccessible, and subject to rockfall, so the Forest Service at first decided to leave him there.

A Crag Rat team was determined to bring his body down, if at all feasible, Wilson Appelgren, Bob Sheppard, Rod Hukari, Glenn Marsh, Jr., and Bill Sheppard, Jr. They arrived at Detroit Ranger Station at 4:00 a.m. the following Thursday and enlisted the company of Ralph Wiese, although he doubted the advisability of trying to retrieve Morley. At Pamelia Lake Morley's mother and sister urged the group to go for the body, if it could be safely done. They cooked the men a breakfast, and they were on their way.

An equipment drop, high on the mountain, was made to them by Ranger Spencer T. Moore of Willamette National Forest, piloted by CAP flier Richard Swift of Salem. The group reached the site of Morley's body and carried it 2,000 feet down the glacier to a waterfall on Milk Creek, a very hazardous operation on a body of ice that is rarely climbed. Darkness forced them to retreat to Pamelia Lake.

On Friday morning they were joined by Norman Hukari, Don Pierson, Ellwood Samuel, Don Marsh, Arne Udelius, George Sheppard, Bill

Bryan, Wolfgang Sterr, Dave Henthorne, John Edmundson, Bill Gale, Ross Hukari, John Arens, and Eino Annala. Several loggers cleared the brush, so the group could carry the litter out to intercept Skyline Trail on Milk Creek. From there the evacution was all on trail to Pamelia Lake, thence out another five miles to the road.

Thus the Crag Rats had made a retrieval after the Forest Service had taken all other groups of rescue personnel off the case. Mrs. William Morley was deeply grateful that her son's body had been brought down, and she wanted to do something to show it.

The Oregon Intermountain Rescue Council had existed for several years, headed by James Simmons who had been prominent in the Mount Hood Ski Patrol. For the most part it never did function unless there was an emergency, then prominent climbers and skiers quickly mobilized to do their job.

However, there were rumblings of dissent because of lack of coordination between Forest Service, sheriffs, military aircraft groups, and the mountain groups. An incident had occurred in a search in the Badger Lake area a short time previously, when aircraft pilots and ground search crews had not been given full information. One of the men involved, Wes Weygandt, had made some pointed remarks about the need for closer co-operation, and somehow the word got back to Mrs. Morley.

Later in the year the Crag Rats received a substantial gift from Louise Morley. By January 1955 there was considerable stirring of interest among the members of the Mountain Rescue Council — The Mazamas, Wy'east Climbers, Trails Club, Red Cross, Crag Rats, Alpinees, Oregon Highway Patrol, Oregon Highway Commission, Cascade Ski Club, and US Forest Service. On February 1, they met in Portland to consider a more comprehensive organization. It was felt that public education about the hazards in skiing, climbing, and getting lost in the back country, could help in cutting down the number of incidents and tragedies.

On February 12, another meeting was held at the William Morley residence on Palatine Hill Road in Portland. Representatives of various clubs attended. On March 12, a large meeting was held at Mazama clubrooms in Portland to further develop the idea of educational programs on safety and survival.

On the weekend of October 1-2 The Mazamas had scheduled a Glacier Rescue training session for Eliot Glacier. It was decided to make it a state-wide event of the rescue groups and to hold an organizational meeting. On Saturday, glacier training was conducted, and that night at Cloud Cap Inn the Mountain Rescue and Safety Council of Oregon (MORESCO) was formed. Articles of incorporation were executed by James M. Simmons, Richard R. Pooley, and John H. Biewener. Directors were chosen from participating clubs; Pooley from The Mazamas, Randall Kester of Wy'east Climbers, Ross Hukari of Crag Rats.

Before the ink was dry Sheriff Terry Schrunk of Multnomah County called for help on a search for two women lost in the Larch Mountain area. They were later found alive on a ledge just below Trails Club lodge in the Columbia Gorge. The Sunday glacier practice was cancelled.

November 10, 1955, MORESCO held its first board meeting in Portland, and elected officers; president Randall Kester, vice-president Ross Hukari, secretary-treasurer John Biewener, education chairman Richard Pooley, and rescue chairman Henry Lewis. The rescue chairman was actually the most important member of the organization, and Lewis had the background of being the first Patrol Chief of the Ski Patrol in 1938, a veteran of many searches and rescues.

Some of the early meetings of MORESCO were: Annual Meeting at Portland, April 28, 1956, Training at Mazama Lodge October 13-14, 1956, Annual Meeting at Mazama clubrooms April 18, 1957, Training at Santiam Pass September 13-14, 1958. At the Annual Meeting of 1957 it was decided that every rescue member must have a basic Red Cross first aid card by 1958 and an advanced card by 1959.

One of the largest training operations ever conducted by MORESCO was a giant meeting at Timberline Lodge on the weekend of June 17-18 of 1961. About 400 people from rescue groups all over the country assembled to hear lectures and watch rescue demonstrations on the steep sides of Salmon River Canyon. John Biewener drove in from Colorado to give one of the principal addresses. Live demonstrations of helicopter use were made, and pilot Edling flew his light plane so close to the ground that he practically handed a package out of the window to show the crowd a simulated air-drop.

Included in the group were professional rescue teams from Southern California, various sheriff's deputy groups from other states, and the sheriffs from several Oregon counties. The Forest Service was prominent on the scene. Many participants remember the hilarious party Saturday evening in the Blue Ox Bar, when rescue personnel jammed the room to unbelievable capacity, and the happy celebrants singing enmasse along with the musical combo on the stage.

MORESCO still functions as an operating unit, but business is down. Multnomah and Clackamas Counties have put rescue personnel on their law-enforcement staffs. Wherein a hiker gets stranded on a ledge, the sheriffs' deputies usually answer the call. Searches are mostly conducted by Explorer Scout units, who have been very well trained in recent years. On Mount Hood's north side the Crag Rats and Alpinee's vie with each other to be on the spot in an emergency, and their performance has been outstanding. Both units are members of MORESCO, but their efficiency usually precludes the need to call for help outside Hood River.

Today's MORESCO organization spends a great deal of effort in public education, trying to prevent accidents and problems before they happen.

PNSA, Organization of Ski Competitors

PACIFIC NORTHWEST SKI ASSOCIATION

In January of 1929, Cascade Ski Club gained recognition with the National Ski Association through their affiliation with Western Amateur Ski Association. This led to competition with other major groups, especially the Hollyburn Ski Club from British Columbia.

Competition was in jumping and cross-country. The Arlberg technique of turning had not been introduced into this country, and skiers were not schooled in high speed turns on steep hillside terrain.

Through association with other clubs, an all-day meeting was arranged to be held at the Multnomah Hotel in Portland on November 23, 1930, to formulate an organization. There were representatives from six ski clubs from Oregon and Washington: Fred H. McNeil, Myron Jones, Judge Fred W. Stadter, and Harald Lee of Cascade Ski Club; J.C. Beeson and J.S. Bresko from Cle Elum; Andy Anderson, R.W. Arens, and Percy F. Bucklin from Hood River Ski Club; Paul Hosmer of Bend Skyliners; C. Stang Anderson and R. Flakstad of Seattle; Walter E. Anderson and D.L. Motteler of Leavenworth.

McNeil was elected chairman of the meeting, and Beeson secretary. A discussion followed as to whether the group should be affiliated with Western Amateur Ski Association or form a division of the National Ski Association. Anderson of Leavenworth and Bucklin of Hood River were appointed to retire from the meeting and resolve the matter, as well as to choose a name. Constitution and by-laws were placed in the hands of a second committee, Anderson of Seattle, Stadter of Cascade, and Hosmer of Bend.

After lunch Bucklin and Anderson came back with the recommendation to name the group the Pacific Northwestern Ski Association and ask for status as a division of the National.

The by-law and Constitution Committee advocated the exchange of jumpers to compete in a circuit of tournaments held by member clubs, with travelling expense the responsibility of the guest contestants and the tournament expenses as the cost of the host club.

An election of officers was held, Fred H. McNeil president, J.C. Beeson first vice-president, Paul Hosmer second vice-president, Judge Fred Stadter secretary, Percy Bucklin treasurer. Other members of the Board of Directors were C. Stang Anderson and Walter Anderson.

McNeil at the time was an officer in The Mazamas and secretary of Cascade Ski Club. He worked on the editorial staff of the *Oregon Journal.* As president of PNSA he had a great many contacts and got the organization off to a powerful and enthusiastic beginning.

One of the first problems was the responsibility to NSA for contestants and support for the 1932 Olympic Winter Sports program. This was accentuated by a depression bank closure that froze $1,900 of funds held by the Norge Club of Chicago, funds that were to have been turned over to the NSA. Loss of this money placed a great deal of pressure on the NSA to keep the Olympic program solvent. At the outset PNSA dues were $30 per year. Each of the six member clubs paid PNSA $25 per year in dues. Later on the National asked for more support for the Olympics.

Meanwhile a parallel organization had been formed in California, and there was some interplay with groups in Canada. Cascade Ski Club was selected as host for the first PNSA championship tournament. On October 29, 1931, the directors met again at the Multnomah Hotel, at a $1 dinner, and made plans for the 1931-2 ski season. Shortly afterward McNeil was reelected and Howard Dalsbo became the secretary.

Alpinee's, Hood River's Serious Climbers

The Alpinee's, Inc. were organized February 3, 1947, for the purpose of operating and maintaining a mountain rescue organization, which would work to promote, develop, and advance general and scientific information and knowledge in mountain climbing and mountain rescue work; also to advance and teach winter sports. Charter members were L.C. (Jack) Baldwin, George Howell, Myron Weygandt, Dick Mansfield, Don Kresse, and Bob Duckwall.

The organizers were young, vigorous men, who had just returned from duty in World War Two. Two were new members of Crag Rats, who wanted more action, greater use of current techniques in mountaineering. The club quickly became aligned with the Mountain Rescue Association in Seattle; Oregon at the time had only an unofficial group that was listed in Ray Conway's desk drawer.

They soon acquired a tragia for evacuation of rescue victims, and developed a very effective cable retrieval system in use to this day. On May 19, 1957, The Alpinees presented an impressive display and simulated rescue on Armed Forces Day at the Portland Air Base. Many other such presentations were made at mountain rescue conferences, such as one at Snoqualmie Pass, Washington, on May 25, 1949. An exhibition was made to the ranger staff at Yosemite National Park on October 2 to 5, 1958, when Jack Baldwin, Roger Getchell, Ernest Hanson, Cranson

Fosberg, Harold Franz, and Phil Tyler visited the park.

Alpinees affiliated with the Senior Member Group of the Hood River Squadron, Civil Air Patrol, Oregon Wing. This is a unique arrangement that resulted in remarkable strengthening of both components. Alpinee activities pumped new life into the waning squadron, and air support gave the club a very effective tool for search and rescue work.

Many of their operations have been in searching for downed aircraft and rescuing possible survivors. Searching rivers for drowning victims has been an important function. In Mountain rescue work they have been extremely active, keyed into radio networks and being ready to go at a moment's notice. The club includes aircraft pilots, experienced climbers, boaters, radio operators, 4-wheel-drive vehicle drivers, skiers, first aid men. In 1954, the National Ski Patrol gave The Alpinee's the authority to act as Mount Hood Ski Patrol on the north side of the mountain.

The club acquired a square acre in the southern outskirts of Hood River. In 1961 they began clearing the timbered plot and planning a building. Jack Baldwin, building contractor, supervised the erection of the Alpinee's home, completed late in 1962. The structure is uniquely suited to the club's use. A 40-foot fireplace was made of stone that can be climbed by several routes. Anchors at the top allow a belayer to protect climbers as they negotiate the pitches. Practice can even be done in walking a loaded akja down the vertical surface in simulated rescue.

As with the Crag Rats, the Alpinees are a closely welded group of individuals. Once each month an indoor lecture and training session is given at the club house. The subjects include advanced work as well as frequent recall of basic mountaineering, first aid, and search techniques. Frequent outdoor practice sessions are scheduled. Training officer at this writing is Carroll Davis.

Membership runs about 100. New members need not have a background of experience, but are expected to learn search and rescue technique as soon as possible. Many of the new members are young, which pressages a continuing vitality in the club. Some of the better mountaineers in the group are Carroll Davis, Kenneth Abendroth, Darryl Lloyd, Dean Kleinsmith, Tom Nash, Bob Newman, Howard Kanable, Jack Baldwin, and James Parr.

Skiyente Women Skiers

Skiyente is a women's ski club, the only one in existence registered through auspices of the National Ski Association. The club was founded in the 1955-56 season, gaining its nucleus from the Associated Women Skiers, which finally dissolved about 1963.

The club is an aggressive affiliate of PNSA, each member belonging individually to PNSA. Club purposes are to support PNSA, ski racing, ski safety, the US ski team, ski patrol, and to advocate Forest Service policy favorable to the sport of skiing.

In respect to racing Skiyente sponsors annual contests sanctioned by PNSA, The Skiyente Cup, and The Memorial Cup. Every third year the club takes its turn in sponsoring the Golden Rose Cup Race, a PNSA event associated with the Portland Rose Festival. The Maryanne Hill Cup Race is held for members only, named for the first president and organizer of the club, who felt that the Associated Women Skiers were too socially oriented and not active enough in skiing. Skiyente also holds an annual Mitey Mite race at Timberline known as the Betty Dodd Kiddies Klassic.

Skiyente's largest social function is the King Winter Kaper Dance in February, honoring each year, the man deemed to have given the most in capability, time, and effort to further the sport of skiing at Mount Hood. Selection is by secret ballot, and only the president and dance chairman know the identity of King Winter until the announcement is made at the dance. Past winners of the honor, all of whom have their pictures hanging at the Ratskeller at Government Camp are:

1956	. Marion Whiting	1966	. Kenneth Low
1957	.. Barnie Becker	1967	... Bill Spencer
1958	.. Jack L. Vidoni	1968	.. Joe Englesby
1959	... Vince Gignac	1969	..... Lee Perry
1960	.... Keith Petrie	1970	Stuart Mockford
1961	.... Kenneth Van Dyke	1971	...... Richard Kohnstamm
1962	.... Bill Keil	1972	.. Duane Bridge
1963	.... Dave Wiley	1973	.. Jack Weigand
1964	. Everett L. Darr	1974	.. Ole Langerud
1965	.... Joe Genoud		

Other club social events include the Christmas Fireside, Old Timers' Night, Installation Party, and a summer picnic. Fund raising functions vary with the year. Planned for the 1974-75 season are a Monte Carlo Night and a spaghetti feast.

The club has been very active in the PNSA organization, always having a member serving as a member of the Board of Directors or chairman of a committee of PNSA. Three times Skiyente has been declared the Outstanding Ski Club of the Year with PNSA. The United States Ski Association once awarded them the award of fourth outstanding club in the nation.

Officers are elected for a fiscal year beginning June 1. Past presidents are:

1955	.. Maryanne Hill	1965	... Betty Dodd
1956	.. Maryanne Hill	1966	Darlene Hatfield
1957	.... Bunny Low	1967	Barbara Bennett
1958	. Joanne Genoud	1968	Sinda Markham
1959	. Delores Curran	1969	.... Judy Perry
1960	... Joyce Harris	1970	. Laurie Newton
1961	. Delores Vidoni	1971	. Leslie Gilsdorf
1962	.... Jody Wiley	1972	Eileen Schurman
1963	...... Jo Bunch	1973	... Nancy Haug
1964	..... Mary Alice Thompson	1974	.... Phyllis Cascadden

MOUNT HOOD SKI CLUB

One of the very early ski clubs was Mount Hood Ski Club, organized with 24 charter members in late 1926 or early 1927. By January of 1928, it had grown to about 100. President was Dr. Guy DuPlessis, vice-president Boyd Summers, secretary Harry Conway, treasurer Ted Emerson, and corresponding secretary Gordon Johnson. Membership was largely men of Norwegian descent who had learned cross-country technique in their army and competed in jumping contests in Norway.

Old-timbers say the club suddenly disintegrated in 1928. Most of their members turned up shortly in the Cascade Ski Club, who held a few more meets at Swim, but settled into regular activity at the site of the present jumping hill on the north side of Multorpor Mountain.

Another ski club of the 1928 vintage was Viking Sports Club, another group of Norwegians. They too, faded out of existence, being mostly absorbed into Cascade Ski Club later on.

CASCADE SKI CLUB

One might say that the father of Cascade Ski Club was Ole Haugen, who secured first rights for the Multorpor Jump Hill in 1928 and developed it with his two brothers, Lars and Seibert. The nucleus of the organization came from a split in the ranks of Mount Hood Ski Club. Both were basically composed of men born in Norway, skilled at jumping and cross-country racing. At some time in 1928 a number of the men of MHSC decided to defect, and the Cascade Ski Club was born. The first officers were:

Reider Hafstad . . . . President
Kaare Schafstad . . . . Vice-president
Ole Haugen . . . . Secretary-treasurer

Their first jumping tournament was held at Multorpor on January 6, 1929. By the end of the month, they had affiliated with the National Ski Association through a membership in the Western Amateur Ski Association. This gave the club immediate sanction in holding first-magnitude tournaments at Government Camp.

Most of the local competition came from Mount Hood Ski Club and Viking Sports Club, which soon folded up. Meets were also exchanged with the men on the north side, Hood River Ski Club, and Guide Ski Club, on the jump hill located at the site of the present-day Cooper Spur Ski Area. Big competition was from Seattle and the Hollyburn Ski Club of Vancouver, British Columbia. The north woods were crawling with Norwegian jumpers ready to compete with the Oregonians. Tournaments often used a combined score for competition in both cross-country and jumping.

Cascade Ski Club maintained an area on the upper floor of the Battle Axe recreational building. They rented from Everett Sickler, but that arrangement lasted only about a year. When Henry Villiger bought Battle Axe Inn, he raised the rent, and the Cascaders moved out.

The officers for the second year were:

Harald Lee . . . . President
Hjalmar Hvam . . . . Vice-president
Reider Hafstad . . . . Secretary
Norman Bruck . . . . Treasurer

There was a great deal of unity in the ski community of those days. Mazamas such as Judge Fred Stadter and Fred McNeil were also members of Cascade. All the old skiers knew each other. At Christmas of 1929, 1,100 winter sports fans crowded Summit, Swim, and Government Camp for a December 23 holiday celebration. S.W. Lawrence in a Santa Claus suit was helped by L.W. Hawn to pass out candy and gifts at a party at Government Camp Hotel. The music was provided by the United Artisan Drum and Bugle Corps. Down at Swim, Boyd Summers threw another Christmas party for his patrons. Hjalmar Hvam won the standing ski jump event with a leap of 84 feet. Kaare Schafstad came in with 74 feet and Ole Langerud 68 feet.

When PNSA was formed November 23, 1930, Cascade Ski Club was one of the six original member clubs and without a doubt the group most influential in founding the association. The secretary of Cascade, Fred McNeil, became the president of PNSA, and the club held the first sanctioned PNSA tournament held on February 1, 1931.

In 1931, the club had two large projects going. One was in shaping up the jumping hill at Multorpor. In October, they borrowed $1,000 and rented a huge gasoline yarder to move dirt. New stands and buildings were erected, and when they were finished Multorpor had jumps for A, B, C, and D competition.

For a short time the club used a shack at the foot of Multorpor for headquarters, but there was

Original Cascade Ski Club building 1932 — Photo Hjalmar Hvam

Cascade Ski Club, August 10, 1947
Photo Maryanne Hill collection

a great push for a club house. This was the same year that the Mazamas were building their log structure northeast of Summit. Cascade Ski Club contacted the school board of Portland District #1 and secured some portable World War One schoolhouses. These were hauled up in sections and erected just south (behind) of the old Government Camp Hotel. The old original Norwegians of the club were right in their element, doing the carpentry and finishing needed to make the place a home. By mid-December all the building was enclosed, with doors and windows set.

It was during that autumn that a tremendous push was made to increase membership. The club held meetings in Portland with films and music. Memberships were sold for a dollar to anyone who wanted to ski, or watch skiers jump, or even watch movies of skiers. On December 10, 1931, McNeil reported a membership of 450, and he met with treasurer Fred VanDyke to plan and order a bookkeeping system with proper cash book, membership ledger, invoice file, and voucher forms. The club was dealing with money in four-figure amounts, and it was time to put it on a business-like basis. A publication was started to keep membership aware of club happenings.

The building programs on the ski hill and the new lodge placed the club in a severe financial position made even more acute by the depression. On February 25, 1932, they were faced with current payables of $1,256, with only $513 in the bank to cover them. In addition there were long-term notes on money borrowed to make the improvements. Needless to say, Cascade Ski Club weathered these hard times and became prosperous in later years.

In the autumn of 1933 the Government Camp Hotel burned to the ground, menacing all the nearby buildings with the intense heat. Local residents worked feverishly, and the Cascade club building was saved.

In January 1934, a new type of skiing was brought to Mount Hood, the downhill and slalom races. The Mazamas sponsored a series of races at timberline. Boyd French, J.J. Jones, and Grant McConnell won the first one. The expert skiers of Cascade Ski Club quickly picked up the art of slalom running and dominated the field. Hjalmar Hvam and Roy Tangen were two of the men who immediately made good showing.

This big change occurred in skiing when such men as Bierly and Boyd French, Sr. came into the area with the new parallel techniques. This al-

LIST OF PRESIDENTS

1928-9	Reider Hafstad
1929-0	Harald A. Lee
1930-1	Harald A. Lee
1931-2	Harald A. Lee
1932-3	Fred W. Stadter
1933-4	Fred H. McNeil
1934-5	Fred VanDyke
1935-6	Corey Gustafsson
1936-7	Harold Hanson
1936-7	Boyd French, Sr.
1937-8	Fred H. McNeil
1938-9	Fred H. McNeil
1939-0	Harold Kelley
1940-1	Guy Talbot, Jr.
1941-2	Hjalmar Hvam
1942-3	George Riggs
1943-4	Vern Caldwell
1944-5	Albert Bullier
1945-6	Gary Gast
1946-7	Wade Cornwell
1947-8	Norman Lindhjem
1948-9	Joe Taylor
1949-0	Ted Wassard
1950-1	David W. Young
1951-2	David W. Young
1952-3	Chester VanHouten
1953-4	Malcom Carter
1954-5	Walter Elmer
1955-6	Bud Christen
1956-7	Paul Roscoe
1957-8	Paul Roscoe
1958-9	Don F. Higgens
1959-0	Don F. Higgens
1960-1	Jack Hilbourne
1961-2	Howard Josephson
1962-3	Ralph Byrne
1963-4	James Ziegler
1964-5	Neil Smyth
1965-6	Don Lofis
1966-7	Bob Fredeen
1967-8	Paul Roscoe
1968-9	Howard Hermanson
1969-0	Hal Pallay
1970-1	Don Robison
1971-2	Paul Nagel
1972-3	Ragnor Gusfafsson
1973-4	Bob Swan
1974-5	David Johanson

lowed far more people to get the most out of skiing as individuals, but it also added a great new dimension in racing. Slalom and downhill races, added to the traditional jumping and cross-country events, created four-way competition. Most competitors specialized, as they do today, but some tournaments were conducted using a four-way combined score. It did not take very many years until slalom and downhill took over the sport. After World War Two jumping and cross-country became practically a legend, seldom run.

Cascade kept a very strong position in maintaining a large stable of racers all through the Thirties. By the time World War Two was over a great many of the original members had retired to the armchair. The clubhouse halls no longer rang with the accents of the old Norwegians who skied and played hard all day and ate and drank far into the night. The new membership consisted of good-to-expert skiers of social prominence who gave the club an aristocratic tone on the mountain.

In 1947, a large new club lodge was built on the north side of the highway, behind Mountain View Inn and Hjalmar Hvam's ski shop. The new building has a large living room for parties or dances, a dining room, drying room, waxing room, locker area, and large dormitories. The exterior was designed in a massive style, very appropriate for the mountain setting. The old clubhouse on the south side of the highway was torn down and the remnants razed. When Mountain View burned in 1955, a very large open area was created, which gives the Cascade club lodge an impressive open snowfield in front of the building.

In the last decade the character of Cascade Ski Club has changed somewhat toward being a group with appeal to families, as the wave of World War Two veterans changed from swashbuckling youth to senior members of the ski community.

Trails Club of Oregon

The Trails Club of Oregon was formed on Larch Mountain on October 15, 1915, the year that the Larch Mountain Trail was dedicated to the public. The first president was Samuel C. Lancaster, the engineer who did the masterful job on the old scenic highway in the Columbia Gorge. Henry R. Hayek was one of the founders. After several years of being the guardian of the trail, the club took on more of the nature of a general outdoor club, incorporating on June 5, 1923.

In 1925 the club built Nesika Lodge in Multnomah Basin, up the trail from Multnomah Falls. The lodge is actually a series of buildings. One serves as kitchen and dining hall, a site for parties. Other buildings provide dormitory space, accommodating 60 women and 50 men. On the edge of the cliffs, a short distance on the trail leading east, is a small open-air amphitheater protected by a rock wall on the cliff side. From that point an awe-inspiring view of the Columbia Gorge lies beyond the breathtaking drop of the cliff.

The club sponsors many trips to the lodge each year, with evening programs and hiking during the daytime. The site is within easy hiking distance of the Franklin Ridge — Oneonta Gorge loop trail or to Larch Mountain.

In 1949, a new lodge was built at Mount Hood, up West Leg Road from Mazama Lodge. This building is used by the club in skiing and climbing activity. It was activated with an opening party on December 3-4 of that year. After a time they named it Tyee Lodge. In 1953 "Tyee Junior" was completed, a small structure to house their electric generating plant. At a later date a big expansion was made on Tyee Lodge. Sleeping accommodations are for 26 women and 25 men.

Trails Club of Oregon has remained as a small, closely knit group. Membership in the 1950's ran from 250 to 325. Emphasis is placed upon trail hiking, especially on the Pacific Crest Trail. The club maintains committees on Lodge, Climbing, Outings, Winter Sports. The Board of Trustees includes nine members. The *Blazer* is the monthly publication.

The list of presidents includes many individuals distinguished in the civic and outdoor world:

PRESIDENTS
TRAILS CLUB OF OREGON

Year	President	Year	President
1916	S.C. Lancaster	1946	Frank Dorsey
1917	Henry R. Hayek	1947	Durward E. Wright
1918	Chester Hogue	1948	Durward E. Wright
1919	Fred H. Kiser	1949	Ray Wybenga
1920	R.J. Grace	1950	Henry Waespe
1921	R.J. Grace	1951	Wm. Spreadborough
1922	D.P. Wells	1952	Samuel Jacobson
1923	George L. Bickel	1953	George Velguth
1924	Fred A. Steeble	1954	John Hook
1925	H.F. Morden	1955	John Hook
1926	H.F. Morden	1956	Una Davies
1927	Martin Deragisch	1957	Una Davies
1928	A.W. Kindorf	1958	Ralph Burrough
1929	George Henderson	1959	Norman Greene
1930	Roy D. Beam	1960	Norman Greene
1931	Herman W. Erren	1961	Pete Stangell
1932	Edward J. Lenz	1962	Pete Stangell
1933	Edward J. Lenz	1963	Edward Hill
1934	Glen A. DeGroff	1964	Paul Riseley
1935	Glen A. DeGroff	1965	Mary Lou Greene
1936	Edward Neubauer	1966	Larry Williams
1937	Edward Neubauer	1967	Anne Bohlen
1938	Melvin Becker	1968	Anne Bohlen
1939	Herb Rasor	1969	Carl Soderback
1940	G.E. Cannon	1970	Carl Soderback
1941	G.E. Cannon	1971	Stanley Goodell
1942	Harold Mace	1972	Stanley Goodell
1943	Kenneth Martin	1973	George Blinco
1944	Ray Cummins	1974	George Blinco
1945	Harold Mace	1975	Jon Vanderbout

Schnee Voegli, Competitive Bon Vivants

In 1942 a group of sophomores and juniors in Portland high schools decided to form a men-only club. Everett Darr let them use the Mountain Shop in Portland for their meetings and permitted them to sleep on the floor of his shop at Government Camp, then called the Ski Pole. There were 13 boys in the original group, with Jack Keep presiding.

World War Two disbanded their efforts, as the armed forces took them and sent them onto the battle front. When the war terminated in 1945, they began to filter home and renew old friendships. Under the leadership of Robert Dooley, the club reformed for the 1947-8 season, and have been a strong factor in skiing at Mount Hood ever since.

In 1948 they became a PNSA sanctioned club, opening the door to holding top racing competition. In 1966 they realized a long-awaited dream by being sanctioned by the United States Ski Association, opening the opportunity to partake in events of the international ski association, FIS.

Schnee Voegli sponsors the Turkey Day Slalom and Portland Day Trail Race each year. They take turns with Skiyente and Cascade Ski Clubs to run the Golden Rose Ski Race once every third year. The Golden Rose is an annual race in June associated with the Portland Rose Festival. The Far West Kahndahar, a major USSA race, comes to Mount Hood about every third year. It has previously been sponsored by Alpine Meadows in California and Alpenthal in Washington. At present only Schnee Voegli is shouldering the immense cost of staging the race. In 1971 chairman Tom Markham had a budget of about $10,000, that had to be raised through local contribution, a little larger than normal amount, because the FW Kahndahar was a qualifying race for Olympic competition. In 1974 chairman Tudor Marks carried the race on, although California and Washington groups ceased to operate their license to stage the race because of high financial burden. Kahndahar races are run in about three or four nations, sanctioned by the Ski Club of Great Britain.

Competition within the club is held annually at the Club Championship Race. Another intra-club race is called the Snowbird Giant Slalom, a late season event which is open only to the members who have never placed in any competitive ski race. The eve of the Snowbird is marked with a big steak fry and calcutta pool, a hilarious evening with plenty of cold beer and iced wine to eliminate any possibility of heat exhaustion among either contestants or spectators.

Another widely famed fun race is the Annual Kahndabeer Race from Timberline Lodge to Government Camp. The racers don hilarious costumes and must consume three cans of beer in the presence of race officials at various stations enroute. The race began in 1947, 1948, and 1949 under the private sponsorship of three Schnee Voegli members in turn, Allan Fischer, Joe Englesby, and Ian McAndie. Then the Mount Hood Ski Club, now defunct, took over until 1960, when Schnee Voegli adopted it as a club race. The Kahndabeer is famed for its broad-minded observance of the rules, with winners often coming in first by virtue of some clever, conniving, underhanded maneuver. Despite the most bitter opposition, one "Lucky" McKenney won the event ten different years.

Aside from the function of ski racing, Schnee Voegli conducts a complete social calendar. Perhaps the best description is to quote Stuart Mockford, club historian in 1970-1971:

"There are several purely social functions for members and often their wives and guests. These include the annual picnic which is an extravaganza fondly looked forward to; sure to be blessed with an outstanding array of bikini-clad damsels; fun and games; quantities of tasty food; and, because of the sunstroke problem, liquid cheer. Every year there are "Blitz Parties" with the cooperation of the local brewery which fully realizes that the Club as a whole probably consumes more beer than any group of similar size in the area. This year we are at Blitz four times. Then there is the "Secret Function" on which no comment will be given or else it wouldn't be a secret any longer.

"Two public dances are sponsored partly as fund-raising functions by the Club at Timberline Lodge each year. These are the "Green Buzzard's Ball" and the "Pray for Snow Dance" and are most popular with the younger set.

"Club meetings are held on the second and fourth Tuesdays of every month except through the summer. The meetings are presently held at the Portland Thunderbird Motel. Most business meetings are noted for incoherent arguments and unique interpretations of Robert's Rules of Order, possibly abated by there being a bar in the room. In spite of the distractions, a great deal of serious business is transacted. Following the meetings it is traditional for the membership to adjourn practically en masse to the favorite tavern of the moment and continue their chivalrous discussions."

The club had maintained a phenomenal esprit de corps. New members are proud to be included in a group that requires high standards of skiing and which places its members in the thick of the excitement of working on the big ski races.

A list of presidents follows:

1942-3 .. Jack Kemp
1947-8 .. Bob Dooley
1949-0 . Jack Munzel
1950-1 .Jerry Fullman
Fred Schmaling
1951-2 ... Bob North
1952-3 Barney Becker
1953-4 ..... Kenneth VanDyke
1954-5 .. Jack Vidoni
1955-6 .... Eugene P. Goodrich
1956-7 ...... Charles Lawton
1957-8 .... Willi Antis
1858-9 .... Matt Greenslade
1959-0 ....David Anderson
1960-1 . .Phillip Ringle

1961-2 . . . . . Les Segal
1962-3 . . Jerry Becker
1963-4 . . Gene Brown
1964-5 . . . . . . William Spencer
1965-6 . . . . James Feldman
1966-7 . . . . Stuart Mockford
1967-8 . Kenneth Low
1968-9 .Roger Sanman
1969-0 . . . Joe Cornell
1970-1 . . . Joe Cornell
1971-2 . . Ed Anderson
1972-3 . . Bob Gilsdorf
1973-4 . . Bob Gilsdorf
1974-5 . . . . Carlo Ottoboni

Seracs on Eliot Glacier

Schools, a Big Business

THE JAYCEE SKI SCHOOL

The Portland Junior Chamber of Commerce sponsored and ran several big ski races in the years just after World War Two. To stage such a race means a lot of organization. There is publicity, providing the trophies, registration of contestants, and rounding up a small army of timers, starters, radio operators, judges, and gate-keepers. In 1947 Chet Bohlman and Ed DeKoning were officials at the top of the course on the Golden Poles Race. Up there at the 10,000-foot level just below Crater Rock, they began reflecting on their activities.

"This gets to be pretty much of an old thing," said DeKoning.

"Yes, it does," replied Bohlman. "But what bothers me is that we are doing all this work just to satisfy a hundred or so hot-shot racers."

"Well, that's what the club wants."

"Not necessarily," said Bohlman. "Suppose we quit running these races and started a ski school for all those bunnies that come up here and break their legs because they don't know how to ski?"

"It would appeal more to me."

Bohlman was director of sports with the Junior Chamber, and he and DeKoning put together a plan for a school to present to the Board of Directors. After several committee meetings they were ready to present a ski school planned for early 1948, and the board endorsed the idea heartily.

The first year about 460 signed up for the school. The next year it was 800, and it grew accordingly. Prominent skiers and racers were drafted to help on the project. It soon became apparent, from examining the accident ratios, that instruction was diminishing the number of broken legs and arms among the casual skiers.

The idea of a free school soon faded and the Jaycees soon found it necessary to give their instructors compensation for their time and expense. But the format remained the same. The idea was to give a good instruction package for as little as possible.

The ski school program won the Portland chapter a national award in the Junior Chamber organization. But the surprising thing was that Jaycee Ski Schools began to open in other states on the basis of the success at Mount Hood. Before the advent of the school the *Oregonian* and the *Oregon Journal* at times cooperated with the ski patrol to hold schools. All that activity ceased when the Junior Chamber Ski School opened its doors.

The school for the 1974-75 season gives four days of instruction, complete with lift rides for a fee of $34. Classes are maintained in Beginner, Intermediate, Advanced, Racing, and Cross-country.

EDWARD A. JOHANN

In 1969, Ed Johann, Mazama leader and expedition climber, began to guide parties on a professional basis. His main assistance has been from his sons, Eddie, Jr. and Joseph, and his son-in-law, Gary Craighead.

Most of his activity has been on Mount Hood, for which his present rate is $18 per climber. Clients are obtained by a few small advertisements and by sending brochures to various places in California. Representation at outdoor shows also steers some business in his direction. In 1975, he took a group of climbers to the volcano area south of Mexico City.

SKI BOWL SKI SCHOOL

The Ski Bowl Ski School was established in 1954, when a modern lift was constructed on the upper Bowl. Owners were Nap Rocqu, Barney Becker, and Robert Strand. The whole instruction staff was only five people.

Later ownership shifted to Strand, Robert Weismann, and Bruce Chenowith. About three instructors operating during the week, mainly on evenings, and 60 instructors are used on weekends.

Instruction is given at levels of Beginner, Intermediate, Advanced, Expert, Cross Country, and Free Style, which is trick skiing. Clientele is school and church groups and clubs such as Multnomah Athletic Club.

TIMBERLINE SKI SCHOOL

Timberline Ski School had its beginnings with the famous Otto Lang, Austrian instructor and author of a book on downhill skiing. Lang had put together a film "Snow Flight," which he showed to American audiences in 1936, and he ran the Hannes Schneider Ski Schools at Mount Rainier and Mount Baker.

One of his employees at Mount Rainier was Ariel Edmiston, a student at University of Washington. When Timberline Lodge opened up in 1938, he sent Edmiston down to take charge of the new operation. Lang made occasional appearances, spreading his supervision between the three mountain ski areas, but Edmiston ran the operation at Timberline in 1938 and in the 1938-9 ski season. He then quit and returned to college at University of Washington, with Hans Sarback taking the post. In the 1940-41 season he returned to Timberline to be co-director with Hans.

After World War Two Sarbach once again resumed the position to be followed by Nap Rocqu in 1947, then Olaf Rodegard and Don Reed. Lee St. John took it in 1953, and Gus Weber in 1954. However, Dave Case says that his brother Don ran the school as a private operation in 1953-4 and 1954-5.

In 1956, the operation of Timberline Lodge was under Dick Kohnstamm, and his school director was Pepi Gable. Ariel Edmiston was one of the instructors. Eric Sailer was appointed director in December, 1957. In the 1965-6 season, Loren O'Conner took the job. Then the present director took charge, Harold "Bud" Nash.

Instruction is held in Beginner, Intermediate, Advanced, Racing, and Cross Country. The staff averages 10 full-time instructors and another 60 weekend instructors. Since 1967 this has increased from six full-time and 18 weekend personnel.

Learn-to-ski packages coupled with lodging account for most of the week-day business. Women's groups come in busloads on Tuesdays, Wednesdays, and Thursdays. Groups from companies, clubs, churches, and schools throw the big bulge of activity onto the school during weekends.

MOUNT HOOD SKI SCHOOL

The Mount Hood Ski School had its beginnings about 1949 at Ski Bowl under the operation of Gary Gast. To understand the background of the change in ownership, it is necessary to review the activities of Donald Case, who was Chief Instructor of the Jaycee Ski School in the 1951-2 season.

In the seasons of 1953-4 and 1954-5, Case ran ski school activities at Timberline Lodge. This was as a concession, as the operator, Charles Slaney, did not run the school as a part of the lodge business. In 1955-6, Case formed Multorpor Ski School with his brother, David, Will Herrington, and Jack Muntzel. In 1956 they bought Mount Hood Ski School from Gary Gast and discontinued the Multorpor name. The new operation held classes at both Ski Bowl and Multorpor, and has done so ever since.

Jack Muntzel was killed in an airplane crash and Don Case moved to California leaving Mount Hood Ski School under the ownership of Dave Case and Will Herrington.

Multorpor Jump Hill — early 1930's

Elk Cove. Mount Hood and Barrett Spur 1931

The peak number of instructors was 105 in 1966, when they held two classes per day. The following year they decreased the number of instructors and began to conduct four classes per day, greatly increasing the output per instructor. The number has climbed back to a present range of 85 to 95. During the week 10 to 15 instructors are on duty. Students are taught in levels of Beginner, Intermediate, Advanced, Racing, and Cross Country. Jumping has been dropped for lack of interest.

Mount Hood Ski School is the only one at Mount Hood which is accredited with the Oregon State Board of Higher Education. Many of the classes are held in conjunction with colleges and high schools so that the students can earn recognized credit in Physical Education. Some of the colleges participating are Portland State College, Lewis and Clark College, Mount Hood Community College, Clackamas County Community College, Chemeketa Community College, Warner Pacific College, and Pacific University. Other group classes include women's clubs and groups from commercial firms.

FAMED CLIMBER BECAME INSOLVENT

Wednesday, February 19, 1975 *The Oregonian* reported that Luther G. Jerstad, an American conquerer of Mount Everest, had filed a petition for involuntary bankruptcy in the US District Court for Lute Jerstad Enterprises, Inc. The corporation ran Lute Jerstad Adventures, Mount Hood Meadows School of Mountaineering, Mount Hood School of Mountaineering, and Mountain Magic.

Lute Jerstad Enterprises listed debts of $110,253. The two major amounts were to the US Small Business Administration for $37,797, and to Adventures Inc. of Wichita, Kansas, for $60,322.

It was in 1971 that Jerstad opened up for business at the 8,600-foot level in a camp in the rocks up above Mount Hood Meadows. On June 22 of that year the famed Tensing Norgay, the Sherpa who made the first ascent of Mount Everest in 1953, visited Jerstad's camp. The operator of a mountaineering school in Darjeeling, India, Norgay was paying a visit to his friend, Jerstad, to observe a five-day session of his school. John West took Norgay and his wife up as high as the snow cat would go. On disembarking, the Sherpa's sleeping bag got away and rolled 1,500 feet down the hill. West went after it with the snow cat.

Hjalmar Hvam on left instructing somersaults
Photo Hvam

At that time, Jerstad had the services of Dick McGowan and Jay Ullin, both well known mountaineers from Washington. McGowan had previously run a school of mountaineering at Mount Rainier. The course was laid out for a five-day session, in which the students learned to handle ice-axe, climbing ropes, and crampons on the Newton Clark Glacier, finishing with a climb of the Wy'east Route. The basics were much the same as offered by The Mazamas or the Seattle Mountaineers in their climbing courses, however the net result was a much more finished climber. First of all, the training was concentrated, with little outside diversion. There was little time to forget from one session to the next. Secondly, the instruction staff was highly trained and professional. They were sufficient in number to give training in depth.

In 1972 the school was moved to the north side of the mountain. A tent city of about 20 brightly-colored mountain tents was set at about 8,600 feet on the Eliot Glacier. Reporter Bill Keil found them there on July 16, Jerstad and nine assistants. Jerstad was eloquent in his commendation for the mountain life, terming his crew as "drop outs". He remarked that they had all been prominent in the eight-a.m.-to-five-p.m.-struggle-for-existence in the city, holding responsible positions, but they had finally "dropped out" to seek a better, more relaxed life.

He remarked about the remote character of the Eliot Glacier. On the Fourth of July, when campgrounds down below were jammed with humanity, only one group appeared. They had walked along the moraine, looked down at the climbers' camp, then gone on their way.

Early in the 1972 season, a fundamentalist Christian group from Los Angeles had attended the Jerstad school. Their aim was to climb Mount Ararat in the Holy Land in search of Noah's Ark. Most of Jerstad's clientele came from California or eastern cities, wealthy men, who could afford an elite approach to learning mountaineering. At the time of Keil's visit to the camp, there were seven students and Jerstad served them with a staff of nine.

Worldwide mountain tours into The Himalaya Range, or perhaps The Alps or Andes, were led by Jerstad personnel. His men also assisted film companies in shooting alpine scenes that required technique. The notice of Jerstad's financial failure was received with sadness in the mountaineering world, because he had been widely admired and respected.

Lute Jerstad first leaped into fame in 1963, when as a member of the American team, he was one of the conquerors of Mount Everest. Later he was well known as a professor at the University of Oregon and at Lewis and Clark College.

U S Forest Service, Guarding Mount Hood

On June 17, 1892, President Benjamin Harrison created the Bull Run Timberland Reserve by executive proclamation. This gave the growing city of Portland protection for 142,000 acres of watershed in an area that has been jealously guarded and closed to the public ever since.

Grover Cleveland used presidential authority on September 28, 1893, to add to the Bull Run by creating the Cascade Range Forest Reserve, a vast area including most of the Cascade Range all through the state of Oregon. Administration was done from Washington D.C., using inspectors and very few employees. As soon as the large reserve was created, the senators and congressmen from Oregon began to spend great effort to destroy it. They did not wish to see large areas taken out of private ownership. They were defeated, and the forest reserve remained inviolate.

The Cascade Range Forest Reserve was split into two sections, North and South. Control was under the General Land Office, which later became the Bureau of Land Management in the Department of the Interior. There was considerable political upheaval in Washington after the election of Theodore Roosevelt in 1901. In some areas there had been considerable scandal and corruption in the General Land Office.

Gifford Pinchot took a very strong stand that forests belonged in the Department of Agriculture. He felt that raising trees was comparable to raising corn or wheat. Eventually he and his supporters had their way, and the transfer was made February 1, 1905. He began to ask for businesslike reports from the District Foresters, and when he did not receive them, many "resignations" were accepted from Foresters who had tenure under the regime of the General Land Office.

A name change was effected March 2, 1907, when the Cascade Range Forest Reserve became Cascade Forest Reserve. On June 30, 1908, the CFR was broken up into several national forests, the one at Mount Hood being named Oregon National Forest. At the same date Bull Run Forest Reserve was combined into Oregon National Forest, and the name was discontinued.

On January 1, 1924, an executive order changed Oregon National Forest to Mount Hood National Forest, which it has been ever since. On July 1, 1933, the Santiam River drainage was removed from MHNF and placed under a newly-created Willamette National Forest. Since that date, the acreage of MHNF has remained quite stable.

MHNF has several ranger districts which are

Percy Shelley and Family at HQ Bull Run District — Photo USFS
This station on Little Sandy River built 1908

remote from the mountain; only two encircle the mountain area. Hood River Ranger District maintains offices on Highway 35, south of Mount Hood Post Office. Until the new office was built, the district had been housed in a complex on the eastern outskirts of Parkdale since 1933.

The Zigzag Ranger District was called Bull Run until 1957. The Bull Run Ranger District first had its headquarters on the Little Sandy River, a stream that runs inside the closed watershed area. It was built in 1908 by George A. TenEyck and C. Berthen; the first ranger to occupy it was Percy Shelley.

In 1908 the Bull Run Ranger District maintained a two-room cabin and a fenced area for livestock at Zigzag. In 1915 the district headquarters moved from the building on the Little Sandy River to Zigzag, where the Forest Service added considerably to the complex. At that time there was a five-room house, a workshop, a barn, pasture, hay field, and a garden. The complex covered about 80 acres.

There had been a Summit Ranger District in early days. Along about 1920 John Calverley was the District Ranger there. The district was later discontinued and placed into other districts. However, in 1953 Summit Ranger District was recreated for a period of 10 years, wherein it was consolidated into the Zigzag district.

FOREST SERVICE REGIONS

Up until 1908 the Forest Service had operated out of Washington D.C., using Forest Inspectors to hold some semblence of organization. H.D. Langille was one of these men, his name appearing later in this chapter. The Forest Inspector had a great deal of authority.

On December 1, 1908, a program of decentralizing went into effect, with the United States being cut up into several Districts, Portland being designated as District 6. A staff was sent out from Washington D.C. that month to set up the first District Office in the Buck Building. The District 6 included Alaska, Oregon, and Washington.

The whole district at that time had an annual expenditure of $457,000; income was $210,018. Sheep and cattle grazing were a big factor in income at that time. Twenty years later, in 1928, expenditures had risen to $2,764,000 and income to $1,238,669, although Alaska had been removed from the District.

ASCHOFF A COLORFUL PIONEER

One of the very colorful men in the first years of the Forest Service was German-born Adolf Aschoff, a settler at Marmot. As well as being the postmaster and operator of a resort hotel at Marmot, he also acted as a mountain guide while holding his position with the Forest Service.

On May 19, 1899, he received confirmation of his appointment as a Forest Ranger from Forest Superintendent S.B. Ormsby in Salem, and ordered to report for work to Forest Supervisor

HOOD RIVER DIST. RANGERS

NAME	PERIOD BEGINNING
Warren M. Cooper	1905
Stanley C. Walters	Feb. 20, 1920
Ross W. Williams	July 1, 1947
Bert E. Holtby	April 1, 1951
Milton D. Andrews	June 6, 1954
Cranson H. Fosburg	Nov. 18, 1956
Richard L. Mueller	Sep. 5, 1965

Warren M. "Barney" Cooper was the son of David Rose Cooper, a homesteader near Mount Hood Post Office and pioneer road builder to timberline. Cooper died in 1920, and Walters was transferred from Summit Meadow to become the new Ranger. Walters moved his headquarters to his own ranch until 1933, when a new district headquarters was built by CCC boys just East of Parkdale.

One man of note in the Hood River District was Van Embree, who began work in 1923. He taught more men in the MHNF how to use the Osborne Firefinder than any other individual.

ZIGZAG DISTRICT RANGERS

NAME	PERIOD BEGINNING
Percey Shelley	Jan. 1, 1908
C.L. "Roy" Henson	Oct. 13, 1910
Raymond E. Smith	July 1, 1922
Harlan Hiatt	April 1, 1929
Harold Engles	Dec. 16, 1936
Charles Thurston	April 1, 1943
James P. Langdon	April 1, 1945
Sherwood C. Trotter	Jan. 27, 1957
David F. Keiser	Sep. 15, 1958
Stanley R. Rapp	June 25, 1961
H. Peter Wingle	May 11, 1963
Richard Buscher	April 9, 1967
Joe Astleford	June 10, 1972
James M. Olson	Aug. 20, 1972

SUMMIT DISTRICT RANGERS

Ralph A. Wiese	July 1, 1953
Bruce M. Kirkland	Nov. 17, 1957
H. Peter Wingle	July 11, 1962
Consolidated to Zigzag	May 10, 1963

Two modern houses were built in 1969, between Timberline Junction on Highway #26 and the Mazama Lodge site, to accommodate the recently created Summit District that was reconsolidated into Zigzag District. In 1965 a new office building was erected at Zigzag.

Government pack horse — Photo USFS
An age-old way of transport

W.H.H. Dufur at Dufur. He was established as Ranger at Marmot. A letter of September 26 noted that Dufur was sending report forms, envelopes, and stationery, as well as asking for a report on how much trail had been built by one of Aschoff's underlings, Morse.

On May 8, 1900, he received a severe letter from Ormsby, one of many he would receive from superiors in his Forest Service career. The government was trying to regain the squatters' land in Summit Meadow, occupied since the death of Perry Vickers by Horace Campbell and his brother. It is not believed that Campbell had ever filed a homestead claim, but that he was merely trying to prove a claim by squatter's rights.

At Oregon City Campbell's claim was witnessed by Stephen Coalman and Stephen Mitchell, who swore that he had begun his residence at Summit Meadow in May, 1889, and had lived there and cultivated the ground until October 1895, except when driven out by snow. He had a half acre in garden, 80 acres cleared and fenced, and improvements were worth $1,500. In October 1895, Campbell had been driven out by a storm, became ill, and was committed to the insane asylum in Salem.

It seems that Aschoff had made a report to Dufur instead of Ormsby, and Ormsby delivered a good chastising by letter. He wanted to know the facts about Campbell at once, along with a list of witnesses.

On June 17, 1901, Ormsby sent another sharp letter to Aschoff, this time to note that Ranger Morse had gone into the Reserve without appointment orders. Morse was to be recalled at once until he took his oath of office. Indications are that Aschoff was working somewhat on a seasonal status, as well as Morse, which required a new appointment and oath of office in the spring.

Strangely enough, the following month on June 26, Aschoff wrote to Ormsby stating that he had taken his oath, but had not received any orders. Three days later Ormsby fired a letter back stating that Aschoff should have known enough to report to Dufur at once.

In 1903 it became evident that the Department of the Interior was beginning to be excited about the ravages of forest fires that had swept the woods year after year, each time chewing into more of the valuable forest resource. This was probably due to Gifford Pinchot, who viewed the forests as an agricultural crop. A General Letter placed in the hands of every ranger was written by J.H. Fimple, Acting Commissioner of the General Land Office. It pointed to the danger of fire and the need for vigilance. Fire posters were to be hung. Campfires of sportsmen and grazing permitees were to be inspected and their makers held liable in case of outbreak of fire. Fire posters were to be hung in prominent places. In case of fire, Rangers were given authority to hire emergency help at once. Rangers were to be held personally responsible for fires escaping into the forest.

The documented story of Aschoff's career with the Forest Service gives a good picture of a Ranger's life in those early days. Despite his wrangles with superiors, he rose to Acting Supervisor with offices at Marmot and Hood River. It cannot be discerned which office was principal. It is noted that Forest Superintendent G.B. Sheller conferred with him at Hood River on March 16-17-18 of 1904. During this time he had talks with the officials of The Dalles concerning their watershed area in the forest, and in May he discussed fencing the watershed with the Water Commissioner. Forest Inspector H.D. Langille, who had spent years at Cloud Cap, paid an official visit to Aschoff from Washington D.C. in May 1904.

Aschoff's May report showed 23 days at headquarters and eight days in the field. He wrote 63 letters and received 81. He, as well as the Rangers under him, were expected to keep detailed records of activities and expenses.

On August 26, 1904, he got a telephone call from Frank Dodge, Superintendent of the water works, telling of a fire that was spreading in Bull Run Reserve. The next morning he left his office at 3:00 a.m. to catch the 4:48 train to Portland. From there he rode the Oregon Water Power and Railway Company car to Boring, then caught a stage to Sandy, and another to Marmot to arrive by 4:00 p.m. It rained all night. The following morning he went to Aims, Walker Prairie, and on to the Bull Run Ranger Station, where he found that the rain had brought the fire into control. Firefighters were controlling burning snags in a few areas. The next morning he was on his way to Sandy to catch the stage and train back to Hood River.

By the end of 1904 Aschoff was disheartened by the slack performance of some of his Rangers. He wrote a letter to Forest Inspector Langille in Washington complaining, "I do know that we have only a few honest workers, and it makes me often bilious to know that more than twice as much work could be easily accomplished, if we had men who would take real interest in the welfare of the Reserve."

Langille did not respond in a very friendly

Aschoff's office at Marmot — Photo USFS

manner. He indicated that the startling statement by Aschoff showed the need of more comprehensive reports. He asked for all the Ranger reports for the past six months, so that he could examine them for lax operation. In this letter of January 23, 1905, he also asked Aschoff to limit his correspondence to the Washington office and to make it brief.

On February 24, 1905, Langille wrote another letter. He had examined the reports Aschoff had sent. Rangers were making a great deal out of a small amount of work. Each one was to state his beginning and ending time of work each day. Rangers were blaming lack of report forms for losing two to three days a month. They were losing too much time travelling, and since they spent too much time hunting their horses, corral fences must be built at once. Making reports and drawing maps should be done on rainy days when men could not work well in the field.

On May 6, 1905, Aschoff stood by while his son underwent surgery in a Portland hospital. On the way home to Marmot, he found his wife lying unconscious in the road between Sandy and Marmot. She had been thrown out of her buggy when her horses ran away. He stayed up with her all night.

The following day being Sunday, he spent the whole day and night looking after her, other than conferring with his Rangers. On Monday he got someone to look after her, and he went on to Forest Reserve business, processing 59 applications for grazing permits. At 10:00 p.m. he quit work and returned to his wife's side, to find her still unconscious.

This went on all week with business as usual. The following Sunday she still had not regained her senses, but his log did not mention her again. It might be assumed that she returned to normal soon after.

On February 1, 1905, Gifford Pinchot finally reached his goal of placing the Forest Service under the Department of Agriculture. On June 16, Aschoff was busy sending out badges to his Rangers, Milton J. Anderson, Joseph H. Trout, William C. Walker, S.E. Browder, Warren "Barney" Cooper, Ila C. Nealeigh, Lewis Johnson, W.C. Ward, D.C. Powell, Arthur B. Lacey, M.D. Markham, W.H. Heseman, Ephraim Henness, William E. Simmonds, and Forest Guards Hayes and Wallace. Aschoff received his own appointment as Forest Supervisor as of June 28, 1905.

BADLY INJURED ON SADDLE HORN

But even before, he was involved in a serious accident that removed him from duty all summer. On Thursday, June 22, 1905, he started out for a trip with riding horse and pack horse over a new trail to Bull Run Lake, Lost Lake, Cloud Cap Inn, and points beyond. That day he rode 20 miles and made camp on the Clear Fork of Sandy River near the present day McNeil Forest Camp.

At 5:00 the next morning he broke camp, saddled, and packed his horses. Upon mounting, the horse reared under him, finally falling backward onto him with all its weight on his left leg. The saddle horn penetrated the flesh of his thigh, creating a hole eight inches deep and four inches wide. He was able to extricate himself and stop bleeding, then tied up the wound with shoestrings and a towel.

The next move was to change saddles and ride the pack horse back home as fast as he could. Home by 2:00 p.m., he dressed the leg and rested. At 6:00 p.m., Rangers O.V. Hickman, John B. Senecal, John W. Staats, and Henry E. Steed, came in from working on trail. All stayed overnight but Hickman.

Just as he had spurned the idea of taking his wife to the hospital when she lay unconscious, Aschoff in a like manner disregarded his own injury. The next day was business as usual, passing out the new badges and assigning tools for building a new lodge and cutting fallen trees on the trail between Bull Run Lake and Lost Lake. Even on Sunday he worked.

On Monday, June 26, the leg was inflamed. In order to avoid pulling off his assistant, Anderson, from work outside, he employed Engineering Supervisor M.P. Isenberg to assist the clerk in the office. The following day he was taken to St. Vincent's Hospital in Portland, where the doctor operated immediately. His stay at the hospital was lengthy, and his reports on the affair were not made until August 9.

No further events in the year 1905 are recorded until December 8, when Aschoff wrote letters to Rangers W.H. Heseman, Ephraim Henness, Lewis Johnson, Arthur B. Lacey, Henry E. Steed, and M.D. Markham, asking them to resign or state their case as to why they should not be discharged from the Forest Service. Reasons varied from negligence and avoidance of duty on various operations, especially the big fire at Detroit. Some were reminded of their dislike of work.

A week later Aschoff sent in his own resignation, evidently disheartened by pressure from both below and above. This immediately resulted in a resignation by Ranger Ila C. Nealeigh in sympathy. On December 21, 1905, Gifford Pinchot wrote to Aschoff, accepting his resignation in terse terms as of January 1, 1906. Evidently Pinchot was glad to see him go. So ended the career of a man who played a big part in the drawing of maps, laying out of early trails, and development of an organization in those early days.

After he left the Forest Service he received a letter of June 16, 1906, from Forest Inspector Daniel Bronson in Washington, asking for an explanation of a permit to build a lodge near timberline on the south side to The Mazamas. He wished to know, "Are you a member of The Mazamas? Is the permit being exercised? What is the annual charge?" Of course, nothing had ever been done by the club, so the letter was anticlimatic.

FOREST SERVICE IN RECREATION

Recreational use in Mount Hood National Forest is indicated by some statistics available for recent years. Organizational camps or lodges have remained about the same since 1959. Ski lifts and size of ski area has increased dramatically during that time, indicating that most of the visitors go to the mountain for daytime trips and do not stay overnight.

The first permit to build a residence for recreational housing was in 1913. By 1928 there were about 400 of them, finally levelling off at the present number.

YEAR	VACATION HOMES	CAMP & PICNIC AREA
1959	581	118
1960	581	121
1961	598	
1962	598	103
1963	597	107
1967	568	115
1970	563	
1971	564	143
1972	564	142
1973	564	142

On March 20, 1940, Regional Forester Lyle F. Watts announced a change in designation from a primitive area to a wild area of the 14,800 acres around Mount Hood. In the wild area no roads, timber cutting or business are allowed, only recreation such as hunting, fishing, or skiing. A strip was excepted to provide for the road and development at Cloud Cap Inn.

Three old-favorite campgrounds have phased out of use, Twin Bridges at the foot of Laurel Hill, and Phlox Point and Nanitch on the West Leg Road below Timberline Lodge.

In 1960 McNeil Forest Camp was started on Old Maid Flat on the Sandy River. On June 24, 1961, it was officially dedicated by Marshall Dana of the *Oregon Journal* giving the main speech. Other speakers were Paul Neff, the Supervisor of MHNF, Herbert Stone the Regional Forester, G.E. Cannon, and David Keiser. Richard R. Pooley stood on McNeil Point high on the west side of the mountain and flashed mirror signals to show its position to those at the campground ceremony.

In 1960 Mud Lake just south of Summit Meadow was changed into a 60 acre lake, named Trillium Lake, by the building of a dam. The lake was stocked with fish, and the following year a large campground was built on the east lakeshore.

Mount Hood from Trillium Lake

Mud Lake before the building of the dam — Photo USFS

The Forest Service estimates the yearly usage by hunters, fishermen, campers, and many other categories, the fact that these figures must be derived from a great deal of educated guessing, leads to the doubt of their validity, but as a general guideline they indicate trends in usage. Figures indicate man-days.

YEAR	HUNTERS	ANGLERS	ALL VISITORS
1959	25,974	203,126	2,139,324
1960	27,800	212,025	1,997,085
1961	32,000	186,900	2,089,800
1962	31,200	176,600	3,316,600
1963	31,800	109,800	
1967			3,601,000
1968			3,634,000
1970			3,329,100
1971			3,368,300
1972	112,000	321,000	3,673,200
1973	107,900	344,300	3,102,500

FIRE CONTROL IN MHNF

Fires were the earliest concern of the Forest Service and have continued to be so. Early-day pioneers and Indians were unbelievably careless of fire, and the summer sky was always filled with a pall of smoke. The system of locating fires originated by Bushnell Osborne Jr. was placed into use about 1914 and quickly expanded to a network of lookouts connected by telephone.

By being able to pinpoint a fire, the Forest Service quickly became much more effective. The building of roads into sustained yield areas gave a great deal more protection than before. After World War Two crews were used to parachute into areas and extinguish fires before they became a threat.

With a system of azimuth indicating lookouts established on high points all over the national forest system, the Forest Service began to change its system again in the Sixties. In 1964 the number of lookouts in MHNF dropped from 27 to only five, as the surveillance was taken over by regular aircraft patrols. Using aircraft spotters cut detection costs considerably. In that same year 80 heliports out of a planned number of 172 were completed in MHNF. An air cargo base was established at Hood River Airport to supply fire-fighting crews.

Shortly afterward suppression of fires was begun by dropping chemical fire retardants from aircraft. In 1967 the air tanker base at Troutdale Airport mixed and dropped 90 loads of 1,000 gallons each. In 1973 the amount was 114,400 gallons. Aircraft used were B-26, B-17, DC-6, and DC-7.

YEAR	NUMBER FIRES	ACRES BURNED	ACRES SLASH BURNED
1959	42	16	5,000
1960	63	88	8,000
1961	140	74	5,451
1962	44	146	7,424
1963	59	68	7,714
1965	136	41	5,100
1966	76	1,458	4,000
1967	192	269	4,300
1968	59	27	4,276
1969	122	161	3,500
1970	365	507	
1972	209	13	
1973	177	7,173	

Logging with donkey engine 1936 — Photo USFS

Firefighters at Herman Creek 1916 fire — Photo USFS

ROADS AND TRAILS OF MHNF

Roads and trails have increased over the years, as has the cost of construction and maintenance. In 1973 the average mile of road cost $44,500 to construct and the average maintenance cost of existing roads was $500 per mile. Forest Service road is graded out, properly drained, and surfaced to what would have been highway standards. To realize the vast change in costs and specifications, one might recall that Samuel K. Barlow borrowed $4,000 for the construction of the whole Barlow Road, ran out of money, and finally spent no more than twice that sum to run a wagon track across the Cascades. Trails at present cost about $80 per mile to maintain. Roads and trails in use in MHNF are as follows:

YEAR	MILES ROADS	MILES TRAILS
1959	1631	1466
1961	1794	1309
1963	1882	1348
1964	1966	1348
1966	2112	1123
1967	2170	1035
1968	2261	1034
1969	2390	1030
1970	2364	1025
1971	2416	1012
1972	2465	1025
1973	2500	1025

The rampant Christmas flood of 1964 proved very destructive to the road and trail system. It was necessary to rebuild six bridges, two trail bridges, and 106 miles of road.

In 1969 a road was planned down White River from the bridge on Highway 35. In 1973 it was completed down to a crossing of the river and the old Barlow Road. In 1974 finishing touches were made at Barlow Crossing to connect with the road S448 that comes back to Highway 26 near Clear Lake. This area will be of interest to cross-country skiers in winter and campers in summer.

Four top USFS men at Herman Creek Fire 1916 — Photo USFS

Chief of FS	W.B. Greeley
Dist. Forester	George H. Cecil
Sup. Oregon NF	Thomas Sherrard
Fire Chief	W.B. Osborne

On August 9, 1935, Supervisor of MHNF A.O. Waha announced that 17 men had been put on trail construction to complete the missing link in the Timberline Trail, an eight mile stretch from Yocum Ridge to Eden Park. It was some time, however, before the work was completed in 1938 or 1939. At that time the trail was touched by road at Timberline Lodge and at Cloud Cap Inn. At the present time the 36.5 mile trail is also accessible at Mount Hood Meadows and at the end of the access road to Ramona Falls.

In 1936 the CCC crews were given the job of running a new ski trail down from Timberline Lodge to Government Camp in anticipation of the demand of future crowds. The job was under the direction of Hjalmar Hvam.

In 1965 MHNF erected a **Job Corps Center**, the equivalent of a modern CCC at Timber Lake just below Ripplebrook Ranger Station on the Clackamas River. The facility was designed to accommodate 200 young men who wanted to learn a trade or skill and had become disenchanted with the academic school world. The camp included seven dormitories, an educational building, office, dispensary, dining hall, ball field, and a trailer court to house the staff. In 1973 MHNF spent

$1,484,660 on the maintenance and operation of Timber Lake Job Corps Center.

LUMBER PRODUCTION IN MHNF

The timber resource of the national forests is at this time one of the prime concerns. The table showing the number of billion feet of standing timber has remained virtually static, indicating that the annual cut is approximately the same as the annual sustained yield, which is estimated at 330 million board feet. In MHNF the number of cattle is small, and the number of grazing permits has decreased from 26 in 1959 to 14 in 1973.

YEAR	STANDING BOARD FT.	MILLIONS BD.FT.CUT	TREES PLANTED
1959	28.0	391.4	1,684,000
1960	28.0	322.1	1,558,000
1961	28.0	310.8	2,800,000
1962	29.6	356.1	1,993,120
1963	26.6	356.8	2,340,000
1964	29.6	354.1	2,076,500
1965	29.6	413.2	1,892,000
1966	29.6	442.2	1,892,000
1967	27.6	350.1	1,541,000
1968	27.6	390.1	1,782,000
1969	27.6	352.7	
1970	29.6	429.0	
1971	29.3	326.0	
1972	29.3	422.0	

OTHER PERTINENT FACTS

The size of MHNF has remained just about the same in recent years, the 1973 acreage being 1,059,240. Cash receipts were high in 1973, a total of $21,620,417. Of this gross amount, 25% is paid to the six counties of the MHNF, proportionate to the area within the county lying in the national forest. Clackamas County received $2,558,294, Hood River $1,068,168, Jefferson $22,972, Marion $344,882, Multnomah $363,030, and Wasco $1,047,756.

Naturally this amounts to a great fluctuation from year to year. It is to be noted that this 25% of gross is paid without respect to costs or expenses of the year.

Watershed is a great factor in MHNF. From its timbered area comes the domestic water for 40% of the people of the state of Oregon.

Carrying lumber to summit house — Photo George Calverley
John Gertson of Fargher Sheep Co. and John Calverley bringing up repair material in 1921.

1925 Map of Loop Highway — Oregon Journal
No roads shown to Timberline Lodge or over Lolo Pass. Note old Barlow Road, old road to Cloud Cap, and Mount Hood Lodge.

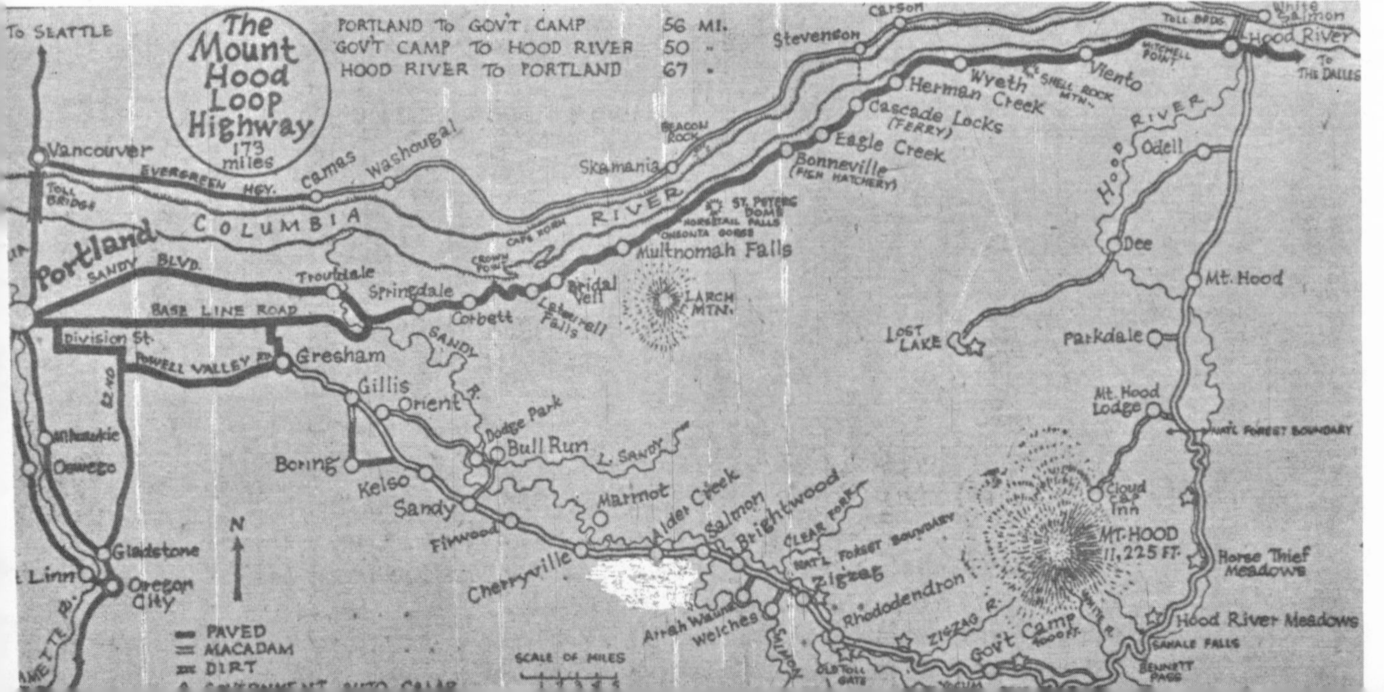

1892 *The Evening Telegram* of October 10, reported a presentation to the Portland Chamber of Commerce by Lieutenant Fred A. Schwatka in support of setting aside Mount Hood as a national park. He proposed that the chamber advance $500 for an expedition to establish boundaries, define needs for roads, and survey the need for trails. A book was proposed to record the interesting features of the mountain, so that it might be circulated to other sections of the country.

On October 20, *The Oregonian* reported on the efforts of the Oregon Alpine Club to set aside areas around Mount Hood for national park use. A letter was received from Assistant Secretary Chandler in Washington D.C., stating that a petition sent by club by special messenger on July 18, has been referred to the Commissioner of the General Land Office. It was noted that through the efforts of W.G. Steel, 12 townships around Crater Lake were set aside in 1886.

For many years the issue of a national park was a hot one. In 1911, the Superintendent of Parks of Portland, E.T. Mische, wrote to the Secretary of Agriculture, asking for status of Mount Hood as a national park, rather than as an area under the Forest Service. Agitation grew strong, both for and against the concept. The Forester of the United States, M.S. Graves wrote to Oregon Representative H.J. Sinnot, stating his reasons why he felt it better to leave Mount Hood as part of the National Forest. In 1916, Oregon's Senator Chamberlain was author of Senate Bill S6397, which would have declared Mount Hood as part of a very large National Park, 688 square miles. A little later, both Senators Lane and Chamberlain were publicly promising to oppose the national park plan as proposed by Secretary of the Interior, Franklin K. Lane. The bill was not passed.

However, the Forest Service was aware that they were in a delicate position, and that the public was demanding roads and development. This probably accounts for the survey of the Loop Highway made in 1915 and its ultimate completion in the Twenties. It accounts for the building of the $175,000 road nine miles up to Cloud Cap Inn in 1925 and the rejection of the idea of a tramway up Cooper Spur by promoters in the late Twenties. It also accounts for the great consideration for climbers and skiers all through the years.

In the late Twenties, Stephen T. Mather, Director of the National Park Service, was giving Mount Hood his personal attention. There was a movement afoot for many years to create a great national park that would join Mount Hood with Mount Jefferson, Mount Rainier, and perhaps Mount Baker.

The issue died down for a number of years until 1939, when Secretary of the Interior, Harold Ickes, began to make a power play. He personally requested Mount Hood as a National Park. The Oregon Winter Sports Association disapproved of that. In April of 1940, Oregon's Senator Charles McNary wired newsman (later senator) Richard Neuberger that Secretary Ickes had again referred to Mount Hood as a good example of an area that should be a national park. Ickes attempted to have the Forest Service transferred from the Department of Agriculture to the Department of Interior. Perhaps World War Two interrupted the play for power, but it never did materialize.

The gang at Summit Ranger Station circa 1919 — Photo George Calverley
Back row from left, Pinky a packer for Fargher Sheep Company, Vernon Calverley, Wilbur Kelly, George Calverley, John Gertsen of Fargher employ, and Al T. Maas.
Front row, John Calverley, two unidentified ladies, and Tommy Kinzel who mined for gold in the area without results.

The Earliest Climbs of Mount Hood

THE THOMAS DRYER PARTY

Who was first to climb Mount Hood? The reader can never know for sure, because confusion and an ancient quarrel cloud the true story. First claimants were Thomas J. Dryer, Wells Lake, and an unknown Indian. Dryer, the publisher of the *Weekly Oregonian*, had climbed Mount Saint Helens in the year before with __________ Wilson, ____________ Smith, and ____________ Drew. His accounts of the climb on Mount Hood go into unbelievably detailed trivia expressed in long-winded, trite language of the day, noting such exciting incidents as losing a hat while riding along on his horse. But the real facts about where his party went were never recorded, seemingly quite an ommission of duty for a journalist.

The trip started from Portland with Dryer and Captain O. Travaillot, merchant and retired seafarer, riding out to Philip Foster's landmark farm at Eagle Creek. This is the same Foster whose farm was such a welcome outpost for the Barlow-Palmer party in 1845. At Foster's they met Wells Lake and William Barlow. Now titled Captain, Barlow had spent several years building and maintaining the original Barlow Road as an aide to his father, Samuel K. Barlow. Joel Palmer was expected to join the Dryer party, however he did not show himself, probably because of petty feelings with young Barlow. Palmer, a general in the Indian Service by that time, had been the first man to make a known exploration of the high slopes of Mount Hood, approaching the area around Crater Rock and Triangle Moraine from Mississippi Head and Zigzag Glacier.

On Saturday, August 4, 1854, the party rode on horseback from Foster's. It was a hot day and guide Barlow evidently had some very green outdoorsmen in his care, from the tone of Dryer's descriptions. It is impossible to know whether the party went up the Barlow Road to Government Camp or the Timberline Trail southeast of Ramona Falls (Upper Sandy Guard Station). In any event Dryer was trying to locate three others to join the party at timberline, Major Granville O. Haller, an unknown Indian, and Judge Cyrus Olney of the Oregon Territorial Bench. Olney was also a news correspondent for Dryer from The Dalles. By building a fire on an exposed mountain ridge, Dryer finally made contact with the three from The Dalles, and all took cover from the bad weather in a canyon below timberline on the night of Monday, August 7. Some effort to leave a message for General Palmer was made, but he never did appear.

It was a cold night, and on the morning of August 8, ice was frozen in tin cups, and dew frozen on the outside of their blankets. Rising before daybreak, they packed the horses and headed for timberline. Barlow stayed with the animals and watched the party through the telescope the rest of the day.

Equipment included creepers (undoubtedly primitive crampons), iron-socket mountain staffs with hooks, rope and food. No thought was given to sunburn protection or dark glasses.

The route took them across Deschutes Branch (White River Glacier) to the snow slope east of Steel Cliff. They followed a ridge that separated White River from Dog River (Hood River which flows from the Newton Clark Glacier). The party started out on different variations, each man holding the opinion he had the best way, but by some miracle they all converged on the steep snow ridge leading up the southeast corner of Mount Hood.

They encountered sun cups which Dryer described as waves on a chopped sea. Major Haller became dizzy and dropped out. Captain Travaillot found blood oozing from his skin (Dryer had tremendous imagination) and quit the climb. After travelling over a slope measured by theodolite at 70.5 degrees (hardly possible at that point), Judge Olney could go no further).

Dryer, Lake, and the Indian proceeded in single file for two hours to what Dryer called the top, arriving at 12:00 noon. He found the top a narrow crescent, facing the southwest. His description of the summit is quoted, "*The sharp ridge on top runs from the southwest to the north, making a sharp turn to the west at the north end. The main ridge is formed of decomposed volcanic substances of a light reddish color, which cones from 20 to 50 feet high at intervals of a few rods. These cones or rocks are full of cracks or fissures, as if they had been rent by some convulsion of nature at a remote period. Between these cones there are numerous holes, varying from the size of a common water bucket down to two or three*

Thomas Dryer, editor, politician, and alpinist. He was first to climb Mount St. Helens and claimed a first ascent of Mount Hood.

inches in diameter. Through these breathing holes — as we shall call them — and through the crevices in the rocks there is constantly escaping hot smoke or gas of a strong sulphuric odor. In passing over the ridge for near half a mile we discovered a large number of these breathing holes; through some the heat was more intense than in others."

The Indian was frightened and retreated from the volcanic vents. Dryer and Lake dropped in stones and found the holes were deep. Dryer reported viewing Jefferson, Three Sisters, McLaughlin, St. Helens, Rainier, Adams, Shasta, and Fremont Peak in the Rockies. Southeast by south he noted a lake he judged to be 40 miles distant, but he made no mention of Lost Lake and Bull Run Lake. While on top they hear the rumble of a section of the glacier settling, at first seeming to be an earthquake.

Detractors of Dryer mentioned that he had not mentioned the lakes in the northwest, Bull Run and Lost. His description of the summit is a good description of the "Crow's Nest" area atop Steel Cliffs. There are no volcanic vents on the summit. He described the ridge as a half mile long; it does not check with the length of this volcanic area. From the point where they said he quit, the tricky traverse and climb up the chute on Wy'east Route add about 350 feet to the elevation. He did mention seeing St. Helens, Rainier, and Adams; to do so, he would have had to stand on the true summit. However, he did claim to see Shasta and Fremont Peak, known impossibilities.

Will Steel in his writing was very blunt in saying Dryer had not reached the top, that the route now known as Wy'east is impossible. At the time Steel was writing all of this, Will Langille was proving him wrong by pioneering the route. Whether the bombastic Dryer did or did not make the full ascent to the summit is a very dubious point. However, it should be noted that to merely reach the Crows Nest, if that were the upper point of his climb, was an accomplishment of great note at that time. He made the first contact with the sulphurous gasses issuing from Hood's crater area.

The measurement of Mount Hood's height was another matter, a ridiculous comic-opera operation using a table made out by Baron de Humboldt, the famous explorer. Keeping in mind the latitude of 44 degrees, 30 minutes, the temperature, the southeast exposure, the depth of the snow at camp, and the meltage of the afternoon, the pseudo-scientists of Dryer's party, Travaillot and Haller came up with a camp elevation of 11,250 and the height on Mount Hood at 18,361. Local jokesters literally tore Dryer to shreds over this potpourri of foolishness. It might be noted that the "scientific" data also included another remark that further prejudices the idea of an ascent to the true summit.

"The side northwest being approximately 500 feet lower than the principal north pinnacle, which is about fifty feet superior to the south pinnacle, which we ascended. The craters exist on both sides." Upon descending the mountain, Dryer must have looked back to reconstruct his path, feeling that he had merely climbed the lesser of two nearly-even pinnacles. However, in his own words he **does** suggest that there was a higher place on the mountain than where he actually stood.

There was no public debate about Dryer's climb until 1857, when the Pittock group climbed Mount Hood. A letter from one of Pittock's companions, James Deardorff, sparked an acid exchange between the editor and himself.

THE BELDEN REPORT

Undoubtedly prompted by the publication of Dryer's story in *The Oregonian*, a Mr. Belden came forth in October 1854, claiming to have climbed the mountain. He proclaimed that "the loftiest of the snow peaks is Mount Hood." Belden found it to be 19,400 feet high, reported respiration very difficult. Above 18,000 feet blood oozed from pores in the skin, eyes bled, and blood rushed from their ears. It made good science fiction, although Mr. Belden has never been credited with anything but a good story.

THE POWELL-PITTOCK PARTY

On **Thursday, August 6, 1857,** the first documented climb was made on Mount Hood by Henry L. Pittock, Professor L.J. Powell, William S. Buckley, W. Lyman Chittenden, and James G. Deardorff.

It was reported in the *Democratic Standard* of August 13, 1857, in a letter to the editor by James Deardorff. Two days later Thomas Dryer, editor and publisher of the *Weekly Oregonian* fired back a withering attack on the party of young men, who dared to suggest that they had been *first* on top. The issues of the *Democratic Standard* of August 13 and August 20 can not be located, although typed excerpts are in one of the scrapbooks of The Mazamas, perhaps put there by William G. Steel. It is known that Steel looked for them for several years, because he begged his readers of *Steel Points* to produce a copy of the *Standard.*

The story is further authenticated by an editorial by Henry L. Pittock in *The Oregonian* of August 2, 1864, in which he stated the date. All details dovetail perfectly. Pittock reported that it took about five and a half hours to reach the summit from timberline, the party reaching the top at about 12:30 p.m.

They expected to find a broad summit, and the precipitous drop on the north side caused them to recoil with fear, at first being afraid to stand. He described the top as a "narrow crag in form of a crescent, the main ridge running from west to east and turning abruptly to the south at the east end. The inner side of which forms the black precipice a thousand feet high (Steel Cliff), always noticed from the city as never being covered with snow."

After eating lunch, they sunk a staff into the

snow and tied on it a handkerchief "which looked a little more like a Turkish crescent than our national ensign." This was left fluttering in the north wind. He reported seeing Mount Rainier, Mount Adams, Mount St. Helens, and Mount Olympus to the north, as well as sections of the Columbia River and two large lakes set in rocky wells. To the south he saw Mount Jefferson, Three Sisters, and Mount McLaughlin. A bank of clouds obscured their view of the ocean. Olympus and McLaughlin are not visible from Mount Hood's summit, nor is the ocean, however Pittock's observations were relatively correct.

Their attention then turned to rolling rocks off the summit to crash down the north side, some smashing to bits on outcroppings below. An hour was spent at that boyish sport, before they left the summit for the descent. The snow was of such consistency that the descent gave no difficulty. Pittock also mentioned climbing down into one of the fumaroles about 30 feet on a rope. He could not see the bottom. The sloping sides (of Crater Rock) inside the fumarole were yellow with sulphur dust. He also noted that from the side of Steel Cliff a fumarole emitted a pulsing jet of steam, as if it had been expelled by a steam engine.

He claimed the time of descent as about two hours. No mention was made of sunburn, although it was the custom for early parties to use no protection and get horribly burned, as well as snowblind. Further details of the trip can be gleaned from Deardorff's letter.

DEARDORFF REPORTS

DEMOCRATIC STANDARD, **PORTLAND, OREGON, THURSDAY, AUGUST 6, 1857**

A letter from James G. Deardorff:

Mr. Editor:

In looking over the columns of your last week's issue, I saw a notice of a party of young men bound for the summit of Mount Hood. Being one of that party, and believing, insomuch as the summit of this loftiest peak in North America has heretofore been considered inaccessible, that a short account of the mountain and its ascent would not be uninteresting to your readers, I have attempted in as brief a manner as possible, to give you a short history of what we saw and experienced.

After equipping ourselves with climbing implements and securing the instruments which we deemed necessary for taking the height and temperature of the mountain, we packed up and started upon our journey, reaching Philip Foster's at the foot of the Cascades, at about 4:00 p.m. Here our horses munched a rich supper and breakfast from Mr. Foster's barn, while we fared no less sumptuously from our well-stored bags of eatables.

Tuesday morning ere the sun had emerged from the east, we were on our way, glad to exchange for a season the putrid, sultry air of the city for the refreshing breezes of the mountains.

We found the settlement, along the emigrant road, to extend as far in the mountains as the first crossing of Sandy. Here we passed a farm, the orchard and the flourishing fields of potatoes and oats bespeak no small degree of agricultural industry and improvement.

From here on we found the road good until we reached the second crossing of the Sandy, from which point it was very much obstructed by fallen timber. After a fatiguing day's travel, both to ourselves and animals, we pitched camp at what is known as Mount Hood Prairie. From this point, early on Wednesday morning, three of our party, Messrs. **Chittenden, Powell and myself,** started to the snowy peak for the purpose of selecting a camp higher on the mountain, Messrs. **Pittock** and **Buckley** volunteering to remain at camp. We reached the snow, which extends down the gulches some distance into the timber, at eight o'clock, having travelled up a tolerably open ridge for about four miles. At this point the trees are generally gathered in small groves or clumps along the banks of the ravines, leaving the ridges open, they being covered with excellent green grass and the most delicate and beautiful flowers.

The strawberry was also here just putting forth its white bloom, while the whole of the green herbage reminded us of the appearance of our own valleys during the months of April and May. Selecting a spot for our camp as high up on the mountain as we could find wood and grass, we returned and soon got our small command under way to the new camp. On unpacking we found to our mortification that our thermometer and other instruments were broken, and our expectations of measuring the mountain consequently frustrated.

Thursday morning, having staked our horses and furnished our pockets with provisions, we commenced the ascent, following the same gulch along which Mr. Powell and myself had ascended two years previous. We all left camp with our heavy coats, but finding mine rather burdensome I left it by the way, trusting in the warmth of my Hudson Bay over-shirt.

After travelling for four hours up the south side we found ourselves on the northeast of a mass of rocks which, dividing into three pinnacles, rise to the height of fifty or seventy-five feet. Out of these piles of rock issues heat and smoke with a strong sulphurous smell. The rocks are not compact and solid, but lie together loosely so that the heat and smoke issues from nearly the whole surface without the formation of any crater. Also to our right, on the main ridge of the mountain, about three hundred and fifty feet below what I shall call the summit ridge, at a point where the ridge turning south forms a crescent, we observed another heap of rocks from which there issued a considerable quantity of heat and smoke.

Between us and this smoke, however, there was

a steep precipice of some two hundred and fifty feet; but, picking our way over the snow, we finally succeeded in reaching this left-handed heap of burnt and cemented rocks where we discovered the entrance into a deep and extensive cave, into which four of our party in turn lowered each other by means of a long rope which we had fortunately provided ourselves with. Each as he descended was delighted and astonished at the beauties before him. Another small opening to the cave some fifty or sixty feet below the one through which we entered admitted sufficient light to reveal to some extent, the beautiful forms which the snow and ice had assumed in melting and freezing. Each one returned from beneath the massive arch regretting that we had not the time and means of exploring it further.

We took dinner at this point, and I can assure you that after toiling for four hours up the snowy declivities, we felt a disposition to do justice to our dried panther, sardines and crackers. After dinner we felt somewhat refreshed, and four of us pushed on for the summit. Mr. Chittenden determining to take a short blow before he commenced the last test. After ascending about 200 feet, we brought up on the edge of a deep crack about 50 feet across, but bearing to the left about a hundred yards, we found it closed for 50 feet and then it opened again, and continued so nearly parallel with the mountain as far as we could see it. We considered this a lucky circumstance, for had the snow below this narrow strip given away and formed a gulch in the sand-mounds, we would undoubtedly been at our journey's end; but passing over this natural bridge and turning back to the right, we soon reached to the summit ridge and peeped over the craggy precipices below.

Passing a few yards to the east we found firm footing on what appears from here the snowy summit, which we found to be about fifteen feet across, with a gentle slope either way. The mountain contracts into a narrow ridge running directly east, on about the same level for a hundred and fifty yards, when it lowers about three hundred and fifty feet very abruptly at the same time turning to the south and forming a crescent already described.

This we believe to be the part of the mountain heretofore described as the summit *(BY DRYER)*, from the fact that it best answers the description; and again from the fact that directly behind the summit ridge from this point, we discovered two quite extensive lakes, which, had the party reached the summit ridge, they could not have helped seeing, and would have been most likely to have described.

While on the summit we felt no inconvenience whatever in breathing; neither did we experience any difficulty from swelling and bleeding, while we could talk and be heard nearly as easy as we could at the base. To the north we saw three snow peaks, the names of which were Mt. St. Helens, Mt. Rainier, and Mt. Olympus *(ADAMS)*; also two lakes already mentioned, lying a little west of northwest, about fifteen miles from the mountain; we should judge them to be about two and a half miles long and a mile and one fourth wide. One of these lakes is most probably drained by Dog *(HOOD)* River *(LOST LAKE)*, and the other by Sandy *(BULL RUN LAKE)*.

The mountains along the north base of Mt. Hood appear much more level than along the south side, and we venture the opinion that the thoroughfare across the mountains will ultimately be located north of Mt. Hood peak. A dense cloud of smoke intercepted our view of the Willamette Valley, but along the range of mountains to the south we could see Mt. Jefferson, the Three Sisters and Shasta Peak *(SHASTA NOT POSSIBLE)*; we also saw two small lakes ten or fifteen miles south of the emigrant road. On the summit we found the rock to consist for the most part of modified granite and neis, while further down the mountain we found an abundance of pumice, land, and ashes.

After planting our flag on the summit, giving nine hearty cheers, and engraving our names on the rock as well as we could with our jack-knives, we commenced the descent, having been on the summit an hour and one fourth. We reached camp in just forty five minutes from the time we left the summit, feeling that we were amply paid for our toil in gaining the dizzy height, and believing that we left something more than our foot-marks there to indicate to others who may visit the spot that we **WERE** on the summit.

Yours respectfully,
Jas. G. Deardorff

DRYER RETORTS

The following editorial written by Thomas J. Dryer, publisher of the *Weekly Oregonian* in the issue of Saturday, August 15, 1857.

MOUNT HOOD

A party of young men have recently returned from a trip to Mount Hood. One of their number* has published in the *Democratic Standard* an account of the trip, and description of their ascent to the summit. This ambitious youth is so anxious for fame, distinction and notoriety, that he has clearly demonstrated the fact to the satisfaction of his own mind that *he* and *his* party are the first that ever reached the summit. This second Humbolt will not believe that Judge Olney, Major Haller, Captain Travalliot, Wells Lake, Capt. Barlow and T.J. Dryer visited Mount Hood and that a part of these gentlemen ascended to its highest peak, two years ago. Oh no, notwithstanding all these gentlemen have published the fact to the world, these panting aspirants for fame have come to the conclusion that Olney, Haller, Lake, Travalliot and Dryer were all guilty of cool, deliberate falsehood, and so they clearly indicate in their account of their late wonderful exploits in gaining the summit; a thing not difficult to accomplish — so he says.

Well, these young gentlemen may learn to their own advantage, that to become great or good men, they must learn the elementary principles that constitute gentlemen; they must not measure the veracity of those far their seniors in years, experience and standing, with *their* panting desire for fame. A little modesty and prudence sometimes saves young men a good deal of trouble, and may win for them "golden opinion from all sorts of people," which should be worth more than the undenied credit of being the first to ascend to the top of Mount Hood.

We commend the following romantic abstract from an unpublished poem, to Master James Deardorff, and recommend its use by him in place of "now I "lie" me down to sleep, etc., etc."

"You'd scarce expect one of my age
To climb so high a mountain
To get a little rabbit skin
To wrap my little footsey-tootsies in"
Chorus — to be repeated three times
"The grass upon the mountain side
Is greener than the vale.
The higher up a monkey climbs
* * * * * * * * * *
How plain he shows his tail."

DEARDORFF ANSWERS DRYER

DEMOCRATIC STANDARD, **PORTLAND, OREGON, THURSDAY, AUGUST 27, 1857**

A letter from James G. Deardorff:

Mr. Editor:

Permit me, through the columns of the *Standard*, to reply to some of the ungentlemanly remarks of Mr. Dryer, who charges a party of "young aspirants," as he calls them, who ascended Mount Hood, of coming to the conclusion that Judge Olney, Maj. Haller, Messrs. Lake, and Travaillot were guilty of cool and deliberate falsehood. Now, as far as regards this party of young men I cannot say: but as to myself, I came to no such conclusion, for I have not seen any statement made by either of these gentlemen that THEY or any other persons were on the summit of Mt. Hood.

But I did come to the conclusion, and I think it was the unanimous conclusion of the party, that the part of the mountain Mr. Dryer describes as the summit is some three hundred and fifty feet below the summit. We found no smoke issuing from the summit whatever, and if Mr. Dryer ascended to this point, why does he so misrepresent it? Why, if with his piercing organs of vision, he could see Fremont's peak, in the Rocky Mountains, could he not see the lakes and country along the northwest base of the mountain on which he stood? — because he did not get up high enough? — or, perhaps, this would not have been of interest to his readers. I opine that every person who visits this mountain must be convinced that he could not have attained with less than three hundred feet of the summit, along the ridge, which, by reading his description, they must naturally infer he ascended.

The great Sir Thomas (DRYER) thinks it beyond his endurance that a party of "young aspirants" should dispute his word — a man of HIS standing and veracity. Certainly, a man who will dispute his word must be a second Humboldt indeed. With regard to your bar-room slang and poetical black-guardism, Mr. Dryer, your character in that line has been so long established that your effusions have become an old song without effect.

James G. Deardorff

DRYER RIDES AGAIN

1858 Thomas Dryer accompanied a party that left Portland on Monday, August 16, and consolidated with others at Philip Foster's. This was primarily a fishing and hunting trip. It is notable because Samuel K. Barlow and Philip Foster were members of the group, also because Dr. Evans and Arthur Warner rode horses up the south side to a point higher than any before reached by horse.

Dryer, Dr. Evans, Warner, Sam Barlow, Captain A.F. Hedges, and Mr. Fisher were the six men who left the main party at Summit Meadow and rode up to timberline. On Friday morning, August 20th they saddled up and rode high on the mountain, not intending to climb to the summit.

Those who remained below were G.E. Robbin, Robert Thompson, A. Myers, J.M. Breck, Frank Holland, S.D. Francis, John Colum, John P. Brooks, and Philip Foster. Later the full party moved south down the Cascade Range to a lake near Clackamas Meadow which had been named Dryer's Lake in 1857 by Barlow, Hedges, and Holland.

DRYER SUCCESSFUL

1859 Thomas J. Dryer, George T. Myers, H.W. Davis, James M. Blossom, Sr., Colonel A.G. Myers, M. McLaughlin, and C. Pickett left for an adventure in the Mount Hood area in July. Several days were spent hunting and fishing in the Welches area, but on Monday July 26, they broke camp and left for timberline, taking the trail up from Government Camp area.

Tuesday morning at 4:00 a.m. all but McLaughlin left for the summit on horseback. After five hours on horses, they tethered them and set out afoot, reaching the summit at 12:30 p.m. They lunched and looked for an hour and started down. The descent was difficult, with repeated belaying with the rope down to the crater area. At that point some walked down, but most did a sitting glissade, reaching camp just at sunset.

Dryer noted the unusual amount of snow on the mountain, snowbanks extending down to Laurel Mountain (Laurel Hill one would suppose). He used a barometer to establish the height of camp at timberline at 10,000 feet and the summit at 18,363, thus confirming the measurements taken by the comic-opera method of his climb of "three years ago" *(actually it was five years ago)* with Lake, Travaillot, Haller, and Olney. Dryer referred to his ascent as his third, counting one in 1858 and the original of 1854.

Since Dryer had just descended the South Side Route a few days before he wrote the article, he should have had the topography of the summit area well in mind. He should have been especially concerned because of his exchange of published remarks with James Deardorff in 1857. He did reiterate the claim that he had climbed the first time **to the summit** with Lake. Adding up this information one can only assume one of the following premises:

1. That he did actually reach the summit in 1854. If this is the case, his reporting was very poor for that of a professional newspaperman.

2. That he knew he had not really reached the summit, but decided to bluff it out even it it had become obvious that he was caught on many prongs of a lie.

3. That he thought he had reached the summit and was such a confused, unobserving individual, that he did not have the faculty to really know where he had been.

Upon analysis, all the possible premises seem far-fetched and leave the investigator of this day completely in the dark.

No mention of the ravages of sunburn were mentioned. Evidently this party took some kind of precaution to avoid it. The rest of the trip was filled with further hunting. An elk and two deer were partially jerked for the homeward trip, partially left to spoil. Bears sniffing around their camp were discouraged by an occasional shot at them with a revolver.

RETURN TRIP IN 1858 BY PITTOCK

On July 10, of 1858, three men of the 1857 party returned for another try at the South Side Route, W. Lyman Chittenden, Professor L.J. Powell, and Henry Pittock. In addition, they brought along Reverend Thomas Wood, Chittenden's sister, Wilbur Cornell, and Dr. J.S. Glenn and his wife. Documentation for this climb is also from Pittock's account in *The Oregonian* of August 2, 1864.

However, most of the details of the climb are presented by Fred McNeil in *Wy'east The Mountain* as information gleaned from the writing of Reverend Thomas Alexander Wood. Wood's manuscript could not be found by the author in 1975, although an intensive search was made. McNeil did make one serious error in confusing the climb with the 1857 success and stating that it was the first ascent.

This group started out evidently from Summit Meadow, getting a start at the late hour of 7:30 a.m. Equipment included thermometers and a spirit lamp for heating water on the summit to make an altitude calculation. They took no sunglasses or greasepaint. Horses were ridden to the snow line, where difficult walking began because of new, soft snow.

Miss Chittenden soon dropped out. Dr. Glenn and his wife quit near Crater Rock, thus giving up the opportunity to be the first woman on the summit. Professor Powell, said by Wood to be the expedition leader, quit somewhere below the top, leaving Pittock, Chittenden, Cornell, and Wood to gain success.

Wood's story related passing through the Big Crevasse, then kicking and chopping steps up the Chute on a two hour climb from the Crater. Rocks were falling from cliffs above, often making them wish to give up the climb. Pittock's account substantiates this, noting that the climb up from the Crater was much more difficult than it had been the previous year, and that it was necessary to dig steps in the hard snow with the iron points of their alpine staves.

Wood said that at 3:00 p.m. they reached the summit. Through a telescope they could see smoke from an Oregon City foundry, the windows in a Portland church, a cluster of houses at Salem, five lakes shining like mirrors, the Blue Mountains, the prairies of Central Oregon, and the peaks of St. Helens, Adams, and Rainier.

Once on top they held a belated 4th of July celebration, according to Pittock. A two-section pole was assembled for a six-foot American Flag, that was left snapping on the breeze atop Mount Hood. They gathered around the flag and gave three cheers, then fired pistols and firecrackers. The flag at last flew upon the summit.

The altitude measurement was not made, because the spirit lamp was in someone's knapsack down below, probably that of Professor Powell. But the can of alcohol was left on the summit and was burned the following year by Carman and Bryant of Clackamas County.

Pittock described the descent to the crevasse as being very dangerous on the steps cut into the hard surface. All were snowblind and were feeling their way cautiously down, while occasional rocks plummeted down the slope. Below Crater Rock they sat down and glissaded, making rapid time.

He also noted that they had excruciating pain in their eyes from the sun, and the following day two of the party could not see. All had swollen faces which later broke into running sores, taking weeks to heal.

Wood commented that the day following the climb was Sunday, a day spent in lamentations and groans over the painful effects of the sun. When they finally arrived in Portland, some of their acquaintances did not recognize them thinking they were Spaniards.

The only discrepancies in the McNeil-Wood version and the Pittock version are as follows:

1. Pittock gave the date as July 10, 1858, which is correct. This checks out with Wood's own comment that the following day was Sunday.

2. McNeil listed James G. Deardorff and William S. Buckley as being on the trip. This was

probably caused by the confusion of his mixing up the 1857 and 1858 climbs.

3. Pittock listed a Mr. Penfield among the eight climbers in 1858. He undoubtedly meant to list Professor Powell.

So much for straightening out an important fact about the first climbs of Mount Hood. Steel had the story straight in 1907, although he did publish some erroneous information a decade earlier. If he had disclosed the source of his information, McNeil would not have been led into a wrong conclusion, and several generations of news reporters would not have repeated the same error over the years.

PITTOCK'S THIRD ASCENT

Pittock returned with Chittenden on August 29, 1859 to climb once more, this time with George Myers and William Stephenson. The top 300 feet below the summit was almost bare. Conditions were even more dangerous than on their previous two ascents, as they picked their way up stones and dirt. Every few steps the leader kicked loose rocks to menace the climbers below him. The mountain was doing its part, too, by sending frequent rockfalls down from above. One member of the party was barely missed by a boulder that would have carried him right down the mountain.

On the ascent they followed the tracks of a wolf, that ran clear to the top and disappeared over the northeast side. The summit was covered with butterflies, some of which they captured and brought home for specimens. On the summit they found a bottle with the names of the Howard party of Clackamas County, who had been there about a week before. On the ridge were remains of the firecrackers they had exploded in 1858, but the flag and pole were gone, perhaps blown over the north side. They left a tin cup with a Pittsburg newspaper and their names under a rock and descended.

PITTOCK SUCCEEDED DRYER

The life of Henry Lewis Pittock is one of the most dynamic stories of the state of Oregon. He was born in London, March 1, 1835, the son of Frederick and Susanna Bonner Pittock. Frederick had previously lived a time in Pittsburg, Pennsylvania, and in 1839, returned there to engage in the printing business. Henry grew up in a print shop, and when he went west at age 18 in 1853, he took that knowledge with him. He and his brother, Robert, went by boat to St. Louis, then west to catch a wagon train. Enroute Robert decided to go to California, and Henry landed at Oregon City on October 15, 1853.

Finding no work there, he proceeded to Portland, tried two other newspapers, and finally got work with Thomas Dryer at the *Weekly Oregonian.* It was printed in a one-story frame building at the corner of First and Morrison, a location menaced by the annual flooding of the Willamette River. Dryer lived next door, and gave Pittock a place to sleep in the print shop.

Pittock's unusual ability soon promoted him from boy's work to more responsible jobs on the *Weekly Oregonian.* Evidently at times Dryer was not paying him and began to owe him more and more money.

Dryer was a fiery politician, spending much time at the Territorial Assembly, and making impassioned speeches in various communities. He was in constant editorial battle with other editors in Oregon. Dryer's appearance was that of a mad sorcerer, stern and fierce. When Pittock's climb of Mount Hood was made public in 1857, causing Dryer much embarrassment, he undoubtedly felt much pressure from his employer. However, the association still stood, and by 1858 Pittock was the foreman at the *Oregonian* shop.

In 1860, Dryer was an elector for the state of Oregon on the Abraham Lincoln ticket, which took him away from Portland for a while. Meanwhile Pittock leased the newspaper and kept on publishing. Dryer was appointed a Commissioner to the Sandwich Islands (Hawaii) and completely passed out of the Oregon scene. Pittock took over the ownership of the paper by virtue of default of the back wages Dryer owed him.

It might be noted that in 1864 Pittock mentioned Dryer's climb of Mount Hood in 1854, but he did state that he did not believe that Dryer had attained the true summit.

Pittock went on to parlay *The Oregonian* into one of the truly great newspapers of the United States, known for the integrity which he had built into it. He later invested in many other businesses, including paper mills, making him one of the greatest industrialists of the west. He participated in the organizational climb of The Mazamas in 1894, becoming a charter member. In 1896-7 he served as president of the club.

THE AYRES PARTY 1864

On July 16, 1864, Edward Ayres climbed Mount Hood. *The Mountaineer* of July 26, quoted him as saying, "we believe it is the first time that the top of the peak has been reached by mortal man." The word *we* indicates that he had company on the climb.

It was this news story in the *Mountaineer* that caused Henry Pittock to summarize the climbing history of Mount Hood in the *Oregonian* on August 2, 1864. If it had not so occurred, the correct history of the first climbs would have been lost forever.

BAD WEATHER BECAME KNOWN

September, 1864 A trio left Portland in beautiful fall sunshine, H.K. Hines, C.T. McConnell, and Judge J.E. Wyche. Upon arriving at the mountain they found that the weather had changed. During their first night at timberline two inches of snow fell, and they waited over one full day to make a start on their climb of South Side Route.

They left their base camp at 6:00 a.m. and went easily upward to the slopes near Triangle Moraine, where there was a hard, icy surface, just under the light covering of new snow. Progress became very difficult, and they sometimes resorted to hands and knees, as they worked from rock to rock on the slippery route.

Hines reached Crater Rock to look back and see McConnell pleading for help about 600 feet behind. When Hines reached the lightly-clad McConnell, he found him suffering from the cold, with ungloved hands numb from pulling himself along on the rocks. Wrapping the hands of the suffering man in flannel, he helped him along to Crater Rock. Soon the three climbers were once again together, standing in the warmth of a fumarole. *(There is reason to believe that volcanic heat was much more noticeable at that time.)*

Soon a dense cloud drifted in against the summit area, enveloping them. The air became very cold, as the wind howled around them, driving snow into their faces. Waiting almost two hours at the only warm spot on the mountain, the three men found ice gathering on their hair and clothing. Hines felt that it was only because of the protection of the fumarole, that they did not perish.

Then the storm abated, and the clouds began to drop, disappearing into the valleys below. Abandoning all ideas about reaching the summit, they took advantage of the improved visibility and headed for their base camp, reaching it about dusk. Later generations of climbers on Mount Hood came to know very well the grim hazard of whiteouts and storms.

HINES, MORELAND, WALTZ

1866 H.K. Hines, J.C.N. Moreland, A. Waltz, and Washington Waltz met by prearranged plan at Revenue's (Sandy) on July 24, for an attempt at climbing Mount Hood. In a letter dated on the summit on July 26, Hines tells his story to the readers of the *Vancouver (Washington) Register.* He noted that the previously dreaded Laurel Hill had been graded to a comparatively easy hill, much simpler to negotiate than the seven or eight times he had previously travelled it. Of the swamps and dense trees near Government Camp he remarked, "there is an inexpressible sense of loneliness in these deep solitudes."

It was 5:00 o'clock Wednesday evening, July 25, when they "emerged from the forest, and stood for the time, appalled, confronting the wonderful body of rock and snow." They selected a camp on the grassy ridge he described as lying between tributaries of the Clackamas and Deschutes Rivers. *It is likely that he was mistaken and they were actually in the Timberline Lodge area, not on the ridge between Salmon River and White River. Also, Salmon River is not a tributary of the Clackamas.*

At 7:00 a.m. they started for the summit on horseback, ascending a mile and a half, where they tied the horses. Description was made of the crevassed jumble of White River Glacier. Then as they approached Crater Rock he wrote "we reached a point of rocks projecting through the snow, from which steam and smoke were issuing, and which were in places so hot that we could not hold fragments of them in our hands."

They then followed up the Hogsback, bypassed the crevasse across it to the left, then climbed directly up to the summit, a route that is being used at the time of printing this book. He described the angle as not less than 65 degrees (a great exaggeration). At 1:00 p.m. they reached the summit. Hines was accurate in reporting all the peaks he did see. He did not let his imagination cause him to report viewing the Pacific Ocean or Mount Shasta as many knowledgeable people were doing as long as 40 years later. Hines, however did state that Mount Hood is the highest peak in the United States, which was a very popular belief of the day. He mentioned that climbing the mountain satisfied an ambition of 13 years.

On the descent they made a detour through an ice cave of the crater, being stopped by a 50 foot vertical wall. He said he would have climbed to the bottom, if he had possessed a rope, but was forced to be content with merely looking into the steaming, smoking mouth of the crater. Certainly the Hines party should have been carrying a rope, but it might have been their undoing, if they had brought one along. In two hours they had reached the timberline camp.

That night they endured the agonies of sunburn. In the morning, Waltz and Waltz were snowblind, and Hines and Moreland were suffering severe pain. At 4:00 p.m. they all mounted horseback and travelled until 9:00. The two blind riders had their horses led along by the two who could see. On Saturday morning they started out once more, one being able to see a little, but the other Mr. Waltz could not open his eyes until a seven-hour ride brought them to Revenue's at 11:00 a.m.

A later report stated that Hines had caught Moreland, when he slipped, preventing him from tumbling down the Chute.

On Monday, August 21, 1865, a group left Portland for what proved to be a very close call with disaster on the high slopes of Mount Hood. William Patterson, Jacob Anderson, Peter Daly, Thaddeus Welch, Ed Albright, and W. Shedd reached Peter Linneman's place, just west of Gresham the first night. Their trip was lubricated a bit with a bottle of **aqua vitae** as they rode along. Shedd and Anderson had held out against temptation, and did not have big heads the following morning, as did the rest.

On Tuesday, progress was slow, as the horses were smooth shod, and the road was slippery. In addition, they evidently made the wrong turn and spent some time progressing in the wrong direction toward Oregon City, the result of asking directions from a shingle splitter they encountered enroute. They finally reached Sandy, and in descending the steep road down toward the river, the wagon slipped off the road, in a close call that might well have killed them all.

They stopped at the home of St. John, east of Sandy, and Wednesday went up over the Devil's Backbone road to Mountain House, where they got feed for the horses. They then descended to Sauvie's Ferry Flat, this time upsetting the wagon while crossing a canyon, but all miraculously escaping injury.

By nightfall, they had reached the Stumpville Hotel, run by Mr. Crawford, and described as east of present-day Rhododendron. They camped there that night, eating a stew that included a hen that one of the men had **innocently** mistaken for a bluejay. On Thursday morning they left the horses and wagon with Crawford and started out on foot.

Laurel Hill was described as being divided by a canyon, with the western side being named Big Laurel Hill and the eastern side Little Laurel Hill. The packs began to weigh heavily upon their backs, but they made their way to **Government Corral,** a place on a ridge covered with burned timber where the road crossed, running in a northeast direction. At that point they plunged off through the woods, reaching timberline a very tired group.

The water supply was sufficient, but it was so milky that they found it necessary to melt snow. The night was spent in "pulling the blankets off each other and trying to find a soft rock to sleep on."

Early Friday morning they left for the summit, each with a stout alpenstock cut in the vicinity. In addition, they had a telescope, a few pieces of rope, and an American flag. The party divided into two teams. Daly, Patterson, and Welch were to try the South Side Route, while Albright, Shedd, and Anderson intended to ascend the southeast slope. After ascending high enough to see into the awesome crossing of the White River Glacier, the latter group decided to give up their idea and join the others on South Side.

Nearing Crater Rock, they could hear many rolling rocks, adding to their discomfort. Arriving at the crevasse which was "thousands of feet deep", they had trouble crossing. Daly slipped twice and was brought up on the rope by his belayer by Shedd. Patterson and Welch also slipped above the crevasse and barely saved themselves by spread-eagling their bodies for maximum friction and clawing desperately with their fingers.

Shedd and Patterson went on up on loose rock, rolling so much in their movement, that Daly and Welch were forced to abandon the climb. Albright and Anderson had quit even sooner. When Shedd and Patterson reached the summit they found the flag staff placed several years before by Henry Pittock and his party. They left the names of all the men of the participants on a paper buried in the rocks and headed on down.

Fear mounted high as they began their descent, but they made it without any more slips. The group had a bite to eat at timberline and walked back to their horses and wagon at Crawford's place that evening. Saturday morning they started home and arrived by Sunday noon.

AN EXPEDITION OF 1866

A group of eight left Portland on Wednesday, August 15, to climb Mount Hood; Dr. W.E. Whitehead, Daniel Harvey, Jr., Professor A. Wood, Reverend James G. Deardorff, D. Dexter Clark, John E. Higgins, George H. Atkinson, Jr., Reverend George H. Atkinson. They were accompanied by Mr. and Mrs. S. Ross and the wife of Captain Metzger, five in a wagon and the rest on horseback.

Dr. Whitehead of Cape Disappointment had arrived the day before on the steamer, John H. Couch, bringing an aneroid barometer, which he hoped to use to get an exact measurement of the elevation of the peak. The US Coast Survey and the Smithsonian Institute had pronounced the inaccuracy of such an instrument in calculating elevation, but the editors of *The Oregonian* assured the members of the climbing party that they were interested in the results.

They camped below, at Government Camp. At daylight on Monday, August 20, they set out for timberline on horseback. It took them until 2:30 p.m. to reach the summit, during which time they met another party descending, Hoyt, Campbell, Wintler, Carey, and Elliot.

Reaching the crevassed area above the crater, Professor Wood noted that the massive walls were solid blue ice terminating below in darkness. Below they could plainly hear the sound of an unseen stream of water. Using five eight-foot alpenstocks and 135 feet of rope, they maneuvered across a narrow crossing of the crevasse, then made their way to the summit. Harvey and Dr. Whitehead stopped at that point and did not complete the climb. Wood described the crevasse as being "a mile" long, an overstatement caused no doubt by the awesome and strange environment. He also described the north side as a mile of vertical columnar rock.

The scientists of the party found that the aneroid barometers would not function at that altitude. Altitude measurement was made by thermometer in boiling water. Finally getting their spirit lamp lighted in the strong wind, they found that the thermometer rose to a maximum of 186 degrees. In this way they calculated the summit at 17,600 feet.

On September 3, Professor Wood gave a lecture at the California Academy of Sciences, stating that Mount Hood was the highest point in the United States, if not in all of North America. The party calculated timberline at about 9,000 feet, and the highest tree observed at 11,009. Professor Wood's pronouncement caused quite a ripple in California, where indignant residents were sure that Mount Whitney was the highest peak. Local scientists in Oregon agreed that the previous estimate of 12,000 feet for Mount Hood's elevation was more nearly correct.

It is interesting to note that four different parties were on Mount Hood in the summer of 1866. The editors of *The Oregonian* expressed the idea that a hotel might be needed at the mountain.

HIMES PARTY

Wednesday, August 28, 1867 An ascent of South Side Route was made by George Himes, Captain W.S. Powell, and John S. Newell. The idea of climbing was an afterthought as their party of five rolled along in their wagon toward a vacation on the Barlow Road. The other two men were Sanford G. Benson and Edward F. Cornell.

As they approached the mountain, they met the successful climbing party which included Frances Case and Mary Robinson, the first two women to climb to the summit. The wagon was hidden in the brush at Government Camp, where no buildings existed at the time, and the five took their horses and camping gear well above timberline.

They cut staves of wood and tempered the points in the fire. For sunburn protection, they smeared charcoal from the campfire upon their faces. No sunglasses were to be had.

As they neared the crater a large boulder came bounding down, narrowly missing three of the men. At that point Benson and Cornell turned back. Crossing the ice bridge over the great crevasse was done in a novel style. Believing it to be too thin, they bolstered it by throwing large blocks of snow under it to jam a narrow aperature in the crevasse.

Once on the summit they found the record of the previous year left by H.K. Hines, J.C. Moreland, and Messers Waltz. It was in descending that Himes ran into trouble. Using their staves as well as possible, and inching down in their smooth soles, they were belaying each other amateurishly, when he slipped. Fortunately, he was able to catch himself with his hand-made alpenstock, just short of the top of the waiting crevasse. Then, as they crossed the snow bridge, Powell and Newell went first. As Himes crossed, teetering above the ugly crevasse, the bridge gave way. He was able to jump just in time to catch the lower lip in safety.

The party reached camp in bad condition, clothing wet from the snow, shoes kicked to pieces in making steps. One of the men was snowblind. But such was generally the experience of those early pioneer groups.

STEEL PARTY

1890 Will Steel led a party of nine up South Side Route on Saturday, August 9. Twenty-one vacationers had left Portland and put in a camp on Salmon River near Welches. They placed a camp at Timberline and bedded down for the night in clear mountain weather, Steel, Louise Dohrmann, Mrs. Brayman and her daughter, Orpha Cranston, Nettie Spencer, F.M. Bennet, R.T. Harrison, and W.C. Alvord.

To save several hundred words of Steel's description it might be simply said that the ladies had considerable difficulty on the climb, and that Miss Dohrmann stopped at the Great Crevasse on the lower part of the Chute. Harrison gave up his chance to attain the summit and stayed with her. Steel found the copper registry box had been crushed by a summit rock which had been dislodged by vandals. Coins had been taken, but Steel took the memorabilia which remained and returned it for safekeeping in Portland. Plans were made for a new summit box.

W.K. CORSON PARTY

1890 A group left The Dalles on August 4, to climb Mount Hood, leader W.K. Corson, Martin Donnell, Hayward Riddell, Edward Wingate, Bert Phelps and Fred Wilson. Riding horseback on very primitive trail, they visited Badger Lake, finally arriving at a campsite in the White River Canyon on Friday, August 15. The following day they pushed on to a higher camp overlooking White River. Corson announced that he was not going to climb, so the remaining five left camp enroute to the summit at 6:00 a.m. Sunday morning.

Ascending the White River Glacier or possibly the western edges of it, they reached the area of Triangle Moraine, where they saw another party ahead. Overtaking them at Crater Rock, they found Mr. and Mrs. Steigler and Mr. Fleck and his 12-year old daughter.

Fleck had climbed once before and took the lead, although shepherding the little girl took most of his attention. At the end of the Hogsback, Mrs. Steigler was too fatigued to go on and sat down on a gunnysack to await the return of the party. They tied the rope around the waist of the girl, and all the others took hold of the rope at intervals. The trip up the Chute and around the crevasse was uneventful until they reached bare rock areas near the summit ridge. All rolling rock was successfully dodged, and they stood on the mountain's top at noon.

Will Steel's notation in the damaged summit box was found, stating that the memorabilia had been taken to the museum of the Oregon Alpine Club. Arriving at base camp at 4:00 p.m., they pushed on to Government Camp and spent two days recuperating before taking the Barlow Road homeward through Wamic.

PROFESSORS' CLIMB

Monday, August 15, 1892 South Side Route was climbed by Professor Young, Professors William N. Ferrin and Whittlesey of Forest Grove, President Prince L. Campbell and Professor W.J. Spillman of Monmouth Normal School, Dr. Ferrin, and G. Haskell Marsh. The climb was preceded by an unsuccessful attempt on Saturday the 13th to climb in bad weather. The effort finally ended on the north end of the Hogsback, the party tied into a 100-foot line and moving in 50-foot visibility. Suddenly the leader was confronted with the crevasse ahead and lay down on the snow in mortal fear of either falling into it or slipping off one side or the other of the Hogsback. A retreat was made to camp.

Monday dawned bright, and the group left from camp at timberline at 6:00 a.m. In the bright sun the slopes and the crevasse were not so frightening. The party left the Hogsback for an exciting climb up the Chute, except for Professor Spillman. He was ahead of the party by an hour. At the Hogsback he turned right and climbed into the floor of the crevasse to eat lunch. Then he went directly upward, not taking the route up the Chute, which lies on the west side of the north summit wall.

Many references were made to the hot sun. The party used veils and burnt cork for their faces. Those who neglected to wear gloves suffered badly sunburned hands and wrists.

Wednesday, July 27, 1892 A party climbed South Side Route from Rainy Camp (see Illumination, July 4, 1888), leaving at 4:30 a.m. and returning in 10½ hours. In party were O.C. Yocum, Dr. Faris, Luther Steel, A.D. Bale, G.U. Weister, and A.L. Parkhurst. This was the third party of the season, and in descending from timberline they met about 40 people coming up. Luther Steel, William G. Steel, and A.V. Bell had ridden up on bicycles from Portland, starting the previous Saturday. On the return trip they rode the 50 miles from the toll gate in about eight hours on Friday.

1892 *The Oregonian* of Sunday, October 23, reported the return of W.G. Steel and O.C. Yocum from an extensive exploration of Mount Hood. They reported that about 75 climbers have signed the register during the year. Above Crater Rock they dug a hole two feet deep in the dirt and inserted a thermometer; it quickly rose to 200 degrees Fahrenheit, the limit of its scale. They fully explored the inside of the crevasse. Note was made of the virtual disappearance of the White River Glacier. (They must have meant a great shrinkage in size, because the glacier is alive and well at the time of printing).

Steel was making the exploration as a correspondent for the *NEW YORK WORLD. The Oregonian* noted that he had explored the mountain more than any other individual, and that it had been proposed that the cliffs to the east of Crater Rock be named Steel Cliff.

LANGILLES AND DELLA WATSON

1893 A climb by Will Langille, Della Watson, and Doug Langille was made on August 10th over what today would be called the Wy'east Route. The significance of the manuscript by Doug Langille, believed to have been written at Cloud Cap Inn on August 9, 1894, is that it gives a description of their climbing the route that Will Steel was claiming to be impossible.

Many scholars of Mount Hood feel that the early guide route of the Langilles, prior to pioneering Cooper Spur Route, would be described as the Newton Clark Headwall Route. Langille's writing seems to describe Wy'east Route instead.

"The morning of August 10th dawned clear and promising, and at 4:00 a.m. we were astir . . . A hearty breakfast eaten, lunch prepared, faces blackened, alpenstocks, ice picks, canteens and ropes procured, we are ready for the start at 5:30. The ascent of Cooper's Spur, a point 9,000 feet in elevation, on the northeast side of the mountain 3½ miles from Cloud Cap Inn . . . is made in two hours.

"We descend a short distance from the summit of the spur, to the immense East Fork or Newton Clark Glacier, which is next to the largest on the mountain. Later in the season this is almost impassable on account of huge crevasses, ice wells, etc., but now we pass safely over it on the deep coat of snow . . . and after an hour and a half of comparatively easy travelling, we reach the opposite side.

"Above us extends a steep slope of loose rolling stone gravel and mud, up which we slowly work to its top, where we meet a snow field nearly 2,000 feet in length, sloping at an angle of nearly 45 degrees. Here the ropes are brought into use, and all are securely tied together. Slowly we climb, upward and upward, until the summit of the ridge is reached at the "Hot Rocks."

"Here more apparent than elsewhere on the mountain, is shown its volcanic origin. The internal fires, which years ago raged within its bosom, are not yet extinct, and numerous vents are still found, from which issue columns of hot, sulphurous fumes of nauseating odor, while the rocks are so hot that the hand is quickly withdrawn from contact with them. Below us is the White River Glacier. . . .

"Leaving this point . . . we ascend the ridge a short distance to the "Finger", the sharp projection which arises from the southeast outline, seeming to point to the not-far-distant summit. . . . Here we linger a few moments to eat our lunch, refill our canteens, and throw sun flashes with a pocket mirror to the eager watchers at the Inn.

"We turn our faces summit-ward and are confronted by a steep, rugged and apparently impossible declivity of treacherous formation, but our previous knowledge of the route made the outlook less forbidding. By carefully choosing our steps, and one travelling at a time, while the others held the line to which each was secured, we progressed slowly along the treacherous route under overhanging cliffs of rock, the least jar which would cause, perhaps, tons to break away from above and go bounding with terrific speed and force down the steep slopes and almost certain death to him who happens in their path.

"These points of danger are safely passed, and we are at the "White Slide" (so named from its chalky appearance), a deep gulch now partly filled with yielding snow, on either side of which rise abrupt cliffs of rock of the same loose formation that we have just passed. . . .

"With the aid of the 200 feet of rope left here previously, securely tied to a large rock at the top, we were soon on the crest of the ridge, here not over a foot in width, then again sloping downward on even a steeper decline than we had just ascended, over the glistening snow to the "Big Crevasse" and White River Glacier below. We follow this narrow crest perhaps 60 feet, feeling the foundation beneath our feet tremble at every step, to where it widens out to the gradual ascent leading upward to the very summit."

Once below the volcanic ridge of fumaroles on the descent they came down the 2000 foot snow field, which they named "Dot's Scoot" in honor of Miss Watson. They arrived at Cloud Cap 11 hours after departure.

MAZAMA ORGANIZATIONAL CLIMB

1894 See THE MAZAMAS for a detailed climb made on July 19, for the purpose of organizing the club on the summit.

Crater Rock and summit in 1894. Note White River Glacier on right, much larger than it is today. The Hogsback between Crater Rock and the summit shows a big buildup, with snow leading almost up to the summit. During the era between 1910 and 1940 the Hogsback diminished to a small snow area, then increased in size again.

WOMAN SLEEPS ON SUMMIT

1894 The success of the organization climb of The Mazamas on July 19, caused several of them to plan another ascent. Thirteen adventurers went back to Camp Mazama (or Camp Drake) on the following day with the idea of taking red fire to Illumination Rock. Word was sent to Portland to expect a display on the night of Monday, July 23.

As they neared Illumination Rock on Saturday, one of the party caused a change in plan and purpose. All agreed to set off the fire on the summit, even though the problems were discussed, the biting wind, the difficulty of climbing the last pitch. The two ladies in the party were in hearty accord, although by Monday morning only Ida McElvain was ready to leave camp, the other lady being ill.

Will Steel furnished kerosene and a large metal lamp, a shovel for digging snow caves. The Monday morning start was at 8:30, late and slow, because they had all day to reach the top. Each took two blankets and a good complement of clothing. Two horses in tandem pulled a share of the load on a sled to a mile below Crater Rock. The next step was to tie 100 feet of rope to the sled and ascend to the end of the rope. Then all would pull the sled up to them. That proved a failure, so they strapped the loads on their backs and toiled up through the soft, slushy snow for hours.

At 5:00 p.m. they had advanced to the base of Crater Rock. Will Steel came down with a party and wished them well, but warning that the wind was blowing a gale on the summit. By 5:45 they reached the Great Crevasse, and by 6:30 they stood on the summit ridge, being assisted up the slope by the powerful wind blowing at their backs.

Over on the northeast corner of the summit they found a sheltered area and dug a snow cave. It was rather tricky to get in and out of it, because one misstep would send a person down over the north side. Loomis and Ross, another pair who had been independent of the group, had been a little ahead, and were already occupying a cave they had dug with a small board.

Taking a moment out to admire an impressive sunset that sent the purple shadows out toward eastern Oregon, they spread blankets on the floor of the snow cave and ate supper. Tea was made over the kerosene lamp, with people jammed wall to wall into the little area.

The next step was to engineer the illumination, a very difficult maneuver in the high wind. Blankets for windbreaks did not a bit of good. The matches blew out before reaching the red powder. Finally one of the nine rockets they had carried up was ignited, but it soared off downward toward the South Side Route.

A little after 10 p.m. they dug a hole in the snow and got ten pounds of red fire burning with kerosene-soaked paper, a blinding display, and the first summit fire set on Mount Hood. At 10:30 the big batch of red fire was ignited, and the illumination made all points of the summit area distinctly visible. Three of the rockets were sent skyward, the rest being duds. At 11:30 they turned in for a long, comfortable night.

Photographer C.C. Lewis rose early to capture the cave on film. By 9:30 other climbers had ascended from below, but the party breakfasted in bed. At 11:30 a.m. they bagan the descent on the icy slope, a hazardous negotiation to the Hogsback. An exploration of a fumarole cave was made at the head of White River Glacier in sickening gas fumes. By 5:30 all were safe at Camp Mazama, just 12 hours ahead of a terrible storm that might have obliterated them.

The party was composed of C.C. Lewis, Eldon Haley, P.L. Campbell, O.P. Hutchinson, Richard Burford, and Mrs. Ida McElvain, the first woman to sleep at the summit of Mount Hood.

SPEED RECORD USING BICYCLES

1895 C.C. Stanley of the Oregon Road Club and H.W. Shreve of the Portland Amateur Athletic Club claimed the record time in leaving Portland on bicycles, ascending Mount Hood, and returning to Portland. Leaving at 5:30 a.m. on Wednesday, August 21, they arrived at Government Camp that evening. Thursday at 5:30 a.m. they started upward, reaching the summit 1:00 p.m. Friday morning they started homeward, arriving in Portland at 5:00 p.m.

VIOLIN ON SUMMIT

1895 On August 26, Professor Charles H. Hamlin climbed Mount Hood, carrying on his back a cherished violin in a green bag. He tuned the instrument and played HAIL COLUMBIA, RED-WHITE-AND-BLUE, STAR SPANGLED BANNER, and WASHINGTON'S GRAND MARCH. All alone the professor, who was over 60 years old, slipped and mashed the violin. However, his musical efforts did not go unheard, as he had thought; another party ascending the chute heard snatches of melody as they climbed.

The second party included H.S. Gibson, superintendent of Clackamas County schools, Fannie G. Porter, Harriett E. Monroe, Bertha M. Gibson, Theodore J. Gary, George L. Story, Nellie Younger, W.G. Beattie, L.T. Anderson, John Weise, Mrs. John Weise, Mary Talbert, and George W. Boylan. They were members of the Clackamas County Teachers' Association heading for a "business meeting" on the summit. Their guide had been O.C. Yocum, but on the way up Yocum encountered Will Steel and Charles Sholes descending. He returned to Government Camp, and they took over guidance of the climb.

Steel wanted to give them a more interesting trip and took them over White River Glacier. He was leading, followed by Harriett Monroe, then W.G. Beattie. Crossing a blind crevasse, their weight broke off a ledge of ice. Steel jumped clear. Beattie shoved Harriett to safety but fell 16 feet to the bottom of the crevasse himself. He had been gallantly carrying a bale of women's coats on his pack, which saved him from all injury but a wrenched knee.

Not having a rope, Steel was unable to help. Beattie finally crawled along the crevasse, taking the dreadful chance of dropping into a deeper, inaccessible area. He was fortunately able to crawl out to an opening in the snow. Steel did not want to let him return to camp alone, so the determined Beattie finished the climb. It took six months of walking with a cane to bring him back to normal.

MAKING LATE ASCENTS

1895 On October 16, Will Langille led a party up Cooper Spur Route, Reverend J.F. Bartmess, Samuel E. Bartmess, Professor George Nauman,

and Perry Taylor. Air was balmy and smoke filled the lower valleys. They believed this to be the latest ascent of the year ever made.

1895 Two bicyclists made the news with their 61-mile trip from Portland to Summit House at Summit Meadow, from where they launched a climb of Mount Hood in the company of two ladies who lived at Summit House, Mrs. Minnie Llewellyn and Miss Lizzie Smith. The two men were Major Edard A. Weed and J.M. Murphy.

When the ladies reached Crater Rock, they quit, and Murphy stayed behind with them. Weed proceeded to the summit, arriving at 4:30 p.m. of October 17, to find that the Langille party of the day before had noted that they would undoubtedly be the last climbers of the season. Weed's descent was altogether alone; the ladies and

These Mazamas slept on top 1894. Front, Prof. O.P. Hutchinson, Richard Burford, C.C. Lewis. Back from left, Prof. P.O. Campbell, Mrs. Ida V. McElvain, Eldon Haley.

Murphy had long departed for Summit Meadow.

He left the summit at 4:50 p.m. and took three hours to reach his horse tethered at timberline. The ride down through the dense forest to Summit House, passing through what is now Summit, was about four miles. Darkness had set in, and Weed depended on the wisdom of his horse to negotiate the road. Down near the bottom two men appeared with lanterns in their hands. They had been sent out to look for the missing Weed.

It was noted that the road from Summit House to timberline had been made by H.S. Campbell and was passable for spring wagons all the way. Whether Campbell built the road, or merely worked on it, or perhaps was merely credited with building the road, can not be fully determined at this time.

1895 A party ascended South Side Route October 26 to establish the record for the latest climb of the fall. They were Reverend B.H. Shankland, T.W. Shankland, B.F. Bullard, and Wilbur Wade. On the eve of the ascent they were soaked by a rain at their timberline camp.

TRIANGLE MORAINE NAMED

1896 The Triangle Club of the Portland YMCA made news on July 10 by a highly publicized climb from Government Camp. Leaving there at 4:40 a.m., they were the first atop the mountain for the year, reaching the summit at 2:45 under the guidance of O.C. Yocum. Triangle Moraine was named in honor of the group and three stayed behind on the moraine to set off an illumination at 9:30 p.m. The party included Hearst Ansley, William M. McGowan, Professor James H. Eaton, Louis Adams, J.L. Mitchell, Dr. Herbert S. Brownton, F.W. Witham, Walter Rogers, J. Prestwood, and Frank E. Ramsey.

FAMED GEOGRAPHERS CLIMB

1896 Henry Gannett, Chief Geographer of the United States Geological Survey, and Richard Goode of the same organization, arrived in Portland on August 30, and left two days later for Cloud Cap Inn. Goode, the supervisor of several survey parties working in the west, wished to study Mount Hood as a possible triangulation point.

The two noted gentlemen climbed the peak with a guide. The excitement of the Killingsworth accident on August 26, caused them to investigate the possibility of rock being dislodged by volcanic pressure. Noting the immense amount of fallen rock below the summit area, they concluded that no volcanic activity had taken place. Smoke from forest fires made any triangulations from the peak an impossibility. Goode was much impressed with the severity of the slope as they descended Cooper Spur Route.

Gannett had his name commemorated on the highest peak in Wyoming. Goode's name is perpetuated by a peak in the North Cascades National Park, just south of Mount Logan. Doug Langille later went to work for the Geological Survey and undoubtedly made his first contact with that group by meeting Gannett and Goode.

CUTTING DOWN THE TIME

1897 The novelty of climbing Mount Hood having definitely lost its edge, more people attempted to shatter records in one way or other. On July 28, four men of the Oregon Road Club left Portland on bicycles at 6:15 a.m. Riding 58 miles to Government Camp, they walked to Timberline and camped. At 4:00 a.m. on Thursday, July 29, they left camp and arrived at the summit at 8:30. Back at Government Camp at 11:15, they rode to Portland by 8:25 p.m., just 38 hours and 10 minutes on the whole trip.

The record breakers were T.M. Stoppenbach, Dr. W.W. Green, T. Birdsall, and C.C. Stanley, who had participated in a similar race against time in 1895. F.A. Heitkemper joined them on the climb from timberline, and the guide was O.C. Yocum.

DELUSIONS ABOUT SHASTA

1900 Dr. Amos, Professor J.A. Lyman, Clarence H. Gilbert, and Reverend H.H. Hoyt climbed Mount Hood on Wednesday, July 00. It was too smoky to see Portland, but they reported seeing the Columbia River near Vancouver and Mount Shasta (Impossibility).

OREGON'S GOVERNOR CLIMBS

1900 On August 4, T.T. Geer, the Governor of Oregon, climbed the mountain in a party of 13 led by O.C. Yocum. Accompanying were his wife, Minnie E. Perley, Colonel S.C. Spencer, Lieutenant Harry Young, L.L. Hawkins, H.O. Rogers, A.J. Bender, John Strout, George Prosser, his daughter May Prosser, and H. Jones. The party signed their names in the new Mazama register box. The old Oregon Alpine Club box was brought down for his museum, the contents having been taken to Cloud Cap by Doug Langille the previous September. The large rock on the left above the crevasse was named Geer Rock. The governor showed great interest in the Barlow Road, over which his father had passed in 1847.

Triangle Club on summit

GIRL BRAVES AVALANCHE

Sunday, July 4, 1915 was the date of a large climb on South Side and Cooper Spur Routes by The Mazamas. On the north side 120 climbers made the summit in a climb that provided a thrill for Ann Dillinger the leader, who had already been prominent in climbing episodes earlier in the year.

The first narrow escape occurred on the ascent while Miss Dillinger was hanging back far to the rear of the party to attend to Gertrude Wiley, ill with altitude sickness. The main party led by Mark Weygandt was approaching the summit, while the two young ladies were still below Crescent Crevasse. To their right they heard an avalanche begin to rumble down the slope, kicked off by the climbers above. Tons of snow and rock poured down to the Eliot Glacier over the classic accident-slide route that claimed so many climbers in later years.

Then Miss Dillinger looked up to see the whole snowfield above Crescent Crevasse shimmering in movement. She pulled Miss Wiley along to the center of the ridge, and plunged both of their alpenstocks deep into the snow. Then standing uphill from Miss Wiley, she braced hard against the alpenstock and waited for the deluge. The snow hit them with a breathtaking rush, building up against Miss Dillinger and fanning out to take a slide path on both sides of them. Miss Wiley's foot was knocked loose, and she was jammed astride the alpenstock.

"How much more is there?" she cried.

"Oh, not much more," Miss Dillinger reassured her, although there was no sign of abatement.

All was covered but their heads when the avalanche stopped. Finally Miss Wiley smiled and commented "I wish our movie man had gotten this." Ann Dillinger took her down to the safety of Cooper Spur, then returned to help the rest of the party on the descent.

Soon one of the young men of the party appeared, sliding in a long sitting glissade. He blithely shot over a depression in the snow near her, and after he had passed there was a cracking noise, and an enormous crevasse that someone dubbed "Lower Albina" opened up to plain view. It was narrow at the top and arched to a great cavern below. It was a struggle the rest of the day to keep other climbers from stepping into it. Weygandt knew the crevasse, but said he had never seen it open so early in the year before.

Falling rock harrassed the party several times. Leaders of the party other than Miss Dillinger were James A. Ormandy, E. Farnham, J.C. Bush, Roy W. Ayer, and A.L. Heyer.

On the south side 118 climbers reached the summit, most of them a part of the large Mazama climb. A great deal of hilarity was added to the day by a group which included Municipal Judge John H. Stevenson, Fred Stadter, who later graduated to the same position, Fred McNeil, Ben Trenkman, and Ted Lansing, the later three being newspaper police reporters. Someone slipped 20 pounds of fireworks in Trenkman's pack, which he discovered after some distance. He removed them and fired the whole batch at once.

On the summit T. Raymond Conway introduced the judge to the whole group of Mazamas, at which point he was forced to give up his anonymity and deliver a Fourth of July speech.

The whole South Side Route climb was menaced in the morning, just before the climbers began arriving in the crater. The steep face of the route just below the summit peeled off in an avalance that exposed two previously unseen crevasses. Lige Coalman made a descent down onto the hard slope and moved the fixed line enough to allow the climbers to ascend to the east of the crevasses. At one time 70 people were clinging to the rope, working their way up the 60° slope.

A great many of The Mazamas were on a climb of Mount St. Helens on the same day. A communication by heliography was planned, and the party on Hood could see several instruments blinking on top Mount St. Helens. There was no way to answer them, because the bearer of the heliograph on Mount Hood had not reached the summit.

On the way down careless climbers at Crater Rock set a boulder in motion that almost got Jerrold Owen. He dodged behind a boulder in front of him, and it was split in two by the flying missile. Another narrowly missed Fred McNeil, and Lansing and Owen had still another close call down lower below Crater Rock.

When one reads of all the close calls, he must regard it as nearly miraculous that there were not many more dead and wounded to pack off the slopes of Mount Hood.

MORE LADIES SLEEP ON TOP

August 8, 1916 Ann Dillinger and her aunt Mrs. C.E. Dillinger, climbed Cooper Spur Route to spend the night on the summit as guests of Lige Coalman. Mark Weygandt was the guide. An electric storm had cleared the air for perfect visibility.

A newspaper account gave the two women credit for being the first women to spend a night on the summit. The writer had obviously not known of the famous climb in July 1894, when Ida McElvain spent the night in a snow cave on the summit.

A week or so after the visit of the Dillinger ladies, Dorothy Ledbetter climbed with her father to spend the night. Soon after that, Martha Spofford of Eugene joined the ranks.

GIRDLING THE MOUNTAIN

Sunday, August 20, 1916 A trip completely around Mount Hood on the glaciers was made by five Hood River men, Hans and Paul Hoerlein, William Marshall, W.B. Arens, and Ned Crawford. Leaving their car at Cloud Cap Inn on the previous afternoon, they put in a base camp near

Cooper Spur. They intentionally waited for dawn, although brilliant moonlight covered the mountainside.

Six inches of new snow gave them good footing as they proceeded across the Eliot, Coe, and Ladd Glaciers. High above them they saw a herd of white goats huddled on a glacial ledge near the summit. Early in the trip Arens caught his foot between two rocks, nearly tearing off his sole, but he continued the trip with the party.

Some of the most difficult terrain of the trip was the descent of Yocum Ridge onto Reid Glacier and the finding of a route through the glacier. One of the Hoerlein brothers was saved by the climbing rope when he slipped and was caught by the others holding fast with their alpenstocks. Many precarious ice bridges were crossed, and the path under a few overhanging seracs caused them to tread lightly and in great fear of collapse.

On the southeast corner of the peak the party could see a herd of goats huddled high above, their horns being clearly visible through binoculars. Mountain goats or sheep had never been seen before on Mount Hood, and the discovery made quite a ripple in scientific circles. The mystery was cleared up on September 9, when P.H. Mohr, a homesteader of the upper valley, announced that the goats were his herd, gone wild.

COLOR PHOTOGRAPHY INITIATED

October, 1916 A group of photographers went to climb Mount Hood with color film, then in its infancy. From a camp at timberline they reached Illumination Saddle about noon, intending to descend to the crevasses of the Reid Glacier. The descent seemed far more difficult than they had expected, and they detoured to the Zigzag Glacier to find crevasses of very respectable size. In the party were Charles A. Benz, Jesse Sill, Frank Ives Jones, L. Wernstedt, M.H. Barnes, and guide Lige Coalman. Jones and Barnes returned to Government Camp in late afternoon.

At sunset Sill and Benz were eating beans heated on a fumarole at the crater. Coalman hurried them along, saying the steps were beginning to freeze. At 6:00 p.m. the party reached the summit. The phone was inoperative, but Coalman signalled the hotel with a lantern to tell them all was well. Wind was blowing a gale at about zero.

Pridemore had climbed with the group and was nearly hit by the window panel on the east side when it was knocked out by the wind. By two a.m. it was so cold that Coalman had to get up and light the stove.

A PHOTO FROM THE AIR

Summer, 1919 The first known photographs to be taken of Mount Hood from an airplane were made by William Bushnell Osborne Forest Examiner of USFS, flying as a passenger in a De Haviland aircraft. The firefighting specialist, who had developed the Osborne fire finder, participated in what was probably the first flight to the elevation of the top of the peak.

The De Haviland was one of the planes being used by the Forest Service in the novel idea of spotting fires from the air. 1919 was undoubtedly the first year of such use of aircraft. Flights around Mount Hood were uncommon enough to rate newspaper space as late as 1925, when two US Army planes made a reconaissance. This particular flight on June 21, had taken over two months to arrange. On several occasions weather had been unfavorable, or one of the planes was not on hand. Permission for the flight had been granted by General Patrick of the Army Aviation Corps.

One aircraft was flown by Lieutenant Oakley G. Kelley, a flier of reknown, and his passenger was photographer Jesse Sill. In the second plane was Sergeant Fred Kelly. His passenger was the mountain veteran and newspaper feature writer, T. Raymond Conway. The second aircraft was flown to Portland from Fort Lewis for the operation.

This successful flight was followed by another, late in the same summer, when a Forest Service fire spotter craft flew right over the summit and tossed out a note to summit guard Smell. Use of aviation by the Forest Service was in its infancy at the time.

MAZAMA TEAMS RACE

Sunday, May 13, 1923 was possibly the beginning of the annual rivalry to be first on top Mount Hood for the year. Two groups of Mazamas raced each other for the honor. The winning team of O.R. Zimmerman, Everett Philpoe, and J.R. Byers made their appearance on top just eight minutes before the other group of Rex Bunnage, Albert and Edward Soderberg, and Leonard Agee.

They were able to drive within two miles of Government Camp. The Bunnage party left timberline about 2:00 a.m., two and a quarter hours before Philpoe's group. They encountered a heavy blizzard down low, but climbed out of it into beautiful weather. Soft snow on the ground made both parties use snow shoes up to the 7,000-foot level.

Bunnage was overcome with mountain sickness for a while and stopped the party. At the Hogsback Philpoe led his group directly up to the summit, shortcutting the Chute Route normally used. Bunnage was already on the Chute, but could not overcome the difference in distance. In later years the rivalry grew more keen, and the mountain was almost always conquered the first week in January.

THE CABIN SAVED THEIR LIVES

February, 1924 First on top in 1924 were T. Raymond Conway, Fred Stadter, and Robert Olson, who left Portland on Friday evening to drive to the mountain and hike in to Timberline Cabin. Snow was high, and they had to enter the cabin by the door under the peak of the roof. At midnight the weather was cloudy and menacing, so that their departure for the summit was at 7:00 a.m.

At the crater they cooked soup over a fumarole, then went on to battle hip-deep snow to the summit. At 6:30 p.m. they arrived on top and found the cabin buried. They dug for two hours with their ice axes to get to the door, which proved to be snowed shut, jammed with snow from the inside. They opened it with a key, then worked it back and forth to get enough space to pass through. Finally one man, the skinniest of the lot, was able to squeeze through a tiny crack and work on the inside of the cabin. Soon they were inside listening to the wind howl across the cupola above, where weather had broken out the windows on the north and west sides.

It had been a rather close call, because they had depended on using the cabin. Turning back at that hour in the deep snow would have been disastrous. The next day they were forced to battle bad weather all the way down the mountain. At 7:00 p.m. they arrived at Mazama Lodge at the foot of Laurel Hill.

One of the purposes of the trip had been to take a Mazama register up to the lookout cabin for the year.

A few weeks later another group was climbing South Side Route in two roped teams. The first men on the Chute were Orville Zimmerman and another. After ascending about a third of the way, an avalance carried them right back down again. Everett Philpoe and Merle Manly were standing down below watching when it happened. Although no one was hurt, the climb was cancelled.

MOTORCYCLES CLIMBED HIGH

Sunday, August 16, 1925 Seth Davidson, riding a Super Excelsior motorcycle, broke Mount Hood's altitude record for an unaided, motor-driven machine. Leaving timberline, Davidson took an early lead against the other riders, who dropped out one-by-one as they maneuvered through the boulders high on the slopes of the mountain. Davidson finally quit at 9,500 feet, virtually burying his machine in soft snow.

The race was sponsored by Wells Bennett, motorcycle dealer. Davidson had ridden up to the timberline with his brother, Jay, in a side car. Before the race he unhooked the side car to make the mountain ride.

CLIMBING EVERY MONTH

Sunday, December 23, 1928 Clem Blakney and Perlee Payton of The Mazamas climbed South Side Route for Blakney's 105th and Payton's 43rd ascent of Mount Hood. With this ascent, Blakney completed a climb on every month of the year, setting a record.

FIRST IN 1929

Sunday, January 6, 1929 The first ascent of the year was made by Paul Callicotte of Cascadian Hikers, John Hallewell of the Adirondack Club, Ole Lien, and James Mount. Observers at Government Camp saw them at the cabin on the summit, and although they had not returned by late Sunday night, they were presumed to be safe.

The Cascadian Hikers was a group that stemmed from a Portland-to-Salem walk staged by the *Oregon Journal.* Mount and Lien later became members of Wy'east Climbers.

FIRST IN 1930

Saturday, January 11, 1930 Paul Callicotte led Ole Lien and Charles F. Anderson on a 16-hour climb of South Side Route, leaving Government Camp at 2:15 a.m. and reaching the top at 4:30

After first ski ascent of Mount Hood — Photo Hjalmar Hvam
From left, Harald Lee, Andre Roche, Arnie Stene, and Hvam.

p.m. Twenty-two inches of new snow forced the use of snow shoes. This was Callicotte's third consecutive year in being first to reach the summit. The party took five hours to descend in the moonlight. Harry Conway watched the progress of the climb through field glasses from below.

Sunday, January 12, 1930 James Mount and Harold Samuelson did South Side Route in 6½ hours from timberline. Mount had been in the first party of 1929 and had made the last climb of the year in December with Ole Lien. Weather was perfectly calm on top.

A NEW TIME RECORD

1930 Paul Callicotte and Charles F. Anderson set a time record for a round trip climb from Portland on July 20. Leaving S.W. 4th and Oak at 12:02 a.m., they reached the summit at 5:45, arrived at Government Camp at 7:38, and returned to the starting point at 8:58. This surpassed the previous record by Perlee Payton in 1928. They passed 79 climbers on their trip and delivered a copy of *The Oregonian* to Mr. and Mrs. McVicar on the summit.

SETTING RECORD ON SKIS

1931 On Sunday, April 26, three members of Cascade Ski Club set a new round trip time record from Portland to the summit. Andre Roch, Hjalmar Hvam, and Arne Stene left 82nd and SE Division at 6:03 a.m. and returned at 2:52 p.m., a total of 8 hours and 49 minutes.

The notable part of the trip was that it was done on skis. They put them on halfway from Government Camp to timberline for a complete ascent and descent, probably the first in history. A strong wind blew at lower elevations, but weather was mild above Crater Rock. They took a half hour out for photography, 25 minutes on the summit, and an hour packing up at Government Camp.

Measuring the South Side Route — Photo USFS

LINCOLN FIRST IN 1935

January 2, 1935 Irving B. Lincoln was first to reach the summit for the year, climbing solo. Others who followed the same day were William Blanchard, Gary Leech, and Joe Daniel. A few weeks later Maxine Faircourt joined a party to be the first woman on the summit in 1935.

ANDERSON SET SPEED RECORD

Sunday, July 21, 1935 A Sherwood, Oregon farmer set the time record from Government Camp to the summit and back again. Charles Anderson started from Rafferty's Tavern (Mountain View Inn) at 6:15 a.m. and was back again in three hours and 52 minutes. The ascent took two hours and 52 minutes, while the descent was done in one hour exactly. This shattered the previous time record set by Gary Leech at 4 hours and five minutes. The trip was strictly done on foot. On the same day about 85 other climbers ascended South Side Route.

LANGERUD SETS RECORD

July 29, 1935 Not to be outdone by his fellow members of Cascade Ski Club, Ole Langerud slashed all previous records by making a round trip from downtown Portland to the top of Mount Hood in 5 hours and 58 minutes. Langerud and Fred Marshall roared out of Portland on motorcycles at 3:48 a.m.

At timberline Marshall waited, nervously at the last, because a blizzard blanked out the mountain. When Langerud appeared out of the fog, he was all covered with ice. However, he immediately mounted his motorcycle, and they rode off to Portland, a living icicle.

FIRST IN 1936

January 7, 1936 Gary Leech and Joe Daniels were first on the summit for the year, fighting their way up through a blizzard, which kept other climbing parties tied down at Timberline Camp.

LARGEST CLIMBING PARTY

On July 9, 1936, Mazama Lynn Darcy led a Mantle Club climb to the summit of 401 people, the largest party in history. Leaders were recruited from the Wy'east Climbers and The Mazamas. Included in the party was Irma T. Springer, 74, believed to be the oldest climber on Mount Hood.

The following Sunday, Paul Callicotte climbed with his son, Harry, 5, believed to be the youngest climber on Mount Hood.

LEECH SET TIME RECORD

August 13, 1936 Gary Leech of Hill's Place at Government Camp set a new round-trip record from Government Camp to the summit of Mount Hood and back. Charles Hill, his employer, timed him at 3 hours, 28½ minutes.

Leech started at 7:00 a.m. and stood on top at 9:36. After a three-minute rest, he sped down, tumbling and falling most of the way in areas sufficiently steep to do so. His steps were often 10 feet apart. It took him 49½ minutes to reach Government Camp. Leech signed in on the summit register and was seen there by Robert Clark, Hubert North, and H.K. Denny.

MEASURING SOUTH SIDE ROUTE

1937 To end the controversy on just how far it is from Timberline Lodge to the summit of Mount Hood, Ranger Harold Engles and a crew made an actual measure. On the descent of the mountain they used a bicycle wheel with odometer to establish the distance at 3.65 miles. Climbers had argued for years, stating everything from two miles to ten.

BICYCLING ON THE SUMMIT

Saturday, August 23, 1947 A group of climbers ascended the South Side Route, pulled the parts of a bicycle out of their packs, assembled it, and rode around the summit of Mount Hood. Mastermind of the stunt was Ty Kearney, 25, who with his fiancee Marianna Sinclair, 23, Jean Sinclair, Walter Holmes, Warren James, Jack Shiley, Fred and Mary Betsworth, and Bonnie James took turns at riding the bike before disassembling it and starting down again.

A GIBBON CLIMBED TO THE SUMMIT

Sunday, July 26, 1964 Kandy, 4, a gibbon from Thailand, climbed to the summit, partly on her own feet, and partly on the back of her owner, Ted Davis of Davis Pet Supply of 2444 SE Hawthorne. Dr. Mathew Mayberry, veterinarian at Portland Zoo, gave Kandy a pre-climb physical examination and pronounced her capable of making the trip.

The operation was sponsored by the Portland Chamber of Commerce and MORESCO to prove the feasibility of using Portland as a convention center for pet organizations. MORESCO MEMBERS on the climb were Jon Marshall, Klindt Vielbig, Charles Adams, and Ron Getchell.

BLIND TEEN-AGERS ON SOUTH SIDE

Sunday, May 13, 1973 Six young people from the State School of the Blind in Vancouver climbed South Side Route in a party of 17, led by Edward A. Johann. The group included Viola Cruz and Teresa Clay, both 12, Dan Davidson and Bernie Buhl, both 14, and Les Robbins and Dean Atkinson, both 18.

The group started in good weather from Timberline Lodge at 2:30 a.m., the youngsters

Mantle Club Climb of August 9, 1936, 411 people led by Lynn Darcy.

noticing the brisk, cold night winds. After the rising of the sun it was necessary to remind them often to apply sunburn cream.

Special protection was given in the Chute by setting lines anchored with pickets in the snow. On top they lunched and rested in the warm sunshine. Johann, a Portland fireman who runs a professional mountain guide service on the side, paid all expenses for the youngsters on the trip.

MOUNT HOOD'S YOUNGEST CLIMBER?

Sunday, September 1, 1974 Penelope White, 5, climbed South Side Route with her family to place a claim to the distinction of being the youngest person to conquer the mountain. She was taken up by her father, S. Sergeant William White of the US Air Force, and her mother, Michael Jane White. Their other daughter, Samantha, 9, was also on the trip. Samantha had made the news a year earlier by climbing Kilimanjaro in Africa.

The ascent on Mount Hood was made at the most dangerous time of the year, because of falling rock prevalent in late summer.

In 1936, Paul Callicotte had taken his son, Harry, also 5, to the summit.

Pioneering Mount Hood's Climbing Routes

FIRST WOMEN TO CLIMB

Monday, August 26, 1867 Frances S. Case and Mary Robinson, two single girls from Salem, climbed South Side Route with a group that left camp at timberline at 7:00 a.m. They reached the top at 1:10 p.m. to spend an hour admiring the view. John M. Garrison reported to *The Oregonian* that the two had been very brave and deserved the status of explorers. They were back to camp at 5:05, excited in being the first women to surmount Mount Hood.

According to quotations from Reverend Thomas A. Wood, Mrs. J.S. Glenn narrowly missed being the first woman on the summit, when she and her husband reportedly quit at Crater Rock on the first recorded successful ascent of Mount Hood in 1857.

The Oregonian did not state who were the male companions of Miss Case and Miss Robinson, other than Mr. Garrison. However, H.L. Thompson and George P. Holman climbed Mount Hood in 1867. Being Salem residents, it is probable that they were members of the party. "Fanny" Case later married F.H. Harvey, and Mary Robinson later became the wife of W.F. Gilkey.

FIRST ON CATHEDRAL RIDGE

In 1887 the north side of Mount Hood was finally conquered by Newton Clark, William J. Smith and Elmer Rand.

A party of eight started on August 11, from the Coopers' tent hotel. They crossed the Eliot and Coe Glaciers, proceeding to the west side of the great Pulpit Rock and then climbing upward. "Bad climbing on steep and slippery talus," caused five of the would-be climbers to quit. Clark, Smith, and Rand continued upward until they topped out high on Cathedral Ridge, then followed it up toward the summit.

They carried a heliograph to the summit with the idea of signalling Hood River, but the atmosphere was obscured by the usual August forest fires. Upon descending they declared the route no climb for tourists and observed that it would probably be the last climb on the north side for some time to come.

FIRST PROBE OF WEST SIDE

1888 The climbing party that reached base camp on Saturday, August 11, (see Heliography) made some significant exploration. They climbed the summit on Sunday, making recordings with the aneroid barometer, thermometers, and attempting to signal Portland by heliograph. On Monday the Portland Superintendent of Schools, W.A. Wetzell teamed up with Lt. J.P. O'Neill to explore the crater and Crater Rock.

On Wednesday Wetzell and Eberhard Caesar made what was probably the first trip along the west side of Mount Hood. The newspaper account indicated that they crossed below Illumination Rock and proceeded either just below or on the lower part of the unnamed Reid Glacier. Over Caesar's objections, they pushed on until they stood alongside the Sandy Glacier, little-visited even today. Two or three mountain men, evidently sheep herders, were accosted on a far ridge. These men said they believed no one had ever come around the route taken that day by Wetzell and Caesar.

Once back in camp the story of their rough journey interested the others. O.C. Yocum and others made the same trip on Friday, August 17, to explore and to make photographs.

Wetzel picked up a carved stick close to the summit of Mount Hood on this expedition, a round piece of wood about 18 inches long. On one end it had been whittled off on both sides. Carved into one side was **H.L. Pittock 1857 1858 1859.** On the other was **E.C. Condon 1870.**

FIRST ON EAST SIDE

1890 Will Langille conquered the east side of Mount Hood on what is today often referred as the Wy'east Route, first climbing to the top of Steel Cliff from the east, then traversing north to a steep chute that leads up to the summit ridge of Mount Hood.

Langille had begun his conquest of the route in 1889, when he was a member of a party consisting of his father, Erkskine Wood, Herbert Nichols, and Will Sayre. The group quit at the Crow's Nest atop Steel Cliff.

On the successful first ascent made in 1890, Langille took along Lewis H. Adams, manager of Cloud Cap Inn, and A.B. McAlpin, photographer. Reaching the chute at the top, he used 200 feet of rope to protect the other two climbers. On reaching the top the group celebrated their history-making feat with a toast of champagne.

FIRST ON NORTH BY A WOMAN

1891 The first ascent of the north side by a woman was made by Miss Carrie Graham of Chicago. Related in a manuscript by H.D. Langille; the round trip took 13 hours, arriving at Cloud Cap at 1:30 a.m. The party was described as being completely exhausted.

PIONEERING WY'EAST ROUTE

The summit register book of the Oregon Alpine Club shows that the route was considered the safest from Cloud Cap Inn. First ascents on Cooper Spur Route and Sunshine Route were followed by descent over the Wy'east Route, because Langille was afraid to do otherwise.

Wy'east Route is a modern name. The Langilles called it the "Adams Route" for Lewis H. Adams, but that name died out during the many years that the route was abandoned. It was also referred to as the "Finger Route". The reader can learn why by reading the account of the climb of 15-year-old Della Watson on August 10, 1893, in the chapter *Climbs Deserving Historical Notice.*

FIRST ASCENT OF COOPER SPUR

August 21, 1891 The summit register book reveals the details of the first ascent of Cooper Spur Route by Will and Doug Langille. Both wrote comments; Will entered the following:

"The undersigned left Cloud Cap Inn at 8:45 a.m. We left with the intention of looking up a feasible route, direct from the inn via Cooper Spur. Yesterday, August 20, we made a partial ascent and determined to go up if possible today. And here we are!

"I have now been here (to the summit) four times, by three different routes, namely via the Crater (South Side) once, via the Finger (Wy'east Route) twice, and via this last way. It is by far the most dangerous and difficult, so much so that we have decided to return via the Adams Route and the Finger. That is bad enough.

"The point we came up is 45 steps down the ridge from this box, where we built a monument. Arrived at 2:55 p.m.

Doug had the following comments about the ascent:

"Weather is very fine and warm with gentle breeze. We find it impossible to return the way we came, and unless anyone is used to climbing, and never loses his nerve, he will find it impossible to ascend at this place. We saw a party of three on Crater Rock."

Author's note — The quotations from the Langilles have been rounded out with a few words to complete sentences or elucidate meanings. No alteration of text has been made, which might affect original meaning.

Once conquered, the Cooper Spur Route did not immediately become the usual "trade route" for guides on the Cloud Cap side. The Langilles still took their clients up the Wy'east Route. On July 18, 1892, Will and Doug made their second ascent of Cooper Spur, described as a "very difficult trip up, and still worse going down. Very cold. The gloves froze on our hands. We stayed about 10 minutes." This is probably the trip described so lucidly by Fred McNeil in a tale of the first ascent. McNeil probably got his data by talking to one of the Langille boys in person in the Thirties which could have resulted in scrambling of dates. His version is summarized in the following two paragraphs:

When they decided to try the route, they passed the big Crescent Crevasse and made good progress toward the summit. Up near the top, Will was chopping steps in very steep ice as Doug suffered below, his feet becoming colder as they inched ahead. The summit ridge provided a real test of mountaineering with a cornice that protruded outward in the configuration of an overhang fashioned by the prevailing southwesterly wind.

Clinging to the near-vertical frozen snow, Will chopped patiently at the overhang until he could force his way up onto the crest of the ridge. The two Langilles soon stood triumphant atop a new climbing route on Mount Hood, one that later saw the footsteps of thousands.

Unless Doug might have led a group on Cooper Spur Route, which is very improbable, (some entries in the summit book do not specify route) the first clients to be guided up the route were Lewis H. Lamberson and Harry Ries. Will brought them up on August 25, 1893, specifically mentioning that they were *his* first clients on the route.

On July 15, 1894, Doug ascended the route with James H. Demmek to set 800 feet of 5/8-inch rope, tying it off on a large boulder near the top. This fixed line was used four days later, when The Mazamas staged their organizational climb of Mount Hood, with Doug leading. At that time the route was being termed the "Mazama Trail." It had also been called the East Route. It is not known when the name Cooper Spur Route was first used.

SUNSHINE ROUTE

September 3, 1892 What is now known as Sunshine Route was first climbed by Will Langille and G.W. Graham. The summit book of the Oregon Alpine Club carried the following description by Langille:

"G.W. Graham and W.A. Langille left Cloud Cap Inn at 7:30 a.m. for the purpose of finding a new route to the summit. We crossed the Eliot

Glacier to the west side and followed up a snow ridge all the way for 800 feet. We cut steps continually, then arrived at a bergschrund that impeded us for a short time. But we soon cut steps across, then went on to the northwest corner (of the mountain) and followed up that backbone of snow to the summit.

"Of four routes, I found this the most like mountain work of any. Weather was warm. I flashed (by mirror) to Inn and received an answer. Summit reached at 3:15 p.m."

They did not descend by the Sunshine Route. They undoubtedly took the Wy'east Route, with which Langille was most familiar. Modern climbers almost always descend Cooper Spur, unless conditions force them to use South Side as an exit.

Langille's description agrees with the present Sunshine Route, a crossing of Eliot to the east edge of Coe Glacier, up past Anderson Rock, across the schrund, up past Horseshoe Rock to the flat security of the Queen's Chair, then up the north snow ridge to the summit ridge. The route gets its modern name of Sunshine Route, because it is fully bathed in morning sunlight.

In 1916 the Guide Mark Weygandt "discovered" the route and became very famous for taking most of his parties over it. However, he took notes and made observations of the route for several years, before beginning to use it. In 1923, he climbed it with Fred Donnerberg and Andy Anderson. Anderson was the first Big Squeek of the Crag Rats and Anderson Rock on the route is named for him.

On June 21, 1925, Weygandt made a public announcement about the safety of the route, noting that it was free of falling rock and never had glare ice before sunset. He pronounced it very easy and made a trip himself in smooth-soled boots without an ice axe. On July 20, he piloted the American Legion climb up the route, taking up 86 climbers, about half women. Many had smooth soles, and fixed ropes were used on about 500 feet of the route. No climbing ropes were used.

Considerable re-evaluation of the hazards of Sunshine Route were made in 1927, when a Mazama rope slid off and killed Dr. Stryker. As a result the Crag Rats began leading the Legion Climbs, Weygandt being somewhat under a cloud for his minimizing of the possibility of danger.

SCHWARZ BROTHERS IN CRATER

Wednesday, August 15, 1900 George and Fred Schwarz climbed South Side with guide O.C. Yocum. They were experienced climbers in their native Switzerland, before coming to the United States. On arriving at the crater, Yocum suggested that they try something a little more sporting, and they elected to ascend the crater wall to the east of the Big Crevasse.

Yocum watched as they skillfully cut steps up the steep ice and finally mastered the route, probably the first to climb it. Their success attracted quite a little attention at the time.

Their trip to Government Camp had been done on bicycles, which in that day had hard rubber tires and a drive-shaft instead of chain and sprockets. They had left Portland at 5:00 a.m. Monday morning and arrived at Government Camp Hotel at 5:30 p.m., a considerably more rigorous ride than a cyclist would have today. Because Yocum was not feeling well, they waited until Wednesday to make their climb.

The grandson of Fred Schwarz, G. Robert Schwarz, carried on the family tradition on May 28-29, 1974, when he and Ray Mosser took 10-speed bicycles from Portland to Timberline Lodge in six hours. Robert Schwarz and Mosser then climbed South Side Route in seven hours, however they used the standard approach to the summit up the Hogsback, not the sporting route which Fred Schwarz said later was the hardest climb of his career.

Grandson Robert Schwarz noted that he was 49 years of age at the time, half again as old as his ancestors at the time of their climb in 1900. He also remarked about the 12% grades on the road from Government Camp to Timberline, noting that he had been the engineer who laid out the road. At present he is a safety engineer with the Bureau of Indian Affairs.

FIRST WINTER ASCENT

The first ascent in wintertime was probably the idea of Ann (Anna C.) Dillinger, who had reached the top of Cooper Spur with H.H. Prouty on December 30, 1914. They perhaps had the summit in mind at that time, but fierce winds made even the ascent of Cooper Spur an ordeal. On February 22, 1915, she was in a party that tried the South Side Route, T. Raymond Conway, Robert Hitch, L. Van Bebber, Lige Coalman, and Mrs. C.E. (Aunty) Dillinger. Weather defeated them.

Conway organized another group immediately, but at the last moment was unable to go. In this group were the two Dillinger women, Van Bebber, Nettie Richardson, W.A. Van Scoy, Charles A. Warner, and Lige Coalman. At Rhododendron the owner of the inn, Emil Franzetti, decided to join them.

On Sunday, March 6, the party left the hospitality of Pridemore and Fox at Government Camp Hotel and started out at 5:00 a.m. in the moonlight. Coalman carried a heavy motion picture camera, and a couple of daylight hours were wasted in shooting film. Van Scoy and Franzetti dropped out at timberline, and Miss Richardson made it another mile. Warner turned back later. Only Ann Dillinger, Van Bebber, and Coalman made it to Crater Rock. Finally all returned to the hotel, and all left for Portland except Warner and Coalman.

Pridemore's poodle dog awakened them at 2:00 a.m., and they were soon on their feet preparing to climb again. By 6:30 they had walked and snowshoed alternately to timberline, Coalman carrying only a light pack. They were dressed in fur-lined parkas such as Warner had used during his years in Alaska. Warner was quite excited, as he had never climbed a mountain before.

"Old man, we are going to make it," he said to Coalman, who was 10 years younger.

"We are," was all that the guide replied.

As they pushed upward, the cold, north wind blew clouds of powdery snow into their faces. Some times they removed the snowshoes during the 5-hour trek to Crater Rock. There they rested on the warm rocks, out of the biting wind. They reached the Big Crevasse, and Coalman hung out over it by holding onto Warner's alpenstock.

"It's 50 feet wide, 150 feet deep, and the snow bridge looks pretty treacherous," he told Warner. They moved to the left and found the crevasse closed.

The snow was soft and loose. It took two hours to battle up through it before they stood on the summit, the first people to climb Mount Hood in the winter. They topped out at 2:30 p.m. on March 8, 1915. A full hour was spent in digging for the summit box, and Coalman signalled Pridemore from the summit to confirm the climb. For Warner it had been quite a distinction to make the first winter ascent while climbing his first mountain.

The descent was a good deal speedier than the ascent. Coalman and Warner left the summit at 4:00 p.m., and at 6:35 were at Government Camp. Warner went on the nine more miles to Franzetti's at Rhododendron before giving up.

The success of the first winter ascent caused Coalman to take another party up two weeks later on March 21. The party included T. Raymond Conway, Ann Dillinger, Dale Simons, George X. Riddell, L.A. Nelson, Frank H. Hilton, George H. Smith, Emil Franzetti, E.W. Howard, L. Van Bebber, and R.H. Atkinson. It was Coalman's 312th ascent of Mount Hood.

From that time on, it became more and more the fashion to be the first on the summit each year, with Warner himself planning a return for the following New Year. This climb started out with some advance publicity about competition from T. Raymond Conway, and ended by Warner almost meeting disaster while making the first winter traverse of the mountain.

FIRST WINTER TRAVERSE

The first winter ascent of Mount Hood by Lige Coalman and Charles E. Warner in March of 1915 whetted their appetite for more accomplishments. It had probably been the first winter ascent in the history of American mountaineering.

Coalman and T. Raymond Conway announced plans for a year end climb of Cooper Spur Route, and so did Warner. A little friendly rivalry began. Conway and Coalman went to the Hood River Valley on Christmas and on December 26, 1915, they started out to conquer Cooper Spur Route. Bad weather forced them to return to Cloud Cap Inn. The next day they made another attempt, only to be driven back by storms again. Since they had a date with a Mazama skiing party at Government Camp for New Year's Eve, they were forced to abandon any further effort and returned to Portland.

William W. Evans, a young Mazama leader, and Warner arrived in Hood River early on the morning of December 29. They caught the 8:00 a.m. train to Parkdale and by chance met Will Langille, who gave them a good deal of advice about the climbing route, before he left the train on the stop before Parkdale. Homer Rogers met them with his sleigh and took them to Mount Hood Lodge, where they spent most of the afternoon enjoying the company of Rogers, Mark Weygandt, and the holiday guests at the lodge.

At 4:30 p.m. they started out on foot for Cloud Cap, Warner, 43, packing 80 pounds on his back, and Evans, 21, carrying 40 pounds. They could see the tracks left the previous day by Coalman and Conway. Before they reached the old trapper cabin below Cloud Cap, Warner had cached his sleeping bag under a tree to lighten the load. The wind was strong and cold, blowing through the unchinked logs and broken windows of the cabin, but by 1:00 Evans was asleep, and Warner stayed up to stoke the fire. At 4:00 a.m. he finally went back for his sleeping bag.

They had a late breakfast, made a scouting trip up toward Cooper Spur, and returned to the cabin. Below timberline, the snow was soft and required snowshoes; above it was hard and icy. They began to feel that they would need an ice axe for the climb, so Evans walked down to Mount Hood Lodge to borrow one from Homer Rogers.

On December 31, they rose at 3:15 a.m. and prepared for their climb. At 5:15 they started out for their historic climb, snowshoeing up past Cloud Cap Inn and following the draw east of the Eliot Glacier Moraine. Below they could see the lights of White Salmon and Parkdale. At dawn they could see the base of Mount Adams and Mount Rainier, beneath a blanket of cloud that hid Mount St. Helens completely. At 7:45 the sun rose for a brief appearance, then was obscured by clouds.

Warner, who had climbed his first mountain only nine months before, had thought that creepers (crampons) would not be needed. As they toiled up the steeper slopes above Cooper Spur in smooth shoes without even the protection of caulks or nails, each step was carefully cut with the ice axe. At 10:00 a.m. a snow storm hit, and they took shelter behind a rock. They then roped up and made it to Paint-Up-Rock (?) and a bit of better weather. Soon they passed Crescent Crevasse, full of snow but detectable.

The surface was ice, covered with a little soft snow. Evans had climbed the route in summer once, but finding the way was confusing. The severity of the slope very nearly drove them back, but they continued up the steep route, feeling a great wave of relief when they saw the anchor rock just below the summit. And there they could see Weygandt's ropes, coiled for use again the next summer.

At 4:15 p.m. they stood on the summit! The summit cabin was covered with such a mass of snow as to make it hard to recognize. One window showed, and they quickly entered. The stove gave them some heat and hot water. They toasted the New Year with unsweetened prune juice. Evans went to sleep in Coalman's sleeping bag, but Warner sat up all night, pumping up the oil stove and listening to the storm howl outside. On a trip outside he tied himself to the climbing rope, remembering the precipitous drop not very far from the cabin door.

At dawn the storm had abated. At 10:00 a.m., they started down the north side, Warner anchoring, and Evans working downward to the end of the 100-foot rope, cutting steps carefully. Then came the steepest part; it seemed slipperier than ever. Fear took over, and the thought of self-preservation gripped them. They retraced their way to the summit for a retreat to the South Side Route. On top of the mountain another storm raged.

Belaying down the slope near Hawkins Rock, Warner caught Evans in a fall, that broke his compass. Evans cut steps all the way to the Big Crevasse, after which they were able to walk down in good footing. They unroped and glissaded down past Crater Rock and Triangle Moraine. An emerging sun brought out the color in Steel Cliff and Illumination Rock. They brought forth a map and prepared to take a compass course; Evans' compass was broken, and Warner's was missing!

Entering fog, they thought they were going too far east and found themselves on the Zigzag Glacier. The clouds lifted, and they could see Government Camp. By 5:20 they were at timberline and on course. The planet Venus rode low in the sky over Government Camp, and they followed it down. They wished for their snowshoes which they had cached on Cooper Spur.

Evans plunged ahead while Warner lagged, preparing himself for the long pull. Two miles above the hotel Evans called, thought Warner was ahead, and began to race below. Reaching the hotel, he found that Warner was still on the trail. A rescue party was sent out with an extra pair of snowshoes.

At the hotel a celebration was held to congratulate Warner and Evans in not only conquering the north side in winter, but in completing a winter traverse. Pridemores, Coalman and Conway, and a group of Mazama skiers took part in the party.

Warner and Evans seemingly had little idea of the long chances they had taken, climbing with only one ice axe, no nails or crampons, only two men on an unknown route that could have very well have obliterated them with one of its frequent avalanches. Warner, who had spent several years in the wilds of Alaska, understood bad weather, but he did not appreciate the dangers of a glacial mountain. On February 22, he was back on the south side with Coalman and four others. Weather was delightful, and the party went all the way to the Big Crevasse on snowshoes.

WY'EAST RE-USED

August 7, 1932 James A. Mount and Everett L. Darr made the first modern ascent of Wy'east Route. The Langille brothers had made a regular practice of taking clients up the south side of the Newton Clark Glacier to gain the top of Steel Cliffs after they pioneered the route in 1890. This was similar to the Wy'east Route of today. But when Mount and Darr tackled the climb, the knowledge of the Langilles had faded into obscurity and they believed that they were attempting a completely new route.

As they traversed north along the east face of the mountain from the top of Steel Cliff, they found the rotted remnant of an old manila rope hanging in a snow chute, undoubtedly a fixed rope used by parties in times past. It seems hardly possible that it could date back to 1893, when the Langilles were climbing the route, but who else would have put it there? Mount and Darr called the new route Wy'east in more or less of a jest to their friends of Wy'east Climbers. It was not long after that they joined the club themselves.

LEUTHOLD COULOIR

September 4-5, 1932 Leuthold Couloir Route was climbed for the first time by James A. Mount and Ralph Calkin, although at the time they referred to it as the Yocum Ridge Route. Shortly after, Everett Darr advocated calling it the Avalanche Route, because of all the rockfall coming down the hour-glass area of the chute. West Side Route was the name used for years until 1970, when the Oregon Geographic Names Board gave official sanction to the name of Leuthold Couloir.

Mount and Calkin were accompanied by Everett Darr on this first ascent. On reaching Reid Glacier, he decided to quit, because he had a cold. Having a day to spend, he began to climb up Hawkins Ridge, up from Illumination Saddle. In time he found himself high on the ridge, overlooking Reid Glacier, below what is usually called Castle Crags.

He crossed one steep couloir, so nearly vertical, that it took him about five minutes to carefully chop steps in the ice and maneuver across to the steep snow on the north side. Downward was the impressive chaos of the Reid Glacier, split by lines of crevasses. Immediately below, about 1000 feet down, the bergschrund grinned at him, a grim warning that one slip would send him into it.

Above he could see the pinnacles of the Castle Crags. Once atop that ridge he should have an easy ascent to the summit and be able to meet Mount and Calkin. **Then came danger!** That side of the mountain is made of what seems to be beds of gravel, loosely cemented together. With a warning roar, one of the ledges above him let go. Darr was directly in thepath of a massive avalanche of rock. It would be sure death in less than a minute.

Back to the south, across the couloir, stood a rock ledge that might give him some protection. His feet hit only once, possibly twice, as he bounded across the couloir like a deer. He dived alongside the rock ledge, held on with his ice axe in the snow, and let the avalanche pass over. With his head on the snow, he could look along past his chest to the bergschrund a thousand feet below on Reid Glacier.

The rocks came; many of them bouncing over his head were the size of automobiles. Then it was all over. He was bleeding from many cuts, and a feeling of dizziness threatened. Somehow he made it down to Illumination Saddle, then stretched out and slept in the warm sun. When he finally rose the sun had set, and he began walking toward timberline.

Soon Mount and Calkin appeared, climbing up to meet him. They had missed him at Government Camp and had come to look for him. He could see them talking, but he heard no words. They considered getting a toboggan, but finally the trip downward was made on foot. When Darr finally recovered from his shaken condition, he realized that he had experienced the most severe climb of the group.

WEST-TO-EAST TRAVERSE

July 15, 1933 The first West-to-East traverse of Mount Hood was made by James Mount, Everett Darr, and Ralph Calkin. They left Timberline Cabin at 2:30 a.m. and topped out on the summit from the Leuthold Couloir Route at 9:30 a.m. The descent was over Wy'east Route to complete the traverse.

ILLUMINATION ROCK

T. Raymond Conway stated that he had climbed Illumination Rock from 10 to 12 times during the years from 1913 to 1930. No climb previous to 1913 is on record.

The first climb ever recorded was by Gary Leech on August 1, 1933, a solo ascent, in which he saw no evidence of any previous climber. Earlier in the same year, Leech had made his first climb of Mount Hood and had been intrigued by the 9,500-foot fin-shaped ridge, which he believed had never been climbed. Ignoring the west approach, because it appeared to be too easy, he first tried the east end. On the east he found a great pile of boulders stacked precariously, moving up them very cautiously to prevent their rolling or shifting. At their top was a 40-foot face of smooth andesite, which he bypassed to the right (north) over a crumbling face to a debris-laden ledge that led past the smooth andesite. After about 60 feet of travel on the ledge, he came to a patch of perpetual ice. Following steep ice upward, he followed chimneys and ledges upward to a steep arete leading to the summit.

To his surprise the arete proved to have a deep trough on its top, which suddenly came to an end at a point where the north side of the trough had fallen away to the Reid Glacier. Negotiating the summit ridge, he found himself ready to surmount the actual summit block, a monolith that hangs over the Reid about six to eight feet. Not a sign of a boot nail scratch could be seen. Leech built a small cairn, feeling that he had made a first ascent.

On June 10, 1934, he returned with Hubert North and Robert Snyder to try the west end of Illumination Rock. Ice on the steeper parts of the cliffs soon made them change their plan to an attempt of the south wall. From the ledges on the southwest side they traversed upward to the east, then up a hazardous climb on the west side of the South Chamber, reaching the easy crest. Near the summit block they found a mushroom of winter ice on top of the knife-edged ridge, admitting defeat just a few feet from the top. On the climb down they explored the south wall, finally leaving

Ralph Calkin 1935 — Photo Joe Leuthold

Illumination Rock on steep snow at the base of South Chamber.

A month later, Leech was exploring on Yocum Ridge, when he was surprised to look over at Illumination Rock and see blue sky through a hole near the top. This hole can be seen from only two places, one a limited area on Yocum Ridge, and the other equally small on the top of Reid Glacier.

On September 9, 1934, Leech was chatting with the guard at Lone Fir Lookout, when A.J. Gilardi and O.R. Lunn descended from a climb of Illumination Rock. The two later made claims of a first ascent.

Leech attempted a traverse on the rock on July 1, 1936. Hubert North and William Blanchard failed to show at Government Camp as planned, so he left for a solo climb, following the route on the south side. On nearing the crest, he was buffeted by a very strong wind. And when he reached the expected hole in the ridge, the combination of gusty wind and the opening falling away to the Reid Glacier came close to scaring him away. From that point eastward the summit ridge was rotten, and many rocks rolled away, as he worked his way along. A year later so much of the loose material had been kicked aside, that a climber could walk along the ridge top.

Soon he stood for the second time atop the overhanging summit block, which he predicted would fall away in ten years. (It is still there to this date.) Then the descent of the east side took him over the narrow arete (Route of the Bicycles) and the Trough, both moderately simple. At the bottom of the first chimney he was forced to chop snow from the ledge. Then from a short sling on a good anchor point, he rappeled downward. Next from a new rappel point he roped down to cross Balancing Slab, a delicately balanced rock, and on down the andesite cliff to the top of the boulder pile. The traverse had been a success!!

On August 18, 1936, he and Hubert North were on the rock again, this time on the west side. On reaching the west side, they were surprised to find a ledge leading down to a point where five routes were obvious. In July of 1937, Leech and Lieutenant John Nance came back to climb the east end, then traverse to a descent on the west.

Leech, who was somewhat of a climbing legend around Government Camp, worked at Hill's Place or on construction jobs until World War Two, climbing Mount Hood or some of its ridges on the least provocation. He wrote the account of his climbs in 1937, but gave them to Everett Darr to remain unpublished until his death. He was killed while working as an electrical lineman near Salt Lake City in 1954, and The Mazamas published his story in the annual of that year.

Gary Leech Washing Clothing at Hill's Place
Photo Maryanne Hill

ELIOT GLACIER HEADWALL

June 28, 1935 Russ McJury of the Wy'east Climbers attacked the Eliot Glacier Headwall Route. The headwall lies between the area of Anderson and Horseshoe Rocks on the west and the great North Face Cleaver on the east. McJury encountered long slopes of very steep ice. The top of the huge rock mass of the North Face Cleaver comes to a point about 200 feet lower than the summit of Mount Hood, known as Cathedral Spire. McJury veered east to the notch between Cathedral Spire and the final summit slope. From that point he was on known terrain, as he had climbed Cathedral Spire at an earlier date with Gary Leech by descending to it from the summit.

As McJury approached the summit, his climb had a little added interest from firecrackers being thrown off the top by Ralph Calkin. Calkin and Joe Leuthold had climbed the inner wall of the crater from the stone shelter cabin, dodging rocks that fell profusely all around, some even passing between their legs.

SANDY HEADWALL

The Sandy Headwall Route was first climbed June 6, 1937 by Joe Leuthold and Russ McJury, members of Wy'east Climbers. They crossed Reid Glacier via Illumination Saddle to the Sandy Glacier. The climb then led directly up the headwall of the glacier to Yocum Ridge and Queen's Chair, a small platform just below the summit of Mount Hood.

The particular day they chose to pioneer the route was a difficult one. The surface in many places was hard ice mixed with bits of sand and gravel. Instead of being able to kick in steps, they were forced to cut steps for a thousand feet on the steep slope, a job that took four long hours. One slip from either would have sent them down in an uncontrolled sliding fall. At one point, a step chopped in frozen rock and ice gave way under Leuthold, but McJury was able to belay him to a safe position. They were using ten-point crampons that lack the two vertical front teeth on the 12-point models used on steep ice in more modern times. The full climb took ten hours.

McJury, on a later climb of the same route, found that snow conditions were much better and safer; the first ascent had been staged on a day which would force many parties to abandon the climb for a less hazardous attempt in the future.

PULPIT ROCK

Between the Ladd and Coe Glaciers stands a great cliff, Pulpit Rock, that was climbed by Irving B. Lincoln in the spring of 1936. Approaching the rock across the Coe Glacier, Lincoln had an experience, always frightening for a solo climber, of breaking through a hidden crevasse and falling to his armpits before catching himself.

The rock had been scanned by many over the years. Newton Clark in his first recorded climb of the north side in 1887, had climbed along the right (west) edge. Lincoln was able to go right up the center, taking advantage of a snow-filled couloir which he was able to negotiate with crampons. No hardware was used. After ascending the rock, Lincoln gained the top of Cathedral Ridge and went to the summit.

NORTH FACE CLEAVER*

Monday, June 19, 1961 The North Face Cleaver, the great ridge of rock that stands above Eliot Glacier, rising to terminate in Cathedral Spire just below the summit, was climbed for the first time by Allen Steck and Dr. Richard D. Long.

The two camped above Cloud Cap Inn Sunday night with Will Siri, Richard C. Houston, and Blanchar Baldwin. All but Baldwin were Californians, members of American Alpine Club who had come to a weekend Mountain Rescue Conference at Timberline Lodge and had then gone around to climb on the north side.

About 2:00 a.m. they left their base camp and climbed to the high end of Eliot Glacier. Baldwin decided to quit and turned back. Siri and Houston veered west and ascended Sunshine Route.

Long and Steck scanned the rock of the North Face Cleaver and decided to try it, not realizing that generations of Oregonians had automatically shunned it as being impossibly rotten rock. They found a good ice bridge over the bergschrund and started up. The bottom was very rotten, but not very steep. Above, where the slope nears the perpendicular, the rock was more solid, and the two proceeded up the full climb with only belay protection on some pitches. No hardware was required. They noted that the top of the Eliot Headwall Route just to their west appeared extremely hazardous. (McJury's route).

*Note — The name North Face Cleaver is not an officially accepted name. It is merely a descriptive term used by the author. At some later date someone may come forth with a name that will be officially accepted.

CASTLE CRAGS ROUTE

September 13, 1933 Gary Leech climbed solo along the rock ridge leading upward from Illumination Saddle. This was confirmed by William "Smoke" Blanchard, a close friend of Leech, who had his personal notes. Russ McJury, David Wagstaff, and David Young climbed the route on July 7, 1951, claiming a first ascent. Leech made many ascents such as this, which were not publicized at the time.

THE IMPOSSIBLE YOCUM RIDGE

Generations of climbers have been tantalized with the idea of climbing Yocum Ridge, for so many years described as the unclimbable route of Mount Hood. The structure is of such fragile rock, that all agreed it would be suicide to even attempt the ridge.

Then, mountaineers got to discussing the idea of climbing in the wintertime, when the precarious beds of gravel are frozen, and some attempts were made. Always the report came back that the ice was loose and feathery, too unstable for setting ice screws.

BECKEY & SCHEIBLEHNER ASCENT

April 9, 1959 Fred Beckey, famed for first ascents, and the Austrian climber, Leopold Scheiblehner, drove to Mount Hood, intending to do some ski mountaineering. As they swung around the last few loops in the road below Timberline Lodge, they began to talk of doing something a bit more demanding.

In the lodge they looked over maps, noting that Yocum Ridge did not show a dotted line. This indicated that it had never been climbed, and **the two decided to do the impossible!** Swinging their packs upon their shoulders, they started off to Illumination Saddle on skis. They camped there that night; weather was good.

The next morning they overslept until 7:00 a.m., but soon after they were roped and quickly crossing the Reid Glacier, dropping elevation at its north side to a point of access to Yocum Ridge. Beckey wrote that the ridge was a mass of ice feathers; not a rock was visible. Leo took the first lead, attaining the ridge with ice picks and use of the front points on the crampons.

From there it was necessary to traverse across walls of fluted ice, praying that neither would slip. There was no way of protection by belaying. Soon after they approached a mushroom tower of ice that stood in the way of progress. Leo took another turn at leading, stepping out to the right and around the corner. Fifteen minutes later he came into view above the mushroom, having cut hand and footholds a long distance up a gully wall.

Proceeding on the ridge, they flanked the worst towers just under the crest, being careful to use a few tiny belay spots that were available on the ridge or behind the towers (gendarmes).

Beckey recalls one pitch of 30 feet up vertical ice. He led it by grasping long columns of ice feathers, and leaning outward to keep his balance, as he kicked in footholds into the unstable structure. He knew that a wrong slash of the ice axe would bring down the whole wall. Looking down, he could see daylight under as much as two feet of the veneer of frost feathers.

A little later Leo led up 12 feet of ice that overhung, cutting holds above his head as he climbed. The usual use of ice screws was out of the question in the unstable ice. Once on the excruciatingly narrow ridge, it was at times necessary to leap down several feet to land on some tiny platform of ice, that could very well crumble upon impact.

The climb went very rapidly for the two, despite the difficulty. At 1:00 they stood on the summit of Mount Hood in a strong breeze. They descended on the South Side to their camp at Illumination Saddle. Donning their skis once more, they were soon back at Timberline Lodge, hardly realizing the import of climbing the IMPOSSIBLE Yocum Ridge Route.

March 1, 1972 Del W. Young, 22, and Terry Hiatt, 24, made a successful climb of Yocum Ridge. Young is a student in psychology at Eastern Washington State College and has acted as chief guide for Lute Jerstad. Hiatt is a gardener in Seattle. Young's own account tells the difficulty of the ascent:

"We camped at Illumination Saddle to get an early start on the ridge, leaving our tent at daybreak, carrying no bivouac gear and hoping to do the climb in a single day.

"We gained the ridge crest about 400 yards east of Beckey's route by climbing two 55 to 60-degree ice pitches up a long, steep gully. The first obstacle was the First Gendarme. This was the crux of the climb, extremely exposed on both sides, with no protection and terrible ice conditions. Once up this gendarme, one is committed to the climb, because a retreat would be almost impossible.

"We then proceeded along an incredibly sharp ridge crest for several hundred feet to the Second Gendarme. It was quite easy. Then, an even more-exposed ridge led from the Second Gendarme toward the peak. Climbing was slow, unbelievably exposed, and spectacular. We rappelled off the north side of the ridge about 50 feet, only to climb back up to the crest in about 100 feet. The day was getting late when we got to the base of the Buttress. Worried about the time, we traversed around the side of the Buttress, dropped down about 50 feet, then ascended to the summit of the mountain. We reached the summit exactly at sunset. Temperature was about zero, and a brisk wind blew. We reached our tent in the last fading light.

"Looking back, I can say that Yocum Ridge was one of the most exciting and spectacular days of climbing I have done. It is the most dangerous climb I have done on Mount Hood, by far. The ice is not real ice, but ice feathers, brittle, fragile, useless for ice screws. The exposure is more profound on the ridge than even on the great walls of Yosemite, where it falls away in only one direction."

Wallalute Falls on Compass Creek.
Now called Middle Fork Falls by USFS.

This chapter covers the tragic side of mountain sport, the accidents, searches and rescues. Considering the extremely large numbers of people who ski and climb on Mount Hood, it would appear to be a very short list. In skiing, the great hazard is in straying away from an area and becoming lost; the number of deaths is very low. The number of accidents, however, is astronomical. Each week a parade of patients returns to Portland with broken bones, torn ligaments, lacerations, and bruises.

In contrast, climbing has resulted in most of the deaths on Mount Hood. The South Side Route has accounted for 13 dead in exposure or direct accident. Of that number, four were killed in two plane crashes. Ski accidents or exposure to hypothermia by lost skiers have taken a toll of six lives. Three more died low on the south side from accidents, one from carbon monoxide, another from a runaway tram car, and the third in a hiking accident.

The west side has taken one life. Two animals have died, a mule on the north, and a horse on the south. Perhaps another horse was lost in a crevasse near Cloud Cap Inn in the 1880's.

The most spectacular site for mountain accidents is the slide from the Chimney area, high on Cooper Spur Route, down the precipitous northeast snow slope of the mountain to the Eliot Glacier. This usually is a slide of 1,500 feet or more. At first glance any good mountaineer would tell you that on such a fall there would be a very slight chance of survival. However, at least ten parties have made this terrible ride, a total of 22 people. Of these, only three people have lost their lives.

The participants of the sixth occurrence of this fall to Eliot Glacier were Colin Chisholm and his son in 1961. This opened the door for jokesters in the mountaineering world to name it the "Chisholm Trail." In addition to the fatalities on the Chisholm Trail, there have been five other deaths on the north side of Mount Hood, one an accident on horseback.

This brings the total of deaths on Mount Hood to 31. No automobile accidents are considered.

The active members of the mountaineering world are appalled at the potential for tragedy created by one-time climbers, who come to the mountain with insufficient clothing. Many "happy wanderers" are seen in the crater area dressed in street shoes, shorts, light shirts or no shirts at all. One climber did South Side route in bare feet. They carry no food or water. They pick their way up to the summit without the protection of ice axe or crampons. Mountain weather often changes dramatically within a short time. A lovely, sunny day can quickly become overcast, then a howling whiteout to trap the unprepared.

This chapter is not just the story of the dead, but the story of tremendous bravery of the living. The necessity of packing out a climber with a broken leg often resulted in ordeals that were cruel and demanding of the rescuers, as well as the victims. In many of these stories, a single sentence encompasses the grim reality of hours of struggling over ice, floundering through powder snow, suffering with the cold, and battling high winds and zero visibility.

DEATHS ON MOUNT HOOD

1896	Frederic Kirn	climbing
1924	Barbara Drum	climbing
1927	Leslie Brownlee	skiing
1927	Stanton Stryker	climbing
1929	Susana Springer	horseback
1932	Glen Gullickson	climbing
1933-4	Charles Newell	monoxide
1934	Victor VonNorman	fumarole
1936	Victor Howell	skiing
1938	Roy Varney	climbing
1938	Russell Gueffroy	climbing
1940	Gerald Herrmann	climbing
1943	Helen Lowry	climbing
1948	Bert Suprenant	skiing
1949	Col. A.Y. Smith	aircraft
1949	Col. W.W. Hodge	aircraft
1949	Sgt. H.E. Sluga	aircraft
1949	Donald Welk	climbing
1949	W.C. Carpenter	tramway
1956	Lynn Kaufman	climbing
1956	Lou Ellen Simko	hiking
1959	David Draper	climbing
1963	R.P. Myers	aircraft
1965	W.S. Davis	skiing
1968	Robert Patterson	climbing
1969	James L. Eaton	skiing
1971	Michael Regan	skiing
1971	Harry B. Carson	climbing
1971	Clinton Carson	climbing
1972	Jack A. Lafeman	climbing
1974	Richard B. Chu	climbing

A MISSING SOLDIER

1883 The first possibility of a climbing tragedy on Mount Hood involved Bernhard, a soldier stationed at Vancouver Barracks. Being a member of a government supply party, he was reported as missing from their camp at timberline. Some of his officers thought he had deserted. His fellow soldiers had the opinion that Bernhard had been overcome with curiosity about the mountain and tried to climb it. Crevasses were more prevalent on the south side in those days; it is very possible that one of them claimed him.

DEATH OF FREDERIC KIRN

1896 Mount Hood's first climbing casualty was Frederic Kirn, Portland grocer of Swiss birth who fell to his death onto the Newton Clark Glacier on Monday, July 12. He arrived at Cloud Cap Inn on Sunday afternoon, an elderly but vigorous man who had walked from the rail station at Hood River. Scanning the mountainside with his field glasses, he asked many questions of guide Will Langille, finally commenting that he could find the way himself and did not need a guide. Many of his questions concerned volcanic phenomena; Langille pointed out some features to him, warning that it would be dangerous to reach them.

Kirn rose at 4:00 a.m., consumed only a cup of coffee, and left the inn a half hour later for his adventure on the slopes that reminded him of his native Switzerland. "Tantsana" watched him occasionally through the telescope, but she lost visual contact. By 5:30 p.m. the Langilles were sufficiently worried to send Will up to look for their guest. He followed the tracks plainly enough to within 700 feet of the summit, where they veered south onto a steep and treacherous rocky area and disappeared. It became obvious that Kirn had trusted a slope of rock that had slid out from under him, perhaps triggered by his own footsteps.

Will Langille carefully followed down the slope of the avalanche for about 300 feet, fearing his own safety most of the time on the high angle of the mountainside. Then he came to the edge of the cliff and saw Kirn's body lying 400 feet below, surrounded by the rocks that had swept him along with them. It was 8:30 p.m. by that time, and the guide knew that there was no chance that Kirn could be alive; he went numbly back to Cloud Cap and called the police in Portland. An officer went to Kirn's home at 853 Albina Avenue and broke the news to his wife and daughter, who at first refused to believe the terrible story, then broke down in shock.

Will took five men the next morning to retrieve the corpse. They climbed over the Newton Clark Glacier from below. Getting to Kirn's badly battered body was very hazardous, as he lay on the very steep ice just above the bergschrund. A slide of a few more feet would have carried him into the bergschrund crevasse, where he probably never would have been found. It took six men until evening to bring the body down to Cooper Spur, where they could lash it to the back of a waiting horse.

Later reports on Frederic Kirn from his family indicated that he had long been intrigued with Mount Hood. He had previously been in the hop business near Gervais, Oregon, and from his home there he could often admire the mountain. He wrote considerable poetry and felt he must visit Mount Hood to better put down his words into meaningful verse. So it was upon this pilgrimage to his beautiful mountain, that he met his own destruction.

His daughter, Eugenie, later had a son, who became prominent in mountaineering and mountain lore, Erwin Rieger. Rieger had the unique experience of spending some of his boyhood in the remote interior of Alaska, shipping back to the states to attend high school and the University of Washington. He followed a career in journalism, being editor of the *Columbian* in Vancouver, Washington, until his recent retirement. Hundreds of Mazamas fondly remember him as their president in 1963-4. He is author of a current book *Up Is The Mountain*, a charming mixture of mountaineering reminiscences and philosophy.

SLIP ON NEWTON CLARK

1891 Will Langille, having made the first ascent of the Wy'east Route in 1890, returned to it with a party of climbers from Cloud Cap, including Anne Lang of The Dalles, Horatio Green, Fred Josselyn, and Will Smith. Near the summit on a steep snow slope 1500 feet above Newton Clark Glacier, they came to a difficult trough that had been gouged out by intermittently falling rock. As a safety precaution the guide cut 12 feet off the 200-foot climbing rope to tie Josselyn and Miss Lang together.

He then carefully led across the trough to the opposite side and anchored the climbing rope. Green, at the rear of the rope, provided the other anchor. Josselyn then started across, Miss Lang right on his heels. Both were using the anchored climbing rope as a hand line. She slipped, knocking Josselyn off his feet, but by some divine miracle she landed on the opposite side of the hand line.

The two shot down the slope until the handline became taut. Fortunately both anchor men did their job well, and the two were saved. Anne Lang hung headfirst over the glacier, dangling helplessly. Josselyn was able to recover his footing quickly, and the two were laboriously hauled back up to the climbing route. The climb was cancelled; only Miss Lang wanted to proceed. This young woman later became Oregon's most distinguished member of the Daughters of the American Revolution.

KILLINGSWORTH ACCIDENT

1896 On Wednesday, August 26, William Killingsworth and his three daughters, Fay, Dora, and Nannie were members of a party of 21 descending from the summit. With a loud cracking noise, a large boulder broke loose above and rolled directly toward them. Fay Killingsworth, about 400 feet below the summit, saw the rock coming for her, but at the last moment it bounded up and over her head. It created a spray of snow so powerful, that she was thrown 15 feet downward and slipped into the crevasse below, being partly buried with snow. It took guide Robert Bigelow several minutes to uncover her.

Frank N. Spicer of Antelope, a strong climber, pulled her from the crevasse. Her face was bleeding and badly cut. Doctors later determined brain concussion. Spicer carried the girl all the way to their camp near timberline. At first she lay limp in his arms, later recovering enough to hold on. Soft snow, melted by the afternoon sun, caused him to sink to a discouraging depth with each step.

They reached the camp well after dark, where a

fire was built. A messenger left for the Bull Run Headworks, the nearest telephone, and called the doctors, C.H. and Dav Rafferty late at night. Dr. C.H. Rafferty gathered his equipment and left at once, reaching Bull Run by Thursday morning. By the end of the day he had reached Miss Killingsworth at the timberline campsite. Friday she was on her way to Portland.

The excitement of the incident caused Killingsworth to report to the Portland newspapers that the rock had been blown out of place by volcanic pressure. Several warnings appeared in the news, telling the great danger of climbing above Crater Rock. O.C. Yocum climbed to the scene of the accident soon afterward to investigate. W.G. Steel and a H.S. Graves of New York City followed the Killingsworth route on September 26, finding no trace of eruption. Killingsworth stated that he would not climb Mount Hood again for a deed to the whole state of Oregon. It was brought out that Bigelow had climbed the mountain on the 25th of July with Steel and had proclaimed himself a guide. Steel was severe in his public criticism of Bigelow.

WILD SLIDE ON COOPER SPUR

1900 In July, Bob Leisure, a new guide at Cloud Cap Inn took a group up Cooper Spur Route. The party was organized by Dorsey B. Smith, who at the time was private secretary to A.L. Mohler, president of Union Pacific Railway. The party included Mohler, his daughter Ruth, Horace Mecklem, Harry Gaylord, Dorsey's brother Otice Smith, John Keating, Dr. K.A.J. MacKenzie, and others.

Ruth Mohler and others quit the climb and remained on the rocks part way up Cooper Spur Route. The party crossed Crescent Crevasse, much more of a hazard in 1900. At Tie-In-Rock, just above the crevasse, Mohler elected to quit. Leisure took the remaining seven clients to the summit. Remaining a bit too long, he found the slope frozen on the descent.

The whole group was tied into one climbing rope, and all were holding on to the life-line (fixed rope) tied near the top of the slope. Leisure should have been at the rear of the string, but for some reason he took the front, letting Mecklem assume the anchor position at the rear. The climbers were mostly inexperienced, and there was much slipping and holding on for dear life as they descended.

Nearing the end of the rope, Keating slipped completely out of control, bowling over Dr. MacKenzie. The whole group began to slide and Harry Gaylord tried desperately to arrest the slide by grasping the fixed line. He later was treated for severely burned hands.

As they passed Tie-In-Rock Dr. MacKenzie called a pitiful farewell to his friend Mohler, as he sped toward almost certain destruction in Crescent Crevasse. At the last moment they were saved by the rough texture of the tracks they had made during the ascent in the morning. Their footsteps had pockmarked the snow with many

holes where the snow stayed soft. Leisure and Mecklem were able to get the party stopped.

A HUMAN TOBOGGAN

1901 An epic rescue was accomplished by members of three different parties climbing the south side on July 15. Professional guide O.C. Yocum was leading a group, Professor F.M. McElfresh, F.D. McLouth, A.L. Knisely, Ethel Nottingham, Jessie Nottingham, Harry Nottingham, F.A. Jones, Frank Jones, J.C. Zinzer, Charles A. Butler, Robert M. Irvine, Arthur Prideaux, George Prideaux, Walter Chown, and C.H. Ames, an Appalachian Club member who wrote a later account of the operation.

Yocum had brought his party near Crater Rock, when Miss Nottingham ran out of energy and had to be supported. The snow had been unusually soft and tiring. The weather had been questionable from the beginning, cold and cloudy. Sleet followed by snow forced them to take cover in the rocks on the north side of Crater Rock. Three men in a separate, unguided group preceded the party up the mountain, and were by that time high on the chute, Elmer Dodd, J.R. Raley, and______________Burdick. Strong wind and snow at blizzard intensity made them abandon their climb and return to join the larger group.

Meanwhile, Charles W. Sholes was bringing up another group below, Mrs. C.W. Nottingham, Henry De Moss, George De Moss, Amelia De Moss, Julia Hall, Talmidge Davis, and Bethel Rawson. Shouts for help were heard from them, and the men from Yocum's party found that Julia Hall was exhausted and Bethel Rawson had collapsed. For no really good reason the two were brought up, instead of down. All effort failed to bring Bethel Rawson to her senses, but lunch and rest had revived all the others. Yocum gave the order to descend. Suddenly five men found themselves alone with the problem of bringing down the unconscious girl, Charles Sholes, Professor McElfresh, Professor McLouth, Henry De Moss, and C.H. Ames.

They carried her in a cradle of interlocking arms down the Hogsback and along the narrow trail that ran just above the crevasse at the top of White River Glacier. An alpenstock jabbed in here and there by one of the party gave the others some measure of stability on the steep snow. When the danger of the crevasse was passed, they rested a moment and reflected on the gravity of their situation. The unconscious girl might die, if they could not get her down quickly. But the strain in getting her just that far had been to the limit of their endurance.

McElfresh produced a wooden box he had been carrying to use as an improvised toboggan. He sat upon it, placed the girl on top of himself, and told them to pull. The wooden box sank into the snow and broke. Then the idea of a human toboggan was advanced. McElfresh lay on the snow with girl ontop, both face up. Sholes had a rope;

they tied the ankles of the two together, leaving two pull-ropes in front and one rope to the rear for stability. The men manned the ropes, and McElfresh tobogganed down the mountain, leaving a deep groove that could be seen from Government Camp several days later.

Ames began to feel the pain of an old ankle sprain and he lagged behind. Soon he came down below the cloud level into better weather. Ahead he could see the rescue group, and further below were spread out the retreating members of Yocum's party. As the slope grew flatter, pulling became harder. Yocum's party tied the climbing rope to McElfresh, and many hands made the trip to timberline very quickly. It had been only 45 minutes since they had left Crater Rock.

Professor McLouth relieved his half-frozen friend, McElfresh, and put the unconscious girl on a horse. He rode back of the saddle, supporting her with the help of men walking alongside. Lower down a horse-drawn carriage took her the rest of the way to Government Camp. It took 5 hours for a physician to bring her to consciousness. It was never publicly reported as to what her problem was, but obviously her health did not merit the climbing of Mount Hood. Her shoes were thin and clothing inadequate as well. As were most of the Sholes party, she was a member of the De Moss Musical Troupe, which had arrived at Government Camp in an historic stage coach.

LIGHTNING STRUCK WEYGANDT

August 27, 1905 M.W. Lyon, Jr., professor of history at Smithsonian Institute, climbed Cooper Spur Route with Mark Weygandt. They left Cloud Cap Inn at 7:30 a.m. and arrived at Lunch Rock just a little past noon, when Mark heard thunder pealing. Continuing upward, they were hit by heavy wind and snow fell as they stood about 100 feet below the summit ridge. Shortly after they were dazed by a bolt of lightning.

In fierce wind and snow on the summit, Weygandt picked up the metal register box. Immediately lightning struck, knocking him off his feet. He quickly replaced the box cover and the two ran off the summit. For the first 1700 feet they had the fixed rope to follow. Wind was so strong that Weygandt was afraid to leave the fixed rope, but the fact that he was wearing only two cotton shirts forced them to descend.

The two stayed tied in to their climbing rope all the way down to Cooper Spur, at which time Lyon urged the guide to go ahead to keep from freezing. Both were safely inside the inn by 4:30, and Lyon praised Weygandt to the newspapers for his pluck, endurance, and steady nerves. Source of this material was the second story written for the newspapers. The first story was very sensational and grossly exaggerated.

TOO FAT TO FALL

1910 An unsubstantiated story mentioned a fall into a crevasse on Newton Clark Glacier by Dr. W.S. Nichol, while ascending Cooper Spur. The crevasse narrowed, and Dr. Nichol was spared the fall into a "bottomless abyss" by his rotund shape. A more slender climber would have fallen through. This is not believed to be Dr. Herbert Nichol, who was prominent in the Snow Shoe Club at that time.

A HEADSTRONG CLIENT

1915 Elijah Coalman met his match when he agreed to take Anne Louise Strong on a South Side Route climb on a Saturday of late October. A daughter of a Seattle minister, she was an employee of the Federal Bureau of Education and had climbed Mount Hood three times in 1915. The party started out from camp at timberline in a gale. Lige advised cancelling the climb; all agreed but Miss Strong. She did change her mind when a gust of wind took her off her feet. That ended the day's climb.

But Sunday morning they were ready again at 3:00 a.m. Even at timberline the surface was glare ice. Lige cut steps with his axe all the way from Triangle Moraine to the summit, a difficult 13-hour trip where any slip could be serious or fatal. He suggested that the party stay in the summit house and descend the following day in daylight. The headstrong girl would have none of that, stating that she was already a day overdue in returning to Washington D.C.

Lige, who had gone through a traumatic experience of falling in the crevasse only three weeks before, should have used his authority. But he allowed the girl to persuade him, and they left at 5:00 p.m. for timberline. Soon his electric headlamp, the only light in the party, burned out. The party inched down, cutting steps in the dark, then feeling for them. They were roped into one string, but a slip could have taken down the whole group. Freezing fog blew in, turning to ice on parkas, hats, and gloves. He hoped that someone at Government Camp Hotel had been watching and knew they were descending.

Others in the party began to lament that they had tried to climb so late in the year and that they had not taken the guide's advice. Anne Strong never wavered, and she finally saw the light of the hotel as they drew out of the fog. To hearten the situation they saw a rescue team with lanterns near timberline. It was too icy for the unequipped searchers to come any higher. Lige could hear their shouts at times, but they could not hear his party against the strong southwest wind. Finally he could see the lantern bearers start downhill once more.

Proceeding painfully slowly on the ice in the dark, the party felt terror strike them as their only hope receded down the hill. Lige rummaged in his pack for combustibles. A few pieces of paper were wadded and soaked in wood alcohol. The wind died momentarily and he lit it while the party yelled together. The lantern carriers stopped, then began to climb up hill again; they had been seen.

Lige sent down the most experienced man from the party to make contact and bring back a lantern. Once he had returned they were able to make much better speed. The light of day was near when they finally reached the hotel. Two women lost emotional control from the anxiety and exhaustion.

HELEN DAVIDSON STRUCK

Friday, August 10, 1917 Guide George Miller led a young group up Cooper Spur Route, Helen Davidson, Wilma Donnell, Helen J. Gray, Chester Huggins, Jr., R. Bain, and Hal Selby. They reached the summit cabin about 11:00 a.m., and after a few pleasant words with Lige Coalman, they started down toward Cloud Cap Inn.

Just below the first steep pitch, a shower of falling rock scattered the party, one piece striking Miss Davidson in the temple and rendering her unconscious. Coalman came down quickly from the summit cabin, agreeing quickly with Miller that she needed a doctor's care. They felt that it was impossible to take her down the severe slopes of Cooper Spur Route, so they carried her to the summit cabin.

David Cooper, Jr. swears that he was in on the rescue and that they broke up a table to get a board for improvising a stretcher to carry the heavy girl. He thought she weighed about 240 pounds. He can recall their lowering her by rope across the three crevasses in the Hogsback, being afraid to put their full weight on the flimsy ladders that bridged the chasms. The *Hood River Glacier* reported that six men carried her down to timberline, where a rescue party waited as a result of an alerting call from the summit cabin.

An additional problem arose about mid-afternoon, when the climbing party realized that they had left Helen Gray behind at Tie-In-Rock on the ascent. Since the full party descended South Side, it was necessary for H.W. Acton, assistant manager of Cloud Cap Inn, to climb up for her. He reached Miss Gray about 5:00 p.m.

When the rescue party evacuated Helen Davidson, she was examined at Government Camp and found to have suffered only a gash on her head, not a fractured skull. She was sent down to Portland on Saturday morning in moderately good condition.

ROCKFALL HIT MISS VAUGHN

1916 A party of Seattle Mountaineers were climbing Cooper Spur Route, observed by Lige Coalman until they passed out of sight below the bulge of the ridge. When they did not appear on time, he sensed trouble and hastened down, first phoning to David Cooper, Jr., at Cloud Cap. The climbing party had gathered around Miss ____________Vaughn with a deep hip wound from falling rock. Lige applied a compress and slid her down to lower elevation, where Cooper waited with a toboggan. At the snow line Cooper had horses ready to take her to the inn.

Climbers at Government Camp Hotel Annex 1915 — Photo Everett Sickler

SEARCH FOR THE EDELFSENS

On arriving at Rhododendron, Anton H. Edelfsen, Portland fuel dealer, became engrossed in the idea of climbing Mount Hood. He and his wife decided to join a Reed College group led by Lige Coalman and assisted by Otto Aschoff. They borrowed warm clothing at Government Camp, but they wore their city shoes that softened in the wet snow.

The climb started from a base camp at timberline at 2:00 a.m. on Sunday, September 24, 1916. Edelfsen wore a business suit and sweater; his wife had knickerbockers and skirt and sweater. Their lack of conditioning began to tell, and they were lagging as the party arrived at Crater Rock. In 1916 a steel cable was set on the rock to aid climbers, and they made it to the top, where Mrs. Edelfsen became ill from sulphur fumes. Coalman told them to wait right there for him until his return from the summit.

However, as time drug by with the fair weather deteriorating, they became uncomfortable in the piercing wind. Below they could see the hotel at Government Camp. When two other climbers returned from the summit, they forgot Coalman's warning and started out with them for timberline.

The two men ahead of Coalman's group did a sitting glissade and left the Edelfsens far behind in minutes. The telephone wire could be seen in the snow for a mile or so, but when the tracks of the two men left the wire, the Edelfsens decided to follow the footprints, a serious mistake. Shortly after, the clouds blew in and cut visibility. Then they lost the tracks near timberline.

Coalman returned with his party to the hotel and found his clients were missing! He quickly returned to timberline and built signal fires to help them locate themselves. Mrs. Edelfsen's shoes were virtually useless. At timberline, rain, sleet and snow hit the lost pair, but Edelfsen was fortunate enough to get a fire started. They spent the night in misery, getting just enough heat to stay alive by the fire.

In the morning he returned to timberline, hoping to find the telephone wire, but failed and returned to the trees for a second night. Huckleberries on the ridges gave them nourishment to keep going. The next task was to rebuild a fire, but only one match remained. With the utmost of caution Edelfsen gathered the driest of twigs. The match stick was slant-grained and broke, the flame end hitting the ground. He grabbed it desperately and saved the flame. Within minutes a fire was leaping through the carefully gathered sticks; their lives had been spared by the tiniest thread.

In the morning searchers found them huddled by their fire, half conscious from hypothermia. The Edelfsens had made the usual error in drifting too far west toward timberline. Tracks were found in Sand Canyon, and the lost climbers were found between Little Zigzag and Big Zigzag Canyons.

FUHRER FELL ON AXE

Sunday, July 29, 1917 Swiss Guide Hans Fuhrer, 29, who later became a very great name in mountaineering at Mount Rainier and in Canada, was the victim of a serious accident, being gored with his own ice axe. Fuhrer had left the summit about noon and had taken the party past the Big Crevasse to the Hogsback. At that point they all sat down in the snow in bobsled fashion for a mass glissade to the lower crater.

The newspaper reported that near the bottom of the run, a grand spill occurred, with the woman riding in tandem behind Fuhrer losing control and catching her foot on his ice axe. The guide was thrown forward and the full seven inches of its point drove into his abdomen, exposing his intestine, a rather delicate medical problem to be met with first aid techniques. Coalman, in his later memoirs, stated that the party had been tipped over by catching the telephone line near the surface of the snow.

Work with the fire-finder on the summit engrossed Coalman at the time of the accident. He finally looked down and saw three men waving hats and sweaters on their alpenstocks to attract his attention. Furhrer's bride of three months was watching through the telescope from Government Camp Hotel, and she saw Coalman leave the cabin, glissade the Chute in one big sweep to the Big Crevasse, jump across it, then run and jump down to the scene of the accident in four minutes. A climbing party two weeks earlier had seen him do exactly the same thing in the course of going down for a load of telephone wire in a mere six minutes.

He placed large pads of gauze on the wound, then bandaged the whole stomach to compress the injury. Then, climbing quickly back to the summit, he telephoned to L.F. Pridemore, owner of the hotel, to come up with help. Ivan M. Woolley, medical student and auto stage driver, had been standing by at the hotel to take the party back to Portland on his scheduled run at 3:30. Pridemore assembled a string of pack animals and started up the mountain.

Coalman then descended to Fuhrer once more, bringing a large packsack which he improvised into a toboggan. He then bodily drug the hefty guide to timberline in an hour's time and placed him on one of Pridemore's horses. Pridemore held the injured man in position as Coalman led the horse down the trail to Government Camp.

Medical student Woolley inspected the bandage, saw no bleeding and loaded Fuhrer in the front seat of the auto for the long trip back to Portland. Driving as gently as he could, Woolley eased along over the miles of corduroy road, easing over bumps and shifting gears through the mud holes as smoothly as he could. West of Gresham, where the pavement started, he pushed the car at top speed, top down and cutout open. Deputy Sheriff Jack LaMonte chased him on a county motorcycle, but never could catch up until Woolley slowed near 82nd and Division. A short conversation soon had LaMonte leading all the way to St. Vincent Hospital, where Dr. Frank Wood was awaiting the case.

Woolley was asked to scrub and assist in the surgery. Both men were surprised at the perfect job Lige Coalman had done in dressing the wound. The intestine had not protruded; soon Fuhrer was walking around Government Camp in good style.

Lige and Hans Fuhrer had often argued about the ice axe. Lige said it should be sheathed while glissading; Fuhrer said otherwise. Actually it was foolish to glissade in a chain as they did, especially considering that they were forced to carry down the ice axe and all the alpenstocks of the party. However, most mountaineers of today would agree that the pick of an axe is used for arresting, and should not be sheathed. A leather sheath is merely used for transporting an axe in a vehicle. One may be assured that Coalman and Fuhrer were not the first men to debate the handling of an ice axe.

AN UNSOLVED MYSTERY

Sunday, June 2, 1918 Lige Coalman and T. Raymond Conway, leading the first party to reach the summit in 1918, spent an hour investigating an apparent tragedy at the Big Crevasse on the South Side Route. Tracks led up to a point 12 feet from the lip and stopped. Signs of a slide into the aperature were noted past that point. They leaned far out over the edge on ropes and called, but there was no one visible from the top. A later questioning around Government Camp turned up no clues. If anyone fell in, his fate is a mystery on Mount Hood until this day.

They continued up with their party of 11, which included Eva Brunnell, Charlotte McDougal, Dorothy Pernot, Julia E. Pratt, Martha Gasch, Jessie Nottingham, Frank Redman, Samuel Fries, and Albert S. Brown, arriving at the summit cabin about 6:00 p.m. to find it snowed in. They entered by a window in the cupola, and soon Coalman was making dinner.

The following morning the plan was to traverse the mountain by descending Cooper Spur Route. Coalman and Conway scouted ahead to Lunch Rock, and feeling that the route was safe, they started the party down at 2:00 p.m. Well before they reached Crescent Crevasse, they were at about the 9,200-foot level, when they encountered a long stretch of glare ice. It proved so dangerous that they reversed the climb, went to the top, and descended the South Side Route again. After a Sunday night at the hotel at Government Camp, they hiked 10 miles to Rhododendron to catch a bus.

MRS. DAVIS HIT BY ROCK

Saturday, July 5, 1919 A group of climbers from Multnomah Athletic Club skirted Crater Rock. One of the leaders dislodged a boulder that bounded down the slope, narrowly missing several of the party, and finally struck Mrs. W.R. Davis. She remained unconscious for several hours, and later examination showed two cracked ribs and internal hemorrhaging.

She was carried slowly down by her husband, Dr. Seeley, Mr. Nelson, Professor Allen, and Dr. Hart. Later in the day the weather turned much worse, and by 8:00 p.m. sleet was falling.

MULE FELL INTO CREVASSE

1922 In early summer, guide Mark Weygandt and packer Walter Davidson with three other men took the fixed ropes up to set them on the summit on Cooper Spur Route, just prior to the second Annual Legion Climb of July 16. They used three pack animals to carry the rope. They reached Cooper Spur and headed west along the ridge, when one of the mules seemed to be affected by the altitude. It laid down, attempted to roll. Then to the horror of the men in the party, it slid right off the ridge and fell to the Eliot Glacier below, sliding down until it disappeared into a crevasse forever.

The Crag Rats plotted the probable rate of travel for several years, and in 1933 they figured it should be showing up in the upper ice-fall of the glacier. They planned to look for it on the Annual Legion Climb on July 16, but the animal's body was not found.

ROCK FATAL TO MISS DRUM

September 3, 1924 Barbara Drum, 35, a graduate student at the University of Washington and hostess at Cloud Cap Inn, joined a party to remove the fixed rope from the summit area on Cooper Spur Route. In the party were guide William Moody, Herbert Reynolds, and Donald

Weygandt party with Legion ropes. A mule slipped into a crevasse shortly after the picture was taken. — Photo Wesley Weygandt

Wright. This annual chore was a strenuous job, and at the end of the day Moody put Miss Drum on the end of his rope while they crossed the top of Newton Clark Glacier.

Suddenly a six-inch boulder came flying down the mountainside and struck her in the small of her back, hurling her off her feet. The rope saved her from a fall into the crevasses of the glacier. The men were afraid to evacuate her from the dangerously-crevassed area and decided to wait until morning. One of them went for blankets at Cloud Cap Inn and relayed the news of the accident. They kept her well-wrapped and warm all night, but she remained in delerium.

On September 4, they brought her down to Cloud Cap Inn, and on September 5, Homer Rogers, operator of the inn, took her to the hospital in Hood River. In a few days she seemed to be recovering, but on September 16, she suddenly died from her injury.

HORSE KILLED ON RESCUE

1924 Mr. and Mrs.________________ from Iowa were climbing south side alone. On the Chute they climbed an avalanche trough, a groove carved by occasionally falling rock. They chose the wrong path, and one more rock came down, breaking his thigh. His wife climbed for help to the summit cabin where Charles A. Phelps was on duty.

Phelps telephoned to Summit Guard Station at Summit Meadows and climbed down to help the victim. All he could do was to chop a platform in the snow with his ice axe and give the man a little comfort. Lige Coalman, working once more as a guide, came to the rescue with George Calverley, both on horseback. Calverley at the time was a guide and also owned a string of pack horses. Both men were unpaid rescuers, using their own equipment as they so often did.

West of Triangle Moraine they approached a crevassed area in an area that is unbroken today. Calverley rode around the end of a crevasse, but it broke through, the rider jumping frantically to avoid falling in. The poor horse was not so fortunate and fell 300 feet to the bottom, jammed in between the sloping walls. Extrication was impossible, and Calverley had no way to put the poor animal out of its misery. They left Coalman's horse on Triangle Moraine and proceeded to the rescue on the chute. With the help of Phelps they alternated carrying the man on their backs down to the remaining horse, after splinting the thigh with strips of thin wood from a packing case.

The following day Calverly was lowered into the crevasse by his brother, Vern, to retrieve the saddle from his dead horse. He brought a large chisel to chip away the ice enough to release the leather straps. A few days afterward the horse had slipped away, out of sight. Perhaps some hiker will find the equine skeleton peeking out from

George Calverley below Timberline Cabin — Photo Calverley

under the edge of receding snow in many years to come.

The Iowa visitor spent some time in a Portland hospital. When he was well enough to drive back home, he had suffered the loss of time, hospital expense, and a bill from George Calverley for the dead horse.

A 700-FOOT ICE SLIDE

June 5, 1926 J.E. Pearson, 23, and Rollin Maddocks, 24, were approaching Crater Rock on Saturday night, roped together and climbing over glare ice. One slipped, causing the two to slide about 700 feet before arresting with their ice axes. They suffered bruises and frozen fingers.

The two started back up, laboriously cutting steps in the ice, and reached the crater about 7:30 p.m. as darkness was falling. They spent the night in comfort, enjoying the heat of the fumaroles and huddling under a blanket. Overhead, a high wind howled in the cliffs and rolled an occasional rock.

Their attempt had been witnessed by Judge Fred Stadter, leader of a Mazama party that had turned back because of bad weather conditions. On Sunday he became concerned about the two men and came back up to Government Camp from Mazama Lodge down below Laurel Hill. No word had been heard by 4:00 p.m. Sunday, so he sounded the alarm that they were missing. They came back through Government Camp at 6:00 p.m., but no one saw them, and a search was made on Monday, until it was found they had already gone home.

VANDA YORK WEDGED IN CREVASSE

Friday, September 10, 1926 Vanda M. York, a Portland girl, arrived in Hood River with the intent of hiking to Government Camp. She reached Parkdale that night, and on Saturday morning had advanced to Cooper Spur Junction.

Curiosity caused her to take a little side trip to J.O. Hannum's Homestead Inn, where the conversation led her to become very interested in climbing Mount Hood. The Hannums discouraged her, telling her that she was not properly outfitted, but she met Mark Weygandt later in the day, and he offered to guide her to the summit.

Herbert Gordon, a young man working at Tilly Jane Camp, wanted to go along, and on Sunday morning the three were ascending the Eliot Glacier on the way to the Sunshine Route. They were working up the last steep slope to the slopes above Langille Crags, Weygandt stopping often to cut steps with his ice axe. On such a pause, Miss York looked around to admire the scenery to the north and suddenly slipped!

They were not only unroped, but Weygandt did not even have a rope with him. The girl picked up speed on the slope. Gordon almost stopped her, then Weygandt took up the chase, almost grasping her as she crossed a crevasse. She stumbled and fell across the lower lip of the crevasse, resting on her chest and arms. Just as the guide thought he had her, she slipped backward and fell 60 feet into the chasm, wedging tightly between the narrowing walls.

The guide raced toward his rope cache, quickly bringing back a coil to the scene. He tied a loop in the end, dropping it to Miss York, and she was able to run it under her arms. Gordon and Weygandt pulled with all the strength they had, but the girl was so tightly wedged, that they could not budge her.

Weygandt knew that he must descend and cut her free, and just as he was considering the problems, he saw a party of climbers descending Cooper Spur. His shouts seemed to have no effect, as they went on their way; he was not aware that they had decided to hurry down for help. Instructing Gordon on handling of the rope, he then climbed down into the crevasse on belay, hoping that the 140-pound boy would be able to hold him on belay.

Before he could reach the girl, the crevasse had become too narrow, and he was forced to chop his way to her, severely impaired in striking good blows at the ice, because of the constriction of the walls. Already the cold had numbed her to unconsciousness, and she was breathing in a very shallow manner. Once he chopped his way close to her, he was able to throw his coat over her to protect her from the falling chips of ice.

Chopping around her body was especially difficult, but he finally saw her form sag toward him. He knew she was at last free! He then signalled to Gordon for a belay and climbed back to the surface of the glacier, chopping steps here and there to stem up the walls of ice. Once more on top, he pulled the girl upward with Gordon's help. The girl outweighed either one of them, and it was a severely difficult pull. Today's glacier rescue techniques were not known at that time.

They wrapped her in coats and succeeded in bringing her back to consciousness. Finally they got her on her feet, and on finding that she had no serious injuries, began walking her slowly down across Eliot Glacier.

Meanwhile the group descending Cooper Spur had brought word to Homestead Inn of the problem. Crag Rats Kent Shoemaker, A.L. Anderson, Harold Davis, and C.V. Jackson were at work brushing out the new ski hill there, and left immediately for Cloud Cap Inn with a timber axe, stove poker, first aid kit, rope, splints, and hot coffee. A call to Don Lamson in Hood River alerted the rest of the Crag Rat organization.

By the time the four reached the glacier, Weygandt and Gordon had walked Miss York down to the edge of the moraine. The Crag Rats then took over, Anderson giving her wool socks and warm shoes, as well as massaging her to increase circulation of blood. By the time they had reached Cloud Cap Inn, Lamson had arrived from Hood River with over 20 Crag Rats.

They took her in an automobile to Homestead

Inn. Miss York had no serious aftermath, only badly swollen hands and feet. On Tuesday Weygandt took her down to catch the train at Hood River, the girl expressing determination to return the following year to complete her climb.

BROWNLEE NEVER FOUND

1927 "Somewhere down there is Brownlee?" How many have asked that question after the fruitless search of New Year 1927? Leslie Brownlee, 21, and Al Feyerabend, his school friend, sought the distinction of being first on the summit in 1927. They left Battle Axe Inn on Friday, December 31, 1926, equipped to the teeth with snowshoes, heavy parkas, flashlights, compass, and hot food in thermal bottles. Skies were overcast, and weather at Government Camp was above freezing. At Timberline Cabin they rested an hour and stepped out at 1:30 a.m. into the beginning of a blizzard.

At 4:00 a.m. they could still see the lights of Portland, but by 5:00 the storm began to dump snow upon them. At 6:00 they were drowsy and lay down to sleep, awakening cold and stiff. With visibility poor, they followed the edge of White River Glacier, expecting to hit the slopes that fall steeply from Crater Rock. Soon they veered west, then tried a compass course due north.

Brownlee showed signs of exhaustion. Feyerabend in his exhuberance failed to realize that there was the last chance to run for their lives. Brownlee turned back with the compass on a course to take him to the timberline area and Government Camp. Feyerabend foolishly continued upward, pride and fear of ridicule being more important than the sense of preservation. He soon gave up and faced the problem of wading through the soft snow, as the howling wind bit his face.

A momentary lift in the clouds showed him later that he was close to the great, dark walls of Mississippi Head, and that he had drifted west, just as so many climbers have done, while descending from Crater Rock in storms. Veering left to the east, he correctly hit the cabin at timberline and was told that four young men had just left for Government Camp. It was natural to assume that one was Brownlee, so it was only after descending to the comfort of Battle Axe Inn, that he found his climbing partner was missing!

A massive search was begun. Loggers and timbermen, Portland police, sheriff deputies from four counties, climbing club members, and many interested onlookers converged at Government Camp to help in the search. Ray Conway, one of the old experts on searches and mountaineering, rose from his sickbed to take charge of the operation at Timberline Cabin. The Forest Service managed to run a telephone line in to the cabin for contact with general headquarters at Battle Axe under the command of L.A. Nelson of The Mazamas. The mountain was combed in planned grids, no possible area being ignored.

The old Timberline cabin pulsed with activity as tired searchers came in to hang clothes to dry and crawl into a bunk as soon as one became empty. Soup and coffee simmered on the battered stove. At Battle Axe the owner, Everett Sickler had to abandon business as all effort turned to the search. Dripping garments hung around the big lobby on the antlers of deer and moose heads, from Indian artifacts and pioneer relics that decorated the wall. Men gaunt from lack of sleep, slumped in chairs or lay on the floor, getting any rest they found possible. A fund to buy food was raised by the Portland Advertising Club.

All too few skis and skiers were available. Most of the search was done on snowshoes through the heavy, wet snow. A probe was sent out to White River Bridge, ten miles from Government Camp on the highway, but snowed in thoroughly on the unplowed loop. After a week Nelson and Conway held a conference with the other leaders who included virtually every man with mountain experience in the northwest, including the guides Coalman and Mark Weygandt. Mazama and Crag Rat leaders all turned out. But they decided that Brownlee could not be found. For years hikers and climbers probed obscure niches on the south side of Mount Hood looking for his body.

HAPPY ENDING FOR WHITE

The Brownlee search was compounded by another that was carried on simultaneously for Calvin White, Jr., 16, a skier who went astray. On the afternoon of New Year's Eve he walked up toward timberline on skis in a group of five boys. Becoming tired, White and two others decided to return to Government Camp. His skis were faster, better waxed, than the others, and he disappeared down the trail ahead of them. When his two friends arrived below, they realized he was missing, and the search was on.

White was thinly clad, had no food with him. The only thing in his favor was that he had started from below timberline, but no trace of him was found all day Saturday and Sunday. On Monday morning Bill Lenz and Dick Scott found faint ski tracks on the west side of Little Zigzag River. About the same time tracks were found on the east side of the same canyon by Kent Shoemaker, William Hukari, and Paul Horlein, all Crag Rats. Since the tracks disappeared, they relayed the information to Conway's headquarters.

Crag Rats William Cochran and John Annala had arrived at Battle Axe Inn at 4:00 a.m. to join the search. On reaching timberline, they were directed toward the recently-found clues. Working on the two opposite sides of Little Zigzag Canyon, they soon had success when Cochran found tracks, then a bed of fir boughs, where White had slept. The footsteps of a stumbling man told Cochran that he must be close. A few shouts brought back a weak response from the boy, who was too weak and cold to move.

Cochran took his own clothing and changed it from the soggy, freezing clothing of White. A drink of warm water gave him some warmth. Two signal shots from Cochran's revolver brought the others hurrying, and a messenger was sent to Battle Axe with the good news. They took him out, first on a sled improvised from skis, then on a toboggan, and finally on a dog sled pulled by a team of dogs and owned by Alaskan explorer, Earl Hammond. White's father, a doctor, lined the sled with hot water bottles.

Government Camp seethed with excitement as the community waited anxiously for the return of the dog sled and the victim found. Hundreds of sightseers and local residents gathered around the hotels. Flares were lighted up on the trail to guide the rescuers in. Newsmen and motion picture crews waited for the arrival. Finally, they could hear dogs barking, and soon the team of excited Huskies flashed by Battle Axe, Hammond braking hard to stop the sled. There were tears in the crowd as they watched the grateful Dr. White greet his haggard son.

Mrs. Brownlee, whose son was also being sought, was a trained nurse. She helped Dr. White in the battle to save Calvin's life. He was taken to Portland the next day. His only serious complication was the loss of two toes from freezing.

Although the massive Brownlee search had been called off after a week, the hunt never did end completely. On January 8, Mark Weygandt and Bill Lenz cut steps in 2000 feet of ice to reach the summit. The cabin was covered with eight feet of ice. Lenz froze a finger on the climb and lost it. Lenz searched again for Brownlee in April as the snow began to melt. On August 26, Ray Conway and L.A. Nelson combed the mountainside with 78 men. Crag Rats, Mazamas, the Trails Club, Knights of Columbus, and the Multnomah Anglers' and Hunters' Association searched every rock and bush and gully on a carefully-planned grid. There was no result. Brownlee's body probably lies at the bottom of a crevasse.

DR. STRYKER KILLED

1927 The Mazama Annual Climb of Mount Hood was under way on July 17, a beautiful, clear Sunday. Early climbers could be seen walking on the summit ridge, as the party of 103 was led across Eliot Glacier by the club president Judge Fred Stadter on the way up Sunshine Route. This was the first time The Mazamas had ever undertaken Sunshine, and they proceeded across the unbroken middle shelf of the glacier unroped.

Suddenly above, a serac, as large as a small office building, collapsed directly above them. Don Onthank remembers well the instant terror that ensued, with the thought of the party being buried under tons of ice blocks. Fortunately one unseen crevasse lay between the party and the serac, which smashed to bits there with a thunderous roar.

Soon after, they approached the Coe Glacier and began to rope up. Harry Krebs was leading 10 climbers on the third rope and gave the call for his team to tie in. Onthank had been walking a little behind, chatting with friends, and upon reaching the rope, he found that only about four feet was left for him at the rear. Since this was insufficient for tying around his waist, he merely tied a loop in the end and held on. At that time it was customary to tie large groups together.

As they traversed up the snowfields near Horseshoe Rock, someone up in the center of the rope slipped, pulling others down. Krebs tried to arrest with his ice axe, then and later, but the initial pull was too strong, and the whole string slid out of control. Onthank suddenly found himself standing there by himself; the rope had been pulled from his hand. Some of the climbers were novices, completely untrained. During the first few seconds several lost their alpenstocks, and the rest were vainly trying to arrest the slide. For about 600 feet the group engaged in crack-the-whip, as first one person, then another, would succeed in partially halting the fall, only to be pulled out of position. Rope leader Krebs almost had it stopped at first. Mary Malloy, W.H. Harris, and Krebs thought they had it stopped at one time, until the weight of falling bodies on the line gave them a hard jerk.

The whole group became a whirling ball of humanity as they approached the end of the 600-foot uncontrolled slide. With screams of terror they dropped over the lip of the bergschrund, falling 30 feet onto soft snow on the lower lip. Their rate of speed fortunately carried them far enough to avoid a direct drop into the crevasse.

Clem Blakney and Perlee G. Payton had been assisting the climb, ascending unroped. The two, quickly followed by Don Onthank and many of the other climb leaders, immediately descended the steep snow to rescue the victims. Blakney pulled Mary Malloy out first, her right ankle broken and chest injured. Then they saw Dr. Stanton Stryker lying there, impaled through the chest with an alpenstock. They pulled it from him and slowed the loss of blood with snow. Stryker was conscious and concerned about the condition of the others. When they asked him if he had any last words, he replied that his affairs were in order; he was at peace with the world.

W.H. Harris rose by himself, nauseated by the shock of a mashed nose, but he was able to help the others. Lieutenant-Colonel Lewis Forester suffered minor injuries. Gerald Moore had head injuries and was irrational. E.M. Bergen fractured both collarbones, had face injury, and was irrational. Gipsy Johnston, a novice, was badly bruised and suffered severe shock. Harry Krebs was injured in chest and abdomen. Miss Elsie Shanahan was able to walk away by herself.

A group of Crag Rats was setting up a course for a summer ski tournament down below on the Eliot Glacier. Others came at once from Cloud

Cap. The accident had been detected at once, because someone had been people-watching from the inn in the ever-popular pastime of following mountainside activity through the telescope. Mazamas made stretchers from alpenstocks and coats and packs. Two small sleds were being carried up to use on the south side descent; they were of good use.

The presence of the Crag Rat groups on the north side that day was a very fortunate situation, because they took over most of the problem of evacuation, across the glacier and down the morainal slopes to Cloud Cap Inn.

Portland doctor C.L. Booth was nearby and quickly saw that Sryker's condition was hopeless. After a half mile of descent the Portland dentist died, the second person to die on Mount Hood from a climbing accident. Dr. C.R. Abraham of Hood River hurried to the mountain with nurses, medication, and stretchers.

Meanwhile, many climbers stood stranded high on the slopes of the Sunshine Route, their leaders having gone below to assist. It was decided very wisely that it would be safer to take them up to the top and down the south side route as by original plan. So this group, mostly women, was shepherded over the top of the mountain by their leaders. Needless to say, the 4:00 p.m. victory dinner planned for the climbers at Government Camp that day was not held.

The shock of this terrible incident prompted a critique of the accident by the club. According to climbing standards of that day, all the normal safety precautions had been made. On today's standards, novices would not be taken on a route as hazardous as Sunshine Route, and climbers are normally limited to three or four on a rope. The climb leaders had conducted some pre-climb training in the handling of rope, alpenstocks, and how to walk on steep snow. Equipment was inspected before the climb started. It is only a miracle that some fatal accident had not overtaken some climbing party many years before.

It might be interesting to note that on that weekend *The Oregonian* reported that 350 people had reached the summit, and that the Mount Hood Loop Highway was jammed bumper-to-bumper with automobiles.

MEANEY BURNED ON SNOW SLIDE

Sunday, June 2, 1929 Clem Blakney, who had often guided on the south of Mount Hood, brought a group of about 40 boys from Grant High School up to the Cloud Cap area for a climb on Cooper Spur Route. It was necessary to hike in from near Homestead Inn, as the road was still under snowcover.

The group got off to a good start in the morning and reached Cooper Spur in good time. But a little higher up, they began to run into hard surfaces that made progress very slow. The group was not roped and had no protection until they reached the bottom end of the fixed line near Lunch Rock. As a result, the group moved very slowly, and it was 4:30 p.m. by the time they had conquered the mountain and had returned once more to Lunch Rock.

One of the boys was William Meaney. He had just let go of the fixed line and had begun to pick his way gingerly downward, when he slipped. Blakney helplessly watched Meaney sliding downward, trying vainly to stop by clawing at the snow with his fingers. At times, he was able to catch ahold a little, but it seemed that in each instance, he tended to veer a bit more to the left, toward the Eliot Glacier. Finally, the group watched in horror as Meaney slid faster and faster, finally disappearing over the headwall toward the glacier. This was the first in the history of 10 different parties to slide over the area, that was in later years jokingly called the Chisholm Trail.

Blakney was sure the boy must be dead. He had difficulty holding back some of the boys, who wanted to follow right down Meaney's track. He sent some of the group immediately to Cloud Cap Inn for help. Meanwhile, Blakney took another portion of the group around to reach the victim on the glacier. When they found him, he was dreadfully burned, his face, head, hands, and arms literally cooked from the frictional heat on the long snow slide. Although unconscious, he was obviously alive.

The messengers reached Cloud Cap Inn in a short while. By 5:30 p.m. the news was in the hands of Dr. J.W. Sifton, who gathered his emergency gear and headed for the mountain. Crag Rats A.L. (Andy) Anderson, T.J. Annala, and Percy Bucklin were reached. They had just returned from some club social event.

Dr. Sifton reached the victim and advised Blakney on how to evacuate him. Then came the long carry to the road. They had reached Ghost Ridge below Cloud Cap, when Anderson, Annala, and Bucklin came up from below, bringing a stretcher. It was already late at night. Loading Meaney onto the stretcher, the group continued downward to the cars, which had been parked near Cooper Spur Junction.

At that point, they loaded him into a truck and rushed him down to the Hood River Hospital, reaching there about 4:00 a.m. The Crag Rats followed and watched over him at the hospital. Percy Bucklin recalls that his burns were extremely severe, and that he smelled like roast pork. The next day, Meaney had still not regained consciousness. Following issues of the *Hood River News* did not mention him again, so it is presumed that he recovered.

MOE DISAPPEARED INTO CREVASSE

July, 1930 While the American Legion climb was being made on Cooper Spur Route, and Hood River Ski Club was conducting a race on Eliot Glacier, another group of Crag Rats were busy on the glacier, shooting a moving picture of a simulated fall and retrieval from a crevasse. When the work was all done, the equipment was packed up ready for the descent, when someone missed Roger Moe, editor of the *Glacier*, a Hood River newspaper.

Someone saw a small hole in the snow, and upon approaching it carefully, they saw Moe 14 feet down in a hidden crevasse. He was braced against the ice, feet on one wall, and back on the other. Luckily for him, the snow bridge, which had collapsed under him, had jammed in the narrowing walls of ice and had held him temporarily. Otherwise, he might have fallen a long way to his destruction.

Crag Rats dropped him the end of a climbing rope and soon had him pulled back to the surface. The only damage was the loss of two pair of glasses by Moe.

GIRL CRUSHED UNDER HORSE

Monday, July 28, 1930 R.H. Springer and his daughter, Susana Springer, 24, came to Cloud Cap Inn from their home in Los Angeles for a vacation. They arrived on Sunday afternoon. Susana became interested in taking a horseback trip to Eden Park with licensed guide Gilbert Edgington. After lunch, she left for the trip with Edgington, he riding his horse ahead of her.

On crossing the narrow bridge across Eliot Creek, her horse suddenly shied from something, causing it to slip off the bridge. Edgington made a routine glance backward and saw the horse floundering in the bed of the turbulent glacial stream. **Miss Springer was missing!** He raced his horse back to Cloud Cap Inn for help, soon returning with Howard Fordyce and Mark Weygandt and Mark's two sons, Wesley and Myron.

Mark Weygandt went immediately down to Stranahan Falls (now labelled Wallalute) to work back upstream. However, Myron Weygandt soon found Miss Springer's body lodged against a boulder, only about 40 feet below the bridge. Her skull had been crushed, where the horse had fallen on her. At first they thought she had drowned, and resuscitation was considered, until they realized that she was dead from the sudden blow. Oddly enough, the horse got to its feet and was able to walk back to the stable on its own.

CALLICOTTE BROKE LEG

Monday, September 22, 1930 Paul Callicotte, climber of note, fell on the Chute on South Side Route and broke his leg. A rescue was not effected until the following morning. Callicotte had been the first on top Mount Hood in 1930, and in July had set a time record for a round trip from Portland to climb Mount Hood.

GULLICKSON KILLED IN FALL

Tuesday, July 5, 1932 Glen Gullickson, of college age, was the last of three men descending the Chute on South Side Route at about 7:30 a.m. The slope was still in the shadow of the cliffs and very icy. The usual fixed rope had not yet been hung in the Chute for the year.

He slipped on hard ice, lost his alpenstock, and tumbled and bounced 800 feet to the bottom, where he fell free about 75 feet to the bottom of a depression. Fortunately, he did not strike the other two as he slid past, because he undoubtedly would have knocked them downward also.

They descended to find him unconscious and bleeding. One of his companions, Wayne Aden, went down to Government Camp, arriving about noon. The other, Gordon Nugent, stayed there with the victim.

At Government Camp Hotel, Perlee Payton, Mazama leader and guide, organized a rescue group at once. MHNF Supervisor, Tom Sherrard, assigned Chester Jones and Carl Hendrickson of Zigzag Ranger Station to the job. In addition there were Vincent Rafferty, Charles Newell, and Everett Morrison.

A storm of the previous day had plastered the mountainside with ice, so that it took the party until 8:00 p.m. to reach Gullickson. They found him dead, with a large wound in the back of his head and a possible broken neck. Bloody foam could be seen around his lips. Bringing the body down the ice-sheathed slopes was difficult, and Payton's group moved slowly. Observers below watched the pinpoints of light as they chopped steps and belayed. They reached Government Camp at 1:25 a.m.

Aden and Nugent said that Gullickson probably slipped because of weakness in one leg, caused by a previous injury in cutting the tendons in his leg with an axe at the Spirit Lake YMCA camp. He had complained about it before starting and remarked that he probably would not have climbed, if Aden and Nugent had known the way. He had previously climbed Mount Hood and Mount St. Helens.

TOWING A SLED PROVED DANGEROUS

Sunday, December 25, 1932 Two boys from Portland were spending Christmas Day at Government Camp, Earl Moore and Bob Meadows. They were riding on a sled near Calverley's at Summit, being towed behind an automobile.

Roger Jensen, the driver of the car, lost control and crashed into a snowbank on the edge of the highway. The sled held its momentum and ran under the car, cutting and battering both boys around the head and shoulders.

They were brought down to Rafferty's Government Camp Hotel for first aid, where Moore came to life quickly. Meadows did not regain consciousness, and he was sent to Portland in an ambulance.

DARR & MORRIS ON YO-YO SLIDE

About 1933 Everett Darr tells the story of an uncontrolled slide on Cooper Spur Route with his climbing companion, Cecil Morris. The two had passed the Chimney on their descent on hard snow, when Morris slipped.

The snow was so hard that Darr could not get

his axe into the snow more than six inches. Morris tried in vain to arrest, but hit the end of the climbing rope and pulled Darr out of belay position. Fortunately, Darr's belay had stopped Morris, and he was able to set a belay as Darr slid lownward. Then, as Darr hit the end of the rope, he pulled Morris out of position, but he was able to set another belay himself. This procedure continued on down the mountain for several rope lengths, first one losing control, then the other.

However, the speed picked up, and the danger grew a little greater each time. It seemed inevitable that they would fall over the north side onto the Eliot Glacier. Finally, Darr saw a crevasse ahead. He decided that no matter how deep it might be, he must drop into it, to arrest their slide. He managed to do so, dropping only about 12 feet to a resting place. Seconds later he saw Morris flying through the air over the top of the crevasse. When Morris hit the end of the rope, the strain did not break the rope, but the sudden snap of the rope was very punishing on their waists.

ESTHER GILMAN BROKE LEG

1933 It was Labor Day weekend, the same one when Don Burkhart was killed on Mount Jefferson. On Mount Hood, Ray Lewis, the summit lookout was spending a quiet Sunday watching Mark and Wes Weygandt bringing up a party over Sunshine Route. Straggling climbers were also visible on the South Side Route.

Harold E. Bangs, his father, Harold W. Bangs, and Albert Wolfe walked up the South Side into the crater. The two older men turned back and young Bangs continued his ascent of the mountain, intending to spend the night in the summit cabin. The fixed rope was iced in partially, but Bangs made it up although he wore only slick-soled shoes. Borrowing crampons from Summit guard Ray Lewis, he returned to the bottom of the chute for a second load of his equipment. Later another lone climber came up; no one can now recall who.

As the sun lowered to the horizon a climber came up from the Weygandt party with bad news. Lewis had suspected something was wrong, because the group should have reached the summit much earlier. While bypassing the bergschrund at the top of Coe Glacier, someone had stepped through the end of a blind crevasse, and the rear three members of the party fell in, Mike Thomas, Eugene Meckley, and Miss Esther Gilman. The rope sawed over rough ice and broke. The two men were able to crawl out, but Miss Gilman broke a leg between knee and ankle.

With only a half mile in distance and 1000 feet in elevation to go, Weygandt elected to try to reach the summit, rather than to try to retrace the route down over hard-frozen slopes broken by many crevasses. The sky was clouded, and a cold wind was increasing. Lewis hurried out over the north side route and saw the party struggling upward, just above Queen's Chair, Mark Weygandt belaying, and his son Wes and Mike Thomas carrying the victim. Returning to the cabin, he, with the assistance of Bangs and the unknown climber, carried out the 1000 feet of fixed rope that had just been pulled off Cooper Spur Route and stored in the summit cabin. With the aid of this long line, they were able to speed the rescue, which was by that time being made in the darkness. The party reached the summit about 10:30 p.m.

Bangs had a first aid card, and he splintered Esther Gilman's leg. The ensuing night was an ordeal. Miss Gilman and another girl occupied the bed; the 11 men fitted themselves in the cupola, on the floor, anywhere they could find in the 12' x 12' cabin. A storm raged all night, plastering the south and west sides of the building with ice, wind moaning in the guy wires.

In the morning about 9:00 a.m. the girl was wrapped in canvas and blankets and lowered down the chute on the south side. At Crater Rock they placed her on the Wy'east toboggan and made much faster time to Phlox Point, where a Forest Service truck waited. The whole party was accommodated free of charge. at Mount Hood Hotel, just six weeks before it burned to the ground.

The failure to appear back at Cloud Cap Inn by the experienced guide, Weygandt, touched off serious fears in the Hood River Valley. The Crag Rats were planning a full-scale search by the time they received news that his group was safe at Government Camp.

The following day, three men went back up the mountain with the toboggan, Ray Lewis, Harold Bangs, and Gary Leech, the climbing fan of Government Camp who ascended Mount Hood at the least excuse, or lack of excuse. Weather appeared bad, so they tied the toboggan firmly to a rock at Triangle Moraine and went on up to the top.

The next day they untied and recoiled the rope they had dropped down for the rescue party two days before. Then Lewis descended the chute on the south side and untied the bottom of the fixed rope. Leech and Bangs pulled it and coiled it. When the ropes were stored and the windows shuttered, Lewis took some personal items and closed the cabin for the year of 1933. It turned out that it was forever; the cabin on the summit was never manned again.

The three men started down the icy chute, now difficult without the fixed rope. Lewis had crampons and did very well. Soon Bangs and Leech were calling down to him to come back to help, if he wanted to get his equipment off the mountain.

The accident of Miss Gilman had an unusually happy ending. She later married Wes Weygandt, becoming Mark's daughter-in-law.

MONOXIDE KILLED NEWELL

Winter of 1933-4 Charles H. Newell, in his thirties, died from carbon monoxide poisoning from a small engine in the service station at Government Camp Hotel. He was found in the wintertime tunnel to the station.

Newell had been very well-known at Government Camp as the cheerful handyman, always singing as he worked. He worked at the gasoline station and rented skis at times, but residents were accustomed to call him to thaw water pipes or do mechanical jobs. He had been involved in several trips onto the mountain to search for lost skiers or to help evacuate rescue victims. Born in New England, he had roved considerably before settling at Government Camp.

DEATH OF VICTOR VonNORMAN

August 27, 1934 Having completed a successful ascent of Mount Hood, Victor VonNorman, a member of a group of University of Washington students, entered the fumarole moat alongside Crater Rock, just as so many others had done. This time it resulted in his death in a very short time. A detailed story is included in the chapter *Deadly Fumaroles, Always Intriguing.*

PAIR INJURED ON CHUTE

Saturday, February 2, 1935 Joe Daniel, 20, and William Blanchard, 19, climbed to the new rock shelter at Crater Rock to spend the night before a Sunday ascent. Daniel was a photographer and wanted to get pictures of a solar eclipse in early morning. On Sunday morning they went on up to the summit and spent considerable time taking the pictures and looking around.

It was 10:00 a.m. by the time they were part way down, when ice and rocks from above plummeted down behind them. A rock struck Blanchard in the back, knocking both off into an uncontrolled slide, that took them below the Hot Rocks on the west side of the Hogsback.

Ole Lien and Maxine Faircourt had left Timberline Lodge at 5:00 a.m. that morning, and had just reached Crater Rock, when they saw the pair fall. Lien hurried to the top of the Hogsback, just in time to meet Daniel coming upward with severe cuts and abrasions all over his body. Blanchard lay below, not moving. Mrs. Faircourt and Lien hurried to him and found that he had suffered fractured ribs, a broken left elbow, internal injury, and a good many lacerations and bruises. Lien was a member of the highly trained Wy'east team, and Mrs. Faircourt was a nurse, so plenty of first aid expertise was available.

Charles Anderson and Ed Aho, two other climbers, also soon reached the scene, and Lien went to the stone shelter for the Wy'east toboggan. The toboggan was not in the best of repair, but they loaded Blanchard aboard and started downward. It was after dark by the time they reached Timberline Cabin, where they rested a while. The trip down to Government Camp took until almost midnight.

Meanwhile another emergency situation had developed during the afternoon. Lester Smith had gone skiing to timberline with three other men. Donald Youmans, Harold Johnson, and Charles Tracy. They had descended Sand Canyon a way, then climbed out. Seeing Smith behind with other skiers, they decided to forge ahead to Government Camp, although Smith was a novice skier. Soon after, Smith slipped on ice and injured his ankle, finding himself all alone. Fortunately he was able to build a fire and have some comfort in the winter night.

As the Blanchard-Daniel rescue party proceeded downward from Timberline Cabin, Ole Lien repeatedly blew a high-pitched whistle, which he usually carried. He hoped that he might intercept some other rescue party who might be looking for them. As it happened, the injured skier, Smith, heard the whistle from his position over to the west in Sand Canyon.

When Lien arrived at Government Camp, the community was in an uproar, as a search party was being formed to search for Smith. Thorlief Reid, the caretaker at Cascade Ski Club, and his friend, Red Hoaglund, were ready to go up the trail on their skis.

With some clues from Smith's skiing friends,

The stone shelter in the crater did not last long.
Photo Joe Leuthold

they soon found him and had him back to Government Camp before daylight. Meanwhile Charles Anderson of the first rescue group had taken Blanchard and Daniel in to a hospital in Portland in his automobile.

HOWELL KILLED IN SKI JUMP

December 19, 1936 Victor Howell, a prominent member of the Hood River Ski Club, was making a landing on Jump Hill at the Cooper Spur Ski Area. He hit a stump, bounced off to strike the square-sawed edge of another. His chest was crushed, the blow killing him instantly. He was an older brother of George Howell.

WY'EASTERS SLIPPED OFF SPUR

1937 On a June 27 climb, Wy'easters Ralph Calkin and Henry Corbett ascended Sunshine Route with Elsie Hall and Jeanne Blake. Taking the usual descent on Cooper Spur Route, they encountered a foot and a half of new snow on the steep slopes. A warm day had accentuated avalanche danger, but they made their way safely down to a point just below the rock chimneys.

At that point an avalanche developed. The two men tried desperately to anchor in the firm snow below the loose covering, but they could not hold. The party picked up speed in a 2,000-foot ride down to Eliot Glacier, falling the last 75 feet in vertical drop. Loose snow had preceded them and piled up a great cushion. Calkin and Corbett had suffered severe burns on arms and hands, trying to arrest the fall. Jeanne Blake was able to walk away on her own, and Elsie Hall had to be carried off the Glacier. The party lost three of their ice axes.

Lee Darling and Roy Varney were bringing a climb of 11 Mazamas behind the unfortunate group. They descended Cooper Spur Route and went down the moraine onto the glacier to help in the rescue.

DEATH OF VARNEY AND GUEFFROY

1938 On Sunday, March 27, a party of Mazamas left Timberline Lodge at 1:00 a.m. for the first winter climb the club had ever scheduled. The climb of 20 was headed by co-leaders Joe Leuthold and William Wood. They had come up to Timberline in a bus from Mazama Lodge. Weather was clear and cold with a breakable crust on the snow. Four of the party were on snowshoes, the rest on skis.

At Triangle Moraine they left their skis and headed for the summit. Weather was moderately pleasant as they tied into two ropes to ascend the chute. Leuthold took his string up first, and as he neared the top, a sleet storm hit the group. The second string did not even start the chute, merely turned around and headed down the mountain. Although only 50 feet from the summit ridge, Leuthold turned the party around. Ice was freezing on their glasses, and a fierce wind drove ice particles into their faces.

Roy Varney, a strong climber and the chairman of the Climbing Committee of The Mazamas, began to fail at Crater Rock. It was later surmised by physicians that he suffered a stroke or heart attack. Although he had not completely recovered from a case of influenza, he was wearing only a cotton work shirt, certainly not sufficient clothing for such an ascent. Dorothy Clark suffering mountain sickness herself recalls lagging back to help him and the last remark that she can remember him saying.

"My God, Dorothy, I can't see." he told her, as she helped him along. Co-leader William Wood and Russell Gueffroy finally took over, and Dorothy pressed on down to Triangle Moraine, where Leuthold was consolidating the string of ten. Gueffroy descended to them and told Leuthold that Wood was proceeding slowly with Varney. At that point Leuthold sent Clyde Hildreth and Max Gatewood back up to assist with Varney, who was stumbling and falling. The first string of climbers complained about the cold and begged to go, so Leuthold sent the rest on down toward the safety of Timberline and started out for a fast trip down on skis, himself.

Leuthold wanted to get to Timberline to use the Snow-Cat to evacuate Varney, but when he got there the keys were gone, probably in the pocket of an operator who had left for town. Efforts to get another set were unfruitful, and Joe Leuthold finally ended up as a first aid case himself in the hands of Ralph Wiese, Ski Patrol First Aid Chief, exhausted from his ordeal on the mountain.

Meanwhile, William Wood, Max Gatewood, and Clyde Hildreth had lashed the incapacitated Roy Varney to a pair of skis. Their progress on foot, struggling through the breakable crust, was very slow. Dorothy Clark, who had left her skis at Triangle Moraine and was walking down, remembers the violent, cold wind. It picked up ice crystals on the surface and hurled them at her face and hands, even infiltrating the inside of her jacket with ice. Gatewood and Hildreth came to the end of their endurance a quarter mile above Lone Fir Lookout. They struck out for Timberline Lodge for self preservation, leaving Wood huddled with Varney. Wood lasted only a few minutes, and left Varney alone. The three straggled into the lodge in falling snow that had cut visibility. They had barely saved their own lives, suffering from exhaustion and exposure to the cold.

District Ranger Harold Engles was watching the situation with intense interest at the lodge. When Hildreth and Gatewood came in with the news about Varney, he quickly took Max Becker and Henry Corbett with him on skis to find him. Engles told Ski Patrol Chief Hank Lewis to stay on patrol work. By 4:30 the storm had closed in severely, dumping much new snow on the breakable crust. Telling Ralph Wiese to take over for him, Lewis left shortly afterward by himself to overtake the Engles party. Visibility ranged about 5 feet; horizontally driving snow made it impossible to tell which way was up.

Lewis groped his way to Lone Fir and with considerable yelling located the Engles party, who had by that time reached the unconscious Varney. Engles had taken two axe handles and wire to lash his and Hank's specially-drilled skis into a toboggan. Then came the nightmare of pulling Varney back to the lodge, a four hour job to descend a mile and a quarter. At one point they fell down a very steep slope, possibly Salmon River Canyon, and had to climb back out again. Then their path brought them down the ridge above the lodge, where for many years lay the Otto Lang Ski Tow.

Finally, the onlookers inside the lodge detected their lights up on the hill. A group charged out into the night to help pull the toboggan down, Ted Coomara, Merritt Cookingham, James Green, Jack Stockman, N.A. Norene, and William Bookmire.

Ralph Wiese worked tirelessly with Varney, giving him artificial respiration long after anyone really had any hope. A physician from Gresham finally arrived by Grayline limousine, which stalled in the heavy snow a mile from the lodge. The doctor walked the last bit holding on to the driver's belt. When he entered, he pronounced Varney dead, despite the efforts of Wiese and the use of a resuscitator from the Gresham Fire Department. The heartsick climbing companions and the searchers made their way back to Portland as road conditions would permit.

The following day someone noticed a car on the highway below Mazama Lodge near Government Camp. It was the automobile of Russell Gueffroy, and a check in Vancouver showed that the Trails Club member had not returned to his home. The search was on once more!

On Monday night the telephone lines in Portland were pulsing with the calls that asked searchers to come to Mount Hood. Hank Lewis was asked to head the operation in the field. On Tuesday morning he, Leuthold, Bill Hackett, Russ McJury, and Ray Lewis drove to Timberline, where Ranger Engles had Boyd Rasmussen, Max Becker, and Boyd French ready to go. Gary Leach came up from Government Camp, and veteran search director Ray Conway came to the lodge to lend his expertise. Conway arranged with the lodge for the feeding of the search crews.

The bad weather persisted, and only Boyd French was permitted to be out alone. Leach and Ray Lewis went to White River, with Hank Lewis, Max Becker, and Al Cohn working another section of the same canyon. Ted Coomara and James Green were sent up past Lone Fir. Harry Johnson and Jack Ferrell looked in Salmon River Canyon.

On Wednesday a human chain was formed with men spaced about 100 feet apart, a group that stretched from Timberline Lodge up the mountain past Lone Fir. Starting east of the lodge, they carefully scanned the mountain side, moving west. With this system they found Gueffroy's skis standing in the snow between Sand Canyon and Little Zigzag Canyon. The moving line was then deployed in a horizontal line sweeping down the slope, but darkness halted operations quickly. As they trooped toward the lodge that night, someone noticed a pattern in the newly fallen snow, a series of dimples that were visible only in the oblique rays of sunset.

Turning a ski pole upside down, they found that under the dimples the crust 18 inches under the new snow had been broken. **Digging down, they found tracks!** Thursday morning they returned early to Sand Canyon to probe the slopes carefully with inverted ski poles. On detecting the broken crust, they cleared away the snow with shovels. A course was established that took them down far into Sand Canyon where it is deep and V-shaped. Russ McJury detected Gueffroy's ski pole, then his pack. One wrist had been broken. They deduced from his position on the crusted base, that he sat down for his fatal sleep not much later than 4:30 p.m. Sunday, the time when the blizzard closed in.

Gueffroy had been known as somewhat of a loner, often skiing away from his group unannounced to cross a ridge or penetrate the forest. Trip-mates were accustomed to waiting for him to

Joe Leuthold in 1938 — Photo Leuthold

Lone Fir Lookout built 1933

arrive late on several occasions. He was knowledgeable of the terrain and a capable skier.

There was some criticism of the leadership of Wood and Leuthold in allowing the party to become segmented, especially by Otto Lang, the ski instructor at Timberline Lodge. This was picked up by *Time Magazine*. However, a full review of the problem reflected the opinion that their decisions actually saved lives. If the full party had been held together to come all the way down with Varney, there would probably have been some who would have perished from hypothermia. Several of the climbers asked permission to proceed by themselves, and permission was granted.

Clothing of that era was not as effective as that of today. Winter climbing parties now are expected to be much better clothed and equipped. Varney was remiss in climbing with insufficient clothing and in venturing onto the mountain while recuperating from illness. In so doing, he exposed the rest of the party to additional hazard and exposure.

Two other disturbing facets of the Varney-Gueffroy incident come from a reliable, but confidential source, not to be disclosed until a later time. One is that a member of the party assured Joe Leuthold and William Wood on Sunday night that all members of the party had been accounted for, the reason that Gueffroy was not missed until later. The other was that Roy Varney was said to have climbed Mount Hood on the day previous to the Sunday ascent to prove his ability, and that this was in spite of the fact that he was under recovery from respiratory ailment.

NELSON COLLAPSED AND DIED

Saturday, May 27, 1938 Milton Robert Nelson, 16, a student at Grant High School, collapsed and died on South Side Route, about 200 feet below the summit. Telore Abendroth, who was tied into the same rope with him, saw Nelson suddenly drop to the snow. By the time he reached him, there was no detectable pulse.

Abendroth started immediately for help at Timberline Lodge, leaving the other three members of the party to stand guard, Gordon Petrie, Jere Lord, and Stanley Greer. While enroute, Abendroth met two engineers from the lodge, Jack Linn and Duane Babcock, who started upward towards the victim. At the lodge Hank Lewis, Patrol Chief of MHSP, and Max Becker of the Forest Service were alerted and went up to the crater with a toboggan. By late afternoon they had brought the body back to the road.

SEATTLE BOY BENIGHTED

Friday, July 1, 1938 William Campbell, 19, of Seattle visited Timberline Lodge and began an ascent of South Side Route on skis. After proceeding a way, he decided the route was too easy and descended. That day he hitchhiked around the Loop Highway to Tilly Jane Camp on the north side.

At that point, he made friends with Donald Brent and another youth, and the three started up Eliot Glacier on Saturday morning. At the top of the glacier, he went ahead with his plan to ascend Sunshine Route as far as possible on skis, and his two acquaintances veered east to return to camp at Tilly Jane.

On that day, a Forest Service party had set a fixed line on South Side Route, and at 5:15 p.m. they saw Campbell ascending at about the 10,000 foot level, just below Horseshoe Rock. They yelled at him, and he answered that he was in no trouble.

On Sunday morning, Brent and his friend went over to Campbell's campsite at Tilly Jane, expecting to find him in his sleeping bag. They immediately notified the Forest Service of the problem. Across the ravine of Tilly Jane Creek at the Legion Camp, three Crag Rats were working on a cleanup detail, Percy Bucklin, Mace Baldwin, and his son Blanchar Baldwin. The time was 8:30 a.m., and they were off at once in search of the missing climber.

Campbell was high on the Eliot Glacier on the steep ice to the left (east) of Horseshoe Rock. He had become trapped by descending from one ice ledge to another, then finding his route cut off by a crevasse below. He did not have the equipment to ascend to the starting point, so he put in one very cold night on the glacier. Bucklin and the Baldwins were able to rescue him from his perch, and they carried him down to a spot near the Langille Glacier.

At that point, a Crag Rat group, who had responded to the Forest Service call for help, met them and took over the transport of the victim to Cloud Cap Inn. He was put to bed for a while, later taken to the hospital in Hood River for observation and treatment.

At Legion Camp after the rescue — Photo Mace Baldwin.
Percy Bucklin, William Campbell, Blanchar Baldwin, Mace Baldwin.

The second Crag Rat group consisted of W.T. Hukari, Arne Hukari, Robert Hukari, Gene Annala, Eino Annala, and Joshua Pierson. A bit of oral legend, handed down by the Crag Rats is that one of the Annala boys asked Campbell, "are you hungry?"

"Yes, I sure am!" he replied.

"Well, good," said the outspoken Annala. "We have plenty. You eat a lot, because when you finish, we are going to kick it all out of you." It is said that the victim was very subdued.

CALLICOTTE INJURED ANKLE

October 1, 1938 Paul Callicotte, writer and well-known climber, was benighted in the crater. The following day he was brought down to Government Camp with an ankle injury. This is believed to be his last appearance in the news of Mount Hood.

LINCOLN FELL INTO CREVASSE

July 31, 1939 Irving B. Lincoln, Portland realtor, was travelling on Eliot Glacier with other companions, when he fell about 50 feet into a crevasse. His party went for help. James DeYoung, forest guard at Tilly Jane organized a party and climbed to the glacier to rescue him. After he was pulled out he was able to walk back to Tilly Jane.

Lincoln had been well known for his photography and also for his solo trips on Mount Hood. He had been the first on top in 1935 on a solo ascent.

A DOUBLE HIT

1939 On Friday, August 11, Vera Hays was hit in the leg by falling rock while on a climb on Cooper Spur Route. Rescuers placed her on a stretcher, and while they were carrying her, she was struck in the head by another rock.

ROCKS HIT YOUNG BOYS

1939 Saturday, August 12, above Crater Rock, four boys in a party of 11 were injured by falling rock. The party of boys from the Multnomah Christian Church were led by El Rey Parrish and Eldon Delashmutt. Rutherford Scott, 9, had a possible leg fracture. Bruises were suffered by Fred Scott, Eugene Starr, and Harold Gratten. Timberline guides, George Henderson and Boyd French helped carry Scott down to the road. The Forest Service recommended that no more climbing be done until snow might fall.

HERRMAN DIED FROM COLD

1940 Gerald (Spike) Herrmann, 28, of Milwaukie, and James (Jay) Lorentz, 19, of Oregon City, left Timberline Lodge for a summit climb at 1:45 a.m. on Sunday, March 31. That night they had not checked in with Dave Babcock. By 1:00 a.m. District Forester Harold Engles ordered a search for Monday morning.

Marshall Stenerson and Joe Leuthold of the Forest Service, Ralph Wiese of the ski patrol, Ralph Calkin, Herbert Rasor, James Simmons, William Wood, Andy Anderson, and Glen Asher divided into two groups to search above the ski lift. A group of skiers probed west to Little Zigzag Canyon, Harold and Al Haroun, Ralph Hadfield, Dean Stapleton, E.P. McKeen-Smith, Willis Caldwell, and Jack Brotherton. In another group, Barry James, Paul Livingston, and Ed Meyer pushed a sortie to White River Canyon. Meanwhile a foghorn on the Lodge and a 1000-watt searchlight at Silcox were used as possible help for the lost climbers.

Harold Engles led a climbing party to the summit. The lost pair had been there and entered "too cold to write," in the summit register. Engles was afraid that they had stumbled off the north side, but Hood River Crag Rats could find no trace of them there. On Monday night the barometer showed a new storm approaching.

On Tuesday, Ralph Wiese led Horace Mecklem Jr., William Hackett, Chester Wilde, and Thomas Hill on a ski trip on the east side to Cooper Spur. Crossing White River and contouring Newton Clark Glacier at the 9500-foot level, they returned to Timberline at 4:00 p.m. with no trace.

But Jack Nelson and John Pfieffer returned in the afternoon from Zigzag Canyon area with the news that their party had found tracks and intended to follow them, perhaps intending to stay out all night. Ole Lien was leading this group of Ralph Hadfield, Steward Mockford, and William Lanahan, and by 2:30 they were successful. In Paradise Park Lanahan came upon Jay Lorentz who collapsed as his rescuer came into sight. Well exposed to hypothermia, he was dazed and snowblind. At the Paradise shelter they gave him food and warmed him as well as possible. Hadfield and Mockford were sent at once to search headquarters at Timberline Lodge to tell them that Lorentz was found. Lorentz was taken down the trail to Twin Bridges for further treatment and transportation.

He told them he had left Herrmann below Crater Rock, too tired to go further. Lorentz shielded him from the wind with snowshoes and both their packs, then headed down for help. Herrmann later rose and started down. Both partners made the same common mistake of drifting too far west in low visibility. Russ McJury and Joe Leuthold finally saw his body from below through field glasses. He lay dead near the east side of Mississippi Head, frozen with head and hands bare.

A SEARCH FOR NOTHING

1940 On April 14, James Ballingall went skiing with Larry Pagter, Bob Phipps, and Donald Carney. Weather was bad so he spent the afternoon playing checkers with some fraternity brothers. His three car-mates reported him missing and moved their car. Unable to find them, he rode home with his checker adversaries.

The resulting search was conducted in blowing

fog and sleet. Joe Leuthold and Ray O'Brien skied down White River Canyon to the bridge and climbed many miles over the ridge to the plowed highway. Dean Stapleton and Al Haroun combed the upper slopes around the ski lift. Steve Treadway, Don McJury, Rod Mangold, and Bob Pickard swept the trails to Government Camp with no result. After risking their own lives that night in vile weather, they finally found that Ballingall was home in his own bed.

A HEAVY RESCUE

August 12, 1940 Grant Ennis, 15, a student at Roosevelt High School, was descending South Side Route in a party of eight. Leaving the Hogsback, the 205-pound boy was well ahead of the rest as he rounded the base of Crater Rock. He slipped on ice and tried desperately to stop with his alpenstock, but he slid off the White River Headwall, finally coming to rest in an island of rock far below.

His companions had seen the fall and ran down the mountain for help. They met Ed Nelson leading a party of Mazamas. Nelson and four others climbed down to Ennis and found him with his back injured. Making a stretcher from alpenstocks and clothing, they started the ponderous carry up to Palmer Glacier near the bottom of Triangle Moraine. The weight of Ennis made it a very difficult job.

Meanwhile another of Ennis's friends had gone below to report the accident to Boyd French, Jr., guard at Lone Fir. French and Max Becker of the Forest Service at Timberline ran for the snow-cat and drove it up as far as possible. When the rescue party came out of the White River Canyon with their victim, they still had three-quarters of a mile to carry him to reach the snow-cat.

SKIERS LOST IN SALMON RIVER

Sunday, January 26, 1941 Three skiers were reported missing in midafternoon, Mary Nyden, Ralph Schulstad, and John Larkin. A wide-spread search was launched by the Ski Patrol out of Timberline Lodge, where they had last been seen.

It was 3:00 a.m. on Monday morning, when they were located far down Salmon River on the Little Fork Trail by Marshall Stenerson, McKeen Smith, and Paul Livingston. Smith hiked a mile out to the highway for help, while the other two built a fire to warm the victims.

On Friday, January 31, three skiers, Atlee Schimelfenig, George Hilt, and Darwin Eagan, went down the Salmon River Canyon to get the skis left behind by Miss Nyden, Schulstad, and Larkin. At 6:15 p.m. they found the girl's skis and were still looking for the other two pair. By 7:15, they realized that night had overtaken them, and they decided to spend the night by the fire, which they built. At daylight they started out, reaching Summit Guard Station by 7:40 a.m. Saturday. The other skis were not recovered.

RESCUE IN WHITE RIVER

1942 Private Charles C. Porter, 36, a medical corpsman from Barnes Hospital in Vancouver, had a miraculous rescue from a crevasse in White River Glacier by Everett Darr and Harry Parker.

Porter had started out at midnight from Battle Axe Inn with R.H. Beagles of Newberg to climb Mount Hood by the South Side Route. He wore smooth-soled shoes, and had only an alpenstock, no crampons. By 5:00 a.m. the two climbers had separated, so Beagles continued to the top, even though Porter had his knapsack and alpenstock. Porter never did appear, so Beagles informed the guard at Lone Fir as he descended.

Word was sent to Summit Guard Station, and Darr and Parker were sent up immediately. On reaching the base of Crater Rock and finding no trace of Porter, they were considering a search of White River and looking over into its cracked surface when they heard a call for help.

They threaded their way through a maze of crevasses and got below the bergschrund to find Porter lying on his back on a snow ledge, 50 feet down in a crevasse. If he had not landed on the ledge, he would have gone much deeper, almost surely to his death. Parker left for Lone Fir to get additional help, and Darr stood by.

James Langdon, Ranger at Zigzag, organized a party of experienced mountaineers, Lou Norene, Ole Lien, and Glen Asher. They, with four Forest Service helpers from Summit, encountered Harry Parker just before he reached Lone Fir Lookout. It was 10:00 p.m. before they reached Darr standing vigil above the victim. By midnight they had removed Porter from the ledge and had him back at Lone Fir.

It was not established as to why he was on the White River Glacier instead of being higher up on the regular South Side Route. He had taken a few steps toward the crevasse to get a better look, then slipped, and fell to the ledge below. He had called for help all day. The fact that he was heard was a miracle.

HELEN LOWRY KILLED

Monday, September 6, 1943 Lu H. Norene, his wife Margaret, Randall Kester, and Portland librarian Helen Lowry, 32, were members of a group at Tilly Jane Camp, who decided to climb Cooper Spur Route. It was not a Mazama climb, although Norene was chairman of the Climbing Committee of The Mazamas and the other three were committee members.

It had been the custom for citizens to help man the Forest Service guard stations, as some of the group had been doing that weekend under the direction of guard Alfred T. Maas.

On the descent of Cooper Spur Route, Miss Lowry slipped and made the usual and classic 2,000-foot slide to the Eliot Glacier, that so many have experienced. In this instance, it resulted in death. Help in the evacuation, in addition to members of the climbing party, were Maas and Boyd French, the operator of Cloud Cap Inn.

BERNIE WERTGEN'S WILD RIDE

1946 It was in mid-May when Bernie Wertgen recalls climbing Cooper Spur Route to the summit all alone, about 14 years of age at the time. On the descent he was glissading in the Chimney, bouncing back and forth on large sun cups, until he fell and found himself sliding very fast.

Repeated attempts at self arrest with his ice axe were futile. Finally the pick of the axe struck something solid; suddenly it was wrested from his hand, breaking the wrist thong. Without an axe he picked up tremendous speed, passing over Tie-In-Rock, then arcing north to the long slide into Eliot Glacier. It had been only three years before, that Helen Lowry had been killed on the same slide.

On the last thousand feet of the long slide, he can remember falling free through the air for hundreds of feet at a time, finally coming in to a gliding contact with the snow at the bottom. This is much the same as an airplane landing or a ski jumper meeting the slope.

Wertgen's wild glide finally ended abruptly in a crevasse, where he lay stunned for an unknown period of time. His watch was gone, but he thought he must have finally roused himself after an hour or more. He was sitting on a ledge about 12 feet below the surface of the glacier. Below him the crevasse dropped away, seemingly bottomless.

He was alone. There was no one else on the mountain. The ice axe, needed for chopping steps up 12 feet of vertical ice, was gone, lost on the mountain. In his pocket was a flashlight. Removing the batteries, he began using the metal case to cut notches in the walls, working slowly upward in a stem position with his feet on the two opposite walls of the crevasse. This finally brought him out on top once more, and he picked his way down the glacier, avoiding crevasses as he went.

A NIGHT IN SAND CANYON

Sunday, June 16, 1947 Four Climbers climbed South Side to Crater Rock, before the deteriorating weather forced them back, Howard J. Richards, a scout leader, Girl Scouts Virginia Wilkes, 17, and Jean Clark 16, and Boy Scout James Earl, 17.

On the descent they veered to the west and hit Sand Canyon. They walked most of the night before hitting the highway near Laurel Hill. On Monday morning they returned to Timberline Lodge and went out to get some of their equipment they had left on the mountain.

ANOTHER SLIDE OFF SPUR

Sunday, June 16, 1947 C.C. White, 25, C.F. White, 29, and E.W. McMillan were in a roped team on Cooper Spur Route. While in the Chute an avalanche swept them down the mountainside 1,500 feet onto the Eliot Glacier. All escaped with only minor bruises. District Ranger Ross Williams warned of the danger of the route.

SUPRENANT DIED IN COLD

1948 On Sunday, February 1, Bert Suprenant, 23, of Portland was reported missing at 4:30 p.m. by his wife Edna Ollin Suprenant. He separated from his ski partner Len Gassner about 3:30 to make one more last run down Pucci's Glade below Timberline Lodge. By 1:00 a.m. Ski Patrol Chief, James Simmons, and ranger James Langdon had directed a sweep of the mountainside from Timberline to Government Camp.

On Monday morning the search was being led by patrolman Randall Kester and recreational guard James Ralph down the West Leg Road. Three apprentice patrolmen in the party found Suprenant at 7:45 a.m., Doug Anderson, Jack Ross, and Lyman Whitney. His frozen body was lightly clad in wool slacks, cotton shirt, air-force flight jacket, and a felt hat without ear covering, not enough to let him survive in the 16-degree temperature and 30-mile winds. Dr. C.A. Nielsen, a physician visiting the area from Seattle, said he had probably died by midnight.

Suprenant had never skied before. His body was found only about 300 feet from Phlox Point, less than 900 feet from where he had abandoned his skis at Alpine Camp, a deserted CCC camp. Patrolman Randall Kester and recreational guard James Ralph had found his skis and poles earlier, but Suprenant had crawled to concealment under a tree. His body posture indicated that he might have tried to build a fire with some of the dry branches above him.

AIR CRASH ON EAST SIDE

Monday, April 12, 1948 Lieutenant Edward J. Kahoun of McChord Field was searching for an A-26 National Guard plane, missing for four days. Downdrafts caused him to crash-land his L-5 Piper aircraft on Newton Clark Glacier just south of Cooper Spur Ridge. The impact knocked out his teeth on the instrument panel, cut his face, and bruised his knees and shins. When Kahoun recovered sufficiently, he started walking, despite instructions in the manual to roll up in his parachute to keep warm until search parties arrived.

At 6:15 a.m. Tuesday morning the Forest Service and Crag Rats reached the wrecked plane and found Kahoun gone. They followed his tracks and found five places where he had stopped to indicate his direction of travel and write "help" in the snow. Then Kahoun's tracks faded out in wind-swept snow, but at 10:30 a.m. pilot Lieutenant Roderick L. Savage saw him on an expanse of snow near Timberline, following the ridge to the north of Newton Canyon. Kahoun was waving frantically for help, and he was given an air drop of food and coffee. The food he could not eat because of his teeth.

Savage was not able to communicate with

ground parties, and Kahoun disappeared into the trees. At one point he lit a fire and stayed with it a short while. Ranger James Langdon ordered a snow-cat to go up Newton Creek, and they found Kahoun late that night. They roared back with him to Timberline Junction, at that time the site of Snowbunny Lodge, where an ambulance was waiting to take him to a hospital.

On September 17, 1962, Don Lowe of The Mazamas found the wreckage of the plane scattered over a wide area on Newton Clark Glacier.

COLLISION ON MISS. HEAD

April 21, 1949 An Air Force B-26 flown by AF Colonel A.Y. Smith, 49, was approaching Portland from Hamilton Field, California. Smith was asking for landing instructions over the radio. The last words that the operator at Portland Air Base heard were that he was at 7,000 feet, flying on instruments. With him were Army Colonel Walter W. Hodge, 45, and Master Sergeant, H.E. Sluga. All were Californians.

A wide air search proved fruitless. Relatives offered a $1,500 reward that was retracted in June. Then, on August 17, Charles Coletti, Air Force veteran and employee at Timberline Lodge, was hiking the trail to Paradise Park with Billie Fowler, lodge maid. Taking a shortcut on the trail, Miss Fowler saw a piece of fiberglass insulation. They then found other bits of wreckage that indicated a downed aircraft.

On returning to the lodge that night they reported the find to James Ralph, Recreational Assistant at Summit. The next morning, Coletti and Ralph went back to Big Zigzag Canyon with walkie-talkie radio. Near the foot of Mississippi Head they could see wreckage. Parts were strewn over the face of the cliff, including three parachutes that had opened by impact. About 500 feet above the ground was a large piece of wreckage, and finally a piece of fabric was found with the numbers of the missing aircraft. Engine vibrations from an Air Force T-26, reconnoitering in the sky above them, caused rolling rock, and they had to cut their investigation short.

The following day, Friday, August 19, a party of 16 left Timberline Lodge to bring back the bodies. Ole Lien of the Forest Service led a team of Air Force rescue men to Mississippi Head, Sergeant Floyd H. Young and Corporal LeRoy LaVigne.

Another group went to the bottom of the canyon under Mississippi Head, Ranger James Langdon, James Ralph, Dr. D.O. Cooke, Ralph Calkin, Joe Leuthold, Everett Darr, Bill Keil, Roy Hickman, Bill Elmstad. Air rescue men from McChord Field were First Lieutenant Paul Nicholas, Sergeant George Patterson. Approach was not easy, and the party satisfied their thirst in the small stream in the canyon bottom. Later they were nauseated when they found Colonel Smith's body decaying in the creek bottom near the base of the cliff.

Everett Darr states that Colonel Hodge's body lay at the base of Mississippi Head. Upon approaching it, they saw his hat atop a pile of what appeared to be dough. This created a very unpleasant job for the retrieval team. After the operation, Darr and Leuthold were roaming around the top of the cliffs of Mississippi Head. Leuthold held out his hand and dropped an object into Darr's; it was a finger with a West Point ring on it. Colonel Hodge had evidently hit atop the cliff and had fallen to the bottom. A newspaper story reported that he had been found on top of the cliff, but Darr refutes it.

Retrieval of the body of Master Sergeant Sluga was the most difficult problem. It dangled from a parachute on the face of Mississippi Head. Darr and Leuthold drove pitons and climbed the rock in Class Six technique. The operation was complicated by rockfall problems, many large boulders delicately balanced and ready to roll with little provocation.

All aircraft had been warned to stay away, but the pilot of an Aercoupe made many passes over the area, dislodging rock several times by the reverberation of his engine. Bill Elmstad was hit a glancing blow with a 50-pound rock, but was not hurt.

The trip out of Big Zigzag Canyon was an ordeal. Two major waterfalls made evacuation a very difficult maneuver. Finally the team had to climb out of the canyon over dangerously steep sand and dirt, holding onto roots or plants.

Examination of the wreckage showed that it was scattered over about 300 acres on the Zigzag Glacier above Mississippi Head, and in the canyon below. The search for the wreck had previously caused the death of a flier, Bruce W. Spalding of Vancouver, who crashed near Vernonia.

DEATH OF DONALD WELK

1949 On Saturday, October 29, Donald Welk, 20, his sister Alice, 17, and Robert Buscho, 24, began the climb of South Side Route just about midnight. Before the sun had risen they had ascended to a point within 300 feet of the summit on hard, icy snow. Welk slipped and yelled, trying in vain to arrest himself with his alpenstock. Quickly, he picked up speed in the Chute, tumbling and cartwheeling, as his sister and Buscho helplessly watched him slide and fall out of sight.

His route took him west of Crater Rock, and he finally came to rest in a depression below Illumination Rock. Buscho started down at once, but by the time he reached Welk he found the body still and cold. He returned to Alice Welk and escorted her down to the top of the ski lift, not yet running at that time of day. A mile of trotting brought him down to Timberline Lodge by 7:30 a.m. to get help with Welk's body.

Lift Supervisor James Carskadon assembled a crew of Timberline Lodge employees, Walter

Aeppli, Ben Lintell, and Lewis Byrne to retrieve Welk. Mel Hardy of the Forest Service also went along. The party reached his body by 11:30 a.m. and strapped him to a toboggan made out of a stretcher and several skis. Their progress was very slow at first across the icy surfaces. By 2:00 p.m. they had returned to Timberline Lodge.

Welk had served 19 months in the US Marine Corps, and was a student at Lewis and Clark College. Alice Welk and Buscho were members of The Mazamas, and the three had planned to attend the Halloween party at Mazama Lodge on Saturday night. None of the group was highly experienced in Mountaineering.

A DEATH ON THE TRAM

Tuesday, December 20, 1949 a death occurred in the construction of the Ski-way, when a construction car ran away and knocked the head of William C. Carpenter, 45, against a steel platform. He and three other men were working off a 12-foot construction car suspended from a cable hung from the tram towers. The three steelworkers were in the process of hanging the cable, when a buildup of slack caused the car to slip and run away from tower #21 down to tower #19.

His fellow-worker Clarence A. Tygart was injured, although Walter Seils and Ivan Harris emerged from the wild ride unscathed. Tower 19 was about halfway up in the line of 38 towers from Government Camp to Timberline. Visitors from the St. Helens Ski Patrol reached the scene first and gave first aid to Tygart. They were Donald Bascom, Richard Jordan, William Hallin, Louis Carter, Tod Deal, and Carl George.

Mount Hood Ski Patrol men brought toboggans from Timberline Lodge to evacuate Carpenter and Tygart. On duty were Joe Leuthold, Keith Petrie, Eldon Metzger, Robert Callicrate, and James Ralph.

MRS. TARTER'S SLIDE ON CHUTE

Sunday, June 3, 1951 It was a good day, with a reported 112 climbers in the summit and crater area. Nancy W. Tarter, 31, began a confident, unroped descent of the Chute with a Trails Club climbing party, led by Teena Lentz. She caught a crampon in a trouser leg and lost control.

Mrs. Tarter understood the principle of self-arrest with the ice axe, but she could not bring it under her chest to exert proper pressure. The axe remained at arm's length as she began to slide faster and switch ends in direction changes. Finally the axe was ripped out of her hand, the strap breaking. Her slide was estimated to be about 1,500 feet, and at the lower end, she began to tumble, as well as slide.

Walter H. Luchs, 36, another member of her party, tried to stop her fall, but he was unable to catch her. A moment later Luchs was struck by a falling rock that Mrs. Tarter had dislodged on her slide. Her trajectory took her past the west side of the Hot Rocks. Dave Wagstaff, a member of Wy'east Climbers, caught her on a steep snow slope with a flying tackle.

Members of a Mazama group were dispersed on the Hot Rocks. It was the Annual Climb, a group of 75 led by Randall Kester and Clark Rhodes. Seeing the victim hurtling down the slope, three of them grabbed ice axes and headed for her position below them, Thaddis Gable, Harold Bangs, and Dr. Leighton Roy.

Gable thrust an axe into the snow to keep Mrs. Tarter from sliding further, and Bangs laid his coat under her. Her face and head had been beaten to a caricature mask, and blood was flowing freely from a hole in the back of her head. Gable was able to stem the flow of blood, while Dr. Roy made a stretcher from makeshift materials. Bangs climbed back up the slope to get a crew working at fielding any rocks that might be falling.

Dean Merton had brought skis up to Crater Rock, and he was sent down to Timberline Lodge to get help. Soon a snow cat was coming up with George North, Bill Keil, and others. An all-out effort was made to bring the cat right up to the gully west of Crater Rock, making it a very short carry with the victim. The evacuation party was under quite a little bombardment from falling rocks. It was said that this was the highest a snow cat was ever driven on Mount Hood.

An unconfirmed newspaper story said that Mrs. Tarter had lost control while attempting a sitting glissade while wearing her crampons.

ADLAI SPILLED IN CAT

Monday, February 13, 1954 Presidential aspirant Adlai Stevenson visited Timberline Lodge and was taken for a ride in the snow cat. Driver John McCone maneuvered too near a cornice and tipped over the machine. He cut the ignition switch, just as it broke through the cornice, so there was no resulting fire.

No one was hurt in the accident. Other passengers were Ralph Wiese of the Forest Service, Alfred Corbett, Arnold Schalyn, and Dennis Stock, a photographer.

HOAX AT TIMBERLINE

Saturday, January 15, 1955 12 members of the Mount Hood Ski Patrol hunted the slopes above Timberline Lodge in a blizzard white-out, looking for a man, who may have never left Portland. In the morning a man identifying himself as Bill Thomas called Summit Ranger Station and said that his friend Michael B. Farrar was missing. He said that Farrar had started out for Crater Rock on skis in a blizzard, Friday at 5:30 p.m. Thomas and his wife and Farrar's wife had waited until 10:30 and come back to Portland. He evaded the question when asked why he had waited so long to report his missing friend.

Ranger Ralph Wiese sent the Ski Patrol out to search the high slopes. While they were out, a man called *The Oregonian* and said that Farrar had returned home. In the conversation he identified himself as a friend, then later as Farrar, himself. Ralph Blank of the Oregon State Patrol went to the address that Bill Thomas had given the Forest Service. Blank was met at the door by Randolph Thompson, who said he had just got home, but that he was sure Farrar was not there; perhaps he was at a friend's house. Thompson refused to let the officer into the house.

Soon after, a woman called to say that Farrar was safe, and that she had heard on television that a search was being made for him. Police and reporters found from neighbors that there had been a great deal of activity and lights snapping off-and-on Friday night. *The Oregonian* sent a radio car to Farrar's address, and the State Patrol went back to check. Again the policeman was met by Randolph Thompson at the door with the same story and the same refusal. While Thompson talked to the officer on the porch, the reporter in *The Oregonian* car called the house on the radio telephone, and Farrar answered.

At that point, he was willing to talk. He said he had left Timberline Lodge after 3:00 a.m. Saturday morning against the advice of other skiers. On his way up the mountain he had fallen in soft snow and had been rescued by two young men and their girls. They had brought him back to Timberline Lodge and wrapped him in blankets to save his life, then brought him to Portland and dropped him at a downtown hotel. He said he had called the ranger station to let them know he was safe.

The police checked with the ranger station and found that he had not called them. He had no wife, as the man, Bill Thomas, had said. Bill Thomas never did come to light, but police surmised that he and Farrar might be one and same. Farrar was found to be 33 years of age and unemployed. The whole affair had all the earmarks of a Marx Brothers comedy.

It was no comedy for the men of the ski patrol, who searched for him in the worst kind of weather. On the edge of the White River Canyon, Dave Hitchcock stepped on a cornice in the whiteout and tumbled down 300 feet on the steep slope toward the glacier. His partners rescued him with a climbing rope, fortunately unharmed. David Wagstaff and Ross Petrie came back from the search with frostbitten faces. There were not many smiles around the ski patrol room that evening.

INJURY OF RUTH PATSCHOWSKI

Friday, August 19, 1955 Ruth Patschowski, 25, of San Francisco, was beginning a descent of the Chute with a Sierra Club party, when she lost a crampon. The party was not roped, and when she lost her footing, she began to cartwheel down the steep snow. Her tumble was short, being stopped by her fall into a 30-foot crevasse. The result was fractured ribs, lacerations, and head injuries.

Franklin L. Gearhart had been watching the climb through binoculars from the camp at Pholx Point. Seeing the accident, he hurried for help to Timberline Lodge. Richard Kohnstamm and James Misko of the lodge tied a toboggan to the snow-cat and quickly drove to the upper limits of the machine at 9,000 feet. Very soon they had reached the crater with the toboggan, ready to evacuate Miss Patschowski.

The Sierra Club party had included three doctors, and she was well attended. Very soon she was delivered to Timberline Lodge and sent on her way to St. Vincent's Hospital, undoubtedly being the fastest evacuation ever made of an injured climber in the crater area.

SEARCH FOR SKIERS

Saturday, May 12, 1956 MORESCO was notified of three lost skiers, Chris Zafaratas, Pat Weller, and Will Sharkey, who had left the Timberline Lodge snow-cat to ski back to the lodge from the 8000-foot level. The call came at 11:10 p.m., and at 3:00 a.m. Sunday the Forest Service asked for air search and a ground search group to leave the lodge at 6:00. Three carloads of MORESCO searchers were recalled a little later, when the lost trio turned up on the highway at the foot of Laurel Hill. They had strayed too far west in the fog and followed Little Zigzag Canyon all the way down. Although they were not well-enough dressed, they were able to build a fire and last through the night.

SEARCH FOR LYNN WATTIER

Thursday, May 24, 1956 Lynn Wattier, an employee at Timberline, became lost while skiing in fog above the lodge. Lodge and Forest Service personnel hunted for her all day, and at 8:50 Friday morning they notified MORESCO. At 2:30 p.m. pilots Ernie Helms and Charles Laveque took to the air for a search. Friday afternoon MORESCO was asked to begin search on Saturday morning. MORESCO placed five teams of men in the field, and the Forest Service placed four. With intensified search Miss Wattier was found at 7:30 a.m. on Saturday.

ALICE NIELSON SEARCH

Sunday, July 8, 1956 a group of Chemeketans led by Jacques Cubilie, started up Cooper Spur Route. At Tie-In-Rock, Alice Nielson, 25, who had been feeling ill for more than an hour before, balked at continuing the climb. Cubilie left her at that point and continued. However, in another hour he was concerned about loose snow and possible avalanche conditions and turned the party back.

Miss Nielson, a secretary from Salem, was nowhere to be seen. Cubilie split the party into two groups, and they searched for her on the way back to Cloud Cap Inn, all to no avail. A large search was begun, and by Monday morning there were 60 or more MORESCO people combing the northeastern slopes of the mountain. Flyers Mel Lindgren and Mel Boyer aided the search from the air.

Miss Nielson had first descended to the tree line, then seeing that she was not at Cloud Cap, she had climbed back up and descended again. Snow was soft with each step sinking to the knee. She was afraid to be without water, and she had followed downward to Cold Spring Creek near a large waterfall, whose thundering roar prevented her from hearing the shouts of rescue teams. An attempt to light a fire failed, because her matches were wet. It was Monday afternoon before Oran Barr and Reuben Sullivan, two young Forest Service men from Parkdale, found her in the canyon.

DEATH OF LYNN KAUFMAN

1956 On Sunday, July 29, Carl Schnoor, 20, college man from Portland, led a group of 19 up South Side Route. They were teen-agers from the east coast, a Youth Hostel group that had made last-minute plans to climb. Schnoor had led several such climbs, although he tied them into one string, closely spaced, considered a very poor practice by mountaineers. Descending the chute **at 3:45 p.m. they slipped.** Schnoor tried unsuccessfully to arrest the fall with his ice axe. Only one or two of the group knew how to react; there were practically none with any experience. Being tied so closely together, they toppled like dominoes and picked up speed.

The slide ended in the moat at the bottom. A moat is the chasm created between rock and melting snow, and this one was filled with the usual boulders and ice blocks. Into this hole the climbers fell one after the other, bodies piled up, a welter of people, ice-axes, and knapsacks in what proved to be the goriest accident of all time on Mount Hood.

A group from Salem of high school age witnessed the accident, Thomas Pfau, Dennis Glasgow, Frank Franklin, Gail Wright, and Louise Pfau. They quickly carried the news to the Timberline cat-driver on Palmer Glacier. At the lodge the Forest Service and lodge personnel went to work. A call to Sandy brought Dr. Elton Leavitt and his partner Dr. William Rohrberg roaring up to the mountain. Timberline operator Richard Kohnstamm quickly became the head snow-cat operator for the rescue. Ralph Wiese and James Langdon of the Forest Service took what help they could get and headed for the Crater.

At 6:00 p.m. John Biewener of MORESCO and his friend Dr. James Owen ate dinner at the Tramway House restaurant in Government Camp, being on their way home from a climb of North Sister. Being told of the accident, they hurried up to make the first appearance for MORESCO. By that time the Doctors Rohrberg and Leavitt were supervising the 12 victims who were laid out on the Hogsback by Forest Service and Timberline personnel. Six victims had already been sent out under their own power.

A New York State girl, **Lynn Kaufman, 13, was dead.** Judith Hart injured her back and broke an ankle. Lawrence D. McCormich broke a hand. Dresel O. Shaw broke a leg and injured an arm. Patricia Shaw had lacerations. Meredith Stebbins had a broken jaw and head cuts. Suzanne Blum had brain concussion and broken back. John Schloss suffered leg injury. Barbara Platto broke both legs. Robert H. Silin cut his leg. Susan Stein fractured her skull. Ronal Heinrich had a broken shoulder. Claire E. Mitchell broke her ankles. Sidney H. Rosenberg injured his leg.

John Biewener conversed with some of the victims. Below, all was dark except for the lights at the Lodge, Government Camp, and an occasional car on the highway. "In 30 minutes you are going to see a solid stream of lights down there on the road," he told them. Sure enough, in a half hour MORESCO members began to crowd the highway from Portland and Hood River, lighting up the timbered slopes below.

The US Air Force sent ambulances, doctors, and medical corpsmen, as well as dropping plasma and drugs from a plane. They set up a medical battle station at the top of the ski lift at Silcox Hut to check in the victims. Coast Guard sent helicopters. The two services put four aircraft and over 25 personnel into the operation. Eighty blankets were stripped from the beds of Timberline Lodge. Everett Darr opened his Mountain Shop at Government Camp and told the rescuers "Take what you need."

By 11:00 p.m. 90 MORESCO men had arrived at the Crater with stretchers, akjas, radios and lights. Thirteen stretchers were carried down that night, the last being the body of Lynn Kaufman. On Palmer Glacier the bobbing flashlights and the lights of the snow cat presented a Martian-like scene from below. At 3:15 a.m. all the stretchers had been brought to the Air Force battle station at Silcox.

The **Timberline Lodge became an emergency hospital** as the victims began appearing below. Doctors and nurses worked throughout the night, 10 physicians being involved in the operation. By morning 16 patients were lodged at Emanuel, Providence, and Good Samaritan Hospitals in Portland.

DEATH OF MRS. SIMKO

September 23, 1956 John L. Simko, 37, and his wife, Lou Ellen, 32, were on a drive and stopped at Timberline Lodge. She suggested they go for a short hike, and they reached a point about a quarter mile below the lodge, when she stumbled on a sharp rock, fell off a 50-foot cliff, and died at once from neck and back injuries. Two University of Oregon medical students who came upon the scene shortly afterward, pronounced her dead. She left two young children.

BERG LOST ON TOBOGGAN

Sunday, February 2, 1957 Max Berg, 18, visiting Timberline Lodge, had a friend in Government Camp and intended to go there to meet him. Berg left the lodge about noon, sliding downward on a toboggan as far as the terrain would permit. He was dressed lightly for the exposure to cold.

The Ski Patrol was alerted and began a search, but it was 7:00 p.m. before Bill Keil and Don Kistner found him off the regular ski trail, huddled on top of the toboggan in an effort to keep warm. He had one shoe off. Weather was about 25 degrees with falling snow. The patrolmen wrapped him in a blanket and rubbed his feet before towing him back to Timberline Lodge. Ralph Wiese of the Forest Service directed the search.

MARTIN LOST & BENIGHTED

Sunday, March 3, 1958 James Martin, 32, of Seattle, left Timberline Lodge at 5:30 a.m. on skis to attempt a summit climb. He was an experienced climber, had climbed Mount Hood seven times and had been on some rescues, himself. He signed out on the climbers' log at Timberline.

He turned back before reaching the summit, because of stormy weather and poor visibility. On the descent he made the usual error of veering too far west, placing him in the area of Mississippi Head. He dug into the snow and got a few hours of sleep during the latter part of the day, but in three different instances the wind blew his snow protection away. This caused him to lose almost all his equipment, except his skiis. Fortunately, he ate a good deal to give him energy, a pound of cheese, a box of raisins, and two peanut-butter sandwiches.

As the temperature dropped to 10 degrees, he was forced to stay awake and keep moving. Finally toes and fingers were no longer pliable, but he kept his legs and arms going.

At 6:00 p.m. Sunday night, the Forest Service noticed that he had not signed back in. They checked and found his automobile still at the lodge. At 8:30, a preliminary search was made by Ranger Bruce Kirkland, Bill Keil, and Bill Kruger. A little later an alert through the MORESCO system brought four teams to Timberline Lodge, ready to start at daybreak.

At 9:00 a.m. on Monday, Martin received a very lucky break. The sun came out, and he was able to warm up in a sheltered spot. For a while he was too cold to put on his skis, but he finally did so and was able to descend about 700 feet. Bruce Kirkland, Ray Conkling, and Howard Veasey saw him on the mountainside about 10:00 a.m., and they made their way to him.

They got him to the snow cat for a quick trip to Timberline Lodge, where he was soon enjoying a cup of hot chocolate, of which he had been dreaming, all through that cold night.

HELICOPTER LANDS ON TOP

August, 1958 A Bell 47-G-2 Helicopter, piloted by W.C. Hartley, landed on the summit of Mount Hood to set survey stakes. Accompanying Hartley was mechanic John Reese.

DEATH OF DAVID DRAPER

Saturday, June 20, 1959 a climbing party of boy scouts and leaders started the descent from the summit on South Side Route at about 1:00 p.m. Amos Smelser and John McClosky, the leaders of the group of over 40 climbers, were in the last rope team to leave the summit. Just ahead of them was a string of two rope leaders, Edward W. Smith, 47, and Don Berger, and three scouts, David Draper, 15, William Halling, 16, and Thomas McCune, 14.

About 200 feet below the summit Smelser noticed a stream of slushy snow pouring off the rocks above, about 18 inches deep and 40 feet wide. **"Anchor in!!"** he yelled, and Berger was able to get a good hold with his ice axe. But the heavy stream hit Smith and the three boys, carrying them right along and ripping out Berger's anchored position. In moments the five had been swept downward into the bottom of the crevasse below.

Smelser and McCloskey moved quickly, to the crevasse to help, but within minutes the slush had frozen into ice, imbedding the victims in unmovable positions. One of the boys was only ankle-deep, and one of the men was immersed to his waist. The other three were covered, with David Draper lying on the bottom of the heap. While Smelser and a crew worked feverishly to chop them free of the ice, word was sent below of the accident, and a MORESCO team led by Keith Petrie assembled to make the evacuation.

Upon reaching Draper on the bottom of the heap, they found him blue and not breathing, although he seemed to try to breathe at first, when they chopped the ice away from his chest. To complicate matters, more of the slush flow came from above at intervals, freezing quickly, and filling the crevasse. By the time they were removing the last victims, so much had poured down, that they were able to climb out on the frozen slush without any direct lifting with climbing ropes.

While he was in the crevasse, and during the period of evacuation, the leaders tried to revive Draper for about four hours. He never did regain consciousness. Smith was able to help himself out of the crevasse after being chopped free of the ice. All were loaded into a snow cat for the trip down to Timberline from the 9,000-foot level. All were sent to the hospital but Berger.

MID-AIR COLLISION

October 22, 1959 two National Guard F-89 Scorpion twin-jet aircraft were practicing radio intercept maneuvers at 27,000 feet, when they collided in a glancing blow in the vicinity of Cooper Spur Junction. All four occupants were immediately ejected and parachuted down. The plane flown by Lieutenant Winfred C. Vinton exploded soon afterward and made a fireball visible for 125 miles.

The explosion at 9:10 p.m. was seen by many people around Parkdale. The Crag Rats were holding a meeting at Cloud Cap Inn and heard a grinding rumble, thought by some to be thunder, and by others to be a sonic boom. Crag Rats, Alpinees, and Civil Air Patrol were immediately called out to search for the fliers.

The weather turned cloudy that night and search was conducted in wet underbrush. Hood River deputies Hardman and Bob Lynch found a piece of aircraft wreckage in the road near Bottle Prairie about seven miles due east of Cloud Cap Inn. At dawn the next morning Crag Rats Bill Bryan and Mark Puddy found another remnant near Mill Creek about three miles north of the first. Soon afterward shots were heard in the Dog River area. Glenn Marsh, Wilson Appelgren, Harold Franz, and a Forest Service man went to investigate and found they had been fired by Lieutenant Jack W. Rayborn, lying with an injured hip. Soon afterward they found his shipmate, Lieutenant Carson McDowell.

To the east a pair of hunters found Vinton. Only his observer, Major Roy Sefton had not been found. Sefton fired signal flares and was sighted in the forest toward Dufur, where ground parties later picked him up.

INJURY OF ALBEN COOK

1960 On Thursday, September 15, two men from Los Angeles, Alben Cook, 31, and Bill Leitzel, 29, started out from Timberline Lodge about 9:00 a.m. for the summit. As they ascended the steep slope at the southeast base of Crater Rock, Cook slipped on loose rock. Rocks rolled over him as he slid and tumbled about 75 feet to a rest.

When Leitzel reached him, Cook could not move his right arm, and his right foot was pinned under a rock. Leitzel freed him and drug him to a rock ledge near an old pile of boards. He then started a fire, made Cook as comfortable as possible, and ran to Timberline Lodge for help.

By 1:00 a.m. the following morning a six-man team had reached him, including a doctor and Forest Service personnel Bruce Kirkland, Bryce Lausch, Don Vandenberg, and Jack Schaefer. Just before daybreak eight more men from MORESCO arrived. It took two hours to reach the top of the chairlift, where they loaded him onto the stretcher-chair for Timberline. By 8:00 a.m. the operation was completed. Cook suffered a dislocated right shoulder, cracked ribs, and sprained ankle.

FALL TO ELIOT BY CHISHOLMS

Sunday, June 25, 1961 Colin Chisholm, 54, a highly-experienced climb leader and past president of The Mazamas, led a party of 26 up the Sunshine Route. In the vicinity of Anderson Rock one of his rope leaders divided the party by taking his string ahead of the leader to the summit. The act was not a normal occurrence, giving the leader the worry over a split party in addition to other leadership problems.

Arriving at the summit, Chisholm found that the rope leader had not waited, but had proceeded down Cooper Spur Route without authority. Grouping his party, he then started down. As customary with a climb leader he took the last rope down, being tied in with his son Douglas, 22.

The two took turns glissading, one anchoring while the other moved down to the end of the slack rope. At a point about 500 feet below the summit, Colin was anchoring, and Douglas began to move too fast, out of control.

At first Colin was not alarmed, but he suddenly realized that they were both sliding too fast, and Douglas was veering to the left toward Eliot Glacier. Their route took them down the steep ice, miraculously missing rocks on both sides. Their speed was sufficient to carry them across the eight-foot bergschrund and out onto the glacier, where a pile of material from previous avalanches stopped their slide.

The slide was observed by Dr. Ted G. Lathrop and his son James, who were tied into the next rope ahead. Dr. Lathrop described the mountainside around Chisholm and his son as a mass of moving snow, indicating that some of the surface had avalanched to prevent their arresting.

Marge Dauelsberg and Ted Meeker, members of Chisholm's party were sent by Lathrop to Cloud Cap Inn for help. Crag Rats Bill Bryan, Elwood Samuel, and Rob and Norm Hukari, who were at Cloud Cap Inn, radioed for help and started up to the scene of the accident. Pilot Bob Edling of The Dalles made an aerial drop of a stretcher and supplies onto Eliot Glacier. Teams of Crag Rats and Alpinees came up for the evacuation, and Dr. W.T. Edmundson examined the Chisholms for injury.

CRASH ON WHITE RIVER

February 2, 1963 Airman 2nd Class Ronald P. Myers left Portland Airport for Williams Air Force Base, Arizona, in a light aircraft. Upon his failure to report in at either Burns, Oregon, or Elko, Nevada, a widespread search was started.

On Sunday, February 11, Russ McJury and Shepard Wilson of the Ski Bowl saw the wreckage of the plane at about the 8,500-foot level on White River Glacier and notified the Forest Service about 1:00 p.m.

District Ranger Peter Wingle led a search team immediately, taking a snow-cat from Timberline Lodge at 2:30. With him were Ray Conkling, Russ McJury, Russ Petrie, and John West. Other Forest Service personnel were Kurt Kessler and Ray Steiger.

They found Myers still strapped to the seat of the aircraft, his body frozen. An akja was used to bring him back to the snow-cat. He had belonged to a flying club at Williams AFB, and had 107 hours of flying time. The wreckage was scattered over several acres.

THREE FALL TO ELIOT GLACIER

Sunday, July 21, 1963 Dr. Eberhard H. Gloekler, Dr. Mark Hanschka, and Robert C. Shoemaker climbed the Cooper Spur Route and got good start downward again. By noon they had most of the steep summit slope behind them when someone slipped and pulled the whole string off in a slide from the 10,000-foot level. The resulting slide carried them down the ice chutes to the Eliot Glacier, more than 1,500 feet below.

Mrs. Gloekler had been waiting for their return at Cloud Cap Inn. By mid-afternoon she was concerned and walked up toward Cooper Spur. She saw a group of climbers hurrying down and assumed they were her husband and companions. The climbers she saw were members of another climbing party who had seen the accident and were running for help below. They bypassed her, and she did not make contact with them to find out about the accident at that time.

By later afternoon MORESCO teams of Crag Rats and Alpinees came to Cloud Cap Inn in response to the call, and by 7:00 p.m. they had reached the victims. The two doctors had suffered simple bone fractures. Shoemaker had fared better, being badly shaken up.

Rescue personnel totalled 49 on an operation that was complicated by high winds, blowing sand, rain, and sleet that added to the problem of working in the dark of night on the glacier. The evacuation was completed by 6:00 a.m. Monday.

FALL TO ELIOT OF KNUTSON

September 5, 1963 Five Reed College students ascended Sunshine Route, Richard Steven Knutson, 21, Mike Templeton, 21, Thomas Link, 21, Gary Payne, 19, and Steve McCarthy, 19. They reached the summit a half hour after noon following an eight and a half hour climb from base camp.

After 45 minutes on top they descended Cooper Spur Route to the base of the Chute at the 10,000-foot level. Knutson, in a string of three, unroped and left the other two still tied in. The two men on the other rope untied completely. Knutson was wearing only one crampon, the other having come off when the parachute-cord binding broke. Disregarding this, he began to glissade, then stopped and began to kick steps down.

At about 2:45 his horrified companions saw him slip, slide on his back. He then tried to self-arrest with his ice axe and disappeared out of sight over the edge toward Eliot Glacier. His fall carried him a thousand feet or more, his axe and pack remaining behind in positions that gave mute evidence of his slide down the ice.

Templeton climbed down Knutson's route, while Link and Payne belayed themselves down to reach the victim. McCarthy ran on down toward Cloud Cap Inn to get help. On the way down he met MORESCO members Albert Combs, John Neal, and Robert Holder a half hour after the accident had happened. They climbed down to the victim while McCarthy and Neal continued toward Cloud Cap Inn.

Templeton reached Knutson first, finding him unconscious in a fetal position, lying on a ledge in a crevasse. Combs and Holder climbed down to him and with the help of the Reed College boys, they moved him up out of the crevasse to a position suitable for helicopter pickup.

Meanwhile, John Neal had driven down to notify the Forest Service, and the sheriff called in a helicopter. The Air Force craft piloted by Captain Chase came in for a landing at Cloud Cap Inn to drop exchange one crew member for Harold Franz, who guided them in to the pickup area. Very shortly after, they were back again to drop Franz, pick up the crewman, and take off for Portland.

Knutson, who showed only signs of abrasions, needed quick attention, and the aircraft changed flight plans enroute to land at Hood River. At the Memorial Hospital they found he had a broken leg, broken breast bone, and a dislocated jaw.

Critique later showed that the members of the climbing party had very limited experience and had been advised by The Mazamas that Cooper Spur Route was dangerous. None had ever been on the route before.

GRAVES BROKE A LEG

April 2, 1964 Crag Rats Bob Sheppard, Mark Thrane, and Don Graves made a trip to Tilly Jane Camp on skis for a snow survey. On the way back down, Graves took a fall on ice and broke his leg below the knee, when the safety binding did not throw. Sheppard and Thrane made a makeshift toboggan with their skis and pulled him for a while. They finally ended by carrying him the rest of the way because of snow conditions.

PRIEST TAKES 2000-FOOT SLIDE

Sunday, June 7, 1964 Roy Edward Thielen, 57, a Catholic priest from St. Joseph's Church in Spokane, left his automobile near Lolo Pass and hiked toward Mount Hood's Western Slopes. He left a note on his car, stating that he would return to it on Tuesday.

The trail leads up to McNeil Point, between Sandy Glacier and Glisan Glacier. Father Thielen's story to the press was not very explicit, but on Tuesday he was still well up on the side of the mountain, hiking on snow slopes, perhaps glacier surfaces. While sliding down a gentle slope, he came to the brink of a steep area and fell. He then rolled and slid about 2,000 feet to the bottom.

He was shaken and had lost his sense of direction, so during the next three days he worked northeast, instead of heading back to the west and his automobile. His food was only a few squares of chocolate. On Friday he finally reached a road near Parkdale, from where he was taken to the hospital.

Father Thielen had climbed previously in Idaho and Montana. From his hospital bed he was already planning an ascent of Mount Whitney in California.

CLAPP BROKE AN ANKLE

Sunday, January 31, 1965 Six Mazamas were climbing South Side. Their route was up the gulley west of Crater Rock, then up the west crater wall, a seldom-used route. John Hoopes was forced to quit the climb because of illness, and Walter Eriksen returned to Timberline Lodge with him. The remaining four were working up the crater wall, Kenneth Winters in the lead, followed by Al Clapp, Elmer McCormick, and Carmie Dafoe. Snow was loose, dry powder on top an icy undersurface.

There was no particular hazard, and Dafoe took a picture just about a minute before McCormick slipped, pulling Winters and Clapp off their feet. Dafoe set his axe to hold the string, but when the full weight hit the end of the line, it pulled him off also. They all slid about 300 feet to the bottom of the slope. McCormick lost his ice axe in the maneuver.

Clapp's crampon had caught, twisted his leg, and broke his ankle. Dafoe at once sent McCormick down toward Timberline Lodge for help. But before he ever arrived, Eriksen at the lodge could see that the party had stopped and were not progressing. He knew something was wrong and tried to get a mountain rescue crew activated. Authorities would not initiate any action until they got a report from above, and so it was necessary for McCormick to appear, before MORESCO was activated. Meanwhile, Eriksen had called down to Mazama Lodge and located William H. Oberteuffer and Carmie Dafoe's brother, Ralph.

In the crater, Dafoe and Winters had placed Clapp in the emergency sleeping bag they carried, then dug a trench to keep him out of the wind. Winters was then sent down to rush along some help. Oberteuffer was the first on the scene, and soon Larry Foster of MORESCO came up, packing one half of the akja on his back. By this time it was 6:00 p.m. and darkness had set in. Weather was clear, about 10 degrees above zero, and the wind was blowing gusts up to 40 knots.

They started the akja down, holding it back on some of the bare, icy slopes with considerable difficulty. The rescue effort was compounded by one of the girls in the Ski Patrol coming up with insufficient clothing. She became so uncomfortable she was hysterical, and her fiance radioed down for another akja for her. It was never used, but the confusion slowed Clapp's evacuation. The snow cat was not able to reach quite as high an elevation as usual, and it was nearly 10:00 p.m. when the rescue team finally reached the safety of the lodge.

Of the party, three are gone in 1975. Eriksen

died in an auto crash near Arlington, Oregon, August 20, 1966. McCormick was killed in a fall off a ledge on Razor Back in Washington's Cashmere Crags in May of 1967. and Clapp died with heart trouble in 1974.

SKI DEATH IN UPPER BOWL

Saturday, February 20, 1965 William Stanley Davis, 16, a member of Lake Oswego High School ski team, was making a run with teammates in the Upper Ski Bowl. Before the eyes of his ski coach, Leonard Alto, Davis came over a rise at about 35 miles per hour, lost control, and hit a stump head on.

The Ski Patrol rushed him to an ambulance. Surgeons performed an emergency operation at Providence Hospital in Portland, but he died shortly afterward.

He had run in competition, along with other members of the team, earlier in the day in the area. At the time of the accident the team was out sharpening their skills and had been photographed on movie film just a few minutes previously.

THREE MORE TO ELIOT

July 17, 1966 Terry Tindall, 19, Sue Davis, 17, and John McDaniels, 18, left Cloud Cap Inn about 8:00 a.m. Weather was good after a stormy night. They followed the route of a party which had left an hour earlier, climbing through the Eliot Ice-fall to the moat-crevasse which divides the glacier from the steep Northeast Face. The earlier party which included Richard R. Pooley, had crossed the moat, and was about three hours ahead on the route.

There was about two feet of soft snow on a wet base. Climbing upward, Sue Davis was following tracks toward a couloir, when an avalanche swept down it in front of her. The party climbed upward between two outcroppings of rock and stopped to eat lunch on one of them. They could see the earlier party very high on the slope. As time passed the climbers left the summit and descended Cooper Spur Route, as did the members of a third party on the north side that day.

McDaniels and his party were climbing hard ice on 40 to 50-degree slope, belaying as they went. Another avalanche swept down the couloir. Then another came down the face about a hundred feet to the right. Moments later, amid warning cries from above, a large avalanche picked them off the side of the mountain and carried them 800 feet down to the Eliot Glacier. The time was about 1:30 p.m. All three had dug into the ice with their axes as well as they could, but they could not stand the blow of the falling snow.

Injuries were minor. All three had been wearing climbing helmets. Sue and McDaniels helped Tindall into his down jacket, and they started back toward Cloud Cap. The other parties gave them assistance when they reached them below

Cooper Spur.

INJURY OF KENNETH EARLY

Sunday, July 31, 1966 Kenneth Early, 34, and Joe Schiebel, 35, experienced climbers from Seattle, were ascending the Chute on South Side Route. It was about 10:00 a.m., and snow conditions were good. Both men were known to be capable, careful climbers.

Early's pack shifted, throwing him off balance. He found himself sliding fast, out of control. Reaching the crevasse, he bounced off the lower wall and fell to the bottom with both shoulders dislocated. Shiebel went for help at Timberline immediately. A group of Mazama teen-agers had seen the accident and kept Early warm with some of their clothing, until the rescue party arrived at 3:00 p.m. It took the five members of the MORESCO party about four hours to bring Early to Timberline Lodge.

SIEGEL AND GIBSON FALL

October 8, 1966 two highly experienced climbers, Charles B. Gibson, Jr., 31, and Louis E. "Bud" Siegel were injured in a fall on Eliot Glacier. Climbing roped at the 8,500-foot level, Gibson was in the lead and slipped as a step gave away.

The surface was icy and Gibson, a very large man, picked up great speed, jerking Siegel out of position when the line grew taut. Gibson's left leg was broken and Siegel had great pain in his ankle. The time was 2:15 p.m. Siegel gave his companion first aid and made him comfortable as possible.

By 6:00 there was no sign of help from any other party, so Siegel started down to Cloud Cap on what proved to be later a broken ankle, at times crawling on the ice. Progress was excruciatingly slow, and the trip which would normally take an hour, lasted until 3:00 a.m., nine hours of agonizing torture in the dark.

Sleeping at Cloud Cap Inn were Bill Bryan of the Crag Rats, Elwood Samuel, and Al and Mary Lou Combs. Combs, a member of MORESCO, left for the scene of the accident at 3:40 a.m. with a sleeping bag and inflatable splints.

MORESCO parties of Alpinees and Crag Rats arrived at the inn and were on their way to Gibson by 6:00 a.m. They brought him down in the akja, using the wheel, when they reached the trail.

Both victims were Mazama climb leaders and MORESCO members. Siegel was a prominent member of Mount Hood Ski Patrol.

SEARCH FOR GATES BROTHERS

Sunday, November 27, 1966 Lonnie Gates, 26, and his brother Lannie Gates, 19, spent Sunday night at the Silcox Hut, preparing for a climb on Wy'east Route. They carried full bivouac gear, tent, gasoline stoves, sleeping bags, and winter clothing. On Monday they left in bad weather, finally pitching their tent on a ledge halfway up the slope east of Steel Cliff.

Tuesday dawned bright and clear, and they were on their way, carrying full packs. As they neared the top, bad weather came in from the west and cut visibility to a few feet. Nearing the summit ridge, they were hit so hard by the wind that they backed off and tried to find a more sheltered route to the summit. When that failed, they descended a short distance and tried to erect the tent, but the wind spoiled their efforts.

The brothers then dug two separate snow caves in the steep sidehill, but once inside they could not get their stoves to light, and they could not keep warm in their sleeping bags. After night had fallen, they abandoned the caves and began descending to keep warm, groping their way in the dark.

On Wednesday their path led them down Clark Canyon. Snow had obliterated the Timberline Trail, and they were not aware that they had crossed it and continued down the canyon. Keith Petrie and Dick Dodd of MORESCO found them in the timber below.

ROBERT PATTERSON DEATH

1968 On Saturday, May 4, six climbers were reported overdue from a climb from Timberline Lodge over the Wy'east Route, Terrance (Terry) Simonitch, his wife Linda, Robert F. Patterson, Terry Riddell, David Roy Skinner and his wife Pam. Another group of climbers thought they had seen them at the 8000-foot level. Weather was good as per forecast, but turned very bad.

That night at 11:00 p.m. Robert Patterson's wife, Wanda, had telephoned to Timberline, asking about her husband's party. She was told to call the Forest Service at Zigzag, but she got no answer there. At 5:00 a.m. Sunday she called Timberline again, reaching Lee, who set the machinery in motion for a search.

On Sunday, five groups totalling 45 men searched to mountainside from Mount Hood Meadows under control of the sheriff of Hood River County. In Clackamas County two groups probed out of Timberline Lodge. Keith Petrie, manager at Mount Hood Meadows, kept the facilities open around the clock. The Maintenance Foreman, John West, used the snow cat as a shuttle bus on the eastern slopes, taking it to an unprecedented 8,200-foot level. Kurt Kessler of the Forest Service managed to get the snow cat up from Timberline to the 8,500 foot level, from where he and Earl Levin managed to slog through the new snow in 15-foot visibility as high as Illumination Rock. James Angell took a small group to Crater Rock.

Blizzard conditions still prevailed at 6:00 a.m. Monday morning, but 75 exhausted rescuers were again on their way to search for the lost six. About 9:00 a.m. the weather let up a little and visibility cleared. A radio message came in from a three-man team alongside Crater Rock.

"They may have been found," reported Al Combs, leader of the team. In snow caves high on the Hogsback, five were still alive. Robert Patterson, 32, had died before dawn of hypothermia.

The group had not seen a cloud until they approached the last steep slopes of the summit on Wy'east Route. Then a storm roared in. By the time they could reach the summit, visibility was 5 feet with wind howling across the top of Mount Hood at 50 miles an hour. Patterson, reaching his first summit, was showing signs of exhaustion, perhaps from not eating sufficiently enroute. Climb leader Terry Simonitch saw that Patterson would not be able to go further, shortly after they left the top. Simonitch, 26, knew that Patterson was falling and stumbling. Using the knowledge accumulated in Odd Bjerke's winter survival course, he dug a cave big enough for four at the top of the Hogsback. He then dug a second cave for himself and his wife, Linda. Two days in the snow caves built up moisture in their clothing. Simonitch knew that if he left the cave and returned, their wet clothing would cause them to freeze quickly.

Patterson's condition was weak to begin with, and his three cave-mates watched him closely, bundling him as well as they could to keep him alive. At the last they gave him mouth-to-mouth resuscitation, but early Monday he was dead.

Al Combs' radio message was received on the high slopes on the east side Monday morning. Three men skied over to the south side and reached the victims soon afterward, crossing the White River Glacier high on the mountain. They were MORESCO members Earl and Jamie Levin and Dr. Cameron Bangs of the University of Oregon Medical School, a specialist in cold weather medicine. Jack Henry converged on the site from near Illumination Rock, where he had been leading a team of Tom Bauman, Ken Jern, and Steve Knutson.

Linda Simonitch, 26, was able to walk down toward the snow cat parked at 8500 feet elevation. Terry Riddell had frostbitten fingers and toes. David Skinner, 27 escaped frostbite, but his body temperature had dropped to a dangerous level.

Skinner's wife Pam, 24, had lost her right glove, and her fingers were frozen. Her feet were frostbitten. Her body temperature was 92 degrees when medical personnel checked her in at Timberline Lodge. Al Combs, Klindt Kielbig, James Dickson, and Bud Siegel changed her wet clothes when they found her, giving her some of their own dry clothing. They warmed her hands and feet by placing them on the bare skin of their own stomachs. She was under administration of pure oxygen for about two hours before they could get her into the snow cat. On the way down to the cat in the akja, Jerry Foster rode under her, holding her in his arms to keep up her body heat.

Under Dr. Bangs' direction at Timberline the frozen hands and feet of the victims were placed in 110-degree water, using a new process developed during years of experiment with arctic patients. The water temperature is very critical, but with the system fingers and toes are saved. All five of the victims were taken to the U of O hospital in Portland.

STOUT SURVIVED IN CREVASSE

1968 Raymond K. Stout, 27, a novice, was led up Cooper Spur Route on September 12, by his friend, Barry Carnley, 27, a beginning climber, who had gone through the basic climbing course of The Mazamas. They left the summit after 5:00 p.m. in deteriorating weather. Carnley decided to descend south side because of wind and decreasing visibility.

Approaching the Hogsback, he found the conditions iced. Stout, a Baptist minister at Hinson Memorial Church, was insecure and reluctant to move forward in the white-out. Carnley, being the more experienced man, should have been the last man down. Instead, he was forced to lead down, knowing that the bergschrund crevasse lay below.

Stout slipped and came hurtling down the slope, pulling Carnley out of his position. Stout went first and Carnley followed right into the waiting crevasse. Carnley was knocked unconscious, but was able to crawl out of the crevasse, badly shaken up. He made it to Timberline Lodge at about 9:00 p.m. to get help.

Ranger Dick Buscher sent a first aid team up at once and a MORESCO party was called from Portland. Stout was found alive in the crevasse, jammed in tight about 25 feet down, right ankle broken, a rib fractured, and his right shoulder dislocated. He had lain 10 hours with his broken ankle jammed up against the ice, but lost no limbs in the accident.

The MORESCO party brought an akja, and they lowered him the first thousand feet. At the snow line they attached the wheel to the akja and rolled along to Timberline Lodge.

A SKI LIFT ACCIDENT

Saturday, March 1, 1969 Six riders on the Pucci Lift at Timberline Lodge were suddenly plunged about 15 feet to the deep snow below, when a bolt snapped on one of the lift towers and allowed a cable to drop. The sudden jolt pitched the riders forward, off their lift seats. Dave Duncan, 35, of Wemme was taken to Providence Hospital for observation for possible back injury.

EATON DIED IN CREVASSE

Saturday, March 1, 1969 A party of five was beginning a ski run from Palmer Glacier, down White River Glacier to the bridge on highway #35. At the 8,400-foot level Jack Vidoni led out toward the White River Canyon, making a turning stop just short of the canyon wall.

Behind him was James L. Eaton, 27, a tool designer at Albina Engine, who worked on weekends as a ski instructor for Timberline Lodge. Eaton suddenly dropped right out of sight into an unseen crevasse, and as Vidoni approached, he could see only Eaton's legs protruding from the snow about 60 feet down.

Vidoni yelled instructions to move his legs, if he were hurt. Vidoni saw Eaton's legs move. Helpless, without a climbing rope, the others quickly went for help. One member of the party skied across and intercepted a snow cat, whose driver radioed for the Ski Patrol. Vidoni headed for Timberline Lodge.

Meanwhile, a climbing group from Seattle came down from above and began rescue efforts. However, it was not before eight ski patrolmen came back in the snow cat, that anyone was able to dig Eaton out. Bud Siegel of MORESCO and MHSP, and Carman Jones of the Seattle group climbed into the crevasse for the final retrieval.

Eaton was not breathing. Despite mouth-to-mouth resuscitation, they could not revive him. He was pronounced dead at the top of the cornice as they loaded him into the snow cat.

A NIGHT IN AN IGLOO

Sunday, December 6, 1970 Dan Bronson, 21, and Ruth Torgerson, 17, left their car at Road 34 on Highway 26, between Rhododendron and Government Camp. Bronson planned to hike to Trillium Lake, although they did not start until 9:00 a.m.

Snow from two to three feet in depth slowed their rate of speed and caused confusion in directions. They found darkness approaching and it was obvious that they could not make it back to the car. Finding a wooden sign **Prevent Forest Fires**, they laid it on the ground for warmth and built an igloo around it. There was wind and a fine mist falling.

The igloo gave them enough protection to save their lives, although they had insufficient clothing to keep warm, and the board was very hard by the time daylight arrived. Miss Torgerson had to keep shaking herself to keep awake, fearing that she would relapse into permanent sleep.

Her mother, Hazel Torgerson of 2141 SW Martha in Portland, called the State Police, but they were helpless after they found the empty automobile on Road 34. It was Monday evening before the two were able to slog out to the highway again. Bronson estimated that they had walked about 11 miles in and another 14 miles back out by another route.

Bronson went to Good Samaritan Hospital for frostbite treatment. Miss Torgerson suffered no more than aching muscles and a bad cold.

MOON-FLANAGAN RESCUE

Sunday, December 27, 1970 two Eugene men, Dale Moon, 32, and Dr. Lathan Flanagan, 34, began a winter ascent at 3:15 a.m. from Timberline in fog and winds of 15-20 knots. They reached the Hogsback in a whiteout, where winds of 40 knots from the east arose. Flanagan led toward the summit, and Moon became aware that they were off course when they entered a series of small chimneys. They reached the summit about 1:00 p.m. and quickly descended. Temperature was about four degrees, and wind had increased to 50 knots.

They feared leaving the visual reference of Crater Rock and followed it south to its end, a route that brought them out onto ledges. They then retreated toward Crater Rock and dug a snow cave at about 4:00 p.m. Moon had a background of survival expertise, and they spent a good night in the cave.

Monday morning they emerged to descend the mountain. Visibility was 10 feet, and the wind blew so hard they had to hold onto each other to stand. Return to the cave was their only option. MORESCO was alerted that afternoon, and Tuesday at 2:00 a.m. James Angell left with a crew to check out the bergschrund on the Chute. Snow was so deep and the weather was so fierce that they were turned back at Silcox Hut. Another attempt was made in late morning to take the snow-cat up, and that failed because of weather.

A hundred MORESCO men showed up at Timberline. In midafternoon one search group went to White River Canyon, and Oliver Fursman took a team to Little Zigzag Canyon. Both returned in about three hours, beaten by the heavy snowfall.

On Wednesday a group of skiers was sent out by snow-cat to try to reach the Hogsback. Two more groups of eight were brought to Silcox Hut by snow-cat to back up the skiers, all wearing snow shoes. Behind them was a fourth group, composed of skiers. The snow-shoe parties fatigued and had to turn back. This took the support away from the skiers, so all teams were pulled back.

MORESCO was then placed on standby status until the weather broke. Two helicopters were ready. On the night of Thursday, December 31, Moon and Flanagan decided to make a desperate run for life, descending by flashlight and compass to the 6,000-foot level in snow drifted to punishing depths. They had drifted west into Little Zigzag Canyon, and could see the lights of Timberline Lodge reflected off the clouds. Wallowing through the snow, each step over the knee, exhausted them so much that they dug into the snow for another night.

New Year's Day dawned bright and clear, and rescue teams once more went up the mountain. Moon and Flanagan emerged from their snow bivouac about 8:00 and started floundering through the deep snow. Their progress was excruciatingly slow, and they were spotted by Bill Keil, scanning Little Zigzag Canyon with his telescope from Government Camp at 9:30 that morning.

The two were rushed to the Oregon Medical School, where they remained under the care of Dr. Cameron Bangs, specialist on frostbite and cold weather survival. Both men were pulled through the ordeal without loss of hands or feet. Both kept their interest in the sport of mountaineering. Moon returned three years later for another similar experience on Mount Hood.

REGAN KILLED IN SKI FALL

Sunday, January 24, 1971 Michael Dennis Regan of Seattle was killed at Timberline Lodge, when he ran over a 20-foot snow bank and fell to the asphalt roadway. The accident happened about noon. Regan was skiing in blizzard conditions in an unmarked area. He died of concussion and head injuries.

Authorities were not able to identify him until the next day. He was carrying a key to a car parked in the lot, which narrowed identification to one of two possible men. Fingerprint analysis confirmed that the body was that of Regan.

IRENE BAER SEARCH

Saturday, June 19, 1971 Irene Baer, 35, was reported lost off a Mazama climb. The leader, Kenneth Haig, had consolidated and counted his party after descending from the summit to the Hogsback. From there the party walked down in small groups, but in tight control between Haig and his assistant in the front of the party. In spite of that, she was able to leave the party, undetected.

Low on the mountain she was missed. The party searched for her for several hours and finally notified the Forest Service at 5:00 p.m. One of her climbing companions had seen her near the base of Crater Rock. Sand Canyon and both Zigzag Canyons were searched. At 7:00 a.m. Sunday MORESCO teams left for White River and Illumination Rock. By 8:30 they were recalled by radio; she had spent the night in the White River area and wandered into Timberline Lodge.

By that time Jack Grauer's MORESCO team had approached the bottom Triangle Moraine. The rest of the team turned back, but Grauer and Dick Getchell continued upward, contouring into the White River Canyon immediately below Steel Cliff. There they saw her tracks, and above were the marks in the snow, threading miraculously through a series of protruding rocks right up to the top of the White River Headwall. Striking any one of the rocks at the speed she was travelling would have killed or seriously injured her.

Up above, about a hundred feet below the regular ascent path below Crater Rock, they found her ice axe, dropped on her first tumble. Miss Baer had intentionally glissaded off the headwall, believing it to be the proper route down. The two MORESCO members celebrated her good luck by climbing to the summit of the mountain.

DEATH OF THE CARSONS

Sunday, August 8, 1971 Harry B. Carson, 42, his wife Joanne, 34, and their sons, Harry, Jr., 13, and Clinton, 12, were involved in a disastrous fall off the Cooper Spur Route onto Eliot Glacier.

Carson, an enthusiastic newcomer to the sport of mountaineering, had enlisted his family for the climb on the north side. While they were descending as a roped-team of four in the Chute or chimney below the summit, Clinton slipped and knocked his father off balance. Harry, Jr. and his mother dug their axes into the snow, but they were pulled out of position when the weight of the other two hit the line.

The four picked up too much speed to arrest, slid 1,000 feet on the slope, then shot down the 900 feet of high-angle ice to the glacier. They were not as fortunate as most of the parties who have made the involuntary slide. They struck protruding rocks part of the way down, then dropped over the lip of the bergschrund onto rocks below.

Harry Carson, Sr. and Clinton were reported dead on arrival at the hospital in Hood River. Joanne Carson suffered a broken leg and pelvis. Harry, Jr. had head and back injuries.

Robert Griffiths, 15, of Hartford, Connecticut, watched the fall, later remarking that they seemed unable to use their ice axes properly for self-arrest. Wes Weygandt, son of the old guide Mark Weygandt, was leading a hiking party below Cooper Spur. He was able to contact an amateur radio operator in Vancouver with his field set. Soon the message was in the hands of Sheriff R.L. Gilmouthe in Hood River. Jerry Bryan and Craig and Bill Sheppard started upward from Cloud Cap, taking along a radio.

Crag Rats, Alpinees, Hood River deputies, and Forest Service men sped to the scene. Two helicopters dropped a rescue party of 17 on a knoll southwest of Langille Crags. Harry Carson, Sr. and Clinton were evacuated, although they were probably dead at the time. But darkness was falling, and the helicopter pilots refused to go back in for the second load.

Sheriff Gilmouthe called on the army at Fort Lewis for a medical evacuation crew. The US Army responded, and Chief Warrant Officer Lindsay Gow, 23, arrived in a Huey helicopter. Bright moonlight helped him bring the aircraft in, but final spotting had to be done by MORESCO men using weak flashlights. Gow set the aircraft down on one runner on the steep snow, hovering while the remaining two victims were hastily loaded aboard. Before the MORESCO teams had groped their way down Eliot Glacier, pilot Gow had landed Joanne and Harry, Jr. at the Hood River airport. By 1:40 a.m. they were safe at the hospital.

Harry Carson, Sr. was a recreation specialist for the Forest Service at the ranger station at Parkdale. He had administered campgrounds and the Mount Hood Meadows Ski Area.

FALL OF MISS SULLIVAN

May 27, 1972 Mary Ellen Sullivan, 22, descending the Chute on South Side Route with a small group, slipped and tumbled 200 feet to the bottom. She sustained a broken right arm and ankle and cuts and bruises.

At the time Ken Hague and Homer Blackburn were leading a Mazama Basic School group upward. Seeing the accident, they hurried to Miss Sullivan's side and gave her first aid. They moved her down to the 9,000-foot level on a stretcher made of ice axes and clothing. A National Guard helicopter carrying Clackamas County deputies and Dr. Cameron Bangs, landed to pick her up for a trip to Willamette Falls Hospital in Oregon City.

The Mazama rescue team went back to the crater and took their 24-person party to the summit.

GIRL SLID INTO CREVASSE

Summer, 1972 Pam Kiel, 19, OSU coed from Coos Bay, was a member of a party of five descending Cooper Spur Route. While in the chimney she slipped and slid into a crevasse just below the foot of the chimney. Her own party carried her down to Tie-In-Rock. Members of Luther Jersted's mountaineering school brought a litter and carried her to the glacier floor.

A message was sent by radio to Cloud Cap Inn where seven Crag Rats were spending the day. They ascended the glacier to get her, and had her back at the Inn by 7:00 p.m. She was not seriously injured.

LAFEMAN DEATH ON WEST SIDE

1972 Jack Alvin Lafeman, Jr., 21, of Vancouver, Washington, attempted Mount Hood on a solo climb on August 25. A climber of limited experience, he was proceeding up Yokum Ridge at the 7300-foot level. He apparently lost his footing on ice and dropped his axe. He fell 60 feet over a cliff and slid another 200 feet or more on snow.

Explorer Scout crews found the body the next day, and a National Guard helicopter took it to Portland. Details were reported by Sergeant Lloyd Ryan, Clackamas County deputy, to the *Oregonian.*

HUNG ON ROPE ALL NIGHT

Friday, February 24, 1974 Jerrit Donald Henderson, 26, James Doherty, 24, and Sarah Burke, 22, left Timberline Lodge at 9:00 a.m. for a two-day climb of South Side Route. The weather deteriorated, and they finally were enveloped in white-out that cut visibility to zero.

In such conditions climbers and skiers often have difficulty knowing which way is up. At the 8,000-foot level, Henderson stepped through the cornice on the White River Glacier, not fully realizing he was falling until he was arrested by the tightening of the climbing rope. The canyon wall where he landed was very steep, and he was hanging on the end of the rope about 50 feet down.

His rope-mates sunk in an ice axe at the top and tied him off. This was then backed up with a snow anchor Sarah was carrying in her pack. Doherty then tried to pull Henderson up, but the weight was too great. No communication was possible with him, because of the howling storm that swept the mountainside. Henderson had the snow shovel in his pack, and he used it to dig a cave in the snow of the canyon wall. There he spent the night.

On top the cornice, Doherty and Miss Burke spent a long, cold night in the storm. Just before dawn they left for Timberline Lodge, arriving there about 10:00 a.m. Saturday morning. When dawn came Henderson came out of his cave and made his way up the rope, but he could not maneuver his way over the cornice without help, finally falling back to his original position.

A Ski Patrol team went up in the snow cat, taking Doherty back to show them Henderson's position. When they finally got him back to Timberline Lodge, authorities had a helicopter ready in the parking lot to fly him directly to Willamette Falls Hospital for treatment of hypothermia and frostbite. Major William Gottlieb was the pilot, and Dr. Cameron Bangs was aboard as the physician.

MOON MAROONED SECOND TIME

Saturday, March 7, 1974 Dale Moon, 35, Clayton Cox, 46, and Lawrence Owens, 29, of Eugene, left Timberline Lodge on skis to put in a base camp at 7,500 feet, not far above Silcox Hut. They had a four-man tent, stove, and adequate camping gear. Weather was calm and fair.

Moon had been involved in a severe survival in a cave on the side of Crater Rock in the last days of December of 1970. He is considered a survival expert by virtue of considerable training.

The trio climbed Mount Hood on Sunday in threatening weather. A severe storm raged, as they descended from the summit, and Moon became confused, going down the wrong side of the Hogsback. At about the 10,400-foot level, visibility was so bad and wind so fierce, that they dug a snow cave and took refuge. Wind was estimated as high as 70 miles per hour and temperature at zero.

For three days and nights the men were pinned down by a storm that did not let up. By Tuesday, Al Combs was organizing a MORESCO search and a helicopter flight was made, proving useless. The first probe Tuesday night found the camp above Silcox Hut. This gave the searchers the information that the lost climbers were holed up in a cave, if they were alive.

Eugene rescue men turned out in force to help their friends. Some of the team were James Blanchard, Mike Seeley, and Wayne Arrington. At 2:00 p.m. on Wednesday, the weather let up, and Moon, Cox, and Owens were able to leave their cave, hurrying down the mountain as fast as possible. They saw the rescue party and the rescuers saw them at about the same time.

Moon refused to regard the operation as a rescue, not wanting to accept a ride in the snow cat until coerced. At Timberline Lodge, Dr. Cameron Bangs waited in a helicopter flown by Captain Herb Sims, Chief Warrant Officer Ron Reade, and Specialist 5 Cliff Conser. Bangs had considerable difficulty in getting the trio to board the aircraft to go to Willamette Falls Hospital in Oregon City for observation for frostbite.

"You are a good survival expert. You have to set a good example," he told Moon. They reluctantly boarded the helicopter.

Dr. Bangs later commented on the 17 mountain victims he had treated since 1973, noting that the whole state of Alaska had only 12 hypothermia victims in the 1973-4 winter season.

The rescue effort had involved about 100 mountaineers, expending from 1,500 to 2,000 man hours of time. Some had commented "Oh, it's Moon again," and refused to join the operation when called. The operation had consumed a reported $6,000 of helicopter time. Lew Russell, Jr. had put his snow cat onto the hill at no charge, and Timberline Lodge had likewise stood the expense of several cats and drivers.

Al Combs of MORESCO noted that there had been 42 people missing in just the month of November, 1973, indicating a tremendous load for law enforcement agencies to bear. Sergeant Tom Cuttsforth of Clackamas County Sheriff's Office had been on the search. He said that he had personally handled about 20 missions during the season.

Moon commented "that he was very embarrassed about the whole thing."

TWO FELL TO REID GLACIER

March 24, 1974 David Henry, 21, of North Bonneville, Washington, and William Magruder, 18, of Stevenson, were attempting to climb the Castle Crags Route up from Reid Glacier. They were tied into a climbing rope and well up the ice and snow cliffs, when one slipped.

The resulting tumble 1500 feet down the ledges to Reid Glacier was devastating, and they lay partly conscious upon the ice for about three hours. The accident had occurred at about 7:00 a.m. About 9:30 a.m. Laurence MacDaniels and John Heak topped Illumination Saddle on their way to cross Reid Glacier and climb the Leuthold Couloir. It was then that they saw Henry and Magruder sprawled out on the surface of the glacier.

Two other climbing groups were camped in the depression east of Illumination Saddle. One group from Salem had done the Leuthold Couloir the day before. One of them had broken his ice axe, therefore he was chosen to descend to Timberline Lodge for help, while the others went to help the injured.

The second group, Mike Volk and a friend, broke up their camp to take foam pads and sleeping bags down to keep the victims warm, following MacDaniels and Heak down to where they lay.

Henry and Magruder were found badly mauled from the pummelling they had taken as they struck repeatedly on the frozen slopes. Had they not been discovered, they would surely have died. Clackamas County deputy Sergeant Lloyd Ryan called for an Oregon National Guard helicopter. Flown by Major William Gottlieb, it came in with Dr. Cameron Bangs to hover on one runner, while the victims were hastily loaded.

At Willamette Falls Hospital in Oregon City they found that Henry had suffered skull fracture, a broken pelvis, and neck damage. Magruder had several fractures and had a loss of memory for a long while. Eventually he returned to normal.

David Henry suffered permanent brain damage. At the last checking in February of 1975, he was barely able to feed himself. He was sent from Oregon City to a nursing home in Vancouver under the care of Dr. Robert Kim, where it is expected he shall remain under permanent care.

CHINESE STUDENT KILLED

1974 Roger Dale Robinson, 20, and Richard Benjamin Chu, 24, left Timberline Lodge at 6:00 a.m. on Sunday, August 18, for a trip around Mount Hood at 7,000 to 9,000-foot elevation. Proceeding clockwise, they were crossing Coe Glacier near Pulpit Rock. Robinson, the more experienced, was at the rear of the 120-foot rope. Chu jumped, landing as intended on the overhanging edge of a crevasse, but the lip broke away, plummeting him to the bottom.

To check the fall, Robinson jumped the opposite direction over a ridge of ice. When he climbed back out, he found Chu lying at the bottom of the crevasse, only an arm and a leg visible, his body covered with congealed snow. Unable to dig him out, Robinson ran for help from a party of climbers under the leadership of Dale Moon, holding a crevasse-rescue training session on Eliot Glacier. It took twenty minutes for four men to dig Chu out of the tremendous weight of ice that covered him.

A physician in Moon's party declared Chu dead. The weight of snow had probably killed him on impact, or else the snow had quickly suffocated him. They carried him down Coalman's Scoot to Timberline Trail. Richard R. Pooley had observed the problem with field glasses from Cloud Cap Inn and radioed the sheriff's office in Hood River. The call was answered by Crag Rats and Alpinees.

A DEADLY TRIP HOME

June 2, 1974 Joanne Conrath, a teacher at Concord Elementary School at Milwaukie, made her first ascent of Mount Hood on a regularly scheduled South Side climb of The Mazamas led by Nancy Icenogle and Ray Snyder.

She found the first mile up to Silcox Hut very punishing, but she later got her stride and topped the summit in a very elated condition. It so happened that Channel 8 Television sent along a cameraman to record the climb as a typical Mazama event, and Mrs. Conrath was interviewed on the summit, speaking very enthusiastically about her first successful ascent.

When the party reached the parking lot at Timberline Lodge after the climb, Nancy Icenogle told her goodbye and chatted with her. Noting that Mrs. Conrath seemed very tired, she said, "the drive home is the most dangerous part of the climb, you know. Don't you want to stop in at Mazama Lodge and sleep a bit?"

Joanne Conrath declined. She wanted to get home, but promised she would stop her automobile and rest, if she got sleepy. These were her last words to any human being. Between Highway 26 and the town of Boring, she ran off the road and died of injuries of the crash.

PTARMIGANS' TWO NIGHTS IN CAVE

Saturday, February 17, 1975 Floyd Whiting, 33 and Henry Berquist, 31, Portland men who are members of the Ptarmigan Club, climbers of Vancouver, Washington, left Timberline Lodge at 6:00 a.m. for a climb of Wy'east Route. After passing Silcox Hut, they ran into soft snow and unfavorable weather conditions.

This caused them to change to the South Side Route, instead of the more difficult Wy'east ascent. About noon they were at 10,000 feet, when a white-out descended upon them. After a short lunch break, they decided to retreat. They descended about 800 feet, then put on their skis, and continued to a lower elevation. Then another white-out enveloped them, so severe that they could not see their feet.

Whiting and Berquist spent two full nights in their cave, about a half mile above Silcox Hut at the 8,000-foot level. By the second day, water began to drip off the ceiling, soaking their clothing. They continued to huddle together and wiggle fingers and toes to avoid freezing. Several times Sunday they looked out of the cave to find the storm still roaring in zero visibility. On Monday morning a rescue crew in a snow cat saw their skis sticking up in the snow, and headed for them.

As Whiting and Berquist heard the machine approach, they dug out to reveal their position. Their discovery was very fortunate. They might very well have been pinned down for several days to become victims of hypothermia.

SKIER KILLED IN WIND STORM

Sunday, March 30, 1975 The first death of a cross country skier occurred on Mount Hood, when Dr. Richard Selden, 32, fell to his death into Newton Canyon at about 4:15 a.m.

On Saturday a group of four had left their automobile at Hood River Meadow, Dr. Selden, Vawter Parker, 29, David Wilson, 29, and John Stevason., 28. Travelling on cross country skis, they followed Clark Canyon upward, planning to camp out and finish their trip on Sunday at Cloud Cap Inn and Cooper Spur Junction. Weather was warm and sunny.

There was a little fresh snow on a hard, crusty base, and they progressed easily, traversing upward on the giant moraine that separates Newton and Clark Creeks. In the afternoon they established a camp at about the 7,000-foot level and pitched their tent. In late afternoon there were mild indications that the weather was changing. A northeast wind was blowing, probably at about 20 knots at 5:00 p.m.

By mid-evening it became obvious that the storm was becoming much worse. Clouds were beginning to show above. About midnight the wind suddenly changed direction, coming in from the southwest at 50 knots with stronger gusts. Their night in the tent was sleepless, as the tent snapped and cracked in the gale. Finally they began to fear that the wind would pick up the tent and blow them into Newton Canyon, so they packed up their gear with the idea of running for lower elevation.

Vawter Parker stated that they began their descent on foot into Clark Canyon, all four abreast in the whiteout, at about 4:00 a.m. During the process of packing up, three of the knapsacks slipped away and were blown into the canyon. Dr. Selden was on Parker's right (west) as they left camp; Wilson and Stevason were to his left.

Selden slipped! Parker heard him yell, but did not note any great distress in his voice. Seconds later there was another cry, then no more contact. Then Parker slipped and found himself sliding downward, controlling a sitting glissade with his ski pole and moving directly down the fall line to the bottom of the Clark Canyon about 300 feet below on slope estimated about 35 degrees.

On coming to a stop, Parker rose and expected to find Selden somewhere on the canyon floor just above him in the gloom, but he had no success. Then, walking down the canyon, he found the physician lying there, still alive, but unconscious. With no flashlight, he used merely the faint reflected light in the enveloping clouds to examine his friend, finding a bleeding head wound, broken right leg, and a left shoulder that seemed dislocated or broken. There was little that Parker could do, and Selden died about a half hour later.

Parker had tried to locate Wilson and Steva-son, but his shouts were muffled by the gale. The white-out had cut visibility to only a few feet. He moved upward a short distance, and was able to detect Selden's path by the blood on the snow, even in that indistinct light. But there was no answer from his friends above, and he assumed that they must have slipped or walked down into the canyon and were already on their way to the automobile. Actually they were in the lee of a giant rock, near the top of the moraine, completely unable to hear his shouts from the short distance below.

The gale-driven pellets of ice scored his face, and Parker decided that he must start downward. Soon the first light of dawn began to help him in picking his way through the storm. Before 8:00 a.m. he was back in his automobile, got it started, and felt the life-saving warmth of the heater on his feet and hands. By 8:30 he had arrived at Mount Hood Meadows to summon help, just as many of the ski patrolmen were reporting in for a stormy Sunday's duty.

Norman McKinnon, manager of the resort, took over the rescue operation until the arrival of Robert Lynch, Sheriff of Hood River County at about 9:30. When Lynch arrived, George Wilson, Jack Mitchem, and Richard Pooley went up to Texas Lift to survey the weather and snow conditions. Slopes were icy and the storm showed little signs of abatement. Wilson took two ski instructors, and skied from about the 8,000-foot level above Texas Lift, crossing the Newton Clark Glacier to a point of descent into Clark Canyon, where Parker's description indicated that the body of the physician lay.

About 9:30 a.m. Pooley, Mitchem, and Mike Gehrman, head of MHM Ski Patrol, left the top of Texas Lift, and began contouring around Heather Canyon on a wall which seemed impossibly steep in the storm. Gehrman took the front of the akja, while Pooley took the rear, fighting their way across the icy slopes, depending on their metal edges for any little bit of grip to be had.

As they neared Clark Canyon the white-out began to lift. George Wilson and his two companions got to the body first and reported in by radio. By about 10:45, Pooley, Mitchem, and Gehrman had reached the scene with the akja and began loading the remains of Dr. Selden, along with knapsacks found in the area, about 250 pounds of load. Still nothing had been seen of the other two lost men, Wilson and Stevason, although they were just above the site of the body. Standing by the rock and yelling, their shouts were lost in the wind, and not a person in the rescue party saw them waving their arms. They were afraid to descend the icy slopes. At one time they thought they had been seen, but no such luck! Both Pooley and George Wilson thought they heard voices, but forgot about it, when Mike Gehrman said it was the radio.

Another party left from the top of Texas Lift, Miles Weaver, James Brischlee, and Stan Harriman, descending into Heather Canyon and onto Heather Ridge. They must have looked right over at Wilson and Stevason , but did not see them, and came on out toward the highway, following the akja team. Rene Farwig and a team of ski instructors from MHM came into Clark Canyon via the top of the yellow chair, following the general route of the Timberline Trail.

A Crag Rat group left Hood River Meadow about 12:45 p.m. to ski up Newton Canyon. This seemed to be the best place to look for the two lost men. The group consisted of Bob Sheppard, Wilson Applegren, Les Hukari, Rob Hukari, Kent Lambert, and James Wells.

Meanwhile, another team had started out the high route from the top of Texas Lift, Rich Morton, James Gunesch, William Gunesch, and Kevin Wiley. This team made the find, seeing Wilson and Stevason by the big rock about 200 feet below the moraine crest. Morton hurried down to Heather Ridge to make the report on Miles Weaver's radio, then finally continued on down, leaving the Gunesch brothers and Wiley waiting for the arrival of climbing equipment to negotiate the icy slope. From the time of the find at about 2:30 p.m. the three waited for about two hours, then finally made a desperate move in side-slipping down on the ice to the two victims. The storm was beginning to move in again, and they knew that action must be taken.

Wiley took the small amount of remaining equipment, and the Gunesch brothers began a descent down the steep ice in a very novel manner. Each of the victims was given a ski pole and told to lie face down on the slope, with his crotch against the skier's leg. James and William Gunesch then began inching down the ice, taking side steps and depending on their metal edges to kick in a new hold before the victims held on the ski poles, just above the baskets.

It was certainly well that Wiley and the Gunesch brothers made their move when they did, because the effort to bring climbing equipment to the scene had failed. Norman McKinnon had outfitted Dave Sheppard, Darval Lloyd, and two other men with crampons, rope, gloves, and face masks, and sent them as high as the snow cat can operate above Texas Lift. But by that time the clear weather, which they had enjoyed since about 10:30 a.m., had disappeared; whiteout once more enveloped the mountain slopes. They sat in the snow cat, waiting for a break in the weather which did not come.

The fast-moving Rich Morton, who is Assistant Manager of Mountain Operations at MHM, had returned to his office, having left Heather Ridge just before 3:00 p.m. He recruited Darrell Lloyd of the Alpinee's and Steve Bratt, Assistant Ski School Director, for another trip to the Newton Clark moraine. They crossed once more from the top of Texas Lift, and came down to the big rock, where the two victims had spent 13 hours waiting for help. But all that remained was one orange parka.

Taking thorough precautions, Darrell Lloyd took off his skis and donned crampons to make a search of the area. The rescue team was well on their way to Hood River Meadow, of course, and he found nothing. But at the end of the search he could not find his skis in the whiteout, so he was forced to walk all the way to the highway, with Rich Morton accompanying him. Steve Bratt skied on ahead and reached the rescue party, just as they were approaching the automobile parking area at Hood River Meadow.

This tale of the recovery of Dr. Richard Selden's body and the rescue of David Wilson and John Stevason has been given in more than the usual detail. Most of the other search and rescue operations in the history of Mount Hood have been equally as complex, with many parties probing the mountainside, then finally bringing out the victims under gruelling conditions. But the author wished to illustrate the typical complexity of such an operation, and here was the opportunity to interview several of the rescue men, while the incident was still fresh on their minds.

As to the unusual nature of this fatal accident, it is surmised that Dr. Selden was actually airborne, as he was falling down the slopes, the wind crashing him headfirst into a rock. Wind velocity was in the 60 knot range with gusts that could have been close to 100.

Richard Polley states that he and two companions personally experienced being airborne on a 1974 ski trip across Newton Clark Glacier and down Cooper Spur. Winds were 80 knots and more, and they hoped to find shelter from the wind after crossing the ridge of Cooper Spur. But such was not the case, and he, Jack Mitchem, and John McCormick were all airborne at times, when wind caught them in bad moments. Their experience was nothing more serious than being crash landed at high speed, but the presence of a rock on the slope could have been disastrous.

It is well to reflect upon the expense of such an operation. Norman McKinnon volunteered the free use of his snow cats, personnel of the ski school, and food and drink during and after the operation, a sizeable chunk of money. The skiers involved had not departed from Mount Hood Meadows and were not his customers in any way. The Gunesch brothers, and many others had crossed the icy slopes, and risked their own lives to save the survivors.

Such response to emergency is of course not new to Mount Hood. Timberline Lodge, since its earliest days, has been on the firing line during such emergencies. Richard Kohnstamm and Everett Darr have often contributed freely to save lives without the slightest hope of being recompensed. Hundreds of Ski Patrol and MORESCO members have risked their own safety to bring in victims. May these brief lines of recognition at least acknowledge the efforts of a few to help the many.

SALLIE HEE KILLED IN AVALANCHE

Saturday, April 26, 1975 Four groups of the Mazama Basic Climbing School were receiving ice and snow training in the Timberline Lodge area. About noon three ropes of the group led by Lawrence W. Stadler departed from the Salmon River Canyon and headed for White River Canyon. After a lunch they began the steep descent into White River Canyon, a drop of about 500 feet.

They descended well toward the bottom of the canyon in roped team travel, three of the instructors remaining unroped and following slightly behind, Larry Stadler, Gary L. Beck, and Edwin J. Weber. The roping order of the first string was Samuel Nebel, 31, Kathleen Hastey, and Sallie C. Hee, 28, an instructor in oceanography at Oregon State University. Miss Hee, a climbing instructor in the group, had a good background of experience in mountaineering, both on snow and rock.

The second rope was at approximately the same altitude and a bit south of the first. Roping order was Barbara McDevitt, Matt Hammerquist, 15, and Craig Peterson. The third was still up at a higher level on the slope, being followed by Weber.

Suddenly a large area of the slope slabbed off and began to move, developing immediately into a full-scale avalanche. All six members of the first two ropes found themselves being carried along in the relentless stream of wet, heavy snow, which slithered silently downward. Kathleen Hastey flailed her arms in a swimming motion, using the technique she had heard mentioned in a lecture a few days before.

When the snow came to rest, Stadler, Beck, and Weber were quickly on the scene, digging furiously to uncover the victims. Hammerquist and Peterson of the second rope quickly emerged and helped in the operation. Barbara McDevitt was quickly located and her head exposed, although she had been buried completely. Samuel Nebel, first on the #1 rope, found himself lying ontop the snow. Near him he could see the bright-colored gloves of Kathleen Hastey sticking out of the snow, and he dug her head out, so that she could breathe.

Only the rope emerging from the snow gave a clue of Sallie Hee's location. Digging along it, the instructors and survivors, located her feet. She rested head down, and about 25 minutes had passed since the beginning of the avalanche. Efforts at resuscitation were fruitless, and she became the first avalanche fatality on Mount Hood, as well as the only fatality of the Mazama Climbing School.

Word was sent of the accident by Matt Hammerquist, who informed Richard Tilschner in another group. But long before he could reach the top, Tilschner had already found out about the accident and sent his wife, Nancy, to the lodge to notify the Forest Service. Failing to receive quick response, Tilschner sent over Al Prilliman, who arranged for the assistance of Lew Russell and his privately-owned snow cat.

Development of Skiing at Mount Hood

MOUNT HOOD'S EARLIEST

The first skiing on Mount Hood was done on home-made boards by pioneers using them in lieu of snow shoes, men such as Vickers, Coalman, the Langilles, Mecklem, O.C. Yocum, and Dick Maupin, forest ranger at Summit Meadows. As these people occasionally received guests on the mountain in winter, the guests began to try on skis also.

An expedition that drew much attention was made in 1903 by Colonel L.L. Hawkins, Martin Gorman, and T. Brook White, all officials of The Mazamas. Hawkins made the skis, ten feet long, and a nine-foot balance pole for each man. Equipped with furs to endure the expected, death-dealing arctic cold, they planned to ascend as high on the mountain as possible. O.C. Yocum put them up at Government Camp and heard White prophesize that "the time would come when more people would visit Mount Hood in the winter, than in the summer." If Mr. White could only have known the size of crowds to come, he would have been staggered.

THE MAZAMAS TRIED SKIING

The story of a Christmas vacation ski trip to Government Camp in 1913 by Anna Shannon Monroe gives much background of the south side at that time. Other participants were Osmon Royal, Jess L. Gilkey, D.Y. Lebb, H.H. Prouty, Dr. C.V. Luther, Jerry E. Bronaugh, Rose Coursen Reed, Edith Ellis, Charles E. Atlas, Catherine Poole, Anne Dillinger, Mrs. C.E. Dillinger, Mildred I. Faubion, and Domenico Maraschino, all Mazamas.

They took the train to Bull Run, then the stage to Rhododendron for a night at the inn. On Tuesday, December 28, Lige Coalman took them to Government Camp. The first five miles was on foot, but there they found sufficient snow to don skis, the first time for most of them. With Coalman's coaching they picked up enough ability to make the four miles up 2,000 feet of elevation in three hours, arriving at Government Camp in a great state of hilarity, a little cold and ravenous for food.

A half-dozen cabins stood there near the great tavern, all white and dead and still in drifted snow. The hotel keepers were not living there that winter, and Lige opened up. The men soon had fires going, and Coalman was in the kitchen making dinner that even included huckleberry pie. A little more skiing in the afternoon filled out the day, and the group enjoyed the evening around the fire.

This was a short ski trip, because the next morning they headed for Rhododendron Inn again, gliding through the forest covered with the snow of the evening before. As they ended the run on skis, Coalman practically had to forcibly remove them from some of the party, enthusiasm was running so high for the new sport. By the time they had walked the five miles back to the inn, everyone was tired.

At Rhododendron, A.R. Hine and R.W. Wilson had arrived to join the group. The management telephoned everyone in the valley, and on New Year's Eve, families began arriving, bringing their children and dogs. Maraschino, the Italian chef at the inn, played his accordian while the group held a big Christmas tree exchange of gifts. Then all hands joined in for a great New Year's dance. As 1913 ended they locked arms and sang Auld Lang Syne, then beating hammers on frying pans or whatever could create noise, they welcomed 1914.

New Year's Day was a happy trip back to Portland, calling on the Faubions at La Casa Monte. At Aschoff's at Marmot, a holiday dinner with roast goose and every other special treat Mrs. Aschoff could set upon the table, greeted them at noon. Harley Prouty, president of The Mazamas then led the group on foot the eight miles to catch the train at Bull Run.

ANOTHER MAZAMA TRIP

Having enjoyed themselves so much the previous year, The Mazamas made their second winter outing to Mount Hood. The leaders were H.H. Prouty and Osmon Royal. The contingent took the train from Portland the Saturday after Christmas, spent the night at Hood River, then caught the Parkdale train. Homer Rogers met them with his big sleigh and four horses to take them to his Mount Hood Lodge.

Some of the more adventurous went up to the hill beyond the John Goldsbury Ranch on the Cloud Cap Road Monday afternoon. The next day the whole party went up to Cloud Cap Inn. Mark Weygandt had prepared the trail a few days in advance by cutting 16 windfall trees out of the

Single Pole Skiers near Mount Hood Lodge
Photo Homer Rogers

road. Both the inn and the Snowshoe Club Lodge were locked, of course, and the party started their slide downward. On the way down they encountered the old cabin of Offield, an earlier-day trapper. Most of the party went on down to Mount Hood Lodge, but Mrs. Rose Coursen-Reed, Miss Ann Dillinger, Miss Hazel Mills, D.G. Lebb, H.H. Prouty, Osmon Royal, and guide Mark Weygandt decided to spend Tuesday night in the deserted cabin.

They had brought up blankets and food, and the cabin protected them well, as the gale howled around the eaves all night. The weather cleared later in the night to show the beauty of the north side in the moonlight. On Wednesday morning Prouty and Miss Dillinger put on their skis and set out for Cooper Spur. The skis could be used only a short distance, and they struggled upward in wind so strong they frequently could not stand against it. They finally topped the ridge at 8,500 feet elevation and sent mirror signals back to Osmon Royal who was following their progress from a viewpoint at Cloud Cap Inn.

All hands then returned to Mount Hood Lodge. Thursday was New Year's Eve, and the day was spent in social calls. Harriet Monroe, a guest at a nearby ranch, entertained them with a taffy-pull, and at 10:30 a holiday supper was held at the Coulter Ranch. Then everyone trouped back to Mount Hood Lodge, where Homer Rogers threw a dance that lasted into the New Year.

The following day Weygandt took another group back to the cabin again, Mrs. Coursen-Reed, Miss Anna Nickell, Miss Hazel Mills, E.F. Peterson, Conrad Sieberts, and Osmon Royal. This time all hoped to reach the top of Cooper Spur. On the way to the cabin a foot of new snow fell as they ascended, dampening the enthusiasm considerably. At 11:00 p.m. the weather cleared and some of the "owls" hiked up to Cloud Cap Inn to spend half the night exploring.

Saturday morning Sieberts, Peterson, and Miss Nickell started out with guide Weygandt. The air was bitterly cold, and they could hardly stand against the fierce wind. The ascent ended before they left the timbered area. A good run was enjoyed on the way back to Rogers'. On Sunday the group said a reluctant farewell to Rogers and took the train back toward Hood River and home.

Many of the skiers on such trips were complete novices. Steering the eight-foot boards was done in gentle arcs, many times resulting in a crash into a snow bank. Balance was maintained with the seven-foot ski pole, a stout cudgel cut in the forest, used to propel by pushing back on one side or the other. Placing the stick between the legs and sitting down on it gave the skier a way to stop.

When one remembers that the original Cloud Cap Road was a much shorter, direct route down to Elk Beds, Goldsbury Ranch, and on to Mount Hood Lodge, he must consider that the road was steep. Those beginning skiers must have had a great many fearful moments as they plunged down those grades on very heavy, very long boards.

The Mazamas were no sooner back in Portland, spreading the word of their great trip, when the Portland Indoor Ski Club held a meeting at the Multnomah Athletic Club and planned a trip for January 22. They also re-elected A.D. Wakeman as president.

Hjalmar Hvooming over Cornice 1937 — Photo Hjalmar Hvam
Later in the day a broken leg.

YMCA SKIERS ON NORTH SIDE

On January 21, 1915, a YMCA group left for a similar week of skiing under the leadership of physical director A.M. Grilley. William McMurray, general passenger agent of the Oregon-Washington Railroad and Navigation Company, took them from Hood River to Parkdale in his private rail car. He then accompanied them to Mount Hood Lodge, where he was a featured dinner speaker during their stay. The group included Frank R. Kerr, J.P. Plagemann, Roy Clark, R.H. Atkinson, H.W. Stone, M.M. Ringler, F.L. Schanz, W.H. Kiles, Si Woodworth, N. Olness, W.M. Umbendstock, and Morris Barnes.

Moving pictures of the trip were taken for the Northwest Weekly. A trip to Cloud Cap Inn gave them a chance to experience thrills at "express train speeds". The members of the Snowshoe Club were holding their own outing at the time and invited them in for hospitality around their fireplace. They stayed after dark and skied down in fogbound blackness. Before the YMCA group returned to Portland they elected Frank Kerr as president for the coming year.

Although the north side had the established rail line that gave transportation very close to Mount Hood, and although Homer Rogers was offering the best in accommodations at his lodge, the south side had some activity. *The Oregonian* reported the first adventurers to reach Government Camp, William W. Evans and Fred J. Neidermeyer, both 20. Going to Pleasant Home by rail, they walked the 28 miles to Rhododendron to spend the night.

The following day the two walked to Government Camp to spend the day skiing and snowshoeing as guests of Pridemore and Fox. Late in the day they walked back to Rhododendron. Evans was to become prominent in the news one year later, when he joined Charles Warner in the first winter traverse over the summit.

RACING ON ELIOT GLACIER

The Crag Rats, Hood River Ski Club, and the American Legion were all composed of many of the same members, not 100%, but close to it. When the Legion ran its annual climb, the Crag Rats took responsibility for leading it. Those, who were not needed, usually took some sort of trip across the Eliot Glacier or went skiing on the glacier.

In 1930 a ski competition was held. The contestants raced across Eliot Glacier up to the point where climbers usually started the Sunshine Route, then ran back down to the starting point. It was somewhat a combination between cross-country and giant slalom. On the same day, another group of Crag Rats was producing a moving picture on the glacier, and one made, disappeared into a blind crevasse.

The success of the competition led Hood River Ski Club to hold it again in 1931. Percy Bucklin headed the activity. At one point, they decided to stretch a rope along a crevasse, which lay below the course a short distance. During the race, Cascade Ski Club's Arne Stene fell on a turn and could not stop himself on the ice. As he shot down toward the crevasse, he grabbed the rope and held it across his chest. It undoubtedly saved his life. Stene rose to come in second in the field of five contestants; first place was won by Nels Skjersaa.

ON SKIS TO THE SUMMIT

1931 See CLIMBS OF NOTE April 26, for the story of the first ascent on skis of Mount Hood. Andre Roch, Hjalmar Hvam, Arne Stene.

APPEARANCE OF THE CHRISTIE

1931 Swiss skier Fritz Bierly appeared on the slopes at Government Camp and astounded local skiers with the first Christiana turns they had ever seen. Within a short time many skiers were doing "christies" and all were managing a poor imitation. This beautiful turn, which was the classic, expert manner of changing direction until well after World War 2, was the sensation of Mount Hood.

A TYPICAL THIRTIES RACE

Sunday, June 14, 1936 A well publicized ski race of national caliber was run in conjunction with the Portland Rose Festival. Newspaper stories written beforehand referred to the race as the Mazama Cup, but the Monday reports did not use that name. It is possible that it was changed the day of the race. The course was set from Crater Rock down to timberline and scored on combined results of downhill and slalom.

Hjalmar Hvam took the honors, although the second place winner, Boyd French, Jr., had a better time on the downhill. The contest drew top-ranking competitors from Seattle and Vancouver, British Columbia. Other local entries were Bob Donaldson of The Mazamas, Roy Tangen of Cascade Ski Club, and Jack Walker of Portland. Adams Carter came from the east to represent Harvard, but broke a ski on his run. Winners Hvam and French represented Cascade Ski Club.

High school entrants ran a course into the Salmon River Canyon. Competition in this age group was just becoming established. Some of the contestants were Ed Berg and Ted Beem of Grant, Tom Terry of Lincoln, Albert Dutton and Bob Schramm of Washington, Ole Herwig and Kurt Aune of Franklin, and 14-year old Don French who had just graduated from Rose City Grade School.

CIRCUIT ON SKIS

1951 Friday, March 23, Ray Conkling and Bill Oberteuffer left Timberline Lodge at 6:00 a.m. for a trip around Mount Hood on skis at the 9000-foot level. On the first day they crossed White River Glacier, Newton Clark Glacier to Cooper Spur. On Elliot Glacier and Coe Glacier they had to go on foot, using ice axes and crampons. The first night was spent at Barrett Spur.

On Saturday they crossed Sandy Glacier, Yocum Ridge, and climbed up Reid Glacier to Illumination Saddle for the camp of the second night. On Sunday they had an easy run down to Timberline Lodge.

Weather was harsh. Of two parties that tried for the summit on Sunday, one turned back because of wind, cold, and ice. The trip revived a custom of the Wy'east Climbers of the Thirties, but it had not been done for many years.

SKIING SAID TO BE SAFER

March 30, 1960 In an address to the American College of Surgeons, Dr. A. Gurney Kimberley declared that skiing is a relatively safe sport and is becoming safer as time goes on.

More lifts are getting more people onto the big hills, he said. Kimberley stated that accident ratio rates are more favorable than they were in 1950, despite the fact that the mountains are full of people gliding down 45-degree slopes, winding through brush, rocks, and stumps, negotiating varying textures of snow and ice in varying weather and light conditions, and attaining speeds up to 60 miles per hour.

He cited the payoff of release bindings, good ski instruction, and teaching the consequences of extreme fatigue. Kimberley warned against the use of hand-straps on ski poles.

AMPUTEES BEGAN COMPETITION

Saturday, April 4, 1964 The first National Amputee Race was scheduled at Timberline Lodge. Wind, rain, and freezing sleet were enough to keep most two-legged skiers off the slopes, but nine contestants entered the race. The course was originally planned alongside the Magic Mile, but bad weather closed the lift. The start of the race was moved down near the lodge, with the finish line in Pucci's Glade.

This entailed a lot of laborious climbing up to the starting line by the one-legged skiers, using ski poles tipped with small skis. Richard Martin placed first, Dr. Herbert Shinn of Bremerton came in second, Colin Caldwell of Leechburg, Pennsylvania third, Calvin Andrews fourth, and Roger Fors fifth. Colette Brenaman, 10, of Longview, Washington, was a contestant. Although not PNSA sanctioned, the race was run by PNSA rules.

The National Amputee Race was run each year thereafter. In 1969 the race was run on the Magic Mile on March 1 with 19 entrants, sponsored by the Flying Outrigger Ski Club of the Northwest. Harold Schroeder of Portland won the Senior A competition. Richard Martin, who had won three of the first four annual races, missed a gate and did not place in the winners' list.

Pat West of Entiat, Washington, won the Senior B title, and Mike Engelman the Senior C. Stephan Carroll of Gresham took the Junior B honors, and John May of Lebanon the Junior C.

SKIING DOWN EASTERN CLIFFS

1971 The skiing world was electrified when Sylvain Saudan, 35, Swiss mountain guide and ski instructor, skied off the precipitous east face of Mount Hood on March 1. Saudan had waited patiently as a guest of Mount Hood Meadows for two weeks in order to get the right conditions for the record breaking run. No advance publicity was released, and the public knew nothing of his plans until newspapers reported the story the following day.

Previous to the day of Saudan's exploit, gale-driven blizzards had dumped four feet of snow on Mount Hood. Monday, March 1, dawned bright, and he made preparations for his run, although the depth of loose, new snow offered the threat of serious avalanche danger. However, the Swiss expert skier decided the snow was firm enough and the temperature sufficiently low to order the helicopter.

Jerry Harchenka of Western Helicopter Service flew Saudan upward and he made a leap onto the summit from the hovering aircraft. Saudan waited for the helicopter to make another trip and drop onto the summit his back-up man, Anselme Boud, ski instructor at Timberline Lodge and old alpine friend from Marzine, France. The run off the peak was made on 210-centimeter skis, a little longer than normal, and he used long poles for his unique style of turning.

Waiting until 4:00 p.m., just as the east side of the peak went into shadow, he skied down the Wy'east snow chute, then veered south to the headwall of Newton Clark Glacier, down across the bergschrund, and then across the glacier to 8,000 foot level, where John West stood by with a crew in his snow-cat. Saudan negotiated the 50-degree course by means of his special "seal turn," a unique manner of sitting far back on the tails of his skis, his head and shoulders almost touching the slope behind him, and planting his poles for a 180-degree change in direction. Using the technique he was able to remain within the confines of the steep glacial headwall chute.

Temperature was about 5 degrees above zero, with a strong wind blowing. In fact, the wind almost whipped off his sunglasses; only his long hair kept them from going. Saudan had two bad moments on the run. One was at the top when his skis triggered an avalance that left the bare ice exposed below the surface; however, he was able to hold with his edges. The other was the pair of snow bridges he crossed after reaching the glacier; they had been undetected on the reconaissance trip in the helicopter.

Boud, the back-up man to aid Saudan in case of emergency, had full mountaineering gear with him. He glissaded the Wy'east Route and quickly reached the group at the snow-cat celebrating Saudan's victory. This glissade was a very remarkable feat in mountaineering, allowing no margin for error above the cliffs of the east side.

Saudan had previously skied the Eiger, 13,000-foot peak in Europe which has claimed so many lives, as well as many other celebrated steep mountain faces of The Alps. He compared the east side of Mount Hood to Spencer's Couloir on Mont Blanc. The expenses for his Oregon exploit were paid by a ski-binding manufacturer and a national magazine. Ironically the magazine photographer, stationed on one of Mount Hood's ridges, found that he had placed himself out of sight of most of the run.

STUDENT REPEATED SAUDAN'S RUN

May 1, 1974 A little-known repeat of the breathtaking ski run off the east side of Mount Hood was made by Brian Raasch, 18, of Route 5, Box 2085, Hood River, Oregon.

Raasch, whose father, Kenneth Raasch, heads instruction and ski patrol activities at Cooper

Spur Ski Area, had been chatting one day with Mr. Harpe, his typing teacher at the high school. Brian commented that he could ski the east side of the mountain; seemingly, neither was aware of Saudan's run in 1971. Supposedly, there were some bets made.

On May 1, Brian and a friend climbed the South Side, his partner remaining at Crater Rock on the ascent. On top, Brian put his 8 mm moving picture in the hands of a climber, who took pictures of the boy on the start of his ski descent of the Wy'east Route.

His route passed over much the same terrain which Saudan had skied, but he used more conventional turns than Saudan's "seal turns." Falling was a life or death matter, because, if he had lost control, he would have plunged down over the cliffs, instead of following the long snow slope that turns toward Mount Hood Meadows.

In Brian Raasch's words, "The slope was very steep, the steepest I have ever skied. The trip was a little scary, because the snow was soft, and I started some small avalanches."

His friend drove around to pick him up at Mount Hood Meadows, and they were back in Hood River early in the day. His father querried, "you ran the face today, didn't you?"

"How did you know?" Brian asked. Kenneth Raasch knew that this was the only way his son could have arrived home so early. Brian has some moving picture footage to prove he made the run.

Lighting Mount Hood, 100-year Tradition

When Perry Vickers first observed July 4 with an illumination of the mountain in 1870, he kindled more than just a bonfire. In later years great efforts were made to use Mount Hood as the base of mass communication, but no one in Portland happened to witness the speck of light on the mountain that evening.

Vickers approached the Celebration Committee in Portland with a plan to light red fire at the very top of the peak for July 4, 1873. The committee could not justify the expense, and too, they believed that no man could withstand the cold and wind at night on the summit. Vickers showed the world it could be done with a small display of burning magnesium on the summit on the night of August 16, 1873, a spectacle viewed well from Summit Meadows by some very respectable witnesses. Still the illumination had not been viewed from Portland, although the spectators at Summit Meadow saw Vickers ignite ten different flares.

In 1877 a group from The Dalles vowed to accomplish the task, taking up torches to ignite on July 4. Nothing more was heard of the effort, but on July 24 a Portland group reached the summit, intending to set off red calcium fire. The group which included Professor Eugene Stebinger, Gerhard Franz, Julius Dilg, W. Linderman, and perhaps P.A. Wickers, left another man below with the horses. They reached the summit at 3:00 p.m., but it was too cold to stay. They did leave a 10' x 15' flag on a pole, which no one could see from Portland. The group hurried down the chute, Linderman slipping and catching himself just short of the menacing crevasse. Professor Stebinger had become snowblind, even before reaching the summit, and had to be led.

Portland residents waited hopefully on that night of July 24. At 10:00 p.m. they saw a light. Many assumed that this was the illumination. It proved to be the planet Mars ascending into the sky near Mount Hood. The idea rested for several years before George Breck and Charles H. Gove left Portland in 1885 with a party of men ready to do the job correctly. There was much fanfare for the project which featured setting the fire off in a delayed action. An alarm clock would go off, jerking a string with its hammer, upsetting a bottle of flammable liquid.

Breck and Gove set a good supply of red powder at the base of Illumination Rock; that is how the rock got its name. At 10:00 p.m. the alarm would do their work. Anticipating great fame, the two climbers began to descend when they thought they heard avalanching rock. Instead, it was the red fire being prematurely ignited in the afternoon sun. A falling rock had hit the bottle.

AT LAST, SUCCESS!

It was two years later, in 1887, that a successful illumination was finally staged. Will Steel lighted a half pound of lycopodium powder on Portland Heights to test whether it could be seen in Vancouver. From that they determined that it would take 100 pounds for a Mount Hood illumination. On Friday, July 1, a highly publicized party left Portland, Will Steel, N.W. Durham, O.C. Yocum, Charles H. Gove, John M. Breck, Jr., Dr. J.M. Keene, and Dr. Charles F. Adams. They rode in two wagons driven by Fuller and John McCuen.

By Saturday at 10:00 a.m. they had paid their way through the toll gate east of Rhododendron. They noted that Laurel Hill was a thing of the past, that a new road took a much gentler path up the canyon and along the hillside slopes. West of Government Camp the drivers had trouble getting the wagons through the snow drifts. Reaching Government Camp at 4:00 p.m., they loaded their dunnage onto the horses and onto their own backs. Walking in the moonlight, they finally established camp on a bare ridge well below the timber line. Before retiring they fired several moss-covered trees to watch the flames shoot skyward in explosive effect.

Early Sunday they were on their way pulling camp gear and the red fire powder in a toboggan.

This proved to be a herculean effort over the partially melted mounds of snow. Often the toboggan slid into tree wells, occasionally upsetting. The job became so oppressive that they sent below for help. Fuller came up from Government Camp with a horse and dragged the toboggan to a camp on bare rock at 7300 feet. Steel and Yocum walked west with a heliograph to signal Sergeant E.J. Glass, who was scanning Mount Hood from the top of the Portland Post Office with the telescope owned by electrician Julius Dilg. The heliograph was broken and inoperative, however they did receive flashes from Glass in Portland.

The camp was cold and windy, with no wood for fire and the only water in a canyon to the west. A glorious sunset was little appreciated, and the adventurers rolled up in their blankets to sleep fitfully on the gale-swept rocky ridge. The sunrise on July 4, was also very little appreciated by men who were chilled and had no food except canned beef and ship's bread.

The red fire was divided into 20-pound portions for back-packing. Steel and Keene, intending to stay above, took along blankets. Crossing the Zigzag Glacier, they encountered many long, deep crevasses. The party tied into a 500-foot line. Veils were used to shield their faces from the sun, and all had sunglasses. Yocum recorded the scene on his ponderous camera. Each step plunged in to the knee, and it was 11:00 a.m. before the party arrived at the 9800 foot level on Illumination Rock. At noon they left Steel and Keen to their lonely vigil and left for the high camp. They were able to get the toboggan back to the camp of Saturday night below timberline.

The gale subsided, so that Keene and Steele spent a pleasant afternoon. Between 7:00 and 8:00 it rose again, making them run back and forth on the ridge to keep warm. At 9:30 they fired a handful of red fire, which was detected in Portland, Forest Grove, and by the party in camp. In fact, it caused considerable confusion in camp. Gove climbed a tree to see better, believing that an accident had caused premature firing of the powder. McCuen, the wagon driver, saw the tree rustling and thought it was a bear. Gove descended the tree to find the party gathered around with guns and clubs.

The scheduled time for the illumination was 11:30. It was a cold wait for the two men on the ridge. Drifting smoke and fog caused them anxiety, but when they saw fireworks in Portland, Vancouver, and eastern Oregon, they knew the red fire would be seen. This first successful illumination of July 4, 1887 was seen in Portland, Canby, McMinnville, Vancouver, Silverton, Salem.

Having done their part in celebrating Independence Day, Steel and Keene hurried for the high camp. At one point they stepped into a crevasse, arresting the fall at waist depth. From the camp they drifted too far west, finally bedding down beside a large fire below timberline. Gove went out to look for them at 3:00 a.m. and fired gunshots that gave them sense of direction. He found them a mile away and had them back in camp by 4:00 a.m.

On the trip home they stopped at the Adolf Aschoff place for dinner, to whom they referred as the "big German." The newspaper reporter Durham started to appropriate a small brass thermometer, which he thought belonged to Steel. Aschoff objected to his taking the thermometer, and a good deal of apology and explanation ensued.

US ARMY ANSWERED

In 1888 the Portland Independence Day Celebration Committee planned to back the Oregon Alpine Club in a second illumination, this time raising the appropriation from $75 to $250. The party was planned to include Will Steel, O.C. Yocum, John M. Breck, Jr., Charles H. Gove, Dr. J.M. Keene, Bailey Avery, William H. Walker, Lt. J.P. O'Neill, and W.A. Wetzell. Steel was trying to promote illumination on Mount Shasta and Mount Rainier.

On Monday, July 2, the party bedded down at "Camp Rain" at timberline, having been transported with horses and mules. On a cloudy Tuesday morning they started out with two mules pulling the toboggan. The mules were soon sent back and eight men did the pulling, three more carrying a ladder for the crevasse in the chute. The party pulled the toboggan in short, tiring spurts, finally reaching Triangle Moraine, which by that time was covered with a descending storm cloud. All hope of climbing to the summit was abandoned, as they cached the toboggan and ladder and ran for the shelter of camp.

Wednesday morning was not a glorious Fourth of July, but as the day wore on, the weather improved immensely. Illumination was scheduled for 10:45 p.m., and excited people in Portland and Vancouver watched expectantly. The minutes ticked away until the lycopodium powder was fired at 11:07. As per arrangement with General Gibbon and Assistant Adjutant-General William J. Volkmar, the United States Army unit at Fort Vancouver fired a salute of bursting mortar shells in answer to the illumination.

The ladder was left at the cache below Crater Rock, the site of the illumination, to be used by subsequent expeditions. John Breck, who at the time was credited with being the most experienced mountaineer of the party, had quit the rainy camp on Tuesday, July 3, in disgust. This was Breck's sixth trip to Mount Hood. Having enough of the cold and rain, he walked to the toll gate and rode a horse to Portland from that point the following day.

JOHN M. BRECK, JR.

Although he made only a half dozen climbs associated with the illumination of Mount Hood, Breck in his way played a significant part in the history of mountaineering on the peak. The

Oregon Alpine Club had been the beginning of any organized activity, and the club members had made a focal point of Breck's Drug Store which stood on the northwest corner of SW 5th and Morrison. The club even stored some of its outing equipment in the basement of the store from year to year.

Breck's climbing had been done at an early age, and the illumination for the Fourth of July of 1888 proved to be his last. A cripple all his life, he always used a crutch, and when he ventured out onto snow, he placed a "shoe" on the end of it to distribute his weight. His climbing record had included Mount Hood, Mount Adams, and Mount Rainier, a remarkable feat for a man on a crutch.

Walking all the way from base camp on the South Side down to the Toll Gate on July 3, then riding 45 miles by horseback into Portland the following day, had serious effects upon his health. Four and a half months later he was dead at age 28, the victim of morphine.

His father, John M. Breck, Sr., reported to the newspapers that on Friday, November 16, 1888, that his son had left the family home at 231 Main Street at about 7:00 p.m. to relieve his brother, George at the drug store. The two brothers were partners. About 10:00 p.m. Frank Miller, a previous employee, came into the store, and John hired him, acting on the advice of his mother, who had asked him to employ some help in order to cut down on the long hours at the store. Frank Miller went to work immediately, and John left in the company of Charles D. Ford, a friend.

The two drank some beer in a saloon on Morrison Street, then returned to the store about 11:00 p.m., where John spent considerable effort in fixing the fire. John then offered Ford a drink of whisky. Into his own drink, John poured two dashes into a graduating glass from a small vial in the prescription case. It was a **solution of morphine.**

Quaffing the whisky, Breck and Ford then left for the Quelle, where they drank beer and listened to the music of some zither players there. Then, proceeding down Stark Street, Ford noticed his companion was trembling in his legs. Breck fell to the sidewalk, and Ford summoned a carriage, taking him to the Holton House, where they checked in at 1:10 a.m. What happened afterward is not known, but the doctors did not arrive until 4:00 a.m.

By 8:00 a.m. the physicians had given him up for dead; Breck had never regained consciousness. However, they kept on working, and about 11:00 a.m. they detected heartbeat and slight breathing. Improvement was short, and Breck died at 5:15 p.m. Ford had left his friend after checking him into the hotel, but did return to call the doctors about 3:00 a.m., leaving somewhat of a mystery in the affair.

Breck was not considered a suicide victim, as he had been cheerful during the evening. His only unusual problem was in being so exhausted from the ordeal of his trip home from Mount Hood the previous July. But Breck was not the only member of that party to figure heavily in tragic drama, as another of the group got his name in the headlines five years later.

UNTIMELY END FOR GOVE

Charles H. Gove, a Portland real estate agent, had taken part in the illuminations of Mount Hood. On Sunday, March 26, 1893, *The Sunday Oregonian* carried a story of his Saturday night shooting of C.J. Smith, then killing himself with his own .38 Smith and Wesson revolver.

Five years previously Gove and Smith had been business associates and Smith was a boarder in the Gove home. Mrs. Gove told her husband that Smith had attempted rape while he was away from home on a business trip. This preyed on Gove's mind for five years, before he broke down mentally and resolved to kill Smith. Smith denied all of this, and people who knew him believed his story.

1894 As a part of the organizational climb of The Mazamas of July 19, Charles Sholes and three men pulled a toboggan toward the summit, but gave up in exhaustion on a moraine part way up. They continued to a bivouac near Crater Rock, but after a poor night of sleep in high winds, they were in no condition to take the red powder to the summit.

Captain H.H. Wells, who went to the summit to spend the night and ignite the powder, came back down on that July 19th, and a display was made from the moraine by T. Brook White that night. The following day, Friday, a group decided to take lycopodium powder to Illumination Rock on Saturday for an illumination Monday night. Enroute they got braver ideas and decided to plan to make their display for the summit. Accordingly, they made a summit climb on Monday, touched off two batches of red fire, and spent the night on the summit. Ida McElvain became the first woman to spend the night on the summit on that adventure, and this was the first illumination from the summit. Full details can be read in the chapter THE MAZAMAS.

1896 The Triangle Club climbed Mount Hood, named Triangle Moraine, and three of their members stayed there until 9:30 on July 10, to stage a red-fire illumination. Strong wind made the task difficult, but the flash was produced right on time. A group in Portland answered their efforts with a red-fire salute, but the Triangle Club members did not see it. Lights in Portland, however, could be plainly seen from Triangle Moraine.

1897 July 31, an Oregon National Guard signal squad set an illumination at Crater Rock at 9:00 p.m., a display lasting two minutes.

1899 The Fourth of July illumination was placed in the hands of The Mazamas, as offered by their president, William G. Steel. It was proposed in honor of the 14th convention of the

Editorial Association of the United States. The Mississippi delegate, R.H. Henry, offered to supply the funds for the red-fire, and to show appreciation, the great cliff at the head of Big Zigzag Canyon was named Mississippi Head.

The party consisted of Steel, Adolf Aschoff, Francis C. Little, E.G. Jones, and Albert Capron. Plans were to use Illumination Rock as the site. On July 3 the weather closed in and howled a gale. A shelter of snow was thrown up at their base camp at timberline with a good supply of wood to keep them warm. Aschoff was sent to Government Camp for camp equipment to weather the storm. They climbed the moraine above camp and set off 10 pounds of powder at 9:30 to show the watchers in Portland that all was well.

By Tuesday morning, July 4, the weather showed a little sun and scudding clouds. Taking 30 pounds of powder apiece, they started for Illumination Rock in soft snow. Placing 50 pounds of powder on the great cliff as they passed, they named it Mississippi Head and recorded their action in a tin can which they buried under a pile of rock. Advancing to Illumination Rock, they placed the powder and left Little and Capron in charge. Steel tried to send flashes to Portland with a mirror, then he and Jones left to take up posts on Mississippi Head. On their way they saw the golden fireball of the sun sink into the waters of the Pacific Ocean (Impossible). Sinking deeply into the soft snow with each step, it took them an hour to reach the cliff.

From Mississippi Head, Steel could see the light in the Oregonian Tower, then fireworks and city lights. By 9:45 fog had obscured the view of the Tower; by 10:30 the lights toward Vancouver were blanked out. The illumination was not seen from Portland by the crowds assembled there.

1901 *The Oregonian* of October 24, quoted W.M. Killingsworth on the need to illuminate Mount Hood for the Lewis and Clark Exposition of 1905. He suggested electrical illumination, noting the great amount of water available for power at the mountain. Nightly display of red and blue lights were his idea, with a giant lighted statue of Lewis on one side of the mountain and another of Clark on the opposite.

August 1, 1904 The Mazamas made their first ascent of Mount Shasta, with Charles H. Sholes leading a party of 23. An illumination was to be made on that peak and on the summit of Mount Hood to settle the question of whether Mount Shasta could be seen from Hood. Lack of knowledge of the route caused Sholes, Rodney Glisan, and C.E. Alford to be the only ones to reach the summit. It was late in the day, and the weather was too ominous for them to remain on top to light the signal fire.

However, Will Steel arrived at the summit of Mount Hood to do his part in the exchange of red fire signals. At the planned hour that night he illuminated the top of Mount Hood in a display that was viewed magnificently by the residents of Portland, a "great bonfire hanging midway between earth and sky."

July 4, 1905 An illumination party climbed Cooper Spur Route to honor the Lewis and Clark Centennial Exposition in northwest Portland. The party consisted of George Weister, E.H. Moorhouse, Horace Mecklem, W. Mark Weygandt, and guide Peter Feldhausen.

They reached the summit at 6:00 p.m. and spent a cold three hours slapping arms and doing war dances in the cold wind. They could plainly see the Oregonian Building and searchlights cutting the sky from the Exposition grounds.

At the appointed hour of 9:00 they fired the red powder, but the strong wind blew the flame downward so much that it was not seen well in Portland. The illumination did show well to viewers in Hood River and The Dalles. The party started on their way down at 9:15 p.m.

Saturday, July 14, 1917 an ignition of 200 pounds of red fire powder on the summit was made at 9:40 p.m. Lige Coalman called below to the Oregon Journal Building by prearrangement to have them darken their tower, a signal to Portland residents that fire would be seen on the summit in 15 minutes. T. Raymond Conway of The Mazamas came up to assist Coalman, as did a group of six climbers with guide Hans Fuhrer, which included one-legged climber Estes Snedecor.

November 1, 1931 To celebrate the dedication of the new Mazama Lodge, Ole Lien and James Harlow climbed high on the south side to set off magnesium flares at 1:00 a.m. The light was clearly seen from Mazama Lodge. Lien and Harlow went on to climb to the summit.

January 27, 1934 The Wy'east Climbers staged a spectacular display of flares at 10:00 p.m. James Mount, presiding on the loud speaker before a crowd at Government Camp, signalled the maneuver with the lighting of a flare. This was quickly answered by flares on the summit by Ralph Calkin, Bill Hiegel, and Hayden Holm. Spaced out on the south slope of Mount Hood were Joe Leuthold, Ole Lien, Hank Lewis, Edith Pierce, and Curtis Ijames. Everett Darr and Ray Atkeson responded from the top of Multorpor Mountain, as did Bob Furrer and Alfred Monner from Tom-Dick-Harry Mountain. The night was cloudless, and a full moon threw a subdued glow on miles of snow-covered slopes.

July 26, 1935 On a beautiful, moonless night the Wy'east Climbers lighted Mount Hood. Ralph Calkin, Everett Darr, Barrie James, Hank Lewis, Alfred Monner, Leon Darling, Curtis Ijames, Joe Leuthold, and Grant McConnell formed the team on the summit and south slope. At Multorpor and Tom-Dick-Harry were Ray Atkeson, Dale Cowen, Ray Lewis, and James Mount. Irene Darling and Jean Wray stood as spectators at a position just above timberline, and they heard plainly the cheers and applause from the crowd assembled at

Government Camp to watch the illumination.

April 1, 1939 The Wy'east illuminated the peak as a stunt for the Oregon Winter Sports Association. Ralph Calkin, Glen Asher, Henry Corbett, Herbert Rasor, William Wood went to the stone shelter in the crater. Calkin and Corbett shared a tent, and the rest used the shelter to sleep from 6:00 p.m. to 9:00 p.m. They then took their stations — Rasor, Wood, and Asher on the summit, Calkin atop Crater Rock, and Corbett in the crater. Joe Leuthold had a post at Lone Fir Lookout. At 10:00 p.m. Dale Cowen signalled the lighting of flares from his position at Timberline Lodge. The following day the group worked on the Ski Patrol.

Saturday, June 15, 1947 Members of the Wy'east Climbers set off 24 army-type magnesium flares for a six-minute display on Crater Rock. The display was directed by James Simmons, chairman of the Golden Poles Ski Tournament, and Bill Temple, manager of Timberline Lodge. It was signalled at 10:15 by a mortar shell fired near the lodge. Not only the illumination was seen plainly in Portland, but the mortar shell as well.

At the Golden Poles Race the next day, two Olympic contestants placed first in their divisions, Gene Gillis and Gretchen Fraser.

MAZAMA DIAMOND JUBILEE

July 19, 1969 The most spectacular mountain illumination of all time was performed by The Mazamas to commemorate the 75th anniversary of the founding of the club. Robert Millus, Ray Snyder, and Pete Unger were at work just after sunrise on Friday the 18th, loading four boxes of rockets and three mortar tubes, ropes and pickets into the snow-cat. The cat gave out at 9,000 feet. They drove a row of pickets to keep the boxes of equipment from sliding back down to timberline, then unloaded the heavy cargo.

The first carry to the top of the Hogsback was accomplished by 12:15 p.m., and a second trip was made by 4:00. Ready to start up with the third load, they looked down to see the second snow-cat load spin out and pile up at the 8,000-foot level, with more helpers to aid in the carry. Neil Olson and James and Richard Trusky came up, carrying bivouac gear and boxes of flares. Millus managed the third carry of 90 pounds, two boxes of rockets and two gallons of punch.

Snyder and Unger had tents set up and dinner ready, and after gazing at the brilliant, starry sky awhile, they all turned in for a night of sleep. Somewhere up above were the three astronauts on space ship Apollo 11, on their way to place the first man on the surface of the full moon, whose beams shined brightly on the party in the crater.

On Anniversary Day they finished breakfast and set fixed ropes all the way up the Chute. Down below, Donald Eastman was leading a party of Mazama climbers, bringing up more ropes and flares. It was a calm, beautiful day enjoyed at leisure by the four South Side Route parties led by Donald Eastman, Neil Baldwin, Chad Karr, and Richard Eaton. Charles Jensen led a group up Cooper Spur as did Nick Dodge. Jensen's party included Luther Jerstad, the famous Mount Everest climber and mountaineering instructor, who took the ascent of little Mount Hood in good-natured stride, although a member of the

Wy'east Climbers Illuminated Mount Hood 1932 — Photo Joe Leuthold

party was presenting problems not acceptable to any climb leader.

Barney Keep of Radio Station KEX in Portland interviewed Jerstad and illumination leader Bob Millus on a live broadcast there on the summit. After a brief commemoration of the 75th anniversary of the founding of The Mazamas, most of the climbers headed down. Then the real work began for the illumination crew, Millus, Snyder, Unger, Albert E. Weese, Keith West, Peg Oslund, Mitch Michaud, who all stayed at the Hogsback.

Each climber was assigned an area to set flares, 150 in circles of eight feet in diameter; there were nine of these. Mortars and rockets were set up. At 10:35 p.m. Barney Keep contacted Governor Tom McCall by radiotelephone.

McCall replied, "This is probably the greatest, most historic honor that has ever befallen a governor of Oregon, or perhaps any governor in the United States. I want to compliment The Mazamas on their 75 valuable years of contribution to a better state, to a better understanding of our great out-of-doors."

"I think it is entirely fitting that these brave, free spirits in The Mazamas are now paying homage to their counterparts, the men of Apollo 11, who have **JUST MADE MAN'S FIRST LANDING UPON THE MOON.**"

"And so it is my historic privilege, one that no governor will ever have again, to declare that this is the hour, this is the minute, this is the second to light the mountain as Oregon's salute to Apollo 11."

The four-inch mortar shot a projectile into the sky with a shattering roar. Quickly the light of 1,500 flares showed the outlines of the mountain. Mortars were depressing into the snow a half a foot with each shot and had to be reset frequently. In 25 minutes 36 rockets had exploded in the sky. The crater glowed red, as if the subterranean fires had surfaced again. The illumination lasted about an hour and 20 minutes, the most impressive display in Mount Hood's long history. It was hoped that the display might be seen from Apollo 11, but it was not. Overhead, six planes circled the summit area.

At the Hogsback someone started brewing tea, and the group chatted until 1:30. It was a big job the following day to gather up all the burned flares; the garbage had to be packed out. Radio KEX supplied some of the cost of the illumination.

Heliography, Communicating by Sun Flash

July 8, 1888 The Oregon Alpine Club planned an expedition to Mount Hood for mid-August. O.C. Yocum suggested the placing of a summit box for registration of successful climbers. On Thursday, August 9, the group left Portland for what the newspapers called a perilous expedition, Lieutenant of the US Army J.P. O'Neill, O.C. Yocum, Hill Beachy, Martin W. Gorman, W.A. Wetzell, Eberhard Caesar, B.C. Towne, Miss ____________Smith. Three farmers joined the entourage enroute. John Breck was noticeably absent, his enthusiasm having been spent in the illumination trip in July.

Lt. O'Neill hoped to exchange heliograph signals with Sergeant E.J. Glass, who stationed himself in the Kamm Tower in Portland. By Saturday the climbing party had reached a base camp at the timberline level below Illumination Rock. O'Neill began signalling to Glass on Saturday from Illumination Rock, receiving some unintelligible flashes from Portland. On Sunday the party climbed to the summit, placing the 10" x 12" copper box into use. Memorabilia from previous climbing parties were transfered to the new official box, including a diary of Perry Vickers indicating he had slept on the summit on August 17, 1872. O'Neill attempted to use the heliograph from the summit, but got no response from Portland.

Despite some talk about building a snow house on the summit and spending the night, the party spent only an hour and a half before starting down. Temperature measurements were taken, and with an aneroid barometer they determined the height of the peak at 11,520 feet.

On Monday, August 13, O'Neill and Wetzell explored the crater. They saw flashes from 2:00 to 5:00 in the afternoon, but could not decipher a single word. O'Neill tried to signal for seven straight days. On Wednesday he saw flashes believed to have been sent from Vancouver. Vancouver was somewhat in the clear, although nearby Portland was covered with smoky haze all of the time the expedition was on the mountain.

Will Steel wanted to burn red fire on the top of Kamm Tower on Monday night, but Sergeant Glass persuaded him to wait until Tuesday night. However, the Portland illumination display was not seen by the Oregon Alpine Club Party at Mount Hood.

PEAK-TO-PEAK FLASHES

The United States Army had long used a mirror system, the heliograph, for communications. The newly founded club, The Mazamas were intrigued with the idea of signalling from mountain tops. In 1895, the year following organization, they planned an ambitious program of signalling all up and down the Cascades. Bad weather is normally characteristic in June; in addition no one savored the idea of carrying the 19-pound heliographs over soft snow. From mid-summer the northwestern sky was normally obscured with smoke from the frequent forest fires. So July 10 was set as a target date for setting up instruments on Mount Baker, Mount Rainier, Mount Adams, Mount Hood, Mount Jefferson, and Diamond Peak.

Mazama Heliographers on Mount Adams 1895
Standing, W.A. Langille, Professor Edgar McClure, L.H. Lamberson
Sitting, T. Brook White, R.S. Farrell

The Mount Baker failed to reach the summit. The Mount Rainier party of six was led by E.S. Ingraham. They blinked for several hours at Mount Adams, but smoky air frustrated their attempt.

The Mount Adams party of 24 was led by T. Brook White, Will Langille, and Charles Sholes. They never did receive the signals sent from Mount Rainier, but a good response was received from Mount Hood. Smoke filled the valleys and lower slopes, with only the peaks being visible. In a short time the gale-like winds in which they had been climbing, shut off the view of Mount Hood.

On Mount Hood five members of the Oregon National Guard, Signal Corps of the First Regiment made the climb under command of Major Samuel M. Mears, accompanied by H.B. Langille, and his brother, H.D. Langille. The party made an early ascent from Cloud Cap Inn and were ready to transmit quickly when they received flashes from Mount Adams.

C.C. Lewis led the Mount Jefferson party, but heliography was impossible because of smoke. Diamond Peak was also obscured.

MAZAMA BIRTHDAY SUCCESS

July 19, 1895 The first anniversary of the Mazama organizational climb, a group of heliographers ascended from Cloud Cap Inn, William G. Steel, Ella Allis Owen, L.H. Lamberson, T. Brook White, and H.D. Langille. They set up their equipment and made contact with T. Marquam, L.L. Hawkins, and W. Baker, operating from Portland Heights.

Using Morse code, the two groups sent their names, made comments about the weather, and gave an estimation of the temperature atop the mountain. The men in Portland sent the results of a horse race to Mount Hood. T. Brook White, a prominent member of The Mazamas, was so impressed with the effective communication, that he tried to promote widespread use of heliography. He wrote an article for the Mazama Annual, exhorting all to learn to read Morse code. Without a doubt, it had been the most successful experiment in communication by mirroring sun flashes from the top of Mount Hood.

SMOKE STOPPED US ARMY

1897 Oregon National Guard signal personnel, Lieutenant W.T. Bird, Corporal ____________ Kaiser, Privates ______________ Buckman and ______________ Kelly, attempted to break the long-distance record for signalling on August 1. A second party had been sent to Mary's Peak near Corvallis, Sergeants ______________ Humphrey, ____________ Lovelace, ______________ Thompkins, and Private ______________ Craft. The attempt was not successful. A third party stationed on Portland Heights was able to communicate sketchily with Mount Hood, the smoke of an intervening forest fire causing problems of vision. The party in Portland consisted of Corporal ____________ Fehrenbacker, and Privates ____________ Breslin, ______________ Johnson, ______________ Toolen, ____________ Foster, ______________ Martin, and ____________ Faber.

The heliograph did find widespread use by the Forest Service in their lookouts. In lookout stations atop peaks such as Mount Hood, Mount St. Helens, and Mount Adams, as well as on the scores of lesser points that were constantly manned in dry summer weather, they used the flashing devices universally. Dick Johnson of Salem, a member of The Mazamas and The Chemeketans, tells of his first climb on Middle Sister in 1935. He began to flash a mirror, and before he was finished, he received heliograph flashes from 17 stations in the Cascades, Central Oregon, and the Coast Range.

Mazamas Roping-up on Cooper Spur Route 1912.

Deadly Fumaroles, Always Intriguing

From the very first attempt to climb Mount Hood the fumaroles have intrigued those who saw them. Dyer in 1854 noted the vents at the Crow's Nest atop Steel Cliff and threw a rock into one to ascertain its depth.

James Deardorff in the climb of 1857 noted the signs of vulcanism at Crater Rock. Four of that party took turns of being lowered on a rope to explore a deep and extensive cave. Each was "delighted and astonished at the beauties before him — and returned from beneath the massive arch (of ice) regretting that he had not the time and means of exploring it further." A small opening below admitted sufficient light to show beautiful forms assumed by the snow and ice in melting and freezing. It was very fortunate that they did not have sufficient time.

In 1866 the party of H.K. Hines, J.C.N. Moreland, A. Waltz, and Washington Waltz were lured by the fumaroles on the descent. They made a detour through an ice cave in the crater. Looking downward over a 50-foot wall, they were stopped for lack of a rope and contented themselves with merely observing the steaming, smoking mouth of the crater.

In August 1867, George H. Himes, W.S. Powell, J.S. Newell, Ed. W. Cornell, and S.G. Benson reported an immense fissure in the old crater that emitted sulphurous smoke and a hissing sound similar to boiling water. They reported it to be about 300 feet below the summit, possibly a crevasse that connected to fumaroles below.

YOCUM EXPLORED FUMAROLES

In an 1894 story for the *Troutdale Champion*, O.C. Yocum related the story of a descent which he and others had made in 1888 into the crater area.

In his own words, "I in company with several others, let ourselves down into Crater Rock *(he means alongside)*, a distance of some 500 feet and passed from there nearly the same distance under the glacier to a point where the smoke and sulphur fumes emanate. We knew our lives were in constant danger, but curiosity led us forward. Once here we secured quite a number of sulphur crystals, some of which I still have, and started to pick our way out, when it occurred to me to toss into the opening a small stone. I'll never do it again. The rumbling, bumbling, sepulchral noise that rock made I never will forget. We didn't know at what moment it might cause an activity of that old volcano which has been extinct for years. The feat of entering under the glacier has never been performed by anyone so far as we know, for the sulphur fumes have been too dense, quite sufficient to smother one at the entrance."

In light of what happened to the party who experimented in entering the fumarole moat at Crater Rock in 1934, it seems very fortunate that Yocum and his party were able to come out alive.

How many parties have tried to investigate the fumaroles, no one knows. Their deadly nature was not really known for 77 years after Deardorff unknowingly flirted with death by entering a fumarole ice cave in 1857. The lethal nature of crater fumaroles was not really understood until an incident in 1934.

EXPLORATION DEEP INTO CAVE

Sunday, July 19, 1931 The deepest known penetration into Mount Hood's fumarole caves was made by a party led by James Mount. Accompanied by James Harlow, Wallace York, Margaret Danks, and Hans Rhiger, he had climbed South Side Route and had returned to the crater by 7:00 a.m.

It was at that point that they decided to explore the opening in the ice along the east side of Crater Rock, undoubtedly very close to the same area that claimed the life of VonNorman in 1934. Mount noticed that there were very few fumes on that day, and they decided to descend. The first rope length followed the sloping contour of the side of Crater Rock, but after about 120 feet or more of descent, the passageway opened up into a giant cavern of ice with a ceiling that ranged from 30 to 40 feet.

They followed the cavern on the downward slope, noting that it began to turn to the right (southward toward White River). It came to an end in a small room, but there was enough space for a person to crawl under, between the ice and the muddy floor. Below that point they could see that the passageway opened wide again and ran downhill as far as they could see with their flashlights. They did not go any further, fearing the sulphur fumes, and climbed back up the sloping floor to Crater Rock and daylight.

THE VONNORMAN DEATH

On August 27, 1934, a group of University of Washington students formed one of the parties climbing the South Side Route. In the party were Victor VonNorman, Edward Tremper, George Zaloudeka, Richard Coffin, and David Frank Reynolds.

Returning from the top, across the Hogsback, they were intrigued by the fumarole on the east side of Crater Rock. Steam had melted a large cavern in the snow, making it possible to climb down the steep lava slope of Crater Rock toward the source of heat. VonNorman, with Tremper trailing 20 feet behind, travelled about 60 feet in, when he abruptly reversed his course. Appearing very distressed, he climbed upward a few feet, faltered, and dropped fifty feet to the bottom of the incline, where his body lodged between the rock and the snow.

Tremper, by that time feeling the effects of the gaseous fumes, was able to climb out and call his companions. The Civilian Conservation Corps was building a shelter that summer in the crater, just north of the Devil's Kitchen fumaroles. Aunnie

Faubion and assistant, Harold Taylor, US Forest Service packers, happened to be at the new stone hut unloading a string of pack animals they had just brought up. The climbers ran the quarter mile to the packers and asked for help.

Faubion grabbed his pack ropes and went with Taylor to the fumaroles. He soaked his shirt in snow water, wrapped his face, and was belayed into the opening by Taylor and Zaloudeka. The rope was too short, however that made little difference, because he quickly became ill. Taylor next tried the descent and was dragged out in hysteria. The others had to restrain him from reentering the cavern.

Faubion sent one man down to Lone Fir Lookout to ask for help. He then descended with his ten pack horses single handed, leaving Taylor and the others at Crater Rock. In an hour and a half the news was in the hands of the 21-year-old guard at Lone Fir, Paul Williams. The time was about 6:00 p.m. Alarm was telephoned down to the Timberline Guard Station at Phlox Point, the end of the old road. Williams and his younger brother Robert J. Williams, left at once for Crater Rock, arriving about 9:00 p.m.

Francis E. Williamson, Jr., forest recreational inspector at Zigzag, sent an army gas mask up to Ralph Olson, guard at Phlox Point, who then took it to the crater. Paul Williams donned the mask and descended nearly to the bottom of the cave before he was forced to retreat. Olson then attempted it and failed even sooner. The air was composed of noxious fumes with no oxygen content. Army gas masks could not supply oxygen, they merely acted as a filter. Olson hurried back to Lone Fir to call for oxygen helmets. Gary Leech, legendary climbing figure of Government Camp, meanwhile arrived on the scene. He, too, was repulsed by the gas.

State police at Government Camp used their radio and summoned the first aid car of the Portland Fire Department. Firemen Captain F.W. Roberts, C.M. Ferris, and E.R. Hornschuh, accompanied by Deputy Coroner, Arnold Bierman, of Clackamas County arrived at Crater Rock midmorning of August 28, with oxygen masks. Gary Leech donned a mask and succeeded in tying a rope around the tightly-wedged body. The weight of the breathing equipment overcame him, and he retreated to the surface. The firemen resuscitated him. Paul Williams then went down and freed the body so it could be hauled up. Feeling that his mask was fogging on him, Williams pulled it back to adjust it, and was overcome. Firemen brought him back to life. It was characteristic of all the rescuers entering the cave, that they wanted to dash back in. Restraint was necessary.

Two days later at Lone Fir, Paul Williams complained of chest pains and foggy vision. His brother, Robert, took him to Phlox Point, where they hauled him to the hospital. Likewise, Gary Leech was a hospital case. Ironically, had Von-Norman been capable of reviving, all the rescue effort might have been for nothing. They loaded his body on a packhorse. On the trip down the mountainside, the horse stumbled and fell on VonNorman's body, breaking many bones.

Pioneers Witnessed Hood's Volcanic Fire

Mount Hood's volcanic activity was almost a thing of the past when white men began to record her antics. A ring-count of a tree, damaged by volcanic ash near Tilly Jane Camp on the north side, substantiates the date of an eruption in about the year 1825. Capt. John Fremont's visit at Methodist Mission at The Dalles in 1843 reported a comment from Reverend Brewer that there were two volcanoes close by. One, of course, was Mount Saint Helens. The other must have been Mount Hood. Judging from later events, it is very probable that some activity must have been observed between 1800 and 1843.

Mount Saint Helens erupted on November 22, 1842, laying down a half-inch of ash as far away as The Dalles. This eruption was verified in 1892 by a letter to Will Steel from Reverend J.L. Parrish of Salem. Parrish in the company of Dr. Babcock, Jason Lee, Alanson Beers, and others had seen it from the old mission house ten miles below (north) Salem. They saw arising from the summit immense clouds and scrolls of white steam. Under the steam was an emission that varied from gray above to black lower down. The next day the mountain was covered in a mantle of black that lasted until the winter snows covered the ash. The eruption was on the southeast slope of Mount Saint Helens about a third of the length of the slope from the top of the mountain. Parrish reported that in travelling down the river a year or so later, he could still distinctly see the fire burning on the mountain side.

The Oregonian August 20, 1859, reported that on the previous Wednesday (August 17) singular clouds had formed over Mount Hood and occasional flashes of fire were seen in the evening. On Thursday night the fire was plainly visible. On the 19th (Friday) examination by telescope from Portland showed that a large mass had disappeared on the northwest side, and an immense amount of snow on the south side was gone.

A month later on September 18, W.F. Courtney witnessed an eruption of Mount Hood from a cattle drovers' camp on Tygh Ridge near the east end of the Barlow Road. A member of a group driving cattle west, he was standing guard over the cattle at 1:30 a.m. with another man. He saw the heavens light up and a column of fire. "With a flash that illuminated the whole mountainside with a pinkish glare, the flame danced from the crater. Suddenly it sank from sight." They watched the volcanic display for about two hours, blazing forth at irregular intervals. In the morning the snow slopes were black with cinders and ashes. Courtney also reported being a member of a party at a later date, wherein they encountered hot cinders on the mountain sides. (*Everett Record*, May 17, 1902.) Courtney's story was not backed up by any more reports from Portland.

Six years passed before Mount Hood showed her subterranean fire to the world. On September 21, 1865, John Dever, Company E, First Regiment, Washington Territory Volunteers, was standing guard from 5 to 7 a.m. Looking east to observe the glory of the coming dawn, he saw the top of the mountain enveloped in smoke and flame. Jets of flame were shooting up, accompanied by what appeared to be fragments of rock being cast high up. After he saw the rock fall there was a rumbling noise similar to distant thunder. Several members of the guard saw the display. Devers wrote a letter to *The Oregonian* published on October 26.

At times unusual amounts of steam have been observed. In 1907 Will Steel commented that he had seen black, sulphurous smoke that year. Sylvester, reporting for *National Geographic*, was camped at Government Camp in 1907, mapping the Mount Hood quadrangle and observing volcanic activity. On August 28 he visited the east side following a report by his field men that an unusual column of steam was seen rising from the summit all day. That evening a glow was seen behind Crater Rock "like a chimney burning out."

MUD SLIDE NOT VOLCANIC

However, a mud slide in August 1921 had people aroused. A wild story out of Government Camp told of hot water and volcanic sand mixed with boulders, a mass too hot to safely approach. Guides Orval Zimmerman and Chester Treichel went to the Zigzag Glacier to affirm the stories, and they quickly found that there was no warmth in the flow.

The lookout in the summit cabin, Clem Blakney, spent an uneasy night as he heard the avalanching material roar into the crater. He said the summit ridge actually quivered. Slides had torn out the telephone line and the "life-line" climbing rope on the chute above the Big Crevasse. Mazamas A. Boyd Williams and T. Raymond Conway acted as investigators. They found the glacier had been cracked by a tremendous force where the mass of mud and water had poured through a narrow opening. Large blocks of ice had been pushed up to lay upon the surface of the glacier. One theory was that a large water reservoir concealed west of the Hogsback had broken loose to precipitate the unusual destructive flow.

MOUNT HOOD AS A THREAT

Mount Hood is a dormant volcano, as is Mount Rainier, Mount Baker, and possibly other peaks of the Cascade Range. From the summit craters of these peaks, one can see steam constantly spewing from fumarole areas. Their future is unpredictable. They may settle down and sleep forever, or one or more may suddenly burst into life. Such a renaissance of energy is usually preceded by earthquake tremors.

Moana Loa on the Island of Hawaii has been erupting at intervals all during the written history of that area. However, it is a different type of volcano than Mount Hood.

Mount Hood is of the acidic variety, similar to Mount Mazama, which blew its top about 6,500 years ago to form Crater Lake. Another of the same species is Mount Pelee on the Carribean island of Martinique. It erupted violently in 1902, expelling a cloud of glowing gas that asphyxiated a community of 30,000 in a half hour's time.

If Mount Hood should blow its top, it probably would be much the same as the eruption of Mount Mazama, wherein glowing gasses shot 40 miles west to annihilate everything growing, according to Dr. Gordon G. Goles, geologist at the University of Oregon. Ashes of that explosion were deposited well up into the state of Washington. Thousands of square miles received deposits of as much as a foot in depth.

Such cataclysmic effects are usually accompanied by violent thunderstorms and torrential rains, that compound the problem of ash by washing it downward into stream beds. All water supply for a vast area of the state would be destroyed, and transportation would be brought to a standstill.

A lesser eruption could occur, similar to the 1825 occurrence near Cloud Cap Inn. Such a display would probably start from a weak spot in the crater or on an external mountain wall, worn thin as the glacier cuts deeper, near the source of molten rock. It might be limited in damage to the spreading of several inches of ash over the countryside, the size of the area depending on the explosion. The reader will recall that the missionaries at The Dalles told Captain Fremont in 1823, that TWO volcanic peaks were in evidence. The work of the small crater near Cloud Cap in about 1825 had left sufficient ash to be noticed. A larger crater could spew enough ash to create havoc with the Portland metropolitan area. Also, fast melting glaciers could cause giant mud flows, another source of trouble.

Geologists feel that there is little chance of the type of eruption wherein molten lava flows down the mountainside to cool. This is the type known at Moana Loa in Hawaii. It does relatively little damage.

The possibility of a volcanic disaster was covered in the *Oregon Journal* on March 14, 1973, in a story by staff writer Marge Davenport.

Marriages on the Summit of Mount Hood

PEARCE-PECHETTE WEDDING

A Sunday wedding in early July, 1915, was held in Lige Coalman's tent on the summit of Mount Hood, uniting Blanche Pechette of Wapinitia and Frank Pearce of Rowe (Rhododendron). The bride's mother, Mary A. Pechette, Pearl Cline Myers, Pearl Priest, H.E. Monroe, Hazel Howard, Laura Schroeder, Margaret Purvine, Helen Strauser, Maybelle Telker, Hugh Knight, M.H. Stainer, and E.O. McGregor were members of the wedding party, guided by Hans Fuhrer and John Myers.

The ceremony was performed by Reverend G.E. Wood, and his wife attended the bride. The best man was the bride's brother, Chester Pechette. The bride wore white silk chiffon with a veil, and carried orange blossoms and lilies of the valley. Afterward Lige Coalman served a wedding breakfast in his tent. Arrangements were made by Pridemore and Fox of Hotel de Government Camp.

BRIDE PREPARED TO STAY

1928 On Monday, July 9, Elva Taylor, economics teacher from New York City, climbed Cooper Spur Route with a minister to marry Robert G. McVicar in a ceremony on the summit. Miss Taylor had climbed Mount Hood the previous year and met the groom, who was manning the summit lookout cabin.

The bride ascended with Reverend M.H. Staines, Terrance Staines, and Joe Temby of Selah, Washington, Philip Parott of Parkdale, and E.C. Moar of Portland. The groom had ascended several days before and was waiting for the wedding with James Neeman and Fred Mahaffey, who had come up the South Side. The couple spent the rest of the summer on the summit, returning each year through the summer of 1931.

Nature Flexes Her Muscles

Any glacial mountain is under a process of crumbling, eventually ending as a humble, rounded heap of rubble, a mere suggestion of its former grandeur. The greatest action comes from the glaciers, greater than most people can imagine, as thousands of tons of ice move slowly downward, gouging the rock or tearing it away. Glacial ice near mountain cliffs freezes and pulls away large chunks and slabs of rock, making the cliffs ever more perpendicular.

All this rock is carried downward, some so fine that it washes downward in the rivers and is carried to the ocean. Much of the heavier rock is deposited in giant moraines that stand as permanent monuments alongside the route of glaciers that were much larger in the past. Moraines are very plainly seen along the sides of Eliot Glacier. In the White River Valley one can see giant moraines near the mountain, as he views the scene from the White River Bridge on Highway 35.

The study of the action of glaciers is Glaciology, a subdivision of the study of Geology, not a subject included in this book. However, observation of unusual or massive changes, also becomes a part of history. Hardly a person has ever climbed Mount Hood without seeing a few rocks fall. Occasionally they are great boulders or whole ledges, as many of the climbing and accident stories in this book will indicate.

The following stories tell of rockfalls or collapsing structure, that were so significant the newspapers felt the need to report them:

DRYER NOTICED ROCKFALL

1858 On Friday, August 20, Thomas Dryer in a horseback party on the south side, noted that a large mass of rock had fallen off since his previous visit and had slid down into the basin of Zigzag Glacier.

AVALANCHE DOWN SUNSHINE

1930 On Tuesday, August 12, a terrible roar on the side of Mount Hood awakened guests at Cloud Cap Inn at 11:30 p.m. The following morning the results of a massive avalanche of rock and ice were plainly visible. Falling from a point high on the Coe Glacier ice fall, the rubble was spread boldly down the mountainside for at least a mile. Guide Mark Weygandt was quoted in saying that it had obliterated the area normally taken by climbers on the Sunshine Route.

GOVERNMENT CAMP AWAKENED

1933 On Sunday night, January 15, a large crashing roar up high on the mountain was heard in Government Camp. No snow had fallen during the night, and when clouds around the summit blew away on Monday, a large black object was plainly visible in the snow. It was obviously a large piece of rock about 50 feet in diameter and high as a two-story building. It had fallen off Crater Rock or Hawkins Cliff and rolled down the gully between them to come to rest well below Crater Rock.

MASSIVE GLACIAL COLLAPSE

1974 On September 14, a large group of Mazamas gathered at Cloud Cap Inn for glacier rescue practice under instruction of Richard R. Pooley, saw the results of a massive cave-in of the surface of Eliot Glacier. An area of ice, an acre in size, had dropped straight down, leaving ice cliffs a hundred feet high exposed on the upper side. The phenomenon had occurred sometime during the previous week. No good explanation was made as to how such a great void could build up under the ice to allow such a collapse.

STORMS

Tuesday, August 26, 1926 About two inches of rain in 24 hours fell on the South Side, melting new snow on the White River Glacier. The canyon underwent a severe flood, causing large boulders to wash down the stream bed and carrying thousands of cubic yards of silt to form a slurry with the water. The White River bridge had been built with damage in mind. At 1:30 a.m. on Wednesday about 40 feet washed out on the west end of the bridge, plus a section of approach fill.

ANOTHER WHITE RIVER WASHOUT

Saturday, October 16, 1926 A warm Chinook wind suddenly melted snow high on the slopes of Mount Hood and caused another wash in the canyon of White River. On Sunday, a large crowd of motorists drove to the scene to look at the damage. Great boulders were still being washed downward in the stream bed.

Fifteen of the bridge piers were undermined or knocked out, although the surface of the bridge remained intact. Although the road was closed, one man in a light roadster ran the barricade and drove across.

April 24, 1931 Heavy winds of nearly cyclone strength hit Mount Hood, downing trees in vast areas. Losses to summer homes up the valley from Brightwood were immense. First reports estimated that between 75 and 100 homes had been crushed by falling trees.

Mazama Lodge, below Laurel Hill, was damaged by a falling tree. The George Prosser cabin at Government Camp was upturned and damaged. At Summit the ski jump and toboggan run were obliterated by falling trees.

The road to Wapinitia was closed by the falling of thousands of trees. In one area it was estimated that fallen timber lay 20 feet deep in a jumble across the road.

THE CHRISTMAS FLOOD OF 1964

Just after mid-month of December, 1964, the weather turned cold and dumped heavy snowfall on the whole Pacific Northwest, a vast area that ranged from Northern California through British Columbia and east into the mountain areas of Montana and Wyoming. Portland was blanketed with snow that had caused serious traffic impedance and problems of snow removal. At Government Camp, Everett Darr reported a record low temperature of 14 degrees below zero.

However, on Saturday, December 19, the weather experts were giving news of warmer weather coming. This was considered cheerful, a welcome break in the punishing cold snap, not a usual occurrence at that time of year. On Sunday, snow was melting, and rain that afternoon began to turn everything to slush. A warm mass of air had hit the Northwest.

The rains persisted, and by Monday night the rivers were very high. Weather experts were predicting very serious flood conditions. If only they could have known **how serious.** Before another week had passed, officials of Oregon, Washington, California, and Idaho realized that in those states alone, the damage had taken a toll of a billion dollars.

Mount Hood and vicinity stood a great deal of loss. On Tuesday, December 22, 1964, Louise Moody at Rhododendron wrote down events that were later published in the newspaper. Her husband left for work in Portland early that morning, as usual. The eight inches of snow, that had been on the ground Sunday, was rapidly disappearing in the unrelenting rain. Wind was blowing in gusts up to 60 miles per hour.

The first problem was the disruption of the community water supply. As the morning wore on, the situation was obviously becoming serious. The postmaster reported that the highway bridge over the Zigzag River was liable to go out. The Oregon State Patrol was taking children and school teachers across the bridge on foot.

Mrs. Moody walked over to the river. It was not so high, but the water was fast, with giant trees being carried along. The river banks had already been heavily eroded, and one house had already fallen in to become a part of the tremendous load of flotsam. As she watched, the river quickly devoured the ground from under the houses and cabins on the shore. The water was taking boulders and all, in its surge of power.

Five houses were undermined on the west bank of the river. On the east end of the bridge, the water was caving off great chunks of earth and rock to be swept away by the stream. It began to appear that the river might cut further and further eastward into the townsite to destroy a good part of it. However, a house lodged against the end of the bridge and changed the course of the flow.

Returning to her home, she walked against the strong wind that set her backward when it gusted heavily. The telephone was dead. The only communication was from the radios in the State Police car and a Portland General Electric truck.

At 2:30 p.m., she went out for another look. On the west bank, four houses were gone, and the fifth hung at a crazy angle over the water. The earth at the bridge approach finally gave way and quickly disappeared into the swirl. Trees 100-feet long churned in the water and clogged the flow of the stream. Maude Krebs was having her furniture moved out, as great gobs of earth caved off under the south side. At 4:00 p.m., the electric power quit.

WILDCAT'S WILDEST MOMENTS

Meanwhile, at Wildcat Creek, about nine miles to the west on Highway 26, another small mountain rill had become a raging monster. The creek carried down logs, mud, and boulders to smash the community, destroying 15 homes in the small area.

Mrs. Robert Vallereux, one of the residents there, was talking on the phone to her neighbor, 75-year-old Harry Engle. She heard a sound similar to that of an approaching locomotive. Dropping her phone, she rushed to her door to see Engle standing in the door of his own home. Suddenly there was a great roar, as a mass of logs and dirt crushed his house. Engle was not seen again. It was presumed that he had been carried off in the debris of his porch by the water of Wildcat Creek to the Sandy River across the highway.

There were screams coming from the Engle home. Mrs. Engle, 81, was trapped inside a bedroom. Thomas Day and Carl Neumann rigged a rope across the creek to avoid being swept away, then forced a crossing in the water, four feet deep. It took them a half hour to make the crossing, but they were able to get Mrs. Engle and get her to safety.

The highway was quickly chewed away by Wildcat Creek, leaving the second major break in Highway 26. Just to the west of Wildcat on the Sandy River, the family of Andy Morlan was forced to suddenly abandon the expensive, new home which they had just completed. Morlan was not even able to retrive his billfold in another pair of trousers, as they ran for their lives.

Homes fell into the Sandy River by the score, especially upriver from Wildcat Creek. One $60,000 home, complete with swimming pool, vanished into the waters. At Alder Creek, Wally Hanlon, whose home sat atop a rock cliff at the turn of the river, watched breathlessly as tremendous trees turned over from end to end, each one threatening to smash the house with one vicious swipe.

On the Sandy River north of Zigzag the water scoured the banks, removing all traces of the new homes that were swept away. To the east of Rhododendron, historic Toll Gate Picnic Area was changed from a lovely wooded plain, covered with small trees, to a great, gaping river bed. Hundreds of thousands of cubic yards of rock and soil had been washed away to bring the river bank within a hundred feet of the highway. A replica of the old toll gate was left hanging uselessly over the stream bed.

Upstream on the Salmon River a road contractor had set several pieces of heavy construction machinery in place in the autumn, planning to get an early start on a project in 1965. Some of it was swept away. Ed Cook of Cook's Motel, saw a large yellow object tumbling in the streambed. It was the engine of an earth mover or perhaps a large crawler tractor. The wheels and external gear had been knocked off and ground off in the wild ride down the river bed, leaving only the central engine body.

One might wonder how it is possible for such a heavy object to be moved several miles down the river bed. But in such cases, the power of the water is beyond comprehension. Cook also told of a boulder about four feet square and eight feet long, that was moved by the Sandy River from near Brightwood to a point near the mount of Wildcat Creek.

DISASTER ON JOHN DAY BRIDGE

On the same Tuesday, December 22, a beautiful new bridge had been put into use across the John Day River, where the Columbia River Highway crosses at its mouth. Dr. Joseph Robert Dickson, 60, of Chinook, Montana, was travelling with his wife, Norma, and his son, George W. Dixon. They had evidently stopped to do some sightseeing at the bridge, when it became obvious that the John Day River was beginning to undermine the piers.

Dr. Dickson was attempting to drive his car to safety, when the structure collapsed, the center spans falling 140 feet to the river. The son leaped into the river, but could not save his father. He was later recuperating in the hospital at Goldendale. A short time later, two construction workers from Rufus, William Wrightman, about 37, and Charles Cromwell, about 45, drove off the span to land in the wreckage below. This brought the death toll on the bridge to three.

WELCHES WAS AN ISLAND

Meanwhile, with the highway cut off at Rhododendron and at Wildcat Creek, a large community became isolated. About a hundred children had to stay at the school at Welches, being cut off from their homes. Gene Bowman housed many refugees at the golf course.

Tuesday's high temperature in Portland had been 58 degrees. On Wednesday, the rain stopped. It had dumped about 16 inches of water in a period of four days. The hills at Government Camp were bare of snow, a large accumulation melted in three days.

At Rhododendron, utility cables were temporarily restored across the Zigzag River. Forrest Anlicher shot an arrow across the stream, carrying a light cord. This was attached to a series of heavier cords and lines, enabling Joie Smith and some other residents of Rhododendron to pull across temporary cable. The worst was over at Mount Hood, and it was merely a matter of waiting for water to recede.

In Portland, Salem, and Oregon City, the worst was yet to come, with the bulge of water slowly working out from the mountains, carrying fantastic amounts of logs, boards, and dead animals. On Christmas day, crews were frantically placing sandbags against the seawall, a maneuver that saved downtown Portland from becoming a lake.

The Willamette River had disappeared. From Salem to Portland it had become a giant lake, cutting new channels and claiming buildings along its shores. In Portland a log raft had broken up, filling the river with logs from the Ross Island bridge on down. Marinas and landings were destroyed, and some 27 houseboats were swept away. The restaurant boat, River Queen, was torn loose from her moorings, but she was saved by tugboat operators. The death toll in Oregon had mounted to 16.

Timberline Lodge was finally cleared on Thursday, December 23. The guests checked out and drove to The Dalles after the road was temporarily opened. It closed again shortly afterward. An unidentified man at Government Camp had a stroke. He was saved by a helicopter bringing in oxygen for him. Helicopters were in heavy use in emergency situations in the mountain area.

RESTORING THE DAMAGE

By Sunday, December 27, the washout at Wildcat Creek had been made passable to emergency traffic. Tourists were asked to stay out of the area. Snow had been falling again at Government Camp, but all ski areas were closed. Trains and busses were still not moving, and large numbers of travellers were marooned in towns such as Bend or Salem.

On Monday morning, work at Rhododendron had begun with big equipment. Three large bulldozers and 18 trucks were at work on the job of replacing 30,000 cubic yards of fill at the bridge. Rogers Construction Company moved in rock drilling equipment by way of The Dalles to the quarry at the foot of Laurel Hill, where they broke up massive pieces of rock needed for the fill. Sergeant ,Thomas Cuttsforth, Clackamas County deputy, was the first one to walk across the temporary structure into the community of Rhododendron.

The following Sunday a moderate group of skiers crossed the temporary bridge on their way to the ski resorts, but the number was not up to normal. In the spring, when the water went down, the US Army Corps of Engineers went to work on the stream beds of the area, reshaping them and lining them with rock. Two very noticeable areas are in the bed of the Sandy River just east of Wildcat Creek, and in the Zigzag River near the bridge at Rhododendron.

TWO-FOR-ONE IN 1915

One summer day in 1915, the people of Salem witnessed a mirage lasting 90 minutes, in which Mount Hood appeared as two mountains, one atop the other. When the phenomenon was first seen at 2:30 p.m., the image in the sky was almost perfect. In a half hour it changed in shape somewhat.

Frank Moore, Chief Justice of the Supreme Court of Oregon, said that it was a mirage, the first he had ever seen in the state. A distinct dividing space separated the two images. Mirages are normally caused by two strata of air at different temperatures.

Band of sheep at Summit Meadow circa 1919, run by Fargher Sheep Company. — Photo George Calverley

BEARS OF GOVERNMENT CAMP

It was a tradition at Government Camp for the hotels to keep a tame bear, an attraction for fascinated tourists who would feed the animal or buy it a bottle of soda. When Albert Krieg and his crew were building Battle Axe Inn in 1925, they became temporary keepers of Teddy, the Government Camp Hotel bear, when owner John Rafferty went on a short vacation.

Teddy weighed over 400 pounds, a big, angular, raw-boned male. The men of the construction crew were fond of wrestling with him, especially Curt Abbott who was part Indian and especially adept at fighting with the animal. Teddy could have killed any man with one powerful swipe of his paw, but he played much as a large dog would.

In 1926 Everett Sickler bought his own bear for Battle Axe Inn, a small, beautifully-rounded female, which they named Minnie. Sickler drove over to Hood River Trout Hatchery at Dee to buy Minnie from the manager, Max Webster. He paid $50 for the bear and loaded her cage aboard his Model T Ford pickup.

The day was hot and Minnie became very restless in her cage. She began to chew little pieces of the wood away, her head being just a few inches away from Sickler's shoulder as he drove. He solved some of her problem by stopping often at creeks and dousing her with water. The cold water made her more comfortable, and she forgot her effort to break out of the cage.

Minnie proved to be a meticulous and gentle creature. She loved strawberry soda, taking a bottle between her paws to drain it, then setting it neatly down in a row with other empties on the ground. It was not unusual for her to drink eight or ten dozen bottles on a busy Sunday. At the end of the day she would hold her stomach and groan with the overload of carbonated beverages. Minnie was often invited to dinner with the family, where she would eat food from a fork, when Sickler proffered it to her. Her bite was so gentle that her lips barely touched the fork.

Minnie was a lady — until the spring of 1929, when Sickler made an unfortunate mistake with her. Those were Prohibition days. One Sunday a group of tourists were gathered around the bear, when a thin-faced man sidled up to Sickler.

"I wonder how she would like a little moonshine?"

"I don't know," replied Sickler. "It might be fun to try it." This was a disastrous mistake that the hotel-keeper later regretted deeply. They mixed the illicit whiskey with some water and sugar and he handed it to her. The bear upended the bottle and took one sip, just as she would have done with a bottle of pop. She set down the bottle, and her breath came in grunting pants of agony, as she backed into her cage. Nothing could lure her out.

That night Sickler came out to feed her, calling her repeatedly in the darkness near her cage. She suddenly came out and made a swipe at him; he could hear the swish of her paw close to his face. She came to the end of her chain and fell back, the only thing that saved his life. A thoughtless prank had cost him the love of this gentle animal; from that time it was unsafe for Sickler to approach her. She had been tricked.

A wildcat moving picture company, sponsored by Phithian and Barker Shoe Company of Portland, came through Government Camp that spring, more-or-less making up their story as they went. Minnie became one of the stars of their film, climbing through a window and stealing a pie, while a frightened cameraman ground out film from a tripod set in the center of the kitchen floor. The movie company bought Minnie for $80 and took her to their studios in an old aircraft hangar about four blocks south of Beaverton High School.

Their money came to an abrupt end, and the moving picture company was bankrupt. Minnie was left chained outside the building without food or water, until someone complained to the humane society. They took her to the Portland Zoo. Sickler visited her there several years later, but the bear gave no sign of recognizing him.

Everett Sickler and Minnie the Bear — Photo Sickler

TEDDY, BREAKOUT ARTIST

Teddy at Government Camp Hotel was a very clever animal. He would get ahold of a four-inch log and chew off a piece a couple of feet long. He would then wind his chain around the wood and start twisting. In time he could break his heavy chain and be free to roam.

One day J.V. Rafferty came running across the street to Battle Axe Inn. "Teddy is loose!" he told Sickler. "He is up in the attic, tearing up flour sacks."

Sickler picked up a stick and went over to Government Camp Hotel to control the bear. He was the only one who could handle him, but with a flick with a stick on Teddy's nose, he could settle him down immediately. Teddy had emerged from the attic after ripping open several sacks of the winter flour supply. When they found him, he was cavorting down the halls, leaving a trail of flour. Whenever he found a bedroom door open, he entered and with a playful swipe pulled the blankets from the beds.

In 1929, eight feet of snow had fallen on the level in Government Camp. Teddy took this as a signal to hibernate, and he dug into a shack, completely covered with snow, staying there until the weather became more pleasant. A skier passed right over his lair and tried to arouse him, but Teddy slept right through.

Teddy finally was sold to Henry Villiger after he bought Battle Axe Inn in 1929. The bear moved across the street for several years to amuse tourists on the north side of the road. No record can be found of what ever happened to Teddy, although he was involved in an incident in perhaps 1932.

A young man and his girl friend were ogling at Teddy outside Battle Axe. He liked to eat cigarettes, and the thoughtless girl handed him a lighted one. The angered bear made a pass at her, tearing the calf of her leg. A year later she had the effrontery to threaten suit, and her claim was settled by Sickler on behalf of the distressed Villiger.

The famed climbing dog, Ranger — Photo Joe Leuthold

BRULE — ST. BERNARD GREETER

Official greeters at Timberline Lodge for many years were Brule and Lady, St. Bernard dogs that gave the area further alpine atmosphere. Lady was a bit snippy when pushed too far, but the giant Brule patiently shook hands with visitors as many times as asked. He withstood the pummelling by small children, the taunting by teen-agers, and the over-affectionate fondling by crowds of women.

Brule weighed as much as two men, and he worked off his fat by bounding up and down the hills around the lodge and lifts. Romping in the heavy snow in the winter was his forte. But World War Two closed Timberline Lodge in November of 1942, and suddenly Brule was a snowbound prisoner inside the building, unable to exercise as he had before. He built up weight quickly. The snowplows got through to the lodge by December 10th that year, but by then he was so fat they had to load him in the truck with the help of four men and take him downhill to the veterinarian. It was too late; the old canine greeter had to be put to sleep.

Brule had never been a true climbing dog, as had been Ranger at Government Camp Hotel. Brule made the news once in 1939 when he got into trouble in the Crater Rock area, out of his normal range of activity. He had to be rescued by Ski Patrol Chief, Hank Lewis.

RANGER WY'EAST MASCOT

July 1, 1940 *The Oregon Journal* carried the story of the death of Ranger, part Australian Shepherd, who belonged to Mr. and Mrs. J.V. Rafferty of Government Camp. Famous as a mountain climbing dog, Ranger had been born in a litter of pups in 1925 under the porch of Government Camp Hotel. His mother was left behind by an Indian woman that year, and was later shot as a marauder around the community.

Ranger and his brother, Laddie, became great friends with Ole Lien. Lien seldom climbed without the dogs, although Laddie was killed by a hit-and-run driver in 1932. Afraid of cars, Ranger trembled in fear when forced to ride to timberline instead of walk. The Wy'east Climbers were fond of the dog, who could usually be found around their cabin on weekends.

Ranger made his last climb in 1938 with Ole Lien. From then on he was only willing to accompany Lien to Blossom Cabin. In 1939 old age reduced him to lying by the stove at Government Camp. James Harlow and Ralph Calkin carried their old friend in a box to the summit of Mount Hood, a suitable grave for the canine mountaineer. The Wy'east Climbers planned a plaque to commemorate their mascot, who had climbed an alleged 500 times.

ANIMALS CLIMBED ALSO

Animal life on the top of Mount Hood has not been as rare as one might imagine. One morning in 1919, a badger showed up at the door of the lookout cabin to greet Lige Coalman and George Maronay. They captured him and kept him in a cage for three days, until he escaped into the cabin. He upset the canned goods in the pantry, ate about a third of the lard supply, then became sick and crawled into one of their beds. Once evicted from the cabin for his bad manners, he stayed only a few days and wandered off down the mountain.

Chipmunks were frequently seen near the summit, and the cabin had its native mice. The largest wild animal on the summit was a huge black bear seen by Charles Phelps the first week of September, 1923. The bear appeared suddenly over the east crest of the summit ridge; it had probably ascended the Cooper Spur Route. It made a tour of the summit area, passing less than 100 feet from the cabin, then disappeared over the west end of the ridge. Hikers on the north side later reported that they had seen it ascending.

Since World War Two, there have been reports of the carcass of another bear, lying north of the ruins of the shelter cabin in the crater. In recent years the snow level has been too great to leave the area uncovered, but it is very probable that it will be seen again.

In 1919, W.L. Finley, biologist for the State of Oregon, offered the theory that animals such as mice and chipmunks probably followed mountain climbers to the top of the mountain to establish homes there. He reported butterflies, bees, and several species of birds.

In the summer of 1919, George Maronay, who spent the summer on top with Lige Coalman, made a discovery of significance, when he unearthed bones in a patch of receding ice near the summit. Melting had exposed an area never seen before, and Maronay dug out 44 bones and some hair. Summer ended before he was able to dig out the head section, and it is believed that no one ever returned to investigate further.

Geologists L.A. Williams, H.M. Parks, C.B. Osborne, and E.G. Sinclair all agreed that the animal had died and the flesh had been destroyed before the bones were frozen into the ice. Initial identification was that of a species of elk by Professor H.B. Torrey of Reed College.

HERR HOODWINKS HOLIDAY SCHMALTZ

A small, long-haired dachshund, "Schmaltz", became a familiar sight on the trails and ski runs, when his owner, Dr. H. Clagett Harding, fitted him to skis in 1967. Harding or his daughter, Margaret, were often seen skiing along with the dog on a leash. The leash was used to keep Schmaltz from overdoing his skiing and running out of control.

At first Harding used one broad ski for the dog's bottom, and two small skis for his two hind feet. Later he fitted the animal with a pair of 42-inch conventional skis. In 1970 the Hardings visited Switzerland and Norway on a trip and took their skiing canine along. He was an honorary member of PNSA and Cascade Ski Club, and Mount Hood Meadows gave him a free lift pass for publicity purposes.

OBSERVATIONS OF EVERETT DARR

Everett Darr claims that wild bears were very plentiful in the Government Camp neighborhood in the Thirties. Three or four at a time would often be seen in the huckleberry fields on Multorpor Mountain. Hunters wantonly murdered them in those years, returning week after week with packs of dogs to tree and shoot the animals. Legislation was made to protect them, but by that time it was too late; the bear population was almost gone.

Darr had one bear that came up to his cabin every day for a handout of food, becoming very tame. Someone shot it. There was a little retaliation in one instance; one of the bear hunters found that someone had shot all of his hunting dogs.

The Cougar, sometimes called Puma or Mountain Lion, has also virtually disappeared, although Darr saw one west of the Ski Bowl a few years ago. Red foxes have been seen on the mountain, some very high up, and at least one on the summit, seen by the party of 11 guided by Arthur Hinsey and Andrew J. Montgomery from timberline on South Side on August 10, 1905.

Darr was hiking with his wife, Ida, and James Harlow in the Thirties in the area of Little Zigzag Canyon, when they saw a wolf below them, carrying a rabbit in its mouth. They yelled at it and rolled rocks toward it. The wolf kept the cool calculation of a human mountaineer. It watched the rocks, dodging them at the very last moment, never relinquishing its hold on the rabbit. When the rocks were gone, it bounded quickly for cover of the trees.

On one of the midwinter climbs of the Thirties, Ole Lien and Darr found three domestic sheep on the summit. Fearing that they would starve, they tried to drive them downward. The animals would run ahead of them down the Chute, then cut back to the side and climb right back to the top again. They finally gave up the attempt, and nothing has ever been noted about the sheep since that time.

Government Camp Hotel 1932 — Photo Joe Leuthold

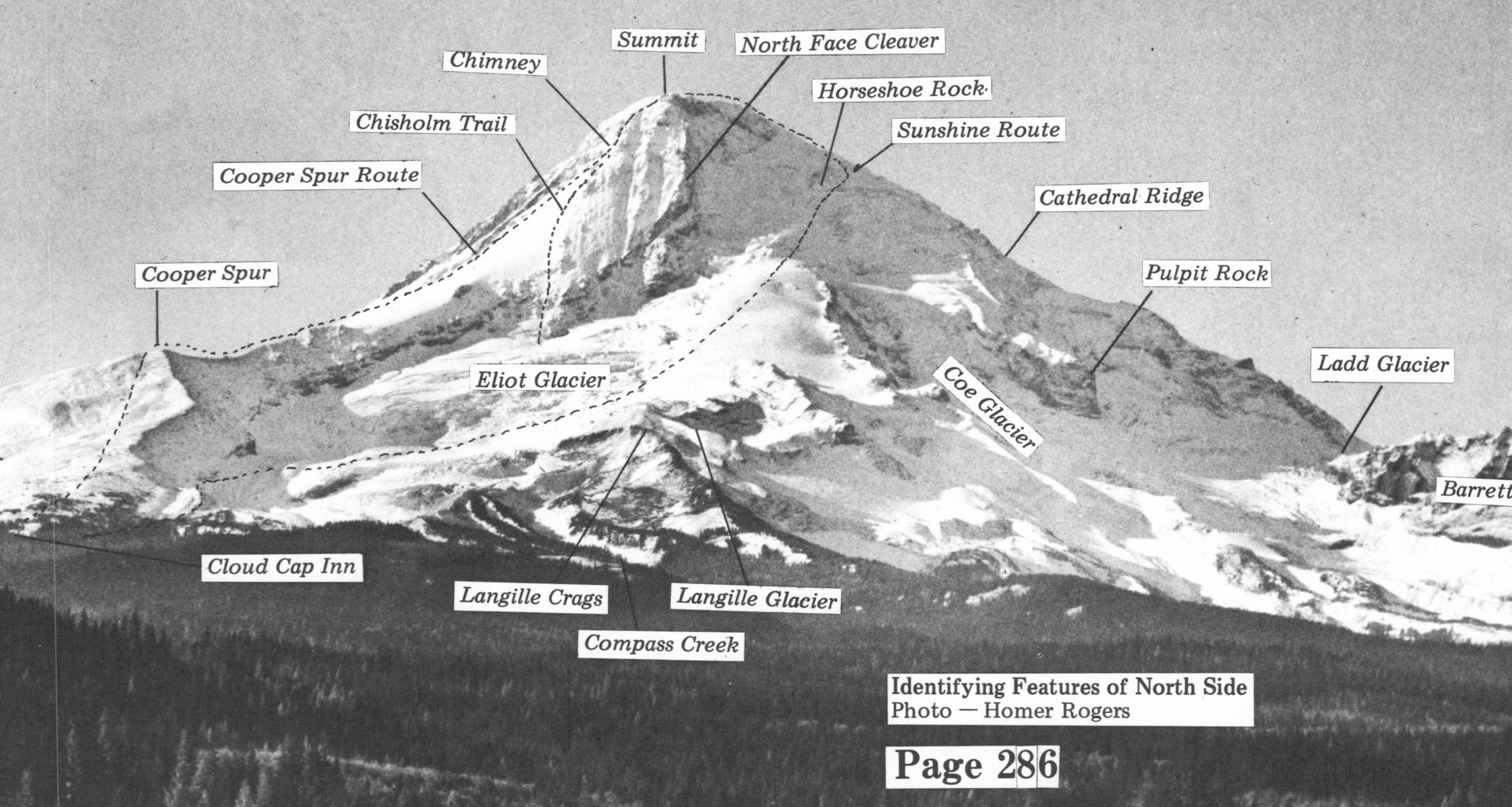

Identifying Features of North Side
Photo — Homer Rogers

Summit
Crow's Nest
Cathedral Spire
North Face Cleaver
(not an accepted name)
Wy'east Route
Cooper Spur
Cooper Spur Route
Newton Clark Glacier
Identifying features of East Side

The summit from Barrett Spur — Photo Homer Rogers 1916

Identifying Glaciers on Hood's Flanks

PALMER GLACIER was for many years regarded as a snow field. In the mild winter of 1923-24 so little snow fell that crevasses began to be revealed. In fact, the following summer George Calverley dropped a horse into a blind crevasse. The glacier lies in the valley below Triangle Moraine and drains into Salmon River. It was known as Salmon River Glacier for a time after the 1924 "discovery".

The Mazamas began investigation and sent a committee to the mountain, Sunday, October 19, 1924, Rodney L. Glisan, L.A. Nelson, Earl A. Marshall, Raymond Smith, Fred McNeil, Everett Philpoe, T. Raymond Conway, and Fred W. Stadter. They concluded that the 4500-foot ice field was definitely a glacier and should be named and included on maps. Since that time, the crevasses have once more disappeared and have never caused an incident again.

ZIGZAG GLACIER originates in the crater between Crater Rock and Hawkins Cliff. It still shows some crevasses below Illumination Rock, but the chaotic broken surface of the old days is gone as the glacier recedes. It is the first glacier on Mount Hood to feel the step of the white man's foot. Joel Palmer climbed the ice cliffs on its lower side, barefooted because of wornout moccasins, on October 12, 1845. He noted fearing the menacing crevasses. Will Steel and Dr. J.M. Keene noted them on July 4, 1887, when they slipped into one at night while descending from an illumination of the mountain. The Zigzag Glacier of today has receded vastly and is largely unbroken. Drainage is into Zigzag River, Lost Creek, and Rushing Water Creek.

REID GLACIER lies between Illumination Ridge and Yocum Ridge, a classic, heavily-crevassed body of ice, that tumbles over an impressive ice fall at the lower end. On Tuesday, July 16, 1901, it was named for Professor Harry Fielding Reid of Johns Hopkins University at a very memorable campfire ceremony at the Mazama outing at Government Camp. Reid was an expert on glaciology, and spent considerable effort studying White River Glacier. Ironically, it

Mount Hood's northwest side

is believed that he never did visit the glacier that bears his name.

Reid Glacier drains into the Sandy River and has left ancient moraine along the south bank for miles where the Zigzag and Reid once converged in the area past Rushing Water Creek. Large, unstable moraines can also be seen up above Ramona Falls.

SANDY GLACIER lies on the west-northwest side of Mount Hood, a large body that is seldom seen. It drains into Muddy Fork of Sandy River.

GLISAN GLACIER named for Rodney L. Glisan, lies northwest of the mountain, draining to McGee Creek. It is a narrow body of ice.

LADD GLACIER, north-northwest of the mountain, is a remote ice area named for William Ladd, one of the builders of Cloud Cap Inn. It drains into Ladd Creek which runs between Cathedral Ridge and Eden Park.

COE GLACIER lies due north of Mount Hood, named for Henry L. Coe, Hood River storekeeper and pioneer developer of the north side area. It is a large, heavily broken glacier that runs up to Pulpit Rock and around Horseshoe and Anderson Rocks. Most of the drainage is through Coe Creek with some flowing through Elk Cove.

LANGILLE GLACIER is a small body of ice lying just west of Langille Crags, draining into the East Fork of Compass Creek.

ELIOT GLACIER named for Thomas L. Eliot, an early explorer of the north side, lies northeast of the summit. It is Mount Hood's most spectacular body of ice, passing over two ice falls in a fantasy of teetering seracs, menacing crevasses, an infinitely broken carving that makes an impressive exit from the mountain between two classic moraines of gargantuan size. Although it has receded greatly, the glacier is still only a short walk from Cloud Cap Inn, making it a very

Looking up Yocum Ridge and Reid Glacier

popular trip for groups of ice climbers. The lower part is well covered with rock and gravel, with ice only discernable to the trained eye.

The full drainage thunders down the deep valley of Eliot Creek.

NEWTON CLARK GLACIER was named for the well-known Hood River surveyor of the 1800's. It falls away from the summit on the east side of Mount Hood to drain into Newton Creek on the north and Clark Creek on the south. Between the creeks lies an immense lateral moraine that suggests that the ice actually formed two major glaciers that threw up the moraine between them.

WHITE RIVER GLACIER lies almost due south of the summit, originating in the crater to the east of the Hogsback. Once much larger, it has receded to the point where the line of continuity is broken in the crater area. The White River is a branch of the Deschutes River, flowing in near Tygh Valley. It has carved out a great sandy valley full of moraines. By the time the river reaches White River Bridge below, water has levelled the bottom to a wide expanse of boulders and sand, almost level. As with Zigzag Glacier, White River has receded vastly since viewed by the Barlow party in 1845. Occasional release of pockets of retained water has produced devastation on the highway at times.

COALMAN GLACIER, named for Elijah Coalman, lies in the chute of the south side. It is a small body of ice, but its configuration changes remarkably. At times it has ramped gracefully down to the Hot Rocks, at others a 40-foot cliff of ice has developed at the same place. Crevasses usually appear across it by early summer.

HOW HIGH IS MOUNT HOOD?

Thomas Dryer's party measured the height of the mountain in a comic-opera attempt in 1854, coming up with 18,361 feet above sea level. They calculated timberline to lie at about 11,250. Dryer reported that blood oozed from the skin of Captain O. Travaillot, and that the stalwart soldier, Major Haller, had become dizzy with the altitude.

A man with an equally good imagination was a Mr. Belden, who wrote a story later in the same year. He claimed to have climbed Mount Hood while on a hunting trip, an unsubstantiated tale. He found the mountain to be 19,400 feet high. Blood oozed from the skin, eyes and ears bled.

Identifying features of South Side — Photo Joe Leuthold

Page 292

By 1866 Reverend G.H. Atkinson had calculated the height at 17,600. A Portland engineer used triangulation and other methods to find the peak to be between 18,000 and 19,000 feet. Maps of the era showed 18,361, and Mitchell's School Atlas gave 19,600 feet as the correct number. Many references were made to Mount Hood as being the highest point in North America.

On August 19, 1867, Colonel Williamson of the US Army at San Francisco went to Mount Hood with 10 men to officially establish the height. He used a cistern barometer reading to 2/1000's of an inch of mercury, with attached wet and dry thermometers, easy to read to 1/10 of a degree. They were all tested at sea level and again at Fort Vancouver. A rough triangulation placed Mount Hood at 12,000 feet.

Williamson presented his report to the California Academy of Natural Sciences, which was presented to the world in the *San Francisco Alta* on September 17. On September 24, *The Oregonian* picked up the story and revealed that Williamson had found the mountain to be 11,225, a very close figure.

On September 24, 1939, Admiral L.C. Colbert, head of the Coast and Geodetic Survey, announced that the true height is 11,245, eight feet less than a survey made in 1916 by the same agency.

Wy'easters on Eliot Glacier
September 18, 1932

White River Canyon

Mississippi Head from trail east of Paradise

alpenstock — a stout pole, often a hoe handle, with a sharp steel tip on the bottom and a thong at top end. Used for walking securely on snow or ice. Little used since the Fifties.

Anderson Rock — a rock protruding from Coe Glacier on the Sunshine Route below Horseshoe Rock. Named for A. L. Andy Anderson of Hood River.

arete — the sharp crest of a rock ridge.

arrest — the act of stopping, when sliding on snow or ice. The act of pulling a falling climber up tight on a belay.

Barrett Spur — rock ridge between Elk Cove and Wiyeast Basin.

belay — the act of safeguarding a climber with a climbing rope, which can be snubbed up tight at once to prevent a fall.

Bennett Pass — the major pass on Highway 35 east of White River. Elevation 4674'.

bergschrund — the major crevasse that normally opens up between a glacier and the summit slopes of a peak.

Bonney Meadows — a meadow under Bonney Butte about five miles southeast of Highway 35 on Roads S21 and S338. Named for sheep rancher Augustus A. Bonney.

CCC — Civilian Conservation Corps hired young boys in Thirties for Forest Service work.

Calverley's — a cafe next to Summit Ski Area in Twenties. Later sold to Wests.

Camp Creek — the creek that flows through Government Camp.

Castle Crags — another name for Hawkins Cliffs, that run up from Illumination Saddle almost to the summit.

Cathedral Ridge — a major buttress on the northwest side, separating Sandy and Ladd Glaciers.

Cathedral Spire — a rock pinnacle near the top of the North Face Cleaver.

chimney — a vertical ravine in rock, usually not more than six feet wide.

Chute — a steep snow slope running to the summit ridge from the Hot Rocks.

class — a measurement of rock climbing difficulty.

Class 1 . . . . walking.
Class 2 . . . . use of hands.
Class 3 . . . . occasional belaying.
Class 4 . . . . constant belaying needed.
Class 5 . . . . hardware for protection.
Class 6 . . . . hardware for direct aid.

Cold Springs Creek — a tributary of East Fork of Hood River draining Elk Meadow and Lamberson Butte.

Cooper Spur — a high point on the ridge running northeast of Mount Hood. Often used in reference to the whole ridge.

Cooper Spur Junction — a community at the point where Road S12 leaves for Cloud Cap Inn from the old highway north of Parkdale.

couloir — an ascending rock ravine.

crampons — sharp steel points mounted on climbing boots for walking on ice.

Crater Rock — the great rock in the center of the crater.

Crescent Crevasse — a forgotten name for a crevasse which always forms on Newton Clark Glacier across the Cooper Spur Route.

crevasse — a large crack in the ice, caused by the glacier moving over uneven subsurfaces.

Crow's Nest — the area on top of Steel Cliff, the point where the real climbing begins on the Wy'east Route.

Devil's Kitchen — the fumarole area in the low spot at the top of White River Glacier, just east of Crater Rock.

Devil's Backbone — a section of the old Barlow Road west of Marmot.

Divers' Creek — named for Joe Divers.

exposure — presence of drop-offs below.

fixed rope — a rope securely tied at the top of a steep or exposed slope. Called the life line in early days.

gendarme — a pinnacle in a rock ridge, causing severe problems in passage. From the French word for policeman.

glacier — a large mass of snow that melts into ice and accumulates sufficient weight to cause the mass to move downhill.

glissade — the act of sliding down a snow or ice

Ghost Ridge

Timberline 1944

surface. A standing glissade is considered much more becoming to an alpinist than a sitting glissade.

Hogsback — the snow ridge running north from Crater Rock toward the summit ridge. Historically it has varied tremendously in height, at present maintaining the very high, built-up curve that was noted in the 1890's.

Homestead Inn — an old inn south of Cooper Spur Junction. Torn down in Thirties.

Hood River Meadow — a lovely alpine meadow on old highway just north of Sahalie Falls.

Horseshoe Rock — on Sunshine Route above Anderson Rock.

Hotrocks — fumarole area at bottom of Chute, northeast of Crater Rock.

hypothermia — incapacitation or death due to loss of body heat. First symptoms are apathy followed by incoherent speech and lack of coordination. Formerly called exposure.

ice axe — a climbing tool now almost universally used. Used for self arrest, chopping steps in ice, and keeping one's balance in steep ice. Shaped like a small pick axe with pick and adze on head.

Illumination Rock — large rock fin on ridge south of Reid Glacier.

Laurel Hill — the old Barlow Road route of descending from the elevation of Government Camp to the Zigzag River at Twin Bridges.

life line — an old term for fixed rope.

Lunch Rock — a high landmark on the Cooper Spur Route.

MHNF — Mount Hood National Forest.

MHSP — Mount Hood Ski Patrol.

Mirror Lake — a small lake a mile south of Yocum Falls by trail.

Mississippi Head — one of Mount Hood's highest cliffs, located at head of Big Zigzag Canyon.

moat — the gap that develops between a glacier and a rock wall.

mogul — a hummock left by skiers carving turns on a ski slope.

MORESCO — Mountain Rescue and Safety Council of Oregon

Multorpor — Government Camp's mountain, named by Will Steel for Multorpor Republican Club of Portland, using the first letters of Multnomah, Oregon, and Portland.

NSPS — National Ski Patrol System.

Neal Creek — named for Peter Neal, near Parkdale.

North Face Cleaver — an unauthorized name, used for lack of any other, for the great rock rib running from the Eliot Glacier to the summit of Mount Hood.

Paradise Park — camp with a shelter house on Timberline Trail at head of Lost Creek. On southwest side of mountain.

picket — a stake driven into snow to secure a climbing line.

piton — an iron pin to be driven in a crack between rocks to secure a climbing rope.

PNSA — Pacific Northwest Ski Association.

Pollalie Creek — formerly Sand Creek.

Pulpit Rock — a cliff that divides Coe and Ladd Glaciers.

Queen's Chair — the moderately-sloping snow shelf at the point where Leuthold Couloir Route, Sunshine Route, and Sandy Headwall Route all meet. There is some disagreement, however; the eminent authority Lewis L. McArthur states that *Queen's Throne* is a prominent rock at the top of Cathedral Ridge.

Ramona Falls — located on the west side of the mountain at about 3480 feet.

Red Hill Lookout — formerly Tony Creek Guard Station.

Robin Hood Forest Camp — on Highway 35. Formerly called Double Three, because it was 33 miles from Hood River.

Rope — a group of climbers tied together and travelling as a unit, usually three or four.

run — a commonly travelled area on skis. The act of travelling from one point to another on skis.

Sahalie Falls — on the old section of Highway 35, northeast of Mount Hood Meadows Junction about a mile.

Sand Canyon — there are two on Mount Hood. The best known is the first major canyon west of Timberline Lodge on the Timberline Trail. The second has been renamed as Pollalie Creek, starting near Tilly Jane and dropping to East Fork of Hood River.

schrund — vernacular term for bergschrund.

serac — a freestanding block of ice created by a glacier splitting up with many crevasses. Usually proliferate at site of ice falls.

scout — to make a test probe of a route prior to an actual climb.

snow cat — a caterpillar-tread vehicle for use over snow and glacier.

Steel Cliff — the major cliff at the top of White River Glacier, to the east of Crater Rock.

stem — a climbing technique on ice or rock, which entails placing the feet on two nearly vertical faces.

string — see rope.

Summit — a recreation and service area just east of the privately-owned land of Government Camp.

Summit Meadow — a grazing area south on Still Creek Road about 1.5 miles from Highway 26.

sun cups — depressions in the snow caused by icing and melting, often creating a stair-step effect on steep slopes.

Swim — once a resort with a swimming pool a bit north of Summit Meadow.

Tamanawaus Falls — a fall accessible by trail up Cold Springs Creek from Sherwood Forest Camp on Highway 35.

Tie-In-Rock — the place on Cooper Spur Route to begin use of climbing rope.

Tilly Jane Camp and Creek — a half mile east of Cloud Cap Inn. Named for nickname of Mrs. William M. Ladd.

Timberline — Timberline Lodge.

timberline — the area around the base of a mountain above which trees can not endure the cold.

Timberline Cabin — built in 1916 west of Timberline Lodge. Now torn down.

Tom-Dick-Harry Mountain — the mountain west of Multorpor Mountain.

Tony Creek — on north side. Named for Langille's pony.

Trillium Lake — created by a dam in Mud Creek, a tributary of Salmon River. A smaller natural pond at the site was called Mud Lake.

Twin Bridges — a section of the old highway, where two bridges were built to cross and recross the Zigzag River. A camp, now abandoned, was maintained at the place.

Umbrella Falls — in East Fork of Hood River just below Mount Hood Meadows.

Veda Lake — just north of Fir Tree Camp on Sherrar Burn Road S32. Named for VErn Rogers and DAve Donaldson.

Wallalute Falls — named by Ann Lang, who was told by Indians that the name meant strong water. Located on Compass Creek. Recently designated for the falls on Eliot Creek in an error by Forest Service. (The falls on Eliot had been known as Stranahan Falls.)

WPA — Works Progress Administration, a federal agency of the Thirties.

Wy'east — the Indian name for Mount Hood.

1944 Looking Down at Crater Rock

Housewarming at Cascade Ski Club — Photo Maryanne Hill
Mrs. Corey Gustafsson on accordion, Charles L. Hill, Anna Rafferty, Sally Hill, Juanita Hagen.

1901, Mazamas on White River Glacier

NW Side from Lost Lake

A List of Advisors

So many people added knowledge to this book. Some of them were:

Jack Baldwin
Mace Baldwin
Harold Bangs
Dr. Cameron Bangs
Fred Beckey
Andy Buxton
Joanne Buxton
Ann Beckman
John Biewener
Ferris Booth
Percy Bucklin
Bill Bryan
George Calverley
Libby Carter
Dorothy Clark
Albert Combs
Harry Conway
Ed Cook
David Cooper
Carmie Dafoe
Everett Darr
Ida Darr
Betty Dodd
Nick Dodge
Ariel Edmiston
Lennis Edwards
Maryellen Englesby
Robert Finn
Thaddis Gable
Max Gatewood
John George
J. Otto George
Thomas Gibbons
Bus Gibson
William Gunesch
Corey A. Gustafsson
Ragnar L. Gustafsson
Steve Guthrie
Reider Hafstad
Alice Haris
Ole Haugen
Maryanne Hill
William Holmes
Hjalmar Hvam
Vera Hvam
Robert Hyslop
Charles Jensen
Edward Johann
Adrian Johanns
David Johanson
Frank Kamph
Maude Krebs
Carl Krieg
Al Kirnak
Richard Kohnstamm
Jean Langley
Ole Langerud
Richard LaPore
Laurita Leuthold
Hank Lewis
Ingrid Malo
Marion Mann
Tom Markham
Ned Marshall
Lewis L. McArthur
Kate McCarthy
John McClosky
Larry McDaniels
Arlie Mitchell
Bob Moller
James Mount
Donald Onthank
Vawter Parker
Thyrza Pelling
Steve Phinney
Richard R. Pooley
Louise Pomeroy
Ross Petrie
Brian Raasch
Carl Reynolds
Erwin Rieger
Frank Branch Riley
Homer Rogers
Howard Rondthaler
Harold Scharback
Everett Sickler
Louis "Bud" Siegel
James Simmons
Amos Smelser
William Spencer
Charles Sperr
Robert Swan
Nancy Tarter
Jack Vidoni
Linda Wagner
Albert E. Weese
Albertine West
Isham West
Wesley Weygandt
Kenneth Winters
Del Young

Mount Hood's
Crater Lake
Circa 1930

Downtown
Rhododendron,
Circa 1928
Inn at right

Lower Right
Beautiful Cairn Basin
Near Ladd Creek
on NW Side 1944

Following Page
Before Timberline
Was Built